Taking Sides on Takings Issues

Public and Private Perspectives

Thomas E. Roberts

Editor

Defending Liberty
Pursuing Justice

Section of State and Local Government Law
American Bar Association

Cover design by Catherine Zaccarine.

The materials contained herein represent the opinions of the authors and editors and should not be construed to be the action of either the American Bar Association or the Section of State and Local Government Law unless adopted pursuant to the bylaws of the Association.

Nothing contained in this book is to be considered as the rendering of legal advice for specific cases, and readers are responsible for obtaining such advice from their own legal counsel. This book and any forms and agreements herein are intended for educational and informational purposes only.

06 05 04 03 02   5 4 3 2 1

Library of Congress Cataloging-in-Publication Data

Taking sides on takings issues : public and private perspectives / Thomas E. Roberts, editor.
        p. cm.
    Includes index.
    ISBN 1-59031-014-4
    1. Eminent domain--United States. 2. Right of property--United States. I. Roberts, Thomas E.

KF5599.T347 2001   2001053871
343.73'0252--dc21

Discounts are available for books ordered in bulk. Special consideration is given to state bars, CLE programs, and other bar-related organizations. Inquire at Book Publishing, ABA Publishing, American Bar Association, 750 North Lake Shore Drive, Chicago, Illinois 60611.

www.abanet.org/abapubs

Summary Table of Contents

CONTENTS

Chapter 3
The Effect of *Palazzolo v. Rhode Island* on the Role of Reasonable Investment-Backed Expectations 41
Gregory M. Stein

**III. DEFINING THE PROPERTY UNIT: TO SEGMENT OR NOT
TO SEGMENT**

Chapter 4
**The Parcel-as-a-Whole Rule and Its Importance in Defending
  Against Regulatory Takings Challenges   75**
Timothy J. Dowling

Chapter 5
Of Parcels and Property   101
John E. Fee

IV. BACKGROUND PRINCIPLES OF PROPERTY AND NUISANCE LAW

Chapter 6

**Background Principles: Custom, Public Trust, and Preexisting
Statutes as Exceptions to Regulatory Takings   125**
David L. Callies and J. David Breemer

Chapter 12
Moratoria and Categorical Takings   307
Daniel P. Selmi

VIII.   *AGINS* "SUBSTANTIALLY ADVANCING STATE INTEREST" TEST: TAKINGS OR DUE PROCESS?

Chapter 16
The "Substantially Advance" Quandary: How Closely Should Courts Examine the Regulatory Means and Ends of Legislative Applications?   371
Douglas W. Kmiec

Chapter 17
Emperors and Clothes: The Genealogy and Operation of the *Agins* Tests   391
Edward J. Sullivan

Chapter 23
**Alternatives to Takings: Procedural Due Process, Equal
    Protection, and State Law Doctrine   551**
Susan L. Trevarthen

XII. REPORTS AND COMMENTS

FOREWORD

The clash between public and private interests over the use of land is intense. With more people demanding new space in a fixed amount of land, the burden on state and local governments to respond to concerns of the people is great. The way government responds has significant social, economic, and environmental implications.

A major consideration that state and local governments face in the adoption and application of land-use regulations is the requirement of the Fifth Amendment to the U.S. Constitution that just compensation be paid for property taken for public use, and the U.S. Supreme Court's holdings that excessive regulation of land use can effect such takings.

Takings law is notoriously complex, and a desire for clarity exists among many of those who must deal with it. For many years, the Section of State and Local Government Law of the ABA has explored takings law in its programs and publication in an effort to aid the bar, planners, public officials, and others interested in understanding this area of the law and working for its improvement. In 1999, the section, in conjunction with the Rocky Mountain Land Use Institute, sponsored a retreat at the University of Denver School of Law to study the current state of takings law. The retreat participants reported to the Council of the Section of State and Local Government Law. Their report provoked significant discussion among those who practice in and study this area of the law. As a follow-up, the section authorized the preparation of this book to explore the widely varying views on the most contentious issues in takings law.

The section owes a debt of gratitude to past chairs Sholem Friedman and Patrick Arey, who led this effort. Particular thanks goes to Peter A. Buchsbaum of the section, who promoted the idea of holding a retreat and became its reporter. Finally, and most important, we thank the many busy practitioners and academics who contributed to this book.

— Daniel J. Curtin, Jr.
Chair, Section of State and
Local Government Law
American Bar Association

ABOUT THE CONTRIBUTORS

Editor
Thomas E. Roberts is a professor of law at Wake Forest University in Winston-Salem, North Carolina. Professor Roberts teaches land-use regulation, natural resources law, and property. He is author of *Land Use Planning and Control Law* (with Julian C. Juergensmeyer) (West 1998) and of *Cases and Materials on Land Use* (with David L. Callies and Robert H. Freilich) (West 3d ed. 1999). He is also the author of numerous articles on land-use and property law. He received his B.A. from Hanover College in 1966 and his J.D. from Ohio State University in 1971.

Contributors
Vicki Been is a professor of law at New York University School of Law, where she teaches land-use regulation, property, and state and local government. She also leads a colloquium on The Law, Economics, and Politics of Urban Affairs. She is the co-author, with Professor Robert Ellickson, of *Land Use Controls* (Aspen Law and Business 2d ed. 2000) and has written extensively about regulatory takings, land-use exactions, the importation of regulatory takings principles into international trade agreements, and environmental justice. Ms. Been received her J.D. in 1983 from New York University School of Law, where she was a Root-Tilden Scholar. She clerked for Judge Edward Weinfeld of the Southern District of New York and for Justice Harry A. Blackmun of the U.S. Supreme Court. She served as an associate professor at Rutgers-Newark School of Law in 1988-1990 and was a visiting professor at Harvard Law School in 1995-1996. Ms. Been filed an amicus brief in *Palazzolo v. Rhode Island* on behalf of the National Wildlife Federation and various other environmental and land-use organizations.

Michael M. Berger is a shareholder in the Santa Monica, California, law firm of Berger & Norton, where he has focused his practice in land use, eminent domain, and other varieties of real property litigation since 1969, after obtaining his LL.M. in real property for work at Yale University and the University of Southern California. A member of the California Academy of Appellate Lawyers, the American College of Real Estate Lawyers, a Fellow of the American Academy of Appellate Lawyers, and an adjunct professor at the University of Miami, Mr. Berger has written and lectured widely on issues of takings and land-use law.

Mr. Berger represented the property owners in *First English Evangelical Lutheran Church v. County of Los Angeles, City of Monterey v. Del*

Monte Dunes, and *Preseault v. ICC*, and filed amicus curiae briefs in support of the property owners in such cases as *Nollan v. California Coastal Commission, Yee v. City of Escondido*, and *Lucas v. South Carolina Coastal Council,* all decided by the U.S. Supreme Court. He currently represents the property owners in *Tahoe-Sierra Preservation Council v. Tahoe Regional Planning Agency*, to be decided by the Supreme Court in 2002.

Fred Bosselman has been a professor of law at Chicago-Kent Law School since 1991. Between 1959 and 1991 he practiced law, and as part of that practice he represented local governments in a number of different states in regard to the preparation and litigation of various development exactions.

J. David Breemer is a 2001-2002 research and litigation fellow at Pacific Legal Foundation. He is co-author with David L. Callies of "The Right to Exclude Others from Private Property: A Fundamental Constitutional Right," 3 Wash. U. J. L & Pol'y 39, and "IOLTA in the New Millennium: Slowly Sinking Under the Weight of the Takings Clause," 22 U. Haw. L. Rev. 221 (2000). He is also coauthor with R.S. Radford of "Great Expectations: Will *Palazzolo* Clarify the Murky Doctrine of Investment-Backed Expectations in Regulatory Takings Law?," 9 N.Y.U. Envtl. L. J. 449 (2001). Mr. Breemer obtained his J.D. from the University of Hawaii.

Peter A. Buchsbaum is a partner in the firm of Greenbaum, Rowe, Smith, Ravin, Davis & Himmel LLP of Woodbridge, New Jersey, and is chair of the firm's Land Use Practice Group. Mr. Buchsbaum concentrates his practice in land-use planning and related environmental, municipal, and real estate issues.

Mr. Buchsbaum is a graduate of Cornell University (1967). He obtained his J.D. from the Harvard Law School in 1970. He began his legal career as law secretary to the Honorable Joseph Weintraub, then chief justice of the New Jersey Supreme Court. A great deal of his work has involved *Mt. Laurel* cases and other efforts to obtain rezoning and regulatory approvals for private development. He has also represented public sector clients as general municipal counsel and on specific issues, which include formulation of redevelopment plans in Long Branch and Atlantic City, New Jersey.

He has served as a member of the legislative and appellate practice committees and as chair of the Land Use Section of the New Jersey State Bar Association. He has been a member of the council of the ABA's State and Local Government Law Section and chaired its largest committee, the Land Use, Planning and Zoning Committee. He also is an adjunct professor at the Rutgers School of Law - Camden and a faculty associate of the Lincoln Institute of Land Policy in Cambridge, Massachusetts.

James Burling is a lawyer with Pacific Legal Foundation, a nonprofit, tax-exempt public interest law firm, which was formed in 1973 to litigate nationwide in defense of individual and economic freedoms and to represent responsible citizens supporting sound environmental and land-use litigation. Mr. Burling has worked with the foundation since 1983, litigating cases from Alaska to Florida. From 1986 through 1988, Mr. Burling established and managed the foundation's Alaska office.

Before becoming a lawyer with the foundation, Mr. Burling attended the University of Arizona College of Law in Tucson, where he served as an editor for the law review and received a J.D. degree in 1983. From 1977 through 1980, Mr. Burling was employed as an exploration geologist. He has been a frequent lecturer at continuing legal education seminars, including those sponsored by CLE International and Law Seminars International. He is a planning co-chair for ALI-ABA's course, Inverse Condemnation and Related Government Liability, and has organized Federalist Society seminars on property rights. Mr. Burling is also a frequent guest lecturer before community and property rights organizations on subjects including regulation of wetlands and endangered species, federal land policy, zoning, regulatory exactions, the public trust doctrine, and the taking of private property. Mr. Burling argued *Palazzolo v. Rhode Island* before the United States Supreme Court.

David L. Callies (A.B. De Paul University, 1965; J.D. University of Michigan, 1968; LL.M. Nottingham University 1969) is the Benjamin A. Kudo Professor of Law at the University of Hawaii, where he has taught property, land use, and state/local government law since 1978. Before teaching, he practiced law, counseling local, state, and national government agencies in land-use management and control, transportation policy, and intergovernmental relations. A member of ALI, the American Institute of Certified Planners, and a life member of Clare Hall, Cambridge University, he is past chair of the ABA's Section on State and Local Government Law and the IBA's Academic Forum. He is presently treasurer of the AALS Section on State and Local Government Law and co-editor with Dan Tarlock of the annual *Land Use and Environmental Law Review*. The author of dozens of articles, his books include *Land Use and Development Regulations in the United States* (in Japanese 1996, and Chinese 1999); *Property, Law and the Public Interest* (1998) (with Hylton, Mandelker & Franzese); *Takings: Regulatory Takings and Land Development Conditions After* Lucas *and* Dolan (ed. 1996); and *Cases and Materials on Land Use* (West 3d ed. 1999) (with Freilich and Roberts). He is the editor (with Kotaka) of an 11-country comprehensive study of eminent domain and town planning law, scheduled for publication by the University of Hawaii Press in March 2002.

Daniel J. Curtin, Jr., of McCutchen, Doyle, Brown & Enersen, LLP, Walnut Creek, California, concentrates his practice on local government and land-use law, representing both private and public-sector clients. Mr. Curtin serves as chair of the State and Local Government Law Section of the American Bar Association. He was past chair of the Land Development, Planning & Zoning Section of the International Municipal Lawyers Association and is a member of its International Committee. Mr. Curtin was honored in 1992 with IMLA's Charles S. Rhyne Award for Lifetime Achievement in Municipal Law. He is the author of numerous publications on land use law, which have been cited frequently by the courts, including *Curtin's California Land Use & Planning Law.*

Timothy J. Dowling is chief counsel of Community Rights Counsel, a public interest law firm that assists local governments in defending against challenges to land-use laws and other community protections. He has filed amicus briefs in several U.S. Supreme Court takings cases, including *Palazzolo v. Rhode Island, City of Monterey v. Del Monte Dunes, Phillips v. WLF*, and *Dolan v. City of Tigard*. He also has participated in takings cases before federal courts and state supreme courts across the country. Before joining Community Rights Counsel, Mr. Dowling worked in the Environment and Natural Resources Division of the U.S. Department of Justice, where he received the John Marshall Award for Outstanding Legal Achievement for his work in formulating the department's position on takings legislation. From 1987 to 1992, Mr. Dowling served at the U.S. Environmental Protection Agency as staff lawyer, judicial officer, and acting judge of the Environmental Appeals Board. Before his public service, he was an associate at the law firm of Hogan & Hartson. Mr. Dowling received his J.D. in 1982 from Georgetown University Law Center, where he was an editor of the *Georgetown Law Journal,* and his B.A. in 1979 from the University of Notre Dame. He is coauthor of the *Takings Litigation Handbook* (American Legal Publishing, May 2000) and numerous articles on takings and land-use issues.

Steven J. Eagle is a professor of law at George Mason University School of Law in Arlington, Virginia. He teaches and writes in the areas of land use, real property, and constitutional law. The second edition of his *Regulatory Takings*, a treatise on the limits of permissible governmental regulation of property, was published in 2001 by Lexis Publishing. Professor Eagle is the author of numerous scholarly and popular works on land-use regulation and property rights. He currently serves as vice chair of the ABA's Committee on Land-Use Regulation. Professor Eagle studied economics at the City College of New York and is a graduate of the Yale Law School. He also has taught at the law schools of Vanderbilt University, Pace University, and the University of Toledo.

John D. Echeverria is the director of the Georgetown Environmental Law and Policy Institute and an adjunct professor at Georgetown University Law Center. The institute conducts research and education on legal and policy issues relating to protection of the environment and conservation of natural resources. Mr. Echeverria is the former general counsel of the National Audubon Society, the former general counsel and conservation director of American Rivers, Inc., and a graduate of the Yale Law School and the Yale School of Forestry and Environmental Studies. He served as law clerk to the Honorable Gerhard Gesell of the U.S. District Court in the District of Columbia. Mr. Echeverria has written extensively on various aspects of the takings issue and other aspects of environmental law and acts as program chair for the annual Georgetown Conference on Litigating Regulatory Takings Claims. He has filed amicus brief on behalf of groups of economists, local governments, and conservation groups in most of the U.S. Supreme Court takings cases over the last decade.

John E. Fee is an assistant professor of law at the J. Reuben Clark Law School, Brigham Young University. He received his B.A. in American Studies from Brigham Young University and his J.D. from the University of Chicago Law School, where he was articles editor of the *Law Review.* Mr. Fee was a law clerk to Judge Frank H. Easterbrook of the Seventh Circuit U.S. Court of Appeals from 1995 to 1996 and to Justice Antonin Scalia of the U.S. Supreme Court from 1996 to 1997. He practiced litigation for three years at Sidley & Austin in Washington, D.C., where he focused on areas of constitutional law, environmental law, and religious freedom. Mr. Fee teaches courses in property, land use, environmental law, and administrative law. It was as a law student, while under the tutelage of Richard A. Epstein and other scholars, that Mr. Fee became interested in the issue of regulatory takings as a primary research interest. His comment, Unearthing the Denominator in Regulatory Taking Claims, has been cited by the U.S. Supreme Court and the D.C. Circuit Court of Appeals, among other courts.

Julian C. Juergensmeyer is currently professor and Ben F. Johnson Jr. Chair in Law at Georgia State University. He is a graduate of Duke University (A.B. summa cum laude and J.D. with honors and Order of the Coif). For 30 years he was professor of law and affiliate professor of Urban and Regional Planning at the University of Florida, where he was also Gerald A. Sohn Research Scholar, director of Growth Management Studies, and director of the LL.M. in Comparative Law Program. Professor Juergensmeyer started working on impact fee programs in the mid-1970s and has published, lectured, and consulted on impact fee issues throughout the United States and Europe. Many of his publications relevant to impact fees are cited in his chapter, coauthored with Professor James Nicholas, in this book. He and Jim Nicholas have participated in formulating many of the impact fee programs that are currently in operation today. They and Professor Arthur C. Nelson of Georgia Institute of Technology are the coauthors of APA's *A Practitioners's Guide to Development Impact Fees.*

Douglas T. Kendall is Community Rights Counsel's (CRC's) founder and executive director. He is also an adjunct professor at the University of Virginia Graduate Planning Program, where he teaches a course on legal issues in land-use planning. As CRC's executive director, Mr. Kendall has represented local government clients in state and federal appellate courts around the country and before the U.S. Supreme Court. He is also co-author of CRC's *Takings Litigation Handbook: Defending Takings Challenges to Land-Use Regulations* (American Legal Publishing 2000). Before forming CRC, Mr. Kendall worked as a litigator in the constitutional practice area at the Washington, D.C., law firm of Crowell & Moring, where his practice included representing local governments in constitutional cases. He also spent several years working on Capitol Hill. His writings on takings/land-use law have appeared in numerous publications, including the *Virginia Law Review*, the *Urban Attorney,* the *Harvard Environmental Law Journal*, *The Zoning and Planning Law Handbook*, the *Virginia Environmental Law Journal,* and the *Boston College Environmental Affairs Law Journal*. He received his undergraduate and law degrees from the University of Virginia.

Douglas W. Kmiec is the dean and St. Thomas More Professor of Law at the Catholic University of America in Washington, D.C. Professor Kmiec, one of America's best-known scholars and popular commentators on the law, came to Catholic University after having taught constitutional law for nearly two decades at the University of Notre Dame and being the inaugural holder of the Caruso Family Endowed Chair at Pepperdine University in California. Professor Kmiec was director of Notre Dame's Center on Law & Government and the founder of its *Journal of Law, Ethics & Public Policy*. Beyond the university setting, he served Presidents Ronald Reagan and George Bush from 1985 to 1989 as constitutional legal counsel, a position previously held by Chief Justice William Rehnquist and Justice Antonin Scalia. He is the author of the two-volume West Group treatise, *Zoning & Planning Law Deskbook* (2d ed. 2001) and coauthor (with legal historian Stephen Presser of Northwestern) of three books on the Constitution—*The American Constitutional Order, Individual Rights and the American Constitution* and *The History, Structure and Philosophy of the American Constitution*. Other works include *Cease-Fire on the Family* (Crisis Books/ Notre Dame 1995) and *The Attorney General's Lawyer* (Praeger 1992), and dozens of published law review articles and popular essays.

Daniel R. Mandelker, AICP, is the Stamper Professor of Law at Washington University in St. Louis, where he teaches land-use law. He is the author of a treatise, *Land Use Law*, a coauthor of *Federal Land Use Law,* and coauthor of a law school casebook, *Planning and Control of Land Development*. He is a frequent lecturer at land-use conferences and has consulted with states and municipalities nationally on land-use issues. Professor Mandelker is the principal consultant to the American Planning Association's Growing Smart project, which is preparing new model planning and zoning legislation to replace the Standard Planning and Zoning Acts, and was coauthor of the association's amicus brief for the Supreme Court in *Suitum v. Tahoe Regional Planning Agency.* He has testified before congressional committees on legislation that would modify the rules that determine when takings cases are ripe for adjudication in federal courts.

Dwight H. Merriam, FAICP, CRE (B.A. cum laude University of Massachusetts, 1968; M.R.P. University of North Carolina, 1974; J.D. Yale, 1978), heads the nationally recognized Land Use Group of Robinson & Cole, LLP, in Hartford, Connecticut, representing developers, landowners, local governments, and advocacy groups in land development and conservation issues. He has published more than 150 articles on land-use law, focusing on the significant decisions of the day, including *Palazzolo, Olech,* and *Del Monte Dunes.* Mr. Merriam is the senior coeditor of *Inclusionary Zoning Moves Downtown* and the coauthor of *The Takings Issue.* He has taught land-use law since 1978 and currently teaches at Vermont Law School. He a past president and fellow of the American Institute of Certified Planners, a Counselor of Real Estate, and a member of the American College of Real Estate Lawyers. He is a former director of the American Planning Association and was chair of APA's Planning & Law Division.

James C. Nicholas, Ph.D., is professor of urban and regional planning and affiliate professor of law at the University of Florida, where he is associate director of the environmental and land-use law program. He has held this position since 1985. Before assuming his present position, he was professor of economics at Florida Atlantic University and acting director of the Joint Center for Environmental and Urban Problems. Dr. Nicholas has written widely on the subject of growth management. Among his publications are *A Practitioner's Guide to Development Impact Fees, Calculating Proportionate Share Impact Fees,* and *The Changing Structure of Infrastructure Finance.* He has authored a number of articles in professional literature, including "The Progression of Impact Fees" in *Journal of the American Planning Association,* "Impact Exactions: Economic Theory, Practice, and Incidence" in *Law and Contemporary Problems*, and "State and Regional Land Use Planning: The Evolving Role of the State" in *St. Johns University Law Review.*

In addition to his academic duties, he has worked with many national, state, and local governments in coping with the problems of environmental and land management. He has assisted the states of Florida, Georgia, Delaware, Hawaii, Massachusetts, New Hampshire, and Washington in developing land management and impact fee programs. He has also worked with many local jurisdictions in implementing growth management and impact fee programs. Most of this work has been in cooperation with Julian Juergensmeyer.

Daniel P. Selmi is a professor of law at Loyola Law School, Los Angeles, where he teaches land-use regulation, environmental law, and torts. He has been a professor at Loyola since 1983 and served as associate dean for academic affairs from 1990 to 1993. From 1993 to 1994, Professor Selmi was a visiting scholar at the Environmental Law Institute, Washington, D.C. Before joining the faculty at Loyola, from 1976 to 1983 he served as a deputy lawyer general in the Natural Resources Law and Environmental Law sections of the California Attorney General's Office. From 1975 to 1976, he served as judicial law clerk to the Honorable Manuel L. Real, U.S. District Judge, Central District of California. Professor Selmi is co-author of *Land-Use Regulation: Cases and Materials* (Aspen Pub. 1999) and *State Environmental Law* (West Group 1988 and yearly supplements). He also is coeditor of the six-volume Matthew Bender treatise *California Environmental Law and Land Use Practice*. He is past chair of the California State Bar Section on Environmental Law and has litigated numerous land-use and environmental cases. He received his B.A. and J.D. from Santa Clara University and a master's degree from Harvard University.

Gregory M. Stein is a professor of law at the University of Tennessee College of Law in Knoxville, Tennessee. He teaches courses in land use, real estate finance, real estate development, property, and law and economics. Professor Stein is a coauthor of *A Practical Guide to Commercial Real Estate Transactions* (with Morton P. Fisher, Jr. and Gail M. Stern, ABA Publishing 2001) and numerous journal articles on land use and real estate finance topics, and is on the executive advisory board of the ABA's *Real Property, Probate & Trust Journal*. Before entering academia, he practiced law in the real estate department of Paul, Weiss, Rifkind, Wharton & Garrison in New York. Professor Stein received his B.A. from Harvard University in 1983 and his J.D. from Columbia University in 1986.

Glenn P. Sugameli is senior legislative counsel with Earthjustice in Washington, D.C. He has written extensively on various aspects of takings, including book chapters and articles in *The Urban Attorney*, *Environmental Law*, *Fordham Environmental Law Journal*, and a *Virginia Environmental Law Journal* article on the Supreme Court's *Lucas* decision that was reproduced in the *1994 Zoning and Planning Law Handbook* (Kenneth Young ed. 1994). He has also authored or coauthored numerous amici curiae briefs on the side of the government in the Supreme Court, Federal Circuit, D.C. Circuit, and in successful appeals from Florida, Michigan, and Wisconsin state court decisions that had found takings.

Edward J. Sullivan is a partner with the Portland, Oregon, office of Preston Gates & Ellis LLP, specializing in planning, administrative, and state and local government law. He also teaches planning law at Northwestern College of Law and Portland State University. He has participated as an editor and author in all four of the Oregon State Bar Continuing Legal Education publications on land use. He was admitted to the Oregon Bar in 1969 and was Washington County (Oregon) counsel and legal counsel to the governor of Oregon before entering private practice in 1978. Mr. Sullivan has written widely on municipal and planning law topics throughout his more than 30 years of practice. He is the chair of the International Municipal Lawyers Association Section on Land Development, Planning and Zoning and co-chair of the Subcommittee on Comprehensive Planning and Growth Management of the Land Use, Planning and Zoning Committee for the American Bar Association Section on State and Local Government.

Cecily T. Talbert is a partner with McCutchen, Doyle, Brown and Enersen, LLP and is chair of the firm's Real Estate Industry Group. Ms. Talbert focuses her practice on land use, real estate, and local government law. She coauthors *Curtin's California Land Use and Planning Law*, a well-known publication that definitively summarizes the major provisions of California's land-use and planning laws, and also speaks regularly on topics involving land-use and local government law. Ms. Talbert graduated Phi Beta Kappa from the University of California, Berkeley, in 1983 and received her law degree with honors from Harvard Law School in 1988.

Susan L. Trevarthen practices law with the firm of Weiss, Serota, Helfman, Pastoriza & Guedes in Fort Lauderdale, Florida. She is board-certified in City, County and Local Government Law by the Florida Bar and primarily represents local governmental entities in the areas of land use, local government, and environmental law. Her practice encompasses litigation, appeals, administrative and public hearings, and general municipal representation, including extensive constitutional law and regulatory taking issues. She also represents private property owners seeking approvals from local governments, and writes and speaks frequently on topics in her area of expertise. Ms. Trevarthen is a member of the American Institute of Certified Planners. She was graduated from University of North Carolina at Chapel Hill (M.R.P. and J.D., 1991) and Duke University (A.B., 1986), and served as an adjunct professor in growth management law for Florida Atlantic University, Department of Public Administration (1992-1993). She is a member of the executive councils of both the Environmental and Land Use Law Section and the City, County and Local Government Law Section of the Florida Bar, and serves as the special editor for the "Inverse Condemnation" and "Impact Fees" chapters of the treatise *Florida Environmental and Land Use Law* (available through www.eluls.org).

Edward H. Ziegler is a professor of law and co-founder and former president of the Rocky Mountain Land Use Institute at the University of Denver College of Law, where he teaches property, land-use planning, and land development and design. He is a frequent speaker and nationally noted scholar on zoning and planning law. Prof. Ziegler has published in professional journals throughout the United States as well as in France, Chile, Colombia, Spain, and Great Britain. His writings, which include the five-volume treatise Rathkopf's *The Law of Zoning and Planning*, are cited and quoted in leading teaching casebooks and widely cited in land-use cases by appellate courts throughout the country. His consulting, research projects, and lectures on land-use planning have ranged from the Port of Dutch Harbor on the Bering Sea and Anchorage, Alaska, to New York City's special zoning districts and Florida's Reedy Creek Improvement District, which manages development of Disney World. He has been involved in research projects or symposia for the Lincoln Institute of Land Policy, The Conservation Foundation, the American Bar Association, the American Planning Association, the Urban Land Institute, the National Association of Home Builders, and the U.S. Environmental Protection Agency. He has also served as a consultant to the U.S. Senate Judiciary and Public Works and the Environment committees on matters related to land use and private property rights. Professor Ziegler is a graduate of the University of Notre Dame, holds a J.D. degree from the University of Kentucky Law School, and received the advanced (LL.M.) degree in public law with highest honors from the National Law Center of George Washington University.

REGULATORY TAKINGS: SETTING OUT THE BASICS AND UNVEILING THE DIFFERENCES

1

THOMAS E. ROBERTS*

§ 1.0 Introduction

Declarations of the intractability, complexity, and obscurity of the doctrine of regulatory takings are common. Solutions—some simple and some complex, some legislative and some judicial—have been suggested, but the complaints remain. This is not surprising or necessarily discouraging, for the issues the law of regulatory takings deals with are some of the most complex and contentious in contemporary America. Intensification of land use to meet the needs of an ever-growing population tests the carrying capacity of the land. Whether these needs are best met by more or less regulation is hotly debated.

We possess fundamentally different perspectives of property in land. Some view land as "things" or "parcels" properly controlled by the individual and used to create wealth.[1] Some view those same parcels of land as interdependent parts of an ecological and social whole, with control by the individual sub-

---

* The material in this chapter is based in part on JULIAN C. JUERGENSMEYER and THOMAS E. ROBERTS, LAND USE PLANNING AND CONTROL LAW, Ch. 10 (1998), and is used with permission of Westgroup.

1

ject to sometimes stringent limitation.[2] These conflicting views result in intense conflict over the extent to which government may affect private property rights for the greater good of society and how the burdens and benefits of regulation should be distributed.

Property rights are protected by the Constitution, but the degree to which they are protected and the degree to which they are limited by the interests of the general public is contested. Some believe that few, if any, limits on private property are justified. For others, private rights are inherently limited to protect the public. While extremists exist at both ends of the continuum, the numbers in those absolutist camps are probably not large. This may be comforting to those who fall in the middle, debating where and how to draw the line. But it may be "pollyanna-ish" to think there is a middle ground. It is perhaps more accurate to think of two factions that are closer to the extremes than they are to the middle.

This book explores the distance between these factions in the context of the law of regulatory takings. It does so by offering the views of writers with divergent views on ten problematical issues that arise frequently in regulatory takings litigation. Many of these issues have recently been before the Court, as, for example, in *Palazzolo v. Rhode Island*,[3] or are pending before the Court in *Tahoe-Sierra Preservation Council, Inc. v. Tahoe Regional Planning Agency*[4] and *McQueen v. South Carolina Department of Health and Environmental Control*.[5]

This introductory chapter offers a background on the basics of regulatory takings law, with the hope that it will be helpful to a fuller understanding of the work that follows. While my personal perspective generally favors the pro-social position on regulation, I attempt to introduce the topic in an objective, value-free manner. I have likely failed in some instances. If my perspective colors the introduction, I apologize. In the essays that follow, however, the authors, for the most part, have different perspectives, half from what I will call the private camp and half from the public camp.

§ 1.1   *Regulatory Takings Basics*[6]

The Takings Clause of the Fifth Amendment provides that private property shall not be "taken for public use without just compensation."[7] Whether—and if so, when—this requirement to pay just compensation when "taking" property should apply to government "regulating" property is the basic issue this book addresses. The physical connotation of the word "take" argues against applying the clause to regulatory impacts. It also seems to be agreed that the founders intended to require compensation only for physical expropriations of property.[8] Yet, as Chief Justice Rehnquist has said, the Court has "not . . . read [the Takings Clause] literally."[9] Most agree that this non-literal interpretation began in 1922 when Justice Holmes said that "if regulation goes too far it will be recognized as a taking."[10]

The claim that a regulation has taken property within the meaning of the Fifth Amendment assumes that the regulation is an otherwise valid exercise of police power and asks that it be converted into an exercise of the power of eminent domain due to its allegedly excessive effect or unwarranted nature. This follows from the fact that the Constitution does not prohibit the taking of property, but calls for a taking to be compensated.

Government normally invokes its eminent domain power by filing a condemnation action against a property owner to establish that the taking is for a public use or purpose and to have just compensation assessed. In contrast to this direct condemnation, the takings issue explored here arises from the consequences of government action with respect to property, unaccompanied by an offer of compensation or an action to condemn. An owner who thinks the action has effected a taking and that compensation ought to be paid has the burden to initiate suit against the government by way of an action in inverse condemnation.[11]

§ 1.1(a) *Physical Takings: The per se* Loretto *Test*

Though we deal here primarily with regulations that may effect takings, physical invasions may also do so. This may occur where a government dam causes flooding of upstream property[12] or where military planes engage in frequent, low-level flights.[13] In the context of land-use regulation, a physical takings issue may arise when a condition attached to a development permit requires that private property be dedicated to public use.

Physical invasions trigger special concern, since the Court treats the right to exclude as the paramount property right. In *Loretto v. Teleprompter Manhattan CATV Corp.*,[14] the Court held that a permanent physical occupation is a per se taking without regard to the strength of the public interest and the overall impact on the property's value. Interpreted literally, *Loretto* raised the issue that conditions imposed in the permitting process that resulted in physical occupations, such as subdivision exactions of land for schools or roads, were per se takings.[15] In *Nollan v. California Coastal Commission*,[16] the Court acknowledged an exception to *Loretto*'s per se test. In *Nollan*, the state coastal commission required the Nollans to deed an easement allowing the public to walk along the beachfront side of their ocean lot in return for permission to build a larger house. A straightforward application of the *Loretto* per se rule would have meant that a taking had occurred in *Nollan* without further inquiry,[17] but the Court said that requiring the easement as a condition for issuing a land-use permit would avoid that conclusion if the state could show that a nexus existed between the effects of the landowner's proposed development and the land that was being exacted for easement use. The nexus was found wanting in *Nollan*, but the principle rescued many land-use controls from the *Loretto* per se rule.[18]

§ 1.1(b)   *When Excessive Regulations Came to Be Recognized as Takings*

In the 19th century, the Court rejected the idea that a regulation could be a taking. In *Mugler v. Kansas*,[19] a brewery owner argued that his property had been taken by a law prohibiting the manufacture of beer. The Court labeled his request for compensation an "inadmissible"[20] interpretation of the Constitution. The position of the Court was that regulations under the police power were not burdened by a requirement of compensation.[21] Exercises of the police power were to be reviewed solely under the substantive due process standard that required the Court to uphold a law if it promoted a legitimate public end in a rational way. If the test was met, that was the end of the matter.

The Court's expansion of the Takings Clause to include regulations is generally viewed as having arisen in the 1922 decision in *Pennsylvania Coal v. Mahon*.[22] A Pennsylvania statute prohibited mining beneath residential areas in such a way as to cause mine subsidence. When a coal company announced its intention to mine under the Mahons' house, they sought an injunction. The coal company claimed the statute was an unconstitutional taking of mineral rights, since it effectively prohibited the company from excavating the coal that it had expressly reserved to itself in conveying the land to the Mahons' predecessor in title.

The Court agreed with the coal company. Writing for the Court, Justice Holmes considered the issue a "question of degree,"[23] and warned that "[w]e are in danger of forgetting that a strong public desire to improve the public condition is not enough to warrant achieving the desire by a shorter cut than the constitutional way of paying for the change."[24] The famous, or perhaps infamous, test he established was that "while property may be regulated to a cert..in extent, if regulation goes too far it will be recognized as a taking."[25] In this case the statute went too far, since it made it commercially impracticable to mine certain coal that had been expressly reserved to advance a purpose that Holmes regarded as predominantly private in nature.

Pennsylvania Coal left numerous problems in its wake; the generality of the "too far" test was one of them. Diminution in value, Holmes said, was one factor to be used to determine how far a regulation could go. However, it was not clear what the diminution was in *Pennsylvania Coal*. The Court also did not say what factors other than diminution in value are relevant. Holmes also did not cite, much less discuss, *Mugler*, leaving its validity unclear and likely extending its life.

Some argue that the decision does not rest on the Takings Clause but on substantive due process grounds, and that it only uses its takings language metaphorically.[26] Since both litigants were private, the entire discussion of the Fifth Amendment Takings Clause, some suggest, may be regarded as dictum.[27] Even treating the case as a takings challenge, the remedy was a denial of an injunction, not compensation. Thus, the issue of the appropriate remedy for a regulatory taking was left hanging until 1987, when the Court held that compensation was the mandatory remedy for regulatory takings.[28]

While the due process test applied in *Mugler* did not consider relevant the degree of loss suffered by the property owner, that factor worked its way into the Court's later statements of the rule. In the 1894 decision of *Lawton v. Steele*,[29] for example, the Court said the validity of a police power regulation depends on whether the measure promotes the public interest by a means reasonably necessary to accomplish the purpose that "is not unduly oppressive upon individuals."[30] The subsequent *Pennsylvania Coal* decision restated the Lawton substantive due process test in takings language.

§ 1.1(c) *Confusion between Substantive Due Process Claims and Takings Claims*

Confusion between substantive due process claims and takings claims exists largely due to the similarity of the tests articulated by the Court. A few years after *Pennsylvania Coal*, the Court decided the landmark case of *Village of Euclid v. Ambler Realty Co.*[31] There, addressing a facial challenge, the Court upheld comprehensive zoning as not violative of the substantive due process guarantee to be free from arbitrary state action. Though the opinion echoed Holmes's idea that the validity of police power measures involve questions of degree, saying that "[t]he line which in this field separates the legitimate from the illegitimate assumption of power is not capable of precise delimitation,"[32] it cited neither the Takings Clause nor *Pennsylvania Coal*.[33]

Two years after *Euclid*, the Court decided another land use case, again failing to cite *Pennsylvania Coal*. In *Nectow v. City of*

Cambridge,[34] the Court looked at zoning as applied to a particular tract and found it invalid on due process grounds. The Court held that the zoning of the tract for residential use did not, under the circumstances, promote the public interest.[35] Despite the lack of reference to the Fifth Amendment in the *Euclid* and *Nectow* opinions, on occasion in recent years the Court has loosely referred to them as takings cases, further confusing the line between substantive due process and takings.[36]

Faced with a regulation alleged to be excessive in its impact on an individual, a court might find that the regulation is unduly onerous and thus void under substantive due process or that it goes "too far" and becomes a taking under *Pennsylvania Coal*, requiring the payment of compensation. Differences in the remedy allowed or mandated and in the standard of review used make the choice critical.[37] Under the due process clause, the remedy may be injunctive relief and/or damages, while just compensation is the sole, but mandatory, remedy under the Takings Clause. Low scrutiny is applied to substantive due process challenges, but, increasingly, higher scrutiny is applied to takings claims.

The apparent choice to sue under the Fifth Amendment or the Fourteenth Amendment may be illusory. The Court has held in other areas that where there is an explicit textual source in the Constitution, it must be used to determine liability rather than generalized notions of substantive due process.[38] If the Fifth Amendment Takings Clause qualifies as sufficiently explicit under this theory, the unduly onerous substantive due process test should be subsumed by it.[39] Given the Court's recognition of the regulatory takings doctrine, there is no justification for a duplicative test under substantive due process.

Substantive due process claims premised on arbitrary state action[40] that allege that an act is an invalid police power control are not duplicative of takings claims and must be distinguished from claims that an action has an unduly onerous economic impact. Though the latter, duplicative claim should fade into obscurity, the former should not, since it is independent from a taking claim. For example, a property owner's complaint that a regulation was adopted solely in response to neighbor prejudices[41] or as retaliation against a developer for seeking judicial review of a city's actions[42] might be held to violate substantive due process due to its arbitrary nature. Lacking legitimate public purposes, such state actions would not be characterized as takings and thus sustainable with the payment of just compensation. Rather, the actions would be invalidated.

Property owners encountering procedural hurdles in pursuing takings claims,[43] may seek alternatives. They may turn to substantive due process, procedural due process, and in some cases, equal protection.[44] State law may also afford relief. Chapters 22 and 23 discuss these options.

§ 1.2   *The* Penn Central *Test*

The modern era of takings law began in 1978 in *Penn Central Transportation Co. v. New York City*.[45] New York City declared Grand Central Station a historic landmark, requiring the owner to seek municipal permission to make changes in the structure. After the designation, Penn Central leased the airspace above the station to a developer who planned to build a 55-story office complex, but the landmark commission denied a certificate of appropriateness. The railroad claimed its inability to build in the airspace was a taking.

The Court admitted that the takings issue was "a problem of considerable difficulty,"[46] and that there was no "'set formula' for determining when 'justice and fairness' require that economic injuries caused by public action be compensated by the government, rather than remain disproportionately concentrated on a few persons."[47] While the Court admitted the test involved "essentially ad hoc, factual inquiries,"[48] it attempted to be more concrete in its analysis than Holmes had been in *Pennsylvania Coal*. It listed three factors for consideration: (1) the economic impact on the claimant, (2) the extent to which the regulation interfered with investment-backed expectations, and (3) the character or extent of the government action.[49]

In weighing these factors, the Court held that the historic preservation ordinance was not a taking because it left the station exactly as it had been. It did not amount to a physical invasion of the property and it did not upset the original investment-backed expectations of the owners. The railroad argued a total loss of use had occurred by focusing on the airspace alone. The Court, however, said the relevant measure was the whole parcel and, with respect to it, the record showed that the railroad was able to earn a reasonable return under its present use. The Court also said there was no proof of loss of all airspace. A smaller tower might be approved and the transferable development rights available to the station owners mitigated the loss.[50]

§ 1.3   *The "Substantially Advances" Test*

§ 1.3(a)   **Agins**

While *Penn Central*'s ad hoc test can be faulted for lack of precision and predictability, the Court further complicated things a few years later in *Agins v. Tiburon*.[51] There the Court framed a takings test as follows:

> [t]he application of a general zoning law to particular property effects a taking if the ordinance does not substantially advance legitimate state interests [citing *Nectow*], or denies an owner economically viable use of his land [citing *Penn Central*].[52]

The Court further explained that "[a]lthough no precise rule determines when property has been taken..., the question necessarily requires a weighing of private and public interests."[53]

The problem with *Agins* is that its first prong relies on *Nectow*, a Fourteenth Amendment substantive due process case, to add a Fifth Amendment constraint on regulations. Commentators disagree,[54] but in my view, the first prong of *Agins*, that the ordinance does not substantially advance legitimate state interests, is an awkward fit in the Fifth Amendment takings inquiry, since it is designed to judge the validity of a law. If a law fails to promote a legitimate end, it is invalid and it makes no sense to proceed to discuss whether compensation is due under the Fifth Amendment.[55] Further, and focusing on the means rather than the ends, it is also unlikely that the *Agins* Court meant that the mere conclusion that a law substantially advances an admittedly valid public interest would save it from being a taking, even if an economically viable use remained.[56] The appropriateness and meaning of the "substantially advancing" test in Fifth Amendment takings cases is further explored in chapters 16 and 17.

§ 1.3(b)   Nollan *and* Dolan

In *Nollan*, the state coastal commission conditioned a building permit on the owner's grant to the public of the right to walk along the beachfront side of the lot on which the rebuilding was to occur. The state-asserted interest was to protect the public's ability to see the beach from the street, to prevent congestion on the beach, and to overcome psychological barriers to the use of the beach resulting from increased shoreline development. The Court had no quarrel with the legitimacy of the state's goals but disagreed that the lateral-access easement along the beachfront would promote them. Stressing the word "substantially" in the *Agins* formula, the Court employed intermediate scrutiny and found that the interests asserted by the state would not have been substantially advanced by the condition imposed. Thus, *Nollan* uses the "substantially advancing" language of *Agins* and *Nectow* to direct the initial focus of a takings challenge to the justification for singling out a property owner to contribute land for public use.

Dolan v. City of Tigard[57] followed *Nollan*. There the owner of a plumbing and electric supply store sought a permit to double the store's size and pave the parking lot. For flood control and traffic management reasons, the city required the owner to convey to it affirmative easements on the portion of her lot lying within the 100-year floodplain adjacent to a creek and on an additional 15-foot strip of land. The latter was for a pedestrian and bicycle path. The two requirements amounted to approximately 10 percent of Dolan's property.

The *Dolan* Court held that once the *Nollan* nexus test is met, the state must show that the extent of the exaction is proportional. The *Dolan* Court agreed that the paving of the parking lot would increase stormwater runoff and exacerbate flooding problems, justifying the city in requiring some mitigation response by the owner. However, it was not clear to the Court why the city asked for an easement permitting the public to use Dolan's floodplain land. Physical access did not seem necessary to achieve the flood control purpose. The Court also agreed that the store's expansion would lead to more traffic, so asking the owner to help the city cope with traffic problems made sense. Yet, the city had required only the pedestrian/bicycle pathway to offset this increased demand. That was not good enough for the Court. The city needed to quantify the traffic increase, at least in some general way, to show that the pathway would offset some of the traffic.

Dolan adopted what it called a rule of "rough proportionality"[58] to set "outer limits" of land-use planning.[59] While the burden is on the government to show a degree of connection, the Court does not demand a "precise mathematical calculation, but [rather] some sort of individualized determination that the required dedication is related both in nature and extent to the impact of the proposed development."[60] Though *Dolan*'s phrasing of "rough proportionality" was new, the Court acknowledged that its test was the same as the dedication test followed by the vast majority of state courts.[61]

The *Nollan* and *Dolan* cases raise several questions. These include whether their tests are to be used for legislatively imposed conditions as well as for adjudicatory ones, whether they apply to regulations that do not cause a physical invasion (such as an impact fee), and, when they apply, what degree of judicial scrutiny is to be used. There are disagreements among the courts and commentators, as chapters 13, 14, and 15 explore in detail.

§ 1.4   The Economic Impact Test: Total and Partial Deprivations

In *Pennsylvania Coal v. Mahon*[62] and *Penn Central Transportation Co. v. City of New York*,[63] the Court treated the economic impact of a regulation as an important, if not primary, factor in determining whether a taking had occurred. Those cases, however, provided little guidance on how much of an impact was tolerable and they left unanswered the question of whether the nuisance-like character of a use justified a total deprivation of economic use.

§ 1.4(a)   *Total Deprivations*

In 1992, the Court established what it called a categorical takings rule in *Lucas v. South Carolina Coastal Council*.[64] The owner of two beachfront lots was unable to build due to the application of a setback rule adopted to deter sand dune loss and beach erosion. Accepting the state trial court's finding that the lots subject to the regulation were valueless, the Court held that where a regulation deprives a property owner of all economically viable use, a taking occurs, unless the state can prove that the regulation does no more to restrict use than what the state courts could do under background principles of property law or the law of private or public nuisance.[65]

The *Lucas* Court's categorical rule is not a rule of absolute liability, but, as is true with the categorical *Loretto* rule regarding permanent physical occupations, it is a burden-switching tool.[66] It means that where a law denies all economically beneficial use, no "case-specific inquiry into the public interest advanced in support of the restraint [occurs]."[67] When the property owner makes the showing of a total deprivation of all economically beneficial use, the burden switches to the government, which, to avoid paying compensation, must show that property or nuisance law justifies the restriction.

In determining whether an economically viable or beneficial use exists, a question arises as to whether the value of the property can be considered. The relationship between use and value is not clear from the caselaw and courts have at times used the terms interchangeably.[68] Land may not have a current beneficial use available, yet may retain real value. Whether there is a constitutionally significant distinction between use and value for the purposes of the per se *Lucas* test is discussed in chapters 18 and 19.

Where a total deprivation of economically beneficial use occurs, the state can insulate itself from paying compensation only if the prohibition "inhere[s] in the title itself, in the restrictions that background principles of the State's law of property and [private or public] nuisance already place upon land ownership."[69] Legislatures cannot impose new limitations on owners that effect total economic deprivations unless the state courts could impose the same limit under the common law. The power of the state courts is not limited to a backward look at what they have held in specific cases pursuant to the common law. Rather, it is the principles, not holdings, of state law that control.

While the *Lucas* opinion makes it clear that the power of the courts under the common law is not fixed,[70] the latitude state courts have to shape their law is limited. The *Lucas* Court warns state courts that they can only engage in "objectively reasonable application[s] of relevant precedents."[71] In one post-*Lucas* case, the Oregon Supreme Court held that the doctrine of custom justified a public right of access on private beach property, precluding the conclusion that a taking had occurred.[72] The Supreme Court allowed that decision to stand.[73] Chapters 6 and 7 explore this matter in detail.

§ 1.4(b) *Partial Deprivations*

If a regulation's economic effect is less than total, a multifactor balancing test derived from *Penn Central* and *Agins* is used.[74] In this case, the burden of proof is on the property owner.[75] In balancing the state interest against the private loss, partial deprivation cases differ from the categorical takings rules of *Loretto* and *Lucas*, where the inquiry into the public interest advanced arises only by way of defense.[76] With partial deprivation cases, the inquiry into the public interest occurs as part of the case in chief.

Penn Central listed the character of the government action as one of three factors to examine.[77] In *Agins*, the Court explained that "[a]lthough no precise rule determines when property has been taken..., the question necessarily requires a weighing of private and public interests."[78] The governmental action factor requires an assessment of the "purpose and importance of the public interest,"[79] which then must be weighed against the loss.[80] Chapters 8, 9, and 10 cover the takings implications of partial deprivations of value.

§ 1.5 *Investment-Backed Expectations*

There is a dispute with respect to the role and meaning of reasonable expectations in takings claims. The Court first expressly used the "distinct investment-backed expectations" term in *Penn Central*.[81] It traced the concept to *Pennsylvania Coal*, where the state's anti-subsidence statute abrogated an express contractual reservation of the right to remove coal free from liability for damage to the surface.[82] The fact that *Pennsylvania Coal* was a private dispute where the surface owner bought the land with notice of the prior severance of the mineral rights suggests a high degree of expectation on both sides of the contract that the coal could be removed without liability for surface damage.[83]

In *Penn Central*, the Court found that the railroad's belief that it could use the airspace did not qualify as a reasonable or distinct investment-backed expectation. It was sufficient for takings purposes, held the Court, that the railroad's primary expectation of using Grand Central Station as a railroad terminal and office building, established by 65 years of use, was unaffected by the landmark designation.[84]

In *Palazzolo v. Rhode Island*,[85] the Court held that the mere transfer of title will not defeat a *Lucas* categorical takings claim based on restrictions that existed at the time of acquisition of title. Prior to *Palazzolo*, a number of courts[86] had held to the contrary based on a reading of *Lucas*, which, *Palazzolo* tells us, was mistaken.

These issues are explored in chapters 2 and 3. Chapter 8 contains a detailed statement of the facts, the state court decision, and the Supreme Court's opinions.

§ 1.6   Defining the Unit of Property: Segmentation

The extent of economic impact of a regulation depends on the unit of property used by a court to measure the loss. The choice of a broad or narrow approach will often determine the outcome. Choosing only the portion of land affected by a regulation increases the prospects of a total diminution in value. That, in turn, invokes the *Lucas* categorical takings rule. The concept of property as a bundle of rights does not necessarily translate into a requirement that each strand in the bundle be regarded as separate for the purposes of the Fifth Amendment. Defining the relevant unit of property is a process bound up with the overall test of when "fairness and justice" require that compensation be paid and is particularly tied to assessing an owner's investment-backed expectations.[87]

In the modern takings era, the Court has used a broad definition for regulatory takings cases involving economic impact.[88] In *Penn Central*, the railroad claimed a total economic loss of its airspace above Grand Central Station as a result of the landmark designation. The railroad, however, was wrong to limit the focus to the airspace above the terminal, for, as the Court said, "'[t]aking' jurisprudence does not divide a single parcel into discrete segments, [but] focuses on the nature and extent of the interference in the parcel as a whole."[89] Viewing the whole parcel, the loss of the airspace still left the railroad with a reasonable use. Since *Penn Central*, the Court has fairly consistently used a broad or whole-parcel approach in both real and personal property cases,[90] though not without dissent.[91]

In recent years property owners have paid increased attention to the segmentation issue, hoping to take advantage of the categorical *Lucas* rule and avoid the balancing test of *Agins* and *Penn Central*. Thus, they have asked courts to adopt the position that the relevant parcel is solely the land for which the permit is sought. The lower courts, however, have refused to do so.[92] Instead, in most cases, the courts have examined the expectations of the owner by reference to the whole parcel.[93] However, the Court in *Palazzolo* reminds us that the issue is a "difficult, persisting question," and that the Court has "expressed some discomfort" with the whole-parcel approach.[94] Chapters 4 and 5 explore the differing views on the subject.

§ 1.7 *Temporal Segmentation: Moratoria*

Interim development controls that may temporarily freeze land use activities raise the segmentation issue in the temporal context. The general rule is that one is guaranteed a reasonable use over a reasonable period of time, and that the mere loss of the present right to use land is not a taking.[95] Under a segmented view, some have argued that a temporary denial of all use is a taking of the present right to use property. This notion was generated in part by a statement of the Court in *First English Evangelical Church v. County of Los Angeles*[96] to the effect that temporary takings that deny all use are like permanent takings. The holding of *First English* was limited:

> We merely hold that where a government's activities have already worked a taking of all use of property, no subsequent action by the government can relieve it of the duty to provide compensation.[97]

On the one hand, the Court, by requiring compensation for the period of time that the regulation effected a taking, refused to accept a broad temporal view that present and future use rights could be joined to deny compensation.[98] On the other hand and at the other end of the time line, the Court suggested that property owners must tolerate normal delays in the land use permitting process without compensation.[99] Thus, the total loss of a right to use the land during the period of reasonable delay is not compensable.

Since *First English*, a number of courts have rejected the narrow severance argument in dealing with moratoria as takings.[100] Yet, the issue of moratoria and temporary takings continues to pose problems, as evidenced in the recent opinion of the Ninth Circuit in *Tahoe-Sierra Preservation Council, Inc. v. Tahoe Regional Planning Agency*.[101] The issue is addressed in chapters 11 and 12.

§ 1.8   Ripeness and Forum Selection

Williamson County Regional Planning Commission v. Hamilton Bank of Johnson City[102] and *First English Evangelical Lutheran Church of Glendale v. County of Los Angeles*[103] impose ripeness and forum selection requirements on Fifth Amendment takings claims.[104] In *Williamson County*, the Court said that an as-applied takings claim is premature until the "government entity charged with implementing the regulation has reached a final decision."[105] Physical takings claims are not subject to the final decision requirement, since the physical invasion itself establishes what has been taken.[106] Likewise, a property owner making a facial takings claim is not subject to the final decision rule, since, by definition, the mere enactment of the law, and not its application, takes the property.[107]

Williamson County also held that takings claims are subject to the requirement that the property owner seek compensation from the state by way of an action in inverse condemnation.[108] The initial impact of this requirement was limited, since, at that time, there were several states that did not have a compensation remedy. In 1987, however, the Court held in *First English*[109] that the self-executing nature of the Fifth Amendment required a compensation remedy. Since a state is constitutionally obligated to have a compensation remedy,[110] the only question is whether the remedy is adequate. In almost all cases it is.[111]

Once a property owner has pursued the compensation remedy, the law of claim and issue preclusion will usually preclude a Fifth Amendment claim from being maintained in federal court. Adjudication of the claim in state court bars a subsequent suit in federal court under the full faith and credit statute.[112] Collateral attack of the state court judgment is not available in federal district court. A property owner who is dissatisfied with the results obtained from the state court is limited to appealing directly to the U.S. Supreme Court. While there is disagreement over whether the action pursued in state court is a federal or state-based claim, under even the latter view, once litigated, rules of issue preclusion likely will bar a suit in federal court on the federal claim, since the issues being tried in state court would be the same. Chapters 20 and 21 contain detailed discussions of ripeness.

§ 1.9   Conclusion

The essays that follow explore in depth the areas of controversy noted above. Whether one view among the varying views will dominate remains to be seen. Also, whether one view ought to dominate is a question that proponents of each view should ask themselves. Minimizing public rights may impair our resources, upsetting critical ecological balances. And yet some contend that individual ownership does a better job of conserving resources.[113] Minimizing private rights may mean destabilizing investment in land[114] and eroding individual liberties.[115] And yet maximizing private rights may cause further inequality of wealth.[116] Perhaps, "in a democratic society the existence of multiple ethics must be accepted."[117]

The coexistence of these conflicting ethics makes it difficult to have predictable rules of law. One hope is that the chapters that follow will unearth areas of common ground.

Notes

1. As Justice Scalia approvingly quoted Lord Coke "'For what is land but the profits thereof'" Lucas v. South Carolina Coastal Council, 505 U.S. 1003 (1992). *See also* RICHARD A. EPSTEIN, TAKINGS: PRIVATE PROPERTY AND THE POWER OF EMINENT DOMAIN (1985).

2. *See* Fred Bosselman, *Four Land Ethics: Order, Reform, Responsibility, Opportunity*, 24 ENVTL. LAW 1429 (1994); Robert C. Ellickson, *Property in Land*, 102 YALE L.J. 1315 (1993).

3. 121 S. Ct. 2448 (2001).

4. 216 F.3d 764, 780 n.22 (9th Cir. 2000), *rehearing en banc denied*, 228 F.3d 998 (9th Cir. 2000), *cert. granted*, 2001 WL 69237.

5. 340 S.C. 65, 530 S.E.2d 628 (2000), *cert. granted and case remanded* for reconsideration in light of *Palazzolo*, 2001 WL 726265, June 29, 2001.

6. Several authors of this book have one and multivolume treatises that include detailed coverage of, or deal exclusively with, regulatory takings. *See* JULIAN C. JUERGENSMEYER & THOMAS E. ROBERTS, LAND USE PLANNING AND CONTROL LAW (1998); DANIEL R. MANDELKER, LAND USE LAW (4th ed. 1997); DOUGLAS W. KMIEC, ZONING AND PLANNING DESKBOOK (2d ed. 2001); EDWARD H. ZIEGLER, JR., RATHKOPF'S THE LAW OF ZONING AND PLANNING (4th ed. rev. 1993 CLARK BOARDMAN CALLAGHAN) (5 volumes); STEVEN J. EAGLE, REGULATORY TAKINGS (2d ed. 2001); DOUGLAS T. KENDALL, TIMOTHY J. DOWLING & ANDREW W. SCHWARTZ, TAKINGS LITIGATION HANDBOOK (2000); and ROBERT MELTZ, DWIGHT H. MERRIAM, & RICHARD M. FRANK, THE TAKINGS ISSUE (1999). With a special focus on California, *see* DANIEL J. CURTIN & CECILY T. TALBERT, CURTIN'S CALIFORNIA LAND USE AND PLANNING LAW (21st ed. 2001).

7. U.S. CONST. amend. V. The takings guarantee applies to the states through the Fourteenth Amendment's due process requirement. Chicago, B. & Q. R.R. Co. v. Chicago, 166 U.S. 226, 235-41 (1897).

8. *See* Lucas v. South Carolina Coastal Council, 505 U.S. 1003, 1015 n.15 (1992).

9. Penn Central Transportation Co. v. New York City, 438 U.S. 104, 142 (1978) (Rehnquist, J., dissenting), *rehearing denied,* 439 U.S. 883 (1978).

10. Pennsylvania Coal v. Mahon, 260 U.S. 393, 415 (1922).

11. *See* United States v. Clarke, 445 U.S. 253 (1980).

12. Pumpelly v. Green Bay Co, 80 U.S. (13 Wall.) 166 (1871).

13. United States v. Causby, 328 U.S. 256 (1946).

14. 458 U.S. 419 (1982).

15. The *Loretto* Court rejected the argument that the cable installations were valid as conditions for residentially leased property. 458 U.S. at 439 n.17.

16. 483 U.S. 825 (1987).

17. The Nollans and amici in the *Nollan* case argued that *Loretto* controlled, rendering the condition a per se taking. The Court rejected this. *See* Gilbert L. Finnell, Jr., *Public Access to Coastal Public Property: Judicial Theories and the Taking Issue,* 67 N.C. L. Rev. 627, 665 n.293 (1989).

18. Sparks v. Douglas County, 72 Wash. App. 55, 863 P. 2d 142, 144 (1993) (invasions of property, such as required dedications, usually are takings under *Loretto,* but permission to develop land may be conditioned on the owner's agreement to dedicate a portion of his property to public use if the regulatory exaction reasonably prevents or compensates for adverse public impacts of the proposed development).

19. 123 U.S. 623 (1887).

20. *Id.* at 664.

21. Fred Bosselman, David L. Callies, and John Banta, *The Taking Issue* 120 (1973).

22. 260 U.S. 393 (1922). The birthdate of the regulatory takings doctrine is debated. Perhaps it was earlier. Professor Ely notes that the Court had intimated that regulations could become takings before 1922. *See* James W. Ely, Jr., *The Fuller Court and Takings Jurisprudence,* 1996 J. Sup. Ct. History, vol. II at 120. Then again, perhaps it was later. Professor Brauneis notes some problems with viewing *Pennsylvania Coal* itself s a taking case. *See* Robert Brauneis, *The Foundation of Our "Regulatory Takings" Jurisprudence: The Myth and Meaning of Justice Holmes's Opinion in Pennsylvania Coal v. Mahon,* 106 Yale L.J. 613 (1996).

23. *Pennsylvania Coal,* 260 U.S. at 415.

24. *Id.* at 416.

25. *Id.*

26. *See* Norman Williams, Jr., et. al, *The White River Junctions Manifesto,* 9 Vt. L. Rev. 193, 208-14 (1984).

27. *Id.* at 209-10.

28. 482 U.S. 304 (1987).

29. 152 U.S. 133 (1894).

30. 152 U.S. at 137 (1894).

31. 272 U.S. 365 (1926).

32. *Id.* at 387.

33. The Court's failure hardly seems like oversight, since the district court in *Euclid* did speak to the takings issue. 297 F. Supp. 307, 310–12 (N.D. Ohio 1924).

34. 277 U.S. 183 (1928).

35. *Id.* at 188.

36. The Court has referred to the 75 percent diminution in value in *Euclid* as evidence of how far a regulation can go without being a taking. Concrete Pipe and Products of California, Inc. v. Construction Laborers Pension Trust for Southern California, 508 U.S.

602, 646 (1993); Lucas v. South Carolina Coastal Council, 505 U.S. 1003 (Stevens, J., dissenting) (1992); Penn Central Transp. Co. v. City of New York, 438 U.S. 104, 131 (1978). Justice Stevens speaks of *Euclid* as fusing due process and takings in *Moore v. City of East Cleveland*, 431 U.S. 494 (1977).

37. Eide v. Sarasota County, 908 F.2d 716 (11th Cir. 1988).

38. Whitley v. Albers, 475 U.S. 312 (1986); Graham v. Connor, 490 U.S. 386 (1989).

39. *See* Armendariz v. Penman, 75 F.3d 1311 (9th Cir. 1996) (issue of a taking for a private purpose must be brought under the Fifth Amendment, not substantive due process). Several other cases discuss the issue in land use matters, without clear resolution. Bickerstaff Clay Product Co., Inc. v. Harris County, 89 F.3d 1481 (11th Cir. 1996) (finding due process claim with respect to public use subsumed by the Fifth Amendment); Miller v. Campbell County, 945 F.2d 348 (10th Cir. 1991); Pearson v. City of Grand Blanc, 961 F.2d 1211 (6th Cir. 1992). *See generally* Thomas E. Roberts & Thomas C. Shearer, *Land-Use Litigation: Takings and Due Process Claims,* 24 URB. LAW. 833, 836 (1992).

40. *See, e.g.*, Village of Euclid v. Ambler Realty Co., 272 U.S. 365 (1926); Nectow v. Cambridge, 277 U.S. 183 (1928); Village of Belle Terre v. Boraas, 416 U.S. 1 (1974); and Moore v. City of East Cleveland, 431 U.S. 494 (1977).

41. Marks v. City of Chesapeake, 883 F.2d 308 (4th Cir. 1989). *But see* Church of Jesus Christ of Latter-Day Saints v. Jefferson County, 721 F. Supp. 1212 (N.D. Ala. 1989).

42. Carr v. Town of Dewey, 730 F. Supp. 591 (D. Del. 1990). *But see* Nestor Colon Medina & Sucesores, Inc. v. Custodio, 964 F.2d 32 (1st Cir. 1992) (retaliation possibly First Amendment violation, but not a violation of substantive due process).

43. *See* Thomas E. Roberts, *Procedural Implications of Williamson County/First English in Regulatory Takings Litigation: Herein of Reservations, Removal, Diversity, Supplemental Jurisdiction, Rooker-Feldman, and Res Judicata,* 31 ENVTL. L. RPTR. 10353 (April 2001).

44. *See, e.g.*, Village of Willowbrook v. Olech, 120 S. Ct. 1073 (2000).

45. 438 U.S. 104 (1978).

46. *Id.* at 123.

47. *Id.* at 124.

48. *Id.*

49. *Id.*

50. *Id.* at 137.

51. 447 U.S. 255 (1980).

52. *Id.* at 260. The seeds for this use of *Nectow* were sown in *Penn Central.* 438 U.S. at 127.

53. 447 U.S. 255, 260 (1980). Further reflecting the mixed confusion, the Court added that the "seminal decision in *Euclid v. Ambler Co.* is illustrative. In that case, the landowner challenged the constitutionality of a municipal ordinance that restricted commercial development of his property. Despite alleged diminution in value of the owner's land, the Court held that the zoning laws were facially constitutional. They bore a substantial relationship to the public welfare, and their enactment inflicted no irreparable injury upon the landowner. " *Id.*

54. *See infra* chapters 16 and 17.

55. *See* Estate and Heirs of Sanchez v. County of Bernaillo, 120 N.M. 395, 398, 902 P. 2d 550, 553 (1995), interpreting the state constitution to avoid a literal reading of its version of the *Agins* test. It held that a taking is not established by simply showing that a

regulation is not reasonably related to a proper purpose. If the case involves no appropriation, it does not implicate the Fifth Amendment unless its significantly affects beneficial
use. Such a regulation may be invalid, but it is not a taking. 902 P. 2d at 552. *See also*
Jarold S. Kayden, *Land Use Regulations, Rationality, and Judicial Review: The RSVP in
the Nollan Invitation* (Part I), 23 URB. LAW. 301, 314 (1991).

56. *See* Del Oro Hills v. City of Oceanside, 31 Cal. App. 4th 1060, 37 Cal. Rptr. 2d
677, 686 (1995), *cert. denied* 116 S. Ct. 86 (1995).

57. 512 U.S. 374 (1994).

58. *Id.* at 391.

59. *Id.* at 395.

60. *Id.* at 395.

61. 515 U.S. at 390, n.7.

62. 260 U.S. 393, 415 (1922).

63. 438 U.S. 104 (1978).

64. 505 U.S. 1003 (1992).

65. 505 U.S. at 1027.

66. In *Nollan*, the Court makes it clear that *Loretto* is not absolute and that a permanent
physical occupation can avoid the finding of a taking if it meets the nexus test.

67. *Lucas*, 505 U.S. at 1015.

68. Tahoe-Sierra Preservation Council, Inc. v. Tahoe Regional Planning Agency, 216
F.3d 764, 780 n.22 (9th Cir. 2000), *rehearing en banc denied*, 228 F.3d 998 (9th Cir.
2000), *cert. granted*, 2001 WL 69237.

69. 505 U.S. at 1029.

70. Thus, the Court acknowledges that new prohibitions may be imposed if deemed
necessary by virtue of changed circumstances or new knowledge. 505 U.S. at 1030-31
(citing RESTATEMENT SECOND OF TORTS).

71. *Lucas*, 505 U.S. at 1032 n.18.

72. Stevens v. City of Cannon Beach, 317 Or. 131, 854 P. 2d 449 (1993), *cert. denied*,
510 U.S. 1207 (1994). *See* David J. Bederman, *The Curious Resurrection of Custom:
Beach Access and Judicial Takings*, 96 COLUM. L. REV. 1375 (1996). The doctrine of
custom was recognized in State ex. rel Thorton v. Hay, 254 Or. 854, 461 P. 2d 671 (1969).

73. Though not without dissent. *See* Stevens v. City of Cannon Beach, 317 Or. 131,
854 P. 2d 449 (1993), *cert. denied*, 510 U.S. 1207 (1994).

74. *Lucas*, 505 U.S. 1003, 1015.

75. Florida Rock Ind., Inc. v. United States, 18 F.3d 1560 (Fed. Cir. 1994).

76. *Loretto*, 458 U.S. 419, 440 (1982) (noting the "multifactor inquiry generally
applicable to nonpossessory governmental activity" is not affected by its decision).

77. *Penn Central*, 438 U.S. at 124. The other two were the economic impact on the
claimant and the extent to which the regulation interfered with investment-backed expectations. *See* Kavanau v. Santa Monica Rent Control Bd., 16 Cal. 4th 761, 941 P. 2d 851,
860, 66 Cal. Rptr. 2d 672, 681 (1997) (listing ten factors).

78. 447 U.S. 255, 260 (1980).

79. Loveladies Harbor, Inc. v. United States, 28 F.3d 1171, 1176 (Fed. Cir. 1994). If
a physical invasion occurs, a taking is more likely to be found.

80. Bernardsville Quarry, Inc. v. Borough of Bernardsville, 129 N.J. 221, 608 A. 2d
1377 (1992) ("whether a regulatory measure effectuates the taking of property requires a
multifactor balancing test that serves to weigh the public interest in enacting the regulation
against private property interests affected by it").

81. 438 U.S. at 124-25.

82. *Id.* at 129 (citing *Pennsylvania Coal*, 260 U.S. 393, 414 1922)).

83. Frank Michelman, *Property, Utility, and Fairness: Comments on the Ethical Foundations of "Just Compensation" Law*, 80 Harv. L. Rev. 1165, 1212 (1967).

84. 438 U.S. 104, 135-37 (1978).

85. 121 S. Ct. 2448 (2001).

86. City of Virginia Beach v. Bell, 498 S. E. 2d 414 (1998); Gazza v. New York State Dept. of Environmental Conservation, 89 N.Y. 2d 603, 679 N.E. 2d 1035, 657 N.Y.S. 2d 555, *cert. denied* 118 S. Ct. 58 (1997); Wheeler v. City of Wayzata, 511 N.W. 2d 39 (Minn. App. 1994); M & J Coal Co. v. United States, 47 F.3d 1148, 1153 (Fed. Cir. 1995); Grant v. South Carolina Coastal Council, 461 S. E. 2d 388 (S. C. 1995); Hunziker v. State of Iowa, 519 N.W. 2d 367 (Iowa 1994), *cert. denied*, 514 U.S. 1003 (1994); Ward v. Harding, 860 S.W. 2d 280 (Ky. 1993), cert. denied, 510 U.S. 1177, 114 S. Ct. 1218, 127 L. Ed. 2d 564 (1994); Kudloff v. City of Billings, 860 P.2d 140 (Mont. 1993). *But see* Vatalaro v. Dept. of Envtl. Regulation, 601 So. 2d 1223 (Fla. App. 1992), *review denied*, 613 So. 2d 3 (Fla. 1992). In *Applegate v. United States*, 35 Fed. Cl. 406 (1996), the court said that the rule of *Lucas* that a buyer assumes ownership subject to regulatory scheme in effect at time of purchase applies only to regulatory takings, not physical takings.

87. Lucas v. South Carolina Coastal Council, 505 U.S. 1003, 1016 n.7 (1992).

88. A narrow view is used for physical invasions like *Loretto* that involve a loss of the right to exclude.

89. 438 U.S. at 130-31.

90. Andrus v. Allard, 444 U.S. 51 (1979) (personal property); Keystone Bituminous Coal Ass'n v. De Benedictis, 480 U.S. 470 (1987) (real property); Concrete Pipe and Products of California, Inc. v. Construction Laborers Pension Trust, 508 U.S. 602 (1993) (personal property).

91. *See* the dissenting opinions in *Penn Central* and *Keystone*.

92. Loveladies Harbor, Inc. v. United States, 28 F.3d 1171, 1182 (Fed. Cir. 1994).

93. Corn v. City of Lauderdale Lakes, 95 F.3d 1066 (11th Cir. 1996); Zealy v. City of Waukesha, 201 Wis. 2d 365, 548 N.W. 2d 528 (1996); Quirk v. Town of New Boston, 140 N.H. 124, 663 A. 2d 1328, 1332 (1995) (agreeing with *Loveladies* that affected portion may at times be used, but generally whole tract is to be the focus); Clajon Production Corp. v. Petera, 70 F.3d 1566 (10th Cir. 1995); Presbytery of Seattle v. King County, 114 Wash. 2d 320, 787 P. 2d 907, *cert. denied*, 111 S. Ct. 284 (1990); Cheyenne Airport Bd. v. Rogers, 707 P. 2d 717 (Wyo. 1987); Broadwater Farms Joint Venture v. United States, 35 Fed. Cl. 232 (1996) (loss of 12 of 27 lots as result of regulatory action not compensable taking); *but see* Clem v. Chrisole, Inc., 548 N.E. 2d 1180 (Ind. App. 1990).

94. 121 S. Ct. at 2465.

95. *See* Williams v. City of Central, 907 P. 2d 701 (Colo. App. 1995); Woodbury Place Partners v. City of Woodbury, 492 N.W. 2d 258 (Minn. App. 1992); McCutchan Estates Corp. v. Evansville Vanderburgh County Airport Auth. Dist., 580 N.E. 2d 339 (Ind. App. 1991), *cert. denied* 488 U.S. 823 (1988); Dufau v. United States, 22 Cl. Ct. 156 (1990) aff'd without opinion, 940 F.2d 677 (Fed. Cir. 1991); Guinnane v. City & County of San Francisco, 197 Cal. App. 3d 862, 241 Cal. Rptr. 787 (1987).

96. 482 U.S. 304, 318 (1987).

97. *Id.* at 321.

98. *First English* generated some confusion by saying that temporary takings that deny all use were like permanent takings. However, when the Court made that analogy, it was not addressing the segmentation issue but the remedy issue.

99. *See* Frank Michelman, *Takings*, 1987, 88 Colum. L. Rev. 1600, 1621 (1988) and

Thomas E. Roberts, "Zoning Moratoria as Regulatory Takings," in *Recent Developments in Environmental Preservation and the Rights of Property Owners*, 20 URB. LAW. 969, 1012, 1017 (eds. Bozung and Alessi). *See also* Margaret J. Radin, *The Liberal Conception of Property: Cross Currents in the Jurisprudence of Takings*, 88 COL. L. REV. 1667, 1675-76 (1988), questioning whether *First English* endorses the severance of the period of time when use is lost by an interim ordinance.

100. *See* cases cited in note 96 *supra.*

102. 216 F.3d 764 (9th Cir. 2000), *rehearing en banc denied,* 228 F.3d 998 (9th Cir. 2000), *pet. for cert. filed,* 69 U.S. L. W. 3505 (Jan. 18, 2001) (No. 001167).

102. 473 U.S. 172 (1985).

103. 482 U.S. 304.

104. Suits brought under the due process and equal protection clauses are generally subject to the final decision rule described below, but not the compensation rule. Thomas E. Roberts, *Ripeness and Forum Selection in Fifth Amendment Takings Litigation,* 11 J. LAND USE & ENVTL. L. 37, 68 (1995); Jeffrey Lyman, *Finality Ripeness in Federal Land Use Cases from Hamilton Bank* to *Lucas,* 9 J. LAND USE & ENVTL. L. 101, 127 (1993).

105. 473 U.S. 172, 186 (1985).

106. Sinaloa Lake Owners Ass'n v. City of Simi Valley, 882 F.2d 1398, 1402 (9th Cir. 1989), *cert. denied,* 494 U.S. 1016 (1990). *But see* Harris v. City of Wichita, 862 F. Supp. 287, 291 (D. Kan. 1994) (stating in dicta that law is unclear).

107. Yee v. City of Escondido, 503 U.S. 519 (1992). *See also* Galbraith v. City of Anderson, 627 N.E. 2d 850 (Ind. App. 1994).

108. *See* Southern Pacific Transportation Co. v. City of Los Angeles, 922 F.2d 498, 505 (9th Cir. 1990). There is some dispute. *See, e.g.,* Christensen v. Yolo County, 995 F.2d 161 (9th Cir. 1993) (court assumes, without discussion, that facial claim is ripe). In *Adamson Companies v. City of Malibu,* 854 F. Supp. 1476 (C.D. Cal. 1994), the court found a facial takings claim ripe in federal court without prong two having been met but did so by mistakenly relying on *Yee v. City of Escondido,* 503 U.S. 519 (1992). In *Yee,* the Court heard a facial takings claim and noted that it was not subject to prong one finality. The Court did not address prong two, which in fact had been met.

109. 482 U.S. 304 (1987). Prior to *First English,* some state courts, notably Florida, New York, and California, rejected money damages as possible relief for regulatory takings.

110. *See* Carson Harbor Village v. City of Carson, 37 F.3d 468, 474 (9th Cir. 1994); Tari v. Collier County, 846 F. Supp. 973, 976 (M.D. Fla. 1994).

111. *See* Thomas E. Roberts, *Procedural Implications of Williamson County/First English in Regulatory Takings Litigation: Herein of Reservations, Removal, Diversity, Supplemental Jurisdiction, Rooker-Feldman, and Res Judicata,* 31 ENVTL. L. RPTR. 10,353 (April 2001).

112. 28 U.S. C. § 1738. See Dodd v. Hood County, 136 F.3d 1219 (9th Cir. 1998) and Roberts, *supra* note 112.

113. Robert C. Ellickson, *Liberty, Property, and Environmental Ethics,* 21 Eco. L. Q. 397 (1994).

114. *See* Carol M. Rose, *A Dozen Propositions on Private Property, Public Rights, and the New Takings Legislation,* 53 WASH. & LEE L. REV. 265, 297 (1996).

115. Robert C. Ellickson, *Liberty, Property, and Environmental Ethics,* 21 Eco. L. Q. 397 (1994).

116. *Id.*

117. Bosselman, *supra* note 3 at 1511.

THE NOTICE RULE IN INVESTMENT-BACKED EXPECTATIONS

2

DANIEL R. MANDELKER

§ 2.0   Introduction

A careless[1] introduction of four puzzling words brought a new confusion to takings law that time has only made worse. In *Penn Central Transportation Co. v. United States,*[2] Justice Brennan added frustration of "distinct investment-backed expectations"[3] as one of several factors courts should consider in land use takings cases. The Court did not use this phrase before, and it implied a new support for landowner takings claims.

This hope has not materialized, and the investment-backed expectations factor has become, instead, a shield for government that protects land use regulations from the Takings Clause. This chapter first discusses the Supreme Court's interpretation of investment-backed expectations in takings cases, and how a notice rule it adopted can defeat takings claims.[4] It then discusses federal court cases that applied the notice rule and how Supreme Court's most recent takings decision might change the treatment of investment-backed expectations takings cases.

§ 2.1   The Origins and Elaboration of the Investment-Backed Expectations Takings Factor in the Supreme Court

§ 2.1(a)   Penn Central: *Introducing the Idea*

The *Penn Central* case, in which the Court adopted the investment-backed expectations takings factor, arose when New York City declared Grand Central Terminal a historic landmark and rejected a proposal to construct a high-rise office building in airspace over the terminal. The Grand Central Station owners claimed a facial and as-applied taking. Justice Brennan disagreed, and introduced the investment-backed expectations factor to help explain the Takings Clause. After noting the Court did not have a "set formula" for deciding takings cases, that "justice and fairness" determine when a taking occurs, and that the application of the Takings Clause depends on the circumstances of each case, he continued:

> In engaging in these essentially ad hoc, factual inquiries, the Court's decisions have identified several factors that have particular significance. The economic impact of the regulation on the claimant and, particularly, the extent to which the regulation has interfered with distinct investment-backed expectations are, of course, relevant considerations. So, too, is the character of the governmental action.[5]

He added that a taking is found more readily when there is a physical invasion rather than "some public program adjusting the benefits and burdens of economic life to promote the common good," a clear suggestion that courts should be less willing to find a taking when regulations restrict the use of land.[6]

Justice Brennan illustrated the investment-backed expectations taking factor by discussing *Pennsylvania Coal Co. v. Mahon*,[7] which was a landmark Supreme Court takings case authored by Justice Holmes. Though Justice Brennan said that *Pennsylvania Coal* was "the leading case" for the investment-backed expectations proposition,[8] this phrase does not appear in that decision, and there is no indication that Holmes intended to introduce it. In *Pennsylvania Coal*, a coal company sold surface rights to property on which a dwelling was constructed but expressly reserved the subsurface right to mine coal. Pennsylvania later adopted a statute prohibiting coal mining that caused residential dwellings to subside. Suit was brought by the coal company against a property owner whose conveyance included this restriction. As Justice Brennan summarized the *Pennsylvania Coal* decision, a taking occurred because the statute "made it commercially impracticable to mine the coal" and "had nearly the same effect as the complete destruction of the property rights" the coal company reserved.[9]

Justice Brennan's reliance on *Pennsylvania Coal* to illustrate the investment-backed expectations taking factor suggests he would apply it only if a regulation extinguished a divisible property interest, at least when a formal deed reservation had created that interest. This conclusion is supported by his rejection of a segmentation rule for determining when a taking occurs. He stated:

> "[T]aking" jurisprudence does not divide a single parcel into discrete segments and attempt to determine whether rights in a particular segment have been entirely abrogated.[10]

This statement appears to mean that some prior, and presumably formal, division of property must occur before a separate property interest can be the basis for a takings claim.

Justice Brennan further limited the investment-backed expectations takings factor by holding that landowners do not have expectations in the right to develop land:

> [T]he submission that [Penn Central and its lessee] may establish a "taking" simply by showing that they have been denied the ability to exploit a property interest they heretofore had believed was available for development is quite simply untenable.[11]

This statement is a little puzzling. Recall that Justice Brennan also held that the owners of Grand Central Terminal did not have a property interest in the airspace they wanted to "exploit." Since this was so, any beliefs they held about the right to develop that airspace should have been irrelevant. Another interpretation is that Justice Brennan meant the right to develop land is a property right that landowners cannot exploit, whether it is airspace or some other type of property. If this explanation is correct, the exploitation rule could write the Takings Clause out of the Constitution. A landowner's claim that she has been denied the right to develop land is at the heart of every takings case.

Justice Brennan put another twist on the exploitation theory in a holding that reflects the facts in *Penn Central* and the admitted profitable use as a terminal. In a reference to this use, he held the landmark law did not interfere with the "primary expectation concerning the use of the parcel" as a railroad terminal.[12] This holding would clearly apply in other situations where a land-owner has a profitable existing use of land, and could eliminate many takings claims. For example, if a developer buys profitable agricultural land zoned at a low residential density and brings a takings claim against this zoning, a court could find she did not have investment-backed expectations because the "primary ex-pectation" concerning the property was its use for agricultural purposes.[13]

The introduction of investment-backed expectations in *Penn Central* thus appears as a puzzling contribution to takings law. Though this takings factor would seem to enhance the protection of property interests, most of Justice Brennan's opinion reduced its importance. Rather than indicating how landowners can use this takings factor to prove takings claims, he suggested ways in which government could use it as a defense. He did not at this time, however, introduce the idea that notice of a land use regu-lation defeats investment-backed expectations. Instead, he intro-duced a finely nuanced set of rules that courts were told to use to decide these claims. Later Supreme Court and lower court cases ignored these nuanced explanations and concentrated, instead, on a notice rule the Court introduced later.

§ 2.1(b) Kirby: *Foreseeability*

Penn Central is best explained as a case where the property owner did not have investment-backed expectations because it already had a productive use of the property. Justice Brennan suggested there might also be a failure of investment-backed expectations when a landowner planned to develop unimproved land, but that was not the case before the Court.

This problem arose in a different but analogous setting in a little-known case, *Kirby Forest Industries, Inc v. United States*.[14] The government filed a condemnation complaint and a notice of lis pendens to take unimproved land for a park. The landowner claimed these actions amounted to a taking because they "had the effect" of preventing it from making any profitable use of the land or from selling it to another private party.

The Court turned to its land use cases for its decision. It noted a zoning ordinance would be a taking if it deprived a landowner of all "economically viable" use of his land,[15] and acknowledged that "under some circumstances" a land use regulation that "se-verely interfered" with a landowner's "'distinct investment-backed expectations' might be a taking."[16] It then discussed the "prin-ciple" underlying "this doctrine." This principle, it said, was an exception to the rule that most governmental burdens must be accepted as part of the advantage of living in a civilized community. However, some are so substantial and unforeseeable, and can so easily be identified and redistributed, that "justice and fairness" require that they be borne by the public as a whole.[17]

This important dictum, almost entirely forgotten, sheds new light on what the Court means by investment-backed expectations. The Court suggests that a landowner has investment-backed expectations entitled to protection only when government acts suddenly and substantially to interfere with his property rights and could have avoided this interference. An example is a drastic downzoning of land to a more restricted use. This is a substantial and unforeseeable change that government could have avoided by adopting a land use plan that showed the land would be downzoned at some future time. The adoption of the plan would have allowed the landowner to adjust to this proposed zoning change before it occurred. The Court has not elaborated on this concept of "substantial and unforeseeable" change, but it stands as a helpful rule for deciding when landowners have investment-backed expectations.

§ 2.1(c) Monsanto: *The Notice Rule*

Kirby is an important case in the interpretation of investment-backed expectations takings because it suggests that notice and foreseeability are important elements in defining what that factor means. A case decided the same term took this idea one step further, and for the first time adopted a notice rule to decide when landowners have investment-backed expectations. This rule became a critical element in the application of the investment-backed expectations factor to takings claims.

In *Ruckelshaus v. Monsanto Co.*,[18] a federal environmental statute authorized an agency to disclose data submitted by applicants seeking registration of a pesticide. Monsanto claimed the statute was a taking of property because it required the disclosure of trade secrets. The Court held that the "force" of the investment-backed expectations taking factor partly defeated the takings claim, even though the Takings Clause protects trade secrets in property. Monsanto did not have reasonable investment-backed expectations in trade secrets disclosed after the adoption of the statute because the statute put Monsanto on notice that it required disclosure. Neither did the disclosure requirement impose an unconstitutional condition on a valuable government benefit. The Court held that Monsanto was aware of the condition, which rationally related to a legitimate governmental interest, and voluntarily submitted data in return for an economic advantage.

This case adopted a rule that, as extended to land use cases, means a property owner does not have investment-backed expectations when she has constructive notice that a land use regulation restricts the use of her property. This holding is circular; it allows government to define the conditions under which a taking can occur. Government can prevent a taking through the adoption of a regulation because it puts the landowner on notice that he is subject to regulation. Government obtains even more leverage in takings cases because *Monsanto* suggested that actual notice of a regulation is unnecessary. Constructive notice is enough.

There is another basis for the *Monsanto* decision, however, that avoids the circularity problem by adding a new dimension to the notice rule. The Court held that Monsanto did not have investment-backed expectations because it was part of a regulated industry and should have anticipated laws that affected its business expectations.[19] The Court has never decided whether land development is a regulated industry, but it did distinguish *Monsanto* in the *Nollan* case, which was the next Court decision to consider the investment-backed expectations problem.

§ 2.1(d)   Nollan: *The Death of the Notice Rule?*

Following *Monsanto*, federal and state courts applied the notice rule to defeat takings claims in a number of cases, often in wetlands cases where landowners claimed that restrictive development regulations were a taking of property.[20] This was the situation when the Court revisited investment-backed expectations a few years after *Monsanto* in a set of cases commonly known as the Takings Trilogy.

One of these cases, *Nollan v. California Coastal Commission*,[21] considered the notice problem. The Nollans applied for a permit to build a home on the California coast in an area covered by the California Coastal Act. This act required a permit from the California Coastal Commission for any new development. The Commission granted a permit to build the home, but conditioned it on the dedication of an easement that allowed the public to cross the beach in front of it. The purpose of this condition was to provide opportunities for public views of the beach, which the new home would impair, but the Court held a taking occurred because there was no link, or nexus, between the condition and its stated purpose.[22]

Justice Brennan dissented. He would have applied *Monsanto*'s constructive notice rule to hold that plaintiffs did not have investment-backed expectations in the approval of their home without the condition. He argued that the landowners were aware when they bought their property that "stringent regulation of development along the coast" had been in place for many years, and that a condition requiring access had been placed on almost all other homes in the area. The Nollans were thus on notice that the Commission would approve development only if they made provision for lateral beach access. They could not have a "reasonable expectation" or an "entitlement" to approval without the access condition.[23]

Justice Scalia, who wrote the majority decision, did not agree. He dealt with the notice problem in footnote 2 of his opinion,[24] where he acknowledged Justice Brennan's application of the rule to the case but distinguished *Monsanto*. There, he explained, a taking did not occur because government "announced" that an application for a "valuable Government benefit" would confer on government a "license" to use and disclose trade secrets the application contained:

> But the right to build on one's own property—even though its exercise can be subjected to legitimate permitting requirements—cannot remotely be described as a "government benefit." And thus the announcement that the application for (or granting of) the permit will cntail thc yielding of a property interest cannot be regarded as establishing the voluntary "exchange" that we found to have occurred in *Monsanto*.[25]

Scalia added that the Nollans' property rights were not "altered because they acquired the land well after the Commission had begun to implement its policy."[26] The government had a mere "unilateral claim of entitlement," not an enforceable property interest.

Justice Scalia did not specifically mention the investment-backed expectations takings factor in his footnote, but he implied that the notice rule adopted in *Monsanto* is limited to voluntary exchanges. He also clearly implied that a voluntary exchange does not occur when a landowner receives permission to develop his property. The conclusion is that Justice Scalia believed a court can find a taking even though a landowner has purchased land subject to a restrictive regulation. It is not clear whether Scalia would take a different view if a landowner at the time of purchase had actual notice of a land use regulation, and government later applied it to frustrate his expectations. Neither is it clear whether Scalia's footnote prohibits courts from even considering constructive notice of a land use regulation in taking cases. Justice Scalia may have meant only that constructive notice of a restrictive regulation in existence at the time of purchase is not an absolute bar to a taking claim. He did not discuss the application of investment-backed expectations when a landowner purchases land before a restrictive land use regulation affecting his land is adopted.

Although *Nollan's* footnote may limit the effect of notice on investment-backed expectations, it is at odds with the Court's treatment of ownership expectations in a different constitutional setting. In *Nordlinger v. Hahn*,[27] a property tax case, the Court rejected an equal protection challenge to California's Proposition 13, an amendment to the state constitution that placed limits on general real property taxes. It upheld a provision that applied the tax limitation only to persons owning property at the time the amendment was adopted, not to persons who bought later. It did so partly because it concluded a new owner who acquires property "does not have the same reliance interest warranting protection against higher taxes as does an existing owner."[28] It added that "an existing owner rationally may be thought to have vested expectations in his property or home that are more deserving of protection than the anticipatory expectations of a new owner at the point of purchase."[29]

Nordlinger was a property tax case brought under the Equal Protection Clause, and it is not clear whether the Court would adopt the same approach in a takings case.[30] The Court noted it had "not hesitated to recognize the legitimacy of protecting reliance and expectational interests"[31] outside the context of the Equal Protection Clause. It cited *Penn Central* but did not indicate whether its analysis of the California property tax limitation applies in land use as well. *Nordlinger* shows, however, that the Court has not been consistent in the constitutional protection it gives reliance and expectation interests in property.

§ 2.2   The Ascendancy of Investment-Backed Expectations in the Post-Trilogy Years

In the years after the Trilogy, the investment-backed expectations takings factor took on added importance. Federal and state courts not only ignored Justice Scalia's footnote in *Nollan* but treated the absence of investment-backed expectations as a decisive element in takings cases.[32] Then more complications were created by a Supreme Court decision, five years after the Trilogy, that set the stage for a merging of investment-backed expectations with property law principles that apply to takings claims. This case also influenced the courts to defeat takings claims through the notice rule because it adopted a draconian per se takings test that threatened important environmental restrictions.

Lucas v. South Carolina Coastal Council[33] was the draconian post-Trilogy case. Lucas bought two lots on a barrier island on which he intended to build homes similar to those on immediately adjacent parcels. At the time of purchase these lots were not subject to any regulation, but a Beachfront Management Act the state adopted later prohibited permanent structures on the property.

Justice Scalia, again writing for the Court, held that a per se taking occurred because the restriction on the Lucas property deprived him of "all economically beneficial or productive use of land." This, Scalia claimed, was an established category of land use cases where restrictive regulations were compensable "without case-specific inquiry into the public interest advanced in support of the restraint," an apparent reference to the *Penn Central* balancing test. The implication, presumably, is that the takings rules adopted in *Penn Central,* including the investment-backed expectations takings factor, do not apply when a per se taking occurs. In addition, if the land use restriction is total, the purpose of the regulation is not important. These elements of the per se rule threaten restrictive environmental regulation, such as wetlands regulation, because their beneficial purpose cannot save their restrictive impact on property values.

For these reasons, a per se takings claim appears absolute because it rests entirely on economic loss. The purpose of the regulation is irrelevant, even though it is beneficial or important. However, Justice Scalia qualified this draconian rule in another part of his opinion.[34] There he held a threshold takings inquiry is to decide, under "'existing rules or understandings'" of state law, whether a landowner ever possessed the property interest she claimed as taken. The purpose of this "logically antecedent inquiry into the nature of the owner's estate" is to determine whether the uses prohibited by the regulation are not part of his "title" but instead are background principles of state law with which the landowner must comply. One example, presumably, is the doctrine that holds a landowner subject to the regulation of land held in public trust. Justice Scalia cited the law of nuisance as another. The difficult question is whether a government regulation existing at the time of purchase defeats a takings claim because it is a background principle that is part of the title. If so, the notice rule Scalia thought he had eliminated has been revived in another form.

§ 2.3   *Federal and State Court Cases*

The stark per se takings rule in *Lucas* put federal and state courts in a bind. A strict application would invalidate many environmental regulations, such as wetlands regulations, that arguably leave a landowner without an economically viable use. The courts, understandably concerned about critical environmental laws, did not take this bait. With few exceptions, they did not follow footnote 2 in *Nollan,* usually without distinguishing it or even explaining why. They applied the notice rule based on *Monsanto* to reject claims of investment-backed expectations, and in some cases used that rejection to defeat a takings claim. They also merged the notice rule with Justice Scalia's exception for background principles of state law, and held that a regulation adopted before a landowner acquired his land was a background principle that defeated a taking. Two cases, one federal and one state, illustrate this tendency.

§ 2.3(a) Good v. United States

Good v. United States[35] was a typical permit denial under the federal Clean Water Act for a residential development in wetlands. The plaintiffs purchased property on a Florida Key shortly after the Clean Water Act was adopted in 1972. They knew they had problems. The sales contract acknowledged possible difficulties in obtaining federal and state approval, but the plaintiffs did not begin efforts to develop the property until 1980, when they hired a consultant to obtain the necessary permits. That contract acknowledged that obtaining the permits was "at best difficult and by no means assured."

A long saga then ensued in which plaintiffs initially obtained the required federal permit from the Corps of Engineers, only to have that permit expire because of delays in obtaining state and local approvals. These delays occurred partly because the state designated the Florida keys as an area of critical state concern, which allowed the state to review local land use regulations and decisions for consistency with state guidelines for the critical area. The critical area designation occurred several years after the Goods bought the property.

By the time the federal permit expired, Congress had adopted the Endangered Species Act, and the Corps finally denied a new permit when endangered species were found on the property. The landowners sued for a taking, the Court of Federal Claims rejected their claim, and the Federal Circuit affirmed.

The Federal Circuit began its opinion by holding that "[f]or any regulatory takings claim to succeed, that claimant must show that the government's regulatory restraint interfered with his investment-backed expectations in a manner that requires government to compensate him."[36] The court quoted from its earlier wetlands cases, which held that an owner who buys with knowledge of a restraint on land use does not have a reliance interest and assumes the risk of economic loss if he does not obtain a permit. In economic terms, a purchaser cannot show a loss on his investment attributable to the restraint because the market discounted the risk of denial in the purchase price.

That was fine as far as it went, but the Goods cited *Lucas* and argued the notice rule did not apply in a per se takings case. The court disagreed. Quoting *Lucas*, it noted its holding that the per se takings rule eliminates only the "case-specific" inquiry into the "public interest" that supports a land use regulation. The *Good* court concluded that *Lucas* does not dispense with an inquiry into a landowner's investment-backed expectations.[37]

Requiring a showing of investment-backed expectations when a landowner claims a per se taking is debatable, but the court also had to face an alternate argument by plaintiffs. They claimed they had reasonable investment-backed expectations because they obtained the necessary permits for their development under the federal statute in effect when they purchased the property. The Endangered Species Act under which the Corps denied the permits was adopted after that date, and they argued it did not affect investment-backed expectations they already had.

The court again disagreed, and adopted (though it did not cite) a theory of regulatory risk I proposed in an earlier article on investment-backed expectations.[38] What impressed the court was that from 1973, when plaintiffs bought the property, to 1980, when they first applied for federal permits, "public concern about the environment resulted in numerous laws and regulations affecting land development." The court noted some of the events mentioned above, such as the enactment of the Endangered Species Act and the designation of the Florida Keys as an area of critical state concern.

The picture that emerged, said the court, was that the landowners had acknowledged the difficulty of obtaining approvals for their project. They waited seven years before taking any action to develop their land, "watching as the applicable regulations got more stringent." Inaction did not bar the takings claim but reduced the ability to "fairly claim surprise." The plaintiffs were aware at the time of purchase that they needed regulatory approval. They must be presumed to have been aware of the "greater general concern for environmental matters" during the seven-year delay before they applied for approval to develop their property.

Good adopted a number of critical holdings that affect the role of the investment-backed expectations takings in takings cases. It held that success in establishing investment-backed expectations is essential to proof of a takings claim, a holding not supported by *Penn Central*. That case listed investment-backed expectations as one of several takings factors courts should consider. *Good*'s treatment of the *Lucas* per se rule is equally startling. It means landowners must show they have investment-backed expectations even when they have been denied all economically viable use of their land.

Good is important because it is a sensitive, fact-based decision that the landowners did not have investment-backed expectations under the facts of that case. The court based this conclusion on the plaintiffs' own acknowledgment at the time of purchase that securing the necessary approvals would be difficult; their confirmation of that difficulty when they decided to develop the land; the purchase of land in a vulnerable ecological environment; the delay in deciding whether to apply for a development permit; and the increasingly stringent regulatory climate during the delay period.

I argued in my earlier article that market signals could alert a would-be buyer that purchase of a property carried a risk of denial under a land use program. This could occur when property values in an area were severely discounted. Landowners would have to accept a regulatory risk that they would be denied permission to develop, and would not have investment-backed expectations that would support a takings claim if this regulatory risk occurred. This argument is an extension of the accepted principle that landowners must accept market risk, and have no takings claim when their property depreciates in value because the market turns against them. *Good* added ad hominem elements in its reliance on the landowner's conduct, but otherwise endorsed the regulatory risk principle.

§ 2.3(b)   Kim v. City of New York

In *Good,* the landowners purchased the property after environmental regulations that affected its development were in effect, but the environmental regulations that prevented its development were adopted after their purchase. *Kim v. City of New York*[39] was a New York Court of Appeals case in which the restriction on the use of the property was in effect before the landowners purchased. The court held that notice of this restriction defeated the landowners' investment-backed expectations and their takings claim.

A city agency raised the grade on a street on which the plaintiffs' property was located, as authorized by the city charter, and filed a map reflecting that legal grade in the appropriate city office. The plaintiffs purchased the property ten years later. It did

not conform to the legal grade, and the court noted they had
"constructive notice" of this fact because of the filed map. Later
the city informed the plaintiffs that it intended to raise the grade
on their property as authorized and offered to do so at no cost,
but stated that the plaintiffs must reimburse the city for this work
if they did not respond. They did not respond, so the city placed
side fill on 2,390 square feet of the plaintiffs' property abutting
the street to raise it to the legal grade. Understandably, the plaintiffs sued for a permanent physical occupation.

This should have been the end of the story, because the plaintiffs clearly pleaded a per se physical taking under *Lucas*. Remember, however, that there is an exception to a per se taking for
limiting background principles of property inherent in the
landowner's title. The court acknowledged there was some "confusion" concerning this exception because the Supreme Court in
Lucas used common-law nuisance doctrine to illustrate these background principles.

The New York court refused to limit the background principles exception to common-law restrictions, however.[40] It found
no "sound reason" to isolate the inquiry into background principles to some "arbitrary earlier time in the evolution of the common law." It would be "illogical and incomplete" to restrict the
inquiry in this manner to identify background principles of state
property law that could limit a landowner's use of land without
compensation. To do so would elevate common law over statutory law, and would be inconsistent with the principle that statutory law can repeal an inconsistent common-law principle. This
holding merges the notice rule that applies to investment-backed
expectations with the background principles exception to per se
takings adopted in *Lucas*. The holding in *Kim* is simply another
way of adopting the conclusion the court reached in *Good,* that
the per se takings rule does not eliminate the need to find investment-backed expectations. The confusions inherent in *Lucas* provide a possible basis for the decision in *Kim,* but this case restores
the circularity introduced by the notice rule. The difference is
that the New York court applied a notice rule by incorporating
local law as part of the background principles that limit an owner's
use of his land.

The New York court was aware of this problem and the objection, based on the *Nollan* footnote, that the notice rule does not
apply in land use cases. The court distinguished *Nollan*, however,
in an important footnote of its own.[41] The *Nollan* footnote, the
court held, is "readily harmonized" with the logically antecedent
inquiry authorized by *Lucas*.[42] There was no existing restriction
on the title in that case because it centered on the state agency's

policy of requiring a public easement as a condition to a building permit. Because the prior owners of the property had neither applied for nor been granted a permit, the government's interest was merely a unilateral claim of entitlement and not an enforceable interest in property. A different question would have been presented in *Nollan* if the property was subject to a conditioned permit when the Nollans acquired it.

Kim's distinction of the *Nollan* footnote may have merit. The court seems to say the notice rule applies only if a public agency takes a restrictive action affecting the land before a landowner acquires title. In *Kim,* that action apparently was the filing of the regrade map. The New York Court of Appeals applied the same reasoning in a companion case to *Kim, Gazza v. New York State Department of Environmental Conservation*, that upheld the denial of a variance under a wetlands regulation.[43] Other cases that applied the notice rule to defeat a takings claim did not adopt this view. *Good* is an example. There the court applied the notice rule to defeat a takings claim although restrictive action prohibiting the development of the land occurred after the plaintiffs acquired title.

Kim's distinction of the *Nollan* footnote may also have merit because the Supreme Court has held that the mere adoption of a land use regulation is not a taking. A taking occurs only when government denies permission to develop under a regulation.[44] If this is true, then a property owner does not have a takings claim to transfer until he has been denied permission to develop under a land use regulation that applies to his property.[45]

§ 2.4   Palazzolo v. State of Rhode Island

§ 2.4(a) *The Decision*

This was the situation when the Supreme Court decided *Palazzolo v. State of Rhode Island*,[46] another wetlands case. A corporation that included Palazzolo as a shareholder purchased a tract of land, most of which was coastal wetland, some time ago. After the purchase, Palazzolo bought out his associates and became the sole shareholder. The corporation made unsuccessful attempts to develop the property over the years and later, in 1971, the state adopted a coastal wetlands law. Sometime thereafter the state revoked the corporation's charter, and Palazzolo became the sole shareholder. He then made several attempts to develop the property and, when rejected by the state coastal agency, filed an inverse condemnation claim in state court.

The Rhode Island court rejected a *Lucas* takings claim, partly by holding he could not challenge a law that predated his acquisition of title. This law was a background principle of state property law that bound the landowner. It rejected a claim of investment-backed expectations under *Penn Central* for the same reason. Both holdings were an application of the notice rule. Palazzolo could not succeed on a takings claim directed at legislation adopted before he took title.

The U.S. Supreme Court reversed on the notice rule but wrote six opinions. The 5-4 majority, in an opinion written by Justice Kennedy, rejected the notice rule as the state court applied it to both the *Lucas* and *Penn Central* claims. Whether this is a concession that the notice rule applies to both types of claims is not clear. It is clear the majority held only that the enactment of a law after a landowner purchases title cannot absolutely bar a takings claim. This is a question of title to property. A landowner could not be "stripped of the ability to transfer the interest which was possessed prior to the regulation." For this proposition, the Court cited and relied on footnote 2 in *Nollan.* Later, however, the majority forgot where it was and talked in terms of the "background principles" that, under *Lucas,* can defeat a takings claim. In this part of the opinion Justice Kennedy noted they had "no occasion to consider the precise circumstances when a legislative enactment can be deemed a background principle of state law."

This statement exposes the ambiguities in the majority opinion, which are reinforced by its holding that Palazzolo did not have a *Lucas* claim because the upland portion of his property had significant value as a building plot for a single home. As a result, Palazzolo was not denied all economically viable use of his land. The Court then remanded the case so the state court could decide the *Penn Central* takings claim, but how the state court should handle the remand is not clear because Justices O'Connor and Scalia, who joined the majority, each wrote separate opinions to explain what the remand meant.

Justice O'Connor made it clear the majority simply rejected the "sweeping" rule the Rhode Island court adopted, that "preacquisition enactment of the use restriction *ipso facto* defeats any takings claim based on that use restriction." For her, the "difficult question" was how to consider the "temporal relationship between regulatory enactment and title acquisition . . . in a proper *Penn Central* analysis." Investment-backed expectations are "one of a number of factors" courts must examine in a *Penn Central* analysis, and "the regulatory regime in place at the time the claimant acquires the property at issue helps to shape the reasonableness of those expectations."

Justice Scalia wrote separately and briefly to disagree with Justice O'Connor. He made it clear that neither a *Lucas* nor a

Penn Central claim is eliminated by a transfer of title. Because Justices Breyer, Ginsburg, Souter, and Stevens wrote or concurred in opinions in which they agreed with Justice O'Connor's explanation of the majority decision, there is a clear majority on the Court for a continued application of some form of the notice rule as part of an investment-backed expectations analysis.

§ 2.4(b)   *Implications*

Palazzalo does not advance takings law much further than it was before the decision. It is now clear that a municipality cannot adopt a land use regulation and argue that its adoption prior to a purchase of title defeats a takings claim. That is an "Emperor's New Clothes" conclusion. Beyond that point, the decision is not clear.

One problem is that the Court backed into investment-backed expectations issues by concentrating solely on an exception adopted in *Monsanto,* which was not a land use case. The Court should have begun its analysis with a description of investment-backed expectations as a takings factor, and what it means. This explanation should have discussed the various meanings placed on this term by Justice Brennan in *Penn Central,* and whether the Court still believed in them, such as the exploitation theory.

The Court should then have continued with a more complete discussion of the notice rule adopted in *Monsanto* and whether it applies in land use cases. Justice Scalia answered this question in the negative in his *Nollan* footnote. The Court agreeably quotes this footnote, but only that part holding that a transfer of title does not extinguish a takings claim. It says nothing about Scalia's rejection of the "announcement" theory, which was a rejection of the notice rule. Moreover, the Court does not discuss the holding in *Kim,* that *Nollan* was distinguishable because the property had not been burdened with an access condition before the Nollans bought it.

Because of these omissions, we really do not know what the Court thinks about the investment-backed expectations takings factor and the notice rule it added later. The Court did not discuss its present understanding of what the investment-backed expectations takings factor means, and did not discuss the notice rule except to hold that a transfer of title does not extinguish a takings claim. Because the Court was silent on these important issues, Justice O'Connor's concurring opinion is the most important statement by the Court. Her opinion is, in effect, the majority opinion because she was joined by Justices Stevens, Breyer, Ginsburg, and Souter.

Unfortunately, Justice O'Connor discussed the takings test adopted in *Penn Central* but did not consider how the Court has applied the investment-backed expectations element that is part of this test. She suggests only that courts should consider the existing regulatory framework when evaluating a takings claim. She did reject *Monsanto's* holding, that a failure to prove investment-backed expectations can defeat a takings claim, by holding that those expectations are only one factor to consider under the *Penn Central* test. We are left to puzzle over what effect the Court's decision in *Palazzolo* will have, and what its effect will be on earlier lower court decisions. This problem is compounded because *Palazzolo* made both a *Lucas* and a *Penn Central* claim, and the majority apparently said its decision on transferability applies to both. Justice O'Connor, however, limited her discussion to the remand of the case under the *Penn Central* analysis.

An initial question is whether cases such as *Kim* and *Good* are overruled by implication by *Palazzolo,* which did not mention them. In both cases the landowner purchased land after a restriction had been adopted—the Clean Water Act in *Good* and the charter amendment and filing of the regrade map in *Kim*. This circumstance would not now be an absolute bar to the Kims' takings claim. The question is whether *Kim's* holding that investment-backed expectations are defeated by a specific action affecting the property, such as the adoption of a regrade map, is acceptable after *Palazzolo*. Another factor is that the city put them on notice it intended to regrade their land, offered to pay for it, and they refused. Justice O'Connor specifically mentioned the concern that landowners receive windfalls under the Takings Clause; it certainly would be a windfall to allow the Kims to receive compensation for a taking after ignoring an offer of reimbursement from the city.

In *Good,* the regulations the court relied on to defeat investment-backed expectations were adopted after the Goods took title, so the transferability of a takings claim was not an issue. *Palazzolo* does not apply, and the question is whether the court's regulatory risk approach is a correct application of the investment-backed expectations takings factor. It may or may not be correct, but *Palazzolo* does not answer this question.[47]

There is one final point. The Court writes as if takings claims go on forever. It should think again. Takings claims are everywhere subject to a statute of limitations, although courts differ on when a takings claim is barred. Some pick the date on which a takings claim ripens, while others pick the day on which a regulation was adopted.[48] Either way, sound public policy dictates that takings claims have a limited life. The notice rule, properly applied, is simply another way of limiting that life.

Notes

1. I use this word advisedly, but apparently not much thought was given to the introduction of this takings factor into takings law. Rumor has it that Justice Brennan's clerk was stumped on how to handle the case and called a friend at the Harvard Law School. His friend advised him to read an article on takings by a Harvard law professor that clearly influenced the opinion.

2. 438 U.S. 104 (1978).

3. The Court now seems to require that investment-backed expectations be "reasonable" rather than "distinct," but there has been no apparent change in the way it applies this concept.

4. This part of the chapter is based on two of my earlier articles, *Investment-Backed Expectations: Is There a Taking?* 31 J. URB. & CONTEMP. L. 3 (1987), hereinafter cited as *Takings I*, and *Investment-Backed Expectations in Taking Law*, 31 URB. LAW. 215 (1995), hereinafter cited as *Takings II*.

5. *Penn Central*, 438 U.S. at 124.

6. *Id.*

7. 260 U.S. 393 (1922).

8. 438 U.S. at 127.

9. *Id.*

10. *Id.* at 130.

11. *Id.*

12. *Id.* at 136.

13. *See, e.g.,* MacLeod v. County of Santa Clara, 749 F.2d 541 (9th Cir. 1984) (denial of right to harvest timber), *cert. denied*, 472 U.S. 1009 (1985).

14. 467 U.S. 1 (1984).

15. *Citing* Agins v. City of Tiburon, 447 U.S. 255 (1981).

16. *Id.* at 14.

17. *Id.*

18. 467 U.S. 986 (1984). By this time the Court was requiring expectations that are "reasonable" rather than "distinct."

19. *Id.* at 1008. *See also* Concrete Pipe & Prods. v. Construction Laborers Pension Trust, 508 U.S. 602 (1993). The Court held the company's collective bargaining agreement did not protect it from an amendment to a federal statute requiring an increase in pension liabilities. Applying earlier decisions, *see* Connolly v. Pension Benefit Guaranty Corp., 475 U.S. 211 (1986), the Court held that anyone who does business in a "regulated field cannot object" if a statute is later amended.

20. *See Takings I, supra* note 4, at 29-30.

21. 483 U.S. 825 (1987).

22. The Court suggested, as an alternative, that the Commission could require a viewing spot on the property and access to the spot.

23. *Id.* at 860.

24. *Id.* at 833 n.2.

25. *Id.* at 833. Justice Brennan argued in his dissent that *Monsanto* applied, and stated that "[if] the Court is somehow suggesting that the 'right to build on one's own property' has some privileged natural rights status, the argument is a curious one." *Id.* at 860.

26. *Id.* The Court added that "[s]o long as the Commission could not have deprived the prior owners of the easement without compensating them, the prior owners must be understood to have transferred their full property rights in conveying the lot."

27. 505 U.S. 1 (1992).

28. *Id.* at 14.

29. *Id.* The Court stated: "A new owner has full information about the scope of future tax liability before acquiring the property, and if he thinks the future tax burden is too demanding, he can decide not to complete the purchase at all." The same observation applies to a landowner who purchases land with notice that a land use regulation covers his property that might frustrate his development expectations.

30. The majority rule is that an increase in a general ad valorem real estate tax is not a taking of property. *See, e.g.,* Superior Oil Co. v. City of Port Arthur, 628 S.W.2d 94 (Tex. Ct. App. 1981), *appeal dismissed,* 459 U.S. 802 (1982).

31. *Id.* at 14 n.4.

32. *Takings II, supra* note 4, at 243-49.

33. 503 U.S. 1003 (1992). *See* Daniel R. Mandelker, *Of Mice and Missiles: A True Account of Lucas v. South Carolina Coastal Council,* 8 J. LAND USE & ENVTL. L. 285 (1999).

34. *See* 503 U.S. at 1027-30.

35. 189 F.3d 1355 (Fed. Cir. 1999), *cert. denied,* 529 U.S. 1053 (2000).

36. *Id.* at 1360.

37. *But see* Palazzolo v. Rhode Island, 121 S. Ct. 2448 (2001), discussed *infra,* text accompanying notes 46-47.

38. *See Takings II, supra* note 4.

39. 681 N.E.2d 312 (N.Y.), *cert. denied,* 522 U.S. 809 (1997). This and three other similar cases decided at the same time are known as the New York Takings Quartet. For an excellent but critical discussion of these cases, see Stephen P. Eagle, *The Regulatory Takings Quartet: Retreating From the Rule of Law,* 42 N.Y.L. SCH. L. REV. 345 (1998). Petitions for certiorari were filed in all four of these cases. The Court's failure to grant certiorari in any of them is unbelievable in view of its later grant of certiorari in the *Palazzolo* case, which raised similar issues but in an impossibly muddled factual situation.

40. *Id.* at 315.

41. 681 N.E.2d at 316 n.3.

42. The court noted the conclusion from my article, *Takings II,* at 35-38, that the *Nollan* footnote does not prohibit inquiry into statutory or regulatory restrictions.

43. 679 N.E.2d 1035 (N.Y.), *cert. denied,* 522 U.S. 813 (1997). In this case the state inventoried the landowner's property as a wetlands under its wetlands law prior to the time the landowner took title. This was apparently enough of an action to make the *Kim* rule apply. This law required a variance before any development of the property could occur, and the court held that after the adoption of these regulations the only permissible development of the property was dependent on securing a variance under the statute. "[The property owner] cannot base a taking claim upon an interest he never owned." *Id.* at 1041.

44. United States v. Riverside Bayview Homes, Inc., 474 U.S. 121 (1986). I am indebted to Kenneth Bley for this suggestion.

45. The Court in the *Riverside* case was talking about the Clean Water Act's dredge-and-fill provision, which requires a permit before development can occur. It did not address the possibility that a land use regulation that does not require a permit can be so restrictive it is a facial taking. One possibility is an absolute restriction on building on steep slopes without a variance opportunity.

46. 121 S. Ct. 2448 (2001).

47. However, on the day after it decided *Palazzolo,* the Court granted certiorari in *McQueen v. South Carolina Coastal Council,* 530 S.E.2d 628 (S.C. 2000), and then vacated the judgment and remanded the case to the South Carolina Supreme Court for further consideration in light of *Palazzolo.* 121 S. Ct. 2582 (2001). The facts in *McQueen* were dissimilar because the landowner bought the property many years before the state enacted a coastal law under which the state denied a permit. The court discussed and relied on the *Good* case to hold that a taking had not occurred. It noted the beachfront property was subject to some kind of development regulation for over a century, that the preexisting permit requirement was relevant to the landowner's investment-backed expectations, and that his "prolonged neglect of the property and failure to seek development permits in the face of ever more stringent regulation demonstrate a distinct lack of investment-backed expectations." *Id.* at 634-35. The South Carolina court will have an opportunity on remand to decide whether *Good'*s regulatory climate rule survives *Palazzolo.*

48. D. MANDELKER, J. GERARD & T. SULLIVAN, FEDERAL LAND USE LAW § 5.05[1][b].

The Effect of *Palazzolo v. Rhode Island* on the Role of Reasonable Investment-Backed Expectations

3

Gregory M. Stein

§ 3.0 Introduction

This chapter seeks to assess the effect that the Supreme Court's recent decision in *Palazzolo v. Rhode Island*[1] will have on the role that reasonable investment-backed expectations play in regulatory takings law. The chapter begins with a brief description of the role of expectations before *Palazzolo*. It then turns to the opinions in *Palazzolo*, including an examination of important features of the concurring and dissenting opinions. Next and most centrally, the chapter describes how *Palazzolo* is likely to affect judicial application of the reasonable investment-backed expectations test. This part of the analysis concludes that the long-term effect of *Palazzolo* is likely to be minimal, with few plaintiffs winning cases today that they would have lost before it was decided. The final portion of the discussion notes some of the important open issues the Court may have to address in future cases.

§ 3.1 Reasonable Investment-Backed Expectations before Palazzolo

The U.S. Supreme Court first discussed the significance of reasonable investment-backed expectations in *Penn Central Transportation Co. v. City of New York*.[2] While noting that regulatory takings claims are fact-specific and necessarily lead to ad hoc resolution, the Court listed several factors lower courts must consider when resolving these cases, including "the extent to which the regulation has interfered with distinct investment-backed expectations."[3] The Court observed that it had previously rejected takings claims when the government action in question "did not interfere with interests that were sufficiently bound up with the reasonable expectations of the claimant to constitute 'property' for Fifth Amendment purposes"[4] and concluded that New York's Landmarks Preservation Law "does not interfere with what must be regarded as Penn Central's primary expectation concerning the use of the parcel."[5] Thus the closer a property right is to core property rights, the more reasonable it is for an owner to develop expectations as to the use of that right and the greater the likelihood a court will find a deprivation of that right to be a taking.[6]

The Court relied heavily on Professor Frank Michelman's influential 1967 essay, *Property, Utility, and Fairness: Comments on the Ethical Foundations of "Just Compensation" Law*,[7] in which Michelman sought to ascertain why courts provide compensation for only some losses. Paraphrasing Bentham, Michelman described property as "the institutionally established understanding that extant rules governing the relationships among men with respect to resources will continue in existence,"[8] a definition that is a precondition for the economically productive use of property. At the same time, "[u]tilitarian property theory, . . . for all its emphasis on security of expectations, easily allows that compensation need not be paid in respect of investments which, when they were made, . . . were of a sort which society had adequately made known should not become the object of expectations of continuing enjoyment."[9] Thus, if you seek to develop a brickyard in a neighborhood that may be destined for residential use, and you do not purchase a buffer zone that is adequate to fend off possible nuisance claims from future neighbors, "you proceed at your own risk when you violate other people's apparently crystallized and justifiable expectations."[10]

Beginning in the late 1980s, the Court began to hint that it might be moving away from a consistent application of the expectations test. In *Nollan v. California Coastal Commission*,[11] the Court noted that the property owners did not obtain a reduced bundle of rights even though they had acquired their land after the state began to implement a more restrictive land use policy.[12] The Court specifically stated, "So long as the Commission could not have deprived the prior owners of the easement without compensating them, the prior owners must be understood to have transferred their full property rights in conveying the lot."[13] Five years later, in *Lucas v. South Carolina Coastal Council*,[14] the Court held that a regulatory taking is compensable whenever it deprives an owner of all economically beneficial use of his land. This later opinion did not import any consideration of an owner's expectations into its analysis except in those exceptional cases where "the proscribed use interests were not part of his title to begin with."[15]

Even as expectations analysis appeared to be in decline at the Supreme Court level, many state courts and lower federal courts continued to emphasize the importance of reasonable investment-backed expectations. In several noteworthy cases, state courts concluded that an owner is deemed to be on notice of all existing laws at the time she acquires property and cannot recover takings compensation when those laws are applied.[16] For example, in *Basile v. Town of Southampton*,[17] the New York Court of Appeals rejected a claim by a post-enactment buyer, holding that "[w]hatever taking claim the prior landowner may have had against the environmental regulation of the subject parcel, any property interest that might serve as the foundation for such a claim was not owned by claimant here who took title after the redefinition of the relevant property interests."[18] The Supreme Judicial Court of Massachusetts reached a similar result in *Leonard v. Town of Brimfield*,[19] holding that "[a]t the time [the plaintiff] purchased the property she had constructive notice of the zoning map, which was available for viewing at the building inspector's office.... [S]he may not complain about the loss of a right she never acquired."[20] The Rhode Island Supreme Court reached a similar result in early 2000, in *Palazzolo v. State* ex rel. *Tavares*.[21]

§ 3.2   *The Court Addresses Expectations Again in* Palazzolo v. Rhode Island

Palazzolo raised the issue of reasonable investment-backed expectations in a specific context. Shore Gardens, Inc. (SGI), acquired approximately 20 acres of coastal property in 1959. The state revoked SGI's corporate charter in 1978 for nonpayment of taxes, and SGI's property passed by operation of law to its sole shareholder, Anthony Palazzolo. During the 19-year period in which SGI owned the property, Rhode Island enacted legislation and regulations significantly curtailing the ability of owners to use certain coastal property, including that owned by SGI.[22] Palazzolo subsequently sought to fill the property, and later re-

quested a permit to build a private beach club. The state's Coastal
Resources Management Council rejected both proposals as violating the state's Coastal Resources Management Program and as
not deserving of a special exception. Palazzolo challenged the
second of these denials in state court, arguing that the state had
inversely condemned his property and seeking compensation of
$3,150,000.[23]

§ 3.2(a)   *The Opinion of the Rhode Island Supreme Court*

The Rhode Island Supreme Court affirmed the trial court's ruling in favor of the state. After concluding that the claim was not
ripe, the court nonetheless went on to reject Palazzolo's claim on
the merits for two different reasons. First, the state supreme court
concluded that Palazzolo had no right to challenge the application of regulations that predated his 1978 acquisition of the property. Second, Palazzolo's argument that he had been deprived of
all economically viable use of his property, in violation of *Lucas*,
was undercut by uncontradicted evidence that the upland portion
of his property could be used and was worth $200,000.

According to the state court, Palazzolo's acquisition of title
with notice of existing land use restrictions undermined his argument in two related ways. Even if Palazzolo had been able to
show that he was deprived of all economically viable use of his
property as required by *Lucas*, his knowledge of the existing land
use regime would demonstrate that "'the proscribed use interests
were not part of his . . . title to begin with.'"[24] Under *Lucas*, such
a showing demonstrates that Palazzolo's estate never included the
right to use the property in the manner he proposed. In other
words, he was not "deprived" of anything. Moreover, Palazzolo's
notice of these laws belied his claim that his reasonable investment-backed expectations were constitutionally impaired under
the more flexible *Penn Central* test. "In light of these [preexist-
ing] regulations, Palazzolo could not reasonably have expected
that he could fill the property . . . ."[25]

§ 3.2(b)   *The Opinion of the U.S. Supreme Court*

The U.S. Supreme Court granted certiorari on three different
issues, a fact that helps explain the convoluted nature of the six
opinions in the case and the difficulties in assessing the Court's
meaning.[26] Three of the Justices would have rejected the
landowner's claims on ripeness grounds without ever reaching
the two other issues. Two of these three dissenters mention the
expectations issue only in passing, in a footnote, and the third
authored just three paragraphs in response to the Court's treat-

ment of the expectations issue. Thus the case affords only an incomplete analysis of this substantive matter. However, five Justices did manage to reach a tense agreement on this question, with two of the five concurring separately to register their respective, and opposing, observations.

After finding the case to be ripe,[27] the Supreme Court rejected the state court's holding that Palazzolo's prior knowledge of legal restrictions acted as an automatic bar to his regulatory takings claim. Before parsing this issue in any detail, Justice Kennedy's opinion for the five-member majority on this issue noted that "[some] enactments are unreasonable and do not become less so through passage of time or title. . . . A State would be allowed, in effect, to put an expiration date on the Takings Clause. This ought not to be the rule."[28] Such an outcome also is unfair to the owner at the time the regulation becomes effective, the opinion noted, because that owner might not survive the process of ripening a claim of his own.

The Court's more detailed discussion of the notice issue begins by comparing direct condemnations with regulatory takings. When the government takes property directly under its power of eminent domain, "any award goes to the owner at the time of the taking, and . . . the right to compensation is not passed to a subsequent purchaser."[29] This is true because at the time of the taking "the fact and extent of the taking are known."[30] In other words, if there has been a direct taking, there is no doubt as to whether or when it occurred or who owned the property at the time. There are strong public policy reasons for not allowing this owner to transfer a ripe claim, and this owner is the only party entitled to receive the resulting compensation. The Court referred directly to *Danforth v. United States*[31] in support of its conclusion that the same analysis applies to inverse condemnations arising from physical occupations.[32]

Inverse condemnation suits challenging the *application* of land use regulations are different. Unlike direct takings or inverse physical takings, inverse regulatory claims do "not mature until ripeness requirements have been satisfied . . . [and] until this point an inverse condemnation claim alleging a regulatory taking cannot be maintained."[33] The owner at the time the law becomes effective, unlike the owner at the time of a direct condemnation, cannot yet assert a takings claim because of the nature of the Court's ripeness requirements. Thus, "[i]t would be illogical, and unfair, to bar a regulatory takings claim because of the post-enactment transfer of ownership where the steps necessary to make the claim ripe were not taken, or could not have been taken, by a previous owner."[34]

Because of the distinction between these two types of claims, a party who acquires property with knowledge of a preexisting limitation in the land use law is not categorically barred from subsequently bringing a regulatory takings claim. The original owner cannot bring a claim because the issue is not crystallized and thus is unripe, so the successor owner may be permitted to step into her predecessor's shoes. However, the Court had "no occasion to consider the precise circumstances when a legislative enactment can be deemed a background principle of state law .... The determination whether an existing, general law can limit all economic use of property must turn on objective factors, such as the nature of the land use proscribed."[35]

Note that the Court's analysis conflates two different, if overlapping, issues. The question of an owner's expectations can arise in the *Lucas* setting, with an owner arguing that she has been deprived of all economically viable use of her property and the government responding that its restriction already formed an inherent limitation on the owner's use of her property when she acquired it.[36] The question *Palazzolo* addresses in the context of *Lucas* is whether the owner's knowledge of some preexisting limitation is sufficient to defeat her claim that she has been deprived of everything she had. The expectations issue also surfaces in claims of less-than-total takings that fall within the *Penn Central* analytical framework. In this distinct setting, the per se *Lucas* rule does not apply, and a court must assess a variety of factors, including the owner's reasonable investment-backed expectations, before reaching its decision as to whether an owner has suffered a taking. The question that *Palazzolo* confronts in a *Penn Central* analysis is what weight the owner's knowledge of existing law should bear. The Court merges these two questions, stating that "the two holdings together amount to a single, sweeping rule."[37] Because the state court considered the *Lucas* issue but Palazzolo never raised the *Penn Central* argument at trial, the Supreme Court was forced to remand the case.

The Court concluded that there may be some circumstances in which a party who buys land with knowledge of a preexisting limitation on her use of the property nonetheless may maintain a takings claim. Palazzolo did not suffer a *Lucas* taking,[38] but because he did not raise the *Penn Central* issue below, the Court remanded the case to the Rhode Island courts for further exploration of this matter. Note that the Court displayed no apparent concern about the federalism questions it raises when it attempts to establish the contours of a private owner's property rights under state law.[39]

§ 3.2(c)   *Concurrences and Dissents in the Supreme Court*

Justice Scalia, concurring, would disregard entirely the state of the law when the owner acquires title. His brief opinion, written to clarify this point and to respond to Justice O'Connor's contradictory concurrence, addresses this point directly: "In my view, the fact that a restriction existed at the time the purchaser took title . . . should have no bearing upon the determination of whether the restriction is so substantial as to constitute a taking."[40] If a prior law takes property unconstitutionally, that impropriety is not cleansed by the passage of title to another owner, whose expectations need not include the enforcement of a law that takes property without compensation. "The 'investment-backed expectations' that the law will take into account do not include the assumed validity of a restriction that in fact deprives property of so much of its value as to be unconstitutional."[41]

Justice O'Connor, concurring with the Court's opinion but disagreeing with Justice Scalia's remarks, zeroes in on this critically important issue at the outset of her separate opinion, noting, "The more difficult question is what role the temporal relationship between regulatory enactment and title acquisition plays in a proper *Penn Central* analysis."[42] In her view, while the fact that an owner acquired property with knowledge of an existing land use limitation is not an automatic bar to a claim, it should figure heavily in a court's deliberations.

> Today's holding does not mean that the timing of the regulation's enactment relative to the acquisition of title is immaterial to the *Penn Central* analysis. Indeed, it would be just as much error to expunge this consideration from the takings inquiry as it would be to accord it exclusive significance.[43]

With Justice O'Connor apparently serving as the central vote on a sharply divided Court, her words, in particular, merit careful attention:

> Our polestar instead remains the principles set forth in *Penn Central* itself and our other cases that govern partial regulatory takings. Under these cases, interference with investment-backed expectations is one of a number of factors that a court must examine. Further, the regulatory regime in place at the time the claimant acquires the property at issue helps to shape the reasonableness of those expectations.[44]

Elaborating on this point, Justice O'Connor observes,

> [O]ur decision today does not remove the regulatory
> backdrop against which an owner takes title to property
> from the purview of the *Penn Central* inquiry. It simply
> restores balance to that inquiry. Courts properly con-
> sider the effect of existing regulations under the rubric
> of investment-backed expectations in determining whether
> a compensable taking has occurred."[45]

Justice O'Connor thus strongly reaffirms *Penn Central's* "reasonable investment-backed expectations" test and notes that the
owner's acquisition of property subject to a restrictive law is one
of the factors a court must consider in determining what the
owner's expectations are and whether they are reasonable.

Justice Ginsburg penned the principal dissent, which was joined
by Justices Souter and Breyer and which disagreed with the Court's
decision primarily on ripeness grounds. In her final footnote,
however, Justice Ginsburg offers some clues as to how these three
Justices might address the expectations issue were it properly presented, perhaps to provide some guidance to the Rhode Island
courts on remand. Justice Ginsburg states, "If Palazzolo's claim
were ripe and the merits presented, I would, at a minimum, agree
with Justice O'Connor, Justice Stevens, and Justice Breyer, that
transfer of title can impair a takings claim."[46] This somewhat
cryptic remark, with its use of the permissive term "can," dis-
tances these three Justices from the concurrence of Justice Scalia,
suggesting that these three members of the Court will factor the
state of the law at the time an owner acquires title into any analysis of the owner's expectations.

Justice Breyer, who joined Justice Ginsburg's dissent, also
wrote separately to emphasize this point. In just three paragraphs,
he stakes out a position on this issue much in line with that of
Justice O'Connor, noting, "[M]uch depends upon whether, or how,
the timing and circumstances of a change of ownership affect
whatever reasonable investment-backed expectations might otherwise exist."[47] Justice Breyer, however, goes further, noting that
while prior knowledge of a limiting law may not serve as an
automatic bar to a takings claim, it is a factor that will matter
greatly when a court must evaluate an owner's expectations as
one of the *Penn Central* factors. "Ordinarily, such expectations
will diminish in force and significance—rapidly and dramatically—as property continues to change hands over time. I believe
that such factors can adequately be taken into account within the
Penn Central framework."[48]

Justice Stevens appears to go at least as far as Justices O'Connor, Ginsburg, Breyer, and Souter in viewing prior knowledge of existing law as an important factor in any takings claim that alleges impairment of the owner's reasonable investment-backed expectations. If the takings claim is facial and ripe, as he believes Palazzolo's claim is,

> the extension of the right to compensation to individuals other than the direct victim of an illegal taking admits of no obvious limiting principle. If the existence of valid land-use regulations does not limit the title that the first postenactment purchaser of the property inherits, then there is no reason why such regulation should limit the rights of the second, the third, or the thirtieth purchaser.[49]

And in cases in which a landowner acquires regulated land but does not yet know how the regulations will be applied, "I would treat the owners' notice as relevant to the evaluation of whether the regulation goes 'too far,' but not necessarily dispositive."[50]

This close reading of the Court's opinions is important, given that the Court directly or obliquely addressed the question of expectations in six difficult, confusing, and inconsistent opinions. Before focusing more closely on the effect of *Palazzolo* on the role of reasonable investment-backed expectations, it is worth emphasizing that five of the Justices reaffirmed the viability of *Penn Central*'s open-ended approach to analyzing reasonable investment-backed expectations. The discussion above already has noted the pertinent remarks contained in opinions joined by five of the six concurring and dissenting Justices. Justice Kennedy's concurrence in *Lucas*[51] indicates that he too supports this argument, although his failure to restate that support in *Palazzolo* raises the question of whether he still adheres to his views of nine years earlier.

§ 3.3   *The Effect of* Palazzolo *on Judicial Analysis of Expectations*

Palazzolo provides property owners, government regulators, lawyers, and judges with one holding, two important insights, and a great deal of residual uncertainty regarding an owner's expectations. The case holds that an owner's knowledge of a limitation contained in land use law at the time she acquires property does not act as an automatic bar to her bringing a takings suit arising from the effect of that preexisting law on her land. The first insight is that the Court still views as viable *Penn Central*'s emphasis on examining reasonable investment-backed expectations as a critical component of the ad hoc analysis appropriate for most regulatory takings cases. The second insight is that different subcategories of takings cases merit different types of analysis, a fact that was true before *Palazzolo* but that this latest case underscores. *Palazzolo* also leaves open many key questions, including the precise definition of "reasonable investment-backed expectations." The best that lawyers and commentators may be able to do in the absence of clarification from the Court is to attempt to break the expectations issue down into its components, identify the factors that weigh heavily into each type of takings case in which expectations are an issue, and seek to assess the relative importance of each.

§ 3.3(a)   *Direct Condemnations*

In a direct condemnation case, the government entity is the plaintiff. It initiates the process of taking property in accordance with state law[52] and names the owner of the property as the defendant. By conceding that it is taking property, the government crystallizes its actions immediately, and the case is ripe from the start. There typically is little disagreement or uncertainty as to what the government is doing and generally no doubt as to which party is entitled to recover as a result. The owner may dispute whether the government entity has the right to take the property at all—perhaps by raising a public use defense[53]—and how much compensation the government owes the owner. But once a valid taking occurs, the owner at the time of the taking is the only party entitled to compensation, and this right does not pass to a successor owner.[54]

The precise moment at which the taking actually occurs is important for a number of reasons: it establishes the identity of the party entitled to compensation; it fixes the date on which the property must be valued; it is the date from which any interest on the award will be measured; and it begins the running of the statute of limitations.[55] If the owner were to transfer the remaining portion of the property after this date but before receiving compensation for the taking, the original owner would be transferring a newly reduced bundle of sticks and would remain entitled to the entire compensation award, and the successor would receive none of it. For this reason, the parties would have to factor the ongoing proceeding for compensation into their respective valuations of the property, and the successor would have to ensure that her offer price reflects only the value of the estate that remains after the taking.

The Court's reasonable investment-backed expectations analysis has focused on inverse condemnations rather than on direct condemnations such as these. But parties' expectations as to direct condemnations are so well settled that application of *Penn Central*'s expectations analysis to a direct condemnation would not lead to surprising or unpredictable results. When it comes to direct condemnations, buyers, sellers, and regulators operate against a background of established law, and there is nothing in *Palazzolo* to suggest that the Court intends to revisit this fairly stable fragment of takings law.[56]

§ 3.3(b) *Inverse Physical Takings*

In most disputed takings cases, the taking is an inverse one: The government acts in a way that falls short of a direct taking, but the owner nonetheless argues that this less direct action effectively takes private property under the Fifth Amendment.[57] In these cases, the owner becomes the plaintiff, contending that the government has inversely condemned her property, and the government defendant contests the very existence of a taking.[58]

The simplest type of inverse condemnation case is one in which the government permanently and physically occupies the owner's property, and the Court long has treated this type of action as a taking for which compensation is due.[59] In an inverse physical taking case, it is the government's intrusion onto the property that effects the taking.[60] This event, like the events that effect a direct condemnation, is easy to identify and prove in court, and ripeness concerns in these cases usually are minimal. The parties may dispute whether these events are permanent enough to rise to the level of a taking,[61] but there ordinarily will be considerably less dispute as to when they commenced.[62] The effective moment of an inverse physical taking serves the same functions as those listed in the discussion of direct condemnations. For the same reasons, the claim remains with the original owner even if that party conveys the land after the occupation occurs, as *Palazzolo* reaffirms.[63] Once again, the law in this area—and thus parties' expectations about that law—is fairly well settled, and *Palazzolo* demonstrates that nothing in that law has changed.[64]

§ 3.3(c) *Facial Inverse Regulatory Takings*

The cases become more difficult when there is no physical occupation by the government to mark the effective moment of the alleged taking. In the most challenging cases that arise today, a government entity may never intrude on the owner's land but instead may seek to enforce a law protecting the environment, a regulation aimed at preserving historically significant structures, or a zoning ordinance designed to segregate different types of uses. If the impact on the owner is severe, she may respond that the government's action effectively deprives her of property unconstitutionally even though there never has been any physical encroachment on the land.

In many cases, it is not clear how burdensome the law is with respect to the owner's land, and the landowner must ripen her claim.[65] But sometimes the law is so specific and far-reaching that its very existence allegedly takes the owner's property, and the owner may bring a facial inverse regulatory takings claim.[66] The owner need not ascertain the particular manner in which the government entity will apply the law to her land, because she is claiming that all possible applications work a taking of her property. The alleged taking thus occurs as soon as the law becomes effective, the claim ripens immediately, and this effective moment has all the repercussions noted above.[67]

Palazzolo notes that in "a direct condemnation action, or when a State has physically invaded the property without filing suit, the fact and extent of the taking are known,"[68] and any takings claim remains with the original owner. In contrast, when the plaintiff raises "[a] challenge to the *application* of a land-use regulation, . . . [the claim] does not mature until ripeness requirements have been satisfied."[69] Because a facial taking—like a direct condemnation or an inverse physical occupation—is a one-time event and not an ongoing process, the opinion suggests that facial claims also will remain with the original owner even if he transfers the property after the new law becomes effective. All three of these "instantaneous" takings should be treated in a similar way, a fact that is not changed by *Palazzolo*.

Facial takings are not common, and cases claiming a facial taking usually fail.[70] Government entities rarely pass blanket laws that are so detrimental to property owners, and even far-reaching land use laws generally allow for variances and special use permits. However, facial takings do occur from time to time,[71] and a court's analysis of a facial taking should proceed just as if the taking were a direct condemnation or an inverse physical taking. Judicial treatment of facial inverse takings is well settled, and the expectations of buyers and sellers should include a recognition of this settled law.

§ 3.3(d) *As-Applied Inverse Regulatory Takings, in General*

Even if a new land use law does not facially take an owner's property, it is possible that the government might apply the law in an individual case in a way that works a taking. These "as-applied" claims are far more common than facial ones, with government entities passing flexible laws and regulations, landowners coming up with diverse plans for different parcels of land, and government bodies then forced to apply these laws to these parcels in individualized ways. A disappointed owner may believe that the government's application of these laws works a taking of her land and may wish to prove this argument in federal court and receive compensation for a taking.

Government entities rarely prohibit all activity on land; more often, they place restrictions on the land that impair the owner's use without depriving the owner of that use entirely. The burden is on the owner to formulate a proposal and see whether the appropriate permitting agency grants or rejects the owner's application.[72] Moreover, a single permit denial does not necessarily imply that the government entity would reject all possible uses of the property. The agency might approve some less intensive use. Finally, the Fifth Amendment does not prohibit takings unless they are uncompensated. The owner cannot claim in federal court that she has been deprived of a constitutional right until an appropriate state forum rejects her claim for compensation.[73]

The Court has developed ripeness requirements that reflect the high degree of discretion inherent in the permitting process. A landowner cannot simply enter federal court and seek compensation. First, she must submit an application to the state or local agency with authority to grant it. If she does not receive consent, the denial is not necessarily final, and she must pursue whatever administrative appeals local procedures provide. Only when all possible appeals have been denied has she received a final administrative decision, and receipt of that final decision is the first step in the ripening process.[74] If her proposal was "grandiose," then the denial alone is insufficient to establish whether a more modest proposal would receive approval, and the owner may have to apply at least one more time and seek final government action on a less extensive proposal.[75] When all the necessary applications have been denied, the dissatisfied landowner next must pursue state remedial procedures and seek the just compensation to which she believes she is constitutionally entitled.[76] Her federal takings claim is not ripe, and she may not enter federal court, until the state denies just compensation.

These ripeness requirements are not merely senseless procedural hoops that an owner must jump through, although there certainly are owners and their lawyers who view them this way. Rather, the Court has recognized that a federal claim does not exist until an alleged taking goes uncompensated at the state level, and an owner cannot seek compensation in a state forum until the local permitting authority has demonstrated with specificity and finality just how the law will be applied to her land. Ripeness, then, is at least partly a jurisdictional prerequisite to any federal takings claim.[77]

The next issue this chapter logically must examine is the manner in which the reasonable investment-backed expectations test operates in as-applied inverse regulatory takings claims after *Palazzolo*. The answer, it turns out, will depend on the extent to which the owner has ripened her claim. The three subsections that follow distinguish among as-applied inverse regulatory takings claims on the basis of their ripeness and attempt to assess the degree to which *Palazzolo* affects the analysis of each of these different types of claims.[78]

§ 3.3(e) *Ripe As-Applied Inverse Regulatory Takings*

The first type of as-applied claim to examine is that in which an owner ripens a federal takings claim in accordance with the Supreme Court's standards and then transfers the property to a third party before pursuing this ripe claim to judgment. To illustrate, assume that this owner acquires the property at a time when the land use law is relatively permissive and then, after the law becomes more restrictive, pursues one or more permit applications to finality and is denied compensation at the state level. His federal claim now is ripe, but he transfers the property to a new owner some time after the state denies compensation. Is the buyer's acquisition of this property on these facts an absolute bar to her pursuit of takings compensation in federal court?

The answer, under *Palazzolo*, seems to be yes. The Court's opinion distinguished between two types of cases. In the first group of cases, a transfer of the property is an absolute bar to the transfer of the takings claim, and only the original owner may pursue takings compensation in federal court. In the second category, a transfer of the property is not an absolute bar, and the Court declined to establish the extent to which the buyer's claim is weakened by her acquisition of the property with knowledge of the limits contained in the existing law.[79]

The first category of cases, in which the successor may not receive compensation, expressly includes "[d]irect condemnation, by invocation of the State's power of eminent domain," and cases in which "a State has physically invaded the property without filing suit."[80] In cases of this type, "any award goes to the owner at the time of the taking, and . . . the right to compensation is not passed to a subsequent purchaser,"[81] as the previous discussion already has explored. This rule is a sensible one, for in these types of cases, the alleged constitutional injury is complete and the state-level claim is ripe before the original owner transfers the property, and the only questions are whether the owner can recover and how much.[82] The factual record is fully developed, the government either has taken property or it has not, and post-transfer events will not affect the success or failure of the claim.[83] If the Court were to allow the buyer to succeed to the seller's right to bring this claim, it essentially would be endorsing sales of lawsuits, and there is a long history, backed by valid public policy reasons, of rejecting transfers of interests in lawsuits.[84] Common law restrictions against champerty and maintenance, for example, remain strong in most states.[85]

Ripe as-applied inverse regulatory takings should fall into this category of non-transferable cases.[86] In holding that Palazzolo's possible future claim, which was unripe when he acquired the property, is not categorically barred by his knowledge of existing restrictions, the Court noted that "[a] challenge to the application of a land-use regulation ... does not mature *until ripeness re-quirements have been satisfied* ...; until this point an inverse condemnation claim alleging a regulatory taking cannot be maintained."[87] SGI, the previous owner, which had not ripened any takings claim, did not possess a mature claim and could not have maintained a federal action, or even an action in a state forum, at the time it transferred the property to Palazzolo. Since SGI could not have brought a claim, the Court reasoned, it would be unfair to Palazzolo—and perhaps a windfall to Rhode Island—categorically to bar Palazzolo from bringing a claim as well.[88]

If SGI had ripened its federal claim before transferring the property, however, the italicized language from the quote above strongly implies that only SGI, and not Palazzolo, could have raised this claim.[89] The line the Court draws between direct condemnations or inverse physical invasions, in which "the fact and extent of the taking are known,"[90] and as-applied challenges, in which the claim "does not mature until ripeness requirements have been satisfied,"[91] suggests that a successor owner cannot bring an inverse takings claim if its predecessor's as-applied claim already was ripe at the time of the transfer.[92] SGI would have met the Court's ripeness requirements and would possess a mature claim, just as if the state had condemned its property directly or taken it inversely by physical occupation. If the claim is mature it cannot be transferred, and a ripe as-applied inverse claim is mature.

The implication of this discussion for the reasonable invest-ment-backed expectations test thus becomes clear. The owner of a ripe as-applied inverse regulatory takings claim cannot transfer that claim to a successor owner, no successor owner can reason-ably expect otherwise, and the successor acquires the property but not the right to seek takings compensation in federal court. With regard to this type of claim, the sole impact of *Palazzolo* is to clarify existing law.

§ 3.3(f)   *As-Applied Inverse Regulatory Takings Claims That Are Unripe under the Compensation Prong*

The analysis becomes still trickier when we examine unripe as-applied claims, and it turns out that the reason the claim has not yet ripened may be critically important to the outcome. As noted earlier, there are two prongs to the ripeness test that federal courts must apply in regulatory takings cases.[93] First, the claimant must receive a denial from the appropriate regulatory agency, this de-nial must be administratively final through all appeals, and, if the proposal is grandiose, the claimant may have to bring at least one more proposal to a final resolution. Second, the claimant must be denied just compensation in the relevant state forum.

In some cases, the original owner of property may clear the first hurdle but not the second before transferring the property to a successor. The logic of *Palazzolo* suggests that the original owner must retain the takings claim in this situation and may not trans-fer it to the successor. The reason *Palazzolo* bars the transfer of claims arising from direct takings, inverse physical takings, and, most likely, ripe as-applied takings is that the facts of the claim already have become finalized. The original owner now owns restricted property and a ripe lawsuit, and only the first of these two assets is transferable.

But if the federal claim is unripe solely because the state has not yet decided whether compensation is due, then the *state* claim is ripe. The second federal ripeness prong requires that claimants seek compensation from the appropriate state court or adminis-trative body. Presumably, the state forum will refuse to entertain claims that are not factually final, which means that state ripeness requirements coincide with only the first of the two prongs that plaintiffs must meet before bringing federal takings claims. The state forum obviously could not require a prior rejection from itself as a prerequisite to its own jurisdiction.[94]

If the state claim is ripe, which is to say that the claimant has met the first but not the second of the two federal ripeness prongs, then the claim is completely developed factually. The federal claim still is unripe under the compensation prong, but the owner has received a final decision. This final decision ripens the state claim for compensation, and *Palazzolo* implies that ripe claims arising from final decisions are not transferable. "[T]he fact and extent of the taking are known,"[95] and the only remaining mystery is whether a state or federal tribunal will view this complete set of events as a violation of the claimant's Fifth Amendment rights.

Palazzolo appears to have no impact at all on the application of the reasonable investment-backed expectations test to a claim that is unripe solely because the original owner failed to pursue compensation in a state forum before transferring the property.[96] The original owner's expectations may be sufficiently grand to support a takings claim, but that claim remains with the original owner even after he conveys the property. The successor should factor the existence of the restrictive law into the price she offers for the property, and the original owner can respond with knowledge that he will retain the right to pursue his ripe state takings claim and his ripening federal claim.

§ 3.3(g)   *As-Applied Inverse Regulatory Takings Claims That Are Unripe under the Finality Prong*

In some cases, an as-applied takings claim will be unripe because the party that owned the property at the time the law became more restrictive has not received a final unappealable decision from the government entity with jurisdiction over the permit application and may not even have applied for a permit yet. It is in cases of this type that *Palazzolo* may have its greatest effect on judicial application of the expectations test. These cases arise when a party acquires land before a use restriction becomes effective and then transfers the property to a successor after that restriction becomes effective but before receiving a final denial from the appropriate government entity. In cases of this type, because "an inverse condemnation claim [by the prior owner] alleging a regulatory taking cannot be maintained,"[97] the successor's acquisition of title with knowledge of the preexisting legal limitation does not act as a complete bar to her successful maintenance of a federal takings claim.

The successor's knowledge of the intervening change in law may not bar her claim entirely, but it is a factor in the success of that claim, and the Justices in *Palazzolo* left open what the relative importance of that factor will be.[98] Parties on both sides of this issue and their lawyers obviously will seek guidance as to when a successor owner may bring a successful federal takings claim after acquiring property for which her seller never received a final permit denial. The reasons why the original owner did not receive a final rejection and the sequence of events in the permitting and sale processes are sure to be of critical importance in answering that question.

In some cases, the original owner will have been well on his way to receiving a final answer. Perhaps he applied for a permit and was denied, appealed that denial unsuccessfully, applied for a permit for a less intensive development and was denied, and was in the process of appealing that denial but had not received a final response when he sold the land. This case may be unripe, but it is awfully close to administrative finality, and a court should impute knowledge of this sequence of events to the successor when assessing the reasonableness of her expectations and the extent to which those expectations are investment-backed.

A successor owner who purchases the property in this thickly clouded state is likely to receive a substantial price discount over what the property would be worth if the original owner had received a permit or if the restriction had never gone into effect. If the new owner argues that she has suffered a taking on these facts, a court should rightly be skeptical. The new owner already should have received a price reduction that reflects the existence of the regulation and the unlikelihood of receiving a permit and will have great difficulty arguing credibly that a post-transfer final denial has deprived her of any expectations that are backed by her investment.[99] And if the new owner overpaid because of an excessively rosy view of the likelihood of receiving a permit (or because of a desire to maximize her chances of prevailing on a subsequent federal takings claim), it is hard to imagine that a court will find these investment-backed expectations to be reasonable.[100]

In cases of this type, the new owner is not categorically barred from bringing a claim arguing that her reasonable investment-backed expectations have been impaired and that this impairment rises to the level of a constitutional violation. But on the range of possible claims that *Palazzolo* leaves open, this one seems relatively weak, a point that at least five of the Justices appear to recognize. Justice O'Connor's concurrence observes that "the regulatory regime in place at the time the claimant acquires the property at issue helps to shape the reasonableness of [that claimant's] expectations,"[101] and Justice Breyer's dissent notes that "much depends upon whether, or how, the timing and circumstances of a change of ownership affect whatever reasonable investment-backed expectations might otherwise exist."[102] Justice Stevens's partial concurrence and Justice Ginsburg's dissent, the latter of which was joined by Justices Souter and Breyer, both express similar views.[103]

In other words, if an as-applied inverse takings claim is unripe because the original owner has never received a final unappealable decision, but the jurisdiction's application of its law to the land so far strongly suggests that no permit will be forthcoming, a successor who obtains title late in the permitting process may raise an inverse condemnation claim but is unlikely to win that claim. Five Justices of the *Palazzolo* Court would allow the claim to proceed, but a different five suggest that it probably will fail.

In contrast, the extent to which the new law may limit the successor owner's use of her land still may be a complete mystery. The law may be relatively new; the change in law may have been relatively unexpected; there may be little history of permit requests for similar projects on similar property in the jurisdiction; and the owner at the time of the new law's enactment may have done little or nothing in pursuit of a permit. The party who owned the land at the time the law changed can fairly claim that he simply has no idea how this new law will be applied to the land and has made no attempt to find out.

If the party who owns the land at the time the law changes were to sell that land under these conditions of uncertainty, the successor owner would have a stronger case than in the previous example.[104] The original owner's sincere uncertainty about the application of the new law gives the successor a higher degree of uncertainty as to how this law will be applied. As a result, the successor has at least some greater cause to be optimistic about the result of the permitting process than in the previous example. This optimism means that the successor is likely to pay more for the property. In other words, the successor reasonably has greater expectations that are backed by her investment. Under *Palazzolo*, this successor is permitted to ripen and bring her claim, and that claim may succeed.[105]

§ 3.3(h) *Summary of the Effect of* Palazzolo *on Judicial Analysis of Expectations*

Palazzolo holds that a party acquiring property after a land use law becomes more restrictive is not automatically barred from bringing a takings claim challenging the application of that law. While most types of takings claims are unlikely to benefit from this holding in any way, as this discussion has attempted to demonstrate, the property owner described in the last factual scenario is the one most likely to gain from the Court's decision. If the original owner's claim was unripe under the finality prong of the ripeness test and that owner and his successor truly had no idea how the government would apply the new law to the land, then there is some chance that the successor's reasonable investment-backed expectations have been constitutionally impaired.

Only some takings cases present successor owners who are bringing claims that their predecessors failed to ripen. Of these, only some are unripe under the finality prong of the Court's ripeness test when the original owner transfers the property. Still fewer of these cases involve parties with little idea as to how the government will apply the new law to the land. And even in these cases, a court still must assess the importance of a wide range of factors. In the end, *Palazzolo*, like *Lucas*, may turn out to be a case that is cited regularly but that changes the outcome of few disputes.

In fact, the most enduring legacy of *Palazzolo* may prove to be its hearty endorsement of *Penn Central*'s expectations test. The Court left little doubt about the continuing vitality of this test nearly a quarter century after the Court first applied it. The reasonable investment-backed expectations of takings claimants will continue to be important factors in the many judicial opinions that are sure to be handed down in the future, including cases in which an owner acquires property with notice of an existing restriction in the land use law.

§ 3.4   *Issues* Palazzolo *Leaves Open*

This chapter already has discussed the principal question that *Palazzolo* fails to answer: the extent to which a new owner who succeeds to an unripe as-applied claim is deemed to be aware of existing restrictions in land use law.[106] Even as the Court reaffirmed the importance of the *Penn Central* expectations test, the Justices were unable to agree on how to apply it in a case presenting facts such as those in *Palazzolo*. The Court left open other questions, as well. The remainder of this chapter will examine three of these questions and offer some insights as to how courts might address them when they arise in the future.

§ 3.4(a) *The Circularity Problem*

The *Penn Central* Court made an oversight when it failed to note that an owner's expectations are shaped by a body of law that includes the Court's statements as to what that owner's expectations may be. In other words, the *Penn Central* analysis is somewhat circular.[107] Justice Kennedy discussed this point in his concurrence in *Lucas*, noting, "There is an inherent tendency toward circularity in [the reasonable investment-backed expectations] synthesis, of course; for if the owner's reasonable expectations are shaped by what courts allow as a proper exercise of governmental authority, property tends to become what courts say it is."[108] This wrinkle is not fatal to the Court's mode of inquiry, however, and "[s]ome circularity must be tolerated in these matters.... [Moreover,... t]he expectations protected by the Constitution are based on objective rules and customs that can be understood as reasonable by all parties involved."[109]

Palazzolo falls victim to the same analytical weakness, but a contrary result in this case would have created the same problem in mirror image. No matter what the Court had held on this question, all owners will take title with notice of the outcome of the case and will factor this outcome into their expectations as to what state and federal property law hold. By ruling as it did, the Court informed those who acquire property with notice of a pre-existing change in the law that they nonetheless can challenge that law as a taking. A buyer's investment-backed expectations now can reasonably include the right to challenge existing laws and, on occasion, receive compensation as a result. This means that buyers should be willing to pay slightly more for recently restricted land (which comes with one additional stick in the bundle of rights: the right to bring this type of takings claim) and that sellers will receive correspondingly more (because they are selling a possible legal victory in addition to the restricted land). The Court has clarified what past expectations include, thereby shaping future expectations.[110]

Had the *Palazzolo* dissenters managed to muster five votes, the result would be equally circular in a reciprocal way.[111] The Court would have informed those who acquire property after a change in the law that their investment-backed expectations may not reasonably include the right to bring a takings claim arising from that change in law. Buyers thereafter would pay less for recently regulated land, sellers would receive less, and the Court's clarification of these parties' expectations would have shaped future expectations in just the opposite way.[112]

As Justice Kennedy's words and the analysis here both imply, this type of recursiveness is not fatal to the Court's approach, and it is difficult to see how any other approach could circumvent this problem. In some senses, property will always be nothing more than what legislatures and courts say it is, and every new judicial opinion that modifies the definition of property is changing all parties' expectations accordingly. The expectations test may imply that there is an immutable body of law inscribed on tablets in the background and that actors must act with knowledge of that law. But neither of the Court's possible outcomes in *Palazzolo* was inherently right or wrong. Every time a court or a legislature speaks, the supposedly immutable body of property law changes, and a party's expectations as to what the law says must thereafter include this modification to the law, along with a recognition that the body of property law will continue to evolve into the future.[113] The tough question, and the one that an awareness of the circularity problem acknowledges but continues to leave partly unanswered, is when those changes amount to takings.

§ 3.4(b)   *How Far Back Do We Go?*

Under *Palazzolo*, an owner who acquires property with knowledge of an existing law is not barred from challenging that law as a taking. The Court held that "a regulation that otherwise would be unconstitutional absent compensation is not transformed into a background principle of the State's law by mere virtue of the passage of title."[114] *Lucas* recognized that background principles of property law may undercut even a claim for a total taking, but "[a] law does not become a background principle for subsequent owners by enactment itself."[115] Moreover, under the more flexible *Penn Central* test, a "claim is not barred by the mere fact that title was acquired after the effective date of the state-imposed restriction."[116] A court's analysis must look backward in time, and this analysis is not stopped short at the time the plaintiff acquired the property.

If a court must look further back than this, how far back should it look? This question arose in two different contexts at the oral argument in *Palazzolo*. In a question to counsel for Palazzolo, Justice Souter asked, "[I]f rights to land use pass from owner to owner like that, how far back does the chain go? . . . [I]t seems to me that there's no logical stopping place until you get back to Roger Williams and the 17th century settlement. So where do we draw the line?"[117] At least in theory, Palazzolo may challenge ancient statutes that impaired the rights of owners long ago, and certainly long enough ago to predate modern land use controls.

A second comment from one of the Justices noted the similar problem that arises when a court must determine what the relevant parcel is for the purpose of calculating the diminution in the value of the property that the law has caused.[118] When a court determines the diminution in value, it must compare the loss to some baseline value of the parcel, and that baseline will differ depending on the time the court selects to look at the property and the size of the parcel at that time. Rhode Island, which wanted this fraction to be as small as possible, argued that a court must look at the history of the property in determining what the relevant parcel is for purposes of making this calculation. One of the Justices pointed out in response that "[e]verything's been whittled down from Lord Fairfax, I mean, in Virginia anyway, nobody would be able to make a takings claim."[119]

The opinions in *Palazzolo* pick up on these concerns but do not resolve them. In rejecting the state's argument for a strong version of the notice rule, the Court held that "[a] regulation or common-law rule cannot be a background principle for some owners but not for others"[120] but then remanded the case on this point. Justice O'Connor's concurrence notes that "the timing of the regulation's enactment relative to the acquisition is [neither] immaterial [nor of] exclusive significance."[121] Justice Scalia, in contrast, would give "no bearing"[122] to this factor.

Justice Breyer, dissenting, would carry Justice O'Connor's point still further. He notes that "[o]rdinarily, such expectations will diminish in force and significance—rapidly and dramatically—as property continues to change hands over time."[123] Justice Stevens "would treat the owner['s] notice as relevant . . . but not dispositive."[124] However, if Palazzolo can assume his predecessor's rights, "there is no reason why such regulations should limit the rights of the second, the third, or the thirtieth purchaser."[125] Finally, Justice Ginsburg, writing in dissent for three of the Justices, "would, at a minimum, agree . . . that transfer of title can impair a takings claim."[126]

All of the Justices, then, recognize that anything other than a categorical ban of Palazzolo's claim opens up a knotty timing issue. The Court does not, however, provide much guidance as to what types of expectations are reasonable in this context. The lack of consensus on the extent to which a current owner may step into the shoes of a predecessor provides little direction to lower courts, including the Rhode Island courts to which Palazzolo must return.

§ 3.4(c)   *Transfers Without Consideration*

The *Penn Central* test requires that constitutionally protected reasonable expectations be backed by an investment. A party that acquires property after a change in the law may have succeeded to title as a result of the death of the prior owner, the foreclosure of a mortgage, a sale in bankruptcy, a sale for nonpayment of property taxes, or the dissolution of a marriage.[127] It seems fair for a court to recognize that these parties' claims should not be weakened simply because they paid nothing, or less than full value, for the property.[128]

These types of parties often are not in a position to negotiate the terms of the transfer of the original owner's claim, to control its timing, or to adjust the purchase price to factor in the existence or nonexistence of any possible takings claim. In addition, their predecessors often had little control over the terms or the timing of the transfer. Successors of this type, to a greater extent than successors who purchase property at arm's length, should be permitted some latitude in enjoying the rights of a predecessor. By holding that notice is not a categorical bar to a successor's claim, the Court allows the lower courts to consider these factors when weighing the significance of the subsequent owner's knowledge of the prior change in law.[129]

§ 3.5   Conclusion

In rejecting a per se rule in *Palazzolo*, the Court acknowledged once again a fact that is readily apparent to property owners, government regulators, lawyers, and legal commentators: Takings law is extraordinarily challenging. It has been nearly a quarter century since the Court famously referred to regulatory takings decisions as "ad hoc, factual inquiries,"[130] a remark that, in its blunt accuracy, has spawned hundreds of reported cases and at least as many law review articles. *Palazzolo* leaves open nearly as many questions as the *Penn Central* opinion did in 1978, but it may be unfair to criticize the Court for failing to resolve an issue that is so difficult to resolve. In all its reported takings cases, the Court has been able to fashion only two firm categorical rules;[131] all else must be thrown on a balancing scale. Time may prove this approach to be the most fair, but it surely provides fodder for those legal realists who believe that the identity of the judge is the determinative factor in any regulatory takings case.

By reaffirming the importance of the reasonable investment-backed expectations test, one of the core analytical elements identified in *Penn Central*, the *Palazzolo* Court guarantees that developers and planners will continue to operate against a background of legal uncertainty and that lengthy and complex litigation will continue to arise from this uncertainty. The best that lawyers and commentators may be able to do in this unsettled atmosphere is to recognize that there are several different subcategories of takings cases, identify the elements that factor into each type of case, and seek to assess the relative importance of each of these factors.

Palazzolo, like so many other recent takings cases, may prove to have less of an impact in the long run than Court-watchers predicted it would as it made its way to the Court.[132] To a large extent, the decision is little more than a reaffirmation of a 23-year-old case, *Penn Central*. Only a single type of successor owner—one who succeeds to a claim that was unripe under the finality prong and to whom the application of the new law to the land remains uncertain—is likely to fare much better after *Palazzolo* than before. This is not to suggest that this claimant will win, for the case had little new to say about when a sequence of government actions amounts to a taking, and one has to believe that Palazzolo's odds of prevailing on remand are not great. One of the effects of *Palazzolo*, however, seems to be that it will allow this type of claim to survive and will afford it at least some chance of success.

Palazzolo nonetheless may have a somewhat greater effect on the broader practice of land use law from the perspectives of both property owners and regulators. The number of owners who believe they fall into this benefited category is likely to exceed the number who actually do, and every one of these potential claimants may be encouraged by *Palazzolo* to bring a case that it might not have brought before the case was decided. Given the *Palazzolo* Court's reaffirmation of its earlier ripeness cases and its resuscitation of the uncertain *Penn Central* standard, most of these plaintiffs still have a long and difficult path ahead of them, and most of them will lose in the end. But any tipping of the scales in favor of plaintiffs, however modest, will encourage more parties to bring claims, will allow some of these claims to survive longer than they would have earlier, and will lead to more landowner victories than before. Most important of all, any change of this type will modify the legal backdrop against which owners file applications, regulators decide how to respond to them, and parties negotiate settlements to their disagreements.

Notes

1. 121 S. Ct. 2448 (2001).
2. 438 U.S. 104 (1978).
3. *Id.* at 124. More particularly, the Court stated,

In engaging in these essentially ad hoc, factual inquiries, the Court's decisions have identified several factors that have particular significance. The economic impact of the regulation on the claimant and, particularly, the extent to which the regulation has interfered with distinct investment-backed expectations are, of course, relevant considerations. So, too, is the character of the governmental action. A "taking" may more readily be found when the interference with property can be characterized as a physical invasion by government than when interference arises from some public program adjusting the benefits and burdens of economic life to promote the common good.

Id. (citations omitted).

4. *Id.* at 125.

5. *Id.* at 136.

6. *See also* Ruckelshaus v. Monsanto Co., 467 U.S. 986, 1005-06 (1984) (noting that mere expectation or need does not rise to level of reasonable investment-backed expectation).

7. Frank I. Michelman, *Property, Utility, and Fairness: Comments on the Ethical Foundations of "Just Compensation" Law*, 80 HARV. L. REV. 1165 (1967).

8. *Id.* at 1212.

9. *Id.* at 1241 (footnote omitted).

10. *Id.* at 1243 (discussing Hadacheck v. Sebastian, 239 U.S. 394 (1915)). *See also id.* at 1239 (noting that "social action which merely . . . brings a deliberate gamble to its denouement . . . raises no question of compensability").

11. 483 U.S. 825 (1987).

12. *Id.* at 833 n.2.

13. *Id.*

14. 505 U.S. 1003 (1992). *See generally* Daniel R. Mandelker, *Investment-Backed Expectations in Takings Law, in* TAKINGS: LAND-DEVELOPMENT CONDITIONS AND REGULATORY TAKINGS AFTER *DOLAN* AND *LUCAS* 119, 124-27 (David L. Callies ed., 1996) (evaluating impact of two cases).

15. *Id.* at 1027 (footnote omitted). Among the Justices who joined in the Court's result, only Justice Kennedy, writing alone in concurrence, asked "whether the deprivation is contrary to reasonable, investment-backed expectations." *Id.* at 1034 (Kennedy, J., concurring).

16. *See generally* Gregory M. Stein, *Who Gets the Takings Claim? Changes in Land Use Law, Pre-Enactment Owners, and Post-Enactment Buyers*, 61 OHIO ST. L.J. 89, 91 n.12 (2000) [hereinafter Stein, *Who Gets the Takings Claim?*] (citing cases).

17. 678 N.E.2d 489 (N.Y. 1997) (mem.).

18. *Id.* at 490-91.

19. 666 N.E.2d 1300 (Mass. 1996).

20. *Id.* at 1303.

21. 746 A.2d 707 (R.I. 2000), *rev'd*, 121 S. Ct. 2448 (2001). *See also* McQueen v. South Carolina Coastal Council, 530 S.E.2d 628 (S.C. 2000), *vacated and remanded sub nom.* McQueen v. South Carolina Dep't of Health & Envtl. Control, 121 S. Ct. 2581 (2001).

22. SGI apparently reacquired five of the 74 lots in issue in 1969, four years after the state enacted its wetlands protection law. Dwight H. Merriam, *The* Palazzolo *Palaestra*, 23 ZONING & PLAN. L. REP. 93, 95 (2000) (summarizing conversation with Anthony Palazzolo).

23. Palazzolo v. Rhode Island, 121 S. Ct. 2448, 2455-57 (2001).

24. *Palazzolo*, 746 A.2d at 715 (quoting Lucas v. South Carolina Coastal Council, 505 U.S. 1003, 1027 (1992)).

25. *Id.* at 717.

26. This chapter will focus almost exclusively on those portions of *Palazzolo* that examine reasonable investment-backed expectations. The opinion also addresses two other critical takings issues—ripeness and segmentation—but space constraints prevent further exploration of those issues here.

27. Ripeness is discussed at *infra* notes 72-78 and accompanying text.

28. *Palazzolo*, 121 S. Ct. at 2462-63.

29. *Id.* (citing Danforth v. United States, 308 U.S. 271, 284 (1939)).

30. *Id.*; *see also* Lucas v. South Carolina Coastal Council, 505 U.S. 1003, 1028-29 (noting that preexisting government easement would constitute limitation on owner's title).

31. *Palazzolo*, 121 S. Ct. at 2463 (citing Danforth v. United States, 308 U.S. 271 (1939)). In *Danforth*, the Court considered a takings claim by an owner whose land became more prone to retaining flood waters as the result of a government-constructed flood-control project. The Court found that there was no direct condemnation because the government had never completed condemnation proceedings and paid compensation to the owner, *id.* at 284-86. There was no inverse physical condemnation by virtue of enactment of the relevant legislation or commencement or completion of construction of the offending levee because any increase in flood water retention was only incidental, *id.* at 286-87. *Danforth* recognizes that the precise effective times of both a direct condemnation and an inverse physical condemnation are easy to pinpoint and that the fact and extent of each type of taking are easy to determine. In each of these straightforward settings, then, there is no reason to abandon the traditional rule that only the owner at the time of the taking is entitled to compensation.

32. *See infra* notes 57-64 and accompanying text. *See also* United States v. Dow, 357 U.S. 17, 25 (1958) (noting that "certainty is not lacking under the rule . . . which fixes the 'taking' at the time of the entry into physical possession—a fact readily ascertainable whether or not the Government makes use of condemnation proceedings, and whether or not it ever files a declaration of taking").

33. *Palazzolo*, 121 S. Ct. at 2463.

34. *Id.*; *see infra* notes 93-105 and accompanying text.

35. *Palazzolo*, 121 S. Ct. at 2464.

36. The Supreme Court's lengthy discussion of expectations in the setting of a *Lucas*-type categorical taking implies that there may be cases in which these expectations could undercut an otherwise categorical takings claim. *Id.* at 2462-64. If so, then *Palazzolo* contradicts the most recent opinion in *Palm Beach Isles Assocs. v. United States*, 231 F.3d 1354 (Fed. Cir. 2000). The Federal Circuit held there that if a plaintiff suffers a *Lucas*-type categorical taking, then the plaintiff "is entitled to a recovery without regard to consideration of initial investment-backed expectations. . . . [They] are not a proper part of the analysis." *Id.* at 1364.

37. *Palazzolo*, 121 S. Ct. at 2462.

38. It is worth noting that the Court rejected a *Lucas*-type claim even though the property may have retained only 6.35 percent of its value. Palazzolo sought compensation of $3,150,000, *id.* at 2456, and accepted the state trial court's finding that the property retained a value of $200,000, *id.* at 2464.

39. *See generally* Phillips v. Washington Legal Found., 118 S. Ct. 1925, 1930 (1998) (holding that existence of private property interest is to be determined by reference to existing rules of state law). The Rhode Island constitution states that a land use regulation for environmental purposes "shall not be deemed to be a public use of private property,"

but this provision dates back only to 1986. R.I. CONST., art. 1, § 16; *see also* Merriam, *supra* note 22, at 6. The Rhode Island Supreme Court has acknowledged, moreover, the subordination of its own laws to the federal Takings Clause. Alegria v. Keeney, 687 A.2d 1249, 1252 (R.I. 1997) (noting that "this section, although firmly evincing a strong Rhode Island policy favoring the preservation and the welfare of the environment, cannot be interpreted by this Court to defeat the mandates of the Federal Constitution").

40. *Palazzolo*, 121 S. Ct. at 2468 (Scalia, J., concurring).

41. *Id.* (Scalia, J., concurring).

42. *Id.* at 2465 (O'Connor, J., concurring).

43. *Id.* at 2465-66 (O'Connor, J., concurring).

44. Id. at 2466 (O'Connor, J., concurring).

45. *Id.* at 2467 (O'Connor, J., concurring). She further notes, "Evaluation of the degree of interference with investment-backed expectations instead is *one* factor that points toward the answer to the question whether the application of a particular regulation to particular property 'goes too far.'" *Id.* (citing Pennsylvania Coal Co. v. Mahon, 260 U.S. 393, 415 (1922)).

46. *Id.* at 2477 n.3 (Ginsburg, J., dissenting) (citations omitted).

47. *Id.* at 2477 (Breyer, J., dissenting).

48. *Id.* (Breyer, J., dissenting).

49. *Id.* at 2472 (Stevens, J., concurring in part and dissenting in part).

50. *Id.* at 2471 n.6 (Stevens, J., concurring in part and dissenting in part) (citing *id.* at 2465-67 (O'Connor, J., concurring)).

51. Lucas v. South Carolina Coastal Council, 505 U.S. 1003, 1034, 1035 (1992) (Kennedy, J., concurring) (noting that "the test must be whether [a] deprivation is contrary to reasonable, investment-backed expectations" and adding that "courts must consider all reasonable expectations whatever their source").

52. The analysis in the remainder of this chapter will focus on takings by states and their subdivisions, as opposed to federal takings, because of the unique ripeness issues that state takings raise when the landowner seeks access to federal court. However, much of the following discussion applies with equal force to federal takings.

53. *See* Hawaii Hous. Auth. v. Midkiff, 467 U.S. 229 (1984) (rejecting public use challenge to takings claim); Berman v. Parker, 348 U.S. 26 (1954) (same).

54. *Palazzolo*, 121 S. Ct. at 2463; United States v. Dow, 357 U.S. 17, 22 (1958); Danforth v. United States, 308 U.S. 271, 284 (1939). *See also infra* notes 59-64 and accompanying text.

55. *See* ROBERT MELTZ ET AL., THE TAKINGS ISSUE 164-65 (1999) (discussing various reasons why identifying effective moment of taking with precision is essential); Gregory M. Stein, *Pinpointing the Beginning and Ending of a Temporary Regulatory Taking*, 70 WASH. L. REV. 953, 960-61 (1995) (same). *See also* Kirby Forest Indus., Inc. v. United States, 467 U.S. 1, 9-15 (1980) (addressing some of reasons why pinpointing effective date of taking is important).

56. In fact, *Palazzolo* reaffirms this law. *Palazzolo*, 121 S. Ct. at 2463 (noting that in direct condemnations, "any award goes to the owner at the time of the taking, and the right to compensation is not passed to a subsequent purchaser").

57. The Fifth Amendment states, in relevant part, "nor shall private property be taken for public use, without just compensation." U.S. CONST. amend. V. This clause has been held applicable to the states. Chicago, B. & Q. R.R. Co. v. City of Chicago, 166 U.S. 226, 235-41 (1897).

58. *See* Agins v. City of Tiburon, 447 U.S. 255, 258 & n.2 (1980); United States v. Clarke, 445 U.S. 253, 257-58 (1980).

59. *See* Loretto v. Teleprompter Manhattan CATV Corp., 458 U.S. 419 (1982); Kaiser Aetna v. United States, 444 U.S. 164 (1979); *cf.* Danforth v. United States, 308 U.S. 271, 286-87 (1939) (considering but rejecting claim of this type). There may be exceptions, such as when a government actor intrudes on an owner's property to abate a nuisance emanating from the property. *See, e.g.*, Hendler v. United States, 38 Fed. Cl. 611, 614-15 (1997), *aff'd*, 175 F.3d 1374 (Fed. Cir. 1999).

60. United States v. Dow, 357 U.S. 17, 21 (1958) (holding that taking occurred when government entered into possession of land, not when it filed declaration of taking three years later).

61. *See, e.g.*, United States v. Dickinson, 331 U.S. 745, 749 (1947) (holding that when government constructs dam that floods property, taking does not occur and statute of limitations does not begin to run until flooding stabilizes); United States v. General Motors Corp., 323 U.S. 373 (1945) (providing compensation for temporary taking of leasehold interest); *Danforth*, 308 U.S. at 286-87 (rejecting owner's claim because intrusion was only "incidental").

62. *Cf. Dickinson*, 331 U.S. at 749 (noting that "there is nothing in legal doctrine[] to preclude . . . postponing suit until the situation becomes stabilized"). *See generally* Boling v. United States, 220 F.3d 1365, 1370-73 (Fed. Cir. 2000) (summarizing difficulties in determining accrual date of takings claim arising from erosion caused by government).

63. Palazzolo v. Rhode Island, 121 S. Ct. 2448, 2463 (2001) (applying same analysis to "a direct condemnation action" and to "[an action] when a State has physically invaded the property without filing suit"). *See also* Lucas v. South Carolina Coastal Council, 505 U.S. 1003, 1028-29 (1992) (reaffirming that government may "assert a permanent easement that was a pre-existing limitation upon the landowner's title"); *Dow*, 357 U.S. at 27 (rejecting claim by successor owner who obtained title after government took physical possession of property). *See generally supra* notes 60-62.

64. If the owner's claim is against a state or local government entity, she still will have to ripen her claim by seeking compensation in the appropriate state forum. *See infra* notes 72-78 and accompanying text (discussing ripeness). *But see* Suitum v. Tahoe Reg'l Planning Agency, 520 U.S. 725, 736 n.10 (1997) (stating that facial claims become ripe upon enactment of offending legislation, without mentioning need to seek compensation).

65. *See infra* notes 72-78 and accompanying text.

66. *See, e.g.*, Keystone Bituminous Coal Ass'n v. DeBenedictis, 480 U.S. 470, 494-95 (1987) (distinguishing between facial and as-applied claims); National Adver. Co. v. City of Raleigh, 947 F.2d 1158, 1163-66 (4th Cir. 1991) (same).

67. *See supra* note 55 and accompanying text (discussing significance of effective moment of taking).

68. *Palazzolo*, 121 S. Ct. at 2463.

69. *Id.* (emphasis added).

70. *See, e.g., Keystone*, 480 U.S. at 495 (referring to "uphill battle" landowners with facial takings claims confront); Hodel v. Virginia Surface Mining & Reclamation Ass'n, Inc., 452 U.S. 264, 296-97 (1981) (rejecting facial claim).

71. Justice Stevens's opinion in *Palazzolo* demonstrates that he thought the petitioner was raising a facial claim, although he would have found for the respondent on the merits. *Palazzolo*, 121 S. Ct. at 2470 (Stevens, J., concurring in part and dissenting in part) (noting that "[t]he most natural reading of petitioner's complaint is that the regulations in

and of themselves precluded him from filling the wetlands, and that their adoption there-fore constituted the alleged taking"). *See also supra* notes 49-50 and accompanying text.

72.   *See, e.g.*, United States v. Riverside Bayview Homes, Inc., 474 U.S. 121, 127 (1985) (observing that, "after all, the very existence of a permit system implies that permission may be granted, leaving the landowner free to use the property as desired").

73.   Williamson County Reg'l Planning Comm'n v. Hamilton Bank of Johnson City, 473 U.S. 172, 194-97 (1985); *see generally* Gregory M. Stein, *Regulatory Takings and Ripeness in the Federal Courts*, 48 VAND. L. REV. 1, 21-22 (1995) [hereinafter Stein, *Regulatory Takings and Ripeness*] (discussing elements of ripeness test).

74.   Suitum v. Tahoe Reg'l Planning Agency, 520 U.S. 725, 733-42 (1997); *Williamson County*, 473 U.S. at 186-94 (1985).

75.   MacDonald, Sommer & Frates v. Yolo County, 477 U.S. 340, 351-53, 353 n.9 (1986); *cf. Palazzolo*, 121 S. Ct. at 2458 (observing that additional applications are unnecessary when "[the] unequivocal nature of the . . . regulations" and "[the] application of the regulations to the subject property" suggest that such attempts would be fruitless).

76.   *Suitum*, 520 U.S. at 733-34; *Williamson County*, 473 U.S. at 194-97.

77.   *Suitum*, 520 U.S. at 734 n.7 (citing Reno v. Catholic Social Services, Inc., 509 U.S. 43, 57 n.18 (1993) and discussing Article III attributes of ripeness); Stein, *Regulatory Takings and Ripeness, supra* note 73, at 11-14 (same).

78.   *See Palazzolo*, 121 S. Ct. at 2470 (Stevens, J., concurring in part and dissenting in part) (treating claim as facial). *See also supra* note 71.

79.   The Court's six opinions express a range of views on the emphasis this factor should receive. *See supra* notes 26-51 and accompanying text.

80.   *Palazzolo*, 121 S. Ct. at 2463.

81.   *Id.*

82.   If the original owner has not yet sought takings compensation for an inverse taking in the appropriate state forum, then her federal claim is not yet ripe. *See* Williamson County Reg'l Planning Comm'n v. Hamilton Bank of Johnson City, 473 U.S. 172, 194-97 (1985); *supra* notes 64, 72-78 and accompanying text. However, the state-level claim for compensation becomes ripe upon receipt of a final decision, *see infra* notes 94-95 and accompanying text, and the landowner is entitled to seek compensation from the state in the state's designated forum.

83.   *See* 2 JULIUS L. SACKMAN, NICHOLS ON EMINENT DOMAIN § 5.02[3] (3d ed. 1998) (distinguishing between claims assigned before and after taking has been effected).

84.   *See, e.g.,* 31 U.S.C. § 3727 (1994) (prohibiting assignment of any part of claim against United States government); Ari Dobner, Comment, *Litigation for Sale*, 144 U. PA. L. REV. 1529, 1543-46 (1996) (discussing history of discouraging trafficking in litigation and noting that, while doctrine has eroded somewhat, champerty remains illegal in most states); Joseph M. Perillo, *The Law of Lawyers' Contracts Is Different*, 67 FORDHAM L. REV. 443, 473-75 (1998) (discussing medieval prohibition on splitting fruits of litigation and noting tension between growth of free assignability of assets and doctrine of champerty); *infra* note 85. *See also* United States v. Dow, 357 U.S. 17 (1958) (discussed at *supra* notes 59-64 and accompanying text); Danforth v. United States, 308 U.S. 271 (1939) (same).

85.   Champerty is defined as "[a] bargain by a stranger with a party to a suit, by which such third person undertakes to carry on the litigation at his own cost and risk, in consid-eration of receiving, if successful, a part of the proceeds or subject sought to be recov-ered." *Black's Law Dictionary* 119 (abridged 5th ed. 1983). An arm's-length purchaser of property would appear to meet this definition, although, in the case of an unripe claim, this

purchaser arguably is acquiring rights from a party to only a *potential* suit. Common law prohibitions on champerty remain strong in most states. *See* Dobner, *supra* note 84, at 1543-46 (noting that champerty remains illegal in most states and criminal in some); *but see* CHARLES W. WOLFRAM, MODERN LEGAL ETHICS 489-92 (1986) (questioning modern need for champerty doctrine).

86. The Court expressed concerns about the "quixotic" effect of the notice rule on older owners or owners who lack the resources to retain their property. *Palazzolo*, 121 S. Ct. at 2463. In the case of takings claims that pass to successors after they have ripened, courts could better address these fairness concerns by creating exceptions to a rule that otherwise bars the transfer of ripe claims. *See infra* notes 127-29 and accompanying text. Unripe claims, under the Court's analysis, merit different treatment. *See infra* notes 93-105 and accompanying text.

87. *Palazzolo*, 121 S. Ct. at 2463 (emphasis added).

88. "It would be illogical, and unfair, to bar a regulatory takings claim because of the post-enactment transfer of ownership where the steps necessary to make the claim ripe were not taken, or could not have been taken, by a previous owner." *Id.*

89. *See* Stein, *Who Gets the Takings Claim?*, *supra* note 16, at 109-12 (suggesting that ripe as-applied claims, like facial claims, should not be transferable).

90. *Palazzolo*, 121 S. Ct. at 2463.

91. *Id.*

92. *See also supra* notes 52-64 and accompanying text (discussing similar rule in context of direct takings and inverse physical takings).

93. *See generally supra* notes 72-78 and accompanying text.

94. *See* Stuart Minor Benjamin, Note, *The Applicability of Just Compensation to Substantive Due Process Claims*, 100 YALE L.J. 2667, 2672 (1991) (stating "[t]he logic of *Williamson County* would suggest that a property owner does not have a ripe [federal] taking claim when she enters state proceedings to obtain just compensation").

95. *Palazzolo*, 121 S. Ct. at 2463.

96. *See* 2 SACKMAN, *supra* note 83, § 5.01[5][d] (noting generally that "if the parcel of land from which the taking is made changes hands after the taking has occurred but before the compensation has been paid, the right to receive the compensation does not run with the land, but remains a personal claim of the person who was the owner . . . at the time of the taking").

97. *Palazzolo*, 121 S. Ct. at 2463.

98. After first noting that "[w]e have no occasion to consider the precise circumstances when a legislative enactment can be deemed a background principle of state law [under the *Lucas* nuisance exception] or whether those circumstances are present here," *id.* at 2464, the Court concluded that "[t]he claims under the *Penn Central* [expectations] analysis were not examined, and for this purpose the case should be remanded," *id.* at 2465. As previously discussed, the concurring and dissenting Justices offer a range of views as to the impact of Palazzolo's knowledge of the intervening change in law. *See supra* notes 40-51 and accompanying text.

99. *See also* Lynda J. Oswald, *Cornering the Quark: Investment-Backed Expectations and Economically Viable Uses in Takings Analysis*, 70 WASH. L. REV. 91, 115 (1995) (describing such claims as "ludicrous"). There is an element of circularity to this argument, of course, as is discussed below. *See infra* notes 107-13 and accompanying text.

100. *See* Stein, *Who Gets the Takings Claim?*, *supra* note 16, at 114-17 (discussing meaning of "reasonable" and "investment-backed" in context of claim by buyer who acquires property after unfavorable change in law). *See generally* Michelman, *supra* note

7, at 1235-45 (discussing impact of prior knowledge of disadvantageous change in law).

101. *Palazzolo*, 121 S. Ct. at 2466 (O'Connor, J., concurring); *supra* notes 42-45 and accompanying text.

102. *Palazzolo*, 121 S. Ct. at 2477 (Breyer, J., dissenting); *supra* notes 47-48 and accompanying text.

103. *See Palazzolo*, 121 S. Ct. at 2471 (Stevens, J., concurring in part and dissenting in part) (noting that "[t]he title Palazzolo took by operation of law in 1978 was limited by the regulations then in place to the extent that such regulations represented a valid exercise of the police power"); *id.* at 2477 n.3 (Ginsburg, J., dissenting) (agreeing with these three other opinions on this issue); *supra* notes 46, 49-50 and accompanying text.

104. *See, e.g.,* RICHARD A. EPSTEIN, TAKINGS: PRIVATE PROPERTY AND THE POWER OF EMI-NENT DOMAIN 154-56 (1985) (arguing that notice rule is unfair to sellers who acquired property before law changed); WILLIAM A. FISCHEL, REGULATORY TAKINGS 194 (1995) (questioning rule that prohibits owner at time law becomes more restrictive from transfer-ring potential takings claim to successor owner); William A. Fischel & Perry Shapiro, *Takings, Insurance, and Michelman: Comments on Economic Interpretations of "Just Compensation" Law*, 17 J. LEGAL STUD. 269, 288-89 (1988) (arguing that rule barring post-enactment buyers from receiving compensation takes property from parties who sold land to them; discussion apparently presupposes unripe as-applied claim); *see also* THOMAS J. MICELI & KATHLEEN SEGERSON, COMPENSATION FOR REGULATORY TAKINGS: AN ECONOMIC ANALYSIS WITH APPLICATIONS 82 (1996) (observing that "the threat of a regulation had to arise unexpectedly at some point in time").

105. *See generally* Daniel R. Mandelker, *Investment-Backed Expectations in Taking Law*, 27 URB. LAW. 215, 232-37 (1995) (discussing extent to which regulatory uncertainty determines strength of investment-backed expectations).

106. *See supra* notes 40-51 and accompanying text (discussing differing views of six Justices).

107. *See* Louis Kaplow, *An Economic Analysis of Legal Transitions*, 99 HARV. L. REV. 509, 522 (1986) (calling reliance arguments circular because they "implicitly assume that it is reasonable to expect laws never to change—a particularly perverse assumption given that laws change quite frequently, and often in predictable ways") (footnote omitted).

108. Lucas v. South Carolina Coastal Council, 505 U.S. 1003, 1034 (1992) (Kennedy, J., concurring).

109. *Id.* at 1034-35.

110. *See also* Anello v. Zoning Bd. of Appeals, 678 N.E.2d 870, 871-72 (N.Y. 1997) (discussing circularity problem).

111. *See* Kaplow, *supra* note 107, at 525 (noting that "the counter-argument [to the reliance argument] . . . is similarly flawed"). *But see* Lynn E. Blais, *Takings, Statutes, and the Common Law: Considering Inherent Limitations on Title*, 70 S. CAL. L. REV. 1, 7 (1996) (arguing that treating preexisting statutes as inherent limitations on title reduces circularity problems).

112. This second approach may be more desirable from a judicial perspective, as it reduces problems of proof. *See* Stein, *Who Gets the Takings Claim?*, *supra* note 16, at 105-09, 111-12, 154-61 (demonstrating benefits of this approach).

113. Good v. United States, 189 F.3d 1355 (Fed. Cir. 1999), *cert. denied*, 529 U.S. 1053 (2000). *Good*, in many ways, serves as a perfect reflection of *Palazzolo*. Under *Palazzolo*, a property owner may prevail even though the law had changed before she acquired the property. Under *Good*, a government body may prevail even though the law did not

change until after the owner acquired the property. The *Palazzolo* holding suggests that plaintiffs in the position that Good was in will have a stronger case under the *Penn Central* balancing test than will plaintiffs in the position of Palazzolo himself. But one of *Palazzolo*'s important lessons is its confirmation of the extent to which the Court disfavors per se rules in takings law. *See* Palazzolo v. Rhode Island, 121 S. Ct. 2448, 2467 (2001) (O'Connor, J., concurring) (cautioning that "[t]he temptation to adopt what amount to *per se* rules in either direction must be resisted").

114. *Palazzolo*, 121 S. Ct. at 2464.

115. *Id.*

116. *Id.*

117. Palazzolo v. Rhode Island, 2001 WL 196990, at *17 (oral argument). The attribution to Justice Souter comes from Peter B. Lord, *R.I.'s Final Arguments—Justices Pepper Lawyers with Questions*, PROVIDENCE J., Feb. 27, 2001, at A1.

118. Pennsylvania Coal Co. v. Mahon, 260 U.S. 393, 413 (1922) (noting importance of "extent of the diminution" in value); *id.* at 419 (Brandeis, J., dissenting) (criticizing this approach). *See also* District Intown Props. Ltd. P'ship v. District of Columbia, 198 F.3d 874, 879-82 (D.C. Cir. 1999) (discussing difficulties in identifying denominator of fraction that represents diminution in value), *cert. denied*, 531 U.S. 812 (2000); *id.* at 885 (Williams, J., concurring) (noting that "[t]he larger the parcel, the greater the chance that the regulated land will retain an economically viable use"); Loveladies Harbor, Inc. v. United States, 28 F.3d 1171, 1180-82 (Fed. Cir. 1994) (discussing denominator problem).

119. Palazzolo v. Rhode Island, 2001 WL 196990, at *41 (oral argument).

120. *Palazzolo*, 121 S. Ct. at 2464.

121. *Id.* at 2465 (O'Connor, J., concurring).

122. *Id.* at 2468 (Scalia, J., concurring).

123. *Id.* at 2477 (Breyer, J., dissenting).

124. *Id.* at 2471 n.6 (Stevens, J., concurring in part and dissenting in part).

125. *Id.* at 2472 (Stevens, J., concurring in part and dissenting in part).

126. *Id.* at 2477 n.3 (Ginsburg, J., dissenting).

127. *See generally* Stein, *Who Gets the Takings Claim?*, *supra* note 16, at 161-63 (discussing these methods of obtaining title).

128. Justice O'Connor recognized this point. *See Palazzolo*, 121 S. Ct. at 2467 (noting that "[w]e also have never held that a takings claim is defeated simply on account of the lack of a personal financial investment by a postenactment acquirer of property, such as a donee, heir, or devisee") (citation omitted); *see also* Steven J. Eagle, *The Rise and Rise of "Investment-Backed Expectations,"* 32 URB. LAW. 437, 440 (2000) (noting that interests of devisees should be protected under expectations test); Richard A. Epstein, Lucas v. South Carolina Coastal Council: *A Tangled Web of Expectations*, 45 STAN. L. REV. 1369, 1370 (1993) (noting that "[t]he government cannot take property from a donee anymore than it can take it from a buyer").

129. *See Palazzolo*, 121 S. Ct. at 2463 (noting that state's proposed rule, when applied in contexts such as these, might be "capricious in effect" and "quixotic"). *See also id.* at 2467 (O'Connor, J., concurring) (suggesting that courts "must attend to those circumstances which are probative of what fairness requires in a given case"); *id.* at 2477 (Breyer, J., dissenting) (noting that "much depends upon whether, or how, the timing and circumstances of a change of ownership affect whatever reasonable investment-backed expectations might otherwise exist"). *Cf.* Anello v. Zoning Bd. of Appeals, 678 N.E.2d

870, 873 (N.Y. 1997) (Wesley, J., dissenting) (noting "interesting alchemy [of notice rule] on the estate of a decedent").

130.   Penn Cent. Transp. Co. v. City of New York, 438 U.S. 104, 124 (1978).

131.   *See* Lucas v. South Carolina Coastal Council, 505 U.S. 1003 (1992) (holding that deprivation of all economically viable use of property is taking per se); Loretto v. Teleprompter Manhattan CATV Corp., 458 U.S. 419 (1982) (holding that permanent physical occupation of property is taking per se); *see also* Hodel v. Irving, 481 U.S. 704 (1987) (holding that right to devise property is valuable property right).

132.   One commentator artfully referred to the Supreme Court's granting of the petition for certiorari in *Palazzolo* as "the chance to see . . . a vigorous contest for some modern-day, Sumo-sized issues surrounding takings claims, issues that are the polemical poles of the interpretation of the Fifth Amendment" and referred to the contest as "worthy of World Wrestling Federation sponsorship." Merriam, *supra* note 22, at 93, 94.

THE PARCEL-AS-A-WHOLE RULE AND ITS IMPORTANCE IN DEFENDING AGAINST REGULATORY TAKINGS CHALLENGES

4

TIMOTHY J. DOWLING

§ 4.0   Introduction

The government generally should prevail in a regulatory takings challenge if it can show that the challenged regulation does not deprive the landowner of all (or virtually all) economically viable use and value of the land. This chapter addresses the threshold question of how to define the relevant parcel of property for takings analysis. It explains why courts examine the impact of a regulation by reference to "the parcel as a whole" and provides government counsel with arguments for ensuring that the relevant parcel for takings analysis includes the entire parcel.[1]

§ 4.1   Defining the Relevant Parcel

Suppose a setback ordinance requires a landowner to locate any permanent structure on the land a certain distance from the street, thereby allowing the landowner to build on the back 90 percent of the parcel but completely devaluing the front 10 percent. The outcome of a takings challenge to the ordinance would depend on whether the court analyzes the economic impact as a 10 percent reduction in value of the entire parcel or a complete devaluation of the restricted portion.

In addition to such physical segmentation of a parcel, it is possible to sever property interests conceptually. Takings caselaw often characterizes property as a bundle of rights, and it describes individual property rights as "sticks in the bundle."[2] Conceptual severance isolates one of the sticks in the bundle. For example, in a takings challenge to a ban on the sale of assault weapons, the claimant might argue for conceptual severance of the right to sell weapons and contend that the ban completely destroys that right, thus taking its property. As shown below, the claimant should lose.

The larger the parcel to be considered, the more difficulty the claimant has showing a dramatic impact on use and value. Accordingly, claimants generally try to define the relevant parcel as narrowly as possible by severing related property interests. They sometimes advocate for an "affected portion" standard, arguing that the relevant parcel should include only the specific property restricted or affected by the challenged regulation. The discussion below will show that such segmentation (both physical and conceptual) is improper and should be rejected.

§ 4.2   The Supreme Court's Parcel-as-a-Whole Rule

§ 4.2(a)   The Parcel-as-a-Whole Rule Defined

The Supreme Court repeatedly has held that the relevant parcel to be examined is not the affected portion of the property but the entire parcel, or what the Court calls the parcel as a whole. This parcel-as-a-whole rule is sometimes called the nonsegmentation or nonseverance rule, because it prohibits a claimant from dividing the whole parcel into discrete segments for takings analysis. The Court has applied the parcel-as-a-whole rule to reject both physical and conceptual severance of one of the sticks in the bundle. Although the Supreme Court resisted segmentation in several early land use cases, it first articulated the parcel-as-a-whole rule in *Penn Central Transportation Co. v. New York City.*[3] There, the City of New York applied historic preservation laws to deny the owners of Grand Central Terminal permission to construct an office building atop it. In rejecting the claimants' argument that the laws took the air rights above the terminal, the Court stated:

> "Taking" jurisprudence does not divide a single parcel into discrete segments and attempt to determine whether the rights in a particular segment have been entirely ab-

rogated. In deciding whether a particular governmental action has effected a taking, this Court focuses rather both on the character of the action and on the nature and extent of the interference with rights in the parcel as a whole—here, the city tax block designated as "the landmark site."[4]

The Court relied on earlier cases upholding height restrictions, mining restrictions, and setback requirements to conclude that takings analysis does not allow claimants to segment their property into discrete property interests to show a complete taking of the severed portion.[5] At first glance, *Penn Central* might be viewed solely as a rejection of physical segmentation (the airspace above the terminal versus the terminal), but it also rejected conceptual severance of one of the sticks in the bundle of property rights (air rights versus the right to use the terminal).[6]

One year later, in *Andrus v. Allard*,[7] the Court again rejected a claimant's attempt at conceptual severance. *Andrus* involved a takings challenge to a ban on the sale of artifacts made from the feathers of bald eagles and other federally protected birds. Although the ban extinguished the claimants' right to sell the artifacts, the Court found no taking: "At least where an owner possesses a full 'bundle' of property rights, the destruction of one 'strand' of the bundle is not a taking, because the aggregate must be viewed in its entirety."[8] Because the claimants retained the right to possess, transport, donate, and devise the property, there was no taking, even though the ban prevented the most (and perhaps the only) profitable use of the property.[9]

In *Keystone Bituminous Coal Ass'n v. DeBenedictis*,[10] the Supreme Court emphatically reaffirmed the parcel-as-a-whole rule as applied to both physical and conceptual severance. There, the claimants argued that Pennsylvania subsidence protections took 27 million tons of their coal required to be left in the ground. This coal comprised less than 2 percent of the total coal in the mines covered by the protections. The Court quoted extensively from *Penn Central* and *Andrus* to reject this physical segmentation argument, concluding that "[t]he 27 million tons of coal do not constitute a separate segment of property for takings law purposes."[11]

The claimants then contended that the subsidence protections took the claimants' support estates, which Pennsylvania law recognizes as a separate property interest.[12] The Court used the parcel-as-a-whole rule to reject this conceptual severance.[13] Again relying on *Penn Central* and *Andrus*, the Court held that "takings jurisprudence forecloses reliance on such legalistic distinctions within a bundle of property rights."[14] The Court also noted that "the support estate has value only insofar as it protects or enhances the value of the estate with which it is associated," which further demonstrates the impropriety of severing it from the rest of the claimants' bundle of rights.[15]

Keystone reflects the Court's strong reluctance to fashion rules of takings liability that would call into question routine land use controls. The Court emphasized that if physical segmentation were allowed, "one could always argue that a setback ordinance requiring that no structure be built within a certain distance from the property line constitutes a taking because the footage represents a distinct segment of property for takings law purposes."[16] This concern harmonizes with Justice Holmes's recognition in *Pennsylvania Coal Co. v. Mahon* that the "[g]overnment hardly could go on if to some extent values incident to property could not be diminished without paying for every such change in the general law."[17]

The Supreme Court applied the parcel-as-a-whole rule again in 1993 in *Concrete Pipe and Products, Inc. v. Construction Laborers Pension Trust*,[18] where a unanimous Court applied the rule to reject a takings challenge to a federal law that imposed liability on employers who withdrew from pension plans. In response to the claimant's argument that the law took its entire property, the Court admonished that takings claimants may not unfairly manipulate their property interests to demonstrate a compensable taking:

> [A] claimant's parcel of property [may] not first be divided into what was taken and what was left for the purposes of demonstrating the taking of the former to be complete and hence compensable. To the extent that any portion of property is taken, that portion is always taken in its entirety; the relevant question, however, is whether the property taken is all, or only a portion of, the parcel in question.[19]

Takings claimants sometimes try to limit the significance of *Concrete Pipe* by noting that it is not a land use case, but the *Concrete Pipe* Court expressly relied on prior land use cases such as *Penn Central* and *Keystone*, and thus its reaffirmation of the parcel-as-a-whole rule applies to regulatory takings cases across the board.[20]

The Court's most recent reaffirmation of the parcel-as-a-whole rule appears in *Dolan v. City of Tigard*.[21] There, a landowner challenged a requirement that she dedicate a portion of her property as a greenway and pathway as a condition to permission to expand her plumbing and electric supply store. Although the Court imposed a new "rough proportionality" requirement for such dedication requirements because they infringe the owner's right to exclude others,[22] it forcefully rejected the suggestion that the dedication denied the landowner all economically viable use of her property. In so ruling, the Court defined the relevant parcel to include the entirety of Dolan's parcel, including the portion on which her store is situated, not just the strip of land subject to the dedication requirement.[23]

The parcel-as-a-whole rule has infused the Court's takings jurisprudence since the turn of the century, well before the clear articulations of the rule in *Penn Central*, *Keystone*, and *Concrete Pipe*. In 1915, the Court rejected a takings challenge to a mining ban despite the 92.5 percent value loss.[24] In 1926, it upheld a zoning ordinance despite a 75 percent value loss.[25] In 1927, the Court sustained a setback requirement that prohibited development on the affected portion of the parcel at issue.[26] All of these rulings and many more are necessarily premised on a consideration of the claimant's entire parcel, not just the regulated portion.[27]

§ 4.2(b) *Caveats*

Notwithstanding the relative clarity of the parcel-as-a-whole rule, certain caveats are necessary, particularly concerning conceptual severance. First, the Court has deemed the right to exclude others from one's property to be "one of the most essential sticks" in the bundle.[28] Therefore, courts routinely segment the right to exclude others in takings analysis, and impairment of that right through government-compelled physical occupation might give rise to a taking.

Second, courts similarly afford special protection to the right to devise property to one's heirs, and abolition of that right might well constitute a taking.[29]

Third, *Andrus* qualifies its nonsegmentation ruling as applying "at least where the owner possesses a full 'bundle' of property rights."[30] If the owner never possessed the full bundle of rights, courts are more willing to engage in conceptual severance.[31]

§ 4.2(c) Lucas *Footnote 7*

Some takings claimants argue for an "affected portion" standard by trying to exploit dicta contained in footnote 7 of *Lucas v. South Carolina Coastal Council*,[32] which is reproduced in the margin below.[33] Some historical background is necessary to understand the significance of this *Lucas* dicta.

In *Penn Central*, the Court noted that *Mahon* arguably treated the support estate in that case as a separate property interest, which raised the issue of whether the *Penn Central* Court should treat the air rights over Grand Central Terminal as a discrete property interest.[34] The *Penn Central* Court rejected this contention, but it failed to make clear whether it was repudiating this reading of *Mahon* or distinguishing it.[35] In *Keystone,* the Court appeared to clarify this ambiguity when it expressly rejected the contention that a support estate should be analyzed apart from the rest of the parcel.[36] The *Keystone* Court read *Mahon* not as allowing segmentation of property interests, but rather as finding that the claimant's entire coal company "could not undertake profitable anthracite coal mining in light of the Kohler Act."[37]

The ambiguity surfaced again, however, in the Court's 1992 ruling in *Lucas*. In footnote 7, the *Lucas* Court contrasted the treatment of the relevant-parcel issue in *Mahon* and *Keystone,* identifying, but not resolving, the apparent tension between the cases.[38] Writing for the majority, Justice Scalia speculated about the possible use of an affected portion standard in certain takings cases.[39] This speculation was clearly dicta, however, because Justice Scalia noted that there was no dispute in *Lucas* over the definition of the relevant parcel.[40] The following year, in *Concrete Pipe*, the Court unanimously reaffirmed the parcel-as-a-whole rule.[41] *Concrete Pipe* appears to have closed the door on the "affected portion" approach to which Justice Scalia alluded.

If a takings claimant relies on the dicta in footnote 7 of *Lucas*, government lawyers should respond that *Lucas*'s mere speculation is entitled to no weight when viewed against the clear holdings in *Penn Central*, *Andrus*, *Keystone*, and, most important, *Concrete Pipe*, a post-*Lucas* ruling joined by the entire Court (including Justice Scalia) that reaffirms the parcel-as-a-whole rule.[42]

Lucas footnote 7 also criticizes the definition of the relevant parcel by the New York Court of Appeals in *Penn Central Transportation Co. v. New York City*,[43] characterizing it as "extreme" and "unsupportable."[44] Some takings claimants argue that this criticism is directed at the parcel-as-a-whole rule. In fact, the New York Court of Appeals considered the claimants' economic return not only from Grand Central terminal, but also from the entirety of their "heavy real estate holdings in the Grand Central area, including hotels and office buildings. . . ."[45] Some of these other parcels are several blocks away from the terminal and separated by major roads and other structures. The *Lucas* Court's criticism of the state court approach suggests only that on the facts of that case, the state court improperly included *all* of the claimants' properties, including non-contiguous properties situated several blocks away, to define the relevant parcel.[46] Significantly, the Supreme Court in *Lucas* did not question its use of the parcel-as-a-whole rule in its own *Penn Central* ruling.

§ 4.2(d)   Palazzolo: Lucas *Footnote 7 Redux?*

The Supreme Court recently touched upon the relevant-parcel issue in *Palazzolo v. Rhode Island*.[47] There, the Court considered a takings challenge to state wetland protections that prohibited Palazzolo from destroying 18 acres of fragile coastal wetlands in Westerly, Rhode Island. The trial court found that Palazzolo's property was worth $200,000 (as of 1986) due to his ability to build a single-family home on the upland portion of the parcel.[48] As a result, the Supreme Court rejected Palazzolo's assertion that he had suffered a per se taking, ruling that "[a] regulation permitting a landowner to build a substantial residence on an 18-acre parcel does not leave the property 'economically idle' [under *Lucas*]."[49]

In rejecting the *Lucas* claim, the Court noted that Palazzolo "refram[ed]" his argument in his brief by contending for the first time that the Court should consider the effect of the wetland protections only on the wetland portion of his parcel, and not consider the value that remains in the upland portion.[50] The Court refused to do so because Palazzolo did not raise this argument in state court or in his petition for certiorari.[51] The Court stressed that "[t]he case comes to us on the premise that petitioner's entire parcel serves as the basis for his takings claim, and, so framed, the total deprivation argument fails."[52]

Notwithstanding its refusal to address Palazzolo's contention, Justice Kennedy's majority opinion contains dicta that refers to the relevant-parcel issue as a "difficult, persisting question."[53] Although Justice Kennedy cited and acknowledged the relevance of *Keystone* to the relevant-parcel issue, he did not describe *Keystone* as a key holding, but instead used more tepid language, stating that "[s]ome of our cases indicate that the extent of deprivation effected by a regulatory action is measured against the value of the parcel as a whole."[54] Justice Kennedy also cited to footnote 7 of *Lucas* for the proposition that the Court "at times expressed discomfort with the logic of this rule."[55] He further observed that certain commentators have also criticized the parcel-as-a-whole rule.[56]

In the wake of this discussion, developers and other takings claimants might well argue that *Palazzolo* has resuscitated the relevant-parcel issue and that the parcel-as-a-whole rule is now in flux. Government counsel have several persuasive responses.

First, and most important, the parcel-as-a-whole rule is based not on mere "indicat[ions]," as suggested by Justice Kennedy, but instead on longstanding, binding rulings by the Supreme Court, including a unanimous, post-*Lucas* ruling in *Concrete Pipe,* which expressly reaffirms the rule.[57] Justice Ginsburg expressly recognized this point in her dissent in *Palazzolo.*[58]

Second, the discussion of the relevant-parcel issue by the *Palazzolo* majority, like *Lucas* footnote 7 itself, is gratuitous dicta because the *Palazzolo* Court, like the *Lucas* Court, expressly declined to address the issue.

Third, Justice Kennedy's description of *Lucas* footnote 7 is hyperbolic. Footnote 7 does not "express discomfort with the logic" of the parcel-as-a-whole rule. Indeed, it does not discuss the "logic" of the rule at all. Instead, footnote 7 observes that the deprivation-of-all-economically-feasible-use rule does not, by itself, offer guidance on how to define the relevant parcel,[59] and it then notes that the relevant parcel might be defined by considering either the affected portion or the parcel as a whole. As noted above, footnote 7 then expresses disagreement with the particular relevant-parcel definition used by the New York Court of Appeals in *Penn Central.*[60] It is noteworthy that in *Lucas,* the Court did not question its own use of the parcel-as-a-whole rule in its *Penn Central* ruling. Footnote 7 then notes that uncertainty regarding the denominator has led to disparate results on occasion, and it suggests that state law might be relevant to the proper definition of the relevant parcel.[61] However, footnote 7 nowhere analyzes, much less criticizes, the "logic" of the parcel-as-a-whole rule.

To be sure, *Palazzolo* signals that certain members of the Court might be receptive to a refinement of the parcel-as-a-whole rule. But it seems highly unlikely that a majority of the Court would repudiate a rule so firmly entrenched in takings jurisprudence and so vital to routine land use regulation. In any event, government counsel should continue to rely on the arguments outlined above to refute any suggestion by takings claimants that *Palazzolo* has undermined the parcel-as-a-whole rule.

§ 4.2(e) *So-called "Temporal Severability"*

Some observers mistakenly argue that the Supreme Court allows for "temporal severability" of property rights. They contend that in *First English Evangelical Lutheran Church v. County of Los Angeles,*[62] the Supreme Court held that takings claimants may divide their property rights into temporal segments and successfully sue for a taking whenever regulation temporarily deprives land of economically viable use.[63] Although a comprehensive analysis of the takings implications of temporary land use restrictions is beyond the scope of this chapter, some clarification is warranted because the concepts of "temporal severance" and temporary takings are so widely misunderstood.

The *First English* Court framed the issue before it as whether a takings claimant could "recover damages for the time before it is finally determined that the regulation constitutes a 'taking' of his property."[64] In other words, is invalidation of the regulation constitutionally sufficient, or must the government also pay compensation for the period of time the regulation was in effect? The Court held that the Constitution compels the payment of just compensation for every regulatory taking, including those that the government chooses to cut short by withdrawing the challenged regulation.[65] The *First English* Court used the notion of a temporary taking to refer to a situation where the government cuts short a permanent taking by rescinding the regulation that gave rise to the taking. Five years later, the *Lucas* Court similarly used the concept of a temporary taking to describe a taking that initially was "unconditional and permanent" but then made temporary through the enactment of new regulations that softened the challenged restriction.[66]

The Supreme Court in *First English* made clear that it was deciding only the remedy issue, stating that the lower courts' disposition "isolate[d] the remedial question" for consideration.[67] It emphasized that it had "no occasion to decide" whether the interim ordinance at issue worked a compensable taking.[68] Nowhere does *First English* state that every temporary denial of economically viable land use—particularly where the denial is known to be temporary from the outset—constitutes a taking.[69] On remand, the California court of appeals concluded that the interim ordinance worked no taking because it advanced public safety, did not deny the claimants all use of the property, and imposed a reasonable moratorium on development until the county could determine which uses were consistent with public safety.[70]

Importantly, *First English* reaffirmed the ruling in *Agins v. City of Tiburon*[71] that good-faith planning activities and other precondemnation activities, even those that reduce land value, do not constitute a taking. "Mere fluctuations in value during the process of governmental decisionmaking, absent extraordinary delay, are 'incidents of ownership,'" and not a taking.[72] The *First English* Court characterized *Agins* and *Danforth* as standing for the "unexceptional proposition . . . that depreciation in value of the property by reason of preliminary activity is not chargeable to the government."[73] The Court went out of its way to note that its holding did not address "the case of normal delays in obtaining building permits, changes in zoning ordinances, variances, and the like."[74]

The *First English* Court used the phrase "temporary taking" to describe "those regulatory takings which are ultimately invalidated by the courts."[75] Its specific holding reiterates this point:

> Invalidation of the ordinance or its successor ordinance after this period of time, though converting the taking into a 'temporary' one, is not a sufficient remedy to meet the demands of the Just Compensation Clause.... We merely hold that where the government's activities have already worked a taking of all use of property, no subsequent action by the government can relieve it of the duty to provide compensation for the period during which the taking was effective.[76]

Far from expanding substantive liability, the concept of a temporary taking actually allows the government to limit its liability. In other words, upon the finding of a regulatory taking by a court, the government may limit its liability by abandoning the regulation and paying only temporary damages for the period of time the regulation was in effect. Indeed, the Court emphasized that "the landowner has no right under the Just Compensation Clause to insist that a 'temporary' taking be deemed a permanent taking."[77] The government has the ultimate choice, however, regarding whether the taking will be temporary or permanent.[78]

Lower courts are virtually unanimous in rejecting takings challenges to temporary restrictions on land use in the absence of extraordinary delay.[79] Similarly, delays in approving a development project may constitute a taking only where extreme and unreasonable.[80]

On June 29, 2001, the U.S. Supreme Court agreed to review *Tahoe-Sierra Preservation Council, Inc. v. Tahoe Regional Planning Agency*,[81] where the Ninth Circuit severely criticized the notion of temporal severance in rejecting a takings challenge to moratoria designed to protect Lake Tahoe. The Supreme Court will hear argument on the question "[w]hether the Court of Appeals properly determined that a temporary moratorium on land development does not constitute a taking of property requiring compensation under the Takings Clause of the United States Constitution."[82] If the Court remains true to its rulings in *Agins* and *First English*, it will reaffirm that a development moratorium does not constitute a taking absent extraordinary delay.

§ 4.3 *Lower Court Application of the Parcel-as-a-Whole Rule*

Although the parcel-as-a-whole rule is easy to articulate, it is sometimes difficult to apply. Some of the most influential relevant parcel rulings arise from challenges to wetland protections because they often raise interesting issues regarding the extent to which associated uplands should be included in the relevant parcel. In *Tabb Lakes, Ltd. v. United States*,[83] a developer challenged a wetlands permit denial by the U.S. Army Corps of Engineers. The Federal Circuit provided a succinct, functional explanation of why the "affected portion" standard is inappropriate:

> Clearly, the quantum of land to be considered is not each individual lot containing wetlands or even the combined area of wetlands. If that were true, the Corps' protection of wetlands via a permit system would, ipso facto, constitute a taking in every case where it exercises its statutory authority.[84]

Another wetlands case frequently cited on the relevant-parcel issue is *Ciampitti v. United States*.[85] After rejecting the claimant's affected portion standard, the *Ciampitti* court listed several factors to use in deciding whether arguably separate properties are in fact part of a single relevant parcel for takings analysis.[86] These factors include "the degree of contiguity, the dates of acquisition, the extent to which the parcel has been treated as a single unit, [and] the extent to which the protected lands enhance the value of remaining lands. . . ."[87] The court made clear that its list is not a comprehensive list, and that "the effort should be to identify the parcel as realistically and fairly as possible, given the entire factual and regulatory environment."[88] Courts from other jurisdictions frequently use the list of factors in *Ciampitti* as a point of departure in defining the relevant parcel.

§ 4.3(a) ***Contiguity and Common Ownership***

Of the various factors listed in *Ciampitti*, contiguity and common ownership typically predominate. For example, in *Zealy v. City of Waukesha*,[89] the Supreme Court of Wisconsin rejected a takings challenge to zoning designed to protect wetlands on 10.4 acres of undeveloped land owned by Zealy.[90] The zoning designated 8.2 acres for agricultural use but allowed the rest of the land to be used for residential and business.[91] The *Zealy* court treated the entire 10.4 acres as the relevant parcel, concluding that *Penn Central*, *Keystone*, and *Concrete Pipe* "do not support the proposition that a contiguous property should be divided into discrete segments for purposes of evaluating a takings claim."[92] The majority of courts appear to follow the *Zealy* court's approach in defining the relevant parcel to include all contiguous property owned by the claimant.[93]

This approach reflects not only the majority rule, but also the modern trend. For example, in a case decided 15 years before *Penn Central*, the New Jersey Supreme Court appeared to consider only the affected portion of the property, excluding other contiguous property owned by the claimant.[94] More recently, however, in *Karam v. New Jersey,* the same court affirmed a lower court ruling that defined the relevant parcel to include all of the claimant's contiguous property.[95] The lower court in *Karam* concluded that recent New Jersey rulings, as well as the decisions of most other jurisdictions, define the relevant parcel to include all of the claimant's adjacent acreage.[96] Adhering to the majority rule, the court defined the relevant parcel to include the claimant's riparian land and adjoining uplands because the land was contiguous, commonly purchased and owned, bound together by a riparian grant, treated as a single unit, and assessed as a single lot.[97] Using the parcel-as-a-whole rule, the court concluded that denial of permission to build a dock on the riparian lands was not a taking.[98] The New Jersey Supreme Court effectively ratified this analysis by affirming "substantially for the reasons expressed" by the lower court.[99]

What happens if persons other than the claimant have a limited ownership interest in part of the property? Do their interests defeat the requisite commonality of ownership? Not necessarily. In *K & K Construction, Inc. v. Department of Natural Resources*,[100] the lower court justified the segmentation of three parcels for takings analysis because one of the three parcels owned by the claimant was subject to an equitable lien. The Michigan Supreme Court disagreed. Notwithstanding the equitable lien, the Michigan high court found sufficient commonality of ownership because at the time of the alleged taking one claimant held title to all three parcels, and that claimant continued to have at least a joint ownership interest in all three.[101]

§ 4.3(b)   *The Claimant's Treatment of the Property*

Another important factor in defining the relevant parcel is the claimant's treatment of the property. If the claimant has used the property as an integrated whole for development or other significant purposes, that action usually justifies treating the entire property as part of the same relevant parcel. In these situations, courts generally forbid the claimant from manipulating the takings analysis by disavowing the claimant's own actions. For example, in *Forest Properties, Inc. v. United States*,[102] the trial court defined the relevant parcel to include all 62 acres of Forest Properties' development project, including 53 acres of developable uplands, not just the 9.4 acres of lake-bottom Forest Properties was prohibited from developing. The court held:

> A property owner who treats a series of parcels as one property for the purposes of development, financing, planning, and utilization cannot then segregate the properties for the purpose of establishing a taking claim.... [I]f a property owner treats a series of properties as one income-producing unit, the value lost to the claimant is not simply the loss of the segregated parcel affected by the Government action, but the decrease in the owner's ability to utilize the unified parcels as one income-generating unit. Any other approach would elevate the style of the transaction over the substance of a property owner's treatment of a parcel.[103]

The Federal Circuit affirmed this ruling, emphasizing that "from the outset, the development was treated as a single integrated project...."[104] Forest Properties argued that the lake-bottom should be severed from the uplands because it held different kinds of title to these properties (equitable vs. fee), it had acquired the properties at different times, different local government authorities regulated the properties, and the two segments could be developed separately.[105] The Federal Circuit rejected all these arguments, ruling that the trial court "properly looked to the economic reality of the arrangements, which transcended these legalistic bright lines...."[106]

The *Ciampitti* court likewise refused to allow the owner to segment property for takings analysis where he had treated the property as a single unit for purchase and financing. The court concluded that it would be improper to allow the owner to "sever the connection he forged when it assists in making a legal argument."[107] The *K & K Construction* court also relied on the claimants' treatment of three parcels as a unified whole in development plans and permit applications to justify including all three in the relevant parcel despite the fact that the parcels were zoned differently.[108] The *Karam* ruling similarly relied in part on the claimants' treatment of wetlands and associated uplands as a unified whole in defining the relevant parcel to include both.[109]

Even where the landowner's treatment of property changes over time, some courts rely on the owner's longstanding, prior use of property as an integrated unit to define the relevant parcel more broadly. In *District Intown Properties Limited Partnership v. District of Columbia*,[110] the claimants bought an apartment building surrounded by landscaped lawns in 1961 and used the property as an integrated whole for 27 years. In 1988, they subdivided the lawns into lots to build townhouses. The District of Columbia denied the development permit under local historic preservation laws. In rejecting a takings challenge to the permit denial, the court defined the relevant parcel to include the entire property, not just the lawns, because the property is contiguous, commonly owned, and had been treated by the claimants as an integrated whole for at least 27 years.[111] Even after subdivision in 1988, there was no evidence that the claimants treated the lawns separately from the apartment for purposes of accounting or management.[112] Although the claimants argued that the District now taxed the subdivided lawn lots separately from the apartment, the court responded that the claimants retained the right to recombine the lots to be taxed as a single parcel.[113]

Where an owner never intended to treat two pieces of property as a single unit, this factor might cut against consideration of the property as a single parcel for purposes of takings analysis. For example, in *Palm Beach Isles Assocs. v. United States*[114] the court found that the relevant parcel consisted of 50.7 acres of wetland and submerged land subject to a permit denial under the Clean Water Act. The court held that it did not include 261 acres previously sold by the owner because the two parcels were never part of a common development scheme, separated by a road and subject to different zoning, and the sale occurred "before the environmental considerations contained in the Clean Water Act came into play."[115]

What if the landowner buys property that is already subdivided, or subdivides the property immediately upon purchase? Does this by itself warrant treatment of the individual lots as separate relevant parcels? In *Keystone*, the Supreme Court ruled that takings jurisprudence precludes reliance on "legalistic distinctions within a bundle of property rights."[116] Accordingly, courts generally ignore parcel and lot designations in defining the relevant parcel.[117] If lot designations controlled the analysis, a landowner could jerry-rig a takings claim by simply subdividing the affected portion of the property. Most courts also seem to agree that a difference in zoning does not by itself justify segmentation.[118]

§ 4.3(c) *Previously Owned, Contiguous Property*

Do the courts evaluate contiguity at the time of the claimant's original purchase or at the time the government imposed the challenged restriction? Stated differently, how do the courts define the relevant parcel if the claimant has developed or sold portions of contiguous property purchased as a single unit? Courts generally prevent developers from enhancing a takings claim by unfairly manipulating their development plans or selling off developable properties.

Courts faced with this issue often begin their analysis with *Deltona Corp. v. United States*,[119] where the court rejected a takings challenge to a federal wetlands permit denial. The court relied, in part, on the claimant's ability to develop other property purchased with and contiguous to the restricted land, even though the claimant had already developed and sold off large portions of the unrestricted property before the permit denial.[120] The court specifically noted that the restricted property contained only 20 percent of the total acreage of the original purchase and only a third of the developable lots.[121] In finding no taking, the court's decision principally rested on the claimant's ability to develop uplands within the restricted parcels.[122] Nevertheless, the *Deltona* court plainly considered the economic impact of the permit denial in view of all contiguous property originally purchased by the developer, regardless of whether the developer owned the property at the time of the permit denial.

Deltona contrasts with the Federal Circuit's more recent ruling in *Loveladies Harbor, Inc. v. United States*.[123] In *Loveladies,* the court distinguished *Deltona* and affirmed the trial court's definition of the relevant parcel, which excluded property that Loveladies had developed before the agency imposed the challenged regulatory restrictions.[124] Loveladies originally purchased 250 contiguous acres in 1958, but it developed 199 acres before the enactment of section 404 of the Clean Water Act and before state authorities sought to restrict its development activities. Prior to the permit denial, Loveladies had sold all but 6.4 of the 199 developed acres.[125] Moreover, in exchange for a state permit, Loveladies promised to convey a deed restriction or conservation easement ensuring that another 38.5 of the 51 undeveloped acres would remain unfilled. When Loveladies wanted to fill 12.5 acres of its undeveloped land, the federal government denied the permit under section 404 of the Clean Water Act.[126] In the takings case, the trial court defined the relevant parcel to include only the 12.5 acres subject to the federal permit denial, found a taking, and awarded $2,658,000 plus interest.[127]

The Federal Circuit affirmed, emphasizing that in defining the relevant parcel, its "precedent displays a flexible approach, designed to account for factual nuances."[128] These factual nuances include "the timing of transfers in light of the developing regulatory environment."[129] The Federal Circuit found no clear error in the trial court's exclusion of the 199 acres developed before the change in the regulatory climate.[130] The appeals court also affirmed the trial court's exclusion of 38.5 acres that Loveladies promised the state to keep undeveloped, stating that "whatever substantial value that land had now belongs to the state. . . ."[131]

Government lawyers should expect claimants to rely on *Loveladies* in arguing for a narrow definition of the relevant parcel. Several responses are available. First, the *Loveladies* ruling is expressly limited to the specific "factual nuances" of that case, and thus should not be read to establish a rule that requires similar exclusions from the relevant parcel in other cases.[132] The Federal Circuit was concerned that Loveladies had been whipsawed by the state, which extracted a promise from Loveladies to keep 38.5 acres unfilled in exchange for the state permit, but then recommended that the federal permit be denied.[133] The state's apparent change in position colored the Federal Circuit's view of the case, for in affirming the exclusion of the 38.5 acres, the Federal Circuit stressed: "It would seem ungrateful in the extreme to require Loveladies to convey to the public the rights in the 38.5 acres in exchange for the right to develop 12.5 acres, and then to include the value of the grant as a charge against the givers."[134] Government lawyers may therefore argue that *Loveladies* has no application beyond the unique factual nuances of that case.

Second, *Loveladies* is poorly reasoned. For example, in distinguishing *Deltona*, the *Loveladies* court described *Deltona*'s takings analysis as having considered only property owned by the claimant at the time of the permit denial.[135] In fact, the *Deltona* court considered all property originally purchased, including property developed and sold before the permit denial.[136] Other courts have criticized and refused to follow *Loveladies*' idiosyncratic analysis.[137]

Notwithstanding the flaws in *Loveladies*, the question remains as to whether the relevant parcel for takings analysis should include parcels sold by the landowner before the challenged regulation took effect. Where the evidence suggests that a landowner, in anticipation of future regulation, sold off property to manipulate the relevant parcel and skew the takings analysis, government counsel should argue that the property should be considered as part of the relevant parcel where the other factors so warrant. Courts should not allow unfair manipulation of land holdings to influence takings analysis. On the other hand, where the owner sells off parcels long before the challenged regulation came into effect and without anticipation of future regulation, the court should consider this factor (along with the other factors) in defining the relevant parcel.

Takings claimants also sometimes rely on a 1986 ruling in *Florida Rock Industries, Inc. v. United States*[138] to argue for a narrow definition of the relevant parcel. There, the Federal Circuit addressed a takings challenge to the denial of a federal permit to fill and mine 98 acres of wetlands, which were part of a 1,560-acre tract. The federal government argued that the relevant parcel was the entire 1,560-acre tract, and that the permit denial did not take the 98 acres because it did not affect the rest of the tract. The Federal Circuit emphasized that this argument "had dignity" and was "of decisive importance" in *Deltona* and other cases, thereby reaffirming the definition of the relevant parcel in those cases as including all contiguous property owned by the claimants.[139] In *Florida Rock*, however, the court found this argument unavailing because the challenged federal law prohibited filling and mining of the balance of the tract.[140] In other words, consideration of the rest of the parcel would not have affected the takings analysis in *Florida Rock* because the owner could not make economically viable use of the rest of the parcel.[141] Government lawyers should have little difficulty distinguishing *Florida Rock* where the claimant enjoys some economically viable use of other contiguous, commonly owned property.[142]

§ 4.3(d) *Is Noncontiguity Fatal?*

If two properties are not contiguous, the lack of contiguity does not automatically defeat a government defendant's effort to treat two properties as a single relevant parcel. For example, in *Ciampitti*, the court defined the relevant parcel to include noncontiguous properties because (1) at the time the claimant bought the properties, he also owned property that linked the noncontiguous properties together, and (2) the claimant treated the noncontiguous properties as a single parcel for purposes of purchase and financing.

In *Town of Jupiter v. Alexander*,[143] the court defined the relevant parcel to include noncontiguous properties—a mainland parcel and an island located about 500 yards away—because the claimant owned them both and intended to use them as an integrated whole. In *Naegale Outdoor Advertising v. City of Durham*,[144] a takings challenge to billboard restrictions, a federal court defined the relevant parcel to include not just the leasehold interest in each sign, as the claimant urged, but all the claimant's billboards in the metropolitan area because the claimant treated its signs as a single unit in charging its customers for advertising in the Durham area. Finally, in *Brotherton v. Department of Environmental Conservation*,[145] a New York court treated property as part of the same relevant parcel even though it was divided by a road.

§ 4.3(e)   *Aberrant Rulings*

Government lawyers should be aware that despite clear Supreme Court precedent, a small handful of lower courts will occasionally engage in impermissible severance. In a particularly troubling ruling, a split panel of a Pennsylvania commonwealth court essentially adopted an affected portion standard for a portion of land that had independent value prior to the challenged government action.[146] As noted by the dissent in that case, the ruling defies *Penn Central* and *Keystone*, and it deserves to be reversed on appeal.[147]

Likewise, on panel rehearing in *Palm Beach Isles*, the Federal Circuit directed the trial court on remand to consider only 1.4 acres of wetlands as a relevant parcel even though the wetlands are adjacent to and, for all intents and purposes, part of 49.3 acres of submerged lands owned by the claimant. The only justification offered by the court for not treating the entire 50.7 acres as a single relevant parcel is that the 1.4 acres of wetland "are not subject to the Government's defenses under the navigational servitude."[148] This definition of parcel based exclusively on the extent to which a particular government defense might apply appears to be unprecedented and is plainly contrary to the Supreme Court's parcel-as-a-whole rule.[149]

Notes

1. This chapter draws heavily from chapter 6 of DOUGLAS T. KENDALL, TIMOTHY J. DOWLING & ANDREW W. SCHWARTZ, TAKINGS LITIGATION HANDBOOK: DEFENDING TAKINGS CHALLENGES TO LAND USE REGULATIONS (American Legal Publishing 2000) (used with permission of the authors). To order the HANDBOOK, call American Legal Publishing at 1-800-445-5588 or go to http://www.amlegal.com/tlh.htm.

2. *See, e.g.,* Dolan v. City of Tigard, 512 U.S. 374, 384 (1994).

3. 438 U.S. 104 (1978).

4. *Id*. at 130-31.

5. *See id.*

6. *See* Keystone Bituminous Coal Ass'n v. DeBenedictis, 480 U.S. 470, 500 (1987) (stating that *Penn Central* precludes reliance on "legalistic distinctions" to sever property rights).

7. 444 U.S. 51 (1979).

8. *Id*. at 65-66.

9. *See id.* at 66-67.

10. 480 U.S. 470 (1987).

11. *Id.* at 498.

12. *See id.* at 500-01.

13. *See id.*

14. *Id.* at 500.

15. *Id.* at 501.

16. *Id.* at 498.

17. 260 U.S. 393, 413 (1922).

18. 508 U.S. 602 (1993).

19. *Id.* at 644.

20. *See id.*

21. 512 U.S. 374 (1994).

22. *Id.* at 388-96.

23. *Id.* at 385 n.6 ("There can be no argument that the permit conditions would deprive petitioner of 'economically beneficial us[e]' of her property as she currently operates a retail store on the lot."); *see also* Clajon Prod. Corp. v. Petera, 70 F.3d 1566, 1577 n.18 (10th Cir. 1995) ("[W]hen considering the economically beneficial use test, *Dolan* clearly indicated that test must be viewed in light of defendant's entire property.").

24. *See* Hadacheck v. Sebastian, 239 U.S. 394, 405 (1915).

25. *See* Village of Euclid v. Ambler Realty, 272 U.S. 365 (1926).

26. *See* Gorieb v. Fox, 274 U.S. 603 (1927).

27. In an influential law review article, Professor Frank Michelman argued that in regulatory takings cases, the economic impact of the challenged government action should not be considered in absolute terms, but instead in comparison to some other quantity. If this comparison were expressed as a fraction, he explained, the loss in value would compose the numerator of the fraction. The critical question concerns the composition of the denominator. If the denominator were the preexisting value of the affected portion of the property, courts frequently would find a taking because the fraction often would be 1, signifying a complete economic wipeout of the affected portion. Professor Michelman argued that a "more relevant" denominator would be the claimant's "whole preexisting wealth or income" because this comparison "would forge a link between compensability and one's ability to sustain uncompensated burdens." Frank Michelman, *Property, Utility, and Fairness: Comments on the Ethical Foundations of "Just Compensation" Law*, 80 HARV. L. REV. 1165, 1192 (1967). Courts apply neither the "affected portion" standard nor the "preexisting wealth or income" standard, and instead examine the parcel as a whole. Due to the continuing influence of Professor Michelman's article, however, many courts refer to the relevant-parcel issue as the "denominator" issue. *E.g.*, Lucas v. South Carolina Coastal Council, 505 U.S. 1003, 1016 n.7 (1992); *Keystone*, 480 U.S. at 497.

28. Kaiser Aetna v. United States, 444 U.S. 164, 176 (1979).

29. *See* Babbitt v. Youpee, 519 U.S. 234, 236 (1997); Hodel v. Irving, 481 U.S. 704, 716-18 (1987).

30. 444 U.S. at 61, 65-66.

31. *E.g.*, Armstrong v. United States, 364 U.S. 40, 48 (1960) (stating that the government's action effectively destroyed and thus took a materialman's lien); Louisville Joint Stock Land Bank v. Radford, 295 U.S. 555, 590, 594 (1935) (holding that a federal law took a mortgagee's property rights in mortgaged farms).

32. 505 U.S. 1003, 1016 n.7 (1992).

33. Footnote 7 of *Lucas* reads as follows:

Regrettably, the rhetorical force of our "deprivation of all economically feasible use" rule is greater than its precision, since the rule does not make clear the "property interest" against which the loss of value is to be measured. When, for example, a regulation requires a developer to leave 90 percent of a rural tract in its natural state, it is unclear whether we would analyze the situation as one in which the owner has been deprived of all economically beneficial use of the burdened portion of the tract, or as one in which the owner has suffered a mere diminution in value of the tract as a whole. (For an extreme—and, we think, unsupportable—view of the relevant calculus, see *Penn Central Transportation Co. v. New York City*, 42 N.Y.2d 324, 333-34, 366 N.E.2d 1271, 1276-77 (1977), *aff'd*, 438 U.S. 104 (1978), where the state court examined the diminution in a particular parcel's value produced by a municipal ordinance in light of total value of the takings claimant's other holdings in the vicinity.) Unsurprisingly, this uncertainty regarding the composition of the denominator in our "deprivation" fraction has produced inconsistent pronouncements by the Court. *Compare* Pennsylvania Coal Co. v. Mahon, 260 U.S. 393, 414 (1922) (law restricting subsurface extraction of coal held to effect a taking) with Keystone Bituminous Coal Assn. v. DeBenedictis, 480 U.S. 470, 497-502, 94 L. Ed. 2d 472, 107 S. Ct. 1232 (1987) (nearly identical law held not to effect a taking); *see also id.*, at 515-20 (Rehnquist, C. J., dissenting); Rose, Mahon *Reconstructed: Why the Takings Issue Is Still a Muddle*, 57 S. Cal. L. Rev. 561, 566-69 (1984). The answer to this difficult question may lie in how the owner's reasonable expectations have been shaped by the state's law of property—*i.e.*, whether and to what degree the state's law has accorded legal recognition and protection to the particular interest in land with respect to which the takings claimant alleges a diminution in (or elimination of) value. In any event, we avoid this difficulty in the present case, since the "interest in land" that Lucas has pleaded (a fee simple interest) is an estate with a rich tradition of protection at common law, and since the South Carolina Court of Common Pleas found that the Beachfront Management Act left each of Lucas's beachfront lots without economic value.

Lucas, 505 U.S. at 1016 n.7.
34. *See Penn Central*, 438 U.S. at 130 n.27.
35. *See id.*
36. 80 U.S. at 500-01.
37. *Id.* at 498-99.
38. *See Lucas,* 505 U.S. at 1016 n.7.
39. *See id.*
40. *See id.*
41. 508 U.S. at 643-44.
42. *See* Zealy v. City of Waukesha, 548 N.W.2d 528, 532-33 (Wis. 1996) (using *Concrete Pipe* to negate the *Lucas* dictum).
43. 366 N.E.2d 1271, 1276-77 (N.Y. 1977), *aff'd,* 438 U.S. 104 (1978).
44. *Lucas*, 505 U.S. at 1016 n.7.
45. *Penn Central*, 366 N.E.2d at 1276-77.
46. District Intown Properties Ltd. P'ship v. District of Columbia, 198 F.3d 874, 880-81 (D.C. Cir. 1999) ("The *Lucas* dictum [in footnote 7] casts aspersions on the state court's elevation of one factor, unity of ownership, over other factors in determining the relevant parcel."), *cert. denied*, 121 S. Ct. 34 (Oct. 2, 2000).
47. 121 S. Ct. 2448 (2001).

48. *Id*. at 2464.

49. *Id*. at 2465.

50. *Id*.

51. *Id*.

52. *Id*.

53. *Id*.

54. *Id*.

55. *Id*.

56. *Id*.

57. *Concrete Pipe*, 508 U.S. at 644.

58. *See Palazzolo*, 121 S. Ct. at 2475 n.2 (Ginsburg, J., joined by Souter & Breyer, JJ., dissenting) (*Palazzolo*'s proposed parcel definition conflicts with "numerous holdings" of the Supreme Court, including *Concrete Pipe*).

59. *Lucas*, 505 U.S. at 1016 n.7 ("Regrettably, the rhetorical force of our 'deprivation of all economically feasible use' rule is greater than its precision, since the rule does not make clear the 'property interest' against which the loss of value is to be measured.").

60. 366 N.E.2d 1271, 1276-77 (N.Y. 1977), *aff'd*, 438 U.S. 104 (1978).

61. *Lucas*, 505 U.S. at 1016 n.7.

62. 482 U.S. 304 (1987)

63. *E.g.*, John E. Fee, Comment, *Unearthing the Denominator in Regulatory Takings Claims*, 61 U. CHI. L. REV. 1535, 1543 (1994) [hereinafter *Comment*] ("*First English* establishes the principle that property rights may be severed into time shares with no apparent restrictions. Insofar as a landowner can show that the property rights of a given parcel have been completely extinguished for an identifiable period of time, a taking has occurred.").

64. *First English*, 482 U.S. at 306-07.

65. *Id*. at 314-22.

66. *Lucas*, 505 U.S. at 1011-12.

67. *First English*, 482 U.S. at 311.

68. *Id*. at 312-13.

69. *See generally* Frank Michelman, *Takings, 1987*, 88 COLUM. L. REV. 1600, 1621 (1988) ("On the interpretation suggested here, the *First English* decision does not reach regulatory enactments, even totally restrictive ones, that are expressly designed by their enacters to be temporary. . . . ").

70. *See First English*, 258 Cal. Rptr. at 896-906. It is surprising how often courts erroneously assert that the Supreme Court found a taking in *First English. E.g.*, Corn v. City of Lauderdale Lakes, 95 F.3d 1066, 1073 n.4 (11th Cir. 1996) (stating that in *First English* the Supreme Court "held that the ordinance effected a temporary taking, requiring the county to pay fair value for the use of the property during that time period.").

71. 447 U.S. 255 (1980).

72. *Id*. at 263 n.9 (quoting Danforth v. United States, 308 U.S. 271, 285 (1939)).

73. *First English*, 482 U.S. at 320.

74. *Id*. at 321.

75. *Id*. at 310 (citations omitted).

76. *Id*. at 319, 321.

77. *Id*. at 317.

78. *Id*. at 321.

79. *See, e.g.*, Tahoe-Sierra Preservation Council, Inc. v. Tahoe Reg'l Planning Agency, 216 F.3d 764 (9th Cir. 2000), *cert. granted*, 121 S. Ct. 2589 (June 29, 2001); Santa Fe

Village Venture v. City of Albuquerque, 914 F. Supp. 478, 483 (D. N.M. 1995); Zilber v. Town of Moraga, 692 F. Supp. 1195, 1206-07 (N.D. Cal. 1988); Smoke Rise, Inc. v. Washington Suburban Sanitary Comm'n, 400 F. Supp. 1369 (D. Md. 1975); Landgate, Inc. v. California Coastal Comm'n, 953 P.2d 1188 (Cal.), *cert. denied*, 119 S. Ct. 179 (1998); Long Beach Equities v. County of Ventura, 282 Cal. Rptr. 877, 888 (Cal. Ct. App. 1991); Williams v. City of Central, 907 P.2d 701, 704 (Colo. Ct. App. 1995); Woodbury Partners v. City of Woodbury, 492 N.W.2d 258, 262 (Minn. Ct. App. 1992); Orleans Builders & Developers v. Byrne, 453 A.2d 200, 208 (N.J. 1982).

80.   Norco Constr., Inc. v. King County, 801 F.2d 1143, 1145 (9th Cir. 1986) ("We recognize a claim might also arise when it is clear beyond peradventure that excessive delay in such a final determination has caused the present destruction of the property's beneficial use."); Landgate v. California Coastal Comm'n, 17 Cal. 4th 1006, 1020 (1998).

81.   216 F.3d 764 (9th Cir. 2000).

82.   121 S. Ct. 2589 (2001).

83.   10 F.3d 796 (Fed. Cir. 1993).

84.   *Id.* at 802.

85.   22 Cl. Ct. 310 (1991).

86.   *See id.* at 318.

87.   *Id.*

88.   *Id.* at 319.

89.   548 N.W.2d 528 (Wis. 1996).

90.   *See id.* at 533-34.

91.   *See id.*

92.   *See id.* at 533.

93.   *See* East Cape May Assocs. v. New Jersey, 693 A.2d 114, 125 (N.J. Super. App. Div. 1997) ("The majority of out-of-state cases which have considered the composition of the denominator of the taking fraction have held that it consists of all of the claimant's contiguous acreage in the same ownership."); *see also* Jentgen v. United States, 657 F.2d 1210, 1213 (Ct. Cl. 1981) (concluding that the relevant parcel consists of 100 contiguous acres owned by the claimant, including 60 undevelopable acres and 40 developable acres); K & K Constr., Inc. v. Department of Natural Resources, 575 N.W.2d 531, 537 (Mich. 1998) ("[C]ontiguity and common ownership create a common thread tying these three parcels together for purposes of the takings analysis"), *cert. denied*, 525 U.S. 819, *reh'g denied*, 525 U.S. 1033 (1998); Bevan v. Township of Brandon Bd. of Appeals, 475 N.W.2d 37, 43 (Mich. 1991) (determining that the relevant parcel includes all "contiguous lots under the same ownership . . . , despite the owner's division of the property into separate, identifiable lots"), *amended by* 439 Mich. 202 (1991).

94.   *See* Morris County Land Improvement Co. v. Township of Parsippany-Troy Hills, 193 A.2d 232, 235-36, 241-44 (N.J. 1963).

95.   *See* Karam v. New Jersey, 723 A.2d 943 (N.J. 1999) (per curiam), *aff'g* 705 A.2d 1221 (N.J. Super. Ct. App. Div. 1998), *cert. denied*, 120 S. Ct. 51 (1999).

96.   *See* Karam v. New Jersey, 705 A.2d at 1226-28.

97.   *See id.* at 1228.

98.   *See id.*

99.   *Karam*, 723 A.2d at 944.

100.   575 N.W.2d 531 (Mich. 1998), *cert. denied*, 525 U.S. 819 (1998).

101.   *See id.* at 537 & n.5.

102.   39 Fed. Cl. 56, 73-75 (1997), *aff'd*, 177 F.3d 1360 (Fed. Cir. 1999), *cert. denied sub nom.* RCK Properties, Inc. v. United States, 120 S. Ct. 373 (1999).

103. *Id*. at 73.

104. Forest Properties, Inc v. United States, 177 F.3d 1360, 1365 (Fed. Cir. 1999).

105. *Id*. at 1366.

106. *Id*.

107. *Ciampitti*, 22 Cl. Ct. at 320.

108. *See K & K Construction*, 575 N.W.2d at 537 n.6.

109. *See Karam*, 705 A.2d at 1228; *see also* Rith Energy, Inc. v. United States, No. 99-5123, 2001 WL 1380899 (Fed. Cir. Nov. 5, 2001) (In a takings challenge to mining restrictions, the relevant parcel included previously mined coal because it would be "artificial" to divide the interests in the claimant's coal lease and focus solely on the coal remaining in the ground.).

110. 198 F.3d. 874 (D.C. Cir. 1999).

111. *See id*. at 880.

112. *Id*.

113. *Id*. at 882.

114. 208 F.3d 1374 (Fed. Cir.), *aff'd on reh'g*, 231 F.3d 1354 (Fed. Cir.), *reh'g en banc denied*, 231 F.3d 1365 (Fed. Cir. 2000).

115. *Id*. at 1381.

116. *Keystone*, 480 U.S. at 500.

117. *E.g.*, Broadwater Farms Joint Venture v. United States, 35 Fed. Cl. 232, 239-40 (1996) (holding that the relevant parcel includes all of claimant's contiguous property owned at the time of the challenged government action even though it was subdivided prior to purchase), *aff'd in relevant part and vacated in part*, 121 F.3d 727 (Fed. Cir. 1997), *reh'g denied*, No. 96-500, 1997 U.S. App. LEXIS 31745 (Fed. Cir. Oct. 14, 1997); *K & K Construction*, 575 N.W.2d at 535-38 ("'[C]ontiguous lots under the same ownership are to be considered as a whole for purposes of judging the reasonableness of zoning ordinances [under the Takings Clause], despite the owner's division of the property into separate, identifiable lots.'") (quoting Bevan v. Township of Brandon Bd. of Appeals, 475 N.W.2d at 43); *Zealy*, 548 N.W.2d at 532-33 (deciding that the relevant parcel includes all contiguous property owned by claimant despite differences in zoning).

118. *See Zealy*, 548 N.W.2d at 532-33 (determining that differences in zoning do not warrant segmentation of contiguous parcels); *K & K Construction*, 575 N.W.2d at 537 (ruling that the difference in zoning across four contiguous parcels owned by claimant did not warrant segmentation). *But cf.* American Savings & Loan Ass'n v. County of Marin, 653 F.2d 364, 371-72 (9th Cir. 1981) (remanding for a determination of whether differently zoned, contiguous properties are part of the same relevant parcel).

119. 657 F.2d 1184 (Ct. Cl. 1981).

120. *See id*. at 1191.

121. *See id*.

122. *See id*.

123. 28 F.3d 1171 (Fed. Cir. 1994).

124. *See id*. at 1181-82.

125. *See id*. at 1174, 1180-81.

126. *See id*. at 1173.

127. *See id*. at 1173, 1181.

128. *Id*. at 1181.

129. *Id*.

130. *See id*.

131. *Id*. at 1181; *see also* Palm Beach Isles Assocs. v. United States, 208 F.3d 1374

(Fed. Cir. 2000), *aff'd on reh'g*, 231 F.3d 1354 (Fed. Cir. Nov. 6, 2000), *reh'g en banc denied*, 231 F.3d 1365 (Fed. Cir. Nov. 13, 2000).

132. *Loveladies Harbor*, 28 F.3d 1181.

133. *See id.*

134. *Id.*

135. *See id.*

136. *Deltona*, 657 F.2d at 1192.

137. *E.g.*, Volkema v. Michigan Dep't of Natural Resources, 586 N.W.2d 231 (Mich. 1998) (denying review of lower court finding of no taking but "disavow[ing]" the lower court's reliance on *Loveladies* to the extent it conflicts with Michigan precedent).

138. 791 F.2d 893 (Fed. Cir. 1986).

139. *Id.* at 904.

140. *See id.*

141. District Intown Properties Ltd. P'ship v. District of Columbia, 198 F.3d 874, 881 (D.C. Cir. 1999) (*Florida Rock*'s definition of the relevant parcel is premised on a finding that mining was prohibited on the entire 1,560-acre tract and that consideration of the rest of the property would not have affected the analysis).

142. In 1994, the Federal Circuit issued *Florida Rock Industries, Inc. v. United States*, 18 F.3d 1560 (Fed. Cir. 1994), which is one of the most disturbing opinions in takings jurisprudence. Although the court reversed a trial court's finding of a taking and remanded for further analysis, the divided panel opined that a compensable taking might occur where government action reduces the value of property by 60 percent. *See id.* at 1570. On remand, the trial court found a taking based on a 73.1 percent value loss. *See* Florida Rock Industries, Inc. v. United States, 45 Fed. Cl. 21 (1999).

The *Florida Rock* theory of liability, often referred to as the partial takings theory, is sometimes viewed as allowing for the conceptual segmentation of a "right" to exploit or derive value from property. The good news for states and municipalities is that *Florida Rock* is aberrational and has had little effect on takings jurisprudence outside the Federal Circuit. *E.g.*, Clajon Prod. Corp. v. Petera, 70 F.3d 1566, 1577 (10th Cir. 1995) (rejecting *Florida Rock*); Front Royal & Warren County Indus. Park Corp. v. Town of Front Royal, 135 F.3d 275, 285-86 (4th Cir. 1998) (reversing a finding of a taking that was based on *Florida Rock*); Maritrans Inc. v. United States, 43 Fed. Cl. 86, 90 (1999) (questioning whether *Florida Rock* accurately represented the law); Wyer v. Board of Envtl. Protection, 747 A.2d 192 (Me. 2000) ("Neither we nor the United States Supreme Court have [sic] allowed recovery for a partial taking and we see no good reason to do so here."). State and local government lawyers should rely on *Penn Central, Keystone, Andrus*, and similar cases to respond to claimants' efforts to narrow the relevant parcel by using *Florida Rock*.

143. 747 So. 2d 395 (Fla. Dist. Ct. App. 1998).

144. 803 F. Supp. 1068, 1073-74 (M.D.N.C. 1992), *aff'd without opinion*, 19 F.3d 11 (4th Cir. 1994).

145. 657 N.Y.S.2d 854, 857 (Sup. Ct. 1997), *aff'd*, 675 N.Y.S.2d 121 (1998).

146. *See* Machipongo Land & Coal Co. v. Pennsylvania, 719 A.2d 19, 28 (Pa. Commw. Ct. 1998), *cert. granted*, No. 112 MAP 2000 (Pa. 2000).

147. *See id.* at 30.

148. *Palm Beach Isles*, 231 F.3d at 1364.

149. A student comment argues that a claimant should be allowed to segment a parcel for purposes of takings analysis unless the segmented portion could not be put to an economically viable use that is independent from the rest of the parcel. *Comment, supra* note 63, at 1557-62. The comment contends that this test would serve as a meaningful

limit on improper severance because "[i]n many situations, an identifiable segment of land may be put to no economically viable use, other than to expand or beautify a building or business operation existing on a neighboring segment of land." *Id.* at 1559. This comment, however, severely underestimates the imagination of landowners who would argue that land subject to setback requirements and other routine land use controls could be put to independent use and thus should be severable. *E.g.*, District Intown Prop. Ltd. P'ship v. District of Columbia, 198 F.3d 874 (D.C. Cir. 1999) (rejecting attempt to sever apartment project lawn where owner wanted to build eight townhouses on the lawn). Given the comment's concession that even the possibility of "operating a magazine stand next to the street" on the segmented portion would be enough to justify segmentation (*id.*), it is difficult to conceive of situations in which the comment's test for severance would not be met. It would lead to severance run amok in direct contravention of the Supreme Court's parcel-as-a-whole rule.

OF PARCELS AND PROPERTY

JOHN E. FEE

5

If you can think about something which is attached to something else without thinking about what it is attached to, then you have what is called a legal mind.

—Thomas Reed Powell[1]

§ 5.0 Introduction

One of the more difficult problems in regulatory taking litigation is to define the relevant parcel of property that is subject to the taking inquiry. The issue arises when courts ask to what extent a law has impaired the usefulness or value of some property interest to determine whether there has been a taking. The smaller the defined property interest, the more likely it is that a court will find a taking by finding that the property has been completely or largely devalued; the larger the defined interest, the more likely it is that no taking will be found because some economic use will remain for the property interest as a whole. How to identify the relevant property interest remains a controversial issue in takings jurisprudence. While the Supreme Court has at times referred to the "parcel as a whole," it has not defined what this critical phrase means. In its most recent taking decision, *Palazzolo v. Rhode Island*, the Court even expressed reservation about whether "parcel as a whole" is the correct formulation.[2] Until there is consensus on how to define the relevant bundle of property, the regulatory taking doctrine will remain a muddle.[3]

In this chapter, I describe the issue of the relevant parcel (or denominator problem) as a definitional problem that cannot be solved by reference to circularities such as "parcel as a whole." In searching for a solution, we should focus on whether a given property interest is significant enough or complete enough that it should be deemed a fully protectable interest under the Takings Clause of the Fifth Amendment. I approach this question by examining property in its various dimensions (horizontal, vertical, functional, temporal) and explore how the relevant property interest is defined in each dimension. Analyzing the Supreme Court's precedent in this way reveals that a number of principles for defining the relevant property interest have already been established, some favoring property owners and some favoring regulators, depending upon the type of property division at issue.

How to define the horizontal boundaries of land for purposes of determining whether there is a regulatory taking—the very issue the Court dodged in *Palazzolo*—is perhaps the most significant unresolved question. I argue that the horizontal boundaries (or minimum horizontal parcel required) should be determined according to the economic viability of the land itself. If some identifiable parcel of land is substantial enough that it could be independently marketed and developed in an economically viable way, it should be protected under the Fifth Amendment as an independent property interest. So if a regulation utterly wipes out the usefulness of that parcel, the owner should be entitled to compensation for it, regardless of whether the owner happens to own other adjacent property. This is not the rule in a majority of courts, although some are moving in this direction.[4] Many courts instead instinctively focus on how much contiguous property is held by a single owner or what is the currently intended use for the property to determine the extent of Fifth Amendment protection. A standard based on independent economic viability, however, better serves the objectives of the Takings Clause in a non-arbitrary way. It also avoids problems of manipulability and market distortions that are associated with other potential rules.

§ 5.1   The Denominator of Regulatory Takings

Disputes over the relevant parcel commonly arise when a restriction on the use of private property applies only to a portion of some land owned by a single owner. The facts underlying *Palazzolo v. Rhode Island* are typical. In 1983, Rhode Island denied Anthony Palazzolo's application to fill 18 acres of wetland property for the purpose of building a beachfront community.[5] Two years later, the state denied a similar application to fill 11 acres of wetlands.[6] Palazzolo owned slightly more than 18 acres altogether, including a small highland parcel.[7] The state's decisions left no foreseeable means for Palazzolo to develop any of his wetland property, depriving that land of all economic use. The government indicated, however, that it would allow Palazzolo to build a single residence on the highland parcel.[8] Palazzolo sued the government, claiming that the restriction amounted to a taking of his property.

The case is similar to *Lucas v. South Carolina Coastal Council,*[9] which held as a categorical rule that "when the owner of real property has been called upon to sacrifice *all* economically beneficial uses in the name of the common good, that is, to leave his property economically idle, he has suffered a taking."[10] David Lucas suffered a taking of two beachfront lots, which he had purchased for the purpose of building homes, when the state coastal commission banned all construction on the property.[11] Because the law left Lucas with no economically viable use for the land, he was entitled to compensation.[12]

Palazzolo's situation differs in that the construction ban applied only to a portion of his property. One might argue, applying the "deprivation of all economic use" test, that this should affect only the amount of compensation owed. Palazzolo suffered a complete loss of numerous housing lots (approximately 73 subdivided lots), just as Lucas suffered a loss of both of his. Under the law of eminent domain, it is accepted in principle that the government must pay for whatever property it takes, even if it is only a fraction of what the owner has.[13] But application of this principle is unclear in the case of restrictions on the use of property. If the relevant property interest is defined as all of Palazzolo's land, including the highlands parcel, the state's actions did not work a categorical taking because some economically viable use remained for the property as a whole (the allowance to build one residence).

Whether there is a taking under the "deprivation of all economically viable use" rule therefore depends precisely upon how broadly to define the relevant property interest. The issue may also be stated as defining the appropriate denominator of the regulatory taking equation.[14] Under *Lucas*, a court must compare the loss of property use resulting from a regulation (the takings numerator) to the sum of all usage rights inherent in a piece of property (the takings denominator). The denominator of the equation is as important to the outcome as the numerator.

The denominator problem also arises in measuring the "diminution in value" of property under the *Penn Central* balancing test, an alternative method of establishing a regulatory taking.[15] Under *Penn Central*, a court balances several factors to determine whether there is a taking, including the character of a regulation, its interference with the owner's investment-backed expectations, and the diminution of property value caused by the regulation.[16] The third factor, which is generally expressed as the percentage of property devaluation caused by regulation, depends precisely upon the amount of property one begins the inquiry with. The larger the relevant property interest, the less significant the comparative effect of the regulation will be. Thus, the Supreme Court has explained: "Because our test for regulatory taking requires us to compare the value that has been taken from the property with the value that remains in the property, one of the critical questions is determining how to define the unit of property 'whose value is to furnish the denominator of the fraction.'"[17]

Unfortunately, *Palazzolo v. Rhode Island* did not settle the legal question of how to define the takings denominator because in that case it was waived. Palazzolo failed to argue in the lower courts that the wetlands parcels were separately taken, but had only claimed a taking of his entire combined interest.[18] On the basis of this single claim, the Supreme Court held that there was no categorical taking of the broadly defined parcel, because some development potential remained for the highland property.[19] The Court explicitly left open how to define the relevant property interest in cases where narrower claims are asserted.[20]

§ 5.2 The Twin Problems of Conceptual Severance and Conceptual Agglomeration

How to define the taking denominator is the flip side of asking what property restrictions go "too far" to be imposed without compensation. Understandably, the law does not allow unlimited property divisions for purposes of identifying regulatory takings, or every restriction on the use of private property could be expressed as a total deprivation. A restriction on the height of buildings could be said to be a complete deprivation of certain airspace rights. A ban on raising pigs in a residential neighborhood could be expressed as completely extinguishing the owner's easement to operate a pigsty. If the relevant property interest were defined narrowly enough, every restriction on the use of private property would qualify as a total taking of something. Margaret Jane Radin has crafted the term "conceptual severance" to describe this loophole strategy.[21] It consists of "delineating a property interest consisting of just what the government action has removed from the owner, and then asserting that that particular whole thing has been permanently taken."[22] Radin's insight of conceptual severance shows that there must be some limit to how narrowly one may define the relevant parcel, unless every property restriction is to require compensation.

Those who favor a narrow interpretation of the regulatory takings doctrine frequently observe the problem of conceptual severance, citing it for why takings law should refuse to recognize narrowly defined segments of property. What is generally missing from such discussions, however, is recognition of the equivalent loophole working in the opposite direction—that of governments avoiding the regulatory takings doctrine by defining the relevant property interests too broadly. Steven Eagle appropriately calls this counter-strategy "conceptual agglomeration."[23] It recognizes that just as a government regulation could always be described abstractly as affecting the "whole" of some discrete property interest, every regulation could similarly be described as affecting only part of some broader set of entitlements.[24] Thus, if the relevant parcel of property were defined broadly enough, the regulatory taking doctrine would be nullified. A regulation that deprives an owner of the use of certain property is not a taking, one could argue, if the owner still enjoys the use of some other property (for example, a personal home, downtown office, stock options, or toothbrush), all of which could in theory be labeled as strands of a single estate or bundle of property rights. Indeed, one could go further by recognizing (as property law does) that ownership of a thing or parcel can be shared by more than one person. Why not define an entire township or county as the whole relevant parcel, of which individual community members each own only mere segments?

While this form of conceptual agglomeration would not make sense for purposes of takings law, it is no more fanciful than that of property owners engaging in unlimited conceptual severance. The law clearly prohibits both extremes. This has been implicit in the law at least since Justice Holmes held in *Pennsylvania Coal Co. v. Mahon* that "while property may be regulated to a certain extent, if regulation goes too far it will be recognized as a taking"[25]—which stakes a compromise between treating every property restriction as a taking and treating no restriction as a taking. The potential loopholes of conceptual severance and conceptual agglomeration demonstrate that there must be some upper and lower limit to the size of the relevant parcel if such a compromise is to be maintained.

But beyond showing the need for rules constraining the size of the denominator, the ideas of conceptual severance and conceptual agglomeration have little usefulness or concrete meaning. As mere tautologies, they demonstrate nothing as to what those constraints should be. This seems to be misunderstood by those who criticize courts for engaging in conceptual severance, as if the mere exercise of conceptual severance proves a court's decision to be flawed. It does not. Every judicial decision assuming some definition of the "relevant parcel" can be described as an act of conceptual severance (since the relevant interest could have been identified more broadly) or as an act of conceptual agglomeration (since the relevant interest could have been identified more narrowly). Whether to call it one or the other simply depends on one's own baseline understanding of what is the "correct" relevant bundle of rights— a key issue that should be examined rather than assumed.[26] Viewed properly as a baseline issue, the real question raised by the denominator problem is not *whether* to sever or agglomerate property interests in defining the relevant parcel, but rather *how* to sever and agglomerate such interests in the most sensible way possible—for it is impossible to define a complete bundle of property rights without in some sense doing both.

§ 5.3   *The Whole Parcel Rule*

Having rejected the idea that any regulation is a taking if it merely extinguishes some narrowly defined right to use property, the Supreme Court has held that a regulation must be examined in light of the whole parcel of property. In *Penn Central Transportation Co. v. New York City*, the Court stated the rule as follows:

> "Taking" jurisprudence does not divide a single parcel into discrete segments and attempt to determine whether rights in a particular segment have been entirely abrogated. In deciding whether a particular governmental action has effected a taking, this Court focuses rather ... on the ... nature ... of the interference with rights in the parcel as a whole.[27]

Some kind of whole parcel rule is necessary to the "deprivation of all economically viable use" and "diminution in value" standards. Without such a principle, even the most minimal restrictions would become takings. But the whole parcel rule abstractly described above does not answer the denominator question, as too many commentators and courts have supposed.[28] Instead, it merely begs the question, what is a whole parcel of property?

Indeed, the Supreme Court has acknowledged the unresolved denominator question since *Penn Central*. In *Lucas*, the Court stated: "Regrettably, the rhetorical force of our 'deprivation of all economically feasible use' rule is greater than its precision, since the rule does not make clear the 'property interest' against which the loss of value is to be measured."[29] The Court went on to discuss an example of a regulation requiring a developer to leave 90 percent of a rural tract in its natural state, stating the law is "unclear" on what would be the relevant property interest.[30] In *Palazzolo*, the Court even questioned whether the whole parcel rule provides the proper baseline, noting that "we have at times expressed discomfort with the logic of this rule, a sentiment echoed by some commentators."[31] The Court continued, "Whatever the merits of these criticisms, we will not explore the point here."[32] If the whole parcel rule were clearly established, and if its meaning in the context of Palazzolo's property were clear, it would have been much simpler for the Court to resolve the denominator question by just applying the rule. Instead, by relying on Palazzolo's waiver of the issue, while noting criticism of the whole parcel rule in dictum, the Court clearly signaled that the denominator issue remains open.

Because some kind of whole parcel requirement is logically necessary, I prefer to examine the issue as a matter of how to apply it, rather than question its legitimacy. At a minimum, the Court's dicta in *Lucas* and *Palazzolo* show that there is no consensus yet on how to distinguish between a mere "discrete segment" and a "parcel as a whole" for taking purposes.[33] (Did Palazzolo own only one whole parcel, or did he own 74 or more of them?) Every definable property interest is at the same time a "whole" of what is defined, and a "parcel" of something larger.[34] Mere statements of the whole parcel principle therefore provide little guidance as to its application.[35]

To understand the Court's precedent, one must look beyond abstract statements to the actual cases the Court has decided and types of property divisions it has rejected and approved. For this purpose, it is useful to consider each of the various dimensions in which property is defined. For real property, four dimensions of the relevant parcel must be considered: horizontal dimensions (geographic area of a parcel, as may be shown on a map or by metes and bounds), vertical dimensions (what air, surface, and subsurface strata are included), functional dimensions (what usage rights are included, as in easements or profits), and temporal dimensions (what past, present, and future interests are included).[36] Examining the Supreme Court's decisions in each of these dimensions, one finds a patchwork of principles that have developed for defining the relevant property interest, which vary depending upon the type of property division at issue.

§ 5.3(a) *Functional Severance*

The Supreme Court has spoken most clearly with respect to functional divisions of property. For purposes of the whole parcel rule, it is established that property may not be severed into every conceivable use to determine whether there has been a taking of any one use. The loss of the most valuable use of property, alone, does not constitute a taking. Thus, in *Andrus v. Allard*,[37] the Court held that a federal ban on the sale of eagle feathers did not work a taking, even though owners of eagle feathers had completely lost their rights to sell. Rather than consider the "right to sell" in isolation, the Court held that "where an owner possesses a full 'bundle' of property rights, the destruction of one 'strand' of the bundle is not a taking, because the aggregate must be viewed in its entirety."[38] In denying the takings claim, the Court went on to discuss other ways the owners were still entitled to use their feathers: "for example, they might exhibit the artifacts for an admissions charge."[39]

It is too simple, however, to say that no functional divisions of property are made for purposes of the whole parcel rule. The Court has recognized certain strands in the bundle of property as so fundamental that they are treated separately, so that deprivations of those rights alone may amount to takings. Among these are the right to exclude others from property[40] and the right to alienate property at death.[41] One might say that these functional rights are completely severed from other property rights for purposes of determining if there is a taking.

The "deprivation of all economically viable use" rule of *Lucas v. South Carolina Coastal Council* also severs a certain category of uses—economically viable uses—from all other potential uses of the property. While all economically viable uses are grouped together for purposes of the rule, they are nevertheless evaluated separately from non-economic uses, as well as from the rights to alienate and exclude. The fact that one might still enjoy the right to use one's property for recreation, deed it to someone else, or exclude others from entering it will not disqualify a property owner from claiming a categorical taking when all "economically viable uses" of the property are prevented.[42] *Lucas* therefore establishes a limited principle of conceptual severance with respect to functional divisions of property rights.

§ 5.3(b) *Vertical Severance*

The Supreme Court has also disallowed vertical divisions of property rights in applying the whole parcel rule. In *Penn Central,* the Court made it clear that air rights are not severable from surface rights. Penn Central, the owner of Grand Central Terminal in New York City, challenged a city landmark ordinance preventing it from constructing a new office tower over the station, claiming it to be a taking of valuable air rights. The Court declined to consider the devaluation of Penn Central's air rights in isolation, explaining that the regulation's effects must be considered in relation to the parcel as a whole—"here, the city tax block designated as the 'landmark site.'"[43] Because Penn Central still enjoyed the valuable use of the existing terminal, there was no taking. *Penn Central* therefore rejects the vertical severance of air rights from surface rights.

The Court has also rejected the conceptual severance of certain subsurface rights. In *Keystone Bituminous Coal Assn. v. DeBenedictis,* Pennsylvania coal companies challenged state regulations requiring 50 percent of the coal beneath certain protected structures to be kept in place to provide surface support.[44] Owners of coal interests argued that this constituted a taking of their "support estate," a separate estate recognized under state law consisting specifically of the right to mine certain coal that supports the surface.[45] The Court rejected this narrow formulation of the denominator, finding it inconsistent with the whole-parcel rule. The Court noted that "in practical terms, the support estate has value only insofar as it protects or enhances the value of the estate with which it is associated. Its value is merely a part of the entire bundle of rights possessed by the owner of either the coal or the surface."[46] Therefore, because valuable rights to mine coal remained in the property, there was not a taking.[47]

It remains an open question after *Keystone* and *Penn Central* whether vertical interests may be severed when the particular interest is significant enough to be independently viable.[48] It also remains an open question whether divided ownership of vertical interests affects the relevant parcel. Would the result have been the same in *Penn Central* if, when the terminal became a landmark, one party owned the air rights and another party owned the surface?[49] These questions aside, *Penn Central* and *Keystone* at least establish that vertical interests generally are bundled together for purposes of defining the relevant property.

§ 5.3(c) *Temporal Severance*

In contrast to functional and vertical severance, Supreme Court decisions support the division of property into time segments for purposes of defining the relevant property interest. This occurs in two ways. First, the Supreme Court routinely severs present and future enjoyment of property rights from past property rights in determining whether there is a regulatory taking. The relevant property interest does not include prior uses of the property. Were this the law, prior economic profits generated from the property would have to be balanced against future losses caused by regulation. Instead, the Court has consistently measured the effect of regulation on prospective property rights alone.[50]

Second, the Court has approved the concept of temporary regulatory takings, another form of temporal segmentation. The leading case is *First English Evangelical Lutheran Church of Glendale v. County of Los Angeles.*[51] First English sought compensation under the Takings Clause for a county ordinance that had prevented it from using certain campground property for a period of several years. The Court held that First English's complaint stated a valid claim for compensation based on the allegation that there was a temporary regulatory taking. "Here we must assume that the Los Angeles County ordinance has denied appellant all use of its property for a considerable period of years, and we hold that invalidation of the ordinance without payment of fair value for the use of the property during this period of time would be a constitutionally insufficient remedy."[52] The Court did not hold that any length of time would suffice to establish a temporary regulatory taking, noting that a different situation may arise "in the case of normal delays in obtaining building permits, changes in zoning ordinances, variances and the like."[53] But *First English* does suggest that the whole property interest can be defined in time segments as short as several years, and need not include the entire fee simple.[54]

§ 5.3(d) *Horizontal Severance*

The Supreme Court has said the least about how to define the relevant parcel horizontally. Yet it is in this context that most of the current denominator disputes seem to arise, as in *Palazzolo.* No rule or presumption against conceptual severance can be established for this dimension because horizontal boundaries are a logical necessity in defining a parcel of land. While it is conceivable to presume that a whole bundle of property rights includes all vertical rights, all functional rights, and all temporal rights of a given parcel (although, as I have explained, the Supreme Court does allow some degree of severance in these dimensions), this only works if the property interest is limited by horizontal boundaries. Take away the horizontal boundaries, and all property interests of all owners would blur into one. Thus, while it is possible to prohibit other types of segmentation, it is not possible in any rational sense to fully prohibit the horizontal segmentation of land. It must instead be prescribed.

Some guidance on the question of horizontal segmentation does appear in the Supreme Court's *Penn Central* and *Lucas* opinions. In *Penn Central*, the Court defined the relevant parcel as "the city tax block designated as the landmark site."[55] Although not indicating why one block was the relevant land area, the decision rejected a broader definition urged by the city: that of including all of Penn Central's real estate holdings in the metropolitan area. The New York Court of Appeals had found this to be the relevant unit of property, rejecting the owner's taking claim in part because of the income it derived from its other real estate holdings.[56] The Supreme Court's *Penn Central* opinion affirmatively rejects this broad definition of the denominator, making clear that common ownership alone does not make disparate holdings a single bundle of property.[57]

In *Lucas*, while acknowledging the problem of defining horizontal interests, the Court also hypothesized as to what the correct rule might be: "The answer to this difficult question may lie in how the owner's reasonable expectations have been shaped by the State's law of property—*i.e.*, whether and to what degree the State's law has accorded legal recognition and protection to the particular interest in land with respect to which the takings claimant alleges a diminution in (or elimination of) value." This quotation seems to suggest a relatively narrow view of the relevant parcel, perhaps even complete horizontal severability.[58] Yet it seems unlikely that the Court would go so far as to say any horizontal division of land, no matter how small, qualifies as an independently protectable interest. Such a rule would draw into question even standard setback ordinances, which necessarily require certain sections of property to remain economically idle.[59] Nevertheless, the meaning of the Court's dictum in *Lucas* remains unclear.

Given the ambiguity of the Supreme Court's decisions, it is not surprising that lower courts have approached defining the relevant parcel in a variety of ways, often inconsistently. In some courts, such as the U.S. Court of Claims (and now Federal Circuit), the standard has evolved toward the recognition of smaller interests but still lacks clarity. Among the factors that courts often rely upon to determine the relevant parcel are common ownership, how the owner treats the property, and how the property is regulated. As explained below, each of these criteria is flawed.

§ 5.4   *The Problem with Focusing on Unity of Ownership*

One way to define the relevant parcel of land is to base it on unity of ownership. The law could provide that all contiguous property under common ownership forms a single parcel for purposes of regulatory takings. The Supreme Court has never held this to be the definition of "parcel as a whole," although some state courts have adopted it.[60] The U.S. Court of Claims also initially applied this rule in wetlands taking cases.[61]

Defining the relevant parcel based solely on contiguous common ownership has an advantage in that it is easy to apply. But it does little to serve the policies underlying the Takings Clause. As a standard of just compensation, it is simply illogical. Why should the law declare that a landowner may not own more than one adjacent "parcel" of land, each independently protected by the Fifth Amendment? A unity-of-ownership standard, for its simplicity, results in arbitrary treatment of landowners and harmful distortions of real estate markets.

One problem with the unity-of-ownership criterion is that it fails to give property the full value of the sum of its parts. Consider the example of Anthony Palazzolo. If the law requires that all contiguous property under common ownership be considered a single parcel, then it must have been a mistake for Palazzolo to purchase both wetlands and highlands together. At a minimum, he should have completed selling off his highland property before attempting to develop the wetlands.[62] By owning both the highlands and wetlands contemporaneously, Palazzolo caused both sets of interests to be worth less. There is no reason that the Takings Clause should make this distinction. Whether Palazzolo should be compensated for his wetlands property should not depend upon whether he happens to own other adjacent property.

The unity-of-ownership test encourages owners to make socially useless splits of property in order to increase its overall compensation value.[63] Justice Brandeis noted the flaw in this rule in his dissenting opinion in *Pennsylvania Coal v. Mahon*:

> The rights of the owner against the public are not increased by dividing the interests in his property into surface and subsoil. The sum of the rights of the parts can not be greater than the rights in the whole.... I suppose no one would contend that by selling his interest above one hundred feet from the surface he could prevent the State from limiting, by the police power, the height of structures in a city. And why should the sale of underground rights bar the State's power?[64]

Determining the relevant property interest based on ownership not only undermines the policies of the Takings Clause because of its manipulability, it is also economically harmful. It
encourages the increasing fragmentation of property interests,
which can significantly increase the transaction costs required to
put property to its best use.[65] This in turn lowers the property's
economic value to the whole community.

Finally, a unity-of-ownership rule unreasonably discriminates
in effect. Some have commented that it turns the Takings Clause
into a deep-pocket rule, making it more difficult for large landowners to receive compensation than small landowners.[66] In fact,
it is even more arbitrary. Whether compensation is required under this rule often depends upon whether various parcels of property happen to be contiguous. An owner in the position of David
Lucas could receive compensation as long as the owner's house
or other property is not located next door to the restricted lots, so
it is not included in the relevant parcel; if the owner's other property does happen to be adjacent, the right to compensation would
be lost. Focusing on contiguous common ownership therefore
makes takings cases turn upon the randomness of whether real
estate interests are contiguous, or instead on the cleverness of
landowners in keeping real estate interests sufficiently fragmented.
If a deep-pocket rule were intended, wouldn't it be more appropriate to focus on the owner's total assets and income stream,
rather than just contiguous real estate?

§ 5.5   *The Problem with Focusing on Actual or Intended*
Use

Because of its flaws, many courts have rejected simple unity of
ownership as the denominator standard,[67] including now the Federal Circuit and U.S. Claims Court. As the Federal Circuit stated
in *Florida Rock Industries, Inc. v. United States*: "Nothing in the
language of the Fifth Amendment compels a court to find a taking *only* when the Government divests the total ownership of the
property; the Fifth Amendment prohibits the uncompensated taking of private property without reference to the owner's remaining property interests."[68]

The factor most commonly relied upon by courts, besides
common ownership, is the owner's actual use or intended actual
use of the property. A court may ask whether the property has
been used and planned as a single functional unit, or whether it
instead consists of economically independent tracts that only happen to be contiguous. Thus, if property is purchased and used for
a common integrated purpose, it will generally be considered a

single unit for takings purposes. For example, in *Forest Properties, Inc. v. United States*, the Federal Circuit found a property
owner's combined 53 acres of uplands and 9 acres of wetlands to
constitute a single 62-acre parcel, because from the time the property was purchased, the owner had planned that all of it would be
developed as a single integrated project.[69]

This is an improvement on simple unity of ownership as a
rule, because owners' expectations with respect to the property
will more closely reflect the property's actual economic potential. In cases where an owner's intended use of property is the
property's only economically viable use, then the functional unity
standard reaches a logical result. Why should a landowner be
allowed to focus on a narrower segment of land for purposes of
the "deprivation of economically viable use" rule, if the segment
could not even be put to profitable use but for combining it with
other surrounding property? Reliance on actual or intended use,
however, also has its problems.

First, the actual use (or functional unity) standard still depends heavily upon common ownership in determining the bounds
of the relevant parcel. Courts that rely upon functional unity generally still implicitly require contiguous common ownership or
balance functional use with common ownership as factors in determining what is the relevant parcel.[70] This then still leads to the
incongruity identified by Justice Brandeis: that of owners making socially useless splits of their property to increase their rights
against the state. Just compensation results can still be manipulated by dividing ownership of land, and for this reason owners
are still encouraged to fragment their interests.

The functional unity standard also encourages owners to fragment the uses of property, causing them often to use property in a
less efficient manner by avoiding economies of scale. Under such a
rule, owners who purchase large tracts of land could increase the
value of property by using the environmentally sensitive portions
(any portions such as wetlands that might conceivably be restricted
in the future) independently from non-sensitive parts of the land,
so in a future inverse condemnation case the tracts would be treated
as separate parcels. Why the law should reward owners for developing wetlands and highlands portions of property separately, when
it is more efficient to develop them jointly, is a mystery. The functional unity standard therefore leads to unjustified results because
of its singular focus on only one potential use for the property: the
owner's actual intended use. Paradoxically, this will generally also
be the property's most valuable use.

Just as the loss of the most valuable use for property should
not be sufficient to claim a taking, there is no reason why the law

should deny compensation to an owner simply because of what has been property's most profitable use. Consider an owner who acquires two adjacent one-acre parcels (lots A and B) in a valuable location, so that the property has multiple profitable uses. The owner could divide lots A and B and develop them as separate projects, each of which would produce a profit of $100,000. Or the owner could combine the two acres in an integrated project for a value of $300,000. Under normal market conditions, the owner would plan the property as an integrated two-acre project because of its higher value. Suppose, then, the state chooses to restrict all development of parcel A. Under the functional unity standard, the owner would not be entitled to compensation because the property was intended as a combined project, making the relevant parcel the combined two acres; the continuing economic viability of parcel B therefore would prevent the owner from receiving any compensation.

The irony in this example is that were it not for the opportunity of earning a greater profit by integrating the uses of parcels A and B, the owner would have received compensation worth $100,000 for the loss of parcel A. By losing more, the owner receives less. If the $300,000 project were not feasible (and hence the property were less valuable to begin with), the owner would have planned to use parcels A and B separately, and would then have been entitled to full compensation for parcel A. In effect, the functional unity standard penalizes owners for what happens to be the most valuable use of their property.

The functional unity standard also suffers from a definitional problem: At what level must development plans for separate tracts of land be "integrated" to be considered functionally one? Courts seem to have rejected the notion that each lot in a planned housing subdivision can be considered a separate project, even though the lots are subdivided, intended to be sold in separate transactions to different buyers, and will each support a home for a separate family. It is not even clear that two neighboring residential subdivisions, which may be developed separately for marketing and zoning purposes, would be enough.[71] As some courts apply the functional unity standard, it seems to require only that the property be acquired at the same time and be used for a somewhat similar purpose.[72] To the extent this is what functional unity means, it is scarcely better than unity of ownership as a rule.

§ 5.6   *The Problem with Focusing on Governmental Action*

An alternative method for defining the relevant parcel looks at how the regulatory scheme in question identifies or treats the property. This factor has been applied in some courts, often balanced with how the owner treats the property.[73] For example, in *Twain Harte Associates, Ltd. v. Tuolumne County,* an owner sought compensation for the rezoning of 1.7 acres as "open space," although the owner held 8.5 acres altogether.[74] The California Court of Appeals held that "the nature of the particular land use regulation" may have the effect of "creating" separate parcels for "taking' purposes."[75] Because the rezoning affected only 1.7 acres, it was presumed to be a separate parcel for summary judgment purposes.[76]

The problem with relying on this factor is that it is highly manipulable by the government. If, as in *Twaine Harte*, one looks at whether the property lies within a single regulatory zone (or how it is identified by the regulatory scheme), the result will often simply depend upon how the regulation is phrased. For example, in *Twaine Harte* the government could have included the restricted open space and the owner's remaining usable property in a single comprehensive zone, defining the open space restriction in relation to the other usable property (like a setback ordinance or height restriction). If changing the form of a regulation is enough to change whether compensation is owed, this approach fails sufficiently to restrain the government. By contrast, if one looks to the substance of a government restriction rather than its form to define the relevant property, the result is complete conceptual severance, which will always favor the owner. If the relevant bundle of property is defined as "that which the regulation prohibits using," by definition it will always be totally abrogated. Focusing upon the criterion of government action, whether alone or in combination with ownership or usage factors, therefore does not seem to make sense.

§ 5.7   A Proposed Solution: Economic Viability of the Land

The criteria most often relied upon by courts to define the relevant parcel—ownership of property, use of property, and regulatory treatment of property—are flawed because such factors are within the complete control of the owner or government. Reliance upon these factors introduces harmful incentives for owners and government, as well as arbitrariness.

Rather than look to factors within the control of landowners and the government, the law should focus on something more objective: the property itself and its relation to the community. Keeping in mind the purpose of the denominator inquiry—which is to provide a baseline against which the constitutional protection of private property is measured—the relevant inquiry ought to be whether a given parcel of land is substantial enough that it should be fully protected under the regulatory takings doctrine. If the parcel is sufficiently large or complete (however the law chooses objectively to define this), it should be considered a "whole parcel" for purposes of determining if there is a taking, regardless of whether the owner happens to hold other adjacent property, how the property was purchased, or how the owner previously intended to use the property. On the other hand, if the interest is not sufficiently complete by objective standards, it should not matter that this is the owner's only sliver of property, for it would have become a worthless sliver in anyone else's hands; the relevant whole parcel should be defined more broadly.[77] Only by focusing on the land itself, rather than on the paper transactions of owners and government, can disparate treatment of landowners be avoided.

There are various ways that the law might objectively define the minimum requirements of a whole parcel. A sensible way seems to be to focus on the economic potential of land. I have therefore proposed the following standard: If an identifiable parcel of land is substantial enough that it could be put to economically profitable use as an independent parcel (but for the challenged regulation), it should be protected as a whole parcel.[78] In other words, a whole parcel is one that is large enough that even if it were the owner's only real property, it would be feasible and profitable to use for some independent enterprise.

The Commonwealth Court of Pennsylvania recently adopted this rule. In *Machipongo Land and Coal Co., Inc. v. Commonwealth Dep't of Envtl. Resources*, coal owners sought compensation for a state regulation designating certain property as unsuitable for surface mining of coal.[79] The principal plaintiff, Machipongo, owned an area comprising 2,037 acres for mining. Pennsylvania subsequently prohibited all surface mining in a designated watershed area, including 157 acres of Machipongo's land.[80] The government sought summary judgment on Machipongo's taking claim, arguing that the relevant parcel consisted of all 2,037 acres of Machipongo's land under the "contiguous land under common owner" approach.[81] The commonwealth court rejected this approach, citing the unfairness and other problems associated with contiguous common ownership.[82] Instead, the court held that the plaintiff could establish a taking on the basis of the 157-acre regulated area, if the following facts could be established: "the regulated land had value prior to the regulation"; "the regulated land has a separate use from the non-regulated contiguous parcel(s)— i.e., . . . it may be profitably used if it is the only parcel"; and "if the regulated land has value separate from the contiguous land, whether all of its benefit is gone."[83] Because these material facts remained in dispute, the court denied summary judgment for the government.[84]

The result in *Machipongo* is a fair one. There is no legitimate constitutional reason to penalize landowners such as Machipongo because they happen to own surrounding property that is not wiped out by regulation, or because they use their property in an integrated way for purposes of achieving economies of scale. By focusing on whether Machipongo's 157 acres were economically viable apart from the other property, the court chose to give the owner, acre-for-acre, the same level of constitutional protection as other potential owners whose only property was affected by the regulation. As the court stated, "This approach is best because it fosters predictability, focuses on the effect of the governmental regulation on the property and not the circumstances of the property owner, and results in fairness because it treats all property owners the same."[85]

The rule of *Machipongo* is also well balanced. Although the holding is generally more favorable to property owners than the contiguous common ownership rule, it does not allow unlimited conceptual severance, not even horizontally. An important requirement of this standard is that a given parcel have economic potential independent of surrounding land interests. There are many "parcels" of property that have economic value, but only for the purpose of enhancing some larger set of property rights. Consider a 10-ft.-wide strip of lawn surrounding an office park. While the owner might complain that it would have been more profitable to build the complex all the way to the street, leaving no open lawn space, the 10-ft. strip alone would not be sufficient to support an independently viable project. Because the land area has no *independent* economic potential (rather, its value is appurtenant to the entire office park), it alone could not be claimed to be a separate parcel for purposes of challenging regulations requiring it to remain open space. Setback ordinances therefore would not generally require compensation under this standard, unless the requirements were so extreme as to deprive an owner of a whole independently viable parcel.[86]

Reliance upon independent economic viability to define the relevant parcel finds support in the Supreme Court's *Keystone Bituminous Coal* decision. In that case, the Court declined to consider the mineral support estate recognized under state law as a separate interest for takings purposes largely because it is not independently viable: "[I]t cannot be used profitably by one who does not also possess either the mineral estate or the surface estate ... Thus, in practical terms, the support estate has value only insofar as it protects or enhances the value of the estate with which it is associated. Its value is merely a part of the entire bundle of rights possessed by the owner of either the coal or the surface."[87] It makes sense to use the same principle for defining the horizontal boundaries of property. Where a given parcel is so small or isolated that it could not be used independently, it would distort the regulatory taking inquiry to treat it as a separate bundle of rights. But in cases where the relevant interest is so substantial that it could stand alone economically, such as Palazzolo's 18 acres of restricted wetlands, there is no legitimate reason to deny compensation on the basis of additional property the owner happens to hold.

Of course, owners should bear the burden of proving that a given parcel of property could be put to viable economic use for some independent project. An "economically viable use" (as under *Lucas*) would have to be more than speculative or merely feasible, but one that could reasonably be expected to produce positive economic returns. In cases where owners claim potential economic uses that differ from their previous actual or intended use of the property, the burden to show that such a use would be economically viable might be a heavy one. It would depend most likely upon showing that similarly sized units of property are regularly traded and developed for similar projects in the vicinity. Notwithstanding the difficulties of proof, owners at least ought to be given the chance to prove independent economic viability. In cases such as *Palazzolo* or *Machipongo,* where the restricted area is so substantial that its independent viability is obvious, this standard produces a sound just-compensation result.

To the extent that this solution increases the fiscal burden of government, it seems to be a fair burden. To be clear, I do not question that environmental programs such as federal wetlands protections or local open space protections are a good thing. The relevant issue is not whether it is in the public interest to preserve natural environments, but whether individual owners such as Anthony Palazzolo should bear the heavy expense of doing so— while the benefits largely go the public. As the Supreme Court has often noted, the Fifth Amendment "is designed 'not to limit the governmental interference with property rights *per se*, but rather to secure *compensation* in the event of otherwise proper interference amounting to a taking.'"[88] Like owners who are deprived of property for roads, hospitals, power lines, and countless other worthy governmental purposes, owners who are deprived of substantial areas of property to support environmental preservation and open space programs should be entitled to compensation under the Fifth Amendment.

Notes

1. Unpublished manuscript, *quoted in* Thurman W. Arnold, *Criminal Attempts—The Rise and Fall of an Abstraction*, 40 YALE L. J. 53, 58 (1930).

2. Palazzolo v. Rhode Island, 121 S.Ct. 2448, 2465 (2001).

3. *See* Carol M. Rose, Mahon *Reconstructed;Why the Takings Issue Is Still a Muddle*, 57 S. CAL. L. REV. 561, 566-69 (1984) (describing the relevant parcel problem as a source of confusion); Richard Epstein, Lucas v. South Carolina Coastal Council: *A Tangled Web of Expectations*, 45 STAN. L. REV. 1369, 1375 (1993) ("Any theory of regulatory takings that openly confesses its inability to come to grips with [the relevant parcel] issue is dead before it is born.").

4. *E.g.,* Machipongo Land & Coal Co. v. Commw. Dept. of Envtl. Res., 719 A.2d 19, 28 (Pa. Commw. 1998). I first proposed the independent economic viability rule in John E. Fee, *Unearthing the Denominator in Regulatory Taking Claims*, 61 U. CHI. L. REV. 1535 (1994).

5. 121 S.Ct. at 2456.

6. *Id.*

7. *Id.* at 2460.

8. *Id.*

9. 505 U.S. 1003 (1992).

10. *Id.* at 1019 (original emphasis).

11. *Id.* at 1009.

12. The Court recognized an exception to the otherwise "categorical rule" for legal restrictions that are inherent in the property title under common law, such as anti-nuisance restrictions. *Id.* at 1027-32. On remand, the South Carolina Supreme Court held that no such common-law principle supported the restriction on Lucas's property. Lucas v. South Carolina Coastal Council, 424 S.E.2d 484, 486 (1992).

13. Loretto v. Teleprompter Manhattan CATV Corp., 458 U.S. 419, 438 n.16 (1982) ("[W]hether the installation is a taking does not depend on whether the volume of space it occupies is bigger than a breadbox.").

14. *See* Frank I. Michelman, *Property, Utility, and Fairness: Comments on the Ethical Foundations of "Just Compensation" Law*, 80 HARV. L. REV. 1165, 1192 (1967); Fee, *supra* note 4, at 1536.

15. *See Palazzolo*, 121 S.Ct. at 2465; *Lucas*, 505 U.S. at 1016 n.8.

16. Penn Cent. Transp. Co. v. City of New York, 438 U.S. 104, 124 (1978).

17. Keystone Bituminous Coal Ass'n v. DeBenedictis, 480 U.S. 470, 497 (1987).

18. 121 S.Ct. at 2465.

19. *Id.* at 2457, 2465.

20. *Id.* While holding that there was no categorical taking, the Court remanded for a determination whether there was a taking under the *Penn Central* test. *Id.*

21. Margaret Jane Radin, *The Liberal Conception of Property: Cross Currents in the Jurisprudence of Takings*, 88 COLUM. L. REV. 1667, 1676 (1988).

22. *Id.; see also* Frank Michelman, *Takings, 1987*, 88 COLUM. L. REV. 1600, 1615-16 (1988) (condemning the strategy of "entitlement chopping").

23. STEVEN J. EAGLE, REGULATORY TAKINGS § 8-2(h) (Michie 1998).

24. As Steven Eagle comments: "Clearly, the creation of tautologies is a game that two can play. In response to the government's assertion that 'anything is 100% of something,' the landowner might with equal plausibility state that 'almost anything does not approach 100% of everything.'" *Id.; see also* Fee, *supra* note 4, at 1550.

25. Pennsylvania Coal Co. v. Mahon, 260 U.S. 393, 415 (1922).

26. If any owner is ever to succeed under the "deprivation of all economically viable use" test, it must sometimes be permissible to define the relevant property as "precisely that which is taken away." The relevant question therefore is not whether conceptual severance should be allowed, but under what circumstances it is allowed.

27. Penn Cent. Transp. Co. v. City of New York, 438 U.S. 104, 130-31 (1978). *See also* Keystone Bituminous Coal Assoc. v. DeBencdictus, 480 U.S. 470, 497 (1987); Concrete Pipe and Prod. of Cal., Inc. v. Constr. Laborers Pension Trust, 508 U.S. 602, 644 (1993); Andrus v. Allard, 444 U.S. 51, 65-66 (1979).

28. *E.g.,* John A. Humbach, *"Taking" the Imperial Judiciary Seriously: Segmenting Property Interests and Judicial Revision of Legislative Judgments*, 42 Cath. U. L. Rev. 771, 796 (1993) (arguing that the *Lucas* Court's hypothetical, in which a rural developer is deprived of all economically viable use of 90 percent of a tract but retains use in the remaining 10 percent, is clearly not a taking under the whole-parcel rule).

29. Lucas v. South Carolina Coastal Council, 505 U.S. 1003, 1016 n.7 (1992).

30. *Id.*

31. 121 S.Ct. at 2465 (internal citations omitted).

32. *Id.*

33. For this reason, it should not be surprising that the Court has, since *Lucas*, repeated *Penn Central*'s general statement of the whole-parcel rule. *See Concrete Pipe and Products*, 508 U.S. at 643-44. While some might prefer to believe that the Court's restatement of the whole-parcel rule in *Concrete Pipe* overruled its prior dicta in *Lucas* concerning the relevant parcel, *see* Timothy J. Dowling, *Reflections on Urban Sprawl, Smart Growth, and the Fifth Amendment*, 148 U. Pa. L. Rev. 873, 885 (2000), it seems instead to be an indication only that "whole parcel" is a flexible concept.

34. *See also* Eagle, *supra,* note 23, § 8-2(h); Fee, *supra* note 3.

35. *See Lucas*, 505 U.S. at 1016 n.7. *See also Keystone*, 480 U.S. at 497 ("These verbal formulations do not solve all of the definitional issues that may arise in defining the relevant mass of property.").

36. I focus here on the dimensions in which real property is generally defined. Other types of property interests raise additional definitional problems with respect to the whole-parcel rule. For example, in *Concrete Pipe and Products* the Court applied the whole-parcel rule to reject a takings claim concerning pension assets. Even in that context, the Court did not fully resolve the scope of the relevant property interest. *See* 508 U.S. at 645 (leaving open the question whether to include assets of affiliated corporations).

37. 444 U.S. 51 (1979).

38. *Id.* at 65-66.

39. *Id.* at 66.

40. *See* Loretto v. Teleprompter Manhattan CATV Corp., 458 U.S. 419, 435 (1982).

41. Hodel v. Irving, 481 U.S. 704 (1987); Babbitt v. Youpee, 519 U.S. 234 (1997).

42 *See* David L. Callies, *Regulatory Takings and the Supreme Court: How Perspectives on Rights Have Changed from Penn Central to Dolan, and What State and Federal Courts Are Doing About It*, 28 Stetson L. Rev. 523, 555 (1999).

43. Penn Cent. Transp. Co. v. City of New York, 438 U.S. 104, 131 (1978).

44. 480 U.S. 470 (1987).

45. *Id.* at 478-79.

46. *Id.* at 501.

47. *Id. Keystone* essentially overruled *Pennsylvania Coal v. Mahon*, which had found a taking on similar facts. *See* Richard A. Epstein, *Takings: Descent and Resurrection*,

1987, Sup. Ct. Rev. 1, 10-15. Nevertheless, *Mahon*'s general formulation of the regulatory taking doctrine remains good law.

48.   For example, what if the regulation in *Keystone* prohibited all subsurface mining but left valuable uses for the surface? In refusing to consider the support estate as a separate property interest, the *Keystone* Court relied heavily on the fact that "it cannot be used profitably by one who does not also possess either the mineral estate or the surface estate." *Keystone*, 480 U.S. at 501. The same would not be true for the entire mineral estate, even if it were owned in common with the surface estate.

49.   In the actual case, Penn Central had in fact leased the air rights to a United Kingdom corporation for development purposes, but not until after the landmark designation. 438 U.S. at 115-16. As I explain in this chapter, determining the relevant parcel based upon ownership boundaries raises a number of conceptual and practical difficulties. It seems to make little sense to make compensation depend upon whether ownership is divided between air and surface rights. *See* Mid Gulf, Inc. v. Bishop, 792 F. Supp. 1205 (D. Kan. 1992) (holding that complete abrogation of subsurface rights is not a taking where surface rights remain viable, even though surface is owned by different party); Pennsylvania Coal Co. v. Mahon, 260 U.S. 393, 419 (1922) (Brandeis, J., dissenting) ("The rights of an owner as against the public are not increased by dividing the interests in his property into surface and subsoil. . . . [W]hy should a sale of underground rights bar the State's power?").

50.   *E.g., Penn Central*, 438 U.S. at 135-38 (examining the effect of the landmark restriction on Penn Central's future use of the terminal).

51.   482 U.S. 304 (1987).

52.   *Id.* at 322.

53.   *Id.* at 321.

54.   The Court did not hold that First English had suffered a temporary taking because the question involved only the sufficiency of its complaint in stating a claim for compensation. But the opinion was clearly written to have substantive effect, and has been interpreted as such. *See* Radin, *supra* note 21, at 1674-76 (describing the opinion as an act of conceptual severance); *see also First English*, 482 at 332-33 (Stevens, J., dissenting) (claiming the decision inconsistent with the whole-parcel rule). The Court at least implies, if not directly holds, that the denial of the use of property for a period of several years, as alleged by First English, would be a temporary taking; otherwise, there would be no need to distinguish shorter periods of delay.

55.   438 U.S. at 131.

56.   *Id.* at 121-22.

57.   In *Lucas*, the Court reiterated its objection to this approach, referring to the New York Court of Appeals' approach in *Penn Central* as "extreme" and "unsupportable." 505 U.S. at 1016 n.7.

58.   The common law has long recognized the creation of new fee simple estates by parceling larger estates, with no apparent minimum acreage that a fee must occupy. As Michael A. Heller writes, "According to the lay intuition, private property is often thought of as a physical thing that can be physically divided. Under this view, Blackacre *itself* is the core of private property. Cut in half, it yields Blackacre and Whiteacre, each equally private property. Cut in half again, the resulting lots are still private property." Michael A. Heller, *The Boundaries of Private Property*, 108 Yale L. J. 1163, 1170 (1999).

59.   Gorieb v. Fox, 274 U.S. 603 (1927) (upholding setback ordinance against due process challenge); *Penn Central*, 438 U.S. at 130-31 (referring to *Gorieb* as exemplary of the whole-parcel rule).

60. *E.g.*, Zealy v. City of Waukesha, 548 N.W.2d 528, 532-33 (Wis. 1996); K&K Construction, Inc. v. Dept. of Nat. Resources, 575 N.W.2d 531, 536 (Mich. 1998); Bevan v. Brandon Township, 475 N.W.2d 37, 43 (Mich. 1991); Jones v. Town of McCandless, 578 A.2d 1369, 1371-72 (Pa. Commw. 1990).

61. Deltona Corp. v. United States, 657 F.2d 1184, 1191-94 (Ct. Cl. 1981); Jentgen v. United States, 657 F.2d 1210, 1213 (Ct. Cl. 1981).

62. In 1959, Palazzolo purchased land including highlands and wetlands, which was subdivided into 80 lots. Six of the highland lots were sold away and developed, leaving Palazzolo with 74 mostly wetland lots. *Palazzolo*, 121 S.Ct. at 2455. Under a unity-of-ownership standard, Palazzolo's critical mistake was in retaining enough highland property for at least one more residence to be built, thwarting his ability to claim a taking of the remaining wetlands.

63. *See* Rose, *supra* note 3, at 568.

64. 260 U.S. at 419.

65. Michael Heller discusses the problem of property fragmentation at length in *The Boundaries of Private Property*, *supra* note 56, including the concept of conceptual severance. *See also* Maureen Straub Kordesh, *"I Will Build My House With Sticks" : The Splintering of Property Interests Under the Fifth Amendment May Be Hazardous to Private Property*, 20 HARV. ENVTL. L. REV. 397 (1996). While I agree with Heller and Kordesh that fragmentation is a concern, unlike these authors I view conceptual severance as a partial solution to it rather than a manifestation of it. Allowing property owners to conceptually split their property for takings purposes (or at least defining the relevant parcel based on something other than ownership) removes the incentive to subdivide the actual ownership of property for purposes of increasing the compensation value of land. By contrast, the unity-of-ownership standard penalizes owners for keeping property interests joined together and rewards them for fragmenting it, contrary to what their incentives should be.

66. *See* Rose, *supra* note, 3 at 568.

67. *E.g.*, Forest Properties, Inc. v. United States, 177 F.3d 1360, 1365 (Fed. Cir. 1999) ("Our precedent displays a flexible approach, designed to account for factual nuances."); Loveladies Harbor Inc. v. United States, 28 F.3d 1171 (Fed. Cir. 1994) ("flexible approach"); Ciampitti v. United States, 22 Cl. Ct. 310, 319 (1991) (balancing various factors, including treatment of property by owner); District Intown Properties Ltd. P'ship v. District of Columbia, 198 F.3d 874, 880 (D.C. Cir. 1999) ("[M]ore should unite the property than common ownership by the claimant."); American Savings and Loan Assn. v. Marin County, 653 F.2d 364, 371 (9th Cir. 1981) (balancing factors); Karam v. New Jersey Dep't of Envtl. Protection, 705 A.2d 1221, 1228 (N.J. Super. A.D. 1998) ("flexible approach").

68. 18 F.3d 1560, 1568 (1994) (original emphasis).

69. 177 F.3d 1360, 1365 (Fed. Cir. 1999).

70. *E.g.*, *Ciampitti*, 22 Cl. Ct. at 318-19 (relevant factors include dates of acquisition by owner and degree of contiguity).

71. *See* Ciampitti v. United States, 22 Cl. Ct. 310, 319 (1991) (combining separate non-adjacent housing projects into "single parcel" for taking purposes because property was purchased and financed as one).

72. *E.g.*, District Intown Properties Ltd. P'ship v. District of Columbia, 198 F.3d 874, 880-82 (D.C. Cir. 1999) (open space maintained for over 25 years, subdivided in 1987 by owner for purpose of building townhomes, considered functionally unified with apartments built in 1961).

73. Twain Harte Associates, Ltd. v. Tuolumne County, 265 Cal. Rptr. 737, 739-40 (Cal. App. 5 Dist. 1990); Ramona Convent of the Holy Names v. City of Alhambra, 26 Cal. Rptr. 2d 140, 145-46 (Cal. App. 2 Dist. 1994); American Savings & Loan Assn. v. Marin County, 653 F.2d 364, 371 (9th Cir. 1981); District Intown Properties Ltd. P'ship v. District of Columbia, 198 F.3d 874, 880 (D.C. Cir. 1999) ("[A] Court must consider how both the property-owner and the government treat (and have treated) the property.").

74. *Twain Harte Associates,* 265 Cal. Rptr. at 739-40.

75. *Id.* at 744-45.

76. *Id.* at 745.

77. An owner who purchases less than a whole parcel of property (as defined for regulatory taking purposes) therefore takes a chance that the interest may be completely extinguished without compensation if other portions of the relevant parcel claimed by other parties remain viable.

78. Fee, *supra* note 4, at 1557-62.

79. 719 A.2d 19 (Pa. Commw. 1998).

80. *Id.* at 22.

81. *Id.* at 27.

82. *Id.*

83. *Id.* at 28.

84. *Id.* at 29.

85. *Id.* at 28.

86. Moreover, even larger whole deprivations could still be imposed as exactions (including large setback requirements, open space, parking lot requirements, even dedications and physical intrusions) without the payment of compensation, as long the Supreme Court's nexus and rough proportionality requirements are satisfied. The independent economic viability standard therefore generally requires compensation only when large deprivations are imposed directly by government, instead of as conditions on development.

87. 480 U.S. at 501.

88. Preseault v. ICC, 494 U.S. 1, 11 (quoting *First English*, 482 U.S. at 315; emphasis in both cases).

BACKGROUND PRINCIPLES: CUSTOM, PUBLIC TRUST, AND PREEXISTING STATUTES AS EXCEPTIONS TO REGULATORY TAKINGS*

6

DAVID L. CALLIES AND J. DAVID BREEMER

§ 6.0 Introduction: Lucas and Background "Principles"

In the 1992 case of *Lucas v. South Carolina Coastal Council*,[1] the U.S. Supreme Court created its now famous "categorical rule" for regulatory takings. The rule requires the government to provide just compensation pursuant to the Fifth Amendment to the U.S. Constitution whenever it denies a property owner all "economically beneficial use" of land.

* This chapter was first presented as a paper at an ALI-ABA course on Inverse Condemnation and Related Governmental Liability on May 4, 2001, in Seattle, Washington. Parts of that paper are drawn from Professor Callies' published research on custom and public trust, in 30 ELR 10,003 (2000) (*Custom and Public Trust: Background Principles of State Property Law?*), and Mr. Breemer's research on state statutes and investment-backed expectations, published in an article co-authored with R. S. Radford (*Great Expectations: Will* Palazzolo v. Rhode Island *Clarify the Murky Doctrine of "Investment-Backed Expectations" in Regulatory Takings Law?* 9 N.Y.U. Env. L.J. 449 (2001).

Neither the purposes behind the denial nor the circumstances under which the land is acquired can diminish the government's liability.[2]

The *Lucas* Court established two exceptions to the otherwise inflexible categorical rule. Specifically, it declared that the rule does not apply (1) if the challenged regulation prevents a nuisance, or (2) if the regulation is grounded in a state's background principles of property law.[3] Since the law of nuisance is full and comprehensive, as well as comprehensible, the first exception presents little difficulty.[4] Leaving nothing to chance, the *Lucas* Court explained that the exception would allow the government to prohibit the construction of a power plant on an earthquake fault line or the filling of a lakebed that was likely to result in flood damage to a neighbor without incurring takings liability.[5] In contrast, the Court was silent with respect to the meaning of the second, "background principles of state property law," exception.

A major and often unexplored trend in takings law is the extent of that background principles exception to the categorical or per se rule established in *Lucas*. The subject is important for two distinct reasons: (1) It is not always easy to discern what such background principles are, and (2) once defined, such principles can seriously erode the basic *Lucas* doctrine meant to provide compensation for regulatory takings that deprive an owner of all economically beneficial use of land, by way of overly expanding the exception. A corollary issue is the extent to which exceptions analysis overlaps with the continuing discussion over the role of investment-backed expectations in *Lucas* situations (there should be none) together with the so-called "notice" issue arguably raised by preexisting state statutes in either total (*Lucas*) or partial (*Penn Central Transportation*) takings analyses.

§ 6.1   Background Principles: An Analysis

In the last decade, it has become clear that at least three sources of state property restrictions may qualify as background principles within the meaning of *Lucas*. These are custom, public trust, and statutory law existing prior to the acquisition of land.[6] This chapter explores these potential background principles, reviewing judicial treatment and critiquing their application to the categorical takings rule. Though *Lucas* failed to provide explicit guidance concerning the definition of the background principles exception, it noted that restrictions premised upon such principles "inhere in landowner's title itself."[7] On the basis of this statement, governments and commentators have turned to state common-law property doctrines to identify underlying title limitations, and thus background principles.[8] From this scrutiny, custom[9] and public trust[10] have surfaced as likely *Lucas* exceptions.

Equally ancient,[11] both custom and public trust theories grant rights in specific parcels of land to certain classes of persons. They are often difficult to detect until asserted, but once found, they operate to engraft an easement-like encumbrance on the affected land title, regardless of the private or public character of the property. Should they become background principles, as courts and commentators suggest, land use restrictions requiring landowners to keep their property so encumbered may be imposed without just compensation.

§ 6.2   Customary Law

If customary law is to represent a background principle, thereby shielding a custom-based land use regulation from takings challenges, it is useful to understand the origins, evolution, and application of custom in the United States. An examination of English custom and a review of what U.S. courts have done when faced with assertions of customary rights provide the necessary background.

§ 6.2(a)   Blackstonian Custom

Customary law is in derogation of common-law possessory property rights, which William Blackstone's *Commentaries on the Laws of England* largely argues to protect.[12] However, in writing what must be considered a polemic in favor of the common law, Blackstone identified three forms of customary law: common law ("general custom"), by which he presumably meant common law as we view it today; court (procedural) custom of particular tribunals or courts; and "particular customs," practiced by and affecting the inhabitants of a defined geographical area. Blackstone carefully defined and delimited this third or "particular" branch of custom, setting out seven criteria that a customary right must meet if it is to be a "good" custom—that is, one that is enforceable against a common-law principle, say, of exclusive possession of private land, a situation in which many of the disputes over custom arose. To be valid, enforceable, and to therefore result in a right of an individual despite common-law principles to the contrary, a custom had to be immemorial,[13] continuous,[14] peaceable,[15] reasonable,[16] certain,[17] compulsory,[18] and consistent.[19]

Even today, the law of custom in England is built around Blackstone's seven criteria.[20] Clearly, for purposes of American adoption and usage, some of the criteria—such as immemoriality as Blackstone would define it—must be modified to fit a country whose common-law experience makes the application of certain criteria somewhat difficult. However, recent U.S. courts have gone far beyond reasonable modification when applying Blackstonian principles to adjudicate customary claims.

§ 6.2(b)   *Early U.S. Decisions*

Until recently, one could characterize U.S. judicial treatment of custom as a source of law as decidedly chilly. Dealing primarily with easements said to derive from customary use, the few early cases found little, if any, reason to support the adoption of the English doctrine of custom. Due in part to the prevalence of recording systems early in the history of the country, unrecorded clouds on title based on immemorial custom would be anathema. John Chipman Gray so aptly commented in his definitive treatise on the rule against perpetuities:

> The objection which exists to allowing profits a pendre by custom really applies, though in a less degree, to allowing easements by custom... In a country like most of America, where a population, sparsely scattered at first, has rapidly increased in density, such rights might become oppressive. The cloud that they would put on the use and transfer of land would far outweigh any advantage that could be acquired from them. Especially it should be remembered that they cannot be released, for no inhabitant, or body of inhabitants, is entitled to speak for future inhabitants. Such rights form perpetuities of the most objectionable character. [21]

Courts were especially troubled by the notion that customary rights were immemorial in nature, for it was thought that "[A]t this day and age, in a government like ours, there can be little need of a resort to such a source as custom for legal sanction."[22] As stated by a Connecticut court in rejecting an attempted assertion of custom:

> The political and legal institutions of Connecticut have from the first differed in essential particulars from those of England. Feudalism never existed here. There were no manors or manorial rights. A recording system was early set up, and has been consistently been maintained, calculated to put on paper, for perpetual preservation and public knowledge, the sources of all titles to or [e]ncumbrances affecting real estate. Nor have we all

the political subdivisions of land that are found in England. Most of these denote forms of communities unknown in this state. Under our statute of limitations, also, rights of way may be established by a shorter user than that required by English law.[23]

Similarly, a New Jersey court refused to grant an easement to permit inhabitants of a town to reach a riverbank, based on custom:

[I]f [this] custom . . . is to prevail according to the common notion of it, these lots must lie open forever to the surprise of unsuspecting owners, and to the curtailing [of] commerce, in its most advanced state, of the accommodation of docks and wharves, when perhaps a tenth part of the lots now open would be all sufficient as watering places; a principle of such extensive operation ought not to be strained beyond the limits assigned to it in law. If [the] public convenience requires high[]ways to church, school, mill, market or water, they are obtainable in a much more direct and rational manner under [] statute than by way of immemorial usage and custom.[24]

Other courts have simply found that the "immemorial" feature of custom could not transfer to America.[25]

A few states adopted some form of customary law, though a close examination reveals less than a full embrace. For instance, in *Galveston v. Menard*,[26] the Texas Supreme Court noted only the possibility of vesting a property right by immemorial custom, but refused to apply it to the case before it or extend its application in Texas. In *Waters v. Lilley*,[27] the Supreme Judicial Court of Massachusetts noted that the right to fish, a right claimed by custom, on another's land was a profit and not an easement that would have made it impossible to claim as a custom in England. A subsequent Massachusetts case, however, confirmed the potential existence of customary easements without specifically finding one in that case.[28]

In two New Hampshire cases, the court initially refused claims of customary rights to enter private property to carry away sand and to collect seaweed on the grounds that both were profits to which the law of custom did not apply (forcing plaintiffs to rely upon prescriptive rights).[29] But the New Hampshire court finally made explicit this implied recognition of the possibility of an easement by custom in *Knowles v. Dow*.[30] The court stated:

"[u]nexplained and uncontradicted [testimony] is sufficient to warrant a jury in finding the existence of an immemorial custom," even if only for something more than 20 years.[31]

§ 6.2(c) *The Rebirth of Custom and Its Rise as a Potential Background Principle*

In the latter half of the twentieth century, U.S. state court judges have been much more receptive to the doctrine of custom than their earlier brethren. Thus, in Idaho, the state's high court clearly recognized that the law of custom was accepted in the state, though it refused to permit the establishment of a customary right unless all of Blackstone's seven criteria were met.[32] In Texas, the courts have upheld state legislation purporting to simply restate existing customary rights to use the beaches of the state, regardless of private "ownership."[33] Yet the most far-reaching and significant treatments come from Oregon and Hawaii. In Oregon, courts "found" a customary right without any fact-finding and extended it to the entire Oregon coast on behalf of the public at large. Hawaii, by comparison, ignored much of its own precedent on the rights of native Hawaiians and extended undetermined rights of access, worship, and gathering over much of the state.

The cases that established customary law and changed property rights in Oregon were decided against a backdrop of legislation that declared that any easement the public had in or on the beach was vested in the state.[34] Based largely on theories of prescriptive rights, the state in *Oregon ex rel. Thornton v. Hay*[35] sought to prevent the landowners, the Hays, from constructing improvements on the dry-sand beach portion of their lot between the highwater line and the upland vegetation line. The Hays appealed an adverse judgment below to the state supreme court. Instead of deciding the case on the grounds won and appealed on, the *Thornton* court, sua sponte, decided it on the basis of custom, stating:

> Because many elements of prescription are present in this case, the state has relied upon the doctrine in support of the decree below. We believe, however, that there is a better legal basis for affirming the decree. The most cogent basis for the decision in this case is the English doctrine of custom. Strictly construed, prescription applies only to the specific tract of land before the court, and doubtful prescription cases could fill the court for years with tract-by-tract litigation. An established custom, on the other hand, can be proven with reference to a larger region. Ocean-front lands from the northern to

the southern border of the state ought to be treated uniformly.[36]

The court cited Blackstone as a basis for its decision and claimed
that the decision "meets every one of Blackstone's requirements."[37]
It therefore held that custom was a valid basis for allowing all the
citizens of the state to go upon all dry-sand areas along the Pacific coast of Oregon, private or not.[38] This decision thus resulted
in the inability of landowners in the affected areas to build anything that would obstruct such access.[39] The court was unmoved
by claims of hardship, noting that "[t]he rule in this case, based
upon custom, is salutary in confirming a public right, and at the
same time it takes from no man anything which he has had legitimate reason to regard as exclusively his."[40]

Twenty-five years later, the Oregon Supreme Court revisited
customary law in *Stevens v. Cannon Beach*,[41] this time explicitly
holding custom to be a *Lucas*-exception background principle of
state law. There, the town of Cannon Beach refused to issue a seawall permit because it would block access to the dry-sand beach in
derogation of the customary public rights established by *Thornton*.
To the Stevenses' Fifth Amendment takings claim, the court responded that the customary law of Oregon was a background principle under *Lucas* and therefore an exception to the *Lucas*
categorical rule governing takings of all economically beneficial
use.[42] In both *Thornton* and *Cannon Beach*, therefore, the right to
exclude the public was never part of the landowners' titles to begin
with. Of course, just when and how the Hays and other similarly
situated landowners were to apprehend that their dry-sand beach
land was subject to a customary easement, given that they purchased the land prior to *Thornton*, the court does not say.

Recent decisions in Hawaii have also recognized and expanded
customary rights, though the situation is more complex because
there is no question that some tradition of customary rights exists, associated with native Hawaiians from the days of the various kingdoms. This tradition predates not only statehood, but
also territorial days and annexation toward the end of the nine-
teenth century. Nevertheless, for much of its history, the state's
high court issued opinions limiting the scope of native Hawaiian
customary rights. In the early case of *Oni v. Meek*,[43] the Hawaii
Supreme Court rejected a claim of pasturage based on pre-1850
customary rights on the ground that an 1850 statute, later codi-
fied in principle as Hawaii Revised Statutes (H.R.S.) 7-1, enumerated all the rights that tenants had in those lands that they did
not "own." A logical conclusion: All other traditional rights, customary and otherwise, were terminated.[44]

Both before and after statehood, courts in the main limited customary law in Hawaii to statutory rights to gather natural products listed in H.R.S. 7-1. An attempt to expand such rights by the state supreme court, by permitting Kamaaina testimony (verbal history by indigenous people) to modify seaward land boundaries of private landowners,[45] was soundly rejected by the federal district court in *Sotomura v. County of Hawaii*.[46] Finding no credible evidence justifying relocation of the seaward boundary, the court observed:

> The Court fails to find any legal, historical, factual or other precedent for the conclusions of the Hawaii Supreme Court, that following erosion, the monument by which the seaward boundary of seashore land in Hawaii is to be fixed in the upper reaches of the waves. To the contrary, the evidence introduced in this case firmly establishes that the common law, followed by both legal precedent and historical practice, fixes the high water mark and seaward boundaries with reference to the tides, as opposed to the run or reach of the waves on the shore.[47]

The district court thus found that there was no evidence of the public use that the state argued ripened into a customary right.

Then in 1995, almost 20 years after *Sotomura*, the Hawaii Supreme Court declared in *Public Access Shoreline Hawaii v. Hawaii Planning Commission* (PASH)[48] that traditional and customary rights of native Hawaiians may be practiced on public and private land, both undeveloped and substantially developed,[49] anywhere in the state. The court also held that government agencies must consider the effect on such customary rights in deciding on applications for development permits. Claiming to build on previous decisions that first limited rights to those enumerated in a statute,[50] the court suggested in dicta that courts could go beyond the statutory enumeration on the ground of custom where the Hawaiian practice does no harm and can be demonstrably shown to be continued within a certain land division. This extension is arguably contrary to the express holding in *Oni*. The court later found that such customary rights could in certain circumstances be exercised outside such a land division if the custom to do so is proven.

With respect to ⁀ᴉe potential conflict between the newly minted customary rights regime and traditional property rights, the court opined that western notions of property law, particularly exclusivity, might not be applicable in Hawaii, particularly when they collide with custom: "We hold that common law rights ordinarily associated with tenancy do not limit customary rights existing under the laws of this state."[51] As to whether the "finding" of such rights in derogation of fundamental "western" concepts of property could be a taking of property without compensation, let the court speak for itself:

> [Property owner] argues that the recognition of traditional Hawaiian rights beyond those established in *Kalipi* and *Pele* would fundamentally alter its property rights. However, [property owner's] argument places undue reliance on western understandings of property law that are not universally applicable in Hawaii. Moreover, Hawaiian custom and usage have always been a part of the laws of this State. Therefore, our recognition of customary and traditional rights . . . does not constitute a judicial taking.[52]

The Hawaii Supreme Court recently clarified some of its conclusion about the scope of customary rights in *Hawaii v. Hanapi*.[53] Alapai Hanapi, a native Hawaiian, was arrested for trespassing on the oceanfront land of his neighbor (a well-known trial lawyer). The land is improved with a single-family residence. The neighbor was engaged in removing illegally deposited fill from the shore and water. Hanapi entered the property without permission to "monitor" the subsequent restoration of the beach and wetland, claiming he was exercising native Hawaiian rights. Hanapi had initiated the original complaint against his neighbor, partly on the basis that the fill was adversely affecting native fishponds adjoining his property, at which he and his family claimed to practice traditional religious, gathering, and sustenance activities. When Hanapi refused to leave, the foreman supervising the restoration called the police, and Hanapi was arrested for trespassing. He was convicted after a trial in which he represented himself.

In sustaining Hanapi's conviction, the court initially noted that one limitation on private property "would be that constitutionally protected native Hawaiian rights, reasonably exercised, qualify as a privilege for purposes of enforcing criminal trespass statutes."[54] However, the court held that Hanapi had failed to establish that his claimed native Hawaiian right was a customary and traditional practice as required. The court stated that Hanapi and others claiming such rights must:

- Qualify as a native Hawaiian within the PASH guidelines (be descendents of native Hawaiians who inhabited the islands prior to 1778)

- Establish that his or her claimed right is constitutionally protected as a customary or traditional native Hawaiian practice (need not be enumerated in statute or constitution, however)
- Demonstrate that exercise of the right occurred on developed or undeveloped or less than fully developed property (not further defined in PASH).[55]

Applying these factors to *Hanapi*, the court held that if property is zoned and used for residential purposes with existing dwellings, improvements, and infrastructure, it is "always inconsistent" to permit the practice of traditional and customary native Hawaiian rights on such property. This represents a retreat from the broader language in PASH. In a footnote, the court noted that "there may be other examples of fully developed property as well where the existing uses of property may be inconsistent with the exercise of protected native Hawaiian rights."[56]

   Hanapi does not, however alter the fact that in Hawaii, as in Oregon and a few other states, custom is growing anew. Indeed, though they do not always express it in such terms, states appear to be using custom as a defense against the categorical takings rule announced in *Lucas* and takings claims in general by way of the *Lucas* "background principles" section. Custom is not, however, the only common-law doctrine that is rising to give meaning to the otherwise vague background principles concept.

§ 6.3   *The Public Trust*

Broadly stated, the public trust doctrine provides that a state holds public trust lands, waters, and resources in trust for the benefit of its citizens, establishing the right of the public to fully enjoy them for a variety of public uses and purposes.[57] Implied in this definition are limitations on the private use of such waters and land, as well as limitations on the state to transfer interests in them, particularly if such transfer will prevent public use. Such definitions and duties flow from the dual nature of title in public trust lands and waters. On the one hand, the public has the right to use and enjoy the land and water—the res of the trust—for purposes such as commerce, navigation, fishing, bathing, and related activities. This is the so-called *jus publicum*. On the other hand, since (according to one source) fully one-third of public trust property is in private rather than public hands,[58] private property rights exist in many such lands and waters. This is called the *jus privatum*.[59] The principal problem is, of course, the extent to which the public trust doctrine can eliminate private property rights without compensation, contrary to the Fifth Amendment.

§ 6.3(a) *The Origins of the Modern Public Trust Doctrine*

The undisputed font of the modern public trust doctrine is *Illinois Central Railroad Co. v. Illinois.*[60] The railroad claimed title to 1,000 acres of submerged lands under Lake Michigan (which it proposed to fill and develop) stretching for nearly a mile along Chicago's shoreline. It obtained title under a specific fee simple grant from the Illinois legislature. Finding that navigable waters and lands under them were held by the state in trust for the public, the Supreme Court held that the state could not convey or otherwise alienate them in fee simple, free of the public trust. The state could, however, sell small parcels of public trust land for uses that would promote the public interest (e.g., docks, piers, and wharves), as long as this could be done without impairing the public's right to make use of the remaining submerged land and water.[61]

Since the Illinois legislature conveyed the submerged land in fee simple in apparent disregard of the public trust, the sale was void. The case now stands for the proposition that only the *jus privatum*, as compared with the *jus publicum*, can be transferred by the state and that, inversely, the *jus publicum* can never be a part of a private title to property. An example of the type of private use that is permissible under the doctrine comes from *Kootenai Envt'l Alliance, Inc. v. State Board of Land Commissioners.*[62] There, the Idaho Supreme Court approved leasing state lands impressed with the trust to a private club for the construction, maintenance, and use of private dock facilities on a bay in a navigable lake. The court specifically held that the lease (not a fee simple transfer) was "not incompatible" with the public trust imposed on the property "at this time."[63]

Nearly a century after *Illinois Central*, the U.S. Supreme Court expanded the reach of the public trust doctrine from submerged lands, like Lake Michigan, to all lands under waters influenced by the ebb and flow of the tides in *Phillips Petroleum Co. v. Mississippi.*[64] In so doing, the Court rejected private fee simple titles extending back to pre-statehood Spanish land grantees that were held by Phillips and its predecessors for over 100 years, and upon which the company had paid taxes as if held in fee simple. Instead, the Court held that title to these lands, often exposed for long periods of time, passed to the state of Mississippi upon its entry into the union under the "equal footing" doctrine.[65] According to the Court, "States have the authority to define the limits of the lands held in public trust and to recognize private rights in such lands as they see fit."[66]

A strong dissent by Justices O'Connor, Scalia, and Stevens expressed alarm that the Court's holding will "disrupt the settled expectations of landowners not only in Mississippi but in every coastal State."[67] By substantially expanding traditional public trust rights beyond navigable waters and bays immediately adjoining them, the decision, argued the dissent, would extend the state's public trust interests to tidal, non-navigable waters, including bodies remote and only indirectly connected to the ocean or navigable tidal waters. The practical effect was that thousands of leaseholders of tidal lands could be displaced because over 9 million acres of land were classified as fresh or saline wetlands, arguably now subject to the state's control under the public trust doctrine.[68]

§ 6.3(b)   *Recent Expansions of the Trust Doctrine: Selected State Cases*

In the last 30 years, many state courts have expanded the geographical reach and substantive scope of the public trust doctrine. In particular, several recent decisions have extended it to cover resources beyond navigable waterways, while also finding that the trust protects public uses in such resources other than the traditional triad of commerce, navigation, and fishing. This trend has precipitated a collision between the newfound rights of the public, under the trust doctrine, and private rights traditionally flowing from private property. Significantly, many courts have rejected the takings claims resulting from this collision.

The most recent and, perhaps, far-reaching extension of the public trust doctrine comes from the Hawaii Supreme Court. In *In re Water Permits*,[69] the court impressed a broad version of the public trust onto the state's fresh-water supply, rewriting Hawaii's legislatively crafted water code and ignoring precedent that limited the role of the public trust in the state's water regime. Finding "a distinct public trust encompassing all the water resources of the state," the court held that "resource protection" was a protected public trust use of such resources. It therefore concluded that the state's water commission was bound by an "affirmative duty to take the public trust into account in the planning and allocation of water resources, and to protect public trust uses whenever feasible."[70] Given the distinct nature of the Hawaii public trust doctrine, this meant that "any balancing between public and private purposes [should] begin with a presumption in favor of public use, access and enjoyment."[71]

A primary basis for the court's expansive interpretation and application of the trust doctrine to non-navigable waters is found in section 1 of Article XI of the Hawaii Constitution, which provides:

[F]or the benefit of present and future generations, the

State and its political subdivisions shall protect and conserve Hawaii's natural beauty and all natural resources, including land, water, air, minerals, energy sources, and shall promote the development and utilization of these resources in a manner consistent with their conservation and in furtherance of the self-sufficiency of the State.[72]

The section further mandates that "all public resources are held in trust for the benefit of the people."[73] In the court's view, these statements "adopt the public trust doctrine as a fundamental principle of constitutional law in Hawaii"[74] and therefore prohibit any derogation from the trust through statutory law. Significantly, the court refused "to define the full extent of Article XI, section 1 reference to 'all public resources,'"[75] arguably leaving open the possibility of further extensions of the physical reach of the doctrine in Hawaii.

In response to a takings objection initiated by private interests concerned that the public trust–based water regime prevented them from utilizing groundwater traditionally considered private property, the court stated:

[T]he reserved sovereign prerogatives over the waters of the state precludes the assertion of vested rights to water contrary to the public trust. This restriction preceded the formation of property rights in this jurisdiction; in other words, the right to absolute ownership of water exclusive of the public trust never accompanied the "bundle of rights" conferred in the Mehele.[76]

Therefore, the "original limitation of the public trust defeats [plaintiff's] claim's of absolute entitlement to water," and consequently, the possibility of an unconstitutional taking.[77]

The extension of the public trust in Hawaii built upon on an earlier water rights case out of California, *National Audubon Society v. Superior Court of Alpine County*.[78] In that case, the California Supreme Court impressed the state's public trust doctrine to non-navigable tributaries of Mono Lake. It too dismissed the ensuing takings claim:

Once again we rejected the claim that establishment of the public trust constituted a taking of property for which compensation was required: We do not divest anyone of title to property; the consequence of our decision will be only that some landowners whose predecessors in inter-

> est acquired property under the 1870 act will, like the
> grantees in [People v. California Fish, 166 Cal. 576 (Cal.
> 1913)], hold it subject to the public trust.[79]

So also the Wisconsin Supreme Court, in *R.W. Docks & Slips
v.Wisconsin*,[80] upheld the denial of a state fill permit to complete
the last phase of a lakeside marina. In upholding the decision of a
state agency to thus protect an "emergent weedbed" that literally
surfaced during (and due to) construction of the earlier phases of
the project, the court held that the public trust doctrine resulted
in state ownership of the subject property, leaving the landowner
with riparian rights of use and access only, subject to the public's
"superior rights."

Expansions of the public trust have not been limited to water
resources. In New Jersey, for instance, courts have expanded the
reach of the doctrine to dry-sand areas in much the same way as
the Oregon courts did in *Thornton* and *Cannon Beach*, but this
time relying on the public trust instead of custom.[81] The most
well-known example is *Mathews v. Bay Head Improvement Ass'n*,[82]
where the New Jersey Supreme Court held that the public trust
doctrine extends to dry-sand beach areas for both access to and
limited use of the ocean and foreshore (traditional trust areas):

> The bathers' rights in the upland sands is not limited to
> passage. Reasonable enjoyment of the foreshore and the
> sea cannot be realized unless some enjoyment of the dry
> [-] sand area is also allowed. The complete pleasure of
> swimming must be accompanied by intermittent periods
> of rest and relaxation beyond the water's edge.... The
> unavailability of the physical sites for such rest and re-
> laxation would seriously curtail and in many situations
> eliminate the right to recreational use of the ocean
> ...where use of the dry sand is essential or reasonably
> necessary for enjoyment of the ocean, the [public trust]
> doctrine warrants the public's use of the upland dry [-]
> sand area subject to an accommodation of the interests
> of the owner.[83]

Although *Mathews* did not consider the takings issue, a more
recent attempt by the state of New Jersey to secure public access
to the Hudson River across non-trust lands was challenged on
Fifth Amendment grounds.[84] In *National Ass'n of Home Builders
v. Department of Envt'l Protection*,[85] a federal district court considered whether a taking arose from a state law requiring landowners to permit a public path along a 17.4-acre piece of land

bordering the river, 11.3 percent of which was "non-public trust property." Reaffirming the vitality of *Mathews*, the federal district court concluded that *Matthews'* "reasonableness" test,[86] rather than the stricter federal standards enunciated in *Dolan v. City of Tigard*,[87] governed the takings claim.[88] Specifically, the court remanded the case for examination of the following factors: "1) the location of the [private] dry sand area in relation to the foreshore; 2) extent of availability of publicly owned upland sand area; 3) nature and extent of the public demand; and 4) usage of the upland area by the owner."[89]

In Washington, the state supreme court applied the state's public trust doctrine to privately held tidelands, part of which were no longer under water, in *Orion Corp. v. State*.[90] There, the landowner planned to build a residential community on dredged and filled tidelands and submerged lands. However, after it purchased the land, the state adopted a series of coastal and tideland laws limiting the landowner's use to recreation and aquaculture. The landowner claimed the restrictions amounted to a regulatory taking.

The *Orion* court applied the then-current federal takings test set out in *Penn Central Transportation Co. v. New York*[91] and held that Orion could have no investment-backed expectations for development. Specifically, it stated that because the state held original title to all of Washington's shoreline, any transfer of shoreline property was impressed with the public trust doctrine, which was, furthermore, inalienable. The court did note that the state's restrictions were more prohibitive than would result from a reasonable application of the public trust doctrine. Therefore, to the extent the regulations only prohibited uses that would be prohibited under the public trust, no taking could occur. On the other hand, the court stressed that, to the extent the regulations were more restrictive, a regulatory taking could occur if they denied all economically viable use.

§ 6.4   *Statutory Law and Background Principles*

In addition to treating the public trust doctrine and customary law principles as exempt from standard federal takings scrutiny, many courts have declared restrictive state environmental regulations to be background principles under which all economically beneficial use of land may be denied.[92] Courts typically recognize statutes as background principles when they predate the acquisition of land and can thus be said to "inhere" in the landowner's title.[93] New York's 1997 regulatory "takings quartet" provides an excellent illustration of this trend.[94] In *Gazza v. New York State*

Department of Environmental Conservation,[95] the New York high court considered whether the denial of a building variance pursuant to a wetlands protection law amounted to a *Lucas* taking. Relying on *Lucas's* observation that a categorical taking is precluded by the "background principles" exception where a "logically antecedent inquiry into the nature of the owner's estate shows that the prescribed use interests were not a part of his title to begin with,"[96] the court declared that "[t]he relevant property interests owned by petitioner are defined by those state laws in effect at the time he took title and they are not dependent on the timing of state action pursuant to such law." [97] The simple enactment of a statutory scheme, even without actual application of the relevant regulations, was therefore sufficient to divest the claimant of a property interest that was previously thought to come with the title.[98] As the court concluded, "the only permissible uses for the subject property were dependent upon those regulations."[99]

In *Kim v. City of New York*, a case decided the same day as *Gazza*, the New York court again stressed that "in identifying the background rules of State property law that inhere in an owner's title, a court should look to the law in force, whatever its source, when the owner acquired title."[100] Providing further insight into the reasons for applying statutes as background principles, the court said, "[I]t would be an illogical inquiry if the courts were to look exclusively to common-law principles to identify the preexisting rules of State property law, while ignoring statutory law in force when the owner acquired title."[101] Apparently, the irrationality derived from the fact that a background principles doctrine that excluded "newly decreed or legislated" rules would "elevate the common law above statute law."[102]

Several other state courts have held that preexisting statutes operate as background principles that defeat a *Lucas* takings claim. The South Carolina Supreme Court, for instance, has held on two occasions that preexisting environmental regulations requiring landowners to obtain permission to fill wetlands defeated the owner's claims to compensation when development was prohibited.[103] In *City of Virginia Beach v. Bell*,[104] the Virginia Supreme Court applied a similar view in considering the constitutionality of a sand dune protection law. There, a corporation partially owned by the Bells purchased two lots seaward of coastal sand dunes for the purpose of erecting residential housing in 1979.[105] After an initial attempt at development failed, title to the lots fell to the Bells as individuals in 1982.[106] The city rejected the Bells' development plans again in 1982.[107] Meanwhile, pursuant to state law, the city passed an ordinance in 1980 that required developers to obtain a dune permit before using or altering sand dune areas.[108] When the Bells sought building permission a third time, the local wetlands board denied the necessary dune permit, prompting the Bells to sue for compensation under the Fifth Amendment.[109]

In rejecting the argument that the permit denial effected a *Lucas* taking, the Virginia Supreme Court characterized *Lucas* as holding that compensation is not required where "the proscribed use interests [are] not a part of [claimant's] use interests to begin with."[110] The court viewed *Lucas* as requiring South Carolina to justify its development restriction on "fundamental" nuisance and property law only because Lucas had taken title prior to the state's enactment of the challenged statute.[111] In *Bell*, on the other hand, the city's dune protection ordinance "predated" the Bells' acquisition of property.[112] Therefore, the city did not have to "prove the existence of any nuisance or property law" to justify its denial of development.[113] Rather, since the Bells took title after passage of the law, they had never possessed the right to develop their land to begin with.[114] Since the property owners could not suffer a taking of rights never possessed, "the City, by enacting the Ordinance, took no property from the Bells."[115] However, following the recent decision of the U.S. Supreme Court in *Palazzolo v. Rhode Island*,[116] these cases must surely be wrongly decided, at least to the extent they purport to be based upon the "background principles" exception to the *Lucas* per se rule. The Court clearly rejected the so-called "notice" rule, as described more fully in the section below.

§ 6.5   *A Critical Look at the Parameters of the Principles*

As the foregoing indicates, courts are clearly willing to identify preexisting statutes as background principles, although a few cases implicitly acknowledge a narrow scope for the background principles exception by rejecting federal law as a basis for a *Lucas* exception.[117] At the same time, they are increasingly acting as if custom and public trust rules also constitute such principles, even when they do not treat the doctrines in those specific terms. At least with respect to public trust and custom, there is much to be said in favor of their apparent status as background principles. Significant difficulties arise, however, in categorically characterizing each of these concepts as *Lucas* exceptions, at least as they are currently applied. The following subsections critique the courts' use of the custom, public trust, and statutory law and suggest that conceptual modifications are required if the emerging law of background principles is to retain logical and precedential consistency.

§ 6.5(a)   *The Limits of Statutory Law*

In contrast to the lower courts' eager adoption of statutes as background principles, the *Lucas* Court itself leaned heavily toward the common law when discussing the meaning of the background principles exceptions. Most significantly, the Court stressed that land use restrictions that deprive a landowner of all economically beneficial use of land cannot be "newly decreed or legislated":

> A law or decree with such an effect must, in other words, do no more than duplicate the result that could be achieved in the courts—by adjacent landowners (or other uniquely affected persons) under the state's law of private nuisance, or by the State under its complementary power to abate nuisances that affect the public generally, or otherwise.[118]

Thus, the only concrete examples of property rules that the Court sanctioned as exceptions to the categorical takings rule were nuisance principles that clearly emanate from the common law.[119] Furthermore, in detailing the circumstances in which the principles could be applied to defeat a takings claim, the Court stated that "[t]he fact that a particular use has long been engaged by similarly situated owners ordinarily imports a lack of any *common-law* prohibition."[120] Finally, the dissenting Justices clearly understood that the majority opinion limited background principles to common law principles, stating:

> [t]he Court's holding today effectively freezes the State's common law, denying the legislature much of its traditional power to revise the law governing the rights and uses of property.[121]

The straightforward conclusion is that statutes may act as background principles only if they codify aspects of the state's common law of property.[122]

The Court resolved all doubts about notice and background principles and what it meant in *Lucas* in *Palazzolo v. Rhode Island*.[123] Briefly, Palazzolo had sought to fill and develop coastal wetlands on his land contrary to a state coastal zone protection statute, of which he had notice before acquiring title to the subject land. The Rhode Island Supreme Court held that the statute was a background principle of state property law and therefore a *Lucas* exception because it predated Palazzolo's acquistion of the property. Characterizing as "sweeping" the rule that a purchaser or successive title holder with notice of an earlier-enacted land use restriction is barred from claiming a regulatory taking, the Supreme Court said, "A blanket rule that purchasers with notice have no compensation right when a claim becomes ripe is too blunt an instrument to accord with the duty to compensate for what is taken."[124] Basing its decision on fundamental principles of the law of property, the Court then held: "[A] regulation that otherwise would be unconstitutional absent compensation is not transformed into a background principle of the State's law by mere virtue of the passage of title."[125] The Court appeared to reject a notice rule not only for total per se takings but also for partial takings: "[the state court] must address, however, the merits of petitioner's claim under *Penn Central*. That claim is not barred by the mere fact that title was acquired after the effective date of the state-imposed restriction."[126]

Aside from its disregard for the Court's own narrow understanding of the background principles concept, the conclusion that preexisting statutes defeat a takings claim incorrectly imputes a general regulatory takings standard into the unique and inflexible categorical rule. To be specific, the statutory background principles trend mimics the modern doctrine of "reasonable investment-backed expectations," which has been held irrelevant to the economically beneficial use standard applied to total or per se takings.[127] Indeed, one recent court decision has aptly described "the concept [as] useless where, as in this case, the alleged taking is 'categorical,' i.e., physical, or involves the denial of all economically viable use of the property."[128] As with the statutory background principles trend, courts routinely ask whether the claimant's property was restricted pursuant to regulations that predated the purchase of property when applying the investment-backed expectations factor. If so, the constructive notice implicit in such preexisting regulations is said to preclude the formation of "reasonable" expectations and thus defeats the takings claim.[129]

As acknowledged by the Court of Federal Claims in *Forest Properties v. United States*,[130] and implicitly recognized in several recent federal[131] and state cases,[132] a background principles concept conflates the exception with the notice-based expectations doctrine when uprooted from its common law foundation.[133] Both concepts preclude landowners from establishing a taking when regulation predates the purchase of property.[134] In *Gazza v. New York State Department of Environmental Conservation*,[135] this conflation was clearly evident when New York's high court held that, in light of preexisting wetlands regulations, a landowner "never had an absolute right to build on his land without a variance,"[136] and in the alternative, that his "'reasonable' expectations were not undermined when the property remained restricted."[137]

The problem is that the circumstances under which a landowner acquires land, and thus the notice rule, may be "keenly relevant to takings law generally," but are inapposite to cases where a landowner is denied all economically viable use. This was made abundantly clear in *Palm Beach Isles Assoc. v. United States*.[138] In *Palm Beach Isles*, a group of investors (PBIA) bought a 311.7-acre parcel of property in 1956, 50.7 acres of which was inundated with wetlands or submerged under shallow water.[139] After years of negotiation with government authorities, the Army Corps of Engineers rejected PBIA's application for a fill permit "on environmental grounds and the requirements of the Clean Water Act,"[140] which was enacted in 1971, long after the property was earmarked for development. The Court of Federal Claims rejected the ensuing takings claim, in part because "the existing statutory regime precluded any reasonable investment-backed expectations of being able to develop the property."[141]

On appeal, the Federal Circuit reversed, holding that the reasonable investment-backed expectations factor, and thus the nature of the underlying regulatory regime, was irrelevant to a denial of all economic use claim under *Lucas*.[142] Then, in rejecting a petition for a rehearing by the panel and en banc, the original panel issued a supplemental opinion [143] that exhaustively reviewed *Lucas* and emphatically concluded that landowner expectations, and therefore regulatory regimes predating the acquisition or attempted development of land, are irrelevant to total takings:

> When the government seizes the entire estate for government purposes, whether by physical occupation or categorical regulatory taking, it is not necessary to explore those [landowner] expectations may have been.[144]

The court continued:

> This does not mean that use restrictions are irrelevant to the takings calculus, even in categorical takings cases. Once a taking has been found, the use restrictions on the property are one of the factors that are taken into account in determining damages due the owner. [citation omitted] It does mean that in the initial analysis of whether a taking, when it is determined that the effect of the regulatory imposition is to eliminate all economic viability of the property alleged to have been taken, the owner's expectations regarding future use of the property are not a factor in deciding whether the imposition requires a remedy.[145]

The use of preexisting statutes as background principles subverts this limitation on the categorical takings analysis by making use restrictions not simply relevant to the takings calculus but often the determining factor in rejected takings claims.[146] Thus, in keeping with the original thrust of *Lucas*, the categorical takings exceptions must be properly restrained by the states' background *common law* of property.

§ 6.5(b) *The Limits of Custom and the Public Trust*

If, as it seems, the Takings Clause is to give way to certain common-law principles, the doctrines of custom and public trust are clearly appropriate candidates for that status. Public rights emanating from these doctrines stand on a footing similar to an easement, leasehold, covenant burden, license, or other recognized private property right in the land of another: a limitation or restriction on the title of and, usually, use by the landowner. Yet the same legal tradition that thrusts these rights forward also hinges their recognition on the existence of several prerequisites.

§ 6.6 *Custom Must Be Returned to the Blackstonian Framework*

It may very well be possible to interpret the common law of the several states (particularly Hawaii) to create rights of access in land without reference to Blackstonian custom (though it is doubtful such creativity could withstand federal takings scrutiny), but the fact remains that courts do not. Instead, Blackstonian custom becomes the ultimate bedrock, the last defense, of each decision. One suspects the courts understand they are on thin ice indeed in breaching the fundamental right to exclude others from private property.[147] Although they are to be commended for attempting to ground such a breach in the valid doctrine of custom, the courts' application of, and reliance on, Blackstone leaves much to be desired.

As we have seen, for a valid custom to exist it must be immemorial, continuous, peaceable, reasonable, certain, compulsory, and consistent. It is these criteria applicable to particular custom (land rights in derogation of common law specific to a particular and limited jurisdiction and definite population) that courts have dealt with and that form the basis still for discussion and categorization of customary law.[148] Unfortunately, while courts that find customary rights have gone through the motions of considering these criteria, they have also for the most part failed to apply all of them or to apply them in the sense they were intended. Thus, in *Oregon ex rel. Thornton v. H*ay,[149] the Oregon Supreme Court took a stab at applying Blackstone's criteria, but mistook the critical requirements of reasonableness and certainty. The court stated:

> The fourth requirement, that of reasonableness, is satisfied by the evidence that the public has always made use of the land in a manner appropriate to the land and to the usages of the community. . . . The fifth requirement, certainty, is satisfied by the visible boundaries of the dry sand area and by the character of the land, which limits that use thereof to recreational uses connected with the foreshore.[150]

This is not by any means what Blackstone meant, nor did cases before, contemporary with, and after his time support such an interpretation. Rather, English cases from Blackstone's time (which presumably he had in mind when writing the Commentaries) and soon after measure the reasonableness of a custom by gauging its impact on private property rights. Thus, one of the most common reasons for declaring a custom unreasonable—and these outnumber the reasonable cases by a fair margin—is that the custom had an unusually burdensome effect on the land over or on which it is exercised.[151] Certainty, on the other hand, comprised three distinct components: certainty of practice, certainty of locale, and certainty of persons. With respect to the latter two, English cases consistently hold that when a specific customary practice is established, its certainty requires limitation to a particular place or locale, like a county, parish, or village (otherwise it approaches the general application and usage that is the hallmark of the common law),[152] and exercise by "individuals of a particular description." It was inconceivable that "all the inhabitants of England" could exercise a custom.

In light of the traditional criteria for custom, the *Thornton* court adopted a version of customary law utterly disconnected from the Blackstonian concept. In particular, by failing to consider the impact of the customary beach use on private property and by eagerly extending customary beach rights to all Oregonians on all parts of the coast, the court applied standards of reasonableness and certainty that cannot be attributed to Blackstone, yet that is exactly what the court did. Indeed, since reasonableness is not a matter of present use but an issue of original legal fairness, the court's statement that "reasonableness is satisfied by the evidence that the public has always made use of the land in a manner appropriate to the land and to the usages of the community"[153] is beside the point, irrelevant, and wrong.

The Oregon court is not alone in misapplying Blackstone's criteria. In *PASH*, the Hawaii Supreme Court also picks and chooses among elements of traditional custom and similarly misapplies the elements of certainty and reasonableness. In "finding" customary rights in 20 percent of Hawaii's citizens over every square foot of land in the state, whether or not developed, and with scant regard for the impact of the rights on private landowners, the Hawaii court follows firmly in the footsteps of *Thornton*, not those of Blackstone.

In sum, custom may indeed be a "background principle" that shields intrusions on private property from scrutiny under the Takings Clause. However, given the potentially severe impact this conclusion could have on property rights in general, and the right to exclude others in particular, it is critical that it comply with specified criteria. Blackstone provides such criteria, not only as a matter of reason but also as a matter of law, since he is almost always cited in the reported American cases on custom and customary law. Unfortunately, up to this point, the modern doctrine of custom bears little resemblance to Blackstone's law of custom. If it remains unrestrained by those traditional bonds, this "background principle" has the potential to completely swallow important private rights in land.

§ 6.7   *The Public Trust Should Be Restricted to Its Traditional Scope*

In traditional terms, as a state-controlled public easement over tidal waters and their lands, it is increasingly clear that the public trust is a background principle. This is not surprising, given that the tidal public trust is a "settled rule of law,"[154] and therefore part of "existing rules and understandings"[155] that constitute background principles.[156] Indeed, the federal circuit has explicitly recognized that the federal navigation servitude—the federal expression of the public trust[157]—is a background principle under *Lucas*.[158] It is fair to say that states can, therefore, prohibit land uses inconsistent with the traditional public trust without paying just compensation.[159] The problem is that there is no uniform public trust doctrine and often no clear doctrinal limits. Thus, as we have seen, the takings issue frequently arises in the context of the public trust when a state court or legislature extends the public's trust "rights" on private property. This occurs when a state "1) imposes restrictions on privately held trust lands; 2) requires public access across private land for access to trust lands or water; and 3) expands the scope of public activities permitted under the guise of public trust rights."[160] The critical public trust question is how far courts can go in redefining the doctrine at the expense of private property rights while still escaping the just-compensation requirement.

It is difficult to identify a bright line beyond which interferences with private property can no longer be legitimately premised upon the public trust doctrine. However, one can say with some certainty that the fit between the public trust and the background principles exception fades as the doctrine drifts from its historical moorings. In contrast to most customary law cases, state courts are often reluctant to reject takings claims simply because a land use restriction is premised on a (expanded) version of the public trust doctrine.[161] For instance, in *Bell v. Town of Wells Beach*,[162] the Maine Supreme Court held that an attempt to expand the state's public trust doctrine to allow the public to traverse private lands to reach public land for recreational purposes resulted in a taking of private property. In the court's view, traditional and permissible access purposes were limited to fishing, fowling, and navigation.

To the same effect is the Massachusetts Supreme Court in *Opinion of the Justices*.[163] There the court refused to expand statutory declarations of public trust to permit so much as access across private land to reach intertidal lands. In holding the proposal to reserve such rights of way a probable taking, the court stated:

> The permanent physical intrusion into the property of private persons, which the bill would establish, is a taking of private property within even the most narrow construction of that phrase possible under the Constitution of the Commonwealth and the United States. . . . The interference with private property here involves a wholesale denial of an owner's right to exclude the public. If a possessory interest in real property has any meaning at all, it must include the general right to exclude others.[164]

Several opinions of the New Hampshire Supreme Court exhibit similar skepticism toward expansions of the public trust that intrude on private property. In *Opinion of the Justices (Public Use of Coastal Beaches)*,[165] the court responded to a new statute that provided for access to tide-flowed public trust shoreline across abutting private land with the following declaration:

When the government unilaterally authorizes a permanent, public easement across private lands, this constitutes a taking requiring just compensation. . . .

. . . Because the bill provides no compensation for the landowners whose property may be burdened by the general recreational easement established for public use, it violates the prohibition contained in our state and Federal Constitutions against the taking of private property for public use without just compensation. Although the state has the power to permit a comprehensive beach activities and use program by using its eminent domain power and compensating private property owners, it may not take property rights without compensation through legislative decree.[166]

The court drove home the same points in the more recent case of *Purdie v. Attorney General.*[167] There 40 beachfront property owners sued the state alleging a taking of their property when the state established a statutory boundary line defining public trust lands further inland from the mean high-water mark. The language of the court is instructive:

Having determined that New Hampshire common law limits public ownership pf the shorelands to the mean high water mark, we conclude that the legislature went beyond the common-law limits by extending public trust rights to the highest water mark. . . . Property rights created by common law may not be taken away legislatively without due process of law. Because [the state statute] unilaterally authorizes the taking of private shoreland for public use and provides no compensation to landowners whose property has been appropriated, it violates the Fifth Amendment of the Federal Constitution against the taking of property for public use without just compensation. . . . *Although it may be desirable for the State to expand public beaches to cope with increasing crowds, the State may not do so without compensating the affected landowners.*[168]

§ 6.8 *Supreme Court Precedent Precludes Redefinitions of Property from the Background Principles Exception*

Constitutional limits on extensions of public trust and custom flow not only from state decisions upholding the fundamental

right to exclude others, but also from several Supreme Court decisions, not the least of which is *Lucas* itself. Of particular interest is the *Lucas* Court's emphatic statement that land use
restrictions premised on the "background principle" exception
"cannot be newly legislated or decreed."[169] Given their long history, the general doctrines of public trust and custom cannot, of
course, be newly decreed. Yet *Lucas* makes clear that the dispositive question is whether the land use restriction itself is part of
"existing rules and understandings" or instead a novel interpretation of state law.[170] As stated by the Court:

> [A]n affirmative decree eliminating all economically
> beneficial uses may be defended only if an *objectively
> reasonable* application of relevant precedents would ex-
> clude those beneficial uses in the circumstances in which
> the land is presently found.[171]

The objective nature of the background principles inquiry was
briefly affirmed by Justices Rehnquist, Scalia, and Thomas in
their concurring opinion in *Bush v. Gore*:[172]

> Similarly, our jurisprudence requires us to analyze the
> background principles of state property law to determine
> whether there has been a taking of property in violation
> of the Takings Clause. That constitutional guarantee
> would, of course, afford no protection against state power
> if our inquiry could be concluded by a state supreme
> court holding that state property law accorded the plain-
> tiff no rights.[173]

In his 1994 dissent to certiorari denial in *Stevens v. Cannon
Beach*,[174] Justice Scalia showed how the objective background
principles limits expansive applications of both custom and the
public trust. In *Cannon Beach*, coastal landowners in Oregon
brought a takings suit against the city of Cannon after it refused
to grant them a permit to build a seawall.[175] In rejecting the claims,
the state's supreme court stressed that the owners had no right to
build on the dry-sand area of their property in a way that would
undermine public beach access.[176] This conclusion was premised
on the 1969 case of *Thornton v. Hay*,[177] which held that the public
had a customary right to traverse over dry-sand areas previously
considered private.[178] In *Cannon Beach*, the court concluded that,
under *Thornton*, the doctrine of custom was a background principle of Oregon property law that precluded the Stevens takings
claim.[179]

When the case was appealed to the U.S. Supreme Court, Justice O'Connor joined Justice Scalia in strongly dissenting to a denial of certiorari.[180] Initially, Scalia emphasized that while a state is generally free to define property rights under state and not federal law, nevertheless:

> [A] state may not deny rights protected under the Federal Constitution ... by invoking a nonexistent rule of State substantive law. Our opinion in *Lucas* ... would be a nullity if anything that a State court chooses to denominate "background law"—regardless of whether it is really such—could eliminate property rights.[181]

To support the proposition that a state cannot avoid a taking simply by asserting that property never existed,[182] Scalia cited to a concurring opinion by Justice Stewart in *Hughes v. Washington*.[183] In awarding natural accretions to a beachfront landowner who took by federal grant, despite a state rule to the contrary, Justice Stewart's *Hughes* opinion emphasized that a retroactive judicial (re)interpretation of riparian rights did not preclude a takings claim:

> Like any other property owner ... Mrs. Hughes may insist, quite apart from the federal origin of her title, that the State not take her land without just compensation. To the extent that the decision of the Supreme Court of Washington ... arguably conforms to reasonable expectations, we must of course accept it as conclusive. But to the extent that it constitutes a sudden change in state law, unpredictable in terms of relevant precedents, no such deference would be appropriate. For a State cannot be permitted to defeat the constitutional prohibition against taking property without due process of law by the simple device of retroactively asserting that the property it has taken never existed at all.[184]

Justice Stewart's opinion in *Hughes* and its sanction in the dissent to denial of certiorari thus signals that the creative construction of custom (or public trust, for that matter) will not constitute a background principle if it is clearly out of line with state precedent.[185]

Scalia's dissent raised several points that show when the use of custom or public trust is an impermissible retroactive alteration of private property rights rather than an application of a "background principle." In concluding that the Oregon court's rejection of the Stevens takings claim on custom principles was not an "objectively reasonable"[186] application of Oregon precedent,[187] Scalia stressed that the court ignored precedent between *Thornton* and *Cannon Beach* that appeared to limit the doctrine of custom.[188] Additionally, he noted that the court improperly interpreted *Thornton*, the underlying basis for the *Cannon Beach* decision,[189] and observed that the Oregon court's "vacillations on the scope of the doctrine of custom...reinforce a sense that the court is creating rather than describing it."[190]

Similar problems are likely to arise if state courts continue to expand the public trust to new areas, or to grant new trust rights (such as environmental preservation) on traditionally impressed lands, since the bulk of state precedent limits the public trust to tidal areas for the interests of commerce, as well as for navigation and recreational activities.[191] Indeed, several state decisions exhibit judicial skepticism of sudden changes in public trust law that infringe on private property. For example, in the 1999 case of *Anderson Columbia Co., Inc. v. Board of Trustees*,[192] a Florida court rejected a state agency's attempt to assert public trust control over filled lands previously granted to private owners in fee simple by the legislature. In so doing, the court emphasized that "[t]he State cannot now by rule or refusal to issue an unqualified disclaimer [of public trust rights] to regain or reclaim any interest in the affected lands. To permit such action would constitute an unlawful forfeiture of private property rights without just compensation."[193]

In sum, background principles are just that: firmly embedded and long-established principles of property law, clearly and unambiguously recognized and universally acknowledged by the citizens of the state in which they are claimed. Newly discovering or expanding such principles in order to protect resources now deemed valuable and in the public interest to preserve or conserve is inconsistent and irreconcilable with the protection of private rights in land traditionally associated with our system of government in the United States. As the court said in *Douglaston Manor, Inc. v. Bahrakis*,[194] in rejecting entreaties to extend the public trust to waters not navigable in fact, "the desirable definiteness attendant upon discrete property rights and principles, along with reliable, predictable expectations *built upon centuries of precedent, ought not to be sacrificed to the vicissitudes of unsupportable legal theories*."[195]

Notes

1. 505 U.S. 1003 (1992).
2. Palm Beach Isles Assoc. v. United States, 231 F.3d 1354 (Fed. Cir. 2000).
3. *Lucas*, 505 U.S. at 1020-32.
4. For nuisance exceptions, *see* Aztec Minerals Corp. v. Romer, 940 P.2d 1025 (Colo. App. 1996) (holding mining company had no right to degrade the environment at one of its mining sites under Colorado nuisance law); M & J Coal Co. v. United States, 47 F.3d 1148 (Fed. Cir. 1995) (holding coal company had no right to conduct nuisance-like activities while surface mining in West Virginia); *see also* Colorado Dept. of Health v. The Mill, 887 P.2d 993 (Colo. 1994) (en banc) (holding federal statutes restricting the disposition of uranium mine tailings fell within the background principles exception so as to deny a landowner use of a 61-acre parcel, even though the applicable statutes were enacted after the landowner acquired the property). For a collection of recent exemption cases (and a summary of takings law generally), see ROBERT MELTZ, ET AL., THE TAKINGS ISSUE, ch. 14 (1999) and David L. Callies, *Regulatory Takings and the Supreme Court: How Perspectives on Property Rights Have Changed from* Penn Central *to* Dolan, *and What State and Federal Courts Are Doing About It*, 28 STETSON L. REV. 523 (1999).
5. *Lucas*, 505 U.S. at 1029.
6. For general discussion of the role of preexisting statutes in regulatory takings analysis, *see* R.S. Radford & J. David Breemer, *Great Expectations: Will* Palazzolo v. Rhode Island *Clarify the Murky Doctrine of "Investment-Backed Expectations" in Regulatory Takings Law?*, 9 N.Y.U. ENV. L. J. 449 (2001).
7. *Lucas*, 505 U.S. at 1029.
8. *See* MICHAEL M. BERGER, ANNUAL UPDATE ON INVERSE CONDEMNATION, ALI-ABA COURSE OF STUDY, INVERSE CONDEMNATION AND RELATED GOVERNMENTAL LIABILITY, SB 14 (October 1996) (noting that "Since *Lucas*, government agencies have been combing their archives in search of arcane matters that might be said to have been a part of a property owner's title and that severely restrict the use of land.").
9. For a thorough analysis of custom, including its application to takings, see David L. Callies, *Custom and Public Trust: Background Principles of State Property Law*, 30 ELR 10,003 (2000); David Bederman, *The Curious Resurrection of Custom: Beach Access and Judicial Takings*, 96 COLUM. L. REV. 1375 (1996); and Paul Sullivan, *Customary Revolutions: The Law of Custom and the Conflict of Traditions in Hawaii*, 20 U. HAW. L. REV. 99 (1999).
10. *See* Katherine E. Stone, *Sand Rights: A Legal System to Protect the "Shores of the Sea,"* 29 STET. L. R. 709 (2000) (arguing that the public trust doctrine can be expanded to restrict development on non-trust lands, for the purpose of preserving public beaches, without triggering a taking); Hope M. Babcock, *Has the U.S. Supreme Court Finally Drained the Swamp of Takings Jurisprudence?: The Impact of* Lucas v. South Carolina Coastal Council *on Wetlands and Coastal Barrier Beaches*, 19 HARV. ENVTL. L. REV. 1 (1995) (arguing that the public trust is a "background principle" that allows regulation of barrier beaches without just compensation).
11. Blackstone suggests that customary law had medieval origins. *See* 1 WILLIAM BLACKSTONE COMMENTARIES 246-47 (Bernard C. Gavit ed., 1941). The public trust doctrine, on the other hand, clearly originates in Roman law, where it was understood that the sea, the rivers, the air and the shoreline were owned by, and accessible to, the people for the purpose of navigation, commerce, and fishing. *See* THE INSTITUTES OF JUSTINIAN 2.1.1 (1870).

12. 1 WILLIAM BLACKSTONE COMMENTARIES *57. Although there are at least 16 editions of the Commentaries, it is generally recognized that the first edition of 1765-1769 was the most influential in the development of common law in the United States. *See* Bederman, *supra* note 9, at 1382.

13. *See* 1 WILLIAM BLACKSTONE COMMENTARIES *76-77. Blackstone defined immemoriality as follows:

> That it have been used so long, that the memory of man runneth not to the contrary. So that if any one can shew the beginning of it, it is no good custom. For which reason no custom can prevail against an express act of parliament, since the statute itself is a proof of a time when such a custom did not exist.

14. *See id.* at *77. With regard to the requirement of continuity, Blackstone stated:

> It must have been continued. Any interruption would cause a temporary ceasing: the revival gives it a new beginning, which will be within time of memory, and thereupon the custom will be void. But this must be understood with regard to an interruption of a *right*; for an interruption of the *possession* only, for ten or twenty years, will not destroy the custom. As I have a right of way by custom over another's field, the custom is not destroyed, though I do not pass over it for ten years; it only becomes more difficult to prove: but if the *right* be any how discontinued for a day, the custom is quite at an end.

15. *Id.* Blackstone defined the requirement of peacefulness in this manner:

> It must have been peaceable, and acquiesced in; not subject to contention and dispute. For as customs owe their original to common consent, their being immemorially disputed at law or otherwise is proof that such consent was wanting.

16. *Id.* In establishing reasonableness as requirement for a "good" custom, Blackstone stated:

> Customs must be reasonable; or rather, taken negatively, they must not be unreasonable. Which as always, as Sir Edward Coke says, to be understood of every unlearned man's reason, but of artificial and legal reason, warranted by authority of law. Upon which account a custom may be good, though the particular reason of it cannot be assigned; for it suffeth, if no good legal reason can be assigned against it. Thus, a custom in a parish, that no man shall put his beasts in the common till the third day of October, would be good; and yet it would be hard to shew the reason why that day in particular is fixed upon, rather than the day before or after. But a custom that no cattle shall be put in till the lord of the manor has first put in his is unreasonable, and therefore bad: for peradventure the lord will never put in his; and then the tenants will lose all their profits.

17. *Id.* at *78. Certainty as described by Blackstone:

> Customs ought to be *certain*. A custom that lands shall descend to the most

worthy of the owner's blood is void; for how shall this worth be determined? But a custom to descend to the next male of the blood, exclusive of females, is certain, and therefore good. A custom, to pay two pence an acre in lieu of tithes, is good; but to pay sometimes two pence and sometimes three pence, as the occupier of the land pleases, is bad for its uncertainty. Yet a custom to pay a year's improved value for a fine on a copyhold estate is good: though the value is a thing uncertain. For the value may be ascertained; and the maxim of the law is, *id. certum est, quod certum reddi potest.*

English cases from Blackstone's time show that the requirement of certainty encompassed certainty of *practice*, of *locale*, and of *persons*. *See* David L. Callies, *Custom and Public Trust: Background Principles of State Property Law?*, 30 ELR 10,003, 10,012-14 (2000).

18. *See* 1 WILLIAM BLACKSTONE COMMENTARIES *78. The requirement that customs be compulsory is so defined:

> Customs, though established by consent, must be (when established) compulsory; and not left to the option of every man, whether he will use them or not. Therefore a custom that all the inhabitants shall be rated toward the maintenance of a bridge will be good; but a custom that every man is to contribute thereto at his own pleasure is idle and absurd; and, indeed, no custom at all.

19. *Id.* Blackstone describes the requirement of consistency as follows:

> Lastly, customs must be consistent with each other: one custom cannot be set up in opposition to another. For if both are really customs, then both are of equal antiquity, and both established by mutual consent: which to say of contradictory customs is absurd. Therefore, if one man prescribes that by custom he has a right to have windows looking into another's garden; the other cannot claim a right by custom to stop up or obstruct those windows: for these two contradictory customs cannot both be good, not both stand together. He ought rather to deny the existence of the former custom.

20. Thus, a recent volume of HALSBURY'S LAWS OF ENGLAND describes the essential attributes of custom as follows:

> To be valid, a custom must have four essential attributes: (1) it must be immemorial; (2) it must be reasonable; (3) it must be certain in terms and in respect both of the locality where it is alleged to obtain and of the persons whom it is alleged to effect; (4) it must have continued as of right and without interruption since its immemorial origin. These characteristics serve a practical purpose as evidence when the existence of a custom is to be established or refuted.

12 (1) HALSBURY'S LAWS OF ENGLAND (1998), ¶ 606, at 160. This entire section on custom is a superb explanation of custom today, prepared by one of the preeminent scholars in legal history, Professor J.H. Baker, Fellow of St. Catherine's College, Cambridge.

21. *See* JOHN CHIPMAN GRAY, THE RULE AGAINST PERPETUITIES § 586 (1942).

22. Delaplane v. Crenshaw & Fisher, 56 Va. (15 Gratt.) 457, 475 (1860).

23. Graham v. Walker, 61 A. 98, 99 (Conn. 1905).

24. Ackerman v. Shelp, 8 N.J.L. 125, 130-31 (1825).

25. *See, e.g.*, Harris v. Carson, 34 Va. (7 Leigh) 632, 638 (1836); *Ackerman*, N.J.L. at 130-31; *Delaphane*, 56 Va. (15 Gratt.) at 475.

26. 23 Tex. 349 (1859).

27. 21 Mass. (4 Pick.) 145 (1826).

28. *See* Jones v. Percival, 22 Mass. (5 Pick.) 485 (1827).

29. *See* Perley v. Langley, 7 N.H. 233 (1834); Nudd v. Hobbs, 17 N.H. 524 (1845).

30. 22 N.H. 387 (1851).

31. *Id.*

32. State *ex rel.* Haman v. Fox, 594 P.2d 1093 (Idaho 1979). Finding six of the seven missing, the court further noted that over half a century of use was not "time immemorial" for the purposes of custom. *Id.* at 1101-02.

33. *See* Moody v. White, 593 S.W.2d 372 (Tex. Civ. App. 1979); Arrington v. Mattox, 767 S.W.2d 957 (Tex. App. 1989), *cert. denied*, 493 U.S. 1073 (1989); *see also* United States v. St. Thomas Beach Resorts, Inc., 386 F. Supp. 769 (D.V.I. 1974), *aff'd*, 529 F.2d 513 (1974).

34. 16 Or. Rev. Stat. § 390.610.

35. 462 P.2d 671 (Or. 1969).

36. *Id.* at 676.

37. *Id.* at 677.

38. *Id.* at 671.

39. *Id.*

40. *Id.*

41. 854 P.2d 449 (Or. 1993), *cert denied*, 114 S. Ct. 1332 (1994).

42. *Id.* at 456.

43. 2 Haw. 87 (1858).

44. *Id.* at 90. Of the asserted custom of pasturage, the court stated: "[I]t is obvious to us that the custom contended for is so unreasonable, so uncertain, and so repugnant to the spirit of the present laws, that it ought not to be sustained by judicial authority." *Id.*; *see also Sullivan, supra* note 9.

45. *See* Application of Ashford, 440 P.2d 76 (Haw. 1968).

46. 460 F. Supp. 473 (D. Haw. 1978).

47. *Id.* at 480.

48. 903 P.2d 1246 (Hawaii 1995), *cert. denied*, 517 U.S. 1163 (1996).

49. *Id.* at 1272.

50. *See* Kalipi v. Hawaiian Trust Co., 656 P.2d 745 (Haw. 1982).

51. *PASH*, 903 P.2d at 1269.

52. *Id.* at 1272.

53. 970 P.2d 485 (Haw. 1998).

54. *Id.* at 492.

55. *Id.* at 494.

56. *Id.* at 495.

57. COASTAL STATES ORGANIZATION, INC., PUTTING THE PUBLIC TRUST DOCTRINE TO WORK 1 (2d ed. 1997).

58. *Id.* at 230.

59. *Id.* at 2.

60. 146 U.S. 387 (1892).

61. *Id.* at 450-64.

62. 671 P.2d 1085 (Idaho 1983).

63. *Id.* at 1094.

64. 484 U.S. 469 (1988).

65. *Id.* at 479-82.

66. *Id.* at 479.

67. *Id.* at 485 (O'Connor, J., dissenting).

68. *Id.* at 493-94.

69. 9 P.3d 409 (Haw. 2000).

70. *Id.* at 453.

71. *Id.* at 454.

72. HAWAII CONST. art. XI, § 1.

73. *Id.*

74. 9 P.3d at 444.

75. *Id.* at 445.

76. *Id.* at 494.

77. *Id.*

78. 658 P.2d 709 (Cal. 1983).

79. *Id.* at 723 (citing City of Berkeley v. Superior Court of Alameda County, 26 Cal. 3d 515, 532 (Cal. 1980)).

80. 244 Wis. 2d 497, 628 N.W.2d 781 (2001).

81. *See* Matthews v. Bay Head Improvements Ass'n, 471 A.2d 355 (N.J. 1984); Lusardi v. Curtis Point Property Owners Ass'n, 430 A.2d 881 (N.J. 1981); Van Ness v. Borough of Deal, 393 A.2d 571 (N.J. 1978); Hyland v. Borough of Allenhurst, 372 A.2d 1133 (N.J. 1977).

82. 471 A.2d 355 (N.J. 1984).

83. *Id.* at 365.

84. National Association of Home Builders v. New Jersey, 64 F. Supp. 2d 354 (D. N.J. 1999).

85. 64 F. Supp. 2d 354 (D. N.J. 1999).

86. *See id.* at 359.

87. 512 U.S. 374 (1994).

88. *Id.* 64 F. Supp. 2d at 359.

89. *Id.*

90. 747 P.2d 1062 (Wash. 1987), *cert. denied*, 486 U.S. 1022 (1988).

91. 438 U.S. 104 (1978).

92. Hunziker v. State, 519 N.W.2d 367 (Iowa 1994) (state statute prohibiting development of lands containing native American burial grounds held a background principle that defeated a takings claim); City of Virginia Beach v. Bell, 498 S.E.2d 414 (Va. 1998); Wooten v. South Carolina Coastal Council, 510 S.E.2d 716 (S.C. 1999) (holding that the existence of statutes requiring landowners to obtain permits to fill wetlands deprived a landowner of Fifth Amendment relief when a permit was denied); Shell Island Homeowners Assoc. v. Tomlinson, 517 S.E.2d 406, 416 (N.C. App. 1999) (quoting *Lucas* in holding that, because a regulatory scheme authorizing such restrictions was on the books at the time a hotel was built, the right to protect the property from natural destruction was "not part of his title to begin with").

93. *See* Glenn P. Sugameli, Lucas v. South Carolina Coastal Council: *The Categorical and Other "Exceptions" to Liability for Fifth Amendment Takings Far Outweigh the "Rule,"* 29 ENVTL. L. 939, 979 (1999) (noting that courts reject takings claims on the basis of preexisting statutes under the background principles exception).

94. *See* Anello v. Zoning Board of Appeals, 678 N.E.2d 870 (N.Y. 1997); Basile v. Town of Southhampton, 678 N.E.2d 489 (N.Y. 1997); Gazza v. New York State Dept. of Envtl. Conservation, 679 N.E.2d 1035 (N.Y. 1997); Kim v. City of New York, 681 N.E.2d 312 (N.Y. 1997); Brotherton v. Department of Envtl. Conservation, 675 N.Y.S.2d 121, 122-23 (N.Y. App. Div. 1998). For an excellent critique of most of these cases, see Steven J. Eagle, *The 1997 Regulatory Takings Quartet: Retreating from the "Rule of Law,"* 42 N.Y. L. Sch. L. Rev. 345 (1998).

95. 679 N.E.2d 1035 (N.Y. 1997).

96. *Id.* at 1039 (quoting *Lucas*, 505 U.S. 1003, 1027 (1994)).

97. *Id.* at 1040-41.

98. *See* Radford & Breemer, *supra* note 6, at 490.

99. *Id.*

100. *Kim*, 681 N.E.2d at 315-16.

101. *Id.* at 315.

102. *Id.*

103. *See* Wooten v. South Carolina Coastal Council, 510 S.E.2d 716, 718 (S.C. 1999); Grant v. South Carolina Coastal Council, 461 S.E.2d 388, 391 (S.C. 1995) (no taking because landowner's "right to use his property did not alter from when he originally acquired title").

104. 498 S.E.2d 414 (Va. 1998).

105. *Id.* at 415.

106. *Id.*

107. *Id.*

108. *Id.* at 398.

109. *Id.* at 415-16.

110. *Id.* at 417 (quoting Lucas v. South Carolina Coastal Council, 505 U.S. 1003, 1027 (1992)).

111. *Id.* at 417-18.

112. *Id.* at 417.

113. *Id.* at 418.

114. *See id.* at 417.

115. *Id.* at 418.

116. 121 S. Ct. 2448 (2001).

117. *See* Forest Properties, Inc. v. United States, 39 Fed. Cl. 56, 71 (1997) (noting that only state law forms *Lucas* background principles); Preseault v. United States, 100 F.3d 1525, 1538 (Fed. Cir. 1996) (concluding that *Lucas* does not support the notion that federal law can serve as background principles).

118. *Lucas*, 505 U.S. at 1029.

119. *Id.*

120. *Id.* at 1031.

121. *Id.* at 1068-69 (Stevens, J., dissenting).

122. *See* Douglas W. Kmiec, *At Last, the Supreme Court Solves the Takings Puzzle*, 19 Harv. J.L. & Pub. Pol'y 147, 152 (1995) (stating that *Lucas* "accepts the property definition implicit in state common law, while rejecting (or at least limiting) its redefinition by state or local legislation").

123. 121 S. Ct. 2448 (2001)

124. *Id.* at 2463.

125. *Id.*

126. *Id.*

127. *See* Palm Beach Isles Assoc. v. United States, 231 F.3d 1354, 1363 (Fed. Cir. 2000). The court held:

> [I]n the initial analysis of whether a taking has occurred, when it is determined that the effect of the regulatory imposition is to eliminate all economic viability of the property alleged to have been taken, the owner's expectations regarding future use of the property are not a factor in deciding whether the imposition requires a remedy.

128. Ultimate Sportsbar Inc. v. United States, 48 Fed. Cl. 540 (2001).

129. For a review of cases in which landowner expectations are undermined by constructive notice of regulation, see Daniel Mandelker, *Investment-Backed Expectations in Takings Law*, 27 URB. LAW 215, 244-45 (1995).

130. 39 Fed. Cl. 56, 71 (Ct. Cl. 1997).

131. *See* Front Royal and Warren County Indus. Park Corp. v. Town of Front Royal, 135 F.3d 275, 287 (4th Cir. 1998) (land development rules at time of purchase established that property owner did not have either expectations or property interests sufficient to establish a takings claim); Outdoor Graphics, Inc. v. City of Burlington, 103 F.3d 690, 694 (8th Cir. 1994) (landowner did not have a protected property interest in maintaining billboards as a nonconforming use because he had no expectation of the use in light of preexisting restrictions).

132. *See* Gazza v. New York State Dep't of Envtl. Conservation, 679 N.E.2d 1035, 1941 (N.Y. 1997) (preexisting wetlands statute undermined expectations and operated as a background principle); Accord Agric. v. Texas Natural Res. Conservation Comm'n, 1999 Tex. App. LEXIS at 13 (1999) (citing *Lucas* for proposition that "owner's reasonable expectations are shaped by uses permitted by state law"); Hansen v. Snohomish County, 1999 Wash. App. LEXIS 1915 (1999) (citing *Lucas*'s background principles discussion for conclusion that, under existing zoning, landowners had no "rightful" expectation in commercial development).

133. For in-depth discussion of the conflation of background principles and "reasonable investment-backed expectations," see Radford & Breemer. *supra* note 6, at 475.

134. *See* Sugameli, *supra* note 93, at 979 (noting that courts reject takings claims on the basis of preexisting statutes under the background principle exception and the reasonable expectations doctrine).

135. 679 N.E.2d 1035 (N.Y. 1997).

136. *Id.* at 1040. Observing that "[t]he relevant property interests owned by petitioner are defined by those state laws in effect at the time he took title," the court concluded that "the only permissible uses for the subject property were dependent upon those [wetlands] regulations." *Id.*

137. *Id.* at 1043. Citing a personal property case, *Ruckelshaus v. Monsanto*, 476 U.S. 986 (1984), the court explained that reasonable expectations are "examined in light of the interference with permissible uses of the land by the subject regulation." *Id.* at 1042.

138. 208 F.3d 1374 (Fed. Cir. 2000).

139. *Id.* at 1377. The 261-acre and 50.7-acre parcels were split by a road. Of the 50.7 acres, 1.4 acres was "shoreline wetlands adjacent to the road, and 49.3 acres [was] submerged land adjacent to the wetlands." *Id.*

140. *Id.* The Corps also considered the effect of PBIA's application on navigation, but concluded that the project should not have a significant adverse effect on navigation, in general." *Id.*

141. *Id.* at 1379. The Court of Federal Claims also held that there was no taking of the submerged 49.3-acre parcel because it was subject to a federal navigational servitude that was a "preexisting limitation upon the landowner's title." *Id.* at 1378. The court concluded that this limitation meant that "the proscribed use interests were not part of the owner's title to begin with." *Id.*

142. *Id.* at 1379. In reaching the conclusion that expectations are irrelevant to a *Lucas* claim, the court relied on an early post-*Lucas* Federal Circuit decision, *Florida Rock Indus. v. United States*, 18 F.3d 1560 (Fed. Cir. 1994). It noted that *Good* appeared to arrive at the contrary conclusion, but concluded that statements of takings law after *Florida Rock* "cannot, of course, change the law (absent a decision en banc), under the doctrine of *South Corp. v. United States*, 690 F.2d 1368 (Fed. Cir. 1982)." *Id.*, n.3.

143. 231 F.3d 1354 (Fed. Cir. 2000).

144. *Id.* at 1363.

145. *Id.* at 1363-64.

146. *See, e.g.,* Gazza v. New York State Dep't of Envtl. Conservation, 679 N.E.2d 1035 (N.Y. 1997) (concluding that preexisting and thus background wetlands regulations defeated a takings claim because "the only permissible uses for the subject property were dependent upon those regulations").

147. *See* Kaiser-Aetna v. United States, 444 U.S. 164 (1979); *see generally* David L. Callies & J. David Breemer, *The Right to Exclude Others from Private Property: A Fundamental Constitutional Right*, 3 WASH. UNIV. J. L. & PUB. POL'Y 39 (2000).

148. 12 (1) HALSBURY'S LAWS OF ENGLAND (1998).

149. 462 P.2d 671 (Or. 1969).

150. *Id.* at 677.

151. *See* Broadbent v. Wilkes, Willes 360 (1742) (rejecting as unreasonable alleged customary right of land tenants to sink pits and mine coal beneath the lands of other tenants because it would "deprive the tenant of the whole benefit of the land"); Wilkes v. Broadbent, 2 Stra 1224 (1745) (upholding Broadbent, with particular emphasis on the great burden on private land); Bastard v. Smith, 2 M & Rob. 129 (1837) (instructing a jury that it could not sanction the reasonableness of an alleged customary right of tin miners to direct water into their mines "unless you find repeated acts of exercise of the custom on the one hand, and of acquiescence on the other"); *see also* Mercer v. Denne, 2 Ch. 534 (1904); 2 Ch. 538 (C.A.) (1905) (upholding custom of fishermen to use a piece of land covered with a shingle to spread and dry their nets "so long as they do not thereby throw an unreasonable burden on the landowner").

152. *See* Parker v. Combleford, Cro. Eliz. 725 (1599) (rejecting custom of lord of a manor to take the best beast of any person dying within the manor as a tribute of goods and chattels payable to the lord at death, because the custom was thus extended to those living outside the geographical area of the manor); Arthur v. Bokenham, 11 Mod. 148, 6 Queen Anne (stating that "the law allows usage in particular places to supersede the common law, and it is the local law, which is never to be extended further than the usage and practice, which is the only thing that makes it law"); Anglo-Hellenic Steamship Co. v. Louis Dreyfous & Co., 108 L.T.R. 36 (1903) (stating that a custom is only good because it "is in effect the common law *within that place* to which it extends, although contrary to the law of the realm") (emphasis added).

153. 462 P.2d 671, 677 (Or. 1969).

154. *Phillips*, 484 U.S. at 474. The Court stated, "[i]t is the settled rule of law in this court that absolute property in, and dominion and sovereignty over, the soils under the

tide waters in the original states were reserved to the several States, and that the new States since admitted have the same rights, sovereignty and jurisdiction on that behalf as the original states possess within their respective borders." *Id.* [citation omitted].

155. Board of Regents of State Colleges v. Roth, 408 U.S. 564, 577 (1972). In that case, the Court concluded that "property" is defined for the purposes of the Fifth Amendment by "existing rules or understandings that stem from an independent source such as state law." *Id.*

156. *Lucas*, 505 U.S. at 1030.

157. *See* Richard J. Lazarus, *Changing Conceptions of Property and Sovereignty in Natural Resources: Questioning the Public Trust Doctrine*, 71 Iowa L. Rev. 631, 636-37 (1986).

158. Palm Beach Isles Assoc. v. United States, 208 F.3d 1374, 1384 (Fed. Cir. 2000). The court stated:

> In light of our understanding of *Lucas* and other cases we have considered, we hold that the navigational servitude may constitute part of the background principles to which a property owner's rights are subject, and thus may provide the Government with a defense to a takings claim. *Id.*

159. *See, e.g.*, Lechuza Villas West v. California Coastal Commission, 70 Cal. Rptr. 2d 399, 418 (Cal. App. 2d 1997), holding Coastal Commission could rely on the public trust to prohibit coastal development that intrudes into areas below the high-water mark without causing a taking).

160. *See* David L. Callies, Preserving Paradise: Why Regulation Won't Work 357 (1994).

161. *See* W.J.F. Realty Corp. v. New York, 672 N.Y.S.2d 1007, 1010-11 (N.Y. Sup. App. 1998) (holding that the Long Island Pine Barrens Protection Act, which was premised on a form of the public trust, was constitutional because it provided a mechanism for compensating property owners whose use of land was restricted under the act); Douglaston Manor, Inc. v. Bahrakis, 89 N.Y.2d 472 (N.Y. Ct. App. 1997) (refusing to extend the public trust to waters not navigable in fact because it would "precipitate serious destabilizing effects on property ownership principles and precedents"); *see also* Purdie v. Attorney General, 732 A.2d 442 (N.H. 1999) (holding that a legislative extension of the public trust to dry-sand areas would cause a taking); Bell v. Town of Wells, 557 A.2d 168 (Me. 1989) (holding that an act allowing public recreation on private intertidal lands amounted to a taking).

162. 557 A.2d 168 (Me. 1989).

163. 313 N.E.2d 561 (Mass. 1974).

164. *Id.* at 568.

165. 649 A.2d 604 (N.H. 1994).

166. *Id.* at 611.

167. 732 A.2d 442 (N.H. 1999).

168. *Id.* at 447 (citing Opinion of the Justices, *supra* note 160) (emphasis added).

169. *Lucas*, 505 U.S. at 1029.

170. *Id.* The Court stated that "[a] law or decree with such an effect must, in other words, do no more than duplicate the result that could have been achieved in the courts— by adjacent landowners (or other uniquely affected persons)—under the State's law of nuisance, or by the State under its complementary power to abate nuisances that affect the public generally or otherwise." *Id.*

171. *Id.* at 1032 n.18 (emphasis added).

172. 531 U.S. 98 (2000).

173. *Id.* at 115 n.1.

174. 510 U.S. 1207 (1994).

175. 854 P.2d 449, 450 (Or. 1993).

176. *Id.* at 456.

177. 462 P.2d 671 (Or. 1969).

178. *Id.* at 676-77. In *Thornton*, the court concluded that its decision opening up private beaches took "from no man anything he had a legitimate right to regard as his," since the right of access was based on ancient practice. *Id.* at 678.

179. *Cannon Beach*, 854 P.2d at 456.

180. 114 S. Ct. 1332 (1994).

181. *Id.* at 1334.

182. *Id.* The dissent stated: "A State cannot be permitted to defeat the constitutional prohibition against taking property without due process of law by the simple device of asserting retroactively that the property it has taken never existed at all." *Id.* (quoting Hughes v. Washington, 389 U.S. 290, 296-97 (1967) (Stewart, J., concurring).

183. 389 U.S. 290, 296-97 (1977) (Stewart, J., concurring).

184. *Id.* at 295-97 (Stewart, J., concurring).

185. For an excellent discussion of the implications of *Hughes v. Washington* with respect to the public trust doctrine, see Geoffrey R. Scott, *The Expanding Public Trust Doctrine: A Warning to Environmentalists and Policy Makers*, 10 FORDHAM ENVTL. L. J. 1, 57-58 (1998).

186. Lucas v. South Carolina Coastal Council, 505 U.S. 1003, 1032 n.18 (1994).

187. *Cannon Beach*, 114 S. Ct. at 1335.

188. *Id.* at 1333.

189. *Id.*

190. *Id.* at 1335 n.4.

191. *See Lazarus, supra* note 152, at 710-16.

192. 748 So. 2d 1061 (Fla. Dist. Ct. App. 1999).

193. *Id.* at 1067.

194. 89 N.Y.2d 472 (N.Y. Ct. App. 1997).

195. *Id.* at 483 (emphasis added).

Threshold Statutory and Common Law Background Principles of Property and Nuisance Law Define if There Is a Protected Property Interest

7

Glenn P. Sugameli*

§ 7.0   Introduction

Only those who own a protected property interest can bring a constitutional claim that their private property has been taken for public use without payment of just compensation by a local, state, or federal government action.[1] As discussed below, the Supreme Court's *Lucas v. South Carolina Coastal Council*[2] decision helped define this threshold issue by explaining how takings can never occur from actions that destroy property from actual necessity and where physical occupation or regulation of property

---

* This chapter is adapted and updated from portions of my article, Lucas v. South Carolina Coastal Council: *The Categorical and Other "Exceptions" to Liability for Fifth Amendment Takings of Private Property Far Outweigh the "Rule,"* 29 Envtl. L. 939 (1999). I filed amici briefs supporting the government in *Lucas, Palazzolo,* and several of the other takings cases discussed here.

is in accord with a variety of statutory or common-law background principles of either property law or nuisance law that define the owner's title to property.[3]

§ 7.1   Background Principles of Property and Nuisance Law

Lucas held that laws cannot take away claimed property "rights" that never existed, such as the "right" to create a nuisance that harms neighboring property or the public.[4] Thus, it is not a taking to forbid uses that are barred by background principles of either property law or of nuisance law, because such forbidden uses were not part of the owner's title to the property to begin with.[5]

§ 7.1(a)   *Destruction of Property by Necessity*

Lucas also recognizes an independent category of immunity from takings claims in its discussion of the government's power to abate nuisances, or "otherwise": "The principal 'otherwise'. . . is destruction of 'real and personal property, in cases of actual necessity, to prevent the spreading of a fire' or to forestall other grave threats to the lives and property of others."[6] The California Supreme Court rejected a takings claim on this basis in a post-*Lucas* decision in which police tracked a felony suspect to a convenience store and, when negotiations failed, apprehended the suspect after lobbing tear gas and mace into the store, causing over $200,000 in damage.[7]

§ 7.1(b)   *Lucas Immunity from Takings Liability Is Truly Categorical*

The only truly categorical rule in Lucas *is a negative one*: If a property restriction repeats limitations inherent in the title to property, as defined by state and federal background principles of property and nuisance law and the necessity exception, the restriction *never* effects a taking.[8] To the extent that a law tracks or can be deemed a background principle, a property owner can have no takings claim even in a rare case where the law deprives the owner of all economically viable use and value of a properly defined parcel as a whole.[9]

Lucas explicitly states that this categorical immunity from takings extends to "physical takings" as well: "[W]here permanent physical occupation of land is concerned . . . we assuredly *would* permit the government to assert a permanent easement that was a preexisting limitation upon the landowner's title."[10] Indeed, the Supreme Court has applied a similar analysis in rejecting a due process claim, holding that: "The first inquiry in every due process challenge is whether the plaintiff has been deprived of a protected interest in 'property' or 'liberty.'"[11]

The background principle analysis examines the extent of the claimant's title.[12] Thus, the source of the preexisting title limitation can be wholly unrelated to the source of the challenged regulation.[13]

It is essential to understand that *Lucas* categorical immunity from takings is a threshold issue. The fact that these negative categories may not apply in a given case in no way satisfies a plaintiff's heavy burden to demonstrate that a taking has occurred.[14] In such a case, the plaintiff only has the right to begin to make the necessary showing that the challenged governmental action has resulted in a taking of private property for public use that requires just compensation.[15]

For example, in a post-*Lucas* case, *Phillips v. Washington Legal Foundation*,[16] the Court decided only one of three issues that would be necessary to require just compensation. The Court held that the plaintiffs had a property interest but explicitly declined to express any view "as to whether these funds have been 'taken' by the State; nor . . . as to the amount of 'just compensation,' if any, due respondents."[17]

The vast majority of post-*Lucas* cases deny takings claims for a variety of reasons.[18] Under *Lucas*, even cases within a so-called affirmative takings liability category do not necessarily require just compensation. In *Hendler v. United States*,[19] the Federal Circuit denied compensation for the value of property that had been physically taken because "the special benefits conferred on the [retained] property as a result of the taking . . . more than offset the value of the easements [taken]—even under plaintiffs' valuation—and hence no compensation therefor is due."[20]

§ 7.2 ## The Supreme Court Has Continued the Lucas Court's Deference to State Courts in Defining Background Principles

Categorical immunity for restrictions that parallel "background principles of the State's law of nuisance and property" reflects the Court's traditional deference to state definitions of the nature and scope of private property interests.[21] The *Lucas* Court characterized this immunity as "surely unexceptional," particularly "[i]n light of our traditional resort to 'existing rules or understandings that stem from an independent source such as state law' to define the range of interests that qualify for protection as 'property' under the Fifth and Fourteenth Amendments."[22] The Court also deferred to the role of the state court in defining these principles: "It seems unlikely that common-law principles would have prevented the erection of any habitable or productive improvements on petitioner's land. . . . The question, however, is one of state law to be dealt with on remand."[23]

The post-*Lucas* Court rejected numerous petitions for certiorari regarding denials of takings claims based on state (and federal) court definitions of general or state-specific background principles. The first of these petitions, in *Stevens v. City of Cannon Beach*,[24] was the only one with a dissent from the denial of certiorari. Seven Justices declined to join Justice Scalia's dissent, which sharply questioned the Oregon Supreme Court's ruling that a developer had no right to build a seawall because the public's "doctrine of custom" to use the dry sand is a background principle of property law under *Lucas*.[25] The Supreme Court subsequently denied a petition for certiorari after the Hawaii Supreme Court cited *Stevens* in ruling that development rights were held subject to preexisting background Native Hawaiian gathering rights.[26]

A 1995 denial of review involved an Iowa Supreme Court decision that a statute protecting an archeological burial site was a background principle as applied to a site that the state archaeologist did not discover until years after the property was purchased.[27] In 1997, the Court separately declined to review four cases in which New York state's highest court ruled that a variety of preexisting statutes and ordinances are background principles that bar takings.[28] In 1998, the Court denied certiorari in *Virginia Beach v. Bell*, in which the Virginia Supreme Court rejected a takings claim because the challenged coastal primary sand dune zoning ordinance had been in effect when the plaintiff acquired the property.[29]

The Court also declined ample opportunities to review federal court decisions that have rejected takings claims based on background principles.[30] Many of these state and federal court decisions held that statutes were background principles under *Lucas*.[31]

My 1993 article[32] noted that the Supreme Court's takings analysis would "likely change upon the retirement of Justice White at the end of the 1992-1993 term. Justice White was the fifth vote for Justice Scalia's bare majority opinion in *Lucas*."[33] I described how "Justice Kennedy, who may now hold the decisive vote on regulatory takings issues, expressed very different views in his *Lucas* concurrence than did Justice Scalia."[34]

The Court's rejection of these certiorari petitions may reflect Justice Kennedy's key role on takings issues and his expression of the need to expand background principles beyond common law in his *Lucas* concurrence.

> The State should not be prevented from enacting new regulatory initiatives in response to changing conditions.... The Takings Clause does not require a static body of state property law.... Coastal property may present such unique concerns for a fragile land system that the State can go further in regulating its development and use than the common law of nuisance might otherwise permit.[35]

The Supreme Court has reiterated the doctrine that: "[b]ecause the Constitution protects rather than creates property interests, the existence of a property interest is determined by reference to 'existing rules or understandings that stem from an independent source such as state law.'"[36] "[A]t least as to confiscatory regulations (as opposed to those regulating the use of property), a State may not sidestep the Takings Clause by disavowing traditional property interests long recognized under state law."[37]

In *Palazzolo v. Rhode Island*, the Court rejected a state supreme court's general interpretation of background principles and held that: "A law does not become a background principle for subsequent owners by enactment itself."[38] As discussed in section 7.9 below, however, the Court carefully limited its holding, stating, "We have no occasion here to consider the precise circumstances *when* a legislative enactment *can be deemed* a background principle of state law *or whether those circumstances are present here*."[39]

§ 7.3 *Background Principles Include Federal and State Limitations*

Limits on state-created property rights may originate in either federal or state law. *Lucas,* which involved a South Carolina statute, understandably focused on state law. Justice Scalia's majority opinion, however, cited, as an example of a background limitation, *Scranton v. Wheeler's*[40] holding that the federal navigational servitude limited a landowner's title:

> [w]here permanent physical occupation of land is concerned, we have refused to allow the government to decree it anew (without compensation), no matter how weighty the asserted public interests involved—though we assuredly *would* permit the government to assert a permanent easement that was a preexisting limitation upon the landowner's title. Compare *Scranton v. Wheeler*, 179 U.S. 141, 163... (1900) (interests of "riparian owner

> in the submerged lands ... bordering on a public navi-
> gable water" held subject to Government navigational
> servitude), with *Kaiser Aetna v. United States*, 444 U.S.
> [164,] 178-180 [(1979)] (imposition of navigational ser-
> vitude on marina created and rendered navigable at pri-
> vate expense held to constitute a taking). We believe
> similar treatment must be accorded confiscatory regula-
> tions, *i.e.,* regulations that prohibit all economically ben-
> eficial use of land. . . . [41]

The U.S. Court of Federal Claims ignored this holding in
rejecting a background principle defense and finding a taking by
relying on this language from a prior Federal Circuit decision
that *Lucas* superseded:[42] "the effect of *Kaiser Aetna v. United
States*, 444 U.S. 164 (1979) is that the old 'navigation servitude,'
often used to excuse what looked suspiciously like takings, is no
longer available for that duty in regulatory takings cases."[43] In a
subsequent case, however, the Federal Circuit held "that the navigational servitude may constitute" background principles,[44] citing the *Lucas* Court's discussion of *Scranton* and a Third Circuit
decision that the federal navigational servitude was a background
principle that precluded a taking from a ban on a coal-loading
facility on a river.[45] Other post-*Lucas* federal court decisions recognize that background principles include federal law limitations
on property owners' state-created property rights.[46]

§ 7.4   Background Principles of Nuisance Law

In denying a takings claim, the Court's 1987 *Keystone* decision
relied in part on the nuisance-type nature of the mining under
homes that was prohibited by state statute.[47] The U.S. Court of
Federal Claims rejected a takings claim under a state nuisance
law analysis that relied upon a state water quality statute that
invoked the public trust.[48]

Other courts have also rejected takings claims when such claims
are precluded by "background principles" of state nuisance law.[49]
As discussed below, the *Palazzolo* Rhode Island trial court denied
a takings claim because filling salt marsh would constitute a public nuisance.[50]

The Florida Supreme Court applied *Lucas* to find that that a
city's six-month closure of a motel with a history of extensive and
persistent prostitution and drug activity abated a public nuisance
and was not a compensable temporary taking of private property.[51]
The court found that the activity had become "part and parcel" of
and "inextricably intertwined" with the motel's operation, but de-

clined to apply a similar analysis to a consolidated case where it found a temporary taking from closure of an "apartment complex solely on a finding that the apartment had been the site of cocaine sales on more than two occasions" and "there was no extensive record indicating that the drug activity had become an inseparable part of the operation of the apartment complex."[52]

§ 7.5   *Background Principles of Property Law*

Lucas background property law limitations on title that preclude a taking include those that have nothing to do with nuisances. For example, courts reject takings claims based on an interest in property relating to government leases or permits because there is no compensable property right extending past the terms of the agreement.[53] Under *Lucas* background principles, wild horses did not take a federal grazing permittee's water rights: "wild horses were present . . . prior to enactment of the Wild Horses Act, and, furthermore, all of plaintiffs' range improvement permits are by their express terms subject to then existing and subsequently approved rules and regulations."[54] Other courts have rejected takings claims for failure to establish a protected property interest, without explicitly utilizing the *Lucas* Court's analysis.[55]

In *Stevens v. City of Cannon Beach*,[56] the Oregon Supreme Court rejected a takings challenge to denial of permits to build a seawall that would allow a motel or hotel development:

> When plaintiffs took title to their land, they were on notice that exclusive use of the dry-sand areas was not a part of the "bundle of rights" that they acquired, because public use of dry sand "is so notorious that notice of the custom on the part of persons buying land along the shore must be presumed."[57]

This application of the doctrine of custom is a *Lucas* background principle of property law and "plaintiffs never had the property interests that they claim were taken."[58]

The Hawaii Supreme Court subsequently cited *Stevens* in ruling that private development rights were held subject to preexisting background Native Hawaiian gathering rights.[59] The Supreme Court denied certiorari even though the Hawaii Supreme Court had concluded that "the Western concept of exclusivity is not universally applicable in Hawaii" and admitted that this "premise clearly conflicts with common 'understandings of property.'"[60]

Under *Lucas*, background principles of property law should include Native American treaty rights. Treaty rights include both outright tribal beneficial ownership[61] and hunting, fishing, and gathering rights on land owned by others. While the Court's 1999 decision in *Minnesota v. Mille Lacs Band of Chippewa Indians*[62] did not discuss background principles, the title that the United States acquired (and subsequently passed along to the state and private landowners) can be seen as never having included the right to exclude Chippewas who are hunting, fishing, and gathering.[63]

Background principles of property law should include a variety of other limitations on title. For example, governments have long regulated fish and wildlife, including hunting and fishing licenses and prohibitions to protect species. Common law (and statutory law) throughout the nation is that "the general ownership of wild animals, as far as they are capable of ownership, is in the state, not as a proprietor, but in its sovereign capacity as the representative and for the benefit of all its citizens in common."[64] These public ownership rights limit private rights and defeat takings claims.[65] Laws protecting and regulating wildlife are a traditional, common component of state property law. State courts have long recognized that all property is subject to the government's power to regulate wildlife.

Thus, limitations that are in accord with background principles of either property or nuisance law cannot be a taking.

§ 7.6　Wetland Laws and Background Principles

One of the *Lucas* Court's examples of background principles embraces at least certain denials of Clean Water Act section 404 permits to dredge and fill lake beds and other wetlands:[66]

> [T]he owner of a lake bed ... would not be entitled to compensation when he is denied the requisite permit to engage in a landfilling operation that would have the effect of flooding others' land.... Such regulatory action may well have the effect of eliminating the land's only economically productive use, but it does not proscribe a productive use that was previously permissible under relevant property and nuisance principles.[67]

Lucas defined nuisances as harms "to public lands and resources, or adjacent private property, posed by the claimant's proposed activities."[68] Nuisance doctrine applies particularly well to congressional protection of specifically limited and defined wetland areas. Courts have recognized that section 404 lessens and avoids harms by preserving wetlands that convey floods, abate storm surges, cleanse polluted runoff, control sediment, provide groundwater recharge and discharge, and prevent loss of rare and endangered species, waterfowl, and other wildlife.[69] Wetland preservation is vital to the survival of many endangered species.[70]

In *Palazzolo*,[71] a Rhode Island trial court denied a wetland takings claim, finding that filling salt marsh would be a *Lucas* background public nuisance because it would reduce shellfish populations and harm filtering mechanisms, resulting in increased nitrate levels in a pond and a threat to the groundwater drinking supply.[72] Because the Rhode Island Supreme Court affirmed on other grounds, the Supreme Court's 2001 decision did not address this issue, although Justices did ask about it at oral argument.[73]

§ 7.7   *Public Trust and* Just v. Marinette County

Both before and after *Lucas*, courts have relied upon the public trust doctrine to deny takings claims, especially as to tidal wetland property.[74] For example, a Florida appellate court rejected a takings challenge to prohibitions on offshore drilling because the public trust doctrine permitted the legislature to exercise without compensation its "authority to protect the lands held in trust for all people."[75] Courts have also recognized that the public trust doctrine limits private rights in a non-takings context.[76]

Background principles should also include a related state law principle first articulated by the Supreme Court of Wisconsin. The landmark *Just v. Marinette County* decision recognized that protection of wetlands is not a taking because "[a]n owner of land has no absolute and unlimited right to change the essential natural character of his land so as to use it for a purpose for which it was unsuited in its natural state and which injures the rights of others."[77]

Other state courts have denied wetlands takings claims in explicit reliance upon this principle, including a 1989 decision in which then-New Hampshire Supreme Court Justice Souter joined.[78] The Supreme Court of Wisconsin has reaffirmed and applied its *Just* decision irrespective of "whether the regulated land is a wetland within a shoreland area, or land within a primary environmental corridor, or an isolated swamp."[79]

The Supreme Court of South Carolina's 1984 *Carter v. South Carolina Coastal Council*[80] decision quoted *Just* in denying a wetland takings claim.[81] *Carter* recognized that "the legislature enacted the Coastal Zone Management Act in response to its recognition of the detrimental effect the uncontrolled use of coastal wetlands would have on the public welfare."[82]

Commentators have cited *Just* as a preexisting limitation on title both before and after *Lucas*. Fred Bosselman, David Callies, and John Banta, in their 1973 seminal work, *The Taking Issue,* discussed *Just* under the heading *Preexisting Title,* as an example of a case in which "governmental agencies can avoid the takings issue . . . by reestablishing a preexisting state interest in the land."[83] Many, but not all, post-*Lucas* legal commentators have cited *Just* as a *Lucas* "background principle."[84] *Just* has been identified as the "leading case justifying the application of natural use limitation as part of the background principles of property law. . . ."[85]

In *McQueen v. South Carolina Coastal Council,*[86] the Supreme Court of South Carolina rejected takings claims because the plaintiff "has failed to demonstrate the distinct investment-backed expectations required,"[87] but stated that *Lucas* had sub silentio overruled the state supreme court's *Carter* ruling on the *Just* issue.[88] The court stated that: "Commentators are divided on whether the [*Just/Carter*] principle . . . is a background principle of state law"[89] and acknowledged that:

> No other court of record has yet squarely addressed the question of whether *Just* is a background principle of state law. One court suggested it is in dicta. *See* City of Riviera Beach v. Shillingburg, 659 So.2d 1174, 1183 (Fla. Dist. Ct. App. 1995) (dismissing takings claim on ripeness grounds, but citing *Just* principle post-*Lucas*); *see also* Zealy v. City of Waukesha, 201 Wis. 2d 365, 548 N.W.2d 528, 534 (1996) (finding no taking on other grounds and declining to reach the issue of whether *Just* is a *Lucas* background principle, but specifically noting that "[n]othing in this opinion limits our holding in *Just* and cases following its rule"); Good v. United States, 39 Fed. Cl. 81, 96 & n.30 (1997), *aff'd,* 189 F.3d 1355 (1999) (noting that status of *Just* line of cases as a background principle of state law is unclear).[90]

No court has agreed with *McQueen* that *Lucas* overruled the *Just/Carter* analysis. Indeed, the issue was reopened in *McQueen* when the Supreme Court granted the plaintiff's petition for certiorari, vacated the judgment, and remanded "to the Supreme Court of South Carolina for further consideration in light of *Palazzolo v. Rhode Island. . . .*"[91]

On remand, the South Carolina high court should reconsider its conclusion that *Lucas* "repudiated the reasoning of *Just*" because the *Lucas* Court stated that regulations "'*requiring land to be left substantially in its natural state* carry with them a heightened risk that private property is being pressed into some form of public service under the guise of mitigating serious public harm.'"[92]

The *McQueen* court's conclusion failed to consider Justice Kennedy's concurring opinion in *Lucas*. It also did not have the benefit of Justice Kennedy's subsequent opinion for the Court in *Palazzolo*, which explicitly left open a possible finding of background principles on remand despite stating that the regulations at issue required the land to be left substantially in its natural state: the Court found that there was "no doubt" that "[o]n the wetlands there can be no fill for any ordinary land use.... And with no fill there can be no structures and no development on the wetlands."[93]

On remand, the Supreme Court of South Carolina should also follow up on its discussion of alternative possible grounds for its rejection of the takings claims:

> Amici Curiae have argued numerous background principles of state law which conceivably bar a property owner from backfilling wetlands. Most significant among these is the public trust doctrine. In South Carolina, the state owns the property below the high water-mark of a navigable stream: this property is part of the public trust. The corollary to this principle is the rule that "lands gradually encroached upon by water cease to belong to the former riparian or littoral owner."[94]

§ 7.8   *Background Principles of Nuisance (and Property) Law Evolve*

In deciding what limits on property uses are in accord with background principles of property and nuisance law, *Lucas* recognized that courts should account for newly recognized environmental dangers: "The fact that a particular use has long been engaged in by similarly situated owners ordinarily imports a lack of any common-law prohibition (though *changed circumstances or new knowledge may make what was previously permissible no longer so....* "[95] The Court cited an example that apparently falls into this category: no compensation would be due to "the corporate owner of a nuclear generating plant, when it is directed to remove all improvements from its land upon *discovery* that the plant sits astride an earthquake fault."[96] Thus, because nuisance law is continuously evolving, *Lucas* can negate compensation when new regulations prohibit uses that were not barred by background principles at the time a parcel was purchased. As nuisance law evolves, it may grow to encompass acts that, under today's standards, are not considered nuisances.[97]

For example, nuisances should include destruction of a species. In 1920, a Justice Holmes opinion for the Court recognized that conservation of endangered species is a "matter[] of the sharpest exigency for national well-being."[98] Since then, as Justice Stevens stated in his dissent in *Lucas*, "[n]ew appreciation of the significance of endangered species ... shapes our evolving understandings of property rights."[99] In rejecting a Commerce Clause challenge to Endangered Species Act protection of a fly that exists only in California, separate opinions by D.C. Circuit Judges Wald and Henderson both relied in part on evidence of such a new appreciation of the significance of endangered species.[100] Judge Wald found that such protection prevents "the channels of interstate commerce from being used for immoral or injurious purposes"[101] and cited legislative history and subsequent evidence of the incalculable value of species as sources of "potential cures for cancer," existing medicines, and genes.[102] Judge Henderson stated that "the effect of a species' continued existence on the health of other species within the ecosystem seems to be generally recognized among scientists."[103]

The *Lucas* Court's reliance on the *Restatement (Second) of Torts* to define nuisance law[104] has additional limiting implications for takings claimants. First, the *Restatement's* evolving definition of nuisance[105] is broader than the definition upon which some lower court decisions have relied.[106] Second, nuisance law, and thus the scope of the immunity from takings liability, varies from state to state.

§ 7.9   Statutes as Background Principles

The *Restatement (Second) of Torts* also recognizes that statutory compliance is a factor in determining whether an activity constitutes a public nuisance.[107] The cases on which the *Restatement* is based rely on state statutes in determining whether a particular use is a nuisance. Therefore, *Lucas* does not foreclose a legislative role in defining nuisance, despite the concerns of Justices Blackmun[108] and Stevens,[109] in dissent. Justice Scalia's majority opinion, however, stated that background principles must be more than merely "the legislature's declaration that the uses [the property owner] desires are inconsistent with the public interest."[110] Justice Kennedy's concurring opinion stated that:

> The State should not be prevented from enacting new regulatory initiatives in response to changing conditions. ... The Takings Clause does not require a static body of state property law ... Coastal property may present such unique concerns for a fragile land system that the State can go further in regulating its develop-

ment and use than the common law of nuisance might otherwise permit.[111]

Justice Kennedy's majority opinion in *Palazzolo v. Rhode Island* expanded on this idea by explicitly recognizing that at least some statutes can be background principles: "We have no occasion here to consider the precise circumstances *when* a legislative enactment *can be deemed* a background principle of state law or whether those circumstances are present here."[112] The highlighted language is critical: *when,* not *if,* a legislative enactment *can be deemed* a background principle, not *can be deemed to track a common-law* background principle. Indeed, Justice Scalia's concurring opinion, which addressed the same section of the majority opinion, described in general terms "a restriction forming part of the 'background principles of the State's law of property and nuisance.'"[113] He did not refer to "a common-law restriction."

Justice Kennedy carefully limited the *Palazzolo* Court's holding: "A *regulation* or common-law rule *cannot be a background principle for some owners but not for others....* A law does not become a background principle for subsequent owners by enactment itself."[114] While this formulation precludes the approach of pre-*Palazzolo* courts that had concluded that by enactment every statute became a background principle, it invites courts to hold that particular statutes and regulations are background principles that bar takings claims by *all* pre- *and* post-enactment owners. Indeed, the Court explicitly did not preclude a statutory or regulatory background principle ruling by the Rhode Island courts on remand, stating that it had "no occasion here to consider ... whether those circumstances are present here."[115]

The *Palazzolo* Court offered some guidance in determining what is a background principle of property or nuisance law, in a passage that avoids any mention of common law while focusing on broad language regarding "a State's legal tradition" and "existing, general law":

> [o]ur description of the concept in *Lucas* ... is explained in terms of those common, shared understandings of permissible limitations derived from a State's legal tradition.... The determination whether an existing, general law can limit all economic use of property must turn on objective factors, such as the nature of the land use proscribed. See *Lucas, supra,* at 1030, 112 S. Ct. 2886 ("The 'total taking' inquiry we require today will ordinarily entail ... analysis of, among other things, the degree of harm to public lands and resources, or adjacent private property, posed by the claimant's proposed activities").[116]

Prime candidates for continued recognition of statutes as background principles include statutory safeguards against coal-mining impacts that include devastating "harm to public lands and resources, or adjacent private property, posed by the claimant's proposed activities." In *Hodel v. Indiana*,[117] the Supreme Court found that a federal statutory "prohibition against mining near churches, schools, parks, public buildings, and occupied dwellings [was] plainly directed toward ensuring that surface coal mining does not endanger life and property in coal-mining communities."[118] In *Keystone Bituminous Coal Ass'n v. DeBenedicits*,[119] the Court rejected a claim that a Pennsylvania law requiring underground coal operators to leave 50 percent of the coal in place beneath protected structures in order to prevent subsidence damage effected a taking. The Court found that subsidence "can have devastating effects,"[120] including damage:

"to buildings, roads, pipelines, cables, streams, water impoundments, wells, and aquifers. Buildings can be cracked or tilted; roads can be lowered or cracked; streams, water impoundments, and aquifers can all be drained into the underground excavations. Oil and gas wells can be severed, causing their contents to migrate into underground mines, into aquifers, and even into residential basements. Sewage lines, gas lines, and water lines can all be severed, as can telephone and electric cables."[121]

The Court found that Pennsylvania had acted "to protect the public interest in health, the environment, and the fiscal integrity of the area."[122] In rejecting the takings claim, the Court held that the operators' contract rights to the coal could not prevent "the Commonwealth from exercising its police power to abate activity *akin to a public nuisance*."[123]

The Federal Circuit recognized, in *M & J Coal Co. v. United States*, that the federal coal mining statute was a *Lucas* background principle of property or nuisance law. When "M & J acquired its mining rights ... it knew or should have known that it could not mine in such a way as to endanger public health or safety and that any state authorization that it may have received was subordinate to the national standards that were established by" the federal law.[124] As discussed above, the U.S. Court of Federal Claims rejected a takings claim under a state nuisance law analysis that relied upon a state water quality statute that invoked the public trust.[125]

In *National Mining Association v. Babbitt*,[126] D.C. Circuit Judge Silberman quoted the plurality Supreme Court opinion in

Eastern Enterprises: "'Congress has considerable leeway to fashion economic legislation, including the power to affect contractual commitments between private parties.'"[127] Judge Silberman indicated that the requirement that coal companies compensate homeowners for damage caused by subsidence from underground mining—thus overriding private agreements—presented a "rather implausible" basis for a takings claim.[128]

Justice O'Connor's majority opinion in *Yee v. City of Escondido*,[129] issued earlier in the 1991-1992 term with *Lucas*, mentioned a ban on coal mining as an example of traditional zoning regulations: "Traditional zoning regulations can transfer wealth from those whose activities are prohibited to their neighbors; when a property owner is barred from mining coal on his land, for example, the value of his property may decline but the value of his neighbor's property may rise."[130] This analysis offers further support for treating coal-mining restrictions as background property law principles of zoning and land use.

Justice Kennedy's majority opinion in *Palazzolo* states:

> The right to improve property, of course, is subject to the reasonable exercise of state authority, including the enforcement of valid zoning and land-use restrictions. *See* Pennsylvania Coal Co. [v. Mahon], 260 U.S. [393, 413 (1922)] ("Government hardly could go on if to some extent values incident to property could not be diminished without paying for every such change in the general law.").[131]

Other "valid zoning and land-use restrictions" should be recognized as background principles that are embodied in statutes and ordinances. For example, the Eighth and Ninth Circuits have denied takings claims because they considered statutes and ordinances in effect when property is acquired to be background principles under *Lucas*.[132] The vacant structure regulation and the billboard ordinance in these cases, however, should be deemed background principles under the *Palazzolo* Court's analysis. Similarly, this analysis should support the Fourth Circuit's citation of *Lucas*'s background principles in holding that when the plaintiff "acquired its title, before annexation by the Town, it had no legitimate expectation that that land came with the public provision of sewer service. Instead, inherent in that title was the implied limitation that the owner would have to provide for its own water and sanitary waste disposal."[133]

Virtually every pre-*Palazzolo* decision on this issue found that the *Lucas* inquiry into "background principles" and limitations inherent in title to property includes "preexisting" state and federal statutes that were in effect when the claimant acquired the property at issue.[134]   Indeed, a pre-*Lucas* Tenth Circuit decision found that the action was not a taking because it abated a nuisance that was proscribed by federal law.[135]

The nature of the statutes at issue and the concerns that many of these courts expressed should lead to a reaffirmation of these decisions on the facts presented, albeit under a *Palazzolo* analysis that recognizes that "a law does not become a background principle for subsequent owners by enactment itself." For example, the Iowa Supreme Court's 1994 *Hunziker* decision ruled that a preexisting state statute authorizing protection of important archaeological burial sites was a *Lucas* background principle of property law governing title to land that was purchased years before the state archaeologist made the significant find.[136] This is analogous to a specific example of a background principle in *Lucas*: no compensation would be due to "the corporate owner of a nuclear generating plant, when it is directed to remove all improvements from its land upon discovery that the plant sits astride an earthquake fault."[137]

Thus, background principles should bar claims based on statututory protection of a species that was not discovered on a parcel until years after the property was purchased. The Federal Circuit reached a similar result in ruling that a developer who purchased land in 1973 shortly before the Endangered Species Act was passed lacked investment-backed expectations needed to claim that a taking resulted from denial of a wetland permit because of a species that was listed in 1990.[138]

Background principles should also include constitutional provisions. The Hawaii Supreme Court denied a taking claim because there was never any absolute ownership of water exclusive of public trust rights that were partially based upon a state constitutional provision.[139] The Supreme Court of Montana should apply a similar analysis in light of its holding that two state constitutional provisions established a fundamental right to a clean and healthful environment, and that state or private action that implicates either provision is subject to strict scrutiny.[140]

In *Palazzolo,* Justice O'Connor provided the necessary fifth vote for the Court's opinion "with my understanding of how the issues discussed in Part II-B of the opinion must be considered on remand."[141] Her concurring opinion stressed that in considering *Penn Central* takings claims, "if existing regulations do nothing to inform the analysis, then some property owners may reap windfalls and an important modicum of fairness is lost."[142] The four dissenters on this issue agreed "that transfer of title can impair a takings claim."[143]

Concerns about windfalls should continue to influence courts to reject takings claims, based at least in part on findings that pre-existing regulations defeat reasonable investment-backed expectations. For example, New York's highest court in *Anello v. Zoning Board of Appeals of Village of Dobbs Ferry* reasoned, "[a]ny compensation received by a subsequent owner for enforcement of the very restriction that served to abate the purchase price would amount to a windfall, and a rule tolerating that situation would reward land speculation to the detriment of the public. . . ."[144]

Notes

1. *See* U.S. CONST. amend. V.
2. 505 U.S. 1003 (1992).
3. Statutes of limitations, laches, and other threshold issues that can defeat takings claims are beyond the scope of this discussion.
4. *Id.* at 1027-29.
5. *Id.* at 1029; *see* James M. McElfish, Jr., *Property Rights, Property Roots: Redis-covering the Basis for Legal Protection of the Environment* [24 News & Analysis], ENVTL. L. REP. (ENVTL. L. INST.) 10,231, 10,247-48 (May 1994); John A. Humbach, *Evolving Thresholds of Nuisance and the Takings Clause,* 18 COLUM. J. ENVTL. L. 1, 7 (1993).
6. 505 U.S. at 1029 n.16 (quoting Bowditch v. Boston, 101 U.S. 16, 18 (1879)); *see also* Miller v. Schoene, 276 U.S. 272 (1928) (state order to destroy cedar trees to prevent spread of disease to nearby apple orchards was not a taking).
7. Customer Co. v. City of Sacramento, 10 Cal. 4th 368, 895 P.2d 900 (1995), *cert. denied,* 516 U.S. 1116 (1996).
8. *See Lucas,* 505 U.S. at 1026-27; David Coursen, Lucas v. South Carolina Coastal Council: *Indirection in the Evolution of Takings Law* [22 News & Analysis], ENVTL. L. REP. (ENVTL. L. INST.) 10,778, 10,784 (Dec. 1992) ("In the guise of articulating one categorical rule—a denial of all use works a taking—the Court has implicitly established another principle that state-imposed [background] limitations on property use always defeat a taking claim.").
9. *See Lucas,* 505 U.S. at 1027-28.
10. *Id.* at 1028-29 (citing Scranton v. Wheeler, 179 U.S. 141, 163 (1900)).
11. American Mfrs. Mut. Ins. Co. v. Sullivan, 526 U.S. 40, 59 (1999) (holding that under a state statute, employees do not have a property interest in payment for medical treatment that has yet to be found reasonable and necessary); *see* U.S. CONST. amend. XIV, § 1 ("nor shall any State deprive any person of life, liberty, or property, without due process of law.").
12. Abrahim-Youri v. United States, 139 F.3d 1462, 1468 (Fed. Cir. 1997), *cert. denied,* 524 U.S. 951 (1998).
13. *See* Rith Energy, Inc. v. United States, 44 Fed. Cl. 366, 366-67 (1999) (denying a takings claim because a federal ban on a mining permit prevented a nuisance under state law: [W]hether the enforcement of these restrictions is accomplished by the state regulatory body or by federal officials acting under the authority of [federal statute] is not an issue), *aff'd on other grounds,* 247 F.3d 1355 (Fed. Cir.), *reh'g denied on other grounds,* 270 F.3d 1347 (Fed. Cir. 2001).

14. *See* Keystone Bituminous Coal Ass'n v. DeBenedictis, 480 U.S. 470, 483 (1987); Meriden Trust & Safe Deposit Co. v. Federal Deposit Ins. Corp., 62 F.3d 449, 455 (2d Cir. 1995).

15. *See, e.g.*, Avenal v. United States, 100 F.3d 933 (Fed. Cir. 1996) (reversing finding that plaintiff never acquired a constitutionally protectable property interest, but affirming holding of no taking because of lack of reasonable investment-backed expectations).

16. 524 U.S. 156 (1998).

17. *Id.* at 172. *See* Washington Legal Found. v. Legal Found. of Washington, ___ F.3d ___, 2001 WL 1412787 (9th Cir. Nov. 14, 2001) (*en banc*) (no taking.)

18. *See* Glenn P. Sugameli, Lucas v. South Carolina Coastal Council: *The Categorical and Other "Exceptions" to Liability for Fifth Amendment Takings of Private Property Far Outweigh the "Rule,"* 29 Envtl. L. 939, 940-56, 978-87 (1999).

19. 175 F.3d 1374 (Fed. Cir. 1999).

20. *Id.* at 1379.

21. *See* Phillips Petroleum Co. v. Mississipi, 484 U.S. 469, 479 (1988) ("States have the authority to define the limits of the lands held in public trust and to recognize private rights in such lands as they see fit.").

22. *Id.* at 1030, *quoting* Board of Regents of State Colleges v. Roth, 408 U.S. 564, 577 (1972).

23. 505 U.S. at 1031. *See* Chevy Chase Land Co. v. United States, 733 A.2d 1055 (Md. 1999) (ruling on certification from the Federal Circuit that a 1911 deed granting an easement for the construction of a branch railway was sufficiently broad to encompass recreational use after railroad operations ceased).

24. 854 P.2d 449 (Or. 1993), *cert. denied*, 510 U.S. 1207 (1994).

25. *See* Stevens v. City of Cannon Beach, 510 U.S. 1207 (1994) (Scalia, J., dissenting, with O'Connor, J., from denial of certiorari).

26. Public Access Shoreline Hawaii v. Hawaii County Planning Comm'n, 903 P.2d 1246, 1268 (Haw.), *cert. denied*, 517 U.S. 1163 (1995).

27. Hunziker v. State, 519 N.W.2d 367, 370-71 (Iowa 1994), *cert. denied*, 514 U.S. 1003 (1995).

28. Kim v. City of New York, 681 N.E.2d 312, 315-16 (N.Y.) (city charter requirement to maintain lateral support for roadway), *cert. denied*, 522 U.S. 809 (1997); Gazza v. New York State Dep't of Envtl. Conservation, 679 N.E.2d 1035, 1039 (N.Y.) (statutory wetlands restriction), *cert. denied*, 522 U.S. 813 (1997); Anello v. Zoning Bd. of Appeals of Vill. of Dobbs Ferry, 678 N.E.2d 870, 872 (N.Y.) (steep-slope ordinance), *cert. dismissed*, 521 U.S. 1132 (1997); Basile v. Town of Southampton, 678 N.E.2d 489, 491 (N.Y.) (state Tidal Wetlands Act), *cert. denied*, 522 U.S. 907 (1997).

29. 498 S.E.2d 414 (Va.), *cert. denied*, 525 U.S. 826 (1998).

30. *See* Marks v. United States, 34 Fed. Cl. 387 (1995) (rejecting on background principle grounds the takings claim for the portion of the property below the high-water mark), *aff'd without opinion*, 116 F.3d 1496 (Fed. Cir. 1997), *cert. denied*, 522 U.S. 1075 (1998); Hoeck v. Portland, 57 F.3d 781, 789 (9th Cir. 1995) (municipal ordinance), *cert. denied*, 516 U.S. 1112 (1996); M & J Coal Co. v. United States, 47 F.3d 1148, 1154 (Fed. Cir. 1994) (Surface Mining Control and Reclamation Act), *cert. denied*, 516 U.S. 808 (1995).

31. The Court also declined to review a decision that reversed on other grounds an intermediate court ruling that preexisting statutes are not background principles. K & K Construction, Inc. v. Michigan Dep't of Natural Res., 551 N.W.2d 413, 421 (Mich. Ct. App. 1996), *rev'd on other grounds,* 575 N.W.2d 531 (Mich.), *cert. denied,* 525 U.S. 819 (1998).

32. Glenn P. Sugameli, *Takings Issues in Light of* Lucas v. South Carolina Coastal Council, 12 VA. ENVTL. L.J. 439 (1993).

33. *Id.* at 462.

34. *Id.* (footnote omitted).

35. *Lucas*, 505 U.S. at 1035 (Kennedy, J., concurring in the judgment).

36. Phillips v. Washington Legal Found., 524 U.S. 156, 164 (1998) (citing Board of Regents of State Colleges v. Roth, 408 U.S. 564, 577 (1972)).

37. *Id.* at 167; *see also Lucas*, 505 U.S. at 1029.

38. 121 S. Ct. 2448, 2464 (2001).

39. *Id.* (emphasis added).

40. 179 U.S. 141 (1900).

41. *Lucas*, 505 U.S. at 1028-29 (some citations omitted); *see also* United States v. Winstar Corp., 518 U.S. 839, 878 n.23 (1996) (Souter, J., with three Justices concurring and three Justices concurring in the judgment) (stating in dicta that the navigational servitude generally relieves the government from paying any compensation at all); United States v. Kansas City Life Ins. Co., 339 U.S. 799, 808 (1950) ("When the Government exercises this servitude, it is exercising its paramount power in the interest of navigation, rather than taking the private property of anyone."). In *United States v. Cherokee Nation of Okla.*, 480 U.S. 700 (1987), the Court stated:

> The proper exercise of this power is not an invasion of any private property rights in the stream or lands underlying it, for the damage sustained does not result from taking property from riparian owners within the meaning of the Fifth Amendment but from the lawful exercise of a power to which the interests of riparian owners have always been subject.

Id. at 704 (citation omitted).

42. Florida Rock Indus., Inc. v. United States, 45 Fed. Cl. 21, 28 (1999).

43. Florida Rock Indus., Inc. v. United States, 791 F.2d 893, 900 (Fed. Cir. 1986) (citation omitted).

44. Palm Beach Isles Assoc. v. United States, 208 F.3d 1374, 1384 (Fed. Cir. 2000). On petition for rehearing, the panel issued an Order that did not alter this holding, 231 F.3d 1354, 1357 (Fed. Cir. 2000), and rehearing en banc was denied, 231 F.3d 1365 (Fed. Cir. 2000).

45. United States v. 30.54 Acres of Land, 90 F.3d 790, 795 (3d Cir. 1996) (citing *Lucas*, 505 U.S. 1003, in which the "Supreme Court explicitly recognized the navigational servitude as a preexisting limitation on riparian landowners' estates"); *see also* Marks v. United States, 34 Fed. Cl. 387 (1995) (background principles bar takings claim for property below high-water mark), *aff'd without opinion*, 116 F.3d 1496 (Fed. Cir. 1997), *cert. denied*, 522 U.S. 1075 (1998); Applegate v. United States, 35 Fed. Cl. 406, 414-15 (1996) ("The holdings of the Supreme Court and the Federal Circuit establish that the Government owes no compensation for injury or destruction of a claimant's rights when they lie within the scope of the navigational servitude.") (citing Chicago, Milwaukee, St. Paul & Pac. R.R., 312 U.S. at 596-97 (1941)); Donnell v. United States, 834 F. Supp. 19, 26 (D. Me. 1993) (no taking from federal order to remove part of wharf, because the wharf owner's state property rights to land submerged under private structures remained subject to "the federal government's control for purposes of navigation and commerce"); Murphy v. Dep't of Natural Res., 837 F. Supp. 1217, 1221 (S.D. Fla. 1993) (recognizing constitutional Commerce Clause–based navigational servitudes, which

enable the federal government to modify navigable waters without incurring obligation associated with similar activities on land to compensate owners of submerged lands), *aff'd*, 56 F.3d 1389 (11th Cir. 1995).

46. *See* M & J Coal Co. v. United States, 47 F.3d 1148 (Fed. Cir. 1994) (federal Surface Mining Control and Reclamation Act), *cert. denied*, 516 U.S. 916 (1995); United States v. Hill, 896 F. Supp. 1057, 1063 (D. Colo. 1995) (no taking because animal parts were inherited after they were already subject to the proscribed conduct under the ESA and other federal wildlife statutes). *See also* Abrahim-Youri v. United States, 139 F.3d 1462 (Fed. Cir. 1997) (no taking from extinguishment of choses in action against Iran), *cert. denied*, 524 U.S. 951 (1998).

47. Keystone Bituminous Coal Ass'n v. DeBenedictis, 480 U.S. 470, 488 (1987).

48. Rith Energy, Inc. v. United States, 44 Fed. Cl. 108, 114 (1999) (citing Tennessee's Water Quality Control Act of 1977 (the Act), TENN. CODE ANN. §§ 693-102 69-3131 (1995 & Supp. 1998), *rehearing denied*, 44 Fed. Cl. 366, 367 (1999) (under state public nuisance law there is no property right to create "'high probability' of introducing acid mine drainage into the Sewanee Conglomerate aquifer"), *aff'd on other grounds*, 247 F.3d 1353 (Fed. Cir.), *reh'g denied*, 270 F.3d 1347 (Fed. Cir. 2001).

49. *E.g.*, Hendler v. United States, 36 Fed. Cl. 574, 585-86 (1996) (suggesting an alternative holding based on *Lucas*'s nuisance background principle grounds, rejecting regulatory takings claim involving governmental access to property near Superfund site), *aff'd on other grounds*, 175 F.3d 1374 (Fed. Cir. 1999); B & F Trawlers, Inc. v. United States, 27 Fed. Cl. 299, 305-06 (1992) (relying in part on *Lucas*'s nuisance discussion to dismiss a takings challenge to Coast Guard's sinking of vessel that threatened navigation); Aztec Minerals Corp. v. Romer, 940 P.2d 1025, 1032 (Colo. Ct. App. 1995) (holding that a state-mandated Superfund cleanup was not a taking because the site was a nuisance); Brown v. Thompson, 979 P.2d 586, 595, 598 (Haw. 1999) (finding that state impoundment of sinking vessel effected a due-process violation, but did not result in a taking because vessel was a nuisance); Kinross Copper Corp. v. State of Oregon, 981 P.2d 833, 840 (Or. Ct. App.) ("[P]laintiff's takings claim is predicated on the loss of a right that it never possessed, namely, the 'right' to discharge mining wastes into the waters of the state."), *opinion adhered to on reconsideration*, 988 P.2d 400 (Or. Ct. App. 1999), *rev. denied*, 944 P.2d 133 (Or.), *cert. denied,* 121 S. Ct. 387 (2000); *see also* Colorado Dep't of Health v. The Mill, 887 P.2d 993 (Colo. 1995) (holding that use restrictions on a uranium tailings disposal site did not constitute a taking).

50. *See also* Gillen v. City of Neenah, 580 N.W.2d 628 (Wis. 1998) (a violation of state public trust doctrine protecting navigable waters is a public nuisance that may be challenged by any person).

51. Keshbro, Inc. v. City of Miami, 2001 WL 776555 (Fla. July 12, 2001).

52. *Id. See also* City of St. Petersburg v. Bowen, 675 So. 2d 626 (Fla. 2d Dist. Ct. App.) (one-year closure of apartment complex to curtail tenant drug use was a temporary taking), *rev. denied*, 680 So. 2d 421 (Fla. 1996), *cert. denied*, 520 U.S. 1110 (1997).

53. *See, e.g.,* Federal Lands Consortium v. United States, 195 F.3d 1190 (10th Cir. 1999) (holding that grazing permits are not property for purposes of either the Takings Clause or the Due Process Clause); Diamond Bar Cattle Co. v. United States, 168 F.3d 1209 (10th Cir. 1999) (holding that state law did not grant property right in federal land); Alves v. United States, 133 F.3d 1454, 1457-58 (Fed. Cir. 1998) (holding that grazing allotments are not a compensable property right under the 5th Amendment); Kunkes v. United States, 78 F.3d 1549, 1550 (Fed. Cir. 1996) (holding that plaintiffs did not have a valid takings claim because they did not follow the statutory requirements to maintain

their mining claim; it was their inaction that caused the forfeiture of the unpatented mining claim); Hage v. United States, 35 Fed. Cl. 147, 171 (1996) (holding that a government grazing permit does not create a property right that allows the holder of the permit to sue for a taking of the property).

54. Fallini v. United States, 31 Fed. Cl. 53, 59 (1994), *vacated on other grounds*, 56 F.3d 1378 (Fed. Cir. 1995) (but affirming rejection of the takings claim).

55. *See, e.g.*, Parella v. Retirement Bd. of the R.I. Employees' Ret. Sys., 173 F.3d 46, 62 (1st Cir. 1999) (retroactive modification of law governing pension rights did not effect a taking because plaintiffs had no clear-cut contractual right to any particular level of pension benefits and thus could not point to any property right); Sebastian v. United States, 185 F.3d 1368 (Fed. Cir. 1999) (in the absence of a statutory or regulatory entitlement, promises made to retired service members did not establish a property interest in health care benefits).

56. 854 P.2d 449 (Or. 1993), *cert. denied*, 510 U.S. 1207 (1994).

57. *Id.* at 456 (quoting State *ex rel.* Thornton v. Hay, 462 P.2d 671 (Or. 1969)). In 1973, *The Takings Issue* cited *Thornton* as an example of a case in which "governmental agencies can avoid the takings issue . . . by reestablishing a preexisting state interest in the land. . . . [C]laims of preexisting title have been most prevalent along the ocean shores, both for sandy beaches and tidal lands." FRED BOSSELMAN ET AL., COUNCIL ON ENVTL. QUALITY, THE TAKINGS ISSUE: A STUDY OF THE CONSTITUTIONAL LIMITS OF GOVERNMENTAL AUTHORITY TO REGULATE THE USE OF PRIVATELY-OWNED LAND WITHOUT PAYING COMPENSATION TO THE OWNERS 309-10 (1973).

58. *Stevens*, 854 P.2d at 456-67.

59. Public Access Shoreline Hawaii (PASH) v. Hawaii County Planning Commission, 903 P.2d 1246, 1268 (Haw.), *cert. denied*, 517 U.S. 1163 (1995).

60. *Id.*; *see also* Samuel J. Panarella, *Not in My Backyard*—PASH v. HPC: *The Clash Between Native Hawaiian Gathering Rights and Western Concepts of Property in Hawaii*, 28 ENVTL. L. 467, 483-85 (1998).

61. *See* Confederated Salish & Kootenai Tribes of the Flathead Reservation v. Namen, 665 F.2d 951, 962 (9th Cir. 1982) (holding that under the Hell Gate Treaty, lakebed is owned by the United States in trust for the tribes). I represented the tribes in this case.

62. 526 U.S. 172 (1999).

63. *Id.* (holding that Chippewa 1837 treaty rights to hunt, fish, and gather on land they sold in the treaty were not extinguished by an 1850 Executive Order, an 1855 treaty, or Minnesota's entry into the Union on "equal footing" with other states); *see also* United States v. Washington, 157 F.3d 630, 647 (9th Cir. 1998) (affirming treaty right of Washington State Indian tribes to gather shellfish from privately owned beaches), *cert. denied*, 526 U.S. 1060 (1999).

64. State of Texas v. Bartee, 894 S.W.2d 34, 41 (Tex. 1994).

65. *See* State of New York v. Sour Mountain Realty, Inc., 714 N.Y.S.2d 78 (2000); *see also* Farris v. Arkansas State Game & Fish Comm'n, 310 S.W.2d 231, 237 (Ark. 1958) (finding no taking from ban on private landowner's sale of game fish raised entirely on private waters on his land; fish farmers had "only a qualified ownership"). The Environmental Policy Project has repeatedly argued that background principles of state ownership of wildlife preclude a finding of a taking. *See* http://www.envpoly.org/takings/courts/briefs.htm (visited Nov. 19, 2001).

66. 33 U.S.C. § 1344 (1988).

67. 505 U.S. at 1029-30.

68. *Id.* at 1030-31.

69. *See, e.g.*, United States v. Riverside Bayview Homes, Inc., 474 U.S. 121, 134-35 (1985) (unanimously endorsing findings on the importance of wetlands to aquatic eco-systems in upholding federal jurisdiction over wetlands not flooded by adjacent waters); Sabine River Auth. v. United States Dep't of [the] Interior, 951 F.2d 669, 672 (5th Cir. 1992) ("Because wetlands are critical to flood control, water supply, water quality, and, of course, wildlife, their rapid disappearance is setting the stage for what may eventually become a significant environmental catastrophe."), *cert. denied*, 506 U.S. 823 (1992). *See also* Blue Water Isles Co. v. Department of Natural Res., 431 N.W.2d 53, 58 (Mich. App. 1988) (denying a takings claim, recognizing that "both the statutes under which the DNR reviewed plaintiff's application and the DNR's denial of plaintiff's request [to dredge and fill 442 acres of marsh lands] are reasonably related to the preservation of the state's natural resources and the protection of the public trust in inland lakes and streams."). *See also* Paul F. Scodari, Environmental Law Institute, Measuring the Benefits of the Federal Wetlands Programs 49-73 (1997) (explaining the varying functions and the social value of wetlands).

70. *See* Sabine River Auth. v. United States Dep't of the Interior, 951 F.2d 669, 672 (5th Cir. 1992), *cert. denied*, 506 U.S. 823 (1992). *See also* Karen Boylan & Don MacLean, *Linking Species Loss with Wetlands Loss*, National Wetlands Newsletter, (Envtl. Law Inst., Wash., D.C.), Nov.-Dec. 1997, at 17 (stating that loss of wetlands will increase the rate of extinction of animals that are dependent on, or associated with, wetlands); Lois Schiffer & Jeremy D. Heep, *Forests, Wetlands and the Superfund: Three Examples of Environmental Protection Promoting Jobs,* 22 J. Corp. L. 571, 588-92 (1997) (citing statistics showing that wetlands have extraordinary economic benefits for com-mercial industries, recreation, and subsistence, and stating that the cost of foregoing wetlands protection is high because wetlands serve to purify drinking water, reduce flood damage, and provide habitats for numerous species).

71. Palazzolo v. Coastal Res. Mgmt. Council, No. C.A. 86-1496, 1995 WL 941370 (R.I. Super. Ct. Jan. 5, 1995); C.A. No. 88-0297 (R.I. Super. Ct. Oct. 24, 1997), *aff'd on other grounds*, 746 A.2d 707 (R.I. 2000), *aff'd in part, rev'd in part, and remanded*, 121 S. Ct. 2448 (2001).

72. 1995 WL 941370 at *3. *See also* Dunwiddie v. Minergy Corp., 580 N.W.2d 628 (Wis. 1998) (a violation of state public trust doctrine protecting navigable waters is a public nuisance that may be challenged by any person).

73. *See* 121 S. Ct. at 2457; www.communityrights.org/PalazzoloOralArg.html (vis-ited Nov. 19, 2001); 2001 WL 196990.

74. *See, e.g.,* Wilson v. Commonwealth, 583 N.E.2d 894, 901 (Mass. App. Ct.) ("[I]f the coastal areas in question are impressed with a public trust . . . the plaintiffs, from the outset, have only qualified rights . . . and have no reasonable investment-backed expecta-tions under which to mount a takings challenge."), *aff'd*, 597 N.E.2d 43 (Mass. 1992); Karam v. NJDEP, 705 A.2d 1221, 1228 (N.J. App. Div. 1998) ("[T]he sovereign never waives its right to regulate the use of public trust property."), *aff'd*, 723 A.2d 943 (1999); Orion v. State, 747 P.2d 1062, 1073 (Wash. 1987) (en banc) (holding that the landowner "could make no use of the land which would substantially impair the [public] trust"), *cert. denied*, 486 U.S. 1022 (1988); *see also* Montana Coalition for Stream Access v. Curran, 682 P.2d 163, 171 (Mont. 1984) (holding that there was no taking of surface waters held in the public trust irrespective of stream bed ownership).

75. Coastal Petroleum v. Chiles, 701 So. 2d 619, 624 (Fla. Dist. Ct. App. 1997), *rev. denied*, 707 So. 2d 1123 (Fla. 1998), *cert. denied*, 524 U.S. 953 (1998).

76. *See, e.g.*, Matthews v. Bay Head Improvement Ass'n, 471 A.2d 355, 363 (N.J.)

(holding that the landowner must provide access to beach areas subject to the public trust doctrine), *cert. denied*, 469 U.S. 821 (1984); National Ass'n of Home Builders v. Department of Envtl. Protection, 64 F. Supp. 2d 354 (D. N.J. 1999) (applying *Matthews* to review of takings claim); National Audubon Soc'y v. Superior Court, 658 P.2d 709, 722 (Cal.) (holding that the public trust doctrine provides an independent basis for challenging water diversions), *cert. denied*, 464 U.S. 977 (1983).

77. 201 N.W.2d 761, 768 (Wis. 1972). *See also id.* ("uses consistent with the nature of the land are allowed and other uses recognized and still others permitted by special permit. . . . The changing of wetlands and swamps to the damage of the general public by upsetting the natural environment and the natural relationship is not a reasonable use of that land."); Zealy v. City of Waukesha, 548 N.W.2d 528, 534 (Wis. 1996) (finding no taking on other grounds, but specifically noting that "[n]othing in this opinion limits our holding in *Just*").

78. Rowe v. Town of North Hampton, 553 A.2d 1331, 1335 (N.H. 1989); *accord* Graham v. Estuary Properties, Inc., 399 So. 2d 1374, 1382 (Fla.), *cert. denied*, 454 U.S. 1083 (1981); New Hampshire Wetlands Bd. v. Marshall, 500 A.2d 685, 689 (N.H. 1985); Claridge v. New Hampshire Wetlands Bd., 485 A.2d 287, 290 (N.H. 1984); American Dredging Co. v. State Dep't of Envtl. Protection, 391 A.2d 1265, 1271 (N.J. Super. Ct. Ch. Div. 1978), *aff'd*, 404 A.2d 42 (N.J. Super. Ct. App. Div. 1979); *see also* Pope v. City of Atlanta, 249 S.E.2d 16, 20 (Ga. 1978) (in rejecting a takings claim regarding river corridor property, the court stated that the *Just* analysis "buttresses our conclusion in this case"), *cert. denied*, 440 U.S. 936 (1979); Usdin v. State Dep't of Envtl. Protection, 414 A.2d 280, 288-90 (N.J. Super. Ct. 1980) (finding that a regulation forbidding construction was "a proper exercise of a police power to prevent a misuse of nature [and not a] compensable taking" when the property was in an area prone to flooding that could harm the public); Chokecherry Hills Estates, Inc. v. Deuel County, 294 N.W.2d 654, 657 (S.D. 1980) (citing with approval *Just*'s statement that the "police power was properly exercised in preventing a public harm by protecting the natural environment of shorelands").

79. M&I v. Town of Somers, 414 N.W.2d 824, 830 (Wis. 1987).

80. 314 S.E.2d 326 (S.C. 1984).

81. *Id.* at 329 (quoting *Just*, 201 N.W.2d at 768).

82. *Id.* at 329 (footnotes omitted).

83. FRED BOSSELMAN ET AL., COUNCIL ON ENVTL. QUALITY, THE TAKING ISSUE: A STUDY OF THE CONSTITUTIONAL LIMITS OF GOVERNMENTAL AUTHORITY TO REGULATE THE USE OF PRIVATELY-OWNED LAND WITHOUT PAYING COMPENSATION TO THE OWNERS 309-13 (1973).

84. ROBERT MELTZ, DWIGHT H. MERRIAM & RICHARD M. FRANK, THE TAKINGS ISSUE: CONSTITUTIONAL LIMITS ON LAND USE CONTROL AND ENVIRONMENTAL REGULATION 377 (1999) ("At least in those states in which the doctrine is well-established, it would seem to qualify" as a background principle); Hope M. Babcock, *Has the U.S. Supreme Court Finally Drained the Swamp of Takings Jurisprudence?*, 19 HARV. ENVTL. L. REV. 1, 4, 45-46 & n.260 (1995); Jan Goldman-Carter, *Protecting Wetlands and Reasonable Investment-Backed Expectations in the Wake of Lucas v. South Carolina Coastal Council*, 29 LAND & WATER L. REV. 425, 447 & n.138 (1993); Glenn P. Sugameli, *Takings Issues in Light of* Lucas v. South Carolina Coastal Council, 12 VA. ENVTL. L.J. 439, 464-65 & n.117 (1993). *But see* Joseph L. Sax, *Property Rights & the Economy of Nature: Understanding* Lucas v. South Carolina Coastal Council, 45 STAN. L. REV. 1433, 1440 (1993); Richard Ausness, *Regulatory Taking & Wetland Protection in the Post-*Lucas *Era*, 30 LAND & WATER L. REV. 349, 403-04 (1995). *See also* Fred P. Bosselman, *Limitations Inherent in the Title to Wetlands at Common Law*, 15 STAN. ENVTL. L.J. 247 (1996);

Michael Blumm, *The End of Environmental Law? Libertarian Property, Natural Law, and the Just Compensation Clause in the Federal Circuit*, 25 Envtl. L. 171, 176 n.37 (1995) ("[B]ackground principles may insulate all wetlands regulation from just compensation claims if courts scrutinize English common law wetland cases. . . . ").

85. James M. McElfish, Jr., *Property Rights, Property Roots: Rediscovering the Basis for Legal Protection of the Environment* [24 News & Analysis], Envtl. L. Rep. (Envtl. L. Inst.) 10,231, 10,244 (May 1994).

86. 530 S.E.2d 628 (S.C. 2000), *vacated and remanded*, 121 S. Ct. 2581 (2001).

87. *Id*. at 635.

88. *Id*. at 632-33.

89. Of the authorities cited in *supra* nn. 83-85, the court cited "*See, e.g*.," Babcock, Goldman-Carter, and "*but see*" Sax, and Ausness. 530 S.E.2d at 632.

90. *Id*. at 632 n.4. The Supreme Court subsequently denied certiorari in *Good*. 120 S. Ct. 1554 (2000).

91. 121 S. Ct. 2581 (2001).

92. 530 S.E.2d at 633 (quoting *Lucas*, 505 U.S. at 1018) (emphasis added by *McQueen* court).

93. 121 S. Ct. at 2459, 2464.

94. 530 S.E.2d at 631 n.2 (citations omitted). James S. Chandler, Jr. of the South Carolina Environmental Law Project and I co-authored the amici brief the court referred to. *See also* Arrington v. Mattox, 767 S.W.2d 957, 958 (Tex. Ct. App.) (finding no taking because public's easement, acquired by custom, across landowner's property to access beach had moved landward with natural movements of vegetation line and line of mean low tide), *cert. denied*, 493 U.S. 1073 (1989).

95. 505 U.S. at 1031 (emphasis added) (citing Restatement (Second) of Torts § 827, cmt. g (1979)).

96. 505 U.S. at 1029 (emphasis added).

97. *See* Zealy v. City of Waukesha, 548 N.W.2d at 535 ("'[W]etlands were once considered wasteland, undesirable . . . But as the people became more sophisticated, an appreciation was acquired that swamps and wetlands serve a vital role in nature and are essential to the purity of the water in our lakes and streams.'") (quoting Just v. Marinette County, 201 N.W.2d 761, 768 (Wis. 1972); *see* Paula C. Murray, *Private Takings of Endangered Species as Public Nuisance:* Lucas v. South Carolina Coastal Council *and the Endangered Species Act*, 12 UCLA J. Envtl. L. & Pol'y 119, 157 (1993) (arguing that most of today's environmental hazards are included in the common-law definition of public nuisance).

98. Missouri v. Holland, 252 U.S. 416, 432-33 (1920).

99. *Lucas*, 505 U.S. at 1069-70 (Stevens, J., dissenting).

100. National Ass'n of Home Builders v. Babbitt, 130 F.3d 1041 (D.C. Cir. 1997), *cert. denied*, 524 U.S. 957 (1998); *see also* Gibbs v. Babbitt, 214 F.3d 483 (4th Cir. 2000), *cert. denied*, 121 S. Ct. 1081 (2001); United States v. Bramble, 103 F.3d 1475, 1481 (9th Cir. 1996).

101. *Id*. at 1048 (Wald, J.).

102. *Id*. at 1051.

103. *Id*. at 1058 (Henderson, J., concurring).

104. 505 U.S. at 1031 (citing Restatement (Second) of Torts § 821B-D (1979)).

105. *See* Restatement (Second) of Torts § 821B-D (1979). "A public nuisance is an unreasonable interference with a common right common to the general public." *Id*. § 821B. "A private nuisance is a nontrespassory invasion of another's interest in the private

use and enjoyment of land." *Id.* § 821D; *see also* Terry W. Frazier, *Protecting Ecological Integrity Within the Balancing Function of Property Law*, 28 ENVTL. L. 53, 92-94 (1998) (defining the "nuisance principle" as allowing use of one's property without interference with the use and enjoyment of neighboring properties).

106. *See, e.g.*, Florida Rock Indus. v. United States, 21 Cl. Ct. 161, 166-68 (1990) (applying a historical analysis to determine whether the landowner's proposed activities constituted a nuisance), *vacated on other grounds*, 18 F.3d 1560 (Fed. Cir. 1994), *cert. denied*, 513 U.S. 1109 (1995).

107. RESTATEMENT § 821B(2)(b) & cmt e.

108. 505 U.S. at 1055-60 (Blackmun, J., dissenting).

109. *Id.* at 1068-71 (Stevens, J., dissenting).

110. *Id.* at 1031.

111. 505 U.S. at 1035 (Kennedy, J. concurring in the judgment). *See also* Sugameli, *Takings Issues in Light of* Lucas, 12 VA. ENVTL. L.J. at 457 n.92 (Any effort to limit background principles to the common law would need to take account of "how the *Lucas* doctrine will be applied to Louisiana's civil law system.").

112. 121 S. Ct. 2448, 2464 (2001) (emphasis added).

113. 121 S. Ct. at 2467, 2468 (Scalia, J., concurring) quoting *Lucas*, 505 U.S. at 1029.

114. 121 S. Ct. at 2464 (emphasis added).

115. *Id.*

116. *Id.*

117. 452 U.S. 314 (1981).

118. *Id.* at 329.

119. 480 U.S. 470 (1987).

120. *Id.* at 474 (footnote omitted). *See also id.* at 474-75 & nn.2 & 3.

121. *Id.* at 475 n.2, quoting Blazey & Strain, *Deep Mine Subsidence—State Law and the Federal Response*, 1 E. MIN. L. FOUND. 1.01, p. 2 (1980).

122. *Id.* at 488.

123. *Id.* (emphasis added).

124. M & J Coal Co. v. United States, 47 F.3d 1148, 1154 (Fed. Cir. 1994), *cert. denied*, 516 U.S. 808 (1995). *Accord* Bowman v. United States, 35 Fed. Cl. 397 (1996). The *Keystone* Court stated that subsidence "presents the type of environmental concern that has been the focus of so much federal, state, and local regulation in recent decades," citing SMCRA in the accompanying footnote. 480 U.S. at 475 & n.3.

125. Rith Energy, Inc. v. United States, 44 Fed. Cl. 108, 114 (1999) (citing Tennessee's Water Quality Control Act of 1977 (the Act), TENN. CODE ANN. §§ 693-102 69-3131 (1995 & Supp. 1998), *rehearing denied*, 44 Fed. Cl. 366, 367 (1999) (under state public nuisance law there is no property right to create "'high probability' of introducing acid mine drainage into the Sewanee Conglomerate aquifer"), *aff'd on other grounds*, 247 F.3d 1353 (Fed. Cir.), *reh'g denied*, 270 F.3d 1347 (Fed. Cir. 2001) (preventing harmful runoff is the type of action typically regarded as not compensable).

126. 172 F.3d 906 (D.C. Cir. 1998).

127. *Id.* at 917 (quoting Eastern Enters. v. Apfel, 524 U.S. 498, 528 (1998) (plurality)).

128. *Id.*

129. 503 U.S. 519 (1992).

130. *Id.* at 529.

131. 121 S. Ct. at 2462. Traditional zoning typically does not constitute a taking. *See* Agins v. Tiburon, 447 U.S. 255 (1980); Village of Euclid v. Ambler Realty Co., 272 U.S. 365 (1926).

132. Hoeck v. Portland, 57 F.3d 781, 789 (9th Cir. 1995) (rejecting a takings claims regarding a city regulation concerning vacant structures), *cert. denied*, 516 U.S. 1112 (1996); Outdoor Graphics v. City of Burlington, 103 F.3d 690, 694 (8th Cir. 1996) (rejecting claim that city's billboard ordinance constituted a taking).

133. Front Royal and Warren County Indus. Park Corp. v. Town of Front Royal, 135 F.3d 275, 287 (4th Cir. 1998). *See also* Superior-FCR Landfill, Inc. v. Wright County, 59 F. Supp. 2d 929 (D. Minn. 1999) (no taking under the Minnesota Constitution because claimant purchased with notice of zoning ordinance; preexisting option to buy did not rescue takings claim).

134. *E.g.,* cases cited in *supra* nn. 27-29; Alegria v. Keeney, 687 A.2d 1249, 1254 (R.I. 1997); Wooten v. South Carolina Coastal Council, 510 S.E.2d 716 (S.C. 1999); Grant v. South Carolina Coastal Council, 461 S.E.2d 388, 391 (S.C. 1995); Board of Supervisors of Prince William County v. Omni Homes, 481 S.E.2d 460, 465 (Va. 1997) (zoning restrictions).

135. United States *ex rel.* Bergen v. Lawrence, 848 F.2d 1502, 1507 (10th Cir. 1988) (citing the Unlawful Inclosures of Public Lands Act, 43 U.S.C. §§ 1061 to 1066).

136. Hunziker v. State, 519 N.W.2d 367, 370-71 (Iowa 1994), *cert. denied*, 514 U.S. 1003 (1995).

137. 505 U.S. at 1029.

138. Good v. United States, 189 F.3d 1355, 1362-63 (Fed. Cir. 1999), *cert. denied*, 120 S. Ct. 1554 (2000).

139. *In re* Water Use Permit Applications, 9 P.3d 409 (Haw. 2000).

140. Montana Envtl. Info. Ctr. v. Department of Envtl. Quality, 988 P.2d 1236 (Mont. 1999).

141. 121 S. Ct. at 2465 (O'Connor, J., concurring).

142. *Id.* at 2467 (footnote omitted).

143. *Id.* at 2477 n.3 (Ginsburg, J., joined by Souter, J., and Breyer, J.) ("at a minimum, agree[ing] with Justice O'Connor, *ante,* at 2465-2467 (concurring opinion), Justice Stevens, *ante,* at 2471-2472 (opinion concurring in part and dissenting in part), and Justice Breyer, *ante,* at 2477-2478 (dissenting opinion), that transfer of title can impair a takings claim."). *See* Rith Energy, Inc. v. United States, 270 F.3d 1347, (Fed. Cir. 2001).

144. *Anello*, 678 N.E.2d at 871. *See also* Front Royal and Warren County Indus. Park Corp. v. Town of Front Royal, 135 F.3d 275, 287 (4th Cir. 1998) (holding that same facts precluded both a title right to and investment-backed expectations of public sewer service); Burgess v. Florida Dep't of Envt'l Protection, 772 So.2d 540 (Fla. Dist. Ct. App. 2000) (holding that the plaintiff's *Lucas* total takings claim was defeated by failure to demonstrate interference with reasonable, distinct, investment-backed expectations), *cert. denied*, 122 S. Ct. __ 70 U.S.L.W. 3194 (Nov. 26, 2001); R.W. Docks & Slips v. State, 628 N.W.2d 781 (Wis. 2001), (no taking where "development of this private marina on the bed and waters of Lake Superior was encumbered by the public trust doctrine and heavily regulated from the get-go."), *cert. denied*, 122 S. Ct. __ 70 U.S.L.W. 3194 (Nov. 26, 2001).

PALAZZOLO AND PARTIAL TAKINGS*   **8**

DWIGHT H. MERRIAM

§ 8.0   *Introduction*

On Monday, June 28, 2001—the very last day for issuing decisions before the 2000 term summer recess—the Supreme Court handed down its decision in *Palazzolo v. Rhode Island*.[1] The Court held, with Justice Kennedy writing for the 5-4 majority, that a landowner's claim that a state's application of its wetlands regulations took his property without compensation in violation of the Takings Clause was ripe for review. The Court further held that the landowner was not barred by his acquisition of title after the regulations' effective date. However, the Court held that he failed to establish a deprivation of all economic use, since the land retained significant development value for construction of a residence.

* This chapter is based upon the author's prior writings on the *Palazzolo* decision, including Dwight H. Merriam, *The* Palazzolo *Decision—Time for Damage Control*, MUN. LAW., Sept.-Oct. 2001; Dwight H. Merriam & Bryan W. Wenter, Palazzolo *Promotes Property Rights*, ZONING AND PLAN. LAW REPORT, V. 24 No.7, July-Aug. 2001; and Dwight H. Merriam, *The* Palazzolo *Palaestra*, ZONING AND PLAN. L. REP., V. 23, No.11, Dec. 2000. The author gratefully acknowledges West Group and the International Municipal Lawyers Association for their permission to use the material in preparing this chapter.

It is no great surprise the Court waited until the term's end. During oral argument, Justices, frustrated by the confused factual and procedural history of the case and muddled arguments, wondered aloud why they took the case in the first place. In reference to the single home site valued at $200,000 the state said it would have approved, Justice Scalia noted, "I thought that was not in the case when we took it. We might not have taken it had I thought it was in the case." No one knew how much land the plaintiff owned, how much "upland" was available for development, or what development might reasonably be approved. The interplay of state and local regulation made things worse all around. But no one ever promised that property rights cases would have four corners, "neat and square," as you might find in a children's story.[2]

§ 8.1 Factual and Procedural History

Before analyzing the Court's decision and hearing what others have to say about it, let me tell you what led up to the Court's decision. In the end, you should have a good sense of how a case like this develops and why the Justices seemed so troubled. I have spent many hours on the telephone and in person with Anthony Palazzolo, who is an engaging and lively man and who has shared with me much of the story not fully set out in the record.

Eighty-year-old retired auto wrecker Anthony "Polly" Palazzolo for years sought to develop wetlands adjacent to Winnapaug Pond in Westerly, Rhode Island. Two decades and numerous permit denials later, Mr. Palazzolo filed an inverse condemnation action against the state of Rhode Island alleging that Coastal Resources Management Council (CRMC) regulations had effectively taken his land without compensation in violation of the Fifth Amendment.[3] Mr. Palazzolo's case, one characterized by some as a David against Goliath showdown and by others as "a title examiner's nightmare,"[4] has its share of interesting factual and legal twists.

In 1959 Natale "Nate" and Elizabeth Urso sold Mr. Palazzolo a one-half interest in the majority of the land, which included 18 acres of wetlands and a disputed amount of "uplands," which Mr. Palazzolo describes as merely a 1,200- to 1,500-foot-long gravel road with a turnaround at one end. According to Mr. Palazzolo, he jumped on board after Mr. Urso sold six lots that he called "Shore Gardens" and four Navy surplus houses were moved to the lots practically overnight. The next day, Mr. Urso and Mr. Palazzolo, Shore Garden's Inc.'s (SGI) sole shareholders, sold the land, comprising three contiguous lots, to SGI.[6] Later that year, SGI subdivided the land into 80 lots.[7] The parcels are located between Atlantic Avenue and Winnapaug Pond, and consist mostly of wetlands and coastal marshlands. Much of the area, according to the state court, is submerged under the waters of Winnapaug Pond, a three-mile long saltwater marsh; other portions are subject to daily tidal flooding and pooling. The land is a refuge and habitat for various species, and it acts as a buffer for flooding and as a filter for runoff that enters the pond.[8] It's a nice place, a truly beautiful place. Mr. Palazzolo refers to it as "The Great Escape"—the name he has painted across the front of his beach house on one of the frontage lots previously sold. A poster of the movie of the same name, with a larger-than-life Steve McQueen depicted on it, hangs in the living room.

The Rhode Island courts indicate that sometime between 1959 and 1961, SGI transferred 11 upland lots to others for development.[9] In 1960, Mr. Urso transferred his SGI shares to Mr. Palazzolo, and Mr. Palazzolo became the sole shareholder. SGI then reacquired five of the 11 previously sold lots in 1969. Thereafter, SGI was the record owner of 74 of the original 80 lots.

Mr. Palazzolo maintains that SGI never had an interest in the 11 upland lots and that he came into the picture after Mr. Urso sold the six Shore Gardens lots. Mr. Palazzolo notes that when he acquired his interest in the 74 lots, Mr. Urso, a lawyer, wanted to incorporate Shore Gardens. Shore Gardens thus became Shore Gardens, Inc., of which Mr. Palazzolo was the first and only president. Mr. Palazzolo further notes that at the time the six lots were sold, Mr. Urso was so busy that he did not get around to completing the deeds until a few months after SGI was incorporated. Mr. Urso signed the deeds under SGI's name, causing confusion on this point in the record. Mr. Palazzolo also maintains that he and Mr. Urso each purchased five lots from SGI, with Mr. Urso selling his five to another party. Mr. Palazzolo later bought those five lots, as an individual owner, and SGI eventually bought Mr. Urso's interest in the remaining 32 lots.

This chronology is important because when Mr. Palazzolo became the owner was critical to his case up until the certiorari petition was filed with the U.S. Supreme Court. Enormous energy was focused on who knew what, when, and at what time during whose ownership, because the "notice defense" provided the government with a chance to cut off the takings claim if Mr. Palazzolo had purchased with knowledge of the restrictive regulations prohibiting his filling of the wetlands. We sometimes glibly refer to the effect of the notice defense on the owner of a regulated marsh who purchased after federal or state wetlands law went into effect as "You bought a wetland, you own a wetland," because we know how hard it is for a landowner to get permission to dredge or fill or to be compensated when someone purchases with knowledge.

But when James Burling of the Pacific Legal Foundation looked at the case, he saw a chance to make lemonade out of the chronological lemons. In drafting the certiorari petition, he conceded something that might not have even been true. He admitted for purposes of the petition that Mr. Palazzolo had owned the property only since 1978, and in doing so, in throw-me-in-the-briarpatch fashion, he accomplished two great things for his client—he avoided having Mr. Palazzolo credited with any of the value of the lots first stripped off, sold, and developed, and he postured the case, like the setter in volleyball, for the Court to take a spike shot at the notice defense. And it worked, although most of us watching from the bleachers guessed it wouldn't.

Besides the importance of the chronology with the notice defense and how it came to drive the posturing of the case before the Supreme Court, the history of this case suggests an important reason why the Court granted certiorari in the first place. Recent takings cases and one on equal protection subtly vibrate with a harmonic undercurrent of the concern of several justices for "fundamental fairness" and the protection of people from governmental "bad faith." Florence Dolan, in her bike path exactions case, presented herself as an elderly widow struggling to make a modest expansion to a mom-and-pop hardware store (though the reality was somewhat different).[10] Mrs. Suitum, another widow, emphasized the years she was forced to wait to be compensated for the restriction on her lot at Lake Tahoe.[11] With the third widow, Grace Olech, the Court found that a three-month delay in connecting her house to public water was enough to allow her to stay in court on an equal protection claim when there was some evidence the municipality was being vindictive for a prior suit she brought against it.[12]

Del Monte Dunes complained of being teased through five applications only to be told it could not have 190 units on a parcel zoned for potentially more than 1,000 units.[13] This was just too much for two Justices, who openly expressed their concern during oral argument for the shabby treatment of the landowner. Justice Scalia, predictably the first to speak to the issue, said: "The landowner here essentially thinks that it was getting jerked around . . . isn't there some point at which . . . you begin to smell a rat, and at that point can't we say . . . this is simply unreasonable."[14] Justice Kennedy wondered: "Even if the property has value, if the city is unreasonable and there is bad faith, isn't the city still liable in damages for that unreasonable treatment of the land-owner?"[15]

On June 29, 2001, the Court granted certiorari in the notorious Tahoe-Sierra Preservation Council, Inc. case. That case has been fought at the administrative level locally and in the courts for 20 years and involves several hundred property owners on Lake Tahoe who have not been able to develop their lots or receive compensation or even get closure to their claims by a final court judgment. Our Supreme Court, with many Justices in their twilight years, may be more sensitive to delay than other tribunals. It is simply human nature that the Justices would be drawn by the people side of some of these cases, and Anthony Palazzolo's story of an 80-year-old retired auto wrecker struggling with a state bureaucracy for 25 years to find a use for his land is certainly an interesting one.

Now you know why the chronology is important.

As the sole shareholder of SGI, Mr. Palazzolo in 1962 sought to dredge Winnapaug Pond and to use the dredge material to fill the wetlands on his parcels. Mr. Palazzolo's application was returned to him because it was missing essential information. Undeterred, in 1963 Mr. Palazzolo submitted an application to build a bulkhead, to dredge Winnapaug Pond, and to fill the land with the dredge material.

In 1965, the Rhode Island legislature adopted an intertidal wetlands law that gave the Coastal Resources Management Council's predecessor authority to regulate the filling of coastal wetlands. Then, in 1966, Mr. Palazzolo submitted his third application to dredge Winnapaug Pond. He again proposed to use the pond's dredge material to fill the wetlands, this time to develop a recreational beach facility.

In 1971, CRMC's predecessor finally approved the 1963 and 1966 applications. The approval gave Mr. Palazzolo two options. He could build the bulkhead and fill the wetland, or he could build the recreational beach facility and fill the wetland. The reason for the approval? In 1938 a hurricane destroyed some sand dunes and silted portions of Winnapaug Pond. There was evidence that deepening the pond through dredging would provide better protection for shellfish during the cold winter months when the pond freezes. However, only 17 days after the 1971 approval (or seven months, according to the Rhode Island Supreme Court), CRMC's predecessor revoked its approval due to environmental concerns. Mr. Palazzolo, who did not appeal the revocation, attributes the revocation to political pressure on the state from a certain environmental group, then in its ascendancy in Rhode Island. No one will likely ever know for sure what happened.

In either 1976 (according to the superior court) or 1977 (according to the supreme court) Rhode Island formed a coastal management program. The program prohibited the filling of coastal wetlands without a special exception.

For most of the period between 1959 and 1978, according to the Rhode Island Supreme Court, Mr. Palazzolo was SGI's sole shareholder. But SGI owned the land as a lawful Rhode Island corporation until its 1978 charter revocation, when it passed to Mr. Palazzolo by operation of law. Despite its charter revocation, SGI remains the record owner and pays the taxes.[16] It was this silent, automatic, and uncelebrated legal event—the revocation of the charter—that technically vested the entire property interest in Mr. Palazzolo.

According to Mr. Palazzolo, he took a greater interest in developing the parcel upon his retirement from the auto-wrecking business in 1979 and the ensuing real estate boom of the 1980s. In an application practically identical to his 1963 application (according to the state supreme court) or to his 1962 application (according to the superior court), Mr. Palazzolo in 1983 applied to build a bulkhead and to fill—but not dredge—18 acres of wetlands. CRMC denied the application, and Mr. Palazzolo did not appeal its decision.

Mr. Palazzolo continued his fight and in 1985 filed another application with CRMC. This application was similar to Mr. Palazzolo's 1966 application, except that it only sought to fill 11 acres of wetlands for construction of a beach club. The U.S. Supreme Court noted that the proposed beach club, with its dumpster, port-a-johns, and trash receptacles, does "not tend to inspire the reader with an idyllic coastal image."[17] CRMC denied this application in 1986. Mr. Palazzolo appealed CRMC's denial but lost at trial in 1995.

It was also about this time, the mid-1980s, that Mr. Palazzolo, the retired auto wrecker, became an expert in land use law. Seriously. He ordered every land use law book out of The West Publishing Company catalogue and studied the law. In a conversation I had with him in his living room at The Great Escape in July 2001, he regaled me with stories of how the Supreme Court Justices had lined up in the leading takings cases. He related details that I had not heard before, and I marveled at his self-taught command of the cases.

In 1988, around the time Mr. Palazzolo's appeal of CRMC's

1986 decision was pending, he filed suit in state court under the state and federal constitutions for inverse condemnation. Mr. Palazzolo sought $3,150,000 in compensation for the profits he expected to earn by filling his wetlands and developing the land as 74 lots for single-family homes.[18]

In 1997 the trial court held that CRMC's rejection of Mr. Palazzolo's 1983 and 1985 applications did not amount to a taking. The trial judge found that Mr. Palazzolo's project would be a public nuisance. He based this finding on evidence that filling the wetlands would negatively affect Winnapaug Pond and thereby reduce species populations and threaten groundwater, and on additional evidence that Mr. Palazzolo's project "would not be suitable for the locality of the subject property."[19]

Mr. Palazzolo appealed to the Rhode Island Supreme Court. The supreme court purportedly decided the case on ripeness grounds, but also "briefly discuss[ed] the merits of Palazzolo's claim."[20] Depending on your viewpoint, the court's discussion of the per se and regulatory takings doctrines, subsequent to its ripeness holding, may be considered either dicta or an alternative holding.

In a de novo review of the trial court's findings on mixed questions of law and fact, the Rhode Island Supreme Court held that Mr. Palazzolo's claim for compensation was not ripe for review. The court's holding rested upon what it characterized as "two crucial facts." First, Mr. Palazzolo never applied to develop a 74-lot subdivision, which meant that he did not receive a "final decision" from the state, as required by *Williamson County Regional Planning Comm'n v. Hamilton Bank of Johnson City.*[21] Second, Mr. Palazzolo did not seek approval for "less ambitious development plans."[22] Mr. Palazzolo's failure to consider "less grandiose" plans defeated his claim that he was denied all beneficial use of his land, because other development might be possible. The court stated that later applications must be "substantially different from the original application."[23] Mr. Palazzolo maintains that he did in fact consider less ambitious uses because his 1985 application sought to develop 11 acres, while his 1983 application was for 18 acres.

The Rhode Island Supreme Court's alternative holding/dicta addressed two issues. First, under *Lucas v. South Carolina Coastal Council,*[24] the court upheld the trial court's finding that there was no per se, categorical taking. CRMC would have approved a homesite on the turnaround at the end of the gravel road on Mr. Palazzolo's parcel. This apparently is the disputed "uplands" portion of the site. Mr. Palazzolo maintains it only amounts to one-tenth of an acre, but no one seems to know for sure. Since there was undisputed evidence, according to the court, that, as developed, the upland portion of Mr. Palazzolo's parcel could be worth $200,000, and the unfilled wetlands were worth $157,000 as an open-space gift, the fact that Mr. Palazzolo could not earn a speculative $3,150,000 did not deprive him of all beneficial use of his land. We note that Mr. Palazzolo's original investment in the land was $13,000,[25] though the number doesn't seem to have been in play in the litigation. But after *City of Monterey v. Del Monte Dunes at Monterey, Ltd.,*[26] in which the developers sold the land for more than they paid for it and the U.S. Supreme Court still upheld a $1.45 million jury takings award, the value issue may not be all that important if the use isn't reasonable or if the Court thinks the landowner was treated unfairly.

When I visited the property in July 2001, I noticed the lot abutting "The Great Escape" to the east on the street and not on the water was for sale. It is on the market for $250,000, so some of the "speculative" numbers may not be far off the mark. The market for coastal properties in New England has been very strong in recent years.

The Rhode Island Supreme Court also affirmed the trial court's finding that Mr. Palazzolo did not become owner of the parcel until 1978, when SGI's corporate charter was revoked. Thus, Mr. Palazzolo took title to the parcel with knowledge of the wetlands laws.

The court's rationale rested in part upon its conclusion that *Lucas* requires reviewing courts to consider whether a landowner originally had the right to engage in the desired use. The court was also concerned that determining that the time of acquisition of title was immaterial might lead to "pernicious 'takings claims' based on speculative purchases in which an individual intentionally purchases land, and then seeks compensation from the state for that 'taking.'"[27] This conclusion would also result in regulatory takings being treated differently from physical takings, since any purchaser of land could claim that a prior regulation was a taking.

Second, after concluding that there was no per se taking of Mr. Palazzolo's land, the Rhode Island court examined the regulatory takings issue under the law established by *Penn Cent. Transp. Co. v. City of New York.*[28] *Penn Central* requires that the court make an ad hoc factual inquiry and consider the character of the governmental regulation, the economic impact of the regulation, and the extent to which the regulation has interfered with distinct investment-backed expectations. The court concluded that Mr.

Palazzolo could not have had investment-backed expectations because he took title to his land in 1978, seven years after the wetlands regulations were in place. In other words, the court concluded that a landowner on "notice" of existing regulations cannot have investment-backed expectations to develop contrary to those regulations.

§ 8.2   *Issues Before the Court*

On June 21, 2000, Mr. Palazzolo, now represented by the Pacific Legal Foundation—the juggernaut of property rights advocacy—petitioned the U.S. Supreme Court for certiorari, which was granted on October 10, 2000. Mr. Palazzolo's petition presented three important unresolved issues:

1. Should a landowner be entitled to compensation if regulations restricting development existed when the landowner took title to the property?
2. If the government has repeatedly denied a landowner's development plans, should the landowner be required to submit a proposal for a "less ambitious" use before claiming that a compensable taking has occurred?
3. How far can government regulations go before they become a taking? In other words, are permissible uses of a parcel of land economically viable solely because a regulated parcel still retains some value greater than zero?

Somewhat related to the third issue is the so-called "numerator-denominator" or "relevant parcel" question, an issue that commentators speculated the Court might address. If the numerator is the property claimed to be taken—the 18 acres (more or less)—what is the denominator? Is it the 18 acres plus that small area of developable "upland," or the larger original parcel from which six lots were sold and developed? Although the parties did not directly put this issue before the Court, the record shows that Mr. Palazzolo previously sold some of his upland lots for development. As we mentioned, Mr. Palazzolo disputes whether he had any ownership interest in the land when the six upland parcels were sold. In its June 28, 2001, decision the Court mused, then refused to address the issue.

According to Mr. Palazzolo, the principal issue is whether he was singled out to provide a public benefit, in which case Rhode Island should compensate him for his loss. Mr. Palazzolo does not challenge Rhode Island's authority to regulate its wetlands.

In fact, in interviews he articulates his support of government regulations, especially to prevent pollution. Mr. Palazzolo says he "only would do what the law would allow, provided I do no harm." But Mr. Palazzolo does challenge whether he should bear the burden of providing the public benefit of wetlands preservation. In response, the state maintained that Mr. Palazzolo's takings claim is not ripe because he never applied for the 74-lot subdivision that is the basis of his takings claim and because he became the owner of the land after regulations were in place. The state further maintained that Mr. Palazzolo has not established a taking under the *Lucas* doctrine because his land still has positive value.

Interest groups filed amicus briefs on both sides. Organizations such as the American Farm Bureau Federation, the National Association of Home Builders, and various property rights groups, including the California Coastal Property Owners Association, the Defenders of Property Rights, the Institute for Justice, and the Washington Legal Foundation, filed briefs on behalf of Mr. Palazzolo. Amicus briefs for Rhode Island came from the United States; 18 states, including New York, New Jersey, Connecticut, and California; several counties; coastal scientists; the American Planning Association; and the National Wildlife Federation, among others.

§ 8.3   Ripeness Through Futility Exception

The June 28, 2001, decision has one of the oddest beginnings for a U.S. Supreme Court opinion in a land use case, though it is certainly entertaining. The first four pages of the decision read like a Fodor's history and guide to Westerly, Rhode Island, describing its settlement in colonial times and commenting on the area's attractiveness as a summer resort with its cool breezes and broad beaches.

Mapping and tracking the Justices' various opinions and positions results in a diagram reminiscent of the Human Genome Project. The *Cliff's Notes*™ version is:

1. Justice Kennedy wrote the majority opinion and was joined by Justices Rehnquist, O'Connor, Scalia, and Thomas.
2. Justices O'Connor and Scalia concurred in the opinion, while sniping at each other in separate opinions on how takings should be analyzed post-*Palazzolo*.
3. Justice Stevens filed a concurring opinion in which he joined in the majority opinion on the ripeness issue but dissented as to the notice defense and the rest of the decision. Justice Stevens made it "pellucidly clear" that he valued the notice defense.

4. Justice Ginsburg dissented and was joined by Justices Souter and Breyer. They thought the case wasn't ripe and that the Court was the victim of a "bait and switch" scam.
5. Justice Breyer filed a separate dissenting opinion in which he focused on the reasonableness of the investment-backed expectations.

The Court's factual summary in section I is good reading and consistent with our description of the background.

To the surprise of some observers, the majority (a bare majority) held that Mr. Palazzolo's claim was ripe and that his acquisition of title *after* the adoption of public regulation affecting his property did not bar his taking claim. The majority also held that his claim was not "categorical" (the *Lucas* total deprivation type) but at most was an ordinary takings claim subject to the multifactor analysis of *Penn Central*. Thus, the case goes back to the Rhode Island courts for adjudication under the multifactor analysis, unless of course the parties can settle. That seems unlikely, however, as Rhode Island Attorney General Sheldon Whitehouse wants to be governor and will probably find it difficult to give an inch. Astonishingly, after an obvious defeat in the U.S. Supreme Court, he simply declared victory. The *Rhode Island Law Tribune* had two articles, one a week after the decision and the second a month later. In the first article, "U.S. Supreme Court Rules Against Palazzolo in Land Dispute," Attorney General Whitehouse says: "We're happy with it. The important point is, under the theory Mr. Palazzolo pursued he lost and he lost flat out."[29] In the second piece, "Bark Worse Than Bite in *Palazzolo* Decision," he offers: "On the underlying legal issues, the state of Rhode Island ... partly won outright; in other areas, the ruling was consistent with Rhode Island's position."[30] Go figure.

On the ripeness issue, the Court fashioned a refinement of the "final decision" ripeness requirement that takes property owners and governments out of the multiple applications box. The Court held that multiple applications for ever-smaller developments are not necessary, even if the first application is "grandiose," if the public regulations are "unequivocal" and the government's application of such regulations leaves no question that a lesser development could or would be approved.[31]

Perhaps what distinguishes the *Palazzolo* case is that the state of Rhode Island suggested all along the way that it might consider different applications. Apparently, if the regulations are unequivocal, and their application is such that an invitation to apply for development is disingenuous, further applications need not be pursued for the claim to be ripe.

It is apparent that the Rhode Island statutes and Coastal Resources Management Plan might be "loosened up" to avoid being construed as unequivocal and thus not foreclose the chance of getting a lesser development approved. The obvious risk for the government, however, is that it would open the door to claims for relief across the board.

In the process of presenting this refinement to the ripeness rule, the Court reiterated support for the general rule that the first of two prongs of ripeness—finality—must be met. Significantly, the Court also identified *Del Monte Dunes* as conditioning the finality rule with a requirement that the government "may not burden property by imposition of repetitive or unfair land-use procedures in order to avoid a final decision."[32] The use of the word "unfair" in describing the holding in *Del Monte Dunes* is intriguing, because it suggests a continuing undercurrent of concern for fundamental fairness in the Court's land use decisions, as I speculated earlier.

The possibility of getting more than one house on the small area of upland at the eastern end of the site "comes too late in the day for purposes of litigation,"[33] in the view of the Court, in large measure because the value of $200,000 was uncontested and cited as fact in the state's brief in opposition.

Remarkably important is the Court's holding that it is not necessary for a property owner to apply for approval of specific activity for a developable portion of the land if the government agrees that such development would not be permitted.[34] The Court expressly disavowed any intent to preclude states from insisting on certain planning procedures, such as applying for local subdivision approval, before applying for state permits.[35] Further, the Court noted that determination of "just compensation" in a takings case does not require rejection of permits at all levels of government, but that valuation is based on fair market value determined by an appraisal, which necessarily includes the regulatory restrictions on the property.[36] In addition, since in this particular case the state based its lack-of-ripeness claim on federal law—*Williamson County*—rather than on any state law ripeness or exhaustion principles, it could not claim that state procedures for the sequencing of applications between the federal and state levels precluded the takings claim from being ripe.

§ 8.4   *Notice Defense Greatly Weakened*

As for the so-called notice defense, the Court held that the effect of the state court's ruling was to create "a single, sweeping rule:

A purchaser or a successive title holder like petitioner is deemed to have notice of an earlier-enacted restriction and is barred from claiming that it effects a taking."[37]

The algorithm inherent in this theory, said the Court, is that because property rights are created by the state, they can be taken by the state through subsequent legislation. Later owners are then barred from claiming any injury, because they purchased or took title with notice of the limitation.[38]

And here comes the most quotable quote from the decision: "The State may not put so potent a Hobbesian stick into the Lockean bundle."[39] "Were we to accept the State's rule, the postenactment transfer of title would absolve the State of its obligation to defend any action restricting land use, no matter how extreme or unreasonable. A State would be allowed, in effect, to put an expiration date on the Takings Clause. This ought not to be the rule. Future generations, too, have a right to challenge unreasonable limitations on the use and value of land."[40]

Some might argue that this is a bit of an overstatement, because the notice defense certainly does not apply to the reasonableness of the application of a restriction. What the Court apparently meant to say, when you take this quote in the context of its total holding, is that there shouldn't be an absolute bar on takings claims based on a mere change in ownership.

The Court's reasoning included several illustrations where the most draconian construction of the notice defense would have pernicious results—an old owner who dies before ripening a claim, a young owner who gets to exercise his rights only because he can live long enough to ripen them, and an owner in strong economic condition who can afford to hold out long enough to ripen his claim as compared to someone who is forced to sell before his claim is ripe.[41] The Court said, "The Takings Clause is not so quixotic. A blanket rule that purchasers with notice have no compensation right when a claim becomes ripe is too blunt an instrument to accord with the duty to compensate for what is taken."[42]

The Court found "controlling precedent" for this holding in *Nollan v. California Coastal Comm'n*:[43] "So long as the Commission could not have deprived the prior owners of the easement without compensating them, 'the prior owners must be understood to have transferred their full property rights in conveying the lot.'"[44] Property rights advocates were doubtless dancing around their campfires on the night of June 28, 2001, while government lawyers held their ears, attempting to block the noise of the joyous celebration.

The Court rejected the state's argument that the wetlands regulation had become a "background principle" of state law.[45] The passage of title could not, said the Court, transform a regulation into a background principle. "A regulation or common-law rule cannot be a background principle for some owners but not for others."[46] Instead, said the Court, to determine whether an existing, general law is a background principle, there must be an inquiry into objective factors, including the nature of the land use proscribed, the degree of harm to the public or to nearby property, and such similar factors.[47] But because this was not a categorical taking, the background principles won't be applied on remand.

§ 8.5   Categorical Takings Limited

While the Court said that leaving a property owner with a "token interest" was not sufficient for the state to escape paying just compensation, it did not appear to the Court that Mr. Palazzolo was left with just a token interest: "A regulation permitting a landowner to build a substantial residence on an 18-acre parcel does not leave the property 'economically idle.'"[48] Mr. Palazzolo's property, according to the Court, still has significant worth.[49]

In its holding, the Court limited the *Lucas*-type categorical taking to the plain language of that decision—"denies all economically beneficial or productive use of land."[50] By holding that the $200,000 development value uncontested by either party was sufficient, either in absolute terms or compared with the claimed $3,150,000, Mr. Palazzolo was not "depriv[ed] of all economic value."[51] In other words, $200,000, or 6.3 percent of the value of the property fully developed, is sufficient to be "substantial" and prevent an inverse condemnation from being categorized as a categorical taking under *Lucas*. A landowner with "substantial" value is subject to the *Penn Central* multifactor analysis.

The Court refused to decide anything in its opinion about the numerator-denominator problem or the relevant parcel rule, because the Court apparently accepted the entire parcel of approximately 20 acres as the relevant parcel, and the area potentially taken as the roughly 18 acres of wetlands exclusive of the small upland area available for development of at least one single-family house. [52]

§ 8.6   *The Other Opinions*

Justice O'Connor, in her concurring opinion, stated that investment-backed expectations are an important part of the three-pronged analysis of *Penn Central* but are certainly not determinative one way or the other.[53] She believes that the timing of a regulation's enactment is relevant under *Penn Central's* reasonable investment-backed expectations analysis.

Justice Scalia, in his concurring opinion, took exception to Justice O'Connor's view that the existence of a regulation at the time of property acquisition is a factor to be considered in determining whether there are investment-backed expectations that would provide support for a valid takings claim. Justice Scalia said: "The 'investment-backed expectations' that the law will take into account do not include the assumed validity of a restriction that in fact deprives property of so much of its value as to be unconstitutional. Which is to say that a *Penn Central* taking [citation omitted], no less than a total taking, is not absolved by the transfer of title."[54]

Justice Stevens, who concurred in part and dissented in part, agreed with the majority that the case was ripe but dissented from the judgment and. in particular, the question of the notice defense. Justice Stevens dwelled on timing: "If the regulations imposed a compensable injury on anyone, it was on the owner of the property at the moment the regulations were adopted. Given the trial court's finding that petitioner did not own the property at that time, [citation omitted] . . . it is pellucidly clear that he has no standing to claim that the promulgation of the regulations constituted a taking of any part of the property that he subsequently acquired."[55] What is pellucidly clear now is that this rigid description of the notice defense is no longer the law. Justice Stevens fears the Court's notice defense holding will result in "a tremendous—and tremendously capricious—one-time transfer of wealth from society at large to those individuals who happen to hold title to large tracts of land at the moment this legal question is permanently resolved."[56]

Justice Ginsburg wrote a dissenting opinion in which Justices Souter and Breyer joined. The dissenters found the Court's holding on ripeness "inaccurate" and "inequitable" because the record was "ambiguous," and because in the state courts Mr. Palazzolo did not seek development of just the upland portion of his land.[57] Mr. Palazzolo cast his claim so that the state had no reason to pursue the issue of upland development. The dissenters said they "would reject Palazzolo's bait-and-switch ploy and affirm" the Rhode

Island court.[58] By "bait-and-switch," the dissenters refer to Mr. Palazzolo changing his claim from a categorical *Lucas*-type taking into one in which the agreed-upon $200,000 value became both the floor and the ceiling on value. The dissenters believe that if the state of Rhode Island had had sufficient opportunity, it might have approved more than one house on the upland, which would have greatly increased the value. For that reason, said the dissenters, the case is not ripe.[59] Finally, the dissenters said that even if the case were ripe in their view, they would agree with Justices O'Connor, Stevens, and Breyer on the notice defense issue that the "transfer of title can impair a takings claim."[60]

Justice Breyer, in his dissenting opinion, agreed with Justice Ginsburg that the takings claim was not ripe, and he agreed with Justice O'Connor "that the simple fact that a piece of property has changed hands (for example, by inheritance) does not always and *automatically* bar a takings claim."[61] He believes the focus should be on the reasonableness of the investment-backed expectations, but that the timing is not dispositive.

§ 8.7   Probable Effects of the Decision

§ 8.7(a)   Effects on Property Owners

What does the *Palazzolo* decision portend for property owners and governments in the future? Property owners will find it somewhat easier to get over the ripeness hurdle where land use regulation is unambiguous, the government has applied the law consistently, and there are no waivers, variances, or exceptions available. The Court clearly articulated the futility exception to the final decision ripeness requirement.

Property owners who purchased with notice of restrictive regulatory programs will not be barred from trying their claims. Actually, the notice rule never was a jurisdictional bar, but it could be used to defeat a claim on motions short of trial or at trial. It is possible that more property owners will bring claims if they perceive a greater chance of success in the absence of the notice defense. I say "perceive" because the notice defense never stopped a property owner from bringing a case and because there is nothing in the decision to indicate that more cases will be won by property owners at trial.

Few takings cases are successful. A rough count from the reported cases is probably 5 percent. No one knows how many cases were never brought because they were deterred by the notice defense, and life is too short to try to count the takings cases that were lost by property owners because of the notice defense alone, independent of any multifactor analysis.

Arguably, the disappearance of the notice defense will encourage more cases to be brought, and some cases that property owners lost, such as *Good v. United States*,[62] might have fared better if they had followed *Palazzolo*. With more cases being brought, more being tried, and more being won by property owners absent the notice defense, there will be an increase in successful claims, but I suspect it will be minimal. For example, a New Jersey appellate court just a month after *Palazzolo* ho-hummed the question of the successors' right to bring a wetlands taking claim ripened in a prior owner in just one sentence, with cites to *Nollan* and *Palazzolo*: "East Cape May is entitled to assert whatever development rights its predecessors would have had."[63] The court upheld the trial court's holding that there was no temporary taking and remanded for the creation of regulations in support of a compromise plan, hinting that such a plan would leave enough value that it would "not necessarily result in a taking."[64] This is likely to be the usual pattern: "Fine, you can make your claim and have your trial, but there is no taking."

However, as a practitioner working both sides of the street, I suspect that with the end of the notice defense with an increase in claims (most brought as section 1983 actions[65] with potential money damages and attorneys' fees) and the heightened threat of plenary trials, government will cave in to property owner pressures a little earlier and a little more frequently, and more cases will settle earlier and for more money and concessions. Regulators are also likely to go easier on property owners at the administrative level. The changes will be subtle, but they are likely to occur, just as we saw after *First English,* when government got the word that it would have to pay money for takings.

Finally, the end of the notice defense has already been used in support of a property owner's application for variances. Maryland's highest court cited *Palazzolo* in response to a claim by neighbors opposing variances granted for a gas station.[66] The variances were necessary to meet the requirements of a special exception. The neighbors argued that a property owner who purchases knowing that he will need variances may not contend that the restrictions constitute a hardship. The court cited *Palazzolo* apparently as authority for the principle that someone can purchase property with knowledge of restrictions and then apply for variances and make claims for hardship. I say "apparently" because the court immediately after the citation points out that the owner purchased without knowledge of the need for variances.[67] Still, it is an interesting point.

§ 8.7(b)   *Decision Effects on Government*

Palazzolo is another small step in the pro-property rights evolution of the takings issue. The movement in that direction began with *First English* and *Nollan* in 1987. Each step in that direction has been met with over-reaction by both property owners and government. One prominent law firm in its instant analysis of the case proclaimed, "The *Palazzolo* decision has a potentially huge impact upon a wide range of environmental regulations."[68] At almost the same time, one of the country's leading land use law professors opined, "*Palazzolo* does not advance takings law much further than it was before the decision."[69] The reality is, like most things, somewhere in the middle, with a noticeably increased burden on the government and a shifting of perceptions at least against cutting-edge, tough regulation.

But government can find real comfort in seeing the ripeness rules unchanged. The two-pronged finality and state compensation requirements of *Williamson County* are still with us. True, the Court reiterated the futility exception more clearly than ever before, but it has been around and used by lower courts for years. Nothing changed on that front. Actually, *Palazzolo* held "school call" for governments while addressing the futility exception. The Court indirectly told governments that if they want to avoid the futility exception they should have flexible and subjective regulations, they should administer them on a somewhat ad hoc basis, and they ought to consider making available broad exceptions and variances ("the instant case does not require us to pass upon the authority of a state to insist in such cases that landowners follow normal planning procedures or to enact rules to control damage awards based on hypothetical uses that should have been reviewed in the normal course... ").[70] Smart governments will want to consider requiring ripeness decisions before takings claims can be brought and enabling or even mandating alternative dispute resolution.[71]

Some solace for governments can be found in the always-comforting arms of the statute of limitations. First, *Palazzolo* reiterated the rule that "when there is a physical taking of property ... in compliance with the law, it is the owner *at the time of the taking* who is entitled to compensation."[72] The Court of Federal Claims cited this passage in *Banks v. United States*[73] for that principle five weeks after *Palazzolo*. In *Banks,* plaintiffs were waterfront owners on Lake Michigan who alleged that maintenance of jetties by the U.S. Army Corps of Engineers from 1950 to 1989 caused erosion of their properties. They sued in 1989. The court granted the government's motion to dismiss. The statute of limitations for filing suit in the Court of Federal Claims is six years.[74] The court held, based on the evidence, that the action accrued in 1989 and the statute ran in 1995.[75] Citing their rules, the court also said that the plaintiffs who acquired after 1989 could not assert the claims of their predecessors that accrued in 1989.[76]

How about using the loss of the notice defense in *Palazzolo* as a basis for *tougher* regulation? Wisconsin, with probably the country's strongest recognition of public trust rights in wetlands and coastal waters,[77] has suggested just that in a recent decision, *ABKA v. Wisconsin Department of Natural Resources.*[78] In *ABKA,* the court of appeals held that the proposed conversion of a 407-boat-slip marina into "dockominiums" (where individuals buy a real property interest in upland with an appurtenant right to occupy a slip) violated the state's public trust doctrine.[79]

Although the court says that none of the parties briefed or argued *Palazzolo* and therefore it would not rely on the decision, the court argued at length that the loss of the notice defense opened the door to claims by dockominium owners in the future if the state ever interfered with their entitlement to their dockominium units.[80] Nice argument—government should not allow property owners to fractionalize their ownership interest in real property and appurtenant riparian rights because it may create future liability for damages.

Unfortunately, as a matter of law the theory doesn't hold water. The sum of the parts is not necessarily greater than the whole, and even if it were, property owners are compensated for increased value created by their good marketing and physical and operational improvements. Unit purchasers of dockominiums can't acquire anything more than the seller owned, so their claims would never be any greater than that of a single marina owner or the members of a nonstock not-for-profit yacht club or any other variation of ownership of the same real property and appurtenant riparian interest.[81] Regardless, it is a clever way to turn *Palazzolo* on its head, and we will doubtless see references to this decision.

The reinforcement of the analysis of investment-backed expectations by Justice O'Connor in her concurring opinion, joined by Justices Stevens, Breyer, Ginsburg, and Souter, puts a majority of the Court behind the case-by-case and fact-by-fact investment-backed expectations analysis of *Penn Central*–type claims. This, I believe, will remain almost as powerful a weapon to attack takings claims as the notice defense was. Professor Mandelker in chapter 2 has a wonderfully detailed analysis of what the Court did not decide on this issue and the opportunity it missed for straightening out some problems.[82]

Categorical takings cases have been more tightly bound by the Court's identification of a threshold of $200,000, or 6.3 percent of value, as being outside the realm of categorical takings.[83] The U.S. Court of Claims, just two months before *Palazzolo*, reviewed its own decisions for *Penn Central* balancing test claims and concluded that it was used where the value lost by regulation was 85 percent or greater.[84] Can it be that there is no regulatory taking up to an 85 percent loss in value and then a possible *Penn Central* analysis up to a 94 percent or higher reduction, and no categorical taking in any event for property valued at at least 6 percent of its pre-regulation level? That is indeed a small subset of all loss-of-value-by-regulation cases.

Unresolved, but likely to develop in the government's favor, is whether legislative enactments and regulatory programs may be construed to be background principles of law that make investment-backed expectations untenable and shift the analysis in favor of the government. Does a state coastal management law, enacted to implement the federal law, embody in any controlling respects the common law of public trust and nuisance, such that it is essentially the codification of background principles? That argument will be hard to make in the face of a history of uncontrolled filling of wetlands before regulation.

The Court confirmed that statutes (even the wetland statute at issue in *Palazzolo*) may constitute background principles that defeat takings liability where the statute is "derived from a State's legal tradition."[85] This "derived from" language suggests that it could include not only statutes that codify common-law nuisance principles but also those that are reasonable extensions of those principles. Some have argued that background principles include only the common law, but *Palazzolo* seems to reject that position.

Local government lawyers should also keep an eye on what happens in the South Carolina Supreme Court decision in *McQueen v. South Carolina Department of Health and Environmental Control*,[86] which the Supreme Court vacated and remanded in light of *Palazzolo*. The South Carolina Supreme Court found that McQueen did not have reasonable investment-backed expectations that he would be able to develop his coastal property. He had owned the property continuously before and after the state regulations were imposed. Glenn Sugameli, senior counsel with the National Wildlife Federation, is quoted in an *Environment Reporter* article on July 6, 2001: "There is plenty of language in *Palazzolo* to allow the South Carolina Supreme Court to reach the same conclusion it did before."

While Glenn Sugameli may be hopeful that the South Carolina Supreme Court will not change its decision, James S. Burling, who represented Mr. Palazzolo before the Court, is quoted in the same article: "The *Palazzolo* decision puts a stop to the idea that the mere passage of time changes the background principles that are taken into consideration when determining whether a property owner's expectations are reasonable." This case will be a good opportunity to see how investment-backed expectations are analyzed in the absence of the notice defense.

§ 8.7(c) *Effects on Mr. Palazzolo*

Our prediction—and you can take this with a large grain of Westerly, Rhode Island, sea salt—is that Mr. Palazzolo and the state of Rhode Island will find it difficult to settle this on remand, at least until Rhode Island Attorney General Whitehouse is done with his bid for governor. If the case is tried under the *Penn Central* multifactor analysis, the Rhode Island courts will find that there is no taking, because upland is available for development and has value, and the U. S. Supreme Court will deny certiorari. On the other hand, it may be that $200,000, or 6.3 percent of the full development value, is not a reasonable economic use under Rhode Island law.

As I finished editing this chapter, Mr. Palazzolo called to tell me he has been denied approval for a one-house septic system on the upland portion of his land. So now he claims he has no use whatsoever.[87]

§ 8.8 *The Partial Takings Issue*

The Supreme Court, as I noted, plucked Mr. Palazzolo's case out of the *Lucas* categorical takings box, which is a very small box indeed, and plunked it squarely in the large field of partial regulatory takings.

Since 1980 there's been some controversy over whether there even is such a thing as a partial regulatory taking because of the decision by the U.S. Supreme Court in *Agins*.[88] Even though I assume here that *Agins* is "virtually" dead (the movie "Weekend at Bernie's" comes to mind, in which a fun-loving group propped up their dead host so the party could go on), the best and brightest land use lawyers are still squabbling over the issue. Michael Berger says in response to my question of whether *Palazzolo* has killed off *Agins*: "I always thought that the *Lucas* categorical rule was a restatement of the *Agins* economically viable prong."[89] David Callies, author of chapter 6, responded to the same question, but with the opposite conclusion: "Yes, and [*Agins*] has been dead for at least a decade," citing *Lucas*.[90] John Delaney disagrees: "I think *Agins* definitely *lives* and is not subsumed into *Penn Central*, if for no other reason than the *Penn Central* test would be awkward to apply in cases involving exactions."[91]

Backing up for a moment to 1978 and the *Penn Central* decision, let me reiterate its three-factor test embraced by the *Palazzolo* Court:

> The *economic impact* of the regulation on the claimant and, particularly, the extent to which the regulation has interfered with *distinct investment-backed expectations* are, of course, relevant considerations. [Citing *Goldblatt*.] So, too, is the *character of the governmental action*. A 'taking' may more readily be found when the interference with property can be characterized as a physical invasion by government... than when interference arises from some public program adjusting the benefits and burdens of economic life to promote the common good. (Emphasis added.)[92]

The Court did not say these factors are exclusive, but it has not expanded on them in later decisions. The lower federal courts and the state courts have applied this test numerous times since.[93] However, the *Agins* decision just two years later in 1980 seemed to include a new and distinctly different constitutional standard for takings:

> The application of a general zoning law to particular property effects a taking if the ordinance does not substantially advance legitimate state interests or denies an owner economically viable use of his land....[94]

In nearly all of the cases where the *Agins* test has been stated, meeting either part of the test is usually considered a taking.[95]

The first prong of the *Agins* test is problematic because it arises out of a substantive due process case and has been applied inconsistently.[96] The next time the Court used language about substantially advancing governmental purposes, it was in a slightly different form in *Dolan v. City of Tigard* with the requirement that governments prove they are "substantially advancing legitimate governmental interests" in imposing permit conditions.[97] Mrs. Dolan claimed a taking when the city of Tigard required her to provide a walkway and bicycle path along the bank of a creek, permitting physical invasion of private commercial property.

But it is really the second prong of the *Agins* test that raised the question of whether partial regulatory takings were still possible. The second prong requires that an owner be deprived of "economically viable use of his land." We find the origins of the second prong in an obscure footnote of *Penn Central*:

> We emphasize that our holding today is on the present record, which in turn is based on Penn Central's present ability to use the Terminal for its intended purposes and in a gainful fashion. The city conceded at oral argument that if appellants can demonstrate at some point in the future that circumstances have so changed that the Terminal ceases to be "economically viable," appellants may obtain relief. See Tr. of Oral Arg. 42-43.[98]

Commentators and the courts have tried to figure out if this second prong of *Agins* is a substitute for the three-part test of *Penn Central* or some equivalent.[99] Another idea is that the second prong of *Agins* requiring the deprivation of all economically viable use comprehends only the economic impact and the investment-backed expectations parts of the three-part *Penn Central* test and not the private burden/public benefit part.[100] It is a doctrinal mess.

This continuing controversy was played out in front of the U.S. Supreme Court when the solicitor general, in his brief in *Del Monte Dunes,* attempted to limit the first prong of the *Agins* rule. He argued in his brief:

> We believe, however, that the [*Agins* "substantially advance language"] may properly be regarded as dictum, and that it is unfounded insofar as it suggests that land-use regulation may be deemed a taking that requires the payment of just compensation if it fails substantially to further a legitimate governmental objective.[101]

During the oral argument of *Del Monte Dunes*, Chief Justice Rehnquist made short work of this attempt to deflate *Agins*:

> Chief Justice Rehnquist: "Was that challenged by the petitioner, the *Agins* rule?"
> Mr. Kneedler: "It was not, Mr. Chief Justice."
> Chief Justice Rehnquist: "Ordinarily we don't accept any new questions or positions from an amicus."[102]

The Court in *Del Monte Dunes* curtly addressed this sleight-of-hand attempt to get *Agins* back before the Court:

> The city did not challenge below the applicability or

continued viability of the general test for regulatory takings liability recited by these authorities [*Agins*, et al.]
and upon which the jury instructions appear to have been
modeled. Given the posture of the case before us, we
decline the suggestions of amici to revisit these precedents.[103]

Palazzolo seems to support the concept that the *Agins* two-
prong test is simply an inartful restatement of the *Penn Central*
three-part test. There are only two references to *Agins* in *Palazzolo*.
Here is the first one:

Since *Mahon*, we have given some, but not too specific,
guidance to courts confronted with deciding whether a
particular government action goes too far and effects a
regulatory taking. First, we have observed, with certain
qualifications,. . . that a regulation which "denies all economically beneficial or productive use of land" will require compensation under the takings Clause. *Lucas*, . . . ;
see also id. at 1035 (Kennedy, J., concurring); *Agins v.
City of Tiburon*, 447 U.S. 255, 261, 65 L. Ed. 2d 106,
100 S. Ct. 2138 (1980). Where a regulation places limitations on land that fall short of eliminating all economically beneficial use, a taking nonetheless may have
occurred, depending on a complex of factors including
the regulation's economic effect on the landowner, the
extent to which the regulation interferes with reasonable
investment-backed expectations, and the character of the
government action. *Penn Central, supra*, at 124. These
inquires are informed by the purpose of the Takings
Clause, which is to prevent the government from "forcing some people alone to bear public burdens which, in
all fairness and justice, should be borne by the public as
a whole." *Armstrong v. United States*, 364 U.S. 40, 49, 4
L. Ed. 2d 1554, 80 S. Ct. 1563 (1960).[104]

Look where *Agins* is cited. The Court is saying that the *Agins*
standard is equivalent to the *Lucas* categorical taking. If a regulation takes away all of the economically beneficial or productive
use of the land, it will be a taking.

The Court in the second half of that paragraph describes the
Penn Central analysis as applying to regulations that limit the use
of property but do so short of eliminating all economically beneficial use. The only other reference to *Agins* in *Palazzolo* is on
the issue of ripeness and contrasts *Agins* with *Williamson County*.[105]

Thus, partial regulatory takings are recognized by the Supreme Court and are subject to the *Penn Central* test. Complete takings of value or reasonable use are categorically takings of the *Lucas* type and are measured by the tests in *Lucas* and in *Agins*. This does not answer the question of the meaning of the first prong of *Agins*, which remains essentially a description of a substantive due process test.

It is unlikely that the Supreme Court sees a need to have economic loss as a necessary and indispensable part of the calculus under the three-part *Penn Central* rule test. It is essential only that there be either a very large loss in value in a partial regulatory taking or no reasonable use remaining in the property.

Del Monte Dunes is a stark example of this latter broad category of reasonable use takings cases in which economic value is not in play. In *Del Monte Dunes,* the property owner sold its property for more than it paid for it before the jury found the taking and equal protection violation and awarded substantial money damages. While it is true that there were substantial costs in simply owning and holding the property, including an environmental cleanup, the property was sold for more than the owners paid for it. And ultimately, the Supreme Court upheld the award of just compensation for the taking.

After *Palazzolo*, it is clear that *Penn Central* rules. The *Palazzolo* decision refers to *Penn Central* 15 times and to *Agins* only once as to the taking issue, and in that one reference, as I noted, it cites *Lucas* first, apparently driving *Agins* deep into the categorical takings corner.

Still, when you have a case like *Del Monte Dunes*, a reasonable use case with a powerful but unstated undercurrent of fundamental fairness and a concern about governmental bad faith, you necessarily have the first prong of *Agins* bridging substantive due process and taking claims.

Remember, the three-part test of *Penn Central* is probably not exclusive. There may be other tests. Remember also that the three-part test of *Penn Central* requires balancing within each of the three tests and between them. It is possible that there may be a little economic loss, a low level of investment-backed expectations but a wantonly unfair burdening of a private property owner for the public's good, and that would be a taking. Mrs. Dolan's bike path case is close to this example. Her 17,000-square-foot hardware and plumbing supply store, which she proposed to expand from 9,700 square feet, had to be moved only a few feet to accommodate the proposed bike path. The bike path would have little or no impact on the value of her property or perhaps even her investment-backed expectations, because it would be below the 100-year flood plain elevation in an area that could not be developed. The bike path did not affect her lot coverage or setbacks or any other development standard, so there was no adverse impact on her. But the Court found that it was patently unfair—today they would say too potent a Hobbesian stick in the Lockean bundle—to require her to give up her right to exclude people from her property so the public could have the benefit of walking and bicycling along Fanno Creek. In *Dolan,* the burden on the private property owner was far too great, especially since it took away the right to exclude others.

On the other hand, there may be instances of very large losses of value damaging substantial investment-backed expectations that are not compensable because the importance of protecting the public is so great—perhaps to the point where the common-law restriction, statute, or regulation rises to the level of a background principle. Prohibiting development on and adjacent to a vernal pool that is the critical habitat for endangered amphibians and subject to a common-law and statutory public trust might be an example of a such a case.[106]

§ 8.9   Conclusions

Post-*Palazzolo*, local government lawyers will still be able to defend against takings claims. The damage of *Palazzolo* is limited to the loss of the notice defense. The U.S. Supreme Court has acknowledged the futility exception, but the two-part ripeness requirement of finality and the pursuit of state compensation remains intact. Property owners will get somewhat better results at the administrative level because of the threat posed by *Palazzolo*. They will get to try more cases and win a few more. They will be able to settle more cases in their favor.

The multifactor *Penn Central* analysis will continue to apply in nearly all regulatory takings cases, and investment-backed expectations analysis is alive and well. The concurring opinions by Justice O'Connor and Justice Scalia are particularly worth reading, because they highlight the debate on the role that investment-backed expectations will have in future takings cases. Much of the time at trial in takings cases will be devoted to a review of those expectations as part of the multifactor analysis required by *Penn Central.*

The sun will continue to rise in the morning and set at night. Our cars will get stuck in the snow. Lovers will quarrel. Babies will make us smile. Someone will bungle the words to *The Star-Spangled Banner* at a baseball game. Life will go on as it has before, even after *Palazzolo*.

Notes

1. 121 S. Ct. 2448 (2001).

2. *See* VIRGINIA LEE BURTON, MIKE MULLIGAN AND HIS STEAMSHOVEL (Houghton Mifflin Co. 1967) (1939).

3. Palazzolo v. State *ex rel.* Tavares, 746 A.2d 707 (R.I. 2000).

4. *Id.* at 715.

5. Palazzolo v. Coastal Res. Mgmt. Council, 1995 WL 941370 (R.I. Super. Ct. Jan. 5, 1995) at *1.

6. *Id.*

7. *Palazzolo,* 746 A.2d at 709.

8. *Id. at* 709-10.

9. *Id.* at 710.

10. Dolan v. City of Tigard, 512 U.S. 374 (1994). *See also* Dwight H. Merriam, with R.J. Lyman, *Dealing With Dolan, Practically and Jurisprudentially,* 17 ZONING AND PLAN. L. REP., (Sept. 1994).

11. Suitum v. Tahoe Reg'l Plan. Agency, 520 U.S. 725 (1997).

12. Vill. of Willowbrook v. Olech, 528 U.S. 562 (2000). *See also* Dwight H. Merriam, *Good and Evil in the Village of Willowbrook: The Story of the Olech Case,* 23 ZONING AND PLAN. L. REP. (May 2000).

13. City of Monterey v. Del Monte Dunes at Monterey, Ltd., 526 U.S. 687 (1999). *See also* Dwight H. Merriam, *The United States Supreme Court's Decision in* Del Monte Dunes: *The Views of Two Opinion Leaders (Part II),* 22 ZONING AND PLAN. L. REP. (Sept.-Oct. 1999); Dwight H. Merriam, *The United States Supreme Court's Decision in* Del Monte Dunes: *The Views of Two Opinion Leaders (Part I),* 22 ZONING AND PLAN. LAW REPORT (Jul.-Aug. 1999); and Dwight H. Merriam, *Will This Mouse Roar? United States Supreme Court Takes a Takings Case,* 21 ZONING AND PLAN. L. REP. (Dec. 1998).

14. U.S. Supreme Court Official Transcript 1998 WL 721087, at *16-17.

15. *Id.* at *19.

16. *Palazzolo,* 746 A.2d at 710.

17. *Palazzolo,* 121 S. Ct. at 2456.

18. *Palazzolo,* 746 A.2d at 711.

19. *Palazzolo,* 1997 WL 1526546 (R.I. Super. Ct. 1997) at *5.

20. *Palazzolo,* 746 A.2d at 714.

21. 473 U.S. 172, 186 (1985).

22. *Palazzolo,* 746 A.2d at 714.

23. *Id.* at 714 n.6.

24. 505 U.S. 1003 (1992).

25. *Palazzolo,* 1997 WL 1526546 (R.I. Super. Ct. 1997) at *1, *6).

26. 526 U.S. 687 (1999).

27. *Palazzolo,* 746 A.2d at 716.

28. 438 U.S. 104 (1978), *reh'g denied,* 439 U.S. 883 (1978).

29. THE RHODE ISLAND LAW TRIBUNE, 1 RILT 21, week of July 4-July 10, 2001, at 6.

30. THE RHODE ISLAND LAW TRIBUNE, 1 RILT 25, week of Aug. 1-Aug. 7, 2001, at 4.

31. *Palazzolo,* 121 S. Ct. at 2458.

32. *Id.* at 2459 (citing *Del Monte Dunes,* 526 U.S. 687, 698).

33. *Id.* at 2460.

34. *Id.* at 2461-62.

35. *Id.* at 2461.

36. *Id.* at 2461-62.
37. *Id.* at 2462.
38. *Id.*
39. *Id.*
40. *Id.* at 2462-63.
41. *Id.* at 2463.
42. *Id.*
43. 483 U.S. 825, 834 n.2 (1987).
44. *Palazzolo*, 121 S. Ct. at 2463-64.
45. *Id.* at 2464.
46. *Id.*
47. *Id.*
48. *Id.* at 2465 (quoting *Lucas*, 505 U.S. at 1019).
49. *Id.* at 2465.
50. *Lucas*, 505 U.S. at 1015.
51. *Palazzolo*, 121 S. Ct. at 2465.
52. *Id.*
53. *Id.* at 2466-67.
54. *Id.* at 2468.
55. *Id.* at 2470.
56. *Id.* at 2472.
57. *Id.* at 2473-74.
58. *Id.* at 2474.
59. *Id.* at 2473-74.
60. *Id.* at 2477 n.3.
61. *Id.* at 2477 (emphasis in original).
62. Good v. United States, 189 F.3d 1355 (Fed. Cir. 1999).
63. East Cape May Assoc. v. State of New Jersey, 2001 N.J. Super. LEXIS 316, at *19 (N.J. Super. App. Div. 2001), 2001 WL 830684.
64. *Id.* at *43-44.
65. 42 U.S.C § 1983.
66. Alviani v. Dixon, 365 Md. 95, 775 A.2d 1234 (2001).
67. 775 A.2d at 1245.
68. *Supreme Court Issues Significant Decision Regarding Regulatory 'Takings,'* Holland & Knight LLP Environmental Law Alert, July 5, 2001, at www.hklaw.com/newsletters.asp?ID=201&Article=1098.
69. D. Mandelker, "The Notice Rule in Investment-Backed Expectations," ALI-ABA Annual Land Use Institute, Aug. 16-18, 2001, at 16; *see also infra* chapter 2 at § 2.4 (b).
70. *Palazzolo*, 121 S. Ct. at 2461.
71. FLA. STAT. ANN. § 70.001 (5) (a), requiring government to "issue a written ripeness decision identifying the allowable uses to which the subject property may be put. . . ." *See also* ME. REV. STAT. ANN. tit. 5, § 3341(3)(A), discussed in John R. Nolon, *Local Land Use Controls That Achieve Smart Growth*, 31 ENVTL. LAW. RPTR. 11,025 (Sept. 2001). *See also* N.J. STAT. ANN. § 13:9B-22b (§ 22b).
72. *Palazzolo*, 121 S. Ct. 2448, 2463 (emphasis in original), *quoting* 2 Sackman Eminent Domain, at § 5.01[5][d][I].
73. Banks v. United States, 49 Fed. Cl. 806, 2001 U.S. Claims LEXIS 145 (2001).
74. 28 U.S.C. § 2501.

75. *Banks*, 49 Fed. Cl at 810.

76. *Id.* at 826, *citing* Rule 17 of the U.S. Court of Federal Claims.

77. *See, e.g.*, Just v. Marinette County, 56 Wis. 2d 7, 201 N.W.2d 761 (1972).

78. 2001 Wis. App. LEXIS 852, 2001 WL 946799 (Wis. App. 2001).

79. *Id.* at 35.

80. *Id.* at 32.

81. My law firm has created over 30 dockominiums totaling over 3,000 slips over the years, so we are somewhat familiar with them as business ventures and forms of ownership.

82. Chapter 2 *infra* at § 2.4.

83. See text *supra* accompanying note 51.

84. Walcek v. United States, 49 Fed. Cl. 248, 271 (2001).

85. *Palazzolo*, 121 S. Ct. at 2464.

86. McQueen v. South Carolina Dep't of Health and Envtl. Control, 340 S.C. 65, 530 S.E.2d 628, *cert. granted, judg. vacated, and remanded*, 121 S. Ct. 2581 (2001).

87. Telephone interview with Anthony Palazzolo, Aug. 30, 2001.

88. Michael M. Berger, *Yes, Virginia, There Can Be Partial Takings,* in ABA, TAKINGS: LAND-DEVELOPMENT CONDITIONS AND REGULATORY TAKINGS AFTER DOLAN AND LUCAS, ch. 7 (Callies, ed. 1996).

89. E-mail from Michael Berger, Berger & Norton, to Dwight H. Merriam, Robinson & Cole LLP (Aug. 25, 2001, 03:01 EST) (on file with author).

90. E-mail from David Callies, Benjamin A. Kudo Professor of Law, University of Hawaii School of Law, to Dwight H. Merriam, Robinson & Cole LLP (Aug. 27, 2001, 02:32 EST) (on file with author).

91. E-mail from John J. Delaney, Linowes & Blocher LLP, to Dwight H. Merriam, Robinson & Cole LLP (Aug. 27, 2001, 3:45 PM EST) (on file with author).

92. *Id.*

93. For a longer discussion of the three tests, *Agins*, and the partial takings issue, see MELTZ ET AL., THE TAKINGS ISSUE 130-39 (1999).

94. 447 U.S. 255, 260 (1980). Significantly, the Court cited *Nectow v. Cambridge*, 277 U.S. 183 (1928), a substantive due process case, as authority for the first criterion and *Penn Central* for the second.

95. At least one lower court has construed the *Agins* test as requiring that *both* elements be satisfied in order to find a regulatory taking. Del Oro Hills v. City of Oceanside, 31 Cal. App. 4th 1060, 1079, 37 Cal. Rptr. 2d 677, *cert. denied*, 516 U.S. 823 (1995). Most courts, however, have read the *Agins* standard in the disjunctive. *See, e.g.*, 152 Valparaiso Ass'n v. City of Cotati, 56 Cal. App. 4th 378, 65 Cal. Rptr. 2d 551 (1997); Seawall Assoc's v. City of New York, 74 N.Y.2d 92, 542 N.E.2d 1059, 1065, *cert. denied*, 493 U.S. 975 (1989).

96. *See infra* chapters 16 and 17—discussion of *Agins* by Doug Kmiec and Ed Sullivan.

97. 512 U.S. 374 (1994).

98. 438 U.S 104, 138 n.36.

99. *See, e.g., City of Waynesville*, 900 F.2d 783, 787 (4th Cir. 1990).

100. Reahard v. Lee County, 968 F.2d 1131, 1136 (11th Cir. 1992), *cert. denied*, 514 U.S. 1064 (1995); *cf.* Florida Rock Indus., Inc. v. United States, 791 F.2d 893, 900 (Fed. Cir. 1986).

101. Brief for the United States as Amicus Curiae Supporting Petitioner In Part, 1998 WL 308006, at *21.

102. Transcript at *23, *Del Monte Dunes II* (No. 97-1235).

103. 526 U.S. 687, 704 (1999).
104. 121 S. Ct. 2448, 2457 (2001).
105. *Id*. at 2459.
106. *See* Danziger. v. Town of Newtown, 2001 Conn. Super. LEXIS 533 (2001), 2001 WL 236758.

DO PARTIAL REGULATORY TAKINGS EXIST?

9

JOHN D. ECHEVERRIA

§ 9.0   *Introduction*

The term "partial taking" appears in no majority Supreme Court opinion involving a regulatory takings challenge to a restriction on the use of private property. The Court has never found a taking when a regulation only limits the use of property but allows some economically beneficial use of the property to proceed. And the Court has never applied the multifactor *Penn Central*[1] test—which ostensibly provides the legal framework for evaluating partial takings claims—to uphold a claim that a regulatory restriction effects a taking.

Notwithstanding this record, there is great interest and concern about the subject of "partial regulatory takings"—as confirmed, for example, by the editor's decision to include three chapters on the subject in this book. Furthermore, some members of the U.S. Court of Appeals for the Federal Circuit and the U.S. Court of Claims have championed the idea, as exhibited in the seemingly endless series of decisions in the case of *Florida Rock Indus., Inc. v. United States.*[2] More significantly, the Supreme Court in the recent case of *Palazzolo v. Rhode Island*[3] rejected a total taking claim under *Lucas v. South Carolina Coastal Council,*[4] but remanded for consideration of a claim under the separate, possibly "partial" test of *Penn Central.* The court on remand in *Palazzolo* as well as other courts trying to make sense of

Palazzolo will have to grapple with the potential existence of a partial taking claim. This chapter seeks to anticipate some of the complexities they will encounter.

The chapter is divided into four parts. The first part focuses on defining terms, trying to make sense of the term total taking and its apparent analog, partial taking. It discusses how a partial taking might potentially be identified and examines the possible alternative remedies in the event of a finding of a partial taking. The second part discusses the backhanded origin of the ostensible *Penn Central* test for partial takings and raises some questions about how it fits into the architecture of takings law. The third part critiques the *Penn Central* test as a possible standard for evaluating partial takings claims. The fourth part collects what appear to be the strongest arguments against the partial taking idea, especially its most expansive versions.

§ 9.1   Defining Terms

It is important to understand the relevant terminology. Following is a review of key terms.

§ 9.1(a)   *What Is a Total Taking?*

The Supreme Court has defined a "total" or "categorical" taking with fair precision. In *Lucas*, the trial court found that the regulation rendered Mr. Lucas's two beachfront lots literally "value-less,"[5] and the Supreme Court had no difficulty concluding that this constituted a "denial of all economically beneficial use" sufficient to constitute a total taking. By contrast, in *Palazzolo*, the opportunity to construct at least one single-family house on the owner's 20-odd acres, consisting of wetlands and a small area of uplands, meant that the property had a market value of at least $200,000. This highly restricted but valuable use was sufficient, the Supreme Court ruled, to take the case out of the *Lucas* category. The Court said that the government could not avoid a *Lucas* taking by demonstrating that the owner "is left with a token interest,"[6] but treated the $200,000 value as more than token. In sum, the *Lucas* rule applies only in those "extraordinary circumstances"[7] when a regulation eliminates essentially all of a property's uses and value. What, then, is a partial taking?

§ 9.1(b)   *Different Kinds of Partial Restrictions*

As a threshold matter, a regulation can be said to partially restrict the use of property in several different senses. First, a regulation can restrict the intensity at which a property might be used. The large-lot zoning at issue in *Agins v. City of Tiburon*[8] represents an example of this type of restriction. Agricultural or forest zoning provides another example.

Second, a regulation can partially restrict use of property because it eliminates or severely restricts the opportunity to use some geographical portion of the property but does not restrict (at least to the same degree) other portions of the property. The *Palazzolo* case is an example of this type of partial restriction. So too is the *Penn Central* case, where the company could continue to use the property for a railroad terminal but was barred from developing the airspace above.

This latter type of restriction raises a partial taking issue, but it also can be viewed as raising the "parcel as whole" question. In *Palazzolo*, the claimant's primary argument was that the restrictions on the use of the entire 20-acre parcel were so severe that they amounted to a taking. Before the Supreme Court, however, plaintiff's counsel also argued that there was a taking because the claim should have been analyzed by focusing on the wetlands and disregarding the uplands. The Court ruled that the parcel issue had been raised too late and had been waived. But in other cases, the partial taking theory and the parcel approach will represent alternative potential approaches for analyzing restrictions that apply to part of the property. At least to date, the Court has insisted on addressing a claimant's taking claim in relation to the property as a whole, rather than by focusing on the specific portion of the property affected by regulation.[9]

The potential parcel argument as applied to property in a geographical sense has an analog in the argument that a taking claimant should be permitted to claim a taking of one or more distinct legal sticks in the bundle of property rights. The claim in *Andrus v. Allard*[10] that the government effected a taking by prohibiting the sale of eagle feathers represents an example of this type of segmentation. So too, in a sense, was the unsuccessful claim in *Penn Central* that there was a taking of the company's legally distinct air rights. Consistent with the established parcel as a whole approach, the Court generally has rejected this argument for subdividing a property holding in order to maximize the possibility of a taking recovery.[11]

Florida Rock, which probably involves the most well-known example of an alleged partial taking, actually involved a partial claim of a rather unusual type. The Army Corps of Engineers denied the owner permission to fill 98 acres of wetlands in Florida. The owner's primary interest in acquiring the property was to mine the underlying limestone. But the denial of the fill permit effectively denied the owner permission to make any economic use of the property. The government defended on the ground that, even though there were no immediate permitted uses of the property, the property retained significant economic value in the marketplace, because speculators would be willing to pay a non-trivial price for the property in the hope that the regulatory restrictions might someday be lifted. In a 1994 ruling, the Federal Circuit credited this argument with precluding the possibility of a "total" taking under *Lucas*, but permitted the case to go forward on the partial taking theory.

This type of partial taking claim raises a number of issues and concerns. First, it is decidedly odd for the government to defend a regulation against a taking claim on the ground that the public may decide to abandon the regulation in the future. According to this logic, the more persuasively the government can show that the public will not back a regulation over the long term, the greater the chances of defeating the claim. Also, market value based on the possibility that some use of the property will be allowed in the future seems distinguishable from market value derived from a permitted, current use of the property, which intuitively provides a more solid basis for rejecting a taking claim. Finally, the restrictions at issue in *Florida Rock* appear similar to the absolute prohibition on development at issue in *Lucas*, which, of course, supported a finding of a "total" taking. It is likely that speculators might have paid at least something for Mr. Lucas's coastal lots; indeed, several Justices expressed skepticism about the trial court finding that the property was "valueless."[12] If speculative value based on possible changes in the rules is sufficient to defeat a total taking claim, it is difficult to see how any total taking claim could be sustained.

§ 9.1(c) *Part of What?*

A total taking claim naturally focuses on the question of what value or use remains as of the date of the alleged taking. However, in the case of an alleged partial taking, the question arises: part of what? Two potential answers point in very different directions.

One alternative is to ask what proportion of the market value or use rights the owner retains under the challenged regulatory regime, as compared to the market value or use rights if the restrictions were not enforced. This question should logically be answered based on estimates of market value as of the date of the alleged taking.

The other alternative is to start with the claimant's original investment in the property and compare that value to the market value of the property subject to the regulatory restrictions. In some cases the value of the restricted property will be less than the original investment, in some cases more, and in some cases the value will be unchanged.

A recent case before the U.S. Court of Federal Claims, *Walcek v. United States*,[13] provides an instructive set of facts. In 1971, plaintiffs paid approximately $117,731 for 14.5 acres of property along the Delaware shore; 13.2 acres were wetlands subject to federal regulatory control. In 1993, the Army Corps of Engineers denied the plaintiffs permission to fill the wetlands in order to develop the entire property. The plaintiffs then sued claiming a taking under the Fifth Amendment. The government defended on the ground that the regulatory restrictions were not so onerous that they rose to the level of a taking. To support its position, the Army Corps contended that it likely would have granted permission for a more limited development that entailed destruction of 2.2 acres of relatively low-value wetlands.

To assess the economic impact of the Army Corps' decision, the court asked the "part of what" question in both ways. First, the court compared the market value based on the plaintiffs' development proposal ($1,485,000) with the value of the property subject to the restrictions the Army Corps intended to impose ($597,000), resulting in an estimated diminution in market value of 59.8 percent. Second, the court compared the plaintiffs' investment in the property ($291,969, based on the $117,731 purchase price augmented by cash outlays to maintain the property) with the value of the property if developed in accordance with the Army Corps' restrictions ($597,000). This calculation indicated that the plaintiffs could more than double their original investment. The court also performed an alternative calculation taking into account the fact that some of the plaintiffs' maintenance expenses yielded tax benefits. This calculation generated a $169,701 figure for the plaintiffs' investment, meaning that the plaintiffs would receive a "profit" of $427,299 under the Army Corps plan, or a 335 percent increase in their original investment.

In sum, the court concluded that the plaintiffs received a profit based on the original investment approach and suffered a loss based on the current market value approach. Weighing the results of both of these calculations along with other facts and circumstances, the court concluded that the plaintiffs had not established a taking. (As this book goes to press, the *Walcek* ruling is on appeal to the Federal Circuit.)

The *Walcek* case also raises an additional wrinkle. While the court adjusted the plaintiffs' original investment to include holding costs, it decided not to make an adjustment to the original purchase price to account for inflation.[14] By contrast, Judge Loren Smith, former chief judge of the Court of Federal Claims, in his latest decision on remand in *Florida Rock*, adjusted the claimant's original investment based on the Consumer Price Index, without explanation.[15] The court in *Walcek* reasoned that an adjustment for inflation is not ordinarily made in calculating the value of an investment for other purposes (such as taxes), that it is unreasonable to assume that the value of an investment will increase in value in lockstep with inflation, and that such an adjustment would raise a whole range of technical complexities.

While the issue of adjusting the original investment based on inflation may seem trivial, it can have an enormous impact on the ultimate resolution of a case. In *Walcek*, factoring in inflation would have eaten up most of the plaintiffs' estimated profit on their original investment. In *Florida Rock*, on the other hand, including inflation accounted for all or most of the plaintiff's supposed loss on its original investment.[16]

Finally, it is noteworthy that the divergence between these two potential measures of economic impact can become enormous if the property has been held for a long time. Real estate prices have escalated rapidly over the last several decades, with some of the most dramatic increases occurring in coastal and other ecologically sensitive areas. In many cases, even highly restricted areas are likely to have market values that far exceed the owners' original investments. Assuming claimants do not benefit from a stepped-up basis based on inflation (at a modest rate of 3 percent, the value of an investment doubles in 24 years), measuring economic impact relative to the owner's original investment will frequently show little if any harm. In a recent case, the Maine Supreme Court rejected a taking claim by an owner denied permission to construct a home on a lot with a market value for development of $100,000.[17] The owner had purchased the property several decades earlier for only $10,000, and the property had value for private, undevelopable open space of $50,000.

At the same time, given the general run-up in real estate values and the tighter restrictions on development in ecologically sensitive areas, the apparent diminutions in property value caused by regulatory restrictions relative to the property's potential unrestricted value are likely to be large. Environmental restrictions have helped preserve the amenity values that make development in environmentally sensitive areas attractive and have restricted the supply of developable land, thereby increasing the value of remaining development opportunities. Thus, calculations based on hypothetical scenarios in which the taking claimant is free from all regulatory restraints are likely to yield misleadingly large estimates of diminutions in market value. In sum, the choice of the benchmark for evaluating the economic impact of regulation means, if not everything in the partial taking analysis, then a very good deal.

§ 9.1(d) *What Would Be the Remedy for a Partial Taking?*

The final preliminary question, assuming for the sake of argument that a partial taking exists, is what the remedy for such a taking would be. Under one view, a taking is an all-or-nothing proposition. A finding of a taking, whether total or partial, means that the government must pay compensation for the taking and will receive full title to the property in return. Thus, although a regulation might fall somewhat short of eliminating all of the property's economic value or use, if it rises to the level of a taking, the entire property has been taken.

Under the alternative view, if a taking is only partial, then the government should only pay compensation for the part affected and should only obtain title to a partial interest. In the *Penn Central* case, for example, under a partial taking theory, the government would only pay just compensation for the airspace and in exchange would receive some kind of easement prohibiting development of the airspace. In *Florida Rock*, the Court of Claims concluded that a finding of a partial taking would lead to government acquisition of some type of "negative easement" prohibiting the filling of the wetlands for mining or other development purposes.[18]

At least in principle, theories of partial regulatory takings could be constructed that would accommodate either type of remedial approach. Nonetheless, the answer to the remedy question is closely related to the issue of the potential scope of the partial taking theory. If the partial taking theory were designed to accommodate only regulatory burdens that, although not eliminating all economic use and value, at least eliminate *substantially* all economic use and value, then the all-or-nothing approach would be entirely practical. Under this view, takings doctrine is confined to cases where government action has effectively appropriated or destroyed private property, and it is reasonable to require the government to acquire the affected property outright.

On the other hand, if partial takings were an expansive concept, the all-or-nothing approach would make less sense. For example, using the *Palazzolo* case as an example, if the coastal restrictions effected a partial taking, would the government acquire the entire 20 acres or only the restricted wetlands? The first option comports with the more traditional approach. But, on the other hand, it seems nonsensical to suppose—assuming Mr. Palazzolo wishes to develop the one upland site and the government is willing to approve it—that the government, based on the wetlands restrictions alone, must acquire the entire property including the upland area.

One obvious concern is that once one accepts partial acquisition as a remedy for a partial taking, there is no principled stopping point. What would distinguish the actual *Palazzolo* case from another case in which the 20 acres were divided into 15 upland acres and five wetlands acres? If a finding of a partial taking is appropriate in the real case, why not the hypothetical one? The obvious judicial interest in avoiding this slippery slope may weigh strongly in favor of finding no taking in *Palazzolo* and similar cases.

One argument for the partial acquisition remedy, and for the idea of partial regulatory takings in general, is that regulatory takings should be analogized to permanent physical takings. In the case of a permanent physical occupation, subject to some qualifications, a court will always find a taking, no matter how small the portion of the property affected by the occupation. By the same token, when a physical-occupation taking takes place, the government logically acquires only the rights in the occupied area, not the entire property. In *Loretto v. Teleprompter Manhattan CATV Corp.*, the finding that Mrs. Loretto's property was physically invaded as a result of the physical placement of a cable television box on her property did not mean that either the government or the cable company obtained ownership of her entire apartment building. Whether the concept of a physical taking supports the idea of a partial regulatory taking depends upon whether the rules governing physical takings can properly be transplanted to the regulatory sphere, a topic I shall address in section 9.2.

§ 9.2   *The Problematic* Penn Central *Test*

Perhaps one of the strongest practical supports for the partial taking theory is the apparent availability of the so-called *Penn Central* multifactor balancing test to evaluate such claims. As with baseball fields amid rows of corn, if the Supreme Court builds a partial regulatory taking doctrine, then partial taking claims apparently must inevitably come.

The *Penn Central* test is based on language from the Court's 1978 decision. The Court began by observing that "[t]he question of what constitutes a 'taking' . . . has proved to be a problem of considerable difficulty," and that "this Court, quite simply, has been unable to develop any 'set formula' for determining when 'justice and fairness' require that economic injuries caused by public action be compensated by the government, rather than remain disproportionately concentrated on a few persons."[19] The Court continued, "We have frequently observed that whether a particular restriction will be rendered invalid by the government's failure to pay for any losses proximately caused by it depends largely 'upon the particular circumstances [in that] case.'" The Court then proceeded to identify "several factors that have particular significance" in "engaging in these essentially ad hoc, factual inquiries":

> The economic impact of the regulation on the claimant and, particularly, the extent to which the regulation has interfered with distinct investment-backed expectations are, of course, relevant considerations. So, too, is the character of the governmental action. A "taking" may more readily be found when the interference with property can be characterized as a physical invasion by government . . . than when interference arises from some public program adjusting the benefits and burdens of economic life to promote the common good.

This language self-evidently provides a slender reed for a determinative takings test. The Court's words, rather than defining an actual test, seem to acknowledge the impossibility of doing so. The Court simply identified several factors that have particular relevance in takings analysis.

Certainly there is no indication the Court was seeking to articulate standards that would govern partial claims. The Court made no mention of any distinction between total and partial takings. Moreover, while Justice Brennan's opinion is notoriously opaque and confusing, it contains strong language rejecting "the proposition that diminution in property value, standing alone, can establish a taking." This seems to contradict, for example, the conclusion by the Court of Federal Claims in *Florida Rock* that a 73 percent diminution in the value of property is sufficient to establish a taking.[20]

Penn Central emerged as the governing standard for partial claims in a decidedly backhanded fashion. Prior to the 1990s, the Court's taking decisions contained no suggestion that regulatory taking doctrine might contain two distinct tiers for analyzing use restrictions.[21] Rather, the issue was always simply whether the regulation resulted in a taking. In 1992, in the *Lucas* case, the Court broke new ground by defining what it called a "total" or "categorical" taking. The Court's novel use of this terminology implied that there was something else that might be labeled a "non-total" or "non-categorical" taking. In a footnote, Justice Scalia reinforced this implication by observing, if "an owner might not be able to claim the benefit of our [new] categorical formulation, . . . we have acknowledged time and again [that] '[t]he economic impact of the regulation on the claimant and . . . the extent to which the regulation has interfered with distinct investment-backed expectations' are keenly relevant to takings analysis generally," citing *Penn Central*.[22] Thus was launched the *Penn Central* partial takings test.

The Court's apparent creation of a two-tier takings analysis in *Lucas* was plainly dictum. The case involved a regulation that eliminated all of the economic value and use of the property and, therefore, plainly met the threshold of economic impact necessary to find a taking under prior Court rulings. There was no need for the Court in *Lucas* to address whether, or according to what test or tests, a taking might be found when a regulation does *not* eliminate all economic value and use. In any event, as a matter of historical fact, the *Lucas* decision represented the spark for the partial regulatory taking idea, including providing the foundation for the Federal Circuit's (in?)famous 1994 *Florida Rock* opinion outlining an expansive theory of partial regulatory takings.[23]

The *Palazzolo* decision reinforces the *Lucas* dictum. In a brief summary of takings doctrine, the Court describes *Lucas* as providing the governing test when a regulation "denies all economically beneficial or productive use of land." The Court then goes on to state that the *Penn Central* test applies "where a regulation places limitations on land use that fall short" of the *Lucas* standard.[24] Significantly, no Justice writing separately took issue with this description of the basic architecture of takings law.

It also fair to observe, however, that *Palazzolo* did not require the Court to address the substance or scope of the *Penn Central* partial takings test or explain how it fits (or does not fit) into takings doctrine. The litigation centered on the *Lucas* claim, which was the focus of the plaintiff's case, and none of the parties raised any fundamental question about the *Penn Central* test. The Rhode Island Supreme Court rejected the *Lucas* and *Penn Central* claims on the ground that the owner's advance notice of regulatory restrictions barred the claims. The U.S. Supreme Court reversed on the ground that pre-acquisition notice cannot be treated as a categorical bar to a taking claim (whether under *Lucas* or *Penn Central*). After resolving the notice issue, the Supreme Court determined that the *Lucas* claim failed because the case did not involve a denial of all economically beneficial use. The Court then remanded the case for consideration of the remaining issues, including the *Penn Central* claim. In a sense, therefore, apart from the notice issue, the *Penn Central* claim passed through the Supreme Court proceedings largely unobserved and unexamined.

While both *Lucas* and *Palazzolo* support an expanded, two-tier version of takings law, there also is a great deal of Supreme Court precedent, some of it in tension with the language in *Lucas* and *Palazzolo,* indicating that takings doctrine remains quite narrow. In a decision issued the year after *Lucas*,[25] the Supreme Court cited with approval decisions rejecting takings challenges to restrictions leading to economic losses as high as 92.5 percent[26] and 75 percent.[27] The rejection of these kinds of "partial" takings claims is consistent with prior Court pronouncements emphasizing the narrowness of regulatory takings doctrine in general, including:

- The basic issue in a regulatory taking case is whether the regulation "has very nearly the same effect for constitutional purposes as appropriating it or destroying it";[28]
- Legitimate takings claims are confined to "extreme circumstances";[29]
- "[M]ere diminution in the value of property, however serious, is insufficient to demonstrate a taking";[30] and
- "Loss of future profits—unaccompanied by any physical property restriction—provides a slender reed upon which to rest a takings claim."[31]

At least in the immediate aftermath of *Palazzolo,* there is no indication from the lower courts that they view the decision as having worked a major change in the scope of regulatory takings doctrine. Indeed, post-*Palazzolo,* several of the states' highest courts have reaffirmed their established, narrow reading of the Takings Clause. For example, the North Dakota Supreme Court recently rejected a taking claim, describing the operative legal standard as follows: "Governmental regulation constitutes a taking for public use only when it deprives the owner of all or substantially all reasonable uses of the property."[32] Similarly, the New Jersey Supreme Court recently rejected a taking claim, in part on the ground that the owner "retained some economically beneficial use of its property."[33]

What, then, is one to make of the ostensible *Penn Central* partial regulatory takings test? First, it was not—and arguably still is not—a necessary conclusion that the architecture of takings doctrine must accommodate two separate tiers. As discussed, the *Penn Central* decision strongly implied that only a severe economic burden would result in a taking. In numerous subsequent cases the Court had suggested that, at least where the claim focuses on economic burden, a regulation will be found to effect a taking only if it "denies an owner economically viable use of his land."[34] *Lucas* arguably represented the exceptional case that proved this rule. Both *Lucas* and *Palazzolo*, while undoubtedly supporting a separate *Penn Central* test, do not grapple with the questions about the legitimacy of the test. Most important, the dictum in *Lucas* and *Palazzolo* notwithstanding, the Court has never applied the multifactor *Penn Central* test to uphold a finding that a restriction on the use of property effects a taking.[35]

Furthermore, assuming some independent *Penn Central* test does exist alongside the *Lucas* test, the test may not focus primarily, if at all, on the problem of partial diminutions in the value of property. The Court has, for example, invoked the *Penn Central* test in cases involving restrictions on the right to devise property;[36] those decisions appear to turn largely on the special nature of the property interest at stake rather than the magnitude of the economic burden. The closest the Court has actually come to using *Penn Central* to conclude that a regulatory statute effected a taking was in *Eastern Enterprises v. Apfel*.[37] In that case, a plurality of the Court applied the *Penn Central* factors to argue that the retroactive effects of the Coal Act amounted to a taking. This suggests that *Penn Central* could have particular application in the context of retroactive legislation. In addition, the *Lucas* rule is apparently confined to real property. Thus, the *Penn Central* analysis might turn out to have primary relevance in personal property claims.

In sum, the very existence and possible scope of the ostensible *Penn Central* test remain open questions.

§ 9.3   *The Incoherence of the* Penn Central *Test*

Apart from its problematic origins and uncertain scope, there are also substantial grounds for questioning whether the *Penn Central* multifactor test represents a coherent standard for evaluating whether regulations amount to takings. It appears, in light of recent Supreme Court pronouncements, that there is something called a *Penn Central* test. It nonetheless seems useful and important to ask whether there is any there there—both for the long term and to provide some comfort to members of the bar baffled by their inability to make sense of this area of the law.

As discussed, the standard formulation of the *Penn Central* test identifies three relevant factors: character, economic impact, and reasonable investment-backed expectations. I will examine each factor in turn to analyze whether these factors demarcate a meaningfully distinct test for so-called partial takings.

§ 9.3(a) *Character*

Character is the most opaque and confusing of the *Penn Central* factors. In *Penn Central* itself, the Court used the term to refer to whether the government action effected a kind of physical occupation of the property. In light of subsequent Supreme Court precedent, however, this interpretation appears nonsensical. In 1982, in *Loretto v. Teleprompter Manhattan CATV Corp.*,[38] the Court established a per se rule that permanent physical occupations, subject to certain narrow exceptions, always result in takings. If the character of a regulation as a physical occupation generally mandates a finding of a taking, then the character factor, at least as originally defined in *Penn Central*, cannot play any role in a multifactor balancing test.

In an attempt to restore some meaning to the "character" factor, some Justices and some judges have interpreted it as requiring consideration of the value or importance of what the government seeks to accomplish. There is some support for this idea. In *Penn Central,* the Court rationalized rejecting the taking claim in part on the basis that the "restrictions imposed are substantially related to the promotion of the general welfare."[39] In addition, in *Lucas* the Court described a "total taking" as being "compensable without case-specific inquiry into the public interest advanced in support of the restraint";[40] this statement obviously implies that weighing the public interest served by a regulation ordinarily *would* be appropriate in other types of cases.

Notwithstanding this support, the interpretation that the character factor relates to the value or importance of the public objective is ultimately implausible. It contradicts the Court's longstanding understanding that a taking claim seeks financial compensation for an "otherwise proper" government action.[41] Stated differently, a viable taking claim presupposes that the government is seeking to advance a legitimate, valuable public purpose. If a taking claim presupposes that the government is acting for a legitimate public purpose, the public purpose served by the government action cannot logically be a factor, to be weighed along with other factors, in deciding whether or not compensation is due under the Takings Clause.

This conclusion also is supported by common sense. The government's liability for a classic exercise of the power of eminent domain obviously does not vary with the importance or value of the public objective. For example, it would be absurd to suppose that the government could deny its obligation to pay compensation when it takes land for a school on the ground that it seeks to meet an important educational need. Moreover, the Takings Clause must have the same basic meaning whether the government initiates a condemnation or an owner brings an inverse condemnation action.[42] If the importance of the public purpose being served cannot be considered in deciding whether payment is due in an eminent domain proceeding, it also makes no sense to consider it in a regulatory taking case.[43]

Indeed, the logic of regulatory takings doctrine suggests that the importance of the public purpose should weigh in favor of paying compensation, not against it. If the government is pursuing an objective that actually succeeds in generating substantial benefits for the public, then the courts, everything else being equal, should logically be more rather than less inclined to shift the burdens imposed by the action to the public.

It seems unlikely that the Supreme Court, when it ultimately decides the question, will embrace the illogical notion that the character factor refers to the value or importance of the public objective. Apart from its bad fit with takings law generally, this interpretation would convert the Takings Clause into a freewheeling tool for judicial reweighing of essentially legislative judgments. It would not comport with the traditional judicial role, for example, for judges to decide wetlands takings cases by balancing the regulation's economic burdens on certain landowners against the water pollution and other harms avoided by preventing wetland destruction. Furthermore, such a test would be essentially standardless, violating the conviction of at least some of the Court's justices that the law should rely on categorical rules rather than balancing tests.[44] In *Palazzolo*, Justice O'Connor embraced a relatively freewheeling version of the *Penn Central* test. There may some significance in the fact that the rest of the justices did not join in her opinion and did not venture independent efforts to make sense of the *Penn Central* test.

§ 9.3(b)   *Economic Impact*

Turning to the economic impact factor, *Lucas* established that a regulation that eliminates all of a property's economic value and use amounts to a presumptive or "categorical" taking. The partial regulatory taking idea suggests that a regulation with less severe economic impact also can support a finding of a taking. It is possible that this type of economic impact, combined with some other factor, may be sufficient to establish a taking. But it is difficult, at a minimum, to rationalize the conclusion that this type of lesser economic impact can have determinative signifi-cance. As discussed, the Court has repeatedly insisted that dimi-nution in property value, standing alone, is insufficient to demonstrate a taking. Recently a unanimous Supreme Court reaf-firmed this principle: "[m]ere diminution in the value of prop-erty, however serious, is insufficient to demonstrate a taking."[45] The Supreme Court might be willing to repudiate this long-stand-ing principle, but absent a radical change in the law, the eco-nomic impact factor does not support a second-tier, partial takings analysis.

§ 9.3(c) *Reasonable Investment Expectations*

The preceding analysis leaves the entire weight of distinguishing between *Lucas* total takings and *Penn Central* partial takings on the reasonable investment-backed expectations factor. This factor is not adequate to support this weight.

It can be contended that the use the owner actually intended to make of the property, in light of the regulatory restrictions in place at the time he made the investment, should be irrelevant in a *Lucas* case but relevant in a *Penn Central* case. This is the con-clusion that can be drawn from Justice Scalia's dictum, on behalf of the Court, in *Lucas*.[46] In *Palazzolo*, however, Justice Scalia, in a separate concurring opinion, advanced an even more radical position—that investment expectations should not matter in ei-ther a *Lucas* case or a *Penn Central* case; in other words, in his view, whether the owner knew about the regulatory restrictions at the time he acquired the property should be irrelevant in any type of takings case. As made obvious by Justice O'Connor's con-curring opinion in *Palazzolo*, a majority of the Justices have re-jected this view, affirming that preacquisition notice matters, at least, in a *Penn Central* case.[47] For several reasons, given the Court's position on investment expectations in a *Penn Central* case, it is likely that the Court will also conclude that investment expectations can matter in a *Lucas* case.

First, Justice O'Connor, probably expressing the views of a majority of the Justices, voiced the concern that if preacquisition notice were not a relevant factor, claimants could reap unfair windfalls at public expense. The concern about windfalls is le-gitimate because investors typically purchase property at a price that reflects current regulatory restrictions; ignoring investment expectations would allow investors to buy low in the private marketplace and sell high in a subsequent taking action against the government. If windfalls are a concern in a *Penn Central* case, however, they should be an even greater concern in the context of an alleged total taking, because the investor may well have bought the property at an even greater discount and may well be seeking an even larger windfall.

Second, Justice Kennedy, who authored the majority opinion in *Palazzolo*, appears to have gone out of his way to preserve the argument that investment-backed expectations, including preacquisition notice, should matter in a total takings case. In *Lucas*, Kennedy wrote a concurring opinion asserting that background principles of state property and nuisance law do not provide the only grounds for defending against a total taking claim. "Where a taking is alleged from regulations which deprive the property of all value," he said, "the test must be whether the deprivation is contrary to reasonable investment-backed expectations."[48] In *Palazzolo* the Court had no need to directly address whether investment expectations might be relevant in a *Lucas*-type case. Nonetheless, Justice Kennedy, speaking for the Court and using carefully chosen language, stated that "we have observed, with certain qualifications . . . that regulation which 'denies all economically or productive use of land' will require compensation under the takings clause." In support of this statement he cited, among other things, his concurring opinion in *Lucas*. At least in the mind of Justice Kennedy, a likely swing vote on this issue, the Supreme Court has not barred consideration of investment expectations in a *Lucas* case.

Finally, it is implausible that preacquisition notice would be relevant in a *Penn Central* case but irrelevant in a *Lucas* case, because investors could so easily manipulate their property holdings in order to evade the first rule and take advantage of the second. If an investor wished to acquire 20 acres of property, including ten acres of uplands and ten acres of wetlands, could the investor avoid the notice rule simply by buying the two pieces in the names of separate corporations? Alternatively, if an investor originally purchased the 20 acres as a unit but wished to manufacture a taking claim with respect to the ten acres of wetlands, could the owner form an independent corporation and convey the ten acres of wetlands to the new corporation? Or, could the investor sell the property to a new purchaser who, hypothetically armed with the legal rule that advance notice of restrictions does not matter, would be willing to pay full market price in the expectation that he could pursue a successful total takings claim? These hypotheticals suggest the implausibility of an absolute rule that advance notice does not matter in a total taking case.

•   •   •

In sum, it is difficult, if not impossible, at least within the confines of existing takings doctrine, to define meaningful legal lines that demarcate a *Lucas* taking claim from the ostensible *Penn Central* claim. The absence of a coherent, independent *Penn Central* test hardly demonstrates that partial regulatory takings do not exist, but it does eliminate one of the major props for this expansive reading of the Takings Clause.

§ 9.4　Seven Brief Arguments Against the Partial Regulatory Takings Theory

Despite the confused origins of the ostensible *Penn Central* partial taking test, and the apparent incoherence of that test based on existing takings precedents and principles, is some type of partial regulatory takings standard nonetheless justified? This section presents seven brief arguments against the partial regulatory taking idea.

§ 9.4(a)　Original Understanding

First, the partial takings theory would lead takings jurisprudence far afield from the original understanding of the Takings Clause. As a result, it would breach the bounds of plausible constitutional interpretation, especially for those justices and judges committed to relying on the drafters' original intentions as a lodestar for constitutional interpretation.

There is virtual consensus that the regulatory taking doctrine has no foundation in the original understanding. No less a supporter of property rights than Justice Scalia has acknowledged the narrow scope of the Takings Clause as a matter of historical fact; as he stated in *Lucas*, "[e]arly constitutional theorists did not believe the Takings Clause embraced regulations of property at all."[49] This conclusion is supported by numerous scholarly investigations including, for example, those by Professor William Michael Treanor[50] and John F. Hart.[51] Noted conservative Robert Bork, while expressing sympathy with the political agenda that would be furthered by Professor Epstein's libertarian rewrite of the Takings Clause, has observed that Epstein's conclusions "are not plausibly related to the original understanding of the takings clause."[52]

As the studies of the original understanding explain, there is no direct evidence of the drafters' intentions in including the Takings Clause in the Bill of Rights. The provision was drafted by James Madison and included in the Bill of Rights at his instigation with no recorded debate. As a result, interpreters of the Takings Clause have been forced to interpret its meaning by investigating historical antecedents in colonial charters, the Northwest Ordinance, and various state constitutions, as well as by studying contemporary understandings of the scope of government regulatory authority. The basic conclusion of this research has been that "the Takings Clause was originally intended and understood to refer only to the appropriation of property."[53]

Since the early part of this century and the Supreme Court's decision in *Pennsylvania Coal Co. v. Mahon*,[54] it has been clear that, notwithstanding the original understanding, some regulations are so economically burdensome that they will be deemed takings. Thus, the Court has already abandoned strict adherence to the original understanding. Nonetheless, unless *Mahon* can be read as a license to completely ignore the original understanding, the evidence about the original understanding must be treated as a powerful argument against the partial taking theory. It is one thing to recognize, as the Court did in *Mahon*, that a regulation can effect a taking if it "has very nearly the same effect for constitutional purposes as appropriating or destroying it";[55] it would be quite another to divorce takings law from the original understanding altogether and conclude that a regulation that leaves an owner some economic value and use constitutes a compensable taking.

§ 9.4(b) *Judicial Deference to Elected Branches*

The partial regulatory taking theory would improperly aggrandize judicial power at the expense of the other branches of government, undermining the system of separation of powers and weakening the authority of the people's elected representatives in addressing environmental, land use, and other matters touched by the Takings Clause.

The Supreme Court has long recognized that an expansive reading of the Takings Clause threatens to intrude on the legislative function. As Justice Oliver Wendell Holmes famously remarked, "Government hardly could go on if to some extent values incident to property could not be diminished without paying for every such change in the general law."[56] In another case, the Supreme Court expanded on this theme: "[G]overnment regulation—by definition—involves the adjustment of rights for the public good. Often this adjustment curtails some potential for the use or economic exploitation of private property. To require compensation in all such circumstances would effectively compel the government to regulate by purchase."[57]

Thus, the partial regulatory taking theory conflicts with the general presumption in favor of the constitutionality of legislative action, a presumption rooted in the doctrine of separation of powers and the general rule that matters of social policy should be decided by government representatives directly elected by the people. Justice Scalia recently described the dangers of what he termed an "imperial judiciary" rendering constitutional decisions on the abortion issue based on "philosophical predilections and moral intuitions" properly left to the political process:

> [B]y foreclosing all democratic outlet for the deep passions this issue arouses, by banishing the issue from the political forum that gives all participants, even the losers, the satisfaction of a fair hearing and an honest fight, by continuing the imposition of a rigid national rule instead of allowing for regional differences, the Court merely prolongs and intensifies the anguish.[58]

These concerns also apply with full force to judicial interpretation of the Takings Clause. The partial taking theory cannot be squared with the traditional function of the judicial branch under our system of separation of powers.

§ 9.4(c) *Givings Matter*

A third rationale for rejecting the partial regulatory takings idea is the pervasiveness of governmental "givings." The basic argument for takings liability is that regulated property owners are subjected to economic burdens that, in all fairness, should be compensated by the public that benefits from the regulation. Givings illustrate that the premise of this argument is highly problematic. In fact, property owners subject to stringent regulation are frequently better off in economic terms than they would be in the absence of the regulation. Furthermore, even if certain regulations impose economic burdens, other government projects and programs confer uncompensated givings; there is no obvious rationale for evaluating the effect of a regulation in isolation as opposed to evaluating the net effect of all the different government activities that affect property values.

A taking claimant typically focuses on the effect of a regulation on the claimant's property, ignoring the fact that the regulation may apply to some or many others in the community. The consequence is that a taking claim tends to highlight the adverse effects of the regulation on the claimant while ignoring the positive effects. A regulation that applies to many owners not only restricts what an owner can do with her property, it also benefits her by restricting what her neighbors can do with their property. In economic terms, a regulated property owner can benefit from the application of regulations to her neighbors in two different ways. First, restrictions on the use of other properties in the community can protect the property from neighboring uses that would detract from its value, for example, by causing pollution or flooding, or by undermining the amenity values in the community as a whole. Second, regulatory restrictions can limit the available development opportunities and thereby increase the scarcity, and hence the value, of remaining development opportunities.[59]

The Supreme Court has pointed to the phenomenon of "reciprocity of advantage" in explaining why takings challenges to zoning regulations, for example, face an uphill battle. As the Court said in *Agins*, land owners subject to a zoning regulation:

> share with other owners the benefits and burdens of the city's exercise of its police power. In assessing the fairness of the zoning ordinances, these benefits must be considered along with any diminution in market value that the [owners] might suffer.[60]

The same reasoning applies to a variety of land use and environmental laws that apply to a significant cross-section of the community. Over the long term, a rough "reciprocity of advantage" is secured for all. Looking at government regulatory activity generally, the obligation to comply with any particular regulation can be seen as "a burden borne to secure the advantage of living and doing business in a civilized society."[61]

The concept of reciprocity of advantage has particular salience in a partial regulatory taking case where the claimant is severely restricted in his use of the property but can obtain permission to conduct some development. In that case there is likely to be direct, tangible evidence of the countervailing benefits of regulation. In *Palazzolo*, for example, the evidence showed that the owner could sell the property for development for 15 to 20 times what he paid for it 30 years earlier, even though there was only a single developable lot on the property. The land's high value was attributable to both the scarcity effect of the coastal regulations and the amenities preserved by protecting wetlands on Palazzolo's property and on adjacent properties. What Palazzolo's property might have been worth in the absence of any regulation applicable to him and his neighbors is unknown and essentially unknowable. The land might have been more valuable, but it also might have been less valuable.

In *Lucas*, the Court explained its new categorical rule in part by observing that reciprocity of advantage was relatively difficult to detect in a total taking case. When a regulation eliminates "all economically beneficial use," the Court said, "it is less realistic to indulge our usual assumption that the legislature is simply adjusting the benefits and burdens of economic life in a manner that secures an average reciprocity of advantage to everyone concerned."[62] If, in fact, the "usual assumption" in a non–total taking case is that there is a rough reciprocity of advantage, that would leave very little room for the supposed partial taking doctrine.

In addition to the phenomenon of reciprocity of advantage, direct governmental "givings" also should be factored into the equation. Publicly funded roads, sewers, and other public facilities, agricultural and other subsidies, and other government tax and spending programs contribute significantly to the value of land. Many empirical studies have documented the large size of these givings.[63] Many givings are, of course, paid for by general tax revenues and provide benefits to society as a whole. It is also true, however, that luck and skillful political activity routinely result in the benefits of givings being concentrated on a small number of landowners. There is no reason to believe that landowners are any more likely to be singled out to bear the burdens of regulatory action than they are to be singled out to be the beneficiaries of governmental givings. If anything, as the country's agricultural policies and flood insurance programs suggest, the opposite is more likely to be accurate. The economic fairness of the burdens allegedly imposed by government cannot be accurately appraised without taking into account the givings as well. Once givings are taken into account, the fairness argument for partial takings appears weak and, at best, uncertain.

§ 9.4(d) *The Analogy to a Physical Occupation Is Flawed*

A frequent argument on behalf of the partial regulatory taking theory relies on an analogy to physical occupation–type takings. When a physical taking is alleged, it is irrelevant whether the physical occupation affects the entire property or only a small portion of it. Advocates of the partial taking idea maintain that a regulatory use restriction should likewise be held to be a taking without regard to the property's remaining value for other, unrestricted uses. As stated by Judge Jay Plager, "The fact that the source of any particular taking is a regulation rather than a physical entry should make no difference—the nature of the legal interests defining the property affected remains the same."[64]

A straightforward doctrinal answer to this argument is that the Supreme Court has never suggested that the Takings Clause applies in interchangeable fashion to use restrictions and to physical occupations. The Court has characterized the physical occupation rule as a "very narrow"[65] principle designed to deal with a special set of circumstances where government has physically invaded, or at least authorized the physical invasion of, private property. Since articulating this special rule, the Court has repeatedly distinguished it from the rule(s) governing takings challenges to use restrictions.

The more fundamental answer is that the per se rule governing physical occupations represents a generous constitutional standard that arguably overcompensates the owner at public expense. There is no disputing the constitutional necessity of complying with the just compensation standard when it applies. But, absent a clear constitutional mandate to extend this standard to so-called partial regulatory takings, an appeal based on fairness and similar treatment of these different types of cases is not compelling.

The just compensation standard requires the government to deal with a citizen subject to a taking on the same basis as would another citizen—that is, by requiring payment of just compensation as measured by the fair market value of the property. If the government were simply another actor in the marketplace, this approach would not be problematic. But the government relates to individual citizens in a distinctive fashion, because it interacts with any individual citizen in myriad ways over the long term. As discussed above, through regulatory and spending programs, the government contributes to the public welfare and supports private property values in a host of ways. When the government takes private property and pays just compensation, a significant amount of the compensation paid represents publicly created value. In short, the just compensation standard, when it applies, requires the taxpayer to overpay for what it is taking.

It is obviously permissible, indeed constitutionally mandated, for the public to overpay when a taking is actually found. On the other hand, something more than the rough comparability of physical occupations and use restrictions is required to justify inventing a new law of regulatory takings that would extend to the regulated community the same kind of public generosity that applies in the case of physical takings. At least to date, the Court's regulatory takings jurisprudence has tended in the opposite direction, emphasizing the "reciprocity of advantage" conferred by government regulations as a reason for not triggering the just-compensation standard. It is possible that the over-generosity reflected in the law governing physical takings is, in a sense, counterbalanced by a similar under-generosity in the case of use restrictions. A more plausible explanation may be that the reciprocal effects of regulatory actions are so pervasive that awarding compensation for every partial restriction would be extravagantly and unreasonably generous to property owners. In any event, the simple fact that a physical occupation, no matter how modest, generally requires payment of compensation does not logically support the conclusion that every restriction on the use of property should be similarly compensated.

§ 9.4(e) *A Decline in Property Value Is Not a Taking*

A further difficulty with the partial regulatory taking idea is the impossibility of translating a reduction in the value of a particular property asset into a constitutional violation. Diminution in market value as a result of regulation, it turns out, provides only an opaque window on the issue of a regulation's fundamental fairness.

First, as a practical matter, the value the property would have in the absence of regulation is virtually impossible to calculate with accuracy. In a typical taking case, the unregulated value of the property is estimated based on the market value the property would have if the challenged regulation were lifted for the owner's property. This approach plainly overestimates the market value of the property, because it gives the owner the benefit of not having to comply with the regulation while simultaneously crediting him with the economic benefit of some or all of his neighbors' compliance with the same regulation. A more accurate assessment of a regulation's actual economic impact would model the effect of not applying the regulation to the owner or to any of his neighbors. Unfortunately, this type of analysis is enormously complex and time-consuming, and would obviously be impossible to perform on a routine basis in every taking case. Thus, litigators and judges are generally left with a comparison between the property's market value if unregulated and its market value if regulated. This approach readily yields an answer, but it is the answer to the wrong question.

There is a more fundamental problem with relying on estimated changes in market value of property to identify compensable takings. The basic justification for any regulatory program is that prices set by the marketplace do not reflect the true economic value of goods and services not effectively supplied or priced by the market. Market failure occurs, according to the standard economic account, because private economic activity generates "externalities" that are not captured by market prices. The very purpose of regulation is to alter the prices that various goods and services would otherwise command in the market. Hence, relying on the market price of property in a hypothetically unregulated state in order to evaluate losses due to regulatory action is caught up in a contradiction; the reason for the regulation itself is the failure of the market and the resulting inaccuracy of price signals.

Finally, it is questionable, based on some of the Court's most recent precedent, whether a reduction in economic value can be equated to an actual taking of property. In *Eastern Enterprises v. Apfel*,[66] Justice Kennedy, joined by four other Justices, rejected the idea that economic loss can be equated with a taking. He observed that the Coal Act imposed a "staggering financial burden"[67] on the plaintiff firm, but nonetheless concluded that it did not create the kind of burden that falls within the scope of the Takings Clause. A properly framed taking claim, he said, challenges a regulation or other government action "as being so excessive as to destroy, or take, a specific property interest."[68] Justice Breyer agreed: "The "private property" upon which the clause traditionally has focused is "a specific interest in physical or intellectual property."[69] When squarely faced with the question, the Supreme Court is likely to confirm that an adverse effect on the value of a property asset is not equivalent to an actual taking of the property itself.

The difficulty of identifying what the government would obtain if it effected a taking based on diminution in value also supports this analysis. A taking claim presupposes that if a taking is actually found, the government will pay compensation and will receive (or at least have the opportunity to receive) title to the property it has taken. Thus, a regulatory taking claim requires identification of some specific property interest to be conveyed to the government in exchange for compensation.[70] However, if the only thing taken is value, it is obviously difficult to know what, if anything, the government has acquired.

§ 9.4(f)   *Partial Takings Liability Would Unreasonably Chill Government Action*

A striking literary flourish in some recent regulatory takings cases is to compare the actions of the government to the actions of a "thief"[71] or a killer.[72] On the surface, the most remarkable aspect of this vocabulary is the notion that government officials should be compared to violent malefactors. On second thought, however, the greater significance lies in the notion that the government is comparable to a private actor. Indeed, it is central to the current effort to invigorate the Takings Clause that the government be made liable on the same basis as a private person. Just compensation, according to the advocates of the takings agenda, much like a private tort damages remedy, seeks to provide redress for harms inflicted and to deter future harms.

For several reasons, the comparison of government officials to private malefactors is misleading. Thieves and killers do not build highways, operate schools, or run sewage control systems; however, governments do these things and much much more. For the reasons discussed, these value-enhancing aspects of government have to be considered to arrive at a balanced interpretation of the Takings Clause. The most critical point for present purposes, however, is that the comparison of government officials to private actors serves to obscure how severely expansive takings liability would chill reasonable and necessary government action.

The principal law and economics argument for subjecting government to expansive liability under the Takings Clause relies on an analogy to the incentives created for private firms by the tort law system. A private factory may discharge pollutants into a river, resulting in harm to public health or the environment. In a competitive economy, a profit-maximizing firm will have little or no incentive to consider these external costs in its internal business accounting. Absent some legal constraint, the factory will continue to pollute despite the fact that this result is not economically optimal for society as a whole. According to standard economic theory, if the firm is required to pay monetary damages to those adversely affected by its operations, it will be compelled to internalize the external costs and total social welfare will be enhanced.

According to some, these ideas can be transferred wholesale into the takings arena. The argument starts from the premise that government "operates with an incentive structure similar to that of a similarly situated private enterprise."[73] The argument also posits that government regulatory actions create costs by imposing economic burdens on certain property owners. Liability under the Takings Clause, the argument continues, would "prevent[] the government from overusing . . . [its regulatory] power."[74]

Contrary to this viewpoint, as a number of scholars have demonstrated, extensive assessments of financial liability against the government under the Takings Clause would not necessarily increase total social welfare. In fact, expansive takings liability could so severely chill government action that it would lead to net declines in total social welfare.

Most important, the argument for extensive takings liability based on cost internalization suffers from a fatal asymmetry.[75] The cost-internalization argument proceeds on the assumption that the costs of government action must be monetized and internalized in order to influence government decision-making. But the benefits of government action represent the other side of the economic equation. Government produces a variety of benefits through regulation, from a safe food supply to nonpolluted air and water to public safety. If the costs of regulatory programs have to be internalized through monetary payments, as taking advocates assert, then the benefits of regulatory programs would have to be internalized in monetary terms as well in order to create balanced incentives. Otherwise, the government calculus would be consistently skewed in favor of minimizing costs, and government decision-making would tend to produce inefficient outcomes.

The reality, of course, is that the benefits of government regulatory action generally are not internalized by government. Furthermore, it is difficult as a practical matter to see how internalization could be accomplished on a broad scale. Thus, a broad takings liability rule would inevitably result only in internalization of costs and would tend to foster government decision-making that does not maximize total social welfare.[76]

§ 9.4(g) The Limitations on the Judicial Role of Counsel Against the Partial Taking Theory

Finally, the partial regulatory taking theory should be rejected because of the need for the law to draw clear and predictable lines in order for the rule of law to be able to function at all. The generally accepted rule that a regulation must eliminate all or substantially all of a property's value and use satisfies this need because it identifies a relatively discrete and easily identified set of cases. If the law were otherwise, and if a taking could be established merely by showing a significant diminution in value, the law of takings would be a highly unpredictable morass for landowners and government officials alike.

Professor Frank Michelman's seminal article, "Property, Utility, and Fairness: Comments on the Ethical Foundations of 'Just Compensation' Law,"[77] spoke powerfully and eloquently to the need for takings doctrine to include clear legal rules. In his article, which probably has been cited more frequently by the Supreme Court than any other work on this subject, Michelman surveyed at great length the various factors that he thought relevant in analyzing the fairness issues at the heart of a taking case. In the concluding section of his article, however, Professor Michelman cautioned that a freewheeling analysis based on fairness was unlikely to supply a suitable judicial standard. He wrote:

> Our question about fairness as an apt standard for judging thus reflects not a suspicion that judicial personnel are less able than other men to understand or apply the

content of the standard, but doubt stemming from a judicial predilection—one which we normally applaud because we deem it healthily responsive to limits we wish to keep in place around the judicial province—to seek an articulate doctrinal packaging for all judgments. The problem is that fairness resists being cast into a simple, impersonal, easily stated formula.

This is not to say that courts cannot usefully be put to work deciding at least some compensability issues; rather it is to suggest abandonment of any idea that courts can or will decide each compensability case directly in accordance with the precept of fairness. Hence, we need to search instead for some workable, impersonal rule believed to approximate in a useful proportion of cases the same result that fairness would dictate. But if that is our choice (or our preferred description of what actually takes place), it is of the utmost importance that we clearly and frankly acknowledge it. The danger here is one of behaving as if courts were doing the whole job when the truth is that they are attentive only to "hardcore" or "automatic" cases. To illustrate: a utilitarian approach to the problem might suggest a judicial rule that compensation is due only when there has been either (a) a physical occupation or (b) a nearly total destruction of some previously crystallized value that did not originate under clearly speculative or hazardous conditions. Such a rule would be workable; it would be internally consistent; and it would be ethically inoffensive as far as it goes. True, its cutoff points are arbitrary, and it completely disregards some significant but less discussable dimensions of fairness. But these attributes in the rule would merely reflect its function as a rule for courts to use in the partial performance of a task for which judicial capabilities are not fully adequate.

§ 9.5   *Conclusion*

The foregoing analysis has hopefully served to demonstrate that the partial regulatory taking idea poses at least as many questions as answers. One of the more interesting questions for the future is to what extent courts will assess the economic impact of regulation by comparing the regulated value to the value of the original investment, on the one hand, and/or to the present unregulated value of the property, on the other. These different calculations may be useful to courts in sorting out whether the alleged "loss" is really disappointment at not achieving a hoped-for appreciation in a speculative investment or whether the regulation has actually resulted in a significant diminution in value. If the regulated value is greater than the original purchase price, even if it is less than the current unregulated value, there is likely a basis for concluding that a good deal of the alleged "loss" in value actually represents the owner's failure to reap a windfall.

Does either approach have a preferred status based on first principles? To the extent the goal of the Takings Clause is to protect the security of investments, the original investment approach seems most sensible. However, if the goal of the Takings Clause is to police redistributions of wealth, the current market-value approach has something to recommend it. Arguably both calculations are relevant and potentially useful.

Another interesting question for the future is how the courts address the question of the remedy for an alleged partial taking. The *Florida Rock* case illustrates some of the problems courts may confront in attempting to award partial relief for partial takings. The Federal Circuit recognized that a finding of taking would entitle the United States to obtain title to the property taken, suggesting that the property interest might be a kind of "negative easement." The court apparently meant that the owner should retain the underlying fee, subject to a prohibition on filling the property for mining or for other development. But what would be the duration of this type of easement? According to the logic of the court's partial takings analysis, which was based on the notion that the property had a positive value based on some possible future use, the easement would presumably be terminable when the owner's (or some subsequent purchaser's) speculative bet paid off and the property became available for development. But this type of easement seems totally incapable of precise definition, as well as an invitation to extraordinary abuse. Would the easement endure for some minimum number of years, or would it simply terminate if and when the regulatory climate shifted, a change in which the landowner would obviously have a major interest and over which it might be able to exercise some influence? Is it possible that an owner could receive compensation for 73 percent of the value of the property and then five years later develop the property or sell it for development, quite possibly at a higher price than the original purchase price? Alternatively, ten or 20 years following the payment of compensation for the taking, and assuming that the regulatory taking climate had not changed, could an owner renew the taking claim on the theory that the speculative bet had, in a sense, matured, but the owner was still being denied the opportunity to develop the property? Under this reasoning, could an owner bring an endless series of takings actions for as long as he held the underlying fee to the property?

Partial regulatory takings, if they exist at all, apparently remain very much a work in progress.

Notes

1. *See* Penn Central Transp. Co. v. City of New York, 438 U.S. 104 (1978).

2. *See* Florida Rock Indus., Inc. v. United States, 8 Cl. Ct. 160 (1985), *rev'd and remanded*, Florida Rock Indus., Inc. v. United States, 791 F.2d 893 (Fed. Cir. 1986), *cert. denied*, 479 U.S. 1053 (1987), *on remand*, Florida Rock Indus., Inc. v. United States, 21 Cl. Ct. 161 (1990), *vacated and remanded*, Florida Rock Indus., Inc. v. United States, 18 F.3d 1560 (Fed. Cir. 1994), *cert. denied*, 513 U.S. 1109 (1995), *on remand*, Florida Rock Indus., Inc v. United States, 45 Fed. Cl. 21 (1999). In the fall of 2001, the parties reportedly settled the entire case for a payment of $21 million.

3. 121 S. Ct. 2448 (2001).

4. 505 U.S. 1003 (1992).

5. *Id.* at 1006.

6. 121 S. Ct. at 2464.

7. *Lucas*, 505 U.S. at 1017.

8. 447 U.S. 255 (1980).

9. In *Palazzolo*, the Court indicated that "we have at times expressed discomfort with the logic of this rule, . . . a sentiment echoed by some commentators." 121 S. Ct. at 2465. It remains to be seen whether anything significant develops from this suggestive remark.

10. 444 U.S. 51 (1979).

11. A notable exception to this rule is the right to devise property, which the Supreme Court has treated as properly divisible from the rest of an owner's property. *See* Babbitt v. Youpee, 519 U.S. 234 (1997); Hodel v. Irving, 481 U.S. 704 (1987). These exceptional cases are generally viewed as resting on the special status of the right to pass on property to one's heirs.

12. *See* 505 U.S. at 1024 (Kennedy, J., concurring in the judgment); *id.* at 1076 (Souter, J., statement).

13. 49 Fed. Cl. 248 (2001).

14. *See id.* at 265-66.

15. *See* 45 Fed. Cl. at 37.

16. Judge Smith calculated that the plaintiff lost about one-half the value of its investment, because the value of the property for speculative investment was $2,822 per acre, whereas the "economic basis" in the property was approximately $6,000 per acre, based on "actual expenditures for purchase price, acquisition interest, and property taxes adjusted for inflation using the consumer price index." 45 Fed. Cl. at 37. But the actual purchase price was only approximately $1,900 per acre, *id.* at 38, meaning that the market value, even with all development prohibited (but not taking into account holding costs), was 50 percent greater than the original investment.

17. *See* Wyer v. Board of Envtl. Protection, 747 A.2d 192 (Me. 2000).

18. *See* 45 Fed. Cl. at 42 n.13.

19. 438 U.S. at 123-24.

20. *See* 45 Fed. Cl. at 40-41.

21. *Cf.* Loretto v. Teleprompter Manhattan CATV Corp., 458 U.S. 419 (1982) (establishing a special per se rule for regulations that effect a permanent physical occupation of private property).

22. 505 U.S. at 1019 n.8.

23. *See* Victoria Sutton, *Constitutional Taking Doctrine—Did Lucas Really Make a Difference?* "18 Pace Envtl. L. Rev. 505 (2001) (providing a similar account of the evolution of takings doctrine post-*Lucas*).

24. 121 S. Ct. at 2457.

25. *See* Concrete Pipe & Prods. of Calif., Inc. v. Construction Laborers Pension Trust, 508 U.S. 602, 645 (1993).

26. *See* Hadacheck v. Sebastian, 329 U.S. 394, 405 (1915).

27. *See* Village of Euclid v. Ambler Realty, 272 U.S. 365, 384 (1926).

28. Pennsylvania Coal Co. v. Mahon, 260 U.S. 393, 414 (1922).

29. United States v. Riverside Bayview Homes, Inc., 474 U.S. 121, 126 (1986).

30. *Concrete Pipe*, 508 U.S. at 645.

31. Andrus v. Allard, 444 U.S. 51, 62 (1979).

32. Braunagel v. City of Devil's Lake, 629 N.W.2d 567, 572 (N.D. 2001).

33. Pheasant Bridge Corp. v. Township of Warren, 2001 WL 868015, at 8 (N.J., Aug. 2, 2001).

34. Agins v. City of Tiburon, 447 U.S. 255, 260 (1980); *see also* Keystone Bituminous Coal Ass'n v. DeBenedictis, 480 U.S. 470, 485 (1987) (applying the *Agins* test).

35. *See* District Intown Props. Ltd. P'ship v. District of Columbia,198 F.3d 874, 886 (D.C. Cir., 1999) (Williams, J., concurring in the judgment), *cert. denied*, 531 U.S. 812 (2000).

36. *See* note 11, *supra*.

37. 524 U.S. 498 (1998).

38. 458 U.S. 419 (1982).

39. 438 U.S. at 138.

40. 505 U.S. at 1015.

41. *See* First English Evangelical Lutheran Church v. County of Los Angeles, 482 U.S. 304, 315 (1987).

42. *See First English*, 482 U.S. at 315.

43. The view that the value or importance of a regulation can defeat a taking claim arguably is consistent with the view, supported by language in certain Supreme Court decisions, that a regulation that fails to "substantially advance a legitimate government interest" should be deemed to effect a taking. If a regulation serves a valuable, legitimate public purpose, it logically must substantially advance a legitimate government interest. As I have argued elsewhere, the "substantially advance" takings test is best viewed as raising a due process issue, not a taking issue. *See* John D. Echeverria, *Does a Regulation That Fails to Advance a Legitimate Governmental Interest Result in a Regulatory Taking?*, 29 Envtl. L. 853 (1999). The position advanced here that the value or importance of the government action cannot legitimately help defeat a taking claim is consistent with the view that the "substantially advance" test is not a legitimate takings test. The substantially advance test has run into strong headwinds in recent Supreme Court cases, and there may be some significance to the fact that the Supreme Court omitted any reference to this ostensible takings test in *Palazzolo*.

44. *See* Antonin Scalia, *The Rule of Law as a Law of Rules*, 56 U. CHI. L. REV. 1175 (1989).

45. *See* Concrete Pipe & Prods. of Calif., Inc. v. Construction Laborers Pension Trust, 508 U.S. 602, 645 (1993).

46. *Compare* 505 U.S. at 1027 (discussing analysis under categorical test) with *id*. at 1019 (discussing analysis under *Penn Central*).

47. *See* John D. Echeverria, *A Preliminary Assessment of Palazzolo v. Rhode Island*, 31 ENVTL. L. RPTR. 11,112 (2001).

48. *See* 505 U.S. at 1034. *See also id*. at 1015 (" The State should not be prevented from enacting new regulatory initiatives in response to changing conditions, and courts must consider all reasonable expectations whatever their source. The takings clause does not require a static body of state property law; it protects private expectations to ensure private investment.").

49. 505 U.S. at 1028 n.15.

50. *See The Original Understanding of the Takings Clause and the Political Process*, 95 COLUM. L. REV. 782 (1995).

51. *See Land Use Law in the Early Republic and the Original Meaning of the Takings Clause*, 94 NW. U. L. REV. 1099 (2000); *Colonial Land Use Law and Its Significance for Modern Takings Doctrine*, 109 HARV. L. REV. 1252 (1996).

52. THE TEMPTING OF AMERICA: THE POLITICAL SEDUCTION OF THE LAW 230 (1990).

53. Hart, 94 NW. U. L. REV. at 1103.

54. 260 U.S. 393 (1922).

55. *Id*. at 414.

56. *Id*. at 413.

57. Andrus v. Allard, 444 U.S. 51, 64 (1979).

58. Planned Parenthood of S.E. Pa. v. Casey, 505 U.S. 833, 1002 (1992) (dissenting).

59. *See generally* C. Ford Runge, *The Congressional Budget Office's Regulatory Takings and Proposals for Change: One-Sided and Uninformed*, 7 ENVTL. L. & PRAC. 5 (1999).

60. 447 U.S. at 262.

61. Andrus v. Allard, 444 U.S. 51, 67 (1979). *See also* Keystone Bituminous Coal, 480 U.S. at 491 ("While each of us is burdened somewhat by . . . [the] restrictions [on the uses individuals can make of their property], we, in turn, benefit greatly from the restrictions that are placed on others.").

62. 505 U.S. at 1017-18.

63. *See* C. Ford Runge, *supra* note 59 (collecting the available empirical evidence).

64. *Florida Rock*, 18 F.3d at 1572.

65. *Loretto*, 458 U.S. at 441.

66. 524 U.S. 498 (1998).

67. *Id*. at 540.

68. *Id*. at 542.

69. *Id*. at 554.

70. *See* Causby v. United States, 328 U.S. 256, 267 (1946) ("[A]n accurate description of the property taken is essential, since that interest vests in the United States.").

71. Osprey Pac. Corp. v. United States, 41 Fed. Cl. 150, 157 (1998).

72. *Florida Rock*, 45 Fed. Cl. at 23.

73. RICHARD A. POSNER, ECONOMIC ANALYSIS OF THE LAW 58 (4th ed. 1992).

74. *See generally* William A. Fischel & Perry Shapiro, *Takings, Insurance, and*

Michelman: Comments on the Economic Interpretations of "Just Compensation" Law, 17 J. LEGAL STUDIES 269, 270 (1992) (arguing that expansive takings liability would serve to "disciplin[e] the power of the state, which would otherwise overexpand unless made to pay for the resources that it consumes").

75.   *See generally* Daryl J. Levinson, *Making Government Pay: Markets, Politics, and the Allocation of Constitutional Costs*, 67 U. CHI. L. REV. 345, 355-57 (2000).

76.   Just as extensive takings liability would chill reasonable government conduct, it also would create a "moral hazard" leading to overinvestment by those who disregard the risk that government regulations might be enacted to shift property to a higher economic use. As stated by Professor Darryl Levinson, "Just as the generous disaster relief for flood victims encourages overbuilding on flood plains, and International Monetary Fund bailouts encourage too much borrowing and fiscal irresponsibility by debtor nations, full indemnification for takings condemnees encourages overinvestment in property." *Id*. at 390.

77.   80 HARV. L. REV. 1196 (1967).

PARTIAL REGULATORY TAKINGS: A PROPERTY RIGHTS PERSPECTIVE

10

EDWARD H. ZIEGLER*

§ 10.0 *Fairness, Causation, and Proportionality Limit the Constitutional Scope of Uncompensated Regulation*

Partial regulatory taking claims may include in the context of land use regulation all taking claims that are not "categorical" or "per se" regulatory taking claims. When so defined, partial taking claims would not include the categorical taking claim that a regulation goes too far by compelling a property owner to suffer a physical invasion of his land[1] or by denying an owner all economically viable use of his land.[2] Recent court decisions make clear that the crystallized lines of categorical taking analysis have not

---

* © 2001 Edward H. Ziegler. Adapted from E. Ziegler, *Partial Taking Claims, Ownership Rights in Land and Urban Planning Practice*, 22 U. UTAH J. LAND RES. & ENVTL. L., No. 1 (2002).

eliminated the Supreme Court's ad hoc multifactored analysis of partial regulatory taking claims.[3] The concepts of fairness, causation, and proportionality, which have in part shaped the lines of categorical taking analysis, are likely to continue to form the critical core analytical elements in the Supreme Court's assessment of partial regulatory taking claims.[4] When analyzed in relation to the policy of horizontal equity reflected in the Takings Clause and in view of owner expectations as shaped by background principles of state property law, these three core concepts appear to provide a coherent and principled basis for limiting the constitutionally permissible scope of uncompensated police power regulation.

§ 10.1 The Supreme Court's Recognition that the Takings Clause Limits the Permissible Scope of Uncompensated Regulation

The Supreme Court has repeatedly ruled that the Fifth Amendment Takings Clause imposes a constitutional limit on the permissible scope of uncompensated police power regulation. This recognition by the Court both reflects and promotes the historical interplay between this country's common-law property rights tradition,[5] the exercise of government police power,[6] and the role of the courts in our constitutional system of protecting individual rights, including private property rights.[7] This compensation principle can be found in the writings of William Blackstone, who noted: "So great moreover is the regard for private property, that it will not authorize the least violation of it; no, not even for the general good of the whole community."[8] James Madison similarly observed: "Government is instituted to protect property of every sort. . . . This being the end of government, that alone is a just government, which impartially secures to every man, whatever is his own."[9]

Courts required compensation for indirect or regulatory destruction of property rights relatively early in this country's constitutional history.[10] Such cases and more recent Supreme Court regulatory taking decisions clearly reject the statist view that all private property and the value thereof are ultimately derived from and dependent upon the grace of the state as mere licenses or privileges.[11] As Douglas Kmiec points out in this regulatory takings context: "American constitutional history declares Jeremy Bentham to be mistaken: property and law are not 'born together.' And they do not die together either. Private property preexists government and is protected not merely because this or that law may be in place, but because it advances the nature of the human person more effectively and directly than alternative forms of property distribution."[12] A similar point is made by constitutional scholar Lawrence Tribe, who notes that the owner expectations protected by the Takings Clause must have their source outside positive law: "These expectations achieve protected status not because the state has designed to accord them protection, but because constitutional norms entitle them to protection."[13]

Modern Supreme Court regulatory taking cases often attribute the origin of regulatory taking analysis to Justice Holmes's opinion in the landmark case *Pennsylvania Coal Co. v. Mahon*[14] where Holmes stated that "[I]f regulation goes too far it will be recognized as taking."[15] The police power "must have its limits," and "when it reaches a certain magnitude, in most if not all cases, there must be an exercise of eminent domain and compensation to sustain the act."[16] Later, Justice Brennan would similarly point out: "Police power regulations such as zoning ordinances and other land-use restrictions can destroy the use and enjoyment of property in order to promote the pubic good just as effectively as formal condemnation or physical invasion of property."[17] More recently, the Supreme Court expressly reaffirmed this position: "If ... the uses of private property were subject to unbridled, uncompensated qualification under the police power, 'the natural tendency of human nature [would be] to extend the qualification more and more until at last private property disappear[ed].'"[18]

§ 10.2 The Supreme Court's Analysis of Partial Regulatory Taking Claims

The Fifth Amendment Takings Clause presupposes the unfairness of the uncompensated taking of private property for public use or benefit.[19] In regulatory taking cases, analysis of fairness in allocation of the burdens imposed, in view of the policy of horizontal equity (the approximation of equal sharing of costs when property is taken by the expenditure of public funds), secures and implements this core policy underlying the Takings Clause. Fairness in this context necessarily requires consideration of the character of the government action and its impact on private owners. Under this analysis, the unfairness of singling out or disproportionately burdening owners by regulation to secure a public benefit that addresses a social problem or need that the targeted owners have not uniquely contributed to or caused triggers the constitutional requirement that compensation be paid for the benefits extracted. This analysis is reflected in a long line of Supreme Court decisions.[20]

This type of ad hoc fairness taking analysis seems to have been applied by Justice Holmes in *Pennsylvania Coal Co. v.*

Mahon.[21] Holmes considered the fairness of uncompensated regulation in view of both the nature of the public interest secured by regulation and the nature of the burden imposed on the private owner.[22] Later, in *Penn Central Transp. Co. v. New York City,*[23] the Supreme Court pointed out that three factors would have particular significance in applying this type of ad hoc multifactored analysis: (1) the character of the government action; (2) the economic impact of the regulation; and (3) interference with reasonable investment-backed expectations.[24] The Supreme Court in *Penn Central*, however, failed to provide any clear explanation of the particular significance of these factors in regulatory taking analysis and failed to identify appropriate lines of analysis that might relate these factors to the Fifth Amendment's core policy of horizontal equity.[25] The Court ultimately upheld the landmark preservation designation in question, ruling that reduction in value does not, standing alone, constitute a taking and that no taking occurred, since *Penn Central* had not shown that it could not earn a reasonable profit on its land considered as a whole.[26]

The multifactored analysis set out in *Penn Central* has been widely criticized as the source of much mischief and confusion.[27] Some later court decisions applied a similar form of analysis in a rather mechanical way, interpreting *Penn Central* to require only that regulation not render land valueless.[28] Under this view of regulatory takings, losses resulting from regulation, short of total destruction of land value, are held to be merely "disappointed expectations," and potentially key criteria for assessing the basic fairness of uncompensated regulation are either casually dismissed or simply ignored.[29] This interpretation of *Penn Central* actually provides no analysis at all of critical core issues related to the concept of horizontal equity underlying the Takings Clause. By eliminating considerations of fairness and justice in allocation of particular regulatory burdens, this type of *Penn Central* analysis fails to provide any coherent or principled basis for adjudging the permissible scope of uncompensated police power regulation.

Penn Central's utilitarian analysis has been largely superseded by numerous Supreme Court and lower federal and state court regulatory taking decisions. More recent Supreme Court decisions repeatedly have rejected the notion that the Takings Clause only requires that land not be rendered valueless.[30] Supreme Court decisions now make clear that common-law ownership rights in land may be held to have been taken by regulation even short of total destruction in value or without regard to the extent of diminution in value.[31] The primary focus in regulatory taking analysis may often not involve diminution in value at all but simply assessment of whether the regulation or permit decision is otherwise within the permissible scope of uncompensated police power regulation.[32] As the Supreme Court reaffirmed in its recent *Del Monte Dunes* decision, the Takings Clause begins where the constitutional scope of uncompensated regulation ends.[33]

Also, the apparent rejection of the argument by the Supreme Court in *Lucas* that nothing short of denial of all economically viable use would constitute a regulatory taking[34] has been picked up in subsequent court decisions that now expressly hold that in such cases, the regulatory taking claim will be resolved by application of partial regulatory taking analysis.[35] As recently stated by the Court of Appeals for the Federal Circuit: "Nothing in the Fifth Amendment limits its protection to only 'categorical' regulatory takings, nor has the Supreme Court or this court so held. Thus there remains in cases such as this the difficult task of resolving when a partial loss of economic use of the property has crossed the line from a noncompensable 'mere diminution' to a compensable 'partial taking.'"[36]

Supreme Court and lower court decisions applying this type of partial "benefit extraction" regulatory taking analysis largely attempt to establish a principled dichotomy between permissible uncompensated police power regulation and impermissible uncompensated benefit extraction.[37] Critical analytical elements in establishing this principled dichotomy are considerations of fairness, causation, and proportionality related to the core policy of horizontal equity underlying the Takings Clause.[38] Assessing the fairness and justice of the regulatory burdens imposed serves to limit the permissible scope of uncompensated regulation consistent with the policy of horizontal equity.[39] Whether the burdens imposed, as a matter of fairness and justice, should be secured by compensation rather than by regulation requires judicial scrutiny of the nature of the government action involved in view of owner expectations as shaped by background principles of state property law.[40]

Landowners may reasonably be held to expect to face the risks of uncompensated police power regulation that serves some arbitration or harm prevention function where the public benefits thereby secured address a social problem caused or generated by the private owner's conduct or proposed use.[41] Partial taking analysis thus recognizes that traditional police power restrictions, including zoning controls on land use and development, generally are permissible forms of uncompensated regulation, since the government can fairly be said to be acting as intermediary between private interests to provide a mutually beneficial environment.[42] Moreover, at some significant level, reciprocal benefits typically accrue to affected owners from the restrictions imposed.

From this analysis has arisen the frequently stated principle that mere diminution in value does not itself effect a taking. As Justice Holmes noted, "Government hardly could go on if to some extent values incident to property could not be diminished without paying for every change in the general law."[43]

Partial taking analysis, however, necessarily distinguishes permissible uncompensated regulation from compensable benefit extraction.[44] Fairness and justice in the allocation of regulatory burdens prohibit the imposition of uncompensated burdens on landowners when they are singled out as simply convenient targets of opportunity for extraction of public benefits that address a social problem that is not caused by the landowners' conduct or proposed use.[45] The nature of the government action involved under this type of regulation is simply the functional equivalent of securing a public benefit by a garden-variety appropriation of private property.[46]

Courts, in applying this type of partial taking analysis, often utilize "fairness" cause-and-effect and proportionality nexus standards to assess the government action involved as it relates to this distinction between uncompensated regulation and compensable benefit extraction.[47] These types of nexus standards have been applied in determining the reasonableness of land use conditions and restrictions by state courts for much of the twentieth century.[48] Commenting on these cases, Professor Dunham points out that there is much authority for the proposition that an owner need not be compensated when land use regulation prevents him from causing a specific problem but that compensation must be paid when regulation simply extracts from him a public benefit:

> Thus it has been held unconstitutional to compel an owner, without compensation, to leave his land vacant to obtain the advantages of open land for the public or to save the land for future public purchase, but it is within constitutional power to compel an owner to leave a portion of his land vacant where building would be harmful to the use and enjoyment of other land (for example, setback line). It is unconstitutional to compel an owner to commit his land to park use to meet the public desire for a park, but he may be compelled to furnish a portion of his land for a park where the need for a park results primarily from activity on other land of the owner. It is unconstitutional to compel him to use his land as a parking lot for the community, but it is within constitutional power to compel him to provide a parking lot for the parking needs of activities on his own land. It is im-

proper to compel a railroad to install grade-crossings for highways to promote the convenience of highway users, but it is permissible to compel the railroad to install grade-crossings to eliminate danger and hazards from the railroad's use of its own property. It is not permissible to compel an owner to hold land in reserve for industrial purposes by restricting his use to industrial purposes only, but it is permissible to exclude industrial development from districts where such development will harm other uses. It is beyond state power to compel an owner without compensation to set aside or give land to the public for a street or highway, but it is within that power to compel him to do so where the need for the streets is related to the traffic generated by the owner's use of his other land. Likewise, the state may compel an owner to furnish other community facilities, such as water and sewer lines, at his own expense where the need for such facilities results in part at least from activities on his other land.[49]

The concepts of causation and proportionality are increasingly recognized as critical elements in applying the core policy of horizontal equity reflected in the Takings Clause.[50] The Supreme Court's decisions in *Nollan*[51] and *Dolan*[52] established just such cause-and-effect and proportionality "substantial nexus" tests for development exactions. Both of these court decisions, which brought to the forefront considerations of causation and proportionality as related to horizontal equity in the allocation of the burdens imposed by regulation, have served to enhance and support application of partial benefit-extraction taking analysis in recent court decisions.[53] Subsequent court decisions have applied these types of nexus standards to a variety of land use conditions and restrictions.[54]

Justice Scalia's opinion in the partial taking case, *Pennell v. City of San Jose*,[55] involving a tenant-hardship rent-control provision, clearly embraces this type of nexus consideration:

Traditional land use regulation (short of that which totally destroys the economic value of property) does not violate this principle because there is a cause-and-effect relationship between the property use restricted by the regulation and the social evil that the regulation seeks to remedy. Since the owner's use of the property is (or, but for the regulation, would be) the source of the social problem, it cannot be said that he has been singled out unfairly. Thus, the common zoning regulations requiring subdividers to observe lot-size and setback restrictions, and to dedicate certain areas to public streets, are in accord with our constitutional traditions because the proposed property use would otherwise be the cause of excessive congestion.[56]

Even in cases where this cause-and-effect nexus standard may be perceived to be satisfied by characterization of the government action as addressing a social harm by preventing the absence of the benefit secured by regulation,[57] the ultimate takings test of fairness and justice in allocation of regulatory burdens, as evidenced by the "singling out" of the particular owners involved and the absence of significant reciprocal benefits, may still result in a finding that a partial regulatory taking has occurred.[58] Preserving, in partial takings analysis, the ultimate distinction between permissible uncompensated police power regulation and compensable benefit extraction reflects ordinary landowner expectations about the scope of the police power and permitted uses of their properties and serves to implement the policy of horizontal equity underlying the Takings Clause.[59]

Outcomes under the Takings Clause are unlikely to be held to turn on simply a question of semantics in describing the purposes of regulation. More important, the ultimate distinction is fundamentally not between harm prevention and benefit extraction. All regulatory actions presumably secure some public benefits. The relevant distinction relates to whether the benefits secured by regulation are obtained by unfairly singling out or disproportionately burdening a targeted group of owners that have not caused or uniquely contributed to the social problem addressed by the benefits extracted.[60]

While there may be no bright line in many cases distinguishing compensable from noncompensable regulation, court decisions applying partial taking analysis suggest consideration of the following factors in assessing whether the burden imposed is one that, as a matter of fairness and justice, should be paid for by the public as a whole: (1) the character of the government action; (2) the nature of the burden imposed; (3) owner expectations as shaped by background principles of state property law; (4) causation and proportionality nexus relationships between the conduct restricted and the social problem addressed by regulation; and (5) whether there are significant reciprocal benefits accruing to burdened owners or whether benefits are widely shared throughout the community while costs are focused on a few. "In short, has the Government acted in a responsible way, limiting the constraints on property ownership to those necessary to achieve the public purpose, and not allocating to some number of individuals, less than all, a burden that should be borne by all?"[61]

Most successful partial taking claims result from the perceived "benefit-extraction" character of the government action involved, particularly when viewed in light of owner expectations as shaped by background principles of state property and nuisance law, often coupled with the lack of any significant reciprocal benefits accruing to the burdened owner or from the failure to demonstrate any causation or proportionality nexus relationship between the social problem addressed and the conduct burdened by regulation.[62] Partial taking analysis reflects and enforces the often-quoted statement of Justice Holmes in *Pennsylvania Coal Co. v. Mahon*, that "a strong public desire to improve the public condition is not enough to warrant achieving the desire by a shorter cut than the constitutional way of paying for the change."[63] Focusing on the concepts of fairness, causation, and proportionality reflected in the policy of horizontal equity, partial taking analysis provides a coherent and principled basis for assessing the limits of uncompensated regulation. Rather than involving courts in an inappropriate judicial weighing of the net social benefits of legislation, partial taking analysis limits the role of courts to determining only whether the constitution requires that compensation be paid to a particular owner to secure the social benefits of government action.

§ 10.3 *Survey of Possibly Successful Partial Taking Claims*

§ 10.3(a) *Direct Taking of Property by Imposition of Development Exactions, Fees, or Conditions*

Partial taking claims have been upheld in cases involving development exactions, fees, or conditions where it is clear that private property is being "taken" by government and no cause-and-effect fairness nexus exists with respect to the exactions imposed. State courts, long before the *Nollan* and *Dolan* decisions of the Supreme Court, had applied this line of partial taking analysis to all manner of development exactions and conditions.[64] This fairness nexus test may be applied by courts to development exactions involving land,[65] money,[66] public improvements,[67] public facilities,[68] or public services[69] when imposed on an owner as a condition of development approval. This line of partial taking analysis expressly rejects the notion that owners wishing to develop land may be singled out to bear regulatory burdens for the purpose of addressing community problems that are not of their making and reflects the ruling in *Nollan* and *Dolan* that the police power may not be exercised by the extraction of unrelated or disproportionate benefits as a condition to development approval.[70]

§ 10.3(b) *Shifting of Burdens to Benefit Favored Persons or Groups*

Partial taking claims have been upheld in cases involving regulatory burdens imposed on an owner's use of land where (1) the owner's property is taken to provide a distinct benefit to another person or group (the legislatively designated beneficiaries) to remedy some perceived social problem or public need and (2) no cause-and-effect fairness nexus exists between the owner who is burdened and the problem or need addressed by the regulation.[71] As stated in a recent court decision: "A proffered State interest, which by definition should serve and protect the general populace on a fairly and uniformly applied basis, should not be countenanced when, as occurs here, the statute instead benefits one special class for an essentially unrelated economic redistribution and societal relationship."[72]

This line of partial taking analysis has been applied to inclusionary zoning and other affordable housing regulatory schemes, including exactions in the form of cash relocation assistance or the provision of, or in lieu of fees for, low-income housing, where no cause-and-effect fairness nexus exists between those persons or activities burdened by the regulation and the social problem addressed by the regulatory scheme.[73] While owners and others burdened by these regulatory schemes may be convenient targets of opportunity for dealing with the problems of persons with low or moderate incomes, they appear to be no more a distinct cause of their economic plight than the butcher, the baker, or the candlestick maker.[74] As Justice Holmes long ago pointed out in the regulatory takings context: "In general, it is not plain that a man's misfortunes or necessities will justify shifting the damages to his neighbor's shoulders."[75]

§ 10.3(c) *Burden Imposed to Subsidize Distinct Government Function or Enterprise*

Partial taking claims have been upheld in cases involving land use restrictions that are clearly imposed to support or subsidize some distinct government function or enterprise (such as the provision of public parks, schools, playgrounds, roads, airports, or flood control projects, etc.), where the burdens imposed are based largely on the accident of ownership of land at a particular location.[76] As Professor Dunham has pointed out, the evil here is that "there is no approximation of equal sharing of cost or of sharing according to capacity to pay as there is where a public benefit is obtained by subsidy or expenditure of public funds. The accident of ownership of a particular location determines the persons in the community bearing the cost of increasing the general welfare."[77] This line of partial taking analysis also would include cases where a distinct group of owners are disproportionately burdened by land use restrictions designed to secure the public benefit of improvements to public sewers, sewage treatment plants, or roads.[78]

§ 10.3(d) *Burdens Directly Benefiting Neighboring Owners: Reverse Spot Zoning*

Partial taking claims have been upheld in reverse-spot-zoning situations where an owner is burdened by restrictions designed to secure a direct benefit to neighboring owners and the absence of reciprocal benefits indicates that the burden is one that, as a matter of fairness and justice, should not be placed solely on the burdened owner.[79] For example, in *Vernon Park Realty Co. v. City of Mount Vernon,*[80] the plaintiff's land, which for a number of years had been used as a commuter parking lot, was specifically zoned for that purpose in contrast to surrounding and nearby property zoned for commercial and office building use. The New York court held this zoning, which was clearly enacted to secure a public benefit, confiscatory as arbitrary and unreasonably burdening the owner of the land in question. The court stated: "However compelling and acute the community traffic problem may be, its solution does not lie in placing an undue and uncompensated burden on the individual owner of a single parcel of land in the guise of regulation, even for a public purpose.[81] These cases suggest that owners may not be singled out by the imposition of regulatory burdens in the absence of either some cause-and-effect nexus or significant mutual reciprocal benefits related to the burdens imposed.[82]

§ 10.3(e) *Substantial Diminution in Value for Social Benefit and Absence of Reciprocal Benefit*

In what is an emerging line of partial taking analysis, some courts have upheld partial taking claims in the context of restrictions designed to secure a generalized social benefit where there is substantial diminution in value (though short of a total taking) and the disproportionate burdens imposed lack significant "direct compensating benefits." Though a cause-and-effect nexus may be satisfied in regard to the preservation of wetlands by a prohibition on the owner's construction thereon, a diminution in value of

91.8 percent (reduction in fair market value from $55,000 to $4,500) was considered a partial taking under an analysis where the ultimate question determined "is upon whom the loss of socially desirable regulations should fall."[83] Partial taking analysis is here stated to include consideration of whether there are "direct compensating benefits accruing to the property, and others similarly situated, flowing from the regulatory environment. Or are benefits, if any, general and widely shared through the community and society, while the costs are focused on a few?"[84]

Under this line of analysis, partial taking claims could apparently be asserted against land preservation restrictions that apply to all similarly situated owners but that lack "direct compensating benefits" where the loss of value is substantial but short of a total taking.[85] Existing court decisions rejecting taking claims based on substantial diminution in value resulting from enactment of typical zoning and similar land use restrictions[86] would not appear to be undermined by this line of partial taking analysis, since such restrictions generally are thought to provide some significant "reciprocity advantage" in securing a mutually beneficial environment.[87]

§ 10.3(f) *Violation of Judicially Formulated Fairness Doctrines Protecting Property Rights in the Regulatory Process*

Partial taking claims have been upheld in cases involving application of judicially formulated doctrines for the protection of individual property rights, derived from judicial balancing of competing interests, that are designed to ensure fundamental fairness in the regulatory process. This line of partial taking analysis may include state court–formulated doctrines intended to protect individual property rights related to permit denials,[88] vested rights,[89] nonconforming uses,[90] and estoppel claims.[91] This line of partial taking analysis now also includes cases where a regulatory taking is based on a finding that the regulation does not substantially advance a legitimate state interest.[92]

§ 10.4   Toward a Conclusion

Throughout most of the twentieth century, partial taking analysis has been largely the subject of state court decision making. Recent decisions of the Supreme Court, however, have refocused attention once again on partial taking claims. As the last frontier (beyond categorical takings) in the regulatory takings paradigm, partial taking analysis resurrects notions of basic fairness in the allocation of regulatory burdens and in reciprocal benefits accruing to affected owners. Under this type of partial taking analysis, the concepts of fairness, causation, and proportionality implement the policy of horizontal equity reflected in the Takings Clause and prohibit the imposition of uncompensated burdens on landowners who are singled out for the extraction of public benefits that address a social problem not distinctly related to the landowners' conduct or proposed use. Also, under present taking jurisprudence, a partial regulatory taking may be found where a regulation or permit decision does not substantially advance a legitimate state interest.[93]

Notes

1. *E.g.*, Loretto V. Teleprompter Manhattan CATV Corp., 458 U.S. 419 (1982). *See* 1 EDWARD H. ZIEGLER, RATHKOPF'S THE LAW OF ZONING AND PLANNING § 6.09 (4th ed. 1999).

2. *E.g.*, Lucas v. South Carolina Coastal Council, 505 U.S. 1003, 1015 (1992). *See* 1 ZIEGLER, *supra* note 1, at § 6.08.

3. *E.g.*, Palm Beach Isles Assocs. v. United States, 231 F.3d 1365, 1367-69 (Fed. Cir. 2000) (Gajarsa, J., dissenting) (expressly discussing this point); Florida Rock Indus. Inc.v. United States, 18 F.3d 1560 (Fed. Cir. 1994), *cert. denied*, 513 U.S. 109 (1995). *And see* cases cited *infra* at note 35.

4. Earlier discussion of the concepts of fairness, causation, and proportionality as related to horizontal equity and partial benefit-extraction taking claims can be found in 1 ZIEGLER, *supra* note 1, at § 6.10 (4th ed. 1993) (as revised 1999); Edward H. Ziegler, "Fundamental Fairness and Regulatory Takings: Judicial Standards of Fairness Shaping the Limits of Categorical and Partial Taking Claims," in 1995 PROCEEDINGS INSTITUTE ON ZONING, PLANNING, AND EMINENT DOMAIN Ch. 11 (Mathew Bender & Co., Inc. 1996).

5. Property in our common-law regime denotes not "things" but intangible "protected rights." *See* United States v. General Motors Corp., 323 U.S. 373, 377-78 (1945) (noting that the word "property" in the Takings Clause "may have been employed in a more accurate sense to denote the group of rights inhering in the citizen's relation to the particular thing, as the right to possess, use and dispose of it.").

6. Common-law property rights are, of course, held subject to the exercise of police power regulation. Since, as courts have repeatedly pointed out, government action in the form of regulation cannot trump the Takings Clause, courts necessarily attempt to establish a principled dichotomy between permissible uncompensated police power regulation and regulation that extracts a benefit for which compensation is constitutionally required. *See* JOHN LEWIS, A TREATISE ON THE LAW OF EMINENT DOMAIN 6 (3d ed. 1909).

7. *See* Lynch v. Household Finance Corp., 405 U.S. 538 (1972):

> Property does not have rights. People have rights. The right to enjoy property without unlawful deprivation, no less than the right to speak or the right to travel, is in truth a "personal" right, whether the "property" in question be a welfare check, a home, or a savings account. In fact, a fundamental interdependence exists between the personal right to liberty and the personal right in property. Neither could have meaning without the other. That rights in property are basic civil rights has long been recognized.

8. WILLIAM BLACKSTONE, 1 COMMENTARIES 135 (1765).

9. 14 Papers of James Madison 266 (Robert A. Rutland et al., eds., 1983).

10. *See* Gardner v. Village of Newburgh, 2 Johns. Ch. 162 (N.Y. 1816) (diversion of stream held a compensable taking); Yates v. Milwaukee, 77 U.S. (10 Wall.) 497, 19 L. Ed. 84 (1870) (law requiring removal of wharf held a compensable taking); Kris Kobach, *The Origins of Regulatory Takings: Setting the Record Straight*, 1996 UTAH L. REV. 1211 (discussing early regulatory taking cases).

11. *See, e.g.*, Lucas v. South Carolina Coastal Council, 505 U.S. 1003, 1024-25 (1992); Nollan v. California Coastal Comm'n, 483 U.S. 825, 833-34 n.2 (1987) (noting that "the right to build on one's own property—even though its exercise can be subjected to legitimate permitting requirements—cannot remotely be described as a governmental benefit."); Dolan v. City of Tigard, 512 U.S. 374, 388 (1994). These Supreme Court decisions make clear that the common-law property right in the use and development of land is not simply a privilege or license that may be restricted or conditioned without judicial scrutiny under the Fifth Amendment Takings Clause.

12. Kmiec, *supra* note 11, at 998-99.

13. LAURENCE H. TRIBE, AMERICAN CONSTITUTIONAL LAW 608 (2d ed. 1988).

14. 260 U.S. 393 (1922).

15. *Id.* at 415.

16. *Id.*

17. San Diego Gas & Elec. Co. v. City of San Diego, 450 U.S. 621, 652 (1981).

18. Lucas v. South Carolina Coastal Council, 505 U.S. 1003, 1015 (1992) (quoting *Pennsylvania Coal*, 260 U.S. at 415 (alterations in *Lucas*).

19. Armstrong v. United States, 364 U.S. 40, 49 (1960).

20. *See* cases cited *infra* note 45.

21. 260 U.S. 393 (1922).

22. *Id.* at 416 ("the question at bottom is upon whom the loss of the [regulatory] changes desired should fall").

23. 438 U.S. 104 (1978).

24. *Id.* at 124-28.

25. *Penn Central* appears to be based on simply the utilitarian rationale that regulation does not constitute a taking if it produces "a widespread public benefit." *Id.* at 134 n.30. *See* Leigh Raymond, *The Ethics of Compensation: Takings, Utility, and Justice*, 23 ECOLOGY L. Q. 577 (1996).

26. 438 U.S. at 129.

27. *Penn Central's* multifactored analysis has been criticized by commentators with quite different ideological views on regulatory taking issues. *Compare* Kmiec, *supra* note 4, at 114-17 (referring to *Agins* and *Penn Central* as "intellectually superseded decisions") *with* John Echeverria, *Is the Penn Central Three-Factor Test Ready for History's Dustbin?*, 52 LAND USE L. & ZONING DIG. 3 (2000) (*Penn Central* analysis "does not represent a meaningful or coherent standard" for regulatory takings).

28. *See, e.g.*, Park Ave. Tower Assocs. v. New York City, 746 F.2d 134 (2d Cir. 1984); William C. Hass v. City & County of San Francisco, 605 F.2d 1117 (9th Cir. 1979) (no taking occurs unless all value is destroyed); Gosnell v. City of Troy, 59 F.3d 654, 658 (7th Cir. 1995) (describing the deferential *Penn Central* "reasonably related to legitimate public purpose test as one where the public purpose" asserted to support regulation leads a court "to break out giggling").

29. This type of deferential standard of review is reflected in Commercial Builders v. Sacramento, 941 F.2d 872, 874 (9th Cir. 1991), *cert. denied*, 112 S. Ct. 1997 (1992) (upholding low-income housing fee on commercial building permits); Holmdel Builders

Ass'n v. Township of Holmdel, 383 A.2d 277 (N.J. 1990) (same). For a critical analysis of this deferential standard of judicial review, see Richard A. Epstein, Lucas v. South Carolina Coastal Council: *A Tangled Web of Expectations*, 45 Stan. L. Rev. 1369, 1374 (1993).

30. Loretto v. Teleprompter Manhattan CATV Corp., 458 U.S. 419, 435 (1982); Nollan v. California Coastal Comm'n, 483 U.S. 825, 837 (1987); Dolan v. City of Tigard, 512 U.S. 374, 395-96 (1994); City of Monterey v. Del Monte Dunes at Monterey, Ltd., 526 U.S. 687 (1999) (affirming jury verdict finding a regulatory taking based on the nexus test that a taking occurs if a regulation or permit decision does not substantially advance a legitimate state interest). *See also* Phillips v. Washington Legal Found., 524 U.S. 156, 170 (1998) (regulatory taking of interest on bank account without regard to extent of diminution in value).

31. *Id.*

32. Five of the six possibly successful partial regulatory taking claims surveyed later herein do not involve any critical analysis of diminution in value. *See infra* at 10.3 "Survey of Possibly Successful Partial Taking Claims."

33. City of Monterey v. Del Monte Dunes at Monterey, Ltd., *supra* note 30. *See also* Chevron USA, Inc. v. Cayetano, 224 F.3d 1030 (9th Cir. 2000) (rejecting an interpretation of "substantially advance" taking test as involving only an inquiry into "what a legislature rationally could have believed" and instead adopting a "heightened scrutiny" of legislative ends and means); Richardson v. City and County of Honolulu, 124 F.3d 1150 (9th Cir. 1997) (rent-control ordinance held a taking, since it would not substantially advance legitimate state interest).

34. Lucas v. South Carolina Coastal Council, 505 U.S. 1003 (1992). Justice Stevens, dissenting in *Lucas*, criticized as arbitrary the notion that "[a] landowner whose property is diminished in value 95% recovers nothing, while an owner whose property is diminished 100% recovers the land's full value." In response, Justice Scalia, writing for the Court, noted that Justice Stevens's analysis "errs in its assumption that the landowner whose deprivation is one step short of complete is not entitled to compensation." *Id.* at 1019 n.8.

35. *See, e.g.*, Florida Rock Indus., Inc. v. United States. 45 Fed. Cl. 21, 22-23 (1999); Creppel v. United States, 41 F.3d 627 (Fed. Cir. 1994); Cienega Gardens v. United States, 33 Fed. Cl. 196 (1995); Bauer v. Waste Mgmt. of Conn., 234 Conn. 221, 662 A.2d 1179 (1995); Tahoe Keys Property Owners' Ass'n v. Water Res. Control Bd., 23 Cal. App. 4th 1459, 28 Cal. Rptr. 734 (Cal. App. 1994); Cannone v. Noey, 867 P.2d 797 (Alaska 1994); Manufactured Housing Communities of Washington v. State, 13 P.3d 183, 197 (2000) (Sanders, J., concurring).

36. Florida Rock Indus., Inc. v. United States, 18 F.3d 1560, 171 (Fed. Cir. 194), *cert. denied*, 513 U.S. 109 (1995).

37. *See supra* note 4.

38. *Id.*

39. *See supra* note 20.

40. Since the meaning of "property" as used in the Takings Clause is largely defined by reference to state law, owner expectations protected in takings jurisprudence are shaped, as the Supreme Court has pointed out, "by the understandings of our citizens regarding the content of, and the State's power over, the 'bundle of rights' that they acquire when they obtain title to property." *Lucas, supra* note 2, at 1027.

In Palazzolo v. Rhode Island, 121 S. Ct. 2448 (2001), the Supreme Court expressly rejected any "notice defense" to regulatory taking cases, holding that enactment of a police power restriction does not itself bar a later owner from asserting a regulatory taking claim with respect to that restriction. The Court pointed out that an exercise of the police power that is so unreasonable or onerous as to compel compensation under the Takings Clause does not become less so through the passage of time or the post-enactment transfer of title—a background principle of state property law that limits an owner's title within the meaning of the Court's *Lucas* decision is not created by mere enactment of a restriction. The Court further noted that post-enactment acquisition of title would not bar a partial regulatory taking claim under a *Penn Central* analysis.

41. The legitimate scope of state police power regulation is generally held to be limited both by considerations related to the sic utere uto principle found in state nuisance law and, at least with respect to uncompensated regulation, by, in appropriate cases, the compensation requirement of the Takings Clause. *See* Village of Euclid v. Ambler Realty Co., 272 U.S. 365, 387 (1926) (discussing the scope of legitimate police power regulation); Manufactured Housing Communities of Washington v. State, 13 P.3d 183, 197 (2000) (Sanders, J., concurring) (providing an extensive discussion of the limits of police power regulation imposed by both state law and the federal Takings Clause).

42. *See* 1 ZIEGLER, *supra* note 1, at 6.03 [3].

43. Pennsylvania Coal Co. v. Mahon, *supra* note 21, at 413.

44. As Professor Ellickson points out: "The intuitive appeal of the traditional harm/benefit test for taking springs from its protection of horizontal equity. When a legislature enacts a standard of conduct that forces some individuals to confer benefits, it is holding them to a standard that most other persons are not only not forced to meet but are known to fall below." Ellickson, *Suburban Growth Controls: An Economic and Legal Analysis,* 86 YALE L.J. 385, 420 (1997). Professor Dunham similarly notes the need to apply this regulation/benefit extraction distinction in the context of land use regulation:

> [T]o compel a particular owner to undertake an activity to benefit the public, even if in the form of a restriction, is to compel one person to assume the cost of a benefit conferred on others without hope for recoupment of the cost. An owner is compelled to furnish a public benefit just as much when his land is taken for the runway of an airport as when he is prevented from building upon his land so that airplanes may approach the runway. In the former the landowner is paid without question; in the latter there is an attempt from time to time to compel the landowner to furnish the easement of flight without compensation by restricting building. The evil of the latter system is that there is no approximation of equal sharing of cost or of sharing according to capacity to pay as there is where a public benefit is obtained by subsidy or expenditure of public funds.

Allison Dunham, *A Legal and Economic Basis for City Planning*, 58 COLUM. L. REV. 650, 655 (1958).

45. *See* text accompanying note 20, *supra*. This taking analysis is found in a number of Supreme Court decisions. *See, e.g.*, Monongahela Navigation Co. v. United States, 148 U.S. 312 (1893) (Taking Clause prevents "the public from loading upon one individual more than his just share of the burdens of government, and says that when he surrenders to the public something more and different from that which is exacted from other members of the public, a full and just equivalent shall be returned to him"); Pennsylvania Coal Co. v. Mahon, 260 U.S. 393, 415-16 (1922) ("a strong public desire to improve the public condition is not enough to warrant achieving the desire by a shorter cut than the constitu-

tional way of paying for the change" and pointing out that "the question at bottom is upon whom the loss of the [regulatory] changes desired should fall"); United States v. Armstrong, 364 U.S. 40, 49 (1960) (the Takings Clause "was designed to bar Government from forcing some people alone to bear public burdens which, in all fairness and justice, should be borne by the public as a whole."); Lucas v. South Carolina Coastal Council, 505 U.S. 1003, 1018-26 (1992) (while regulation often may be interpreted as either "harm-preventing" or "benefit-conferring," there must be heightened judicial review of the nexus between the conduct restricted and the social problem addressed by regulation in situations where there is "a heightened risk that private property is being pressed into some form of public service under the guise of mitigating serious public harm"); Eastern Enterprises v. Apfel, 524 U.S. 498, 528-29, 537 (1998) (plurality opinion) (Takings Clause requires assessment of fairness in burdens imposed related to concepts of causation and proportionality).

46. *See, e.g.*, ERNST FREUND, THE POLICE POWER 511 (1904) (noting regulation/benefit extraction distinction); 1 JOHN LEWIS, A TREATISE ON THE LAW OF EMINENT DOMAIN 6 (3d ed. 1909) (to the same effect); FRED BOSSELMAN ET AL., THE TAKING ISSUE 206, 292 (1973) (to the same effect).

47. *See* 1 ZIEGLER, *supra* note 1, at § 6.10 (citing and discussing federal and state court decisions).

48. *See* 5 ZIEGLER, *supra* note 1, at § 64.04 (citing and discussing federal and state court decisions); 3 ZIEGLER, *supra* note 1, at § 40.04 (citing and discussing state court decisions).

49. Allison Dunham, *A Legal and Economic Basis for City Planning*, 58 COLUM. L. REV. 650, 666-67 (1958).

50. *See, e.g.*, John J. Costonis, *Presumptive and Per se Takings: A Decisional Model for the Taking Issue*, 58 N.Y.U. L. REV. 465, 488 (1983); William Stoebuck, *Police Power, Takings, and Due Process*, 37 WASH. & LEE L. REV. 1057, 1061 (1980); Raymond R. Coletta, *Reciprocity of Advantage and Regulatory Takings: Toward a New Theory of Takings Jurisprudence*, 40 AM. U. L.REV. 297, 351 (1990); Edward H. Ziegler, *Partial Taking Claims and Horizontal Equity: Making Sense of Fundamental Fairness and Development Restrictions*, 19 ZONING & PLAN. L. REP. 53 (1996); Douglas W. Kmiec, *Inserting the Last Remaining Pieces into the Takings Puzzle*, 38 WM. & MARY L. REV. 995 (1997); Jan G. Laitos, *Takings and Causation*, 5 WM. & MARY BILL OF RIGHTS J. 359 (1997).

51. Nollan v. California Coastal Comm'n, 483 U.S. 825, 837 (1987) (describing the imposition of unrelated conditions as "an out-and-out plan of extortion" and ruling that there must be substantial nexus between "nature" of development exaction and some specific problem related to or need generated by a particular development proposal).

52. Dolan v. City of Tigard, 512 U.S. 374, 395-96 (1994) (there must be "rough proportionality" between "amount" of development exaction and extent of specific problem related to or need generated by particular development proposal).

53. *See* Manocherian v. Lenox Hill Hospital, 84 N.Y.2d 385, 643 N.E.2d 479, 483 (1994) (finding a regulatory taking where owners were required to provide renewal leases to nonprofit hospitals). The court therein noted: "[T]here is no basis in *Nolan* itself for concluding that the Supreme Court decided to apply different takings tests, dependent on whether the takings were purely regulatory or physical. The Court promulgated a principle for all property and land-use regulation matters." *Id.* at 483.

54. *See, e.g.*, Storm v. City of Oakland, 255 Neb. 210, 583 N.W.2d 311 (1998) (on-site improvements related to soil erosion); Burton v. Clark County, 91 Wash. App. 505, 958

P.2d 343 (1998) (on-site road improvements); Benchmark Land Co. v. City of Battle-ground, 14 P.3d 172 (Wash. App. 2000) (financing of off-site road improvements); Curtis v. Town of South Thomaston, 708 A.2d 657 (Me. 1998) (on-site pond for fire protection); River Birch Assoc. v. City of Raleigh, 326 N.C. 100, 388 S.E.2d 538, 543 (1990) (open space set aside); Paulson v. Zoning Hearing Bd., 712 A.2d 785 (Pa. Cmwlth. 1998) (hours of operation); McNulty v. Town of Indialatic, 727 F. Supp. 604 (M.D. Fla. 1989) (setback); Ehrlich v. City of Culver City, 12 Cal. 4th 854, 911 P.2d 429 (Cal. 1996) (impact fees); Adamson Cos. v. City of Malibu, 854 F. Supp. 1476, 1502 (C.D. Cal. 1994) (rent control ordinance); Aspen-Tarpon Springs Ltd. P'ship v. Stuart, 635 So. 2d 61 (Fla. Dist. Ct. App. 1994) (conditions on change of use of mobile home park); Outdoor Systems, Inc. v. City of Mesa, 997 F.2d 604 (9th Cir. 1993) (restrictions on signs); State Dept. of Transp. v. Heckman, 644 So. 2d 527 (Fla. Dist. Ct. App. 1994) (waiver of platting requirement in return for conveyance of right-of-way).

55. 485 U.S. 1 (1988).

56. 485 U.S. at 19 (Scalia, J., dissenting).

57. *See* Penn Cent. Transp. Co. v. New York City, 438 U.S. 104, 133 n. 30 (1978) (harm may be characterized as simply the absence of benefit secured by regulation). Despite this ruling in *Penn Central*, more recent U.S. Supreme Court decisions indicate that this line will be drawn in appropriate cases to prevent government from circumventing the constitutional takings guarantee by mere declaration of legislative intent or clever characterization of the purposes for regulation. *See* Nollan v. California Coastal Comm'n, 483 U.S. 825, 836 n. 4 (1987); Lucas v. South Carolina Coastal Council, 505 U.S. 1024, 1025 ("We think the Takings Clause requires courts to do more than insist upon artful harm-preventing characterizations.").

58. *See Lucas*, 505 U.S. at 1026 (the absence of this distinction "would essentially nullify *Mahon's* affirmation of limits to the uncompensable exercise of the police power"); Bowles v. United States, 31 Fed. Cl. 37, 49 (1994); Florida Rock Indus., Inc. v. United States, 18 F.3d 1560, 1571 (Fed. Cir. 1994), *cert. denied*, 115 S. Ct. 898 (1995).

59. As Professor Tarlock points out, the harm/benefit dichotomy as a test for validity may be "so susceptible to abuse as to be useless," at least when not applied in view of ordinary and widely shared expectations about the risks that a landowner faces from public regulation of his land use choices and when the underlying policies of horizontal equity—treating like people alike—are ignored. Tarlock, *Regulatory Takings*, 60 CHI.-KENT L. REV. 23, 31 (1984).

60. *See, e.g.*, cases cited *supra* notes 45 and 54.

61. Florida Rock Indus. v. United States, 18 F.3d 1560, 1571 (Fed. Cir. 1994), *cert. denied*, 513 U.S. 109 (1995).

62. In *Barancik v. County of Marin*, 872 F.2d 834 (9th Cir. 1989), the court upheld a 60-acre per dwelling restriction intended to preserve the "beautiful rural landscape" in the Nicasio Valley. The valley had been designated a distinct planning area, and the regulatory scheme included the use of transfer development rights within the valley and imposed an overall limit on density. Such a regulatory scheme, with its obvious direct reciprocal benefits to owners within the valley, would likely be upheld under the type of "partial taking" analysis discussed herein.

63. 260 U.S. 393, 416 (1922).

64. *See* 5 ZIEGLER, *supra* note 1 at § 65.04 (discussing pre-*Nollan* and pre-*Dolan* state court decisions).

65. *E.g.*, Onge v. Donovan, 71 N.Y.2d 507, 522 N.E.2d 1019 (1988) (discussing long line of cases on point).

66. *E.g.*, Andres v. Village of Flossmoor, 15 Ill. App. 3d 655, 304 N.E.2d 700 (1973) ($1,000 per building for village general fund).

67. *E.g.*, Cupp v. Board of Supervisors, 227 Va. 580, 318 S.E.2d 407 (1984) (road construction unrelated to development).

68. *E.g.*, Plote, Inc. v. Minnesota Alden Co., 96 Ill. App. 3d 1001, 422 N.E.2d 231 (1981) (village cultural center).

69. *E.g.*, Triesman v. Town of Bedford, 132 N.H. 54, 563 A.2d 786 (1989) (holding invalid a condition that privately owned helicopters be used by town's police and fire department).

70. *See Nollan,* 483 U.S. at 837. *And see* Volusia County v. Aberdeen, 760 So. 2d 126 (Fla. 2000) (impact fee for public schools on adults-only mobile home park held a taking).

71. *See, e.g.*, Property Owners Ass'n v. Township of North Bergen, 74 N.J. 327, 378 A.2d 25 (1977) (ordinance requiring subsidization of senior citizen rents by their land-lords and other tenants); Seawall Assocs. v. City of New York, 74 N.Y.2d 1059, 542 N.E.2d 1059, 1069 (1989) (buyout and other burdens imposed on single-room-only housing to address problems of homeless); Guimont v. Clarke, 121 Wash. 2d 586, 611-13, 854 P.2d 1 (1993), *cert. denied*, 114 S. Ct. 1216 (1994) (relocation assistance for low-income tenants); Robinson v. Stuart, 635 So. 2d 61 (Fla. Dist. Ct. App. 1994) (requirement that mobile park owners buy tenants' homes or pay relocation costs); Manufactured Housing Communities of Washington v. State, 13 P.3d 183 (Wash. 2000) (statute grant-ing right of first refusal to mobile home park tenants held a taking); Boorman v. Board of Supervisors, 584 N.W.2d 309 (Iowa 1998) (statute granting immunity from nuisance suits in agricultural areas held a taking).

72. Manocherian v. Lenox Hill Hospital, 84 N.Y.2d 385, 643 N.E.2d 479, 484-85 (1994) (requirement that owners provide renewal leases to nonprivate hospitals based on primary residency status of hospital's employee-subtenant).

73. *See* cases *supra* note 71. *But see* Garneau v. City of Seattle, 897 F. Supp. 1318 (W.D. Wash. 1995) (upholding exaction of cash relocation assistance for low-income tenants); Gagne v. City of Hartford, 1994 Conn. Super. LEXIS 61 (unreported) (requiring replacement of, or in lieu fees for, low-income housing, and cases cited therein); Com-mercial Builders v. City of Sacramento, 941 F.2d 872 (9th Cir. 1991) (upholding impact fee for low-income housing); Holmdel Builders Ass'n v. Township of Holmdel, 583 A.2d 277 (N.J. 1990) (same).

74. Application of this type of benefit-extraction taking analysis is reflected in then–California Chief Justice Rose Bird's dissenting opinion in *Yarborough v. Superior Court*, 39 Cal. 3d 197, 216 Cal. Rptr. 425, 702 P.2d 583 (1985) (not reaching the taking issue of whether a court-appointed lawyer must be compensated for services rendered): "No crystal ball is necessary to foresee the public outrage which would erupt if we ordered grocery store owners to give indigents two months of free groceries or automobile dealers to give them two months of free cars. Lawyers in our society are entitled to no greater privilege than the butcher, the baker and the candlestick maker, but they certainly are entitled to no less."

75. Pennsylvania Coal Co. v. Mahon, 260 U.S. at 416. *See also* Laitos, *supra* note 50, at 364 (pointing out that partial benefit-extraction taking analysis as related to redistribu-tive legislation is generally consistent with John Rawls' theory of "justice" in the alloca-tion of burdens to secure public goods that others primarily enjoy).

76. *See, e.g.*, New Products Corp. v. City of North Miami, 271 So. 2d 24 (Fla. Dist. Ct. App. 1972) (zoning of land for public park); Ripley v. City of Lincoln, 330 N.W.2d 505 (N.D. 1983) (zoning of land for public school); City of Plainfield v. Borough of Middlesex,

69 N.J. 136, 173 A.2d 785 (1961) (zoning for land for public playground); Joint Ventures, Inc. v. Dept. of Transportation, 563 So. 2d 622 (Fla. 1990) (road reservation map restriction); Sneed v. City of Riverside, 218 Cal. App. 2d 205, 32 Cal. Rptr. 318 (1963) (overflight easement); Panhandle Eastern Pipeline Co. v. Madison County Drainage Bd., 898 F. Supp. 1302 (S.D. Ind. 1995) (partial taking found where utility was required to bury its pipelines deeper in the ground to facilitate county drainage project), *citing* Panhandle Eastern Pipeline Co. v. State Highway Comm'n, 294 U.S. 613, 618 (1935); Hager v. Louisville & Jefferson County Planning & Zoning Comm'n, 261 S.W.2d 619 (Ky. 1953) (holding confiscatory amendment to master plan designating owner's land as temporary storage basin in connection with a county flood control project).

77. Allison Dunham, *A Legal and Economic Basis for City Planning*, 50 COLUM. L. REV. 650, 655 (1958).

78. *See, e.g.*, Stevens v. Salisbury, 240 Md. 556, 214 A.2d 725 (1965) (traffic controls); Charles v. Diamond, 41 N.Y.2d 318, 360 N.W.2d 1295, 392 N.Y.S.2d 594 (1977) (sewerage treatment problems); Westwood Forest Estates v. Village of S. Nyack, 23 N.Y.2d 424, N.E.2d 700, 297 N.Y.S.2d 129 (1969) (village may not uniquely burden individual owners as a result of general problem with sewer system); Ozolos v. Henley, 81 A.D.2d 670, 438 N.Y.S.2d 349, 351 (1981) (denial of subdivision approval because of inadequacy of town road).

79. *See, e.g.*, Christopher Lake Dev. Co. v. St. Louis Cty., 35 F.3d 1269 (8th Cir. 1994) (application of design criteria singling out owner to provide drainage system for entire watershed area); Heck v. Zoning Hearing Bd., 39 Pa. Commw. 570, 397 A.2d 15 (1979) (holding invalid denial of permit to construct one-floor addition to a shoreline structure solely on the ground that the addition would obstruct view of a lake); Sheerr v. Township of Evesham, 184 N.J. Super. 11, 445 A.2d 46 (L. Div. 1982) (holding confiscatory regulation that conferred a benefit to the public only to the extent that the plaintiff's trees would provide an appealing vista); Viso v. State, 92 Cal. App. 2d 15, 154 Cal. Rptr. 580 (1959) (rezoning to "general forest" classification of land surrounded by commercial uses held confiscatory).

80. Vernon Park Realty Co. v. City of Mount Vernon, 307 N.Y. 493, 121 N.E.2d 517 (1954).

81. 121 N.E.2d at 519.

82. *See, e.g.*, Paradyne Corp. v. State, 528 So. 2d 921 (Fla. Dist. Ct. App. 1988) (construction of access road to benefit neighboring property held a taking); Unlimited v. Kitsap County, 50 Wash. App. 723, 750 P.2d 651 (1988) (grant of right-of-way to neighboring owner held a taking); Luxembourg Group, Inc., Snohomish County, 76 Wash. App. 502, 887 P.2d 446, 448 (1995) (condition benefiting neighbor must be attributable to problem caused by development).

83. Bowles v. United States, 31 Fed. Cl. 37, 52-53 (1994) (alternative holding).

84. Florida Rock Indus., Inc. v. United States, 18 F.3d 1560, 1571 (Fed. Cir. 1994), *cert. denied*, 513 U.S. 109 (1995). *See also* Walcek v. United States, 2001 WL 334254 (Fed. Cl.) (providing an extensive discussion of the relevant parcel "segmentation" issue related to diminution in value and also discussing calculation of the related issue of measuring return on original investment).

85. *See* Florida Rock Indus., Inc. v. United States, 45 Fed. Cl. 21 (1999) (wetlands preservation restriction that reduced property value of owner's land by 73.1% constituted a compensable partial taking). This line of partial taking analysis would appear to limit the scope of the Supreme Court's earlier decision in *Penn Cent. Transp. Co. v. New York City*, 48 U.S. 104, 130 (1978) (upholding landmark preservation ordinance where owner had

economically viable existing use of the land and substantial diminution in value did not interfere with reasonable investment-backed expectations but only ability to "exploit" market value of the property) to cases involving substantial diminution in the "exploitation" or speculative market value of land as opposed to cases where the substantial loss of value interferes with an owner's reasonable investment-backed expectations relating to the original use or development of lands preserved from development by regulation.

86. *See, e.g.*, Village of Euclid v. Ambler Realty Co., 272 U.S. 365 (1926) (75% diminution in value); Hadacheck v. Sebastian, 239 U.S. 394 (1915) (87% diminution in value).

87. *See* Florida Rock Indus., Inc., 18 F.3d at 1570 (supporting this analysis). *And see* Tahoe Keys Property Owners' Ass'n v. Water Res. Control Bd., 23 Cal. App. 4th 1459, 28 Cal. Rptr. 2d 734, 746-47 (1994) (wherein the court rejected a partial taking claim relating to pollution mitigation fees for the Tahoe Basin based, in part, on the "special benefits" conferred on landowners in the area).

88. Whitehead Oil Co. v. City of Lincoln, 515 N.W.2d 401 (Neb. 1994) (permit denial as taking).

89. Pace Resources, Inc. v. Shrewsbury Twp., 808 F.2d 1023, 1033 (3d Cir. 1987) (recognizing vested rights claim).

90. Ailes v. Decatur County Area Planning Comm'n, 448 N.E.2d 1057 (Ind. 1987) (nonconforming use taking claim).

91. Offen v. County Council, 625 A.2d 424 (Md. Ct. Spec. App. 1993) (recognizing zoning estoppel where egregious action prevented acquisition of vested rights), *cert. granted*, County Council v. Offen, 332 Md. 480, 632 A.2d 446 (1993), *rev'd*, County Council v. Offen, 334 Md. 499, 639 A.2d 1070 (1994) (the Court of Appeals determined that the Court of Special Appeals had abused its discretion in raising, sua sponte, the doctrine of zoning estoppel and reversed the lower court).

92. *See* text and accompanying notes 31-33, *supra*.

93. *Id.*

WHAT'S "NORMAL" ABOUT PLANNING DELAY?

11

MICHAEL M. BERGER*

§ 11.0 Introduction

In First English Evangelical Lutheran Church v. County of Los Angeles,[1] the U.S. Supreme Court held that the Fifth Amendment guarantees just compensation for all takings, physical or regulatory, permanent or temporary. But then the Court hedged its holding. After concluding that the moratorium ordinance before it—which forbade all use for two years—could constitute a taking, the Court noted that its opinion did "not deal with the quite different questions that would arise in the case of normal delays in obtaining building permits, changes in zoning ordinances, variances, and the like...."[2]

That innocent disclaimer would—as the Court should have realized—lead to an entire substructure of the law, as government lawyers strove to portray *all* delays as "normal." Some courts bought it;[3] others did not.[4] The issue remains in turmoil. For example, in the most recent chapter in the *Tahoe-Sierra* litigation,[5] a panel of the Ninth Circuit refused to apply *First English*, opting instead for Justice Stevens's dissent in that case.[6] The confusion in the

* A shareholder in Berger & Norton in Santa Monica, California, I have spent virtually my entire career since graduating from law school in 1967 representing property owners in litigation against government agencies. Some of the views expressed here may have been colored by the fact that I represented the property owners before the U.S. Supreme Court in both *First English* and *Tahoe-Sierra*, which play important roles in this discussion.

law, wrought by lawyers and academics who refuse to accept the idea that the temporary prohibition of use requires compensation, is the subject of this chapter. The focus here will be on the kind of temporary taking resulting from so-called moratoria, i.e., regulations that prohibit all use for a period of time.[7]

§ 11.1   First English *and the Concept of Temporary Takings*

It is impossible to discuss the topic of temporary takings without parsing the U.S. Supreme Court's opinions in *First English*. The plural is necessary because Justice Stevens's dissenting views help to illuminate what the majority decided.

First, it is important to understand that *First English* was a case about a *temporary* planning moratorium. Heated scholarly discussions often focus on whether a "temporary" taking was always designed to be temporary or merely describes the impact of a regulation intended to be permanent but struck down as illegal. These discussions lose sight of the fact that the only thing before the Court in *First English* was the constitutional consequence of an ordinance that was avowedly designed to be in effect for a limited period of time to provide the county's planners time to react to a flood that had caused severe damage in the vicinity of the subject property. Rather than allowing the First English Evangelical Lutheran Church to simply rebuild the camping facility that it lost in a storm, Los Angeles County enacted a moratorium that, under California law, could not exceed two years.[8] Thus, the temporary use prohibition was always intended to be of finite duration, and everyone knew the maximum length it could be.

Also pertinent is the *Agins* litigation, which preceded *First English*, and on which the latter was based. In *Agins v. City of Tiburon*,[9] the California Supreme Court held that compensation was not available as a remedy for a regulatory taking. Thus, as the U.S. Supreme Court acknowledged, the landowner's claims in *First English* "were deemed irrelevant [by the California Court of Appeal] solely because of the California Supreme Court's decision in *Agins* that damages are unavailable to redress a 'temporary' regulatory taking."[10] The challenge in *Agins*, like that in *First English* and *Tahoe-Sierra*, was *not* directed at a "permanent" regulation rendered "temporary" because a court struck it down. Dr. and Mrs. Agins complained about the impact of the city's examination of its options to condemn the property for a public park and its subsequent downzoning. The study period was plainly temporary, and the downzoning was never struck down.

Second, given the finite length of the *First English* moratorium, it would seem inescapable that the Court intended its decision to apply to planning moratoria that were designed to be in effect for only a limited period of time. Knowing that the suit dealt only with the two-year planning moratorium (rather than the permanent development ban that replaced it),[11] the Court said it was dealing with a use prohibition that lasted for "a considerable period of years."[12] The Court also noted that, in that context, deprivation of use was the equivalent of condemning a leasehold interest in the property for that period of time, an interest that "may be great indeed."[13]

Third, the Court contrasted that "considerable period" with the "normal delays in obtaining building permits, changes in zoning ordinances, variances, and the like. . . ."[14] Although the Court went no further in explicating "normal" delays in the planning process, the carefully chosen illustrations would seem to have no impact on moratoria. Each of them illustrates a process in which a landowner is participating with the expectation—or at least the possibility—of obtaining development permission at the conclusion. However, the situation must be otherwise where the regulation is a total development freeze. That "delay" cannot, by any stretch, be considered "normal" for developers working their way through the planning process.[15] In that case, it is not a "delay" at all, but an outright denial of use.

Fourth, in finally deciding the remedy question that had dogged the Court (and the rest of us) for the better part of a decade,[16] the Court obviously believed that a planning moratorium enacted for a finite period of time *could* require compensation under the Fifth Amendment. Otherwise, why pick this vehicle to decide the remedy question, and why remand it to the lower courts for further proceedings?[17] Given its track record, the Court surely could have found a reason not to decide *First English* if the Justices believed that the underlying substantive claim could not result in a Fifth Amendment taking as a matter of law.[18] However, they did not, thus acknowledging, at least by implication, that the substantive claim exists.

Fifth, the cases on which the Court chiefly relied to establish the right to recover for a temporary regulatory taking were direct condemnation cases in which the government condemned the right to use property for a finite period of years. Thus, in concluding that a moratorium enacted for a specific and finite time could be a taking, the Court invoked a line of cases that framed the issue this way:

> The problem involved is the ascertainment of the just compensation required by the Fifth Amendment of the Constitution, where, in the exercise of the power of emi-

nent domain, *temporary occupancy* of a portion of a leased building is taken from a tenant who holds under a long term lease.[19]

The time periods involved were all less than three years with options to renew.[20] *That* is what the Court contemplated in *First English* when it discussed temporary takings. *That* is the kind of time element the Court envisioned when it noted, with dry understatement, that "[t]he United States has been required to pay compensation for leasehold interests of shorter duration than this [i.e., the period of non-use suffered by the church]."[21] *That* is what the Court had in mind when it said that "[t]hese [direct condemnation] cases reflect the fact that 'temporary' takings which, as here, deny a landowner all use of his property are not different in kind from permanent takings, for which the Constitution clearly requires compensation."[22]

Sixth, one cannot overlook the intriguing relationship between the majority opinion, the dissent, Justice Brennan's dissent in *San Diego Gas*, and a contemporaneous polemic called *The White River Junction Manifesto*.[23] In *San Diego Gas*, a five-Justice majority found that the matter was not final and thus not subject to Supreme Court review. Justice Brennan dissented on behalf of the remaining four, concluding that the matter was not only ripe, but that the property owner ought to be compensated for the impact of a confiscatory regulation. What scared the regulatory world was that Justice Rehnquist, although providing the fifth vote on lack of finality, wrote separately to indicate his essential agreement with the substance of Justice Brennan's dissent.[24] As a consequence of being both "appalled" and "astounded" that others around the country could count to five and attribute significance to Justice Brennan's analysis,[25] the authors of the *Manifesto* set out to prove him wrong.

The *Manifesto* attacked Justice Brennan from every angle imaginable (and some that were rather hard to fathom)[26] in an effort to dissuade the Court from turning that dissent into a formal majority. They failed. But they did convince Justice Stevens, who relied on their analysis, particularly their discussion of temporary takings and planning moratoria.[27] With respect to the latter, it must have caused great chagrin among the *Manifesto*'s authors that the case chosen by the Court to announce its temporary taking rule involved a planning moratorium. Here's what they had to say in their effort to save the moratorium:

If a "temporary taking" is at least the deprivation of all beneficial use for a defined period of time, *are develop-*

ment moratoria now to be "temporary takings?" They certainly look like a "temporary taking." So another unanticipated application of Brennan's proposed constitutional rule is that the payment of compensation for any temporary interference with the use of land would be required, a consequence that conflicts with years of established jurisprudence without explanation. If the Brennan dissent is to be the rule, then a way must be found to avoid tossing development moratoria on the judicial ash heap.[28]

While Justice Stevens's dissent placed its reliance on the *Manifesto*, the majority repeatedly cited Justice Brennan's *San Diego Gas* dissent as authoritative.[29] Thus, with Justice Brennan rejecting any substantive difference between temporary and permanent takings,[30] the *First English* majority elevating the Brennan *San Diego Gas* dissent to a Court holding,[31] the *Manifesto* bemoaning the potential impact of compensation on the effectiveness of planning moratoria,[32] and the *First English* dissent accepting that point of view,[33] the clear message of the decision is that planning moratoria that take substantially all economically productive use of property for a period of years must be accompanied by compensation. To emphasize the disagreement, Justice Stevens (in a portion of his dissent in which no other justice concurred) concluded that a temporary regulatory taking should be recognized only when the "temporary" period consumes "a significant percentage of the property's useful life."[34] But that's not what the Court held.

§ 11.2 *A Tale of Two Cases*

And then came *Tahoe-Sierra*. If you are not from California, you may not realize the near-religious significance that Lake Tahoe holds for the natives. You simply worship it, even if local nabobs have been permitted to build lavish waterfront mansions there.[35]

§ 11.2(a) *The Facts of the Tahoe-Sierra Litigation*

Many have sung the environmental praises of Lake Tahoe;[36] none disputes its glories. It is evidently unique in the depth of its clarity—and therein lies both its blessing and its curse. Because of concerns that lakefront developments were compromising the lake's clarity, Congress (in 1969) approved a compact between California and Nevada that created the Tahoe Regional Planning Agency (TRPA) to control development around the lake.

The compact was amended in 1980 to strengthen TRPA's mandate. Thereafter TRPA, evidently heedless of the distinction between regulation and confiscation, began a series of rolling moratoria/prohibitions that has precluded all economically productive use of each of the homesites owned by the 449 landowners remaining in the suit.[37]

Ordinance 81-5 was the first in the unremitting series of rolling prohibitions. Effective Aug. 24, 1981, it prohibited residential use—the use for which the properties were zoned and for which the landowners intended to use them—in parts of the Lake Tahoe region involved in the litigation, i.e., lands classified as either "high hazard" (because of steepness or geology) or "stream environment." The moratorium was to remain in effect until TRPA adopted amendments to the regional plan. A year later, on Aug. 26, 1982, TRPA established environmental threshold carrying capacities, which would determine the maximum capacity for development of each lot in the area. The compact required TRPA to complete its work on the regional plan within one year of that date. As time passed, TRPA recognized that it could not meet that goal, and so, a year later, on Aug. 26, 1983, it adopted Resolution 83-21 (a 90-day temporary moratorium), suspending all permitting activities pending completion of the new regional plan.

The 90-day moratorium that rolled on through Resolution 83-21 was not enough, and TRPA informally allowed it to keep rolling from Nov. 26, 1983, until April 26, 1984, when it finally adopted its new regional plan.[38] The 1984 plan (Ordinance 84-1) made no change in the use prohibition inflicted on these landowners. Although it appeared to permit development elsewhere in the Tahoe Basin, all of the homesites in the *Tahoe-Sierra* litigation remained untouchable. The prohibition simply continued to roll indefinitely.

The state of California (TRPA's staunch ally and defender in this case) sued TRPA when the 1984 plan was adopted, because it felt the parts of the new plan dealing with other landowners did not comply with the restrictive/protective demands of the compact. Shortly thereafter, Judge Garcia, of the Eastern District of California, enjoined TRPA from approving any building projects.[39] That injunction remained in force until TRPA promulgated another revised regional plan in 1987.

But the only effect of Judge Garcia's injunction was to prevent TRPA from allowing those other landowners, not the *Tahoe-Sierra* litigants, to develop their properties. Had there been no such injunction, the 1984 plan would have precluded all development on the properties in the litigation anyway. The injunction thus had no impact on these landowners. It "prevented" TRPA from issuing permits to people who could not have obtained permits in any event for reasons unrelated to the injunction. In short, the prohibition on use of their properties that had started in 1981 continued on, unabated, through 1987 and beyond.

For these landowners, the impact of the 1987 plan was to continue what had gone before. The use prohibitions that previously had been labeled "temporary" simply rolled on. Thus, under none of the various ordinances, resolutions, informal moratoria, or formal plans TRPA issued beginning in 1981 was there anything economically beneficial or productive that these landowners could do with any of their individual homesites. Through this series of rolling enactments, TRPA has effectively blocked construction of their homes for the past two decades, and that prohibition has become permanent. The only thing left for the landowners to do is to continue holding bare legal title to something that cannot be productively used or sell it at fire sale prices to entities established by the two states and the federal government for a salvage operation, while paying property taxes and bearing all other obligations of property ownership in the interim[40]—or suffer foreclosure.

The district court found liability for a temporary taking from 1981 through 1984, relying on the Supreme Court's holdings in *Lucas*, for the proposition that a regulation that deprives a landowner of all economically beneficial or productive use is a compensable taking, and in *First English*, for the proposition that a temporary taking during a planning moratorium requires compensation the same as a permanent taking. The district court denied any compensation for the impact of the 1984 plan, erroneously asserting that it was Judge Garcia's injunction that prevented permits from issuing, not the 1984 plan.[41] Finally, the district court denied any relief from the 1987 continuation of the use prohibitions on these lots on the ground that the statute of limitations had run out by the time the landowners amended their complaints to seek compensation for the effects of the 1987 event.[42]

The Ninth Circuit affirmed insofar as the district court denied relief and reversed the limited relief the district court had granted. The Ninth Circuit simply refused to follow *First English*. Although both *First English* and *Tahoe-Sierra* involved temporary planning moratoria in effect for a finite period of years, the court asserted that it was "flatly incorrect" that *First English* had any impact.[43] Then, viewing each period separately, the court held that each of the properties retained substantial value (because the life of property is theoretically infinite and there could be use left at the end of the moratorium), and therefore there could be no taking, even "assum[ing] arguendo [in light of the district court's findings] that the moratorium prevented all development in the period during which it was in effect."[44]

Needless to say, the Ninth Circuit's bizarre analysis ignores the fact that, while the "life of the land" may be indefinite, the lives of its mortal human owners are not, and using this approach simply strips human owners of all they own and enjoy. As Justice Holmes put it, the Just Compensation Clause of the Constitution "deals with people, not with tracts of land."[45] More recently, the High Court reaffirmed this concept by stressing that "[p]roperty does not have rights. People have rights."[46]

The landowners' timely Petition for Rehearing and rehearing en banc were both denied. Five active circuit judges dissented in an opinion that demonstrated the Ninth Circuit's conflict with *First English*, *Lucas*, and other decisions. Their dissent concludes:

> The panel does not like the Supreme Court's Takings Clause jurisprudence very much, so it reverses *First English Evangelical Lutheran Church v. County of Los Angeles*, 482 U.S. 304 (1987), and adopts Justice Stevens' *First English* dissent.[47]
>
> The panel's desire to ease local governance does not justify approving means that violate rights secured by the Fifth Amendment as authoritatively interpreted by the Supreme Court.[48]
>
> By voting not to rehear, we have neglected our duty and passed the burden of correcting our mistake on to a higher authority.[49]

§ 11.2(b) *The Ninth Circuit's Holding—That a "Temporary" Planning Moratorium Can Never Constitutionally Require Compensation—Is Flatly Contrary to* First English

The Ninth Circuit's holding, that a "temporary" planning moratorium can never constitutionally require compensation, is flatly contrary to *First English*

The dissenters got it right; the Ninth Circuit doesn't like the Supreme Court's takings jurisprudence. Its decisions in the *Tahoe-Sierra* litigation have, bit by bit, undermined the landowners' case. In its first contact with this litigation, the nominal dissenter, in a strange three-opinion decision,[50] noted that the per curiam opinion appeared to harbor "thinly disguised contempt" for the landowners' plea that their Bill of Rights concerns be accorded the same respect as other Bill of Rights concerns.[51] In the latest Ninth Circuit decision in the case, the panel went so far as to de facto "reverse" decisions of the Supreme Court in order to deny relief. But its latest decision simply goes too far in its effort to nullify *First English* and *Lucas*.

To rationalize its deviance from *First English*, the Ninth Circuit concocted a theory it called "conceptual severance," and concluded that such "severance" of different property interests (here, a taking for a period of years) could not legally be done; i.e., unless it is a permanent deprivation, it *cannot* be a taking. The short answer to that assertion is that it defies *First English*, where the Court concluded: "Nothing in the Just Compensation Clause suggests that 'takings' must be permanent and irrevocable."[52] Moreover, government agencies routinely condemn various interests in land for temporary periods.[53] Temporary easements are taken almost daily to facilitate road construction, but no one has ever had the temerity to suggest that the temporary nature of such takings somehow renders them noncompensable.

That the Ninth Circuit's decision conflicts with *First English* requires little more than comparing it with the dissent in *First English*. Although the Ninth Circuit opinion never cites the *First English* dissent, it bears what Judge Kozinski called such "an uncanny resemblance" to that dissent[54] that it caused him to suggest plagiarism.[55] Here is what the Ninth Circuit's opinion looks like when laid side-by-side against the *First English* dissent:

First English dissent	*Tahoe-Sierra* opinion
"Regulations are three dimensional; they have depth, width, and length. As for depth, regulations define the extent to which the owner may not use the property in question. With respect to width, regulations define the amount of property encompassed by the restrictions. Finally, and for purposes of this case, essentially, regulations set forth the duration of the restrictions. It is obvious that no one of these elements can be analyzed alone to evaluate the impact of a regulation, and hence to determine whether a taking has occurred. . . . [I]n assessing the economic effect of a regulation, one cannot conduct the inquiry without considering the duration of the restriction. . . . Why should there be a constitutional distinction between a permanent restriction that only reduces the economic value of	"Property interests may have many different dimensions. For example, the dimensions of a property interest may include a physical dimension (which describes the size and shape of the property in question), a functional dimension (which describes the extent to which an owner may use or dispose of the property in question), and a temporal dimension (which describes the duration of the property interest). . . . A planning regulation that prevents the development of a parcel for a temporary period of time is conceptually no different than a land-use restriction that permanently denies all use on a discrete portion of property, or that permanently restricts a type of use across all of the parcel. Each of these three types of regulation will have an impact on the parcel's value. . . . There is no

the property by a fraction—perhaps one-third—and a restriction that merely postpones the development of a property for a fraction of its useful life—presumably far less than a third?"[56]

plausible basis on which to distinguish a similar diminution in value that results from temporary suspension of a development."[57]

The reason the Ninth Circuit went to such lengths to immunize TRPA was that, from the start, the opinion was a goal in search of a justification. The opinion makes no bones about its desire to protect government planning agencies from the consequences of their own decisions. Calling land-use planning in general "necessarily a complex, time-consuming undertaking," and the specific tool of a moratorium on development "crucial" to the process,[58] the Ninth Circuit announced that courts should be "exceedingly reluctant" to rule in ways that would "threaten [the moratorium's] survival."[59] And so, instead of performing its historic role as the defender of the Bill of Rights, the court chose to protect those impinging on the constitutional guarantee. It thought that providing constitutional protection here would provide property owners with a "weapon" to "penalize local communities for attempting to protect the public interest."[60]

That idiosyncratic Ninth Circuit notion goes far toward explaining the result. It went beyond turning the Fifth Amendment's protection of property rights into a "poor relation" of other constitutionally protected rights;[61] the court declared such rights to be subservient to the wishes of constitutional violators. Takings litigation is not about "penalizing" anyone, any more than complying with the *Miranda* rule is about penalizing the police or the community by making it easier for criminals to ply their trade with impunity. Nor when citizens demand enforcement of their Fourth Amendment rights are they wielding a "weapon" with which to "penalize" the community for its effective law enforcement practices.

Takings litigation is only another instance of "protect[ing] the public interest" by requiring obedience to the Constitution. As Justice Brennan put it, "After all, if a policeman must know the Constitution, then why not a planner?"[62] Neither police officers nor planners are above the law, and requiring them to toe the constitutional mark does *not* "penalize the community." Quite the contrary—it is disregard of the Bill of Rights that penalizes the citizenry.

The Ninth Circuit's erroneous focus on defending all possible planning tools in order to preserve the flexibility of planners is flatly contrary to *First English*, a conclusion easily drawn by comparing its opinion with *First English*:

First English	*Tahoe-Sierra*
"We realize that even our present holding will undoubtedly lessen to some extent the freedom and flexibility of land-use planners and governing bodies of municipal corporations when enacting land-use regulations. But such consequences necessarily flow from any decision upholding a claim of constitutional right; many of the provisions of the Constitution are designed to limit the flexibility and freedom of governmental authorities, and the Just Compensation Clause of the Fifth Amendment is one of them."[63]	"In reaching this conclusion, we preserve the ability of local governments to do what they have done for many years—to engage in orderly, reasonable land-use planning through a considered and deliberative process. To do otherwise would turn the Takings Clause into a weapon to be used indiscriminately to penalize local communities for attempting to protect the public interest."[64]

§ 11.2(c) *Aside from its Conflicts with Decisions of the U.S. Supreme Court, the Ninth Circuit's Decision Conflicts with Decisions of Other Lower Courts, Creating Confusion That All but Asked for Certiorari to Be Granted*

As if direct conflict with Supreme Court decisions were not enough, the opinion below conflicts with other lower court opinoins as well. For example, in *Tabb Lakes, Ltd. v. United States*,[65] the Court acknowledged that, under *First English*, "a taking, even for a day, without compensation is prohibited by the Constitution."

Other courts agree with *Tabb Lakes*. For example, in *Cumberland Farms, Inc. v. Town of Groton*,[66] the town denied a variance. Notwithstanding that the property owners retained some use of the service station on their property, the Connecticut Supreme Court held that they could pursue compensation for a temporary taking of their property during the time that it took to litigate the invalidity of the town's denial. The court expressly noted that the town's argument was "contrary to the holding of *First English*. . . ."[67]

In *Eberle v. Dane County Bd. of Adjustment*,[68] the county denied an access permit. The Wisconsin Supreme Court held that the owners could pursue compensation for a temporary taking, notwithstanding that they regained full use of their property when that court eventually overturned the permit denial. The court expressly concluded that the county's argument against compensation was contrary to both *First English* and *Lucas*.[69]

Likewise, in *Whitehead Oil Co. v. City of Lincoln*,[70] the Nebraska Supreme Court rejected the city's argument—that it should not be liable for a temporary taking because all use of the property had not been taken—by referring to "the line of cases which recognizes relief is possible from regulatory takings which do not deprive the owner of all economic use of the property."[71] Finally, on remand from the Supreme Court's decision in *Lucas*, the South Carolina Supreme Court held that a temporary taking had occurred as a matter of law.[72] This, in spite of the fact that Mr. Lucas could still "picnic, swim, camp in a tent, or live on the property in a movable trailer."[73]

To the extent that some courts have been persuaded to reach a different conclusion,[74] that only emphasized the conflict of decision and set the stage for the Supreme Court's grant of certiorari. There is a resolute need for clarity in this field that, to date, has been sorely lacking. As a matter of practical reality, all who deal with it are having difficulty. As a recent appraisal commentary summed it up, "There is almost universal consensus in the prodigious takings literature that takings theory is a 'muddle,' 'chaotic,' 'unsatisfactory,' 'unpredictable,' lacking in 'doctrine,' and a 'mess.'"[75] There is no reason to add to that litany, and every reason to rectify it.

§ 11.3   *With Apologies to Gertrude Stein, a Taking Is a Taking Is a Taking. It Doesn't Matter How or Why or for How Long, They All Require Compensation*

Once one is able to leave behind the politician's pursuit of a free lunch, the law underlying takings litigation should be simple. Most young children are able to understand the concept that if one of their playmates exerts dominion over something of theirs, they have been subjected to a taking. The victims will either take direct action to retrieve it or seek intervention from a supervisor. That's all that is involved in regulatory taking cases, except that we try to discourage the victims from self-help. The problem is that the players have aged and have overlaid political theories on the simple concept of keeping your hands off that which belongs to others, unless you are willing to compensate them for it.

The jurisprudence of "temporary" takings can be summed up simply: It's the same as for all other takings. The fact that government says it is using police power, rather than eminent domain power, is irrelevant. All that matters constitutionally is the impact of governmental action on private property owners.The impetus for the government's action does not even matter. In fact, the more legitimate the reason, the greater the reason for compensation.

The temporary nature of a freeze on land use is constitutionally irrelevant and merely impacts the amount of compensation due. As usual, Justice Brennan put his finger squarely on the issue, even though he did so 20 years ahead of schedule:[76]

> The fact that a regulatory "taking" may be temporary, by virtue of the government's power to rescind or amend the regulation, does not make it any less of a constitutional "taking." Nothing in the Just Compensation Clause suggests that "takings" must be permanent and irrevocable. Nor does the temporary reversible quality of a regulatory "taking" render compensation for the time of the "taking" any less obligatory. This Court more than once has recognized that temporary reversible "takings" should be analyzed according to the same constitutional framework applied to permanent irreversible "takings."[77]

Justice Brennan's views in *San Diego Gas* became the heart and soul of the majority opinion in *First English*. His ideas about the nature of takings show that the concept of temporary is intellectually and constitutionally beside the point, as the government *always* has the power to make any taking "temporary" by returning what it took,[78] but that does not eliminate the need for compensation.

§ 11.3(a) *All Takings Require Compensation*

Aside from direct condemnations, there are two kinds of takings, labeled by the manner of their imposition. One is caused by direct physical invasion,[79] the other by regulation.[80] However, convenient as they may be for descriptive purposes, these labels are a constitutional irrelevancy; either form requires Fifth Amendment compensation.[81]

In his celebrated dissent in *San Diego Gas*,[82] Justice Brennan expounded what might be called a unified field theory of takings jurisprudence. His opinion drew upon all sorts of takings without differentiation to demonstrate the common constitutional denominator uniting them all, something he aptly called the "essential similarity of regulatory 'takings' and other 'takings.'"[83]

To illustrate his point, Justice Brennan's analysis randomly linked a permanent direct condemnation case[84] with flooding cases (both intended[85] and unintended[86]), a navigable servitude case,[87] an aircraft overflight case,[88] a mining regulation case,[89] and temporary direct condemnation cases,[90] among others.[91] In his pragmatic view, born of a bedrock belief in the Bill of Rights as the individual's shield against governmental overreaching,[92] Justice Brennan viewed all these impositions on private property owners as requiring compensation. The fact that some of them may have been for temporary periods of time merely affected the amount of compensation that would be due.[93] The genius of this formulation is that it makes the law clear and relatively straightforward to apply.[94] When little or no damage is done, then landowners will either not file suit (this type of litigation is neither pleasant nor inexpensive)[95] or recover little or nothing after trial. Legally, however, it recognizes a freeze on use for what it is: a taking for the duration of the freeze.

In Justice Brennan's view, the language of the Fifth Amendment was clear and not to be tampered with. When government action severely interfered with the ability of private property owners to use their land in an economically viable manner, then a taking had occurred, and compensation must be paid:

> The language of the Fifth Amendment prohibits the "tak[ing]" of private property for "public use" without payment of "just compensation." As soon as private property has been taken, whether through formal condemnation proceedings, occupancy, physical invasion, or regulation, the landowner has *already* suffered a constitutional violation, and the self-executing character of the constitutional provision with respect to compensation is triggered. This Court has consistently recognized that the just compensation requirement in the Fifth Amendment is not precatory: Once there is a "taking," compensation *must* be awarded. (450 U.S. at 654; citations and internal quotation marks omitted; emphasis in original].)

Six years later, the Court adopted Justice Brennan's theory as its own in *First English*—and it did so with rigor. It analyzed and applied the same mix of takings cases—direct condemnations, along with a variety of physically invasive and regulatory inverse condemnations, permanent and temporary[96]—and reached the same conclusion: All forms of taking require compensation under the Fifth Amendment. Indeed, the Court emphasized the similarity between direct condemnations for short periods and regulatory takings for similar time periods, and concluded that the two are "not different in kind."[97]

In one of the first lower court applications of *First English*, the Eleventh Circuit Court of Appeals concluded that "[i]n the case of a temporary regulatory taking, the landowner's loss takes the form of an injury to the property's potential for producing income or an expected profit."[98] That is an apt description of what happens during a moratorium. Regulations that permit no use plainly take the property's potential for whatever period of time they are effective.

Lucas v. South Carolina Coastal Council[99] brought it all together.[100] That case involved South Carolina's effort to protect and preserve its shoreline. After all but two lots in an exclusive oceanfront residential subdivision had been built upon, a new law prevented any further construction. The Court held that the owner of the last two vacant lots was entitled to compensation if the new law precluded all economically beneficial or productive use of his land. As long as the law prevented such use, the taking was termed "categorical."[101] On remand, the South Carolina Supreme Court found a temporary taking as a matter of law and ordered compensation.[102]

From his vantage point in academia, Professor Tribe read this caselaw as meaning that ". . . forcing someone to stop doing things with his property—telling him 'you can keep it, but you can't use it'—is at times indistinguishable, in ordinary terms, from grabbing it and handing it over to someone else."[103] Professor Epstein, viewing things from the opposite end of the ideological spectrum, agrees: "What stamps a government action as a taking is what it does to the property rights of each individual who is subject to its actions: Nothing more or less is relevant."[104] Proceeding from the scholarly to the mundane, the idea that deprivation of the right to use property is a serious infringement of ownership may be found in even the most general of texts:

> Property is composed of certain constituent elements, namely, the unrestricted rights of use, enjoyment, and disposal of the particular subject of property. Of these elements the right of user is the most essential and beneficial; without it all other elements would be of little effect, since *if one is deprived of the use of his or her property, little but a barren title is left in his or her hands.*[105]

"Barren title" is precisely what moratoria leave landowners. When they take everything else, regardless of the time period, they become obligated to compensate those whose property is commandeered for the general public good.

§ 11.3(b) *A Seizure of the Right to Use Property—Even Temporarily—Requires Compensation*

The Fifth Amendment's just compensation guarantee is not concerned with the niceties of legal form, but with the practical impact of government actions on the owners of private property.[106] For "the Constitution measures a taking of property not by what a state says, or by what it intends, but by what it *does*."[107]

If a government agency were to condemn property temporarily for a passive use, as it does regularly, no one would seriously suggest that compensation should not be paid.[108] In like vein, when regulations have the same effect (of denying owners the use of their land) through the exercise of police power, there is no functional difference between the two modes of government action.[109] As Justice Brennan explained:

> Police power regulations such as zoning ordinances and other land-use restrictions can destroy the use and enjoyment of property in order to promote the public good just as effectively as formal condemnation or physical invasion of property. From the property owner's point of view, it may matter little whether his land is condemned or ... whether it is restricted by regulation to use in its natural state, if the effect ... is to deprive him of all beneficial use of it.[110]

Either way, the owners are deprived of the use and enjoyment of their land, and it is that deprivation, not the formal acquisition of title by the government, that is the mechanism of the taking.

> [T]he deprivation of the former owner rather than the accretion of a right or interest to the sovereign constitutes the taking. Governmental action short of acquisition of title or occupancy has been held, if its effects are so complete as to deprive the owner of all or most of his interest in the subject matter, to amount to a taking.[111]

Four decades later, Justice Marshall would explain for a unanimous Court that this bedrock precept had not changed:

> We have frequently recognized that a radical curtailment of a landowner's freedom to make use of or ability to derive income from his land may give rise to a taking within the meaning of the Fifth Amendment, even if the government has not physically intruded upon the premises or acquired a legal interest in the property.[112]

Justice Brennan's analysis also showed that there is no constitutional content in the temporariness of a taking. In essence, he concluded, *all* takings are temporary, because the government can always revoke a regulation, cease a physical invasion, or surrender possession.[113] Decades earlier, the Court had noted the unfairness that can occur "when the government does not take [a property owner's] entire interest, but by the form of its proceeding, chops it into bits, of which it takes only what it wants, however few or minute, and leaves [the property owner] holding the remainder, which may be altogether useless to him. . . ."[114] That perfectly describes the situation under development moratoria, where agencies chop off the right to use land and leave the owners holding a very useless remainder.

Thus, the real question is whether a taking has occurred, and that depends on the impact of the governmental action on the ability of the landowner to make economically productive use of the land. Justice Holmes put it quite bluntly near the turn of the last century, saying, "The question is, 'What has the owner lost?'"[115]

In *Lucas*, where the Court considered the Fifth Amendment implications of a South Carolina regulation that precluded all economically productive use of two subdivided residential parcels, it aptly noted "the practical equivalence in this setting of negative regulation and appropriation."[116]

Most recently, in *City of Monterey v. Del Monte Dunes*,[117] the Court upheld a jury's award of compensation for a temporary taking after a city repeatedly denied permission to develop houses on residentially zoned land. The taking, which might otherwise have been permanent, became temporary when another government agency (the state of California) bought the property for a bargain price during the litigation.

Thus, whether a taking is permanent or temporary is really something of a straw issue. The Constitution makes no such distinction. Courts and commentators err when they seek to carve out a species of regulatory taking and immunize it from the constitutional mandate of compensation.

§ 11.4 From a Landowner's Point of View,[118] Government Imposition of a Freeze on All Economically Productive Uses, Albeit Temporarily, Is the Equivalent of a Temporary Condemnation of Such Land. In Either Event, the Rightful Owner's Use of the Land Has Been Taken, and Just Compensation Is Due

Cases about moratoria involve deliberate legislative decisions to freeze the use of undeveloped land for the greater good of the general public. In practical terms, that studied and thoughtful action is no different than a decision to condemn the right to use that same land for a period of years or forever.

§ 11.4(a) A "Police Power" Freeze and an "Eminent Domain" Taking Are Functionally—and Constitutionally—the Same

In a typical regulatory taking case, a government agency enacts a regulation that severely restricts the ability of landowners to use their land productively. This could be by way of a down-zoning, a permit denial, a variance denial, or the like.[119] However, such negative impact is generally not the raison d'etre of the regulation. In such cases, the regulations are primarily designed to readjust the uses of, and relationships among, public and private lands. Even so, when the impact of such well-intended regulations is so severe that it denies private landowners economically productive use of their land, then compensation must be paid.[120]

By contrast, when a government agency enacts a freeze (or moratorium) on development, the *sole* purpose of that action is to foreclose (for either a finite or indefinite period of time) the landowners' ability to make *any* use of their land. The reason behind such a freeze may be to permit a "time out" in the face of changed conditions so that local planners can study the potential uses of the land without having development take place during their study period. The reason also could be to delay further development until public facilities are adequate to serve it or to preclude development indefinitely under the guise of a facility shortage.[121]

Sometimes moratoria are abused by local agencies, mouthing the words of planning propriety while intending all along to prevent use forever, or at least as long as possible.[122] Without any constitutional consequences, such actions will not stop. This does not mean that all moratoria are ill-motivated. Nonetheless, without a constitutional counterweight, government agencies—however motivated—are unable to employ an appropriate cost-benefit analysis to their actions. And that, after all, is the essence of democratic choice: The people should be able to decide whether they (or their planning representatives) "need" to impose severe restrictions so much that they are willing to pay a substantial price to do so.[123]

But, in the end, the reason is irrelevant. The Fifth Amendment is concerned with the regulation's impact, not its rationale or its drafters' rationalizations.[124]

Notwithstanding the Ninth Circuit's view that such moratoria are an essential part of the planning process that should be vigorously protected by the judiciary so that planning agencies can pursue their actions without cost to the general public,[125] the situation is jurisprudentially the reverse.

If, a fortiori, under cases like *Lucas*, compensation is due even where the government does *not* intend to deny productive land use (but the impact of its regulation does so anyway), the need for compensation should be all the more apparent when prohibition of use is the sine qua non of the regulation. The more clearly the government intends to take the use of the land for a period of time, the more clear is the need for Fifth Amendment compensation. The Court long ago held that private property cannot cavalierly be commandeered without payment simply "because the public wanted it very much." (*Pennsylvania Coal Co. v. Mahon*, 260 U.S. 393, 415 (1922).)

> The protection of private property in the Fifth Amendment presupposes that it is wanted for public use, but provides that it shall not be taken for such use without compensation. . . . When this seemingly absolute protection is found to be qualified by the police power, the natural tendency of human nature is to extend the qualification more and more until at last private property disappears. But that cannot be accomplished under the Constitution of the United States.[126]

Those who defend the transmogrification of the moratorium from a limited-use planning tool, reserved for special occasions, into a routinely applied government technique for stultifying all reasonable private land uses trench on that basic constitutional doctrine.

§ 11.4(b) *"Eminent Domain" and "Police Power" Are Really Two Sides of the Same Coin*

The power of eminent domain and regulatory police power are closely related. As one commentator put it, Justice Holmes's *Pennsylvania Coal* opinion demonstrated that eminent domain power and police power "were really two ends of a continuum that can be called 'governmental power.'"[127] Others viewed Justice Brennan's *San Diego Gas* dissent as an updating of Justice Holmes's theory:

> Stripping away empty formalisms, [Justice Brennan] implicitly disputed what is sometimes called the two-track theory, whereby police and eminent domain powers follow separate tracks that, by definition, never intersect. Instead, he introduced the pragmatic notion of

a "*de facto* exercise of the power of eminent domain," sensibly suggesting that an overzealous exercise of the police power may concurrently be an exercise of the eminent domain power.[128]

As if to illustrate the point, the Supreme Court has repeatedly invoked the just compensation provision of eminent domain to validate police power actions that—without compensation—would be unconstitutional.[129] These cases build on the hornbook proposition that, when examining a legislative enactment for constitutionality, that construction should be applied that renders the enactment constitutional rather than void.[130] The Court's solution consistently has been to require the use of the eminent domain concept of compensation to validate legislative exercises of the police power that impaired private property rights.[131] When, for example, Congress decided to establish the Point Reyes National Seashore in Northern California, it provided no timetable for the acquisition and seemed in no hurry to appropriate money for that purpose. The U.S. Court of Claims allowed an inverse condemnation action, a process of which Congress was aware, and that "was available in case the convergent pressures on any landowner became great beyond its expectation," a process that had "saved the day in many another sticky situation."[132]

That solution properly defers to legislative bodies on matters of policy. In *Tahoe-Sierra*, for example, TRPA made a policy decision that it was necessary and in the public interest to freeze the use of hundreds of parcels of residentially zoned and subdivided, but undeveloped, land. Rather than interfere with that policy by enjoining it or overturning it at the instance of the affected landowners, the proper judicial role is to ensure fairness to the landowners by mandating compensation for the period of the freeze. That way, the government gets what its policy makers ordered, but the cost is shouldered by those who benefit, rather than the random owners of targeted land.[133]

In similar fashion, when examining the validity of eminent domain actions, the Court has held that the determination of whether property is taken for a public use involves "what traditionally has been known as the police power."[134] The Court's blending of the concepts in order to validate each of them demonstrates the wisdom of Professor Beuscher, who noted several decades ago that "those wri.ers who emphasize the separate airtight, nonoverlapping character of the two basic powers—police power and eminent domain—have been too glib."[135]

Thirty years after *Berman*, the Court reaffirmed its conclusion. What was then being considered was whether the Hawaii legislature could authorize the use of the eminent domain power to end a land oligopoly. Most of the private land in Hawaii was owned by a few large estates that leased residential lots to tenants who then built and owned homes on those lots. The Hawaii legislature decided to use the power of eminent domain to condemn the underlying fee title and transfer it to the tenants. The question was whether that was a "public use" that could satisfy the constitutional limitation on the use of this "most awesome power"[136] of government. Speaking for a unanimous eight-Justice Court, Justice O'Connor concluded that in eminent domain law, "[t]he 'public use' requirement is thus coterminous with the scope of a sovereign's police powers."[137]

With that simple declarative sentence, the Court unified the juridical underpinnings of eminent domain power and police power and laid the groundwork for concluding that moratoria are takings that require compensation. When a legislative body exercises its discretion to use eminent domain power, the deference accorded that decision is nearly conclusive.[138] In other words, the conscious decision of a legislative body to take property is a decision committed to its sound discretion, and that decision automatically invokes the self-executing command to pay just compensation for whatever property is taken in the process.[139]

In like manner, the conscious decision of a legislative body to exercise its police power by deliberately freezing the ability of selected landowners to make any use of their land—for whatever time and whatever reason—is a decision generally committed to that body's discretion. Such a conscious decision—to the extent the impact is pragmatically the same as that of a decision to condemn for a temporary period—should carry with it the same consequence as the conscious decision to authorize condemnation: compensation for any private property taken in the process. In other words, the substantive law of takings turns on the substance of what the government does and how its actions affect the landowner, not on what alternative label the government chooses to affix to its action.

§ 11.4(c) *Good Intentions Do Not Vitiate the Need for Compensation—In Fact They Reinforce It*

The Fifth Amendment is not concerned with the propriety or virtue of the regulators' purpose in freezing the use of private property or the exigency of the situation that gave rise to the perceived need for it. For a proper exercise of police or eminent domain power, the underpinning of such a beneficent purpose must exist; otherwise the action is ultra vires and void. That much was plainly settled no later than 1922, when the Supreme Court examined a statute designed to stop land subsidence caused by underground coal mining and concluded that the prerequisites for exercise of both police power and eminent domain were present:

> We assume, of course, that the statute was passed upon the conviction that an exigency existed that would warrant it, and we assume that an exigency exists that would warrant the exercise of the power of eminent domain. But the question at bottom is upon whom the loss of the changes desired should fall.[140]

Pennsylvania Coal was merely one in a long line of decisions in which the Court—speaking from varied points on its ideological spectrum—patiently and consistently explained to regulatory agencies that the general legal propriety of their actions and the need to pay compensation under the Fifth Amendment present different questions, and the need for the latter is not obviated by the virtue of the former.[141]

In *Loretto v. Teleprompter Manhattan CATV Corp.*,[142] New York's highest court upheld a statute as a valid exercise of police power, and therefore dismissed an action seeking compensation for a taking. But commendable goals, such as good intentions, are no substitute for adherence to the just compensation guarantee. The Court (through Justice Marshall) put it this way as it reversed:

> The Court of Appeals determined that § 828 serves [a] legitimate public purpose . . . and thus is within the State's police power. We have no reason to question that determination. *It is a separate question, however, whether an otherwise valid regulation so frustrates property rights that compensation must be paid.* (*Loretto*, 458 U.S. at 425; emphasis added.)

Similarly, in *Kaiser Aetna v. United States*,[143] the Corps of Engineers had decreed that a private marina be opened to public use without compensation. The Court disagreed, and explained (through Justice Rehnquist) the relationship between justifiable regulatory actions and the just compensation guarantee of the Fifth Amendment:

> In light of its expansive authority under the Commerce Clause, there is *no question* but that Congress *could* assure the public a free right of access to the Hawaii Kai Marina if it so chose. *Whether a statute or regulation*

that went so far amounted to a taking, however, is an entirely separate question.[144]

In a similar vein are cases like *Preseault v. I.C.C.*,[145] *Ruckelshaus v. Monsanto Co.*,[146] *Dames & Moore v. Regan*,[147] and the *Regional Rail Reorganization Act Cases*.[148] In each of them, the Court was faced with the claim that Congress, in pursuit of legitimate objectives, had taken private property in violation of the Fifth Amendment. The governmental goal in each was plainly legitimate (respectively, the creation of recreational trails, the licensing of pesticides, dealing with the aftermath of the Iranian hostage crisis, and widespread railroad bankruptcy). Nonetheless, the Court did not permit those proper legislative goals to trump the constitutional need for compensation when private property was taken in the process.[149] In each, the Court directed the property owners to the Court of Federal Claims to determine whether these exercises of legislative power, *though substantively legitimate*, nonetheless required compensation to pass constitutional muster.[150] This bedrock principle of the law of constitutional remedies goes back to the unanimous decision in *Hurley v. Kincaid*,[151] where the Court held that the remedy for a taking *resulting from valid governmental action* is just compensation, not judicial second-guessing of governmental policies and decisions through disruptive injunctions.

In *Nollan v. California Coastal Commission*,[152] the Court (through Justice Scalia) examined California's plan to exact easement dedications from all coastal property owners from Mexico to Oregon. That such a publicly owned stretch of beach might serve the general interests of Californians, and thus be proper for the commission to seek, was seen as a different question than the means by which to achieve the goal:

> The Commission may well be right that it is a good idea, but that does not establish that the Nollans (and other coastal residents) alone can be compelled to contribute to its realization. Rather, California is free to advance its 'comprehensive program,' it if wishes, by using its power of eminent domain for this 'public purpose,' see U.S. Const., Amdt. 5; but if it wants an easement across the Nollans' property, it must pay for it.[153]

And, of course, that concept is the underpinning for the Court's categorical rule that if regulation denies all economically beneficial or productive use of private land, it is a per se taking, no matter how beneficial it may be.[154] That is why, under *Lucas*, a

taking *always* occurs when economically productive use is prevented, "*without* case-specific inquiry into the public interest advanced in support of such a restraint."[155]

In *City of Monterey*, the Court (through Justice Kennedy) reaffirmed its position by affirming an award of compensation notwithstanding that the city's purpose in rejecting development was
environmental protection.[156] Also, in last term's decision in
Palazzolo v. Rhode Island,[157] the Court remanded for further consideration a case in which development had been rejected in order to protect coastal wetlands.

Thus, for a taking to occur, it matters not whether the regulators acted in good or bad faith, or for good or bad reasons.[158]
What matters is the impact of their acts, not the purity vel non of
their motives. Indeed, if their motives are benign, that only for-
tifies the need for compensation by confirming that the taking is
truly for a public use as required by the Just Compensation Clause
of the Fifth Amendment.[159]

§ 11.5   Conclusion

It is hard to improve on the Supreme Court's conclusion in *First
English:*

> ... "temporary" takings, which, as here, deny a land-
> owner all use of his property, are not different in kind
> from permanent takings, for which the Constitution
> clearly requires compensation.[160]

Part of the problem in engaging in serious discourse on the
subject of moratoria is the insistence by some of its defenders
that municipalities "have to have it" in order to properly perform
their planning functions. The problem with that defense is that it
encourages municipal procrastination and flies in the teeth of standard Fifth Amendment law that has been with us for generations.
The fact that the government wants something very much does
not mean that it can steal it.[161]

And so it is with moratoria. This chapter has dealt with that
tool in the sense that it prevents all economically productive use
for a period of time. Mere delay in the processing of permit applications that can actually lead to the issuance of development
permits presents a different and, I suggest, less significant problem. It is one that many states have dealt with through "permit
streamlining" legislation, and that some jurisdictions are approaching through "one-stop" permit centers. But a deliberate freeze on

the ability to use undeveloped land is a different creature altogether.[162] Such a conscious decision is the functional equivalent of the adoption of a resolution to condemn property for a temporary period of time. In either case, the government—for what it believes are good and substantial reasons—feels the need to take from property owners the right to use their land. In so doing, the government has slashed through the classic bundle of sticks that represent rights in property, taking a part of each stick and mandating compensation.

It is really very simple: If you take it, you pay for it, and if you take it temporarily, you may pay less. But either way, the cost of the taking must fall somewhere, and it is economically, ethically, and doctrinally sound to make sure that the cost is fairly distributed among members of the populace who benefit from the taking. The Supreme Court's commentary is now more than four decades old, but its constitutional doctrine is sound. The Fifth Amendment, the Court held, was "designed to bar government from forcing some people alone to bear burdens which, in all fairness and justice, should be borne by the populace as a whole."[163] And so it is. A taking is a taking, whether it be physical or regulatory, whole or partial, permanent or temporary. Compensation to those whose rights are taken for the benefit of the rest of us—regardless of the time period—is wholly in keeping with long-standing constitutional philosophy.

Notes

1. 482 U.S. 304 (1987).

2. *Id.* at 321 (emphasis added).

3. California went so far as to conclude that *litigation* is merely part of the planning process, thus extending the "normal" planning process by several years. Landgate v. California Coastal Comm'n, 17 Cal. 4th 1006 (1997), *cert. den.*, 525 U.S. 876 (1998).

4. Wisconsin, for example, expressly refused to adopt California's *Landgate* holding on the ground that it is directly contrary to the U.S. Supreme Court's decision in *First English*. Eberle v. Dane County Bd. of Adjustment, 595 N.W.2d 730, 742 n.25 (Wis. 1999).

5. Tahoe-Sierra Preservation Council, Inc. v. Tahoe Reg. Plan. Agency, 216 F.3d 764 (9th Cir. 2000), *rehearing en banc denied over five-judge dissent*, 228 F.3d 998 (9th Cir. 2000), *cert. granted*, 121 S. Ct. 2589 (2001). That was the fourth published 9th Circuit opinion in the case. For the earlier decisions (bearing the same name), *see* 911 F.2d 1331 (9th Cir. 1990), *cert. denied*, 499 U.S. 943 (1991); 938 F.2d 153 (9th Cir. 1991); 34 F.3d 753 (9th Cir. 1994), *cert. denied*, 514 U.S. 1036 (1995). Including those from the district court, this latter-day *Bleak House* has now produced at least 11 published opinions.

6. For a line-by-line comparison of the *Tahoe-Sierra* analysis and Justice Stevens' *First English* dissent, see 228 F.3d at 1000-01 (Kozinski, J., dissenting).

7. Those who advise government agencies note that the most defensible moratoria do not prohibit all use, but leave the property owners with something to do other than mark

off days on a calendar. *E.g.,* ROBERT MELTZ, DWIGHT H. MERRIAM, & RICHARD M. FRANK, THE TAKINGS ISSUE 278 (1999).

8. *See* CAL. GOV. CODE § 65,858.

9. 24 Cal. 3d 266, 598 P.2d 25 (1979), *aff'd in part*, 447 U.S. 255 (1980).

10. 482 U.S. at 312.

11. 482 U.S. at 313 n.7.

12. 482 U.S. at 322.

13. 482 U.S. at 319.

14. 482 U.S. at 321.

15. Moreover, it would seem that such "normal" delays would be less than the two years in *First English*, as that one had been described as "considerable." There is, however, legislative guidance as to normal planning parameters. Such expressions are found in so-called permit streamlining acts, which appear in many states. Such statutes deem projects approved by operation of law if applications are not acted on in a specified period of time. *See generally* 5 ZIEGLER, RATHKOPF'S THE LAW OF ZONING AND PLANNING § 66.04 (4th ed. 2001); 4 YOUNG, ANDERSON'S AMERICAN LAW OF ZONING, SUBDIVISION CONTROLS, § 25.16 (4th ed. 1996). Such statutes were enacted to provide incentives to end governmental sloth. As one commentary put it:

> Perhaps even a worse result for an applicant than the disapproval by a zoning board of an application for a permit, subdivision approval, variance, or the like, is procrastination by the board before reaching its decision. . . . [W]here the board neglects to make its decision, the developer is left in limbo, without any guidance on whether to go forward with the proposed activity. (Annot., *Zoning: Construction and Effect of Statute Requiring That Zoning Application Be Treated as Approved if Not Acted on Within Specified Period of Time*, 66 A.L.R. 4th 1012, 1023.)

While California grants government agencies a leisurely year to review projects (CAL. GOV. CODE § 65,950), the norm elsewhere is 30 to 60 days. For discussion and application of representative statutes, *see, e.g., American Tower, L.P. v. City of Grant,* 621 N.W.2d 37 (Minn. App. 2001) (60 days); *Gunthner v. Planning Board,* 762 A.2d 710 (N.J.S. 2000) (45 days); *Romesburg v. Fayette County Zoning Hearing Bd.,* 727 A.2d 150 (Penn. Comm. Ct. 1999) (45 days); *City of Birmingham Planning Comm'n v. Johnson Realty Co., Inc.,* 688 So. 2d 871 (Ala. App. 1997) (45 days); *Pope v. De Paola,* 574 N.Y.S.2d 869 (1991) (30 days); *Marandino v. Planning & Zoning Comm'n,* 573 A.2d 768 (Conn. App. 1990) (65 days). It would seem appropriate to utilize such statutes as guidelines for what is "normal" in the planning process, as they contain legislative determinations about how long the planning approval process ought to take. They are, however, irrelevant where the case involves a total freeze on productive use, rather than the processing of some sort of development application.

16. For those who either didn't live through those times or have conveniently forgotten, the Court found itself unable—for various reasons now lumped together and called "ripeness" (*see* Suitum v. Tahoe Reg. Plan. Agency, 520 U.S. 725, 736 (1997))—to decide whether the Fifth Amendment's just compensation guarantee applied to any regulatory takings or only physical ones. Agins v. City of Tiburon, 447 U.S. 266 (1980); San Diego Gas & Elec. Co. v. City of San Diego, 450 U.S. 621 (1981); Williamson County Reg. Plan. Comm'n. v. Hamilton Bank, 473 U.S. 172 (1985); MacDonald, Sommer & Frates v. Yolo County, 477 U.S. 340 (1986). And see the somewhat embarrassed recita-

tion of this history in *First English*, 482 U.S. at 310-11. *See generally* Michael M. Berger, *Vindicating the Rights of Private Land Development in the Courts*, 32 URBAN LAW. 941, 943-57 (2000).

17. That the California Court of Appeal found another way to dismiss the case on remand (First English Evangelical Lutheran Church v. County of Los Angeles, 210 Cal. App. 3d 1353, 258 Cal. Rptr. 893 (1989) (holding as a matter of law that pitching tents and building campfires is an economically viable use of private property); *but see* Lucas v. South Carolina Coastal Council, 505 U.S. 1003 (1992) (building a deck and holding picnics not sufficiently viable to defeat taking claim)) is not a reflection of the Supreme Court's intent, but rather of California's well-earned reputation for hostility toward the rights of property owners. That reputation has been noted by scholars from around the country, regardless of their beliefs as to the propriety of government liability for regulatory takings. *E.g.*, Joseph F. DiMento, et al., *Land Development and Environmental Control in the California Supreme Court: The Deferential, the Preservationist, and the Preservationist-Erratic Eras*, 27 U.C.L.A. L. REV. 859, 872 (1980); WILLIAM A. FISCHEL, REGULATORY TAKINGS: LAW, ECONOMICS, AND POLITICS 226 (Harvard U. Press 1995); David L. Callies, *The Taking Issue Revisited*, 37 LAND USE LAW & ZONING DIGEST 6, 7 (July 1985); Gus Bauman, *The Supreme Court, Inverse Condemnation, and the Fifth Amendment*, 15 RUTGERS L.J. 15, 70 (1983); 1 NORMAN WILLIAMS, AMERICAN LAND PLANNING LAW § 6.03 at 184 (1974); DENNIS J. COYLE, PROPERTY RIGHTS AND THE CONSTITUTION 11 (State U. of N.Y. Press 1993); RICHARD BABCOCK & CHARLES SIEMON, THE ZONING GAME REVISITED 293 (Lincoln Inst. of Land Policy 1985).

18. Counsel for the county had urged the Court to decide that there was no taking (transcript of oral argument, 36-37; 482 U.S. at 312-13), so it cannot be said that the option escaped unnoticed. Nor could it be said that the Court was unaware of this ploy, as it had used it to duck the issue in *San Diego Gas*, 450 U.S. at 633.

19. United States v. General Motors Corp., 323 U.S. 373, 374-75 (1945) (emphasis added).

20. *Id.*; United States v. Petty Motor Co., 327 U.S. 372, 374 (1946); Kimball Laundry Co. v. United States, 338 U.S. 1, 3 (1949). See also *United States v. Causby*, 328 U.S. 256 (1946), in which the government leased an airport for one year, with options to renew until the end of the war. The Court agreed that overflights from the airport took flight easements over neighboring property but remanded the matter for the trial court to determine whether they were permanent or temporary and to award compensation accordingly. Thus, the time of the inverse taking was keyed to the temporary nature of the lease by which the United States occupied the facility.

21. 482 U.S. at 319.

22. *Id.* at 318.

23. Co-authored by five well-known land-use scholars, Norman Williams, Jr., R. Marlin Smith, Charles Siemon, Daniel R. Mandelker, and Richard F. Babcock, and published at 9 VT. L. REV. 193 (1984), the *Manifesto* was openly designed as "a brief opposing the theory that regulation which 'goes too far' constitutionally requires compensation." 9 VT. L. REV. at 245. For the antidote, see Michael M. Berger & Gideon Kanner, *Thoughts on* The White River Junction Manifesto: *A Reply to* The "Gang of Five's" Views *on Just Compensation for Regulatory Taking of Property*, 19 LOY. L.A.L. REV. 685 (1986). Both were cited in the *First English* dissent, 482 U.S. at 335-36 n.13.

24. 450 U.S. at 633-34.

25. 9 VT. L. REV at 193.

26. *See, e.g.*, Berger & Kanner, *supra* n.24 at 712-20.

27. *See* 482 U.S. at 330-31.

28. 9 Vᴛ. L. Rᴇᴠ. at 218 (emphasis added).

29. 482 U.S. at 315, 316 n.9, 318.

30. 450 U.S. at 657.

31. 482 U.S. at 318.

32. 9 Vᴛ. L. Rᴇᴠ. at 218.

33. 482 U.S. at 330-31.

34. 482 U.S. at 331.

35. For a vivid depiction, see the motion picture "The Godfather—Part II."

36. *See, e.g.*, Tahoe-Sierra Preservation Council v. Tahoe Regional Plan. Agency, 34 F. Supp. 2d 1226, 1230 (E.D. Cal. 1999), referring inter alia to Mark Twain, President Clinton, and Vice President Gore.

37. When the suit began in 1984, there were some 700 plaintiffs. Some of them died, and their estates chose to bury the claims with them. Others simply tired of the litigational travail and voluntarily chose to spend their remaining time, energy, and money elsewhere.

38. The staff, realizing it could not meet the Nov. 26, 1983 deadline, informed TRPA's board that unless the board directly ordered otherwise, the staff would simply refuse to process permit applications until the new plan was completed by staff and adopted by the board. The board said nothing, and the moratorium rolled on—quite illegally, it would appear.

39. Unpublished 1984 opinion, *aff'd sub nom.* People *ex rel.* Van de Kamp v. Tahoe Reg. Plan. Agency, 766 F.2d 1308 (9th Cir. 1985).

40. Because of the impact of TRPA's rolling use prohibitions, the majority of the landowners succumbed and sold their parcels for far less than fair market value to one of these scavenging agencies. The agencies paid only the bare residual value of unusable land. The petitioners seek the difference so they may be made constitutionally whole, a result similar to the one upheld in *City of Monterey v. Del Monte Dunes*, 526 U.S. 687 (1999).

41. This, of course, ignored the indisputable fact that these landowners *could not have obtained permits with or without the injunction*, because the 1984 plan forbade development on their lots. The injunction prevented TRPA from granting development permits to *other* landowners, not these. As Judge Noonan expressed it at the oral argument of the third in the appellate series, "It seems to me this is like a situation where the culprit pushes a person off the top of a high-rise building, and while the body is falling, someone else reaches out a window and shoots a bullet into the falling body." The analogy is apt. By the time the injunction was issued, the 1984 plan had already killed the ability of these landowners to use their land. Assuming the injunction applied at all, it merely maimed the corpse.

42. This analysis can hold true only if the 1987 plan is viewed as an entirely separate "event," rather than a continuation of the use prohibition that TRPA had enforced on these lots since 1981. It also required both the district court and the Ninth Circuit to disregard an earlier Ninth Circuit panel's decision (on which both rehearing en banc and certiorari had been denied) that TRPA was wrong on the one statute of limitations issue it pressed fervently and that it had waived the rest. Tahoe-Sierra Preservation Council v. Tahoe Reg. Plan. Agency, 34 F.3d 753 (9th Cir. 1994).

43. Tahoe-Sierra Preservation Council v. Tahoe Reg. Plan. Agency, 216 F.3d 764, 777 (9th Cir. 2000).

44. *Id.* at 780 n.20.

45. Boston Chamber of Commerce v. Boston, 217 U.S. 189, 195 (1910).

46. Lynch v. Household Fin. Co., 405 U.S. 538, 552 (1972).

47. 228 F.3d at 999.

48. *Id.* at 1003.

49. *Id.* at 999.

50. The first appeal in the series, 911 F.2d 1331, was heard by Judges Fletcher, Reinhardt, and Kozinski. It contains a per curiam opinion (apparently by Judge Reinhardt, who also authored the most recent opinion), a special concurrence by Judge Fletcher, and a nominal dissent by Judge Kozinski, which the dissenter characterized as more of a disagreement, given the fact that there were not two votes on the issue he disagreed with.

51. 911 F.2d at 1346. It is more than merely noteworthy that the Supreme Court's opinion in *Dolan v. City of Tigard*, 512 U.S. 374 (1994), agreed with Judge Kozinski's analysis by concluding that the property rights protected by the Fifth Amendment should not be treated as the "poor relations" of other Bill of Rights guarantees (512 U.S. at 392).

52. 482 U.S. at 318.

53. *See* Kimball Laundry Co. v. United States, 338 U.S. 1 (1949); United States v. General Motors Corp., 323 U.S. 373 (1945).

54. 228 F.3d at 1000.

55. *Id.* at 1001.

56. 482 U.S. at 330-32.

57. 216 F.3d at 774.

58. I do not mean to disparage the task of planners in today's regulatory environment. But the complexity of their task is no justification for the excessive delays that frequently are multiples of the time it took this country to fight and win World War II. Moreover, there is simply no justification for protracted, multidecade bureaucratic delays that have unfortunately become a staple of these cases. *E.g.*, City of Monterey v. Del Monte Dunes, 526 U.S. 687 (1999) (five years, five planning submissions, 19 site plans—all rejected; 18 years of litigation); Agins v. City of Tiburon, 447 U.S. 255 (1980). It took Mrs. Agins 30 years to finally receive permission to build four homes on her five-acre parcel. Charles Gallardo, *After 29 Years, Tiburon House Going Up: Home OK'd But Not for Original Owner*, [MARIN] INDEPENDENT JOURNAL, Oct. 21, 1997, at B-6. As noted even by knowledgeable commentators who are sympathetic to the regulators, such unfortunate behavior patterns have become all too common. *See* Rodney Cobb, *Land Use Law: Marred by Public Agency Abuse*, 3 WASH. U.J.L. & POLICY 195 (2000); Orlando Delogu, *The Misuse of Land Use Control Powers Must End: Suggestions for Legislative and Judicial Responses*, 32 ME. L. REV. 29 (1980); Melville Branch, *The Sins of City Planners*, 42 PUB. AD. REV. 1 (1982).

59. 216 F.3d at 777.

60. *Id.* at 782.

61. *See Dolan*, 512 U.S. at 392.

62. San Diego Gas & Elec. Co. v. City of San Diego, 450 U.S. 621, 661 n.26 (1981) (dissenting opinion).

63. 482 U.S. at 321.

64. 216 F.3d at 782. Ironically, it was *precisely* that reasoning of the California Supreme Court in *Agins v. City of Tiburon*, 24 Cal. 3d 266, 276-77 (1979), *aff'd on other grounds*, 447 U.S. 255 (1980), that the Supreme Court branded as an incorrect interpretation of the Fifth Amendment in *First English*, 482 U.S. at 317. Moreover, to characterize a 20-year process of rolling prohibitions of all uses of the petitioners' lands as "orderly" and "reasonable" does violence to the *First English* language.

65. 10 F.3d 796, 800 (Fed. Cir. 1993).

66. 247 Conn. 196 (1998).

67. 247 Conn. at 196.

68. 227 Wis. 2d 609 (1999).

69. 227 Wis. 2d at 633.

70. 515 N.W.2d 401 (Neb. 1994).

71. 515 N.W.2d at 407.

72. Lucas v. South Carolina Coastal Council, 424 S.E.2d 484 (1992).

73. *Lucas*, 505 U.S. at 1044 (Blackmun, J., dissenting). *See also* Sintra, Inc. v. City of Seattle, 829 P.2d 765, 774 (Wash. 1992) ("a temporary taking is compensable under the Fifth Amendment, and *Sintra* need not prove that the property remained unusable after the [regulation] was invalidated. (Citing *First English*.)"); 614 Company v. Minneapolis Community Dev. Agency, 547 N.W.2d 400, 406-07 (Minn. App. 1996) (reduced occupancy of building sufficient to state claim for temporary taking where complaint alleged that remaining uses were not economically viable); Lomarch Corp. v. Mayor of Englewood, 237 A.2d 881 (N.J. 1968) (denial of all use of land for a limited period of time is a taking and is tantamount to the purchase of an option on the land); Peacock v. City of Sacramento, 271 Cal. App. 2d 845 (1969) (denial of all use of land for 3½ years to facilitate the city's decision whether to acquire it for an airport is a de facto taking); Steel v. Cape Corp., 677 A.2d 634 (Md. App. 1996) (moratorium based on facilities shortage was a taking).

74. *E.g.*, Woodbury Place Partners v. City of Woodbury, 492 N.W.2d 258 (Minn. App. 1992), and other cases cited in the introduction to this volume, ch. 1, n.96, as well as ch. 12. And, of course, California—always at the outer edge—believes that litigation to overturn an unconstitutional regulation is merely part of the "normal planning process." (Landgate v. California Coastal Comm'n, 17 Cal. 4th 1006 (1998)).

75. Walter, *Appraisal Methods and Regulatory Takings: New Directions for Appraisers, Judges, and Economists*, 63 APPRAISAL J. 331 (1995).

76. Intriguingly, Justice Brennan wrote this opinion at the very time—early 1981—that TRPA was adopting Ordinance 81-5, the first of the series of rolling moratoria in *Tahoe-Sierra*. Perhaps TRPA should have paid attention.

77. San Diego Gas & Elec. Co. v. City of San Diego, 450 U.S. 621, 657 (1981) (Brennan, J., dissenting on behalf of four Justices, but expressing the substantive views of a majority). Justice Rehnquist concurred with four other Justices that the case was not ripe, but then noted his agreement with Justice Brennan's group of four on the merits. 450 U.S. at 633 (Rehnquist, J., concurring). Six years later, in *First English Evangelical Lutheran Church v. County of Los Angeles*, 482 U.S. 304 (1987), Chief Justice Rehnquist wrote the opinion for a six-Justice majority that adopted and applied Justice Brennan's *San Diego Gas* dissent.

78. In *Kirby Forest Indus., Inc. v. United States*, the Court explained that the government may, if it chooses, even abandon a formal condemnation proceeding.

79. *E.g.*, Loretto v. Teleprompter Manhattan CATV Corp., 458 U.S. 419 (1982); United States v. Causby, 328 U.S. 256 (1946).

80. *E.g.*, *First English*; City of Monterey v. Del Monte Dunes, 526 U.S. 687 (1999).

81. Lucas v. South Carolina Coastal Council, 505 U.S. 1003 (1992).

82. *First English* repeatedly cites Justice Brennan's *San Diego Gas* dissent as authoritative (482 U.S. at 315; 316 n.9; 318).

83. 450 U.S. at 651.

84. Berman v. Parker, 348 U.S. 26 (1954).

85. United States v. Dickinson, 331 U.S. 745 (1947).

86. Pumpelly v. Green Bay Co., 13 Wall. (80 U.S.) 166 (1872).

87. Kaiser Aetna v. United States, 444 U.S. 164 (1979).

88. United States v. Causby, 328 U.S. 256 (1946).

89. Pennsylvania Coal Co. v. Mahon, 260 U.S. 393 (1922).

90. Kimball Laundry Co. v. United States, 338 U.S. 1 (1949); United States v. Petty Motor Co., 327 U.S. 372 (1946); United States v. General Motors Corp., 323 U.S. 373 (1945).

91. 450 U.S. at 651-53, 656-60.

92. *See* CHARLES M. HAAR & JEROLD S. KAYDEN, LANDMARK JUSTICE 191 (1989).

93. 450 U.S. at 658-60.

94. That would be a welcome respite from the welter of criticisms traditionally heaved in the direction of takings law. See, e.g., comments collected in GIDEON KANNER, HUNTING THE SNARK, NOT THE QUARK: HAS THE U.S. SUPREME COURT BEEN COMPETENT IN ITS EFFORT TO FORMULATE COHERENT REGULATORY TAKINGS LAW? Institute on Planning, Zoning, and Eminent Domain ch. 10 at 10-3 n.7 (Sw. Legal Found. 1998).

95. The Supreme Court's records reveal the lengths to which such litigation can go. *Tahoe-Sierra*, for example, was filed in 1984 and resulted in four separate trips to the Ninth Circuit before arriving in the Supreme Court. *City of Monterey v. Del Monte Dunes*, 526 U.S. 687 (1999), began its administrative proceedings in 1981 and its litigation in 1986 before concluding in 1999. Another currently active case, *A.A. Profiles v. City of Fort Lauderdale*, 253 F.3d 576 (11th Cir. 2001), began in 1981 and is still going.

96. 482 U.S. at 314-19.

97. *Id.* at 318.

98. Wheeler v. City of Pleasant Grove, 833 F.2d 267, 271 (11th Cir. 1987).

99. 505 U.S. 1003 (1992).

100. Even commentators who believed *Lucas* established nothing new had to concede that it had synthesized and recompiled much of what had gone before. *E.g.*, Jerold S. Kayden, *Old Wine in New Bottles*, 46 LAND USE LAW & ZONING DIGEST 9 no. 9 (Sept. 1992).

101. 505 U.S. at 1015.

102. Lucas v. South Carolina Coastal Council, 424 S.E.2d 484 (S.C. 1992). For a discussion of the amusing aftermath, in which the state—which had fought Mr. Lucas's development desires through the highest court in the land—insisted that, after it purchased the lots, it had to resell them in order to recoup its investment, see Gideon Kanner, *Not With a Bang, But a Giggle: The Settlement of the* Lucas *Case*, in ABA, TAKINGS: LAND-DEVELOPMENT CONDITIONS AND REGULATORY TAKINGS AFTER *DOLAN* AND *LUCAS*, ch. 15 (Callies, ed., 1996).

103. LAURENCE TRIBE, AMERICAN CONSTITUTIONAL LAW § 9-3 at 593 (2d ed. 1988).

104. RICHARD EPSTEIN, TAKINGS: PRIVATE PROPERTY AND THE POWER OF EMINENT DOMAIN 94 (1986).

105. 63C Am Jur 2d, Property § 3 at 68-69 (1997) (emphasis added).

106. *See* United States v. Dickinson, 331 U.S. 745, 748 (1947) ("Constitution is intended to preserve practical and substantial rights, not to maintain theories. . . . ").

107. Hughes v. Washington, 389 U.S. 290, 298 (1967) (Stewart, J., concurring) (emphasis in original); *see also* Davis v. Newton Coal Co., 267 U.S. 292, 302 (1925). "The taking was for a public use. The incantation pronounced at the time is not of controlling importance; our primary concern is with the accomplishment."; Yuba Goldfields, Inc. v. United States, 723 F.2d 884, 889 (Fed. Cir. 1983).

108. *See* the Court's discussion in *First English*, 482 U.S. at 318, applying this direct condemnation concept to regulatory takings and showing the applicability to regulatory takings of the wartime condemnations of temporary use in *Kimball Laundry Co. v. United States*, 338 U.S. 1 (1949), *United States v. Petty Motor Co.*, 327 U.S. 372 (1946), and *United States v. General Motors Corp.*, 323 U.S. 373 (1945).

109. In *First English*, 482 U.S. at 319, the Court likened a regulatory taking for a period of years to the condemnation of a leasehold, something that could not be done without compensation: "The value of a leasehold interest in property for a period of years may be substantial, and the burden on the property owner in extinguishing such an interest for a period of years may be great indeed."

110. San Diego Gas & Elec. Co. v. City of San Diego, 450 U.S. 621, 652 (1981) (dissenting opinion).

111. *General Motors*, 323 U.S. at 378.

112. Kirby Forest Indus., Inc. v. United States, 467 U.S. 1, 14 (1984); *see also* Hawaii Housing Auth. v. Midkiff, 467 U.S. 229, 244 (1984) ("government does not itself have to use property to legitimate the taking. . . .") (O'Connor, J., for a unanimous eight Justices).

113. 450 U.S. at 657, 659-60.

114. United States v. General Motors Corp., 323 U.S. 373, 382 (1945).

115. Boston Chamber of Commerce v. Boston, 217 U.S. 189, 195 (1910).

116. 505 U.S. at 1019.

117. 526 U.S. 687 (1999).

118. "From the property owner's point of view, it may matter little whether his land is condemned or . . . whether it is restricted by regulation to use in its natural state, if the effect . . . is to deprive him of all beneficial use of it." San Diego Gas & Elec. Co. v. City of San Diego, 450 U.S. 621, 652 (1981) (Brennan, J., dissenting).

119. *See, e.g.*, Penn Central Transp. Co. v. City of New York, 438 U.S. 104 (1978); Agins v. City of Tiburon, 447 U.S. 255 (1980); San Diego Gas & Elec. Co. v. City of San Diego, 450 U.S. 621 (1981); Williamson County Reg. Plan. Comm'n v. Hamilton Bank, 473 U.S. 172 (1985); MacDonald, Sommer & Frates v. Yolo County, 477 U.S. 340 (1986).

120. Lucas v. South Carolina Coastal Council, 505 U.S. 1003, 1015 (1992).

121. *See, e.g.*, First English Evangelical Lutheran Church v. County of Los Angeles, 482 U.S. 304 (1987); Lockary v. Kayfetz, 917 F.2d 1150 (9th Cir. 1990).

122. *See, e.g.*, MARK L. POLLOT, GRAND THEFT AND PETIT LARCENY: PROPERTY RIGHTS IN AMERICA xviii (1993).

123. *See* Michael M. Berger, *The State's Police Power Is Not (Yet) the Power of a Police State*, 35 LAND USE LAW & ZONING DIGEST 4, no. 5 (May 1983).

124. *E.g., Lucas*, 505 U.S. at 1015.

125. 216 F.3d at 777.

126. *Pennsylvania Coal*, 260 U.S. at 415.

127. Gus Bauman, *The Supreme Court, Inverse Condemnation and the Fifth Amendment: Justice Brennan Confronts the Inevitable in Land Use Controls*, 15 RUTGERS L.J. 15, 38 (1983).

128. CHARLES M. HAAR & JEROLD S. KAYDEN, LANDMARK JUSTICE 41 (1989).

129. *See, e.g.*, Regional Rail Reorganization Act Cases, 419 U.S. 102, 134 (1974); Dames & Moore v. Regan, 453 U.S. 654, 689 (1981); Ruckelshaus v. Monsanto Co., 467 U.S. 986, 1013 (1984).

130. Fletcher v. Peck, 6 Cranch (10 U.S.) 87, 128 (1810); *Regional Rail*, 419 U.S. at 134.

131. *See* Hurley v. Kincaid, 285 U.S. 95 (1932).

132. Drakes Bay Land Co. v. United States, 424 F.2d 574 (Ct. Cl. 1970).

133. *See* Armstrong v. United States, 364 U.S. 40, 49 (1960).

134. Berman v. Parker, 348 U.S. 26, 32 (1954).

135. Joseph Beuscher, *Notes on the Integration of Police Power and Eminent Domain by the Courts: Inverse Condemnation*, in J. BEUSCHER & R. WRIGHT, LAND USE 724 (1969). *See also* Bauman, *supra*, 15 RUTGERS L.J. at 53: ". . . as the 'police power' is adapted to more and increasingly complex applications, the police power/eminent domain dichotomy becomes less useful and more anachronistic." (Collecting citations to numerous commentators who share that view.)

136. *See* City of Oakland v. Oakland Raiders, 174 Cal. App. 3d 414, 419, 220 Cal. Rptr. 153 (1985); Winger v. Aires, 89 A.2d 521, 522 (Pa. 1952).

137. Hawaii Housing Auth. v. Midkiff, 467 U.S. 229, 240 (1984).

138. *Id.* at 240-41.

139. *First English*, 482 U.S. at 315; Jacobs v. United States, 290 U.S. 13, 16 (1933).

140. Pennsylvania Coal Co. v. Mahon, 260 U.S. 393, 416 (1922). *See also* Florida Rock Indus., Inc. v. United States, 18 F.3d 1560, 1571 n.28 (Fed. Cir. 1994): "It is necessary that the Government act in a good cause, but it is not sufficient. The takings clause already assumes the Government is acting in the public interest. . . . " More than that, it assumes that the government is acting pursuant to lawful authority. If not, the action is ultra vires and void. Youngstown Sheet & Tube Co. v. Sawyer, 343 U.S. 579 (1952).

141. Emphasizing the point, the dissenting opinion in *Pennsylvania Coal* had argued the absolute position that a "restriction imposed to protect the public health, safety or morals from dangers threatened is not a taking." 260 U.S. at 417. Eight Justices rejected that proposition.

142. 458 U.S. 419 (1982).

143. 444 U.S. 164 (1979).

144. *Id.* at 174 (emphasis added; citations omitted).

145. 494 U.S. 1 (1990) (Brennan, J.).

146. 467 U.S. 986 (1984) (Blackmun, J.).

147. 453 U.S. 654 (1981) (Rehnquist, J.).

148. 419 U.S. 102 (1974) (Brennan, J.).

149. In earlier years, the Ninth Circuit understood this:

> We cannot agree that any legitimate purpose automatically trumps the deprivation of all economically viable use, such that whenever a regulation has a health or safety purpose, no compensation is ever required even if the landowner is thereby denied all use of his property. (McDougal v. County of Imperial, 942 F.2d 668, 676 (9th Cir. 1991))

150. That is why the Fifth Amendment's just compensation guarantee has been held self-executing. The availability of compensation validates and constitutionalizes the otherwise unlawful government action. United States v. Clarke, 445 U.S. 253, 257 (1980).

151. 285 U.S. 95 (1932) (Brandeis, J.).

152. 483 U.S. 825 (1987).

153. *Nollan*, 483 U.S. at 841-42. *See also* Griggs v. Allegheny County, 369 U.S. 84, 89-90 (1962) (airport operator must pay for noise-impacted property beyond the ends of its runway).

154. Lucas v. South Carolina Coastal Council, 505 U.S. 1003, 1015 (1992). *See Florida*

Rock Indus., Inc. v. United States, 18 F.3d 1560, 1571 n. 28 (Fed. Cir. 1994), in which the court noted with understatement: "In *Lucas*, the South Carolina Supreme Court had held that the State's purpose in protecting oceanfront ecology excused the State from liability for its regulatory imposition. The Supreme Court held that was not the correct criterion for takings jurisprudence."

155. *Lucas*, 505 U.S. at 1015 (emphasis added).

156. City of Monterey v. Del Monte Dunes, 526 U.S. 687 (1999).

157. 121 S. Ct. 2448 (2001).

158. Indeed, it has long been settled that courts will not inquire into the motivation of political decisions to take private property, thus making their bona fides judicially off limits. *See, e.g.*, Rindge Co. v. County of Los Angeles, 262 U.S. 700, 709 (1923); Mugler v. Kansas, 123 U.S. 623, 661 (1887).

159. *Cf.* Stanley v. Illinois, 405 U.S. 645, 656 (1972):

> [T]he Constitution recognizes higher values than speed and efficiency. Indeed, one might fairly say of the Bill of Rights in general, and of the Due Process Clause in particular, that they were designed to protect the fragile values of a vulnerable citizenry from the overbearing concern for efficiency and efficacy that may characterize praiseworthy government officials no less, and perhaps more, than mediocre ones.

160. 482 U.S. at 318.

161. Pennsylvania Coal Co. v. Mahon, 260 U.S. 393, 415 (1922).

162. See Wendy U. Larsen & Marcella Larsen, *Moratoria as Takings Under* Lucas, 46 LAND USE LAW & ZONING DIGEST 3, n.6 (June 1994).

163. Armstrong v. United States, 364 U.S. 40, 49 (1960).

MORATORIA AND CATEGORICAL TAKINGS

12

DANIEL P. SELMI

§ 12.0   Introduction

Every clarification of takings jurisprudence seems to breed new uncertainties, and the U.S. Supreme Court's handling of the "temporary takings" issue is no exception. Almost as soon as the Court decided *First English Evangelical Lutheran Church v. County of Los Angeles*[1] in 1987, observers began disputing whether the decision meant that a local government enacting a moratorium, one of the most venerable land-use tools, would be liable for a "temporary taking." Almost 15 years later the discussion continues, sharpened by the Court's 1994 decision in *Lucas v. South Carolina Coastal Council*[2] and, most recently, by the Supreme Court's grant of certiorari in *Tahoe Sierra Preservation Council v. Tahoe Regional Planning Agency.*[3]

The discussion below examines the question of whether a governmental regulatory agency that enacts a land-use moratorium has thereby taken private property for the period of the moratorium and must compensate the property owner. To date, a large part of the debate on this issue has centered on the meaning of *First English*. Ultimately, however, that debate is inconclusive and, from the perspective of the development of takings theory, beside the point. Instead, the appropriate question is whether the rationale for adopting a categorical takings rule applies to the situation of a moratorium. An inquiry into this issue must focus not on *First English* but on *Lucas*, the principal decision articulating that rationale.

Accordingly, this chapter starts by examining the reasons set forth in *Lucas* for adopting the rule on categorical takings. It then analyzes whether extending takings liability to include moratoria would be consistent with those reasons.

Those advocating the view that a moratorium is a taking, referred to below as the "takings proponents," usually portray such a conclusion as a logical extension of *Lucas*. They also imply that this extension will have little impact on the bulk of the Supreme Court's takings jurisprudence, particularly the balancing test found in *Penn Central Transportation Co. v. City of New York*.[4] In fact, however, applying the categorical taking rule of *Lucas* to moratoria would be inconsistent with a number of settled principles in the Court's takings jurisprudence. For example, such an application would conflict with the theory underlying the Court's longstanding requirement that a landowner's takings case must fully ripen before a court may consider it. The extension also would intrude into a sensitive area of local government discretion— government's power to determine whether a particular land-use problem is affecting the ability of local governments to plan and regulate in the public interest.

This chapter argues that extending the *Lucas* categorical takings principle to include moratoria would be inconsistent with the Court's takings jurisprudence. Moreover, such an extension also would have a pernicious effect on land-use planning. It would deter the use of moratoria in those situations where they are most needed: when impending developments present serious environmental or other types of planning problems.

§ 12.1   First English, Lucas, *and the "Play on Words"*

First, some terminology and background are needed. A moratorium is a regulatory prohibition on development for a specific period of time.[5] During this specific period, the government agency engages in a planning effort that is intended to lead to new regulatory controls.[6] The purpose of the moratorium is to ensure that, during this interim period, development will not take place that could exacerbate the problems that led to the planning effort or that could be inconsistent with the new controls when they are enacted. The moratorium is one of the oldest tools in the panoply of land-use regulations.[7] Until the Supreme Court's decision in *First English*, few people had argued that a moratorium constituted a taking for which the local agency must pay compensation.

In *First English*, the Supreme Court addressed the question of the proper remedy when a government regulation is found to take private property. The Court held that if a regulation has taken the property, the government agency is required to pay damages for the period of time that the regulation remains in effect.[8] Thus, even if the government thereafter rescinds the regulation after a taking is found, the government remains liable for interim damages. As the Court put it, "[W]here the government's activities have already worked a taking of all use of property, no subsequent action by the government can relieve it of the duty to provide compensation for the period during which the taking was effective."[9] The Court termed this situation a "temporary taking."[10]

Almost immediately after the Court handed down *First English*, litigators and some commentators began arguing that a land-use moratorium necessarily constitutes a "temporary taking" under *First English* and thus requires compensation.[11] This argument, however, became more credible after the Court's 1994 decision in *Lucas*.

In *Lucas*, the Court explicated its theory of a "categorical taking" when a land-use regulation either physically occupies property or deprives a landowner of all reasonable use of the property.[12] Because the South Carolina Coastal Council's regulation deprived the landowner, Lucas, of all reasonable use of his property, a categorical taking had occurred. In *Lucas,* the Court held that the landowner was entitled to full compensation for the value of the property unless the government could prove that the use had not been part of the landowner's title to the property in the first instance.[13]

A moratorium often denies a landowner the right to develop property during some interim period. As such, the claim that a moratorium necessarily constitutes a taking of property flows from *First English* and *Lucas*. If a moratorium deprives a landowner of all reasonable use of the property for a period of time, the takings proponents argue that it triggers the *Lucas* categorical taking rule. The fact that the moratorium is temporary, so the argument goes, is irrelevant under *First English*.[14] Under that decision, even though the regulation ultimately is rescinded (i.e., is temporary), the jurisdiction still must pay damages.

The takings proponents also point to Justice Stevens's dissent in *First English*, in which he reasoned that no taking had occurred because of the short length of time that the regulation was in effect. The majority responded to this point by declaring that "temporary takings . . . are not different in kind from permanent takings, for which the Constitution clearly requires compensation."[15] The takings proponents cite this passage as confirming their view that moratoria are temporary takings.

Nonetheless, the conclusion that a moratorium effects a categorical taking does not align with the facts of *First English*. The takings proponents claim that any complete deprivation of use, even for less than a permanent period, is a "temporary taking" within the meaning of *First English*. In that case, however, the Court attached the label "temporary taking" to a specific factual circumstance: the situation in which the government rescinds a permanent regulation after it has been found to take property. The government is then liable for a "temporary taking," i.e., a taking for the period of time that the originally permanent regulation remained in effect.[16]

Thus, the term "temporary taking" was intended to illustrate a means by which the government could minimize its takings liability. By rescinding the regulation, the government can put a cap on the takings damages. It seems unlikely that, in coining a remedial term designed to illustrate how the government could minimize its liability, the Court actually intended to establish a much broader principle of substantive takings liability, one that would include a moratorium as a temporary taking.

At a minimum, it is at least clear that the actual holding in *First English* does not require courts to treat moratoria as temporary takings. The claim that *First English* decided that a moratorium is a "temporary taking" is, to use Justice Scalia's terminology,[17] merely a "play on words." It uses the phrase "temporary taking" to mean something other than the Court used it for in *First English*.[18] Most lower courts have rejected this invitation to reconfigure the holding in *First English*.[19]

Two other aspects of the holdings in *First English* and *Lucas* make it unlikely that the Court intended *First English* to extend this far. First, in *First English*, the Court never even reached the question of whether a taking had occurred. In fact, it explicitly disclaimed such an analysis, noting that it had "no occasion to decide whether the ordinance at issue actually denied [the] appellant all use of its property."[20] The Court could not have held that a moratorium is a taking if it did not decide this question.

Second, the Court in *Lucas* commented that the instances in which the government is liable for denying all economically beneficial or productive use of land are "relatively rare."[21] Since moratoria are *not* rare, it seems unlikely that the Court intended to extend liability to moratoria.

Nonetheless, an argument exists that the combined effect of *First English* and *Lucas* can support a conclusion that a moratorium is a taking. The argument would emphasize the impact of the regulation on the landowner. From the landowner's standpoint, the effect of a moratorium is precisely the same as the effect when a regulation, such as the one under review in *Lucas*, takes property, but the government then rescinds the regulation. In both situations, the landowner is deprived of all reasonable use of the property for a finite period of time. The landowner would argue that a deprivation of all use is just that, whether caused by a prospectively temporary moratorium or a permanent regulation later rescinded.[22]

At this point in the development of takings law after *First English*, it is clear that the question of whether a moratorium constitutes a taking cannot be resolved by further inquiry into the text of that decision. Instead, the analytical debate must center on whether the rationale for the categorical takings rule applies in the situation of a short-term moratorium. The pivotal case in resolving that question is *Lucas*, not *First English*. It was *Lucas* that set forth the Court's reasons for applying a categorical rule when a regulation deprives the landowner of all reasonable use of the property. Thus, the critical question should be: Is the proposed extension of the *Lucas* categorical takings principle to encompass short-term moratoria consistent with the Court's reasons in *Lucas* for adopting that principle?[23]

§ 12.2   *Moratoria and the* Lucas *Rationale*

The Supreme Court's majority in *Lucas* offered four reasons why a regulatory deprivation of all reasonable use of property should be treated as a categorical taking. The application of each of these reasons to moratoria is examined below.

§ 12.2(a) *Adjusting the Benefits and Burdens of Regulation*

The first *Lucas* rationale focuses on whether the Court should presume that a local legislative body acted in good faith when it adopted a land-use regulation. The opinion postulates that, in the "extraordinary circumstance" when a regulation permits no productive or economically beneficial use of land, "it is less realistic to indulge our usual assumption that the legislature is simply 'adjusting the benefits and burdens of economic life'. . . in a manner that secures an average reciprocity of advantage to everyone concerned. . . ."[24] In other words, the legislative body's choice to allow no use of the property nullifies the usual deference given to that body's decisions. As a result, the reasons for adopting the regulation become irrelevant, and a full weighing of the public interest involved against the detriment imposed on the landowner is no longer required.

In the situation of a moratorium, however, the legislative body has not yet made the type of regulatory choice about future use of the property that triggered the categorical rule in *Lucas*. To the contrary, the very purpose of the moratorium is to afford time to make that choice. The moratorium allows the public agency to undertake its decision making without interim development that could impair the planning agency's efforts even before the final decision is made.

As a result, applying this part of the *Lucas* rationale to moratoria makes no sense. Such an application would amount to a judicial declaration of a taking before the full benefits and burdens of the regulation were even available for analysis. That type of judicial action is far different from one, as in *Lucas*, that declares a categorical taking after the legislative body has acted to impose a permanent regulation that leaves the property without economic use.

§ 12.2(b) *Functional Effect on Government*

The second rationale in *Lucas* concerns the possible effect of a categorical taking rule on the government's ability to regulate. The Court first identified what it termed the "functional basis" for permitting government regulation that affects property values: that "[g]overnment hardly could go on if, to some extent, values incident to property could not be diminished without paying for every such change in the general law. . . ."[25] However, the Court then concluded that this functional basis for regulation "does not apply to the relatively rare situations where the government has deprived a landowner of all economically beneficial uses."[26] The Court thus apparently concluded that adoption of a categorical taking rule in this situation would not impair the functions of government simply because the rule would apply so rarely.

In the case of moratoria, however, the application of the categorical taking rule would have a much greater impact upon governmental functions for two reasons. First, while a moratorium is not an everyday occurrence, it is still a land-use regulatory tool that has been employed for decades. As a practical matter, in many jurisdictions moratoria play an important role in land-use regulation. They cannot be labeled "rare" and, on that basis, casually dismissed as relatively insignificant.

Second, imposing categorical liability on moratoria will substantially interfere with the government's ability to regulate land use effectively. By definition, moratoria are adopted only when a significant land-use problem exists. In practice, imposing a categorical takings rule will mean that local governments will not adopt moratoria because of the potential liability. Instead, they will leave the existing regulations in place while completing the public process of making the regulatory changes necessary to respond to the perceived problem. During this interim period, the prospect of impending regulatory changes will impel landowners to attempt to secure vested rights under the existing regulatory regime. If these efforts are successful, new development undertaken pursuant to the newly vested rights is likely to exacerbate the very problems that led the public agency to consider new regulations.

The net effect of these occurrences will be a markedly less effective planning regime. Thus, in terms of the second *Lucas* rationale, applying the categorical taking rule to moratoria *will* impair the functional basis of government regulation.

§ 12.2(c) *Risk of Impressing Property into Public Service*

The third rationale for the *Lucas* categorical rule focuses on the risk that the regulation's real purpose may be impermissible. The Court declared:

> [A]ffirmatively supporting a compensation requirement is the fact that regulations that leave the owner of land without economically beneficial or productive options for its use . . . carry with them a heightened risk that private property is being pressed into some form of public service under the guise of mitigating serious public harm.[27]

This rationale reflects the actual wording of the Fifth Amendment, which prohibits the taking of property for "public use" without compensation.[28] As the Court has said on many occasions, the purpose of that amendment is to "bar government from forcing some people alone to bear public burdens which, in all fairness and justice, should be borne by the public as a whole."[29] The *Lucas* opinion assumes that, as the regulatory burden increases, the risk also increases that the burden is imposed to accomplish some sort of public use. The opinion also offered a "typical" example of such a regulation: one that requires land to be left in its natural state.[30]

The very example used by the Court, however, demonstrates the inapplicability of this third *Lucas* rationale to moratoria. The Court's point was that, by requiring land to be left in its natural state, the legislative body was preventing use of the property so that it could capture a benefit for the public. Such a purpose contrasts with allowable regulatory action, which achieves benefits for the public *and* for the landowner—the much-heralded "reciprocity of advantage" to everyone concerned.[31]

In the case of a moratorium, however, the risk cited by the Court to justify the categorical takings rule is not present. The local government is not disabling the owner's use of the property to impress it into a public use. Instead, the local government is acting to protect the planning process that will decide the ultimate uses of that property. Furthermore, a primary function of that process is to *decide* whether there are serious public harms.

Accordingly, until the completion of this short-term process, there is no reason to assume that the government is using its land-use powers as a "guise" for pressing property into public use, the third rationale for the *Lucas* categorical rule. There is, in short, no reason to assume that a "heightened risk" exists.

The Court's reasoning in *United States v. Riverside Bayview Homes, Inc.*,[32] which presents an analogous factual situation, supports this conclusion. In *Riverside* the plaintiff argued that the issuance of a cease-and-desist order, which stopped the filling of a wetlands without a permit, constituted a taking. The Court disagreed, reasoning that requiring a person to obtain a permit before engaging in a certain use "does not itself 'take' property in any sense."[33] After all, said the Court, permission to use the property may later be granted, and even if it is not, other viable uses may be available to the owner. A taking will occur only if, at the end of this process, the agency has denied the owner any economically viable use of the property.[34]

A landowner subject to a temporary moratorium is in the same position in regard to the regulatory system as the plaintiff in *Riverside*. The agency is deciding what uses to allow, and some of those uses may well be consistent with the landowner's preferences. Moreover, even if they are not, the uses allowed may be viable and thus prevent a taking. Until the public agency makes its ultimate planning choice, however, the landowner will not know the regulatory impact on the land, and the Court will not be in a position to evaluate that impact, much less conclude that the government is using its powers as a "guise."

§ 12.2(d) *Equivalency to a Physical Appropriation*

The last *Lucas* rationale links the rule on categorical takings for loss of all economic use to the Court's rule on physical occupation takings, pronounced earlier in *Loretto v. Teleprompter Manhattan CATV Serv.*[35] In *Loretto*, of course, the Court held that the physical occupation of private property was a categorical taking no matter how small the occupation.[36] The *Loretto* holding drew on Justice Brandeis's foundational reasoning in *Pennsylvania Coal*, in which he declared that regulatory takings "very nearly have the same effect for constitutional purposes as appropriating or destroying [property]."[37] The Court in *Lucas* later cited *Loretto* to support its extension of the categorical rule to cases involving regulations causing the loss of all economic use. It reasoned that "total deprivation of beneficial use is, from the landowner's point of view, the equivalent of a physical appropriation."[38]

Of the four *Lucas* rationales, this last one comes closest to offering some logical support for the extension of the *Lucas* rule to moratoria. From the landowner's perspective, the reason he or she cannot use the property is largely irrelevant. Whether the government physically occupies the land or adopts a regulation prohibiting its use, the effect on the landowner is much the same.

At the same time, however, this analogy between physical takings and moratoria is incomplete. The analogy ignores the unique features of a physical appropriation and the governmental compulsion that form the logical foundation of the categorical rule for physical occupations.[39] As the Court emphasized in *Loretto*, the right to exclude others is "one of the most treasured strands" in the "bundle of rights" that make up private property rights.[40] Even the smallest physical occupation violates this sensitive right. Physical occupation *is* an "appropriation" of property in the literal sense. Furthermore, the government regulation itself affirmatively compels the landowner to submit to this physical occupation.[41]

The analogy between interim moratoria and physical occupations is weak for other reasons. The purpose of a moratorium is to allow the completion of a rational planning process to decide what uses the landowner will make of the property. In contrast to this relatively limited interference with property ownership, a physical occupation affects virtually every strand in the "bundle" of property rights, including the ability to sell the land for value. Additionally, a moratorium does not confer the direct benefit on the appropriator that is found in the physical occupation situation. In short, making the landowner wait for a period of time while the land use decision is made is far different from physically ousting the landowner from part of the property for that period of time.

To summarize, none of the four *Lucas* rationales for the categorical takings rule applies convincingly in the moratorium context. They provide no support for extending the categorical takings rule to moratoria.

§ 12.3   *Treatment of Delay in Using Land*

Unlike permanent regulations, such as the one at issue in *Lucas* and in many physical appropriation cases, moratoria—which by definition are temporary—will end. Indeed, state statutes may well constrain the length of time that a moratorium remains in effect.[42] Furthermore, the long-term regulatory limitations on the property become clear only when the moratorium ends and a new land-use regulation is enacted. Thus, from the perspective of a landowner seeking to develop property, a moratorium delays but does not, in and of itself, finally prevent development.

Accordingly, any decision extending the *Lucas* categorical takings rule to include moratoria must consider the consistency of such a decision with the Supreme Court's previous holdings concerning the treatment of regulatory delays in the development of land. As demonstrated below, such a decision would be inconsistent with those holdings.

§ 12.3(a) *Delay in the Permit Process*

The land-use regulatory process normally requires users of land to apply for and secure from the government a permit or other regulatory approval, such as a rezoning, before developing. Subdivision regulation is likewise premised on the local government's approval of an application. The local government's consideration of these applications necessarily entails delay during which no new use can be made of the property, and the Supreme Court's jurisprudence has addressed the legitimacy of that type of delay.

In holding that paying damages is a remedy for a temporary taking, the Court in *First English* carefully noted that it was not addressing the "quite different questions that would arise in the case of normal delays in obtaining building permits, changes in zoning ordinances, variances, and the like."[43] In earlier cases, the Court had explicitly recognized the concept of "temporary harms" caused by delay in the regulatory process. It noted the distinction between these "temporary harms"[44] and "temporary takings," labeling the former as normal "incidents of ownership."[45]

The delay caused by a short-term moratorium is directly analogous to the types of regulatory delay mentioned in *First English* and categorized as a "normal incident of ownership." In all of these instances, any change in the use of the property is temporarily deferred until the regulatory body decides whether to approve it. Judicial confirmation of the government's ability to legitimately plan for land uses—and of the structure of government regulation fashioned to carry out that planning—necessarily endorses some delays in use. These delays are analytically similar to the delays caused by moratoria, and the two types of delay should be treated identically for purposes of takings analysis.[46]

§ 12.3(b) *Delay Under the Ripeness Doctrine*

The Court's ripeness decisions are also directly relevant to the determination of how to treat regulatory delay under the Takings Clause. While the outer contours of the ripeness doctrine can be debated, the Court unquestionably has required that a landowner seek more than one government approval before bringing a takings claim.[47] Only then will the full extent of the regulatory burden be known.[48] For example, in *Williamson County Regional Planning Commission v. Hamilton Bank of Johnson County*,[49] the county rejected the developer's revised subdivision plat for numerous reasons. Nonetheless, the Court held that the developer's takings action was not ripe, for the developer had not sought variances that would have allowed it to develop the property according to its proposed plan.[50]

The ripeness doctrine allows—indeed, mandates—the same type of delay as that caused by short-term moratoria. In both instances, the landowner cannot develop until the agency determines the specific type of regulation that should apply to the property.[51] Just as under the ripeness doctrine, the landowner subject to a short-term moratorium will not know the full extent of the regulatory burden placed on his or her property until the regulatory process is completed. Accordingly, no principled basis justifies treating delay under the ripeness doctrine differently from delay caused by short-term moratoria.

§ 12.3(c) *Delay Caused by Pre-condemnation Activity*

A third type of delay addressed by the Supreme Court's takings precedents arose in *Agins v. City of Tiburon*.[52] In that case, the landowner claimed that the city's planning activities, undertaken to decide whether the city should condemn the landowner's property, constituted a taking. A unanimous Court disagreed:

> The State Supreme Court correctly rejected the contention that the municipality's good-faith planning activi-

ties, which did not result in a successful prosecution of an eminent domain claim, so burdened the appellants' enjoyment of their property as to constitute a taking. . . . Even if the appellants' ability to sell their property was limited during the pendency of the condemnation proceeding, the appellants were free to sell or develop their property when the proceedings ended. *Mere fluctuations in value during the process of governmental decisionmaking, absent extraordinary delay, are "incidents of ownership." They cannot be considered as a "taking" in the constitutional sense.*[53]

The reasoning in *Agins* is significant for several reasons. First, the Court refused to find a taking for "good-faith planning activities," the same type of activities at issue in claims that short-term moratoria constitute takings. Second, the Court observed that even if those activities limited the landowner's ability to sell or develop, the landowner could do so after the condemnation proceeding ended. The Court thus viewed the period for determining loss of value as including the time after the city's condemnation actions had ended.

The moratorium situation is analogous. While the landowner cannot develop or sell the property during the moratorium, he or she certainly is free to do so after the moratorium expires. Under the reasoning of *Agins*, the value of the land is considered over the long run; it is not segmented by isolating the loss of value during the short period of the moratorium.

Finally, the Court referred to the fluctuation of value during the process of government decision making as an "incident of ownership." This concept is quite similar to the phraseology found in *Lucas*, in which the Court established one exception to its categorical taking rule for loss of all economic use: There is no taking where the uses prevented were not within the landowner's title originally.[54] Changes in value caused by temporary planning moratoria are likewise mere incidents of ownership. An owner of land must expect that government will regulate the use of his or her land—that much has been settled for the better part of a century—and with legitimate regulation comes at least some delay in making use of property.

In short, losses caused by planning activities are not compensable takings when the activities are undertaken for the purpose of actually acquiring property. If those losses are not compensable, losses caused by a moratorium designed to determine future uses of the property likewise should not be compensable.

§ 12.4 *Interference With Governmental Discretion*

The previous discussion in this chapter showed why the reasons given in *Lucas* for the adoption of a categorical taking rule, while perhaps justifiable in the context of the permanent taking found in *Lucas*, are unconvincing when applied to short-term moratoria. It also showed that a categorical rule for moratoria would conflict with other parts of the Court's takings jurisprudence. In addition to the *Lucas* rationale for the categorical rule, however, other aspects of the Supreme Court's takings jurisprudence must be weighed in determining whether moratoria should fall under a categorical takings rule.

§ 12.4(a) *Impact on Legislative Discretion*

One of the most important factors to be considered is the extent to which such a rule would interfere with the legitimate discretion exercised by municipal elected officials. Since 1987, the direction of the Supreme Court's takings jurisprudence has been to decrease the deference given to legislative discretion in making land use decisions. The *Lucas* decision is a prime example; it imposes liability for certain actions regardless of the reasons why those actions were taken. In contrast, where the categorical rule does not apply, the courts employ the three-part test from *Penn Central*. One part of that test expressly requires the court to examine the "character of the governmental action,"[55] a factor that focuses on the reasons for the government's action[56] and, therefore, on the basis for its exercise of discretion.

The *Lucas* categorical rule eliminates that factor from the takings equation. The court is only concerned with the impact of the regulation. It does not weigh the nature of the government's action or the benefits that might accrue from it, or otherwise evaluate the reasons for that exercise of discretion.[57] This is one reason why critics of *Lucas*, including a stinging dissent by Justice Stevens in that 5-4 decision, accuse the majority of reviving an approach to judicial review grounded in the substantive due process principles of *Lochner v. New York*.[58]

The *Lucas* Court was careful to describe its categorical rule as a rare exception to the normal instance where the Court would carefully consider the character of the governmental action.[59] If the rule were applied to moratoria, however, refusal to consider the reasons for the government's exercise of discretion would become much more widespread.

Additionally, the extension of the *Lucas* categorical rule to moratoria would significantly impact legislative functions. The rule would intrude into one of the most sensitive areas of legislative discretion: the judgment about when a land-use problem has reached such a critical mass that interim action is needed to effectively craft a solution for it.

The recent litigation over the moratorium at Lake Tahoe provides a striking example. Lake Tahoe is unquestionably one of the most important natural resources in the world because of the remarkable clarity of its water and the beauty of its setting. Over the past 50 years, however, the clarity of the water has degraded rapidly.[60] The scientific evidence is abundant that development around the lake is a large contributor to the problem.[61] In response, Congress passed amendments to the bi-state Tahoe compact that called for a moratorium while planning to protect this world-class resource took place.[62]

The caselaw on moratoria is replete with similar instances in which the legislative body enacting a moratorium is responding to a demonstrated problem. This body of law includes moratoria designed to save lives,[63] to respond to serious environmental problems,[64] and to allow time to secure permanent preservation. It also includes cases where development patterns have simply brought unforeseen problems.[65]

Application of the *Lucas* categorical rule to this situation means that the legislative judgment concerning the need for planning to avoid or mitigate environmental damage receives no weight in the judicial evaluation of whether a taking has occurred. The Court ignores the "character" of the government action: a legislative judgment that short-term prevention of development is appropriate given the scope of the problem when that problem is largely caused by the same type of development being delayed. It also ignores the downside risk of not acting, which is the risk of continued destruction of the resource or exacerbation of the problem. Temporary interference with the right to develop automatically trumps that risk. In effect, the Court rebalances the benefits and burdens of the moratorium to ensure that the scale tips in favor of the landowner and against the legislative judgment.

By their nature, categorical rules elevate specified policy concerns to a dominant position while, at the same time, ignoring other concerns. Given the important concerns that moratoria address, however, the Court should not be quick to adopt a rule that would override legislative judgments that underlie short-term moratoria.

§ 12.4(b) *Impact on Land-Use Planning*

In the usual situation, deference is owed to a legislative judgment because the legislature is carrying out its essential task of adjusting the benefits and burdens of regulation. If those benefits would accrue without imposing the burden on the landowner, a court might be justified in disregarding the benefits and in institutionalizing that disregard in its takings jurisprudence.

However, in the case of a moratorium, imposing costs on the landowner is necessary to attain the unquestionably legitimate goal of effectuating land-use planning. Moratoria can prevent very real harms. They are needed precisely because, without them, landowners will rush to develop before the government can complete the steps needed to adopt and implement regulatory solutions to the perceived problem. As more than one court has noted, people will move quickly to develop their property before the government can take further regulatory steps, and in doing so, they "may cause the very harm the plan is meant to protect [against]."[66]

If a short-term moratorium is held to effect a categorical taking, the government will face a Hobson's choice: (1) accept the additional impacts that will occur before it can enact a new land-use regulation responding to the problem, or (2) pay to prevent the very injury that it is now undertaking land-use planning to avoid. Given the precarious financial state of local governments, the choice will likely be to suffer the harm, and in such a situation, important benefits of professional land-use planning will be jeopardized.

§ 12.5   *Effects on Takings Theory*

Extending *Lucas* and *First English* to cover moratoria also implicates two larger issues in takings theory. To make the extension, the Supreme Court must segment the "bundle" of property rights along a time continuum, and it must decide that the Takings Clause primarily protects land use, not land value. If taken, both jurisprudential steps will increase the already anomalous features of takings law.

§ 12.5(a) *Conceptual Segmentation of Property Rights*

In evaluating the effects of a moratorium, a court can only be sure of the property's allowable economic use during the period of the moratorium. To conclude that a moratorium has effected a taking, the court must ignore the possibility—indeed, perhaps the likelihood—that the property will have economic use once the moratorium ends and thus retains substantial value during the moratorium. Accordingly, for the Supreme Court to apply the *Lucas* categorical rule in the moratorium context, it must conceptually sever the moratorium time period from the subsequent regulatory period and separately examine each period for purposes of takings analysis. It also must focus the takings analysis solely on loss of use, not on loss of value.

There are significant problems in taking the step of conceptually segmenting time. First, it would contradict the view that the Supreme Court's takings jurisprudence has adopted toward regulation and property ownership. In *Penn Central*, the railroad asked the Court, for takings purposes, to treat its air rights above Grand Central Station as conceptually distinct from its existing building on the site. The Court refused, flatly declaring that "[t]akings jurisprudence does not divide a single parcel into discrete segments and attempt to determine whether rights in a particular segment have been entirely abrogated."[67] As recently as 1993, in *Concrete & Prods. Inc. v. Construction Laborers Pension Trust*, the Court repeated its holding that a "claimant's parcel of property could not first be divided into what was taken and what was left" to show a taking.[68]

The takings proponents might respond that conceptual severance along a time continuum is different from severing the property geographically, as the Court refused to do in *Penn Central*. But conceptual time severance is even less logical than geographical severance. It is inconsistent with the Court's very recognition of the government's authority to implement land-use regulation, an authority that dates back to the seminal opinion in *Village of Euclid v. Ambler Realty*.[69]

By definition, regulatory processes have periods of delay built into them. The concept of regulation requires that the landowner await a decision on a permit, and during that waiting period, he or she is necessarily deprived of the envisioned use of the property. As Justice Stevens recognized in *Williamson County*, "Temporary harms are an unfortunate but necessary by-product of disputes over the extent of the government's power to inflict permanent harms without paying for them."[70] Recognition of this regulatory power cannot logically be squared with conceptual severance of time in takings analysis.

§ 12.5(b) *Value Versus Use*

Extension of the *Lucas* categorical takings rule to moratoria also directly raises the issue of whether takings law protects against loss of use or loss of value. The question arises because, in the case of short-term moratoria, the property usually will retain considerable value if that value is considered over the long run, the normal period used in determining market value. The mere existence of a short-term moratorium does not portend that the government regulator will allow no use when the moratorium expires.

In most cases, the moratorium is followed by a new set of land-use controls that allows some use of the property. Thus, to find that a short-term moratorium has taken all economic use of a property, the Court must examine use to the exclusion of value.

Other chapters in this book address the use-versus-value debate.[71] The point to be made here is simply that a short-term moratorium cannot be found to take property unless the Court is willing to ignore the usually considerable value remaining in the property during that moratorium. The property does not just regain lost value when the moratorium ends; rather, it retains value during the moratorium and can be sold during that period. The effect of the moratorium is only to prevent immediate building on the property, a fact that caselaw and other authorities recognize.[72] Thus, if the Court concludes that a moratorium is a per se taking, it will ignore the financial reality of the value that inheres in property during a moratorium.

In doing so, the Court's holding also will have the unfortunate consequence of increasing the anomalous nature of takings law. For example, a downzoning can reduce property value by 75 percent or more, but such a loss is not usually a taking.[73] Notably, the loss of value in *Village of Euclid* was on that order, but no compensation was required.[74] In contrast, a moratorium usually will take less of the property's overall value, but it would be deemed a categorical taking requiring compensation. Indeed, under the *Lucas* categorical takings rule, an extremely short moratorium—theoretically, even one day—would effect a taking and thus require compensation.

Another incongruous aspect of such a holding is shown by comparing the time delay caused by a moratorium to the delay inherent in the permit power. In some instances, moratoria will be of shorter duration than the usual permitting process. This outcome is particularly likely if an applicant must re-apply for regulatory approval in order to ensure that a takings claim is ripe. Yet normal permit delay is not a taking, while the takings proponents argue that *any* delay caused by a moratorium effects a taking.

In a complex area of constitutional law such as takings jurisprudence, some anomalies must be expected.[75] At some point, however, the anomalies created by the rules reach such a level as to discredit the rules themselves. With respect to takings law's treatment of use and value, the extension of the *Lucas* categorical takings rule to moratoria would cast even further doubt on the coherence of the takings rule structure.

§ 12.6   Need for a Corrective Rule

§ 12.6(a) Policing Regulatory Abuse

One justification for a categorical takings rule might be that local governments have abused moratoria through overuse and that only the Court, by adopting a categorical takings rule, can effectively deter such abuse. For example, when local governments impose exactions, the potential for governmental overreaching is apparent. Local governments, short on money, have an incentive to impose a variety of requirements as conditions on developments, thereby requiring developers to fund infrastructure improvements. The Court noted this incentive in *Nollan* and *Dolan*, dramatically referring to the possibility of the "extortion" of improvements from developers in holding that the exactions in those cases were takings.[76] Some might suggest that governmental misuse of moratoria requires a similar expansion of takings liability to deter government abuse.[77]

Exactions and moratoria, however, present quite different situations. To begin with, municipalities do not have the same monetary incentive for adopting moratoria as they do for imposing exactions. Unlike exactions, moratoria do not necessarily shift costs of institutional improvements from government to private individuals. Additionally, there is no conclusive evidence that moratoria have been consistently misused.[78]

Equally important is the fact that courts are not the only governmental body able to effectively police the use of moratoria by local government. In recent years, state legislatures have been active in this area, shaping legislation that balances the rights of property owners against the regulatory needs of government.[79] For example, state legislation has imposed time limits on moratoria,[80] mandated substantive[81] and procedural limitations on them,[82] and demonstrated at least some sensitivity to the costs that moratoria impose on landowners.

This legislative activity ought to give the Supreme Court pause before it extends the categorical takings rule to include moratoria. A moratorium does not present a situation where, unless the Court acts, landowners cannot expect any other government branch to recognize the costs that moratoria can impose. The adoption of a categorical takings rule for moratoria cannot be justified as a necessary prophylactic measure to prevent governmental abuse.

§ 12.6(b) Abnormal Delay

The cases concluding that short-term moratoria are not takings have been careful to differentiate delays caused by moratoria from "abnormal delay." For example, in deciding *First English* on remand from the Supreme Court, the California Court of Appeal concluded that a taking could occur "if these interim measures are unreasonable in purpose, duration, or scope."[83] The Supreme Court itself declared in *Agins* that "extraordinary delay" in the land-use planning process can result in a taking.[84] Furthermore, even where the delay from a moratorium is not abnormal, if the government does not use that time to address the planning problem that gave rise to the moratorium, a court can find a taking.[85]

These outcomes are certainly appropriate. If, in light of the problem at hand, a government agency takes a clearly excessive amount of time to complete its activities, its action in imposing the moratorium is not rationally related to the legitimate public purpose of planning.[86] But a fact-specific inquiry is needed to conclude that, in a particular instance, a moratorium is abnormally long. There must be careful examination of the problem at hand and of the government's reasons for the delay. The fact that there have been so few cases finding unreasonable delay of this nature suggests that, in most instances, governments are using moratoria appropriately. All of these considerations support the conclusion that categorical rules are unsuited to the adjudication of the constitutional consequences of moratoria.

§ 12.7   *Conclusion: First Principles*

Courts have approved of short-term moratoria almost since the advent of zoning. While constitutional doctrine can change, a court should not lightly declare that a moratorium, a land-use tool well accepted for three quarters of a century, suddenly effects a compensable taking.

Such a conclusion would take a further step away from first principles. As scholars have documented,[87] the framers of the Constitution did not intend that the Takings Clause would require compensation. In *Lucas*, Justice Scalia recognized this research but concluded that it was too late in the day to retreat from the principle that a taking requires compensation.[88]

Perhaps that conclusion is true. But the history and original intent of takings law counsels against radical steps that move takings doctrine even further from its origins. Applying the *Lucas* categorical rule to moratoria would be just such a radical, unwarranted step.

Notes

1. 482 U.S. 304 (1987).
2. 505 U.S. 1003 (1992).

3. 216 F.3d 764 (9th Cir. 2000), *reh' g and reh' g en banc denied*, 228 F.3d 998 (9th Cir. 2000), *cert. granted in part*, 121 S. Ct. 2589 (June 29, 2001) (No. 00-1167). In the court of appeal, I authored an amicus curiae brief on behalf of various scientists in support of the defendant in this case. The chapter was submitted just after the Supreme Court's grant of certiorari in the case.

4. 438 U.S. 104 (1978).

5. *See* JULIAN C. JUERGENSMEYER & THOMAS E. ROBERTS, LAND USE PLANNING AND CONTROL LAW § 9.5 (1998) ("Moratoria are legally authorized periods for the delay or abeyance of some activity.").

6. *Id.* ("The adoption of a building permit or development approval moratorium is an increasingly frequently used approach by local governments to halt or slow growth until new growth management programs, new comprehensive plans and/or new zoning ordinances can be adopted and implemented.")

7. *See, e.g.*, Miller v. Board of Public Works, 234 P. 381 (Cal. 1925); Downham v. City Council of Alexandria, 58 F.2d 784 (E.D. Va. 1932); Fowler v. Obier, 224 Ky. 742, 7 S.W.2d 219 (1928).

8. *First English*, 482 U.S. at 322.

9. *Id.* at 321.

10. *Id.* at 318 ("[A] governmental body may acquiesce in a judicial declaration that one of its ordinances has effected an unconstitutional taking of property; the landowner has no right under the Just Compensation Clause to insist that a 'temporary' taking be deemed a permanent taking.").

11. *See* Scott v. City of Sioux City, 432 N.W.2d 144 (Iowa 1988) (plaintiff alleged that in the aftermath of *First English*, an interim ordinance constituted a taking, but the court held that the statute of limitations barred the action). *See also* Kass & Gerard, *Excessive Sound, Fury Over Land Use Ruling*, N.Y.U. L. REV. § A1 (1987). Even before *First English*, some commentators had suggested that moratoria were vulnerable to takings claims if the Court ultimately adopted the reasoning in Justice Brennan's dissent in *San Diego Gas & Electric Co.*, 450 U.S. 621, 636 (1981). *See* Williams et al., *The White River Junction Manifesto*, 9 SUP. CT. REV. 193, 218 (1984) (in the event that Justice Brennan's dissent is adopted, "a way must be found to avoid tossing development moratoria on the judicial ash heap.").

12. *Lucas*, 505 U.S. at 1016.

13. *Id.* at 1031-32.

14. *See* Williams v. City of Central, 907 P.2d 701, 704 (Colo. App. 1995) (plaintiff "claims that, under *Lucas* and *First English I*, a categorical compensable taking occurred because the suspension of special-use permit applications deprived him of all economically viable use of the Belvidere Theater during the 10 months the moratorium was in effect.").

15. *First English*, 482 U.S. at 318-19.

16. *See* Linda Bozung & Deborah Alessi, *Recent Developments in Environmental Preservation and the Rights of Property Owners*, 20 URB. LAW. 969, 1016 (1988):

> The phrase "temporary taking," however, is a label given to a remedy. It is simply a way to describe the option of rescission given to governing authorities once it has been determined that a regulation effects a taking. If the government wants to keep the ordinance in effect, it must pay compensation reflecting a permanent loss. If, however, the government wishes to reduce the amount of compensation

due, it may abandon the ordinance and pay only for the time while the now-rescinded ordinance took property.

17. *Nollan*, 483 U.S. at 838 ("Rewriting the [Coastal Commission's] argument to eliminate the play on words makes clear that there is nothing to it.").

18. For a more complete discussion of the meaning of *First English*, see Thomas E. Roberts, *Moratoria as Categorical Regulatory Takings: What* First English *and* Lucas *Say and Don't Say*, 31 ENVTL. L. RPTR. 11,037 (Sept. 2001).

19. *See, e.g.*, Woodbury Place Partners v. City of Woodbury, 492 N.W.2d 258, 262 (Minn. App. 1993) ("The apparent reach of *First English* is to retrospectively temporary takings (e.g., regulations subsequently rescinded or declared invalid), not prospectively temporary regulations. . . ."); Santa Fe Village Venture v. City of Albuquerque, 914 F. Supp. 478, 483 (D. N.M. 1995) (two-and-a-half-year moratorium not a compensable taking); Zilber v. Town of Moraga, 692 F. Supp. 1995, 1206 (N.D. Cal. 1988) ("A one-and-a-half-year development moratorium in order to develop a comprehensive scheme for regulating open space seems neither unreasonable nor, standing alone, sufficiently burdensome to require compensation."). A number of cases have reached the opposite conclusion. *See* Eberle v. Dane County Bd. of Adjustment, 227 Wis. 2d 609 (1999); Whitehead Oil Co. v. City of Lincoln, 515 N.W.2d 401 (Neb. 1994). In *City of Seattle v. McCoy*, 101 Wash. App. 815, 4 P.3d 159 (2000), the Washington Court of Appeal held that a trial court's order abating the operation of a restaurant and lounge under a drug nuisance statute constituted a compensable temporary taking, citing *First English*. In *Keshbro, Inc. v. City of Miami*, __ So. 2d __, 2001 WL 776555 (Fla. 2001), another nuisance abatement case, the Florida Supreme Court first concluded that the Supreme Court in *First English* had used the term "temporary taking" to refer to the period before a regulatory taking "is invalidated by the courts." __ So. 2d __. It then held, however, that a temporary regulation could be a categorical taking under *Lucas. Id.* at __. Finally, it noted that:

> [T]he courts refusing to extend *First English* beyond its remedial genesis to prospectively temporary regulations have done so in the land-use and planning arena, where an entirely different set of considerations are implicated from those in the context of nuisance abatement.

Id. For takings purposes, the Florida court thus attempted to distinguish temporary regulations in the "planning arena" from other types of temporary deprivations.

20. 482 U.S. at 313.

21. 505 U.S. at 1018.

22. *See* Landgate, Inc. v. California Coastal Comm'n, 17 Cal. 4th 1006, 1026, 953 P.2d 1188, 1200 (1998) ("From the would-be developer's point of view, the impact of ordinary delay due to a governmental mistake on the one hand, and denial of all feasible use on the other, may be identical. . . . ").

23. Judge Kozinski put it slightly differently in his dissent to the denial of rehearing in *Tahoe Sierra*: "The question is whether there is something special about a finite moratorium that relieves the government from the duty to compensate." 228 F.3d 998, 999 (9th Cir. 2000), *cert. granted*, 121 S. Ct. 2589 (June 29, 2001) (No. 00-1167).

24. *Lucas*, 505 U.S. at 1017.

25. *Id.* at 1003 (citing Pennsylvania Coal Co. v. Mahon, 260 U.S. at 413).

26. *Id.*

27. *Id.* at 1018.

28. U.S. CONST. amend. V.

29. *See, e.g., First English*, 482 U.S. at 318-19.

30. 505 U.S. at 1018.

31. *Pennsylvania Coal Co.*, 260 U.S. at 415.

32. 474 U.S. 121 (1985).

33. *Id.* at 127.

34. *Id.* at 126-27.

35. 458 U.S. 419 (1982).

36. *Id.* at 421.

37. 260 U.S. 393, 414 (1922).

38. 505 U.S. at 1017.

39. *See* Palazzolo v. Rhode Island, __ U.S. __, 121 S. Ct. 2448, 2457 (2001) ("The clearest sort of taking occurs when the government encroaches upon or occupies private land for its own proposed use.").

40. *Loretto*, 458 U.S. at 435.

41. *See* Yee v. City of Escondido, 503 U.S. 519, 527 (1992) ("The government effects a physical taking only where it requires the landowner to submit to the physical occupation of his land. 'This element of required acquiescence is at the heart of the concept of occupation.' FCC v. Florida Power Corp., 480 U.S. 245, 252, 107 S. Ct. 1107, 1112, 94 L. Ed. 2d 282 (1987) . . . ").

42. *See, e.g.,* ARIZ. REV. STAT. § 9-463.06 subd. E (West 2001) (a moratorium not based on a shortage of essential public facilities 'shall not remain in effect for more than one hundred twenty days, but such a moratorium may be extended for additional periods of time of up to one hundred twenty days. . . "); IDAHO CODE § 67-6523 (Matthew Bender & Co. 2000) ("An emergency ordinance or moratorium may be effective for a period of not longer than one hundred and twenty (120) days."); ME. REV. STAT. ANN. tit. 30-A § 4356 (West 1999) ("The moratorium must be of a definite term of not more than 180 days," with certain extensions allowed); OR. REV. STAT. § 197.520 (1999) (moratorium not based on a shortage of public facilities "shall be effective for a period [not] longer than 120 days" with certain extensions "for a period [not] longer than six months"); WASH. REV. CODE ANN. 36.70A.390 (West 2000) ("A moratorium . . . may be effective for not longer than six months, but may be effective for up to one year if a work plan is developed for related studies providing for such a longer period," and other extensions are possible.).

43. *First English*, 482 U.S. at 321.

44. Williamson County v. Hamilton Bank, 473 U.S. 172, 203-04 (1985) (Stevens, J., concurring).

45. Agins v. City of Tiburon, *supra*, 447 U.S. at 263 n.9.

46. A number of courts have reached this conclusion. *See, e.g.*, S.E.W. Friel v. Triangle Oil Co., 76 Md. App. 96, 104, 543 A.2d 863, 867 (1988); Guinnane v. City and County of San Francisco, 197 Cal. App. 3d 862, 869, 241 Cal. Rptr. 787, 791 (1987), *cert den.*, 488 U.S. 823 (1988).

47. *See, e.g.,* Agins v. City of Tiburon, *supra*, 447 U.S. at 260 (challenge to the application of a zoning ordinance was not ripe because the property owners had not yet submitted a plan for development of their property); Hodel v. Virginia Surface Mining & Reclamation Assn., 452 U.S. 264, 297 (1981) (rejecting takings claim because appellees did not avail themselves of the opportunities provided by the Surface Mining Control and Reclamation Act to obtain administrative relief by requesting either a variance or a waiver).

48. The distinction between administrative activities leading to regulation and the actual effect of regulation has been recognized even by state court judges who otherwise would extend the categorical takings doctrine. In *Landgate, Inc. v. California Coastal Comm'n*, 17 Cal. 4th 1006, 95 P.2d 1188 (1998), the Coastal Commission erroneously asserted jurisdiction over a development. The plaintiff brought a takings claim seeking compensation for the period during which the Commission stopped the plaintiff's efforts to develop the property. A majority of the court found no taking. Justice Brown dissented. However, even she recognized a difference between the situation where the government has made its regulatory choice and one in which it has not:

> It is that administrative flexibility that lies behind and justifies the prudential ripeness rule in the takings context. Those concerns simply have no bearing in this case, however, *where the commission made clear the extent to which it would permit plaintiffs to develop their lot.* 17 Cal. 4th at 1028 (Brown, J., dissenting) (emphasis added).

49. 473 U.S. 172 (1985).

50. *Id.* at 188.

51. *See* Palazzolo v. Rhode Island, __ U.S. __, 121 S. Ct. 2448, 2459 (2001) ("Under our ripeness rules a takings claim based on a law or regulation which is alleged to go too far in burdening property depends upon the landowner's first having followed reasonable and necessary steps to allow regulatory agencies to exercise their full discretion in considering development plans for the property. . . ").

52. 447 U.S. 255 (1980).

53. 447 U.S. at 263 n.9 (emphasis added).

54. 505 U.S. at 1026.

55. Penn Cent. Transp. Co. v. City of New York, 438 U.S. 104, 124 (1978).

56. *See* Palazzolo v. Rhode Island, __ U.S. __, 121 S. Ct. 2448, 2466 (2001) (O'Connor, J., concurring) (discussing the three-part *Penn Central* test and noting that "[t]he purposes served, as well as the effects produced, by a particular regulation inform the takings analysis.").

57. *Lucas*, 505 U.S. at 1015.

58. *Id.* at 1069 (Stevens, J., dissenting) ("As Justice Marshall observed about a position similar to that adopted by the Court today: 'If accepted, that claim would represent a return to the era of *Lochner v. New York*, 198 U.S. 45 . . . (1905) when common-law rights were also found immune from revision by State or federal Government . . . It would allow no room for change in response to changes in circumstances. . . . '") (citing PruneYard Shopping Center v. Robins, 447 U.S. 74, 93 (1980) (concurring opinion)).

59. 505 U.S. at 1018.

60. Tahoe-Sierra Preservation Council, Inc. v. Tahoe Regional Planning Agency, 216 F.3d 764, 766-67 (9th Cir. 2000), *cert granted in part*, 121 S. Ct. 2589 (June 29, 2001) (No. 00-1167) ("Since mid-century, however, the lake has been undergoing 'eutrophication,' a process by which the nutrient loading in the lake increases dramatically.").

61. *Id.* at 767 ("The dramatic increase in Lake Tahoe's nutrient levels has been caused by the rapid development of environmentally sensitive land in the Lake Tahoe Basin.").

62. Pub. Law 96-551, 1980 H.R. 8235 art. VI(c) ("The legislatures of the states of California and Nevada find that in order to make effective the regional plan as revised by the agency, it is necessary to halt temporarily works of development in the region which might otherwise absorb the entire capability of the region for further development or

direct it out of harmony with the ultimate plan.") The law then explicitly sets forth the moratorium.

63. *See, e.g.,* First English Evangelical Lutheran Church v. County of Los Angeles, 210 Cal. App. 3d 1353, 1367, 258 Cal. Rptr. 893, 902 (1989) ("Given the serious safety concerns demonstrated by the May 1978 flood, the County might well have been justified in prohibiting entirely any human occupancy or other use whatsoever of Lutherglen until it had completed a thorough study and determined precisely what, if any, occupancy and uses were compatible with the public safety.").

64. *See* Union Oil Co., 512 F.2d 743, 752 (9th Cir. 1975) (suspension of operations under leases after offshore oil spill).

65. *See, e.g.,* Matson v. Clark County Bd. of Comm'rs, 904 P.2d 317 (Wash. App. 1995) (temporary ban on new cluster subdivisions in agriculture and forest zoning districts).

66. Williams v. City of Central, 907 P.2d at 706. *See also* Schafer v. City of New Orleans, 743 F.2d 1086, 1090 (5th Cir. 1997) ("Interim zoning or a moratorium may be necessary to prevent a plan's defeat before it is formulated."); DANIEL R. MANDELKER, LAND USE LAW § 6.09 (4th ed. 1997).

67. *Penn Central*, 483 U.S. at 130.

68. 508 U.S. 602, 644 (1993).

69. 272 U.S. 365 (1926).

70. 473 U.S. 172, 203-04 (1985).

71. *See* chapters 18 and 19, *infra.*

72. *See, e.g.,* Growth Properties, Inc. v. Klingbeil Holding Co., 419 F. Supp. 212, 217 (D. Md. 1976) (calculating the fair market value of a parcel subject to a moratorium); City of Jersey City v. Township of Parsippany-Troy Hills, 16 N.J. Tax 504 (1997) (applying a "moratorium discount" to the value of land during a five-year building moratorium).

73. Lucas v. South Carolina Coastal Council, 505 U.S. 1003, 1019 n.8 (1992) (noting that takings law is full of "all-or-nothing" situations in which a small difference in regulatory deprivation makes the difference between a taking, with full recovery, and no taking.

74. Village of Euclid, Ohio v. Ambler Realty Co., 272 U.S. 365, 384 (1926) ("The bill alleges that the tract of land . . . has a market value of about $10,000 per acre, but if the use be limited to residential purposes, the market value is not in excess of $2,500 per acre").

75. *See Lucas*, 505 U.S. at 1018 ("It is true that in at least *some* cases the landowner with 95 percent loss will get nothing, while the landowner with total loss will recover in full. But that occasional result is no more strange than the gross disparity between the landowner whose premises are taken for a highway (who recovers in full) and the landowner whose property is reduced to 5 percent of its former value by the highway (who recovers nothing). Takings law is full of these 'all-or-nothing situations.'").

76. Dolan v. City of Tigard, 512 U.S. 374, 387 (1994) (quoting *Nollan* for the proposition that the absence of a nexus between the regulation and the problem it was attempting to solve "converted a valid regulation of land use into an 'out-and-out plan of extortion.'"). *See also* Ehrlich v. City of Culver City, 12 Cal. App. 4th 854, 876, 911 P.2d 429, 444 (1996) (legislatively imposed fees on a broad class of property owners "may indeed be subject to a lesser standard of judicial scrutiny than that formulated in *Nollan* and *Dolan* because the heightened risk of the 'extortionate' use of the police power to exact unconstitutional conditions is not present.").

77. Notably, however, when the Supreme Court expanded the liability for exactions in *Nollan* and *Dolan*, it did not establish a per se rule.

78. Takings proponents have tried to argue that moratoria have been abused. For example, the petition for certiorari in *Tahoe-Sierra* cites three articles by allegedly pro-government authors as recognizing abuses. *See* Petition for Certiorari, 19 n.21 ("As noted by knowledgeable commentators who are sympathetic to regulators, such unfortunate behavior patterns have become common." The articles cited are Rodney Cobb, *Land Use Law: Marred by Public Agency Abuse*, 3 WASH. U.J.L. & POL'Y 195 (2000) (suggesting that land-use law generally is marred by public agency abuse); Orlando Delogu, *The Misuse of Land Use Control Powers Must End: Suggestions for Legislative and Judicial Responses*, 32 ME. L. REV. 29, 35 (1980) (suggesting that moratoria are "often undertaken without regard to whether present public facilities are or will be overstressed and in circumstances where the total population is not high and ample land for new development still exists"); and Melville Branch, *The Sins of City Planners*, 42 PUB. AD. REV. 1, 2 (1982) ("Interim zoning or a moratorium on zone changes can be employed as a tactic of deliberate delay. . ."). While charging abuse, none of the articles purports to present systematic evidence that moratoria are abused.

79. James Kushner, *Smart Growth: Urban Growth Management and Land-Use Regulation Law in America*, 32 URB. LAW. 211, 222 (2000).

80. *See, e.g.*, VT. STAT. ANN. tit. 24, § 4407 (19)(B) (2000) (moratorium on the siting of wireless telecommunications facilities "shall run for no more than 180 consecutive days"); N.J. STAT. ANN. § 40:55D-90 (2001) ("in no case shall the moratorium or interim ordinance exceed a six-month term").

81. *See, e.g.*, N.J. STAT. ANN. § 40:55D-90 (2001) ("No moratoria on applications for development or interim zoning ordinances shall be permitted except in cases where the municipality clearly demonstrates on the basis of a written opinion by a qualified health professional that a clear imminent danger to the health of the inhabitants of the municipality exists."); N.H. REV. STAT. ANN. § 674:21 subd. V(h) (2001) ("The adoption of a growth management limitation or moratorium by a municipality shall not affect any development with respect to which an impact fee has been paid or assessed as part of the approval for that development.").

82. *See, e.g.*, ME. REV. STAT. ANN. tit. 30-A, § 4356 (2000) (moratorium may be extended for an additional 180-day period only if the municipality finds that "[t]he problem giving rise to the need for the moratorium still exists" and "[r]easonable further progress is being made to alleviate the problem giving rise to the need for the moratorium"); CONN. GEN. STAT. § 8-30g(1)(2) (2001) (moratorium shall not apply to certain types of affordable housing applications); COLO. REV. STAT. § 24-68-105 (vested property right precludes a local government from imposing a moratorium on development); CAL. GOV'T CODE § 65584(d)(2) ("If a moratorium is in effect, the city or county shall, prior to a revision . . . adopt findings that specifically describe the threat to the public health and safety and the reasons why construction of the number of units specified as its share of the regional housing need would prevent the mitigation of that threat.").

83. First Evangelical Lutheran Church of Glendale v. County of Los Angeles, 210 Cal. App. 3d 1353, 1373, 258 Cal. Rptr. 893, 906 (1989).

84. 447 U.S. at 263 n.9.

85. Q.C. Construction Co. v. Gallo, 649 F. Supp. 1331 (D. R.I. 1986).

86. Robert A. Heverly, *Interim Development Controls* in ZONING AND LAND USE CONTROLS § 22.03 (Rohan, ed. 2000):

[M]unicipalities have an obligation when using interim hold techniques to maintain the freeze for only so long as necessary and to expeditiously plan and put into effect a permanent scheme. If a municipality fails to do that, an ordinance may be declared unconstitutional on substantive due process grounds or as a taking under the Fifth Amendment.

87. *See, e.g.,* William M. Treanor, *The Original Understanding of the Takings Clause and the Political Process*, 95 COLUM. L. REV. 782 (1995).

88. Lucas v. South Carolina Coastal Council, 505 U.S. 1003, 1028 n.15 (1992).

APPLYING *NOLLAN/ DOLAN* TO IMPACT FEES: A CASE FOR THE *EHRLICH* APPROACH

13

DANIEL J. CURTIN, JR. AND CECILY T. TALBERT*

§ 13.0   *Introduction*

In the complex realm of land-use takings jurisprudence, the emergence of the *Nollan/Dolan* two-prong nexus test created a framework around which the various governmental exactions giving rise to takings claims could be assessed. The *Nollan* requirement—which calls for a nexus between the project's impact and the legitimate governmental interest justifying the exaction—limits the nature of the government's demands on developers, while the *Dolan* requirement of rough proportionality defines the necessary extent of that nexus. In essence, the two-prong test posits a simple quality/quantity analysis that facilitates a determination of the reasonableness of any government action. While the equation may appear simple, it nevertheless fails to obviate the need for subtle distinctions and factual nuances in its application to the myriad exactions demanded

*The authors wish to express their appreciation for the substantial contribution to this chapter made by Elizabeth M. Naughton, a land-use associate in the Walnut Creek office of McCutchen, Doyle, Brown & Enersen, LLP.

of developers by local governments. This article examines the application of the *Nollan/Dolan* test to impact fees levied on developers by local governments as conditions of permit issuance and concludes that the approach adopted by the California Supreme Court in *Ehrlich v. City of Culver City*[1] represents the most reasoned interpretation of the application of the *Nollan/Dolan* test to such fees.

§ 13.1   *The* Nollan/Dolan *Nexus Test*

In *Nollan*, the California Coastal Commission approved the construction of a two-story beachfront house, subject to the condition that the owners dedicate a public access easement across a portion of their property along the beach. The governmental interest purportedly justifying the dedication was facilitation of the public's viewing of the beach and assisting the public in overcoming a perceived "psychological barrier" to using the beach. The owners challenged the easement, claiming that the condition violated the Fifth and Fourteenth Amendments' prohibitions against taking private property for public use without just compensation. The U.S. Supreme Court held that although protection of the public's ability to see the beach was a legitimate governmental interest, no nexus or connection existed between the identified impact of the project (obstruction of the ocean view) and the easement condition (physical access across the beach). Thus, the exaction constituted a taking of private property without just compensation. The Court did, however, state that requiring the dedication of a viewing spot on the *Nollan* property might have been legal, since there would be a nexus.

In emphasizing the importance of a nexus between the governmental exaction and the burden being imposed by the new development, the *Nollan* Court placed strictures on the nature of governmental demands on developers. Having determined in that case that the demand for a dedication did not have the required connection to the project's impact on the public's view of the ocean, the Court did not need to determine the required extent of such a connection. Thus, while local governments now knew that their demands on developers must answer a need created by the project in question, they did not know how close that connection must be.

In *Dolan v. City of Tigard*,[2] the Court finally answered the open question regarding the closeness of the connection between governmental exactions and the impacts created by development projects. A sharply divided Court held that local governments must prove that development conditions placed on a discretionary permit have a "rough proportionality" to the development's impact in order to defeat a takings claim. In that case, Florence Dolan owned a plumbing and electrical supply store located along Fanno Creek, which flowed over the southwestern corner of the lot and along its western boundary. Dolan applied to the city for a building permit to further develop the site. Her plans called for nearly doubling the size of the store and paving a 39-space parking lot. The planning commission granted Dolan's permit application subject to conditions imposed by the Tigard Community Development Code, which contained the city's Comprehensive Plan. The commission required that Dolan dedicate the portion of her property lying within the 100-year flood plain for improvement of a storm drainage system along Fanno Creek and that she dedicate an additional 15-foot strip of land adjacent to the flood plain as a pedestrian/bicycle pathway. The commission made a series of findings concerning the relationship between the dedicated conditions and the projected impacts resulting from development of the Dolan property.

Dolan requested variances and appealed to the Land Use Board of Appeals (LUBA) on the grounds that the city's dedication requirements were not related to the proposed development and constituted an uncompensated taking. LUBA found a "reasonable relationship" between the proposed development and the requirement to dedicate land along Fanno Creek for a greenway. It also found a reasonable relationship between alleviating the impact of increased traffic from the development and facilitating the pedestrian/bicycle pathway as an alternative means of transportation. The Oregon Appellate Court and the Oregon Supreme Court affirmed the decision. In her petition to the U.S. Supreme Court, Dolan urged that the Court conclusively establish that a precise fit is constitutionally required between an exaction and the impacts of proposed development, instead of the reasonable relationship test used in Oregon and other states, including California. The Court granted certiorari "to resolve a question left open by its decision in *Nollan v. California Coastal Comm'n*[3] of what is the required degree of connection between the exactions imposed by the city and the projected impacts of the proposed development." [4]

In reversing the Oregon courts' decisions, the *Dolan* Court acknowledged the standard rule that a land-use regulation does not effect a taking if it "substantially advances a legitimate state interest" and does not "deny an owner economically viable use of his land."[5] Significantly, the Court noted that in this case it was not dealing with a legislative determination regarding land-use regulations, but rather with a city having made "an adjudicative decision to condition an application for a building permit on an individual parcel."[6] Also, the Court noted that "the conditions imposed were not simply a limitation on the use that [the] petitioner might make of her own parcel, but a requirement that she deed portions of the property to the city."[7]

In evaluating a takings claim under the Fifth Amendment, the Court stated that it must first determine whether an "essential nexus" exists between the "legitimate state interest" and the permit condition exacted by the city. If it finds that a nexus exists, the Court must then decide the required degree of connection between the exactions and the projected impact of the proposed development. The Court noted that it was not required to address this question in *Nollan*, because no nexus existed between requiring the dedication of a lateral public easement and the legitimate governmental interest of reducing the ocean-view obstruction caused by construction of a larger house. In *Dolan*, however, the Court found that the required nexus in fact existed. However, under the second part of the analysis, the Court was obliged to determine whether the *degree of exaction* demanded by the city's permit conditions bore the *required relationship* to the projected impact of the development proposed. Since state courts had a long history of dealing with this question, the Court then reviewed several representative state court decisions. The Court noted that the decisions fell into three categories: first, a very generalized nexus requirement, which the Court determined to be too lax;[8] second, a very exacting nexus described as the "specific and uniquely attributable test" (the so-called *Pioneer Trust* Rule from Illinois), which the Court rejected; and third, an intermediate position of a "reasonable relationship" nexus (highlighted in *Jordan v. Menomonee Falls*[9] and other cases).

The *Dolan* Court noted that the intermediate "reasonable relationship test" adopted by the majority of states (including California) was closer to the federal constitutional norm than the other two tests. However, the Court stated, "we do not adopt [the reasonable relationship test] as such, partly because the term 'reasonable relationship' seems confusingly similar to the term 'rational basis,' which describes the minimal level of scrutiny under the Equal Protection Clause of the Fourteenth Amendment."[10] The Court then coined the term "rough proportionality" to summarize what it holds to be required by the Fifth Amendment.[11] The Court stated, "No precise mathematical calculation is required, but the city must make some sort of individualized determination that the required dedication is related both in nature and extent to the impact of the proposed development."[12] The

Court then reviewed the two dedications demanded of Florence Dolan and found that the city had not met its burden of demonstrating the required relationship. After analyzing the findings upon which the city relied, the Court stated that the city had not shown the "required reasonable relationship" between the floodplain easement and the petitioner's proposed new building.[13] With regard to the pathway, the Court held that although dedications of streets and other public ways are generally reasonable exactions to avoid excessive congestion from a proposed property use, the city had not met its burden of demonstrating that the additional number of vehicle and bicycle trips generated by Dolan's development reasonably related to the city's requirement of a dedication of a pedestrian/bicycle pathway easement.[14]

Clearly, the U.S. Supreme Court has put some limitations on a city's exercise of its police power to require dedication of land as a condition for issuing a development permit. The *Dolan* decision requires a city to document the connection between the dedication and the projected impact of the proposed development. Not only must the required nexus exist, but findings must justify the reasonable relationship between the dedication and the impact. This now requires a two-part inquiry to determine the essential nexus between the project and both the type of condition and the burden of the condition. The "type of impact" nexus test requires that the type of condition imposed must address the same type of impact caused by the development (*Nollan*), and the "burden created" test determines whether the condition is in reasonable proportion to the burden created by the new development (*Dolan*).[15]

§ 13.2   *Applying the* Nollan/Dolan *Test to Impact Fees:* Ehrlich v. City of Culver City

In *Nollan* and *Dolan*, the government conditioned a development permit on the property owner's dedication of land. What if a city or other local agency requires payment of an impact fee? Does the *Nollan/Dolan* nexus test apply? The California Supreme Court conclusively answered that question in *Ehrlich v. City of Culver City*.[16] The *Ehrlich* court held that if a city bases a development or impact fee on an ordinance or rule of general applicability, the fee will be within the city's police power and will not be subject to the heightened constitutional scrutiny of the *Nollan/Dolan* nexus test.[17] However, if an impact fee is adjudicatively imposed on an individual property owner, it will be subject to heightened scrutiny under the *Nollan/Dolan* test.

§ 13.2(a) *Factual Situation*

In the early 1970s, Ehrlich acquired a vacant 2.4-acre lot in Culver City. At his request, the city amended its general plan and zoning and adopted a specific plan to provide for the development of a privately operated tennis club and recreational facility. In 1981, in response to financial losses from operating the facility, Ehrlich applied to the city for a change in land use to construct an office building. The application was abandoned when the planning commission recommended against approval on the grounds that the existing club provided a needed commercial recreational facility within the city. In 1988, Ehrlich closed the facility because of continuing financial losses and applied for amendments to the general plan and the specific plan along with a zoning change to allow construction of a 30-unit condominium complex valued at $10 million. At that time, the city expressed interest in acquiring the property for operation as a city-owned sports facility. After the city completed a feasibility study, the idea was dropped. The city found it lacked the funds to purchase and operate the club. At the same time, the city council rejected Ehrlich's application based on concerns about the loss of a recreational land use needed by the community. Ehrlich then tore down the existing improvements and donated the recreational equipment to the city.

After denial of his application, Ehrlich filed suit and entered into discussions with the city to secure the necessary approvals to redevelop the property. After a closed-door meeting, ostensibly to discuss the pending litigation, the city council voted to approve the project conditioned upon the payment of certain monetary exactions, including a $280,000 recreation mitigation fee for the loss of the private tennis facility, payment of $33,200 for art in public places and a $30,000 in-lieu parkland dedication fee. The $280,000 fee was to be used "for partial replacement of the lost recreational facilities" occasioned by the specific plan amendment. The amount of the fee was based upon a city study which showed that the replacement costs for the recreational facilities "lost" as a result of amending the specific plan would be $250,000 to $280,000 for the pool, $135,000 to $150,000 for the paddle tennis courts, and $275,000 to $300,000 for the tennis courts. After formally filing a protest pursuant to Government Code sections 66020 and 66021, Ehrlich challenged the $280,000 recreation fee and the in-lieu art fee but not the parkland dedication fee.

§ 13.2(b) *Judicial Proceedings*

After the trial court struck down the conditions, the appellate court upheld them.[18] The U.S. Supreme Court, after granting a writ, then remanded the matter back to the court of appeal to be re-examined in light of its recent decision in *Dolan*. Following the remand, the court of appeal, in an unpublished opinion in 1994, again upheld both fees. The California Supreme Court then granted a petition to consider the important and unsettled question concerning the extent to which *Nollan* and *Dolan* applied to development permits that exact a fee as a condition of issuance, as opposed to the possessory dedication of real property at issue in both *Nollan* and *Dolan*. The justices unanimously upheld the public art fee, and five justices upheld the right of the city to impose a "mitigation fee" based on a "rezoning" application but rejected the ad-hoc recreational fee.

§ 13.2(c) *A New Distinction: Legislatively Formulated v. Ad Hoc Development Fees*

In arriving at its decision, the *Ehrlich* court reviewed the *Nollan/Dolan* decisions and the two-part nexus test. Citing *Nollan*, the *Ehrlich* court expressed concern that adjudicative, ad hoc conditions on development present "an inherent and heightened risk that local government will manipulate police power to impose conditions unrelated to legitimate regulatory ends, thereby avoiding what would otherwise be an obligation to pay just compensation."[19] The court emphasized the "extortion[ary]" danger of this "form of regulatory 'leveraging.'"[20] In response to this concern, the court drew a distinction between legislatively formulated development fees imposed on a class of property owners and individually imposed conditions.

The court held that in the "relatively narrow class of land use cases" that involve individual "land use 'bargains' between property owners and regulatory bodies . . . where the individual property owner-developer seeks to negotiate approval of a planned development . . . the combined *Nollan/Dolan* test quintessentially applies."[21] In the more common situation when exactions are imposed pursuant to a general legislative act or rule, cities act within their traditional police powers. The court stated that the discretionary aspect of conditioning an individual approval heightens the risk that the city may manipulate police power to impose conditions unrelated to legitimate land-use regulatory ends. On this point, the court stated:

It is the imposition of land use conditions in individual cases, authorized by a permit scheme which by its nature allows for both the discretionary deployment of the police power and an enhanced potential for its abuse, that constitutes the *sine qua non* for application of the . . . standard of scrutiny formulated by the court in *Nollan* and *Dolan*.[22]

The court next considered whether the *Nollan/Dolan* test applies to general development fees in addition to dedications. The court noted that the courts in *Blue Jeans Equities W. v. City and County of San Francisco*[23] (transit fees) and *Commercial Builders of N. Cal. v. City of Sacramento*[24] (affordable housing fees) held that "any heightened scrutiny test contained in *Nollan* is limited to possessory rather than regulatory takings."[25] The *Ehrlich* court distinguished and clarified these cases because they both involved "legislatively formulated development assessments imposed on a broad class of property owners," and therefore did not require heightened scrutiny.[26] The court then rejected the city's argument that the *Nollan/Dolan* test applies only to possessory dedications and not to fees. Instead, the court found that the applicability of the *Nollan/Dolan* test to a fee depends on whether the fee is an ad hoc determination or a legislative regulation.[27]

§ 13.3   *National Treatment of the* Ehrlich *Approach*

The *Ehrlich* court found the middle ground in the application of the *Nollan/Dolan* test to impact fees. Since that ruling, California courts have enjoyed the luxury of a bright-line rule, shunning the heightened scrutiny of the *Nollan/Dolan* nexus test in the case of legislatively imposed fees, while invalidating individually imposed development fees that do not satisfy the requirements of a nexus and rough proportionality.[28] Nationally, a trend has emerged favoring the *Ehrlich* approach as well. Some states have held that the test applies to both legislative and adjudicative determinations,[29] and a few have held that the test does not apply to fees at all.[30] However, a substantial number of states facing this issue have concurred in the *Ehrlich* court's conclusion that only the ad hoc imposition of development fees is characterized by the level of discretion and potential for extortionate abuse of police power that requires more than a generalized determination of reasonableness. Following is a brief overview of cases in which states other than California have adopted the *Ehrlich* approach or applied an *Ehrlich*-like approach:

- *Home Builders Ass'n of Central Arizona v. City of Scottsdale.*[31] In this case, the Arizona Supreme Court cited *Ehrlich* in declining to apply *Dolan* to a legislatively imposed water resources development fee. In so doing, the court stated, "the

California court suggested that the *Dolan* analysis applied to cases of regulatory leveraging that occur when the landowner must bargain for approval of a particular use of its land. The risk of that sort of leveraging does not exist when the exaction is embodied in a generally applicable legislative decision."

- ***Waters Landing Limited Partnership v. Montgomery County.***[32] Preceding *Ehrlich*, the Court of Appeals of Maryland concurred in the approach, declining to apply *Dolan* to a development impact fee that was imposed by legislative enactment and not by adjudication.

- ***Arcadia Development Corp. v. City of Bloomington.***[33] The Minnesota Court of Appeals held *Dolan's* rough proportionality test inapplicable to a requirement that landowners choosing to cease operation of a mobile home park compensate tenants with a relocation fee. The court stated that because such a fee was a citywide, legislative land-use regulation, *Dolan's* "rough proportionality" test did not apply.

- ***Henderson Homes v. City of Bothell.***[34] Although declining to cite *Nollan/Dolan* and preceding *Ehrlich*, the Washington court nevertheless declined to uphold development fees "voluntarily" paid by individual landowners as a condition of permit issuance, holding that the local government had failed to make a finding that the fees were reasonably necessary as a direct result of the proposed development.

- ***Krupp v. City of Breckenridge.***[35] The court refused to apply *Nollan/Dolan* to a legislatively imposed mandatory plant investment fee, holding that the case did not fall into the narrow class of exactions, such as that imposed in *Ehrlich*, in which the exactions stem from adjudications particular to the landowner and the parcel, and therefore was not subject to a takings analysis.

§ 13.4   *Conclusion*

The application of the *Nollan/Dolan* test to impact fees, like the totality of takings jurisprudence, is an ever-evolving area of the law. As local governments increasingly rely on impact fees to mitigate the effects of burgeoning development, many states will face the challenge of resolving disputes alleging the constitutional invalidity of such fees. California has set a worthy example of a reasoned interpretation of the *Nollan/Dolan* test to impact fees that will continue to resonate nationally. Hopefully, states facing this issue will continue to look to the *Ehrlich* court for guidance, thereby facilitating the development of a consistent and cohesive body of takings law.

Notes

1. 12 Cal. 4th 854 (1996).
2. 512 U.S. 374 (1994).
3. 483 U.S. 825 (1987).
4. Dolan v. City of Tigard, 512 U.S. 374, 377 (1994).
5. *Id.* at 385 (citing Agins v. Tiburon, 447 U.S. 255, 260 (1980)).
6. *Id.*
7. *Id.*
8. Billings Properties, Inc. v. Yellowstone County, 394 P.2d 182 (1964).
9. 28 Wis. 2d 608, 137 N.W.2d 442 (1965).
10. *Dolan*, 512 U.S. at 391.
11. *Id.* After coining the term "rough proportionality," the Court, in its majority opinion, never used that term again in applying its analysis to the facts; instead it continued to use the words "required reasonable relationship" or "reasonably related."
12. *Id.*
13. *Id.* at 395.
14. *Id.*
15. JAMES LONGTIN, LONGTIN'S CALIFORNIA LAND USE, §§ 8.22[2], [3] (Local Government Publications 2000 Update).
16. 12 Cal. 4th 854 (1996).
17. *Id.*
18. Ehrlich v. City of Culver, 15 Cal. App. 4th 1737 (1993).
19. *Ehrlich*, 12 Cal. 4th at 869.
20. *Id.* at 867.
21. *Id.* at 868.
22. *Id.* at 869.
23. 3 Cal. App. 4th 164 (1992).
24. 941 F.2d 872 (9th Cir. 1991).
25. *Id.* at 875 (quoting *Blue Jeans*, 3 Cal. App. 4th at 171).
26. *Id.* at 876.
27. Id. at 906. *See also* Loyola Marymount Univ. v. Los Angeles Unified Sch. Dist., 45 Cal. App. 4th 1256 (1996) (applying *Ehrlich* to hold that the *Nollan/Dolan* test did not apply to a fee imposed pursuant to the Sterling Act (EDUC. CODE §17620; GOV'T CODE §65995)). It should be noted that despite the California Supreme Court's definitive holding, the U.S. Supreme Court remains in flux with regard to the applicability of the Fifth Amendment Takings Clause to regulations that affect private property other than real property. In *Eastern Enterprises v. Apfel*, 524 U.S. 498 (1998), which did not address land use but rather explored the various constitutional challenges that could potentially be applied to allocation of retirement fund liability under the Coal Industry Retiree Health Benefit Act, the plurality took the position that such an allocation was constitutionally invalid under the Fifth Amendment Takings Clause. The dissenters declined to find a taking, instead upholding the law under the Due Process Clause on the grounds that the case involved an ordinary liability to pay money rather than an interest in physical or intellectual property, which have traditionally been the exclusive realm of takings claims. Justice Kennedy, concurring with the plurality, supported invalidation of the act under the Due Process Clause, stating that the act does not involve the type of property to which the Fifth Amendment has traditionally applied. However, despite this leaning toward limiting the applicability of the Takings Clause, Justice Kennedy implied that it should not be so

limited as to exclude land development conditions. His concern was rather curtailing the reach of the Fifth Amendment so as to ensure it does not apply to "all governmental action."

28. *See, e.g.,* Loyola Marymount Univ. v. Los Angeles Unified School Dist., 45 Cal. App. 4th 1256 (1996) (relying on *Ehrlich* in declining to apply *Nollan/Dolan* heightened scrutiny to legislatively imposed school development fees); Breneric Associates v. City of Del Mar, 69 Cal. App. 4th 166 (1998) (declining to apply *Nollan/Dolan* based on the *Ehrlich* court's admonition that such heightened scrutiny is inapplicable to traditional land use regulations that are legislatively imposed).

29. Benchmark v. City of Battle Ground, 14 P.3d 172 (holding *Nollan/Dolan* applicable to impact fees but failing to distinguish between legislatively determined and adjudicatively imposed fees); Northern Illinois Homebuilders' Ass'n v. County of DuPage, 165 Ill. 2d 25 (1995) (holding that two legislatively imposed impact fees were valid under *Nollan/Dolan*, but that the second, more general fee failed to meet the higher standard of "specifically and uniquely attributable" that the Illinois Supreme Court had articulated in Pioneer Trust v. Village of Mount Prospect, 22 Ill. 2d 375 (1961)); Trimen Dev. Corp. v. King County, 124 Wash. 2d 261 (upholding legislatively imposed parkland development fees under the *Nollan/Dolan* test); Home Builders Ass'n of Dayton and the Miami Valley v. City of Beaver Creek, 89 Ohio St. 3d 121 (2000) (applying *Nollan/Dolan* to invalidate a legislatively imposed impact fee).

30. McCarthy v. City of Leawood, 257 Kan. 556 (1995) (holding that a traffic impact fee was subject to the "reasonable relationship" test and not the heightened scrutiny of *Nollan/Dolan* because it did not involve the dedication of land).

31. 930 P.2d 993 (1997).

32. 650 A.2d 712 (1994).

33. 552 N.W.2d 281 (1996).

34. 124 Wash. 2d 240 (1994).

35. 19 P.3d 687 (2001).

DOLAN WORKS 14

FRED P. BOSSELMAN

§ 14.0   Introduction

In my personal opinion, the so-called *Dolan* test[1]
should be applied to all forms of development exaction. My rationale is simple: The test is logical and it
works. Whether it can be intepreted from the Constitution, I leave for others to decide. Given our
highly fractionated Supreme Court, when any five
Justices happen to agree on a workable, logical rule
for one little piece of the law, we should be grateful.
So I will confine my commentary to two issues: the
logic of the *Dolan* test and the experience with it.

§ 14.1   All Forms of Development Exaction Should Be Treated Equally

To understand the logic of the *Dolan* test, we need to
think about the business transaction to which it applies. On the one hand, we have a developer who wants
to build something. On the other hand, we have a
local government that is in the business of providing
services and facilities. In the vast majority of cases,
they both want to make a deal and will welcome rules
that facilitate the deal-making process.[2]

Why does the developer need the government? Because most developers seek to produce a product that will have long-term market value. That value will be greatly affected by the nature, quality, and cost of the services and facilities available to the users of the development. It is in the developer's interest to obtain the kind of services that the market will demand and to obtain them at a low cost. Usually, the local government can provide those services most efficiently through economies of scale.[3]

The city (or some other form of government) also wants to make a deal. It wants to encourage development that will pay taxes and bring jobs. However, it also wants to avoid complaints about the type and quantity of services and ensure that existing residents feel they are getting good service at a fair price.

A key element of this business deal is an assessment of the benefits and burdens the development will create for the community in order to determine the nature and amount of services and facilities for which the developer should be responsible. These are the "development exactions."[4]

As far as fairness to the developer is concerned, the key question—indeed usually the only important question—is how much the exaction will cost.[5] The relevant cost is the net cash outlay of the exaction itself, plus any limitation on the profitability of the development created by the exaction, less the value added to the development as a result of the services provided by the exaction.

For example, if a subdivider puts in an additional lane of roadway at the entrance to the subdivision, his cost is what he pays his contractor to build the roadway, plus (if the roadway reduces the amount of development that would otherwise occur) the income expected from lost development, less any added value of a higher stream of income the development would generate because of the more convenient entrance.

From the developer's perspective, whether the exaction is in cash, land, or services, it is the cost of the exaction that counts, not the form of it. From the city's standpoint too, it is the value of the exaction to the city that is important, not the form of the exaction. Therefore, if the *Dolan* test works, it should be applied similarly to all forms of exaction.

Two different arguments have been made for limiting the *Dolan* test to certain forms of exaction: (1) apply it only to mandatory dedications of land,[6] or (2) apply it only to ad hoc exactions, not to those that are legislatively predetermined.[7] I don't believe that either argument makes sense in the business context in which development exactions take place.[8]

§ 14.1(a) *Land Deserves No Preference*

From a constitutional perspective, land should be treated the same as any other form of property. Early constitutional history clearly rejected the position advocated by some large landowners that land should be treated as a preferred form of property.[9] And today, as we increasingly generate larger shares of wealth in the form of intangibles—intellectual property, computer software, "cyber-property," and so forth—it is increasingly ludicrous to give the "old money" that owns land a sort of aristocratic constitutional preference.

My experience suggests that when a developer is asked to contribute land, he is concerned only with the bottom line. We can imagine a rare case like Chekhov's cherry orchard where the sentimental attachment to the orchard might enter into the equation, but these examples are rare. And in any event, despite Professor Rabin's eloquent arguments, the courts usually have not included such values in awarding compensation.[10]

Far more common is a situation in which the developer *prefers* to dedicate land, rather than put up an equivalent amount in cash. For example, by donating specific pieces of land, the developer often can ensure that the city's facilities will be located on that land, thus giving maximum benefits to prospective buyers of the new development. If the developer pays cash, he or she might have less assurance about how and where the money is spent.

Another example: Many large tracts of land contain areas that are expensive to develop but have significant conservation value. It may be advantageous for both parties to encourage the developer to donate these areas rather than pay cash into a fund for acquisition of land elsewhere. The ability to negotiate complicated exactions such as these is one of the reasons development agreements have become popular vehicles for negotiating large developments in the states where such agreements are permitted.[11]

Another reason the developer may prefer to donate land is because the developer has the land, or an option on it, at the time of the exaction, but is often short of cash or needs to borrow it at construction loan rates. From a cash flow standpoint, dedicating land may be much more advantageous to the developer than providing cash.

Consequently, applying the *Dolan* test only to land dedications would encourage cities to switch to fees rather than dedications and would be highly disadvantageous to the developer.

In addition, the city also would be disadvantaged. It is to the city's benefit to be able to employ development exactions in the form of either fees or dedications without worrying about legal distinctions between them. Because the dedication of land is often beneficial to the developer, the city frequently can negotiate a greater net benefit if all or part of the exaction is in the form of land.

I don't mean to suggest that land dedication is always superior to impact fees from the standpoint of either the developer or the city. In many instances, the fees have great advantages. However, it is in the interest of both parties to be able to negotiate for fees, dedications, or services in kind without worrying about pointless legal distinctions among them.

§ 14.1(b) *The Legislative-Adjudicative Distinction Is Irrelevant*

The second argument against a uniform application of the *Dolan* test is that it should apply to ad hoc exactions, but not to a legislatively established schedule of "impact fees." This argument derives from anecdotal instances in which cities have demanded successive waves of increasingly larger exactions in order to discourage a development they didn't like.[12]

Since the Court clearly is applying the *Dolan* test to ad hoc exactions, to fail to apply it to legislatively exacted fees would be unfair to both the city and the developer for two reasons: (1) It would encourage cities to believe that they could impose impact fees without the careful cost-benefit analysis the *Dolan* test requires, which may produce arbitrary results for the developer, but also may reduce the amount the city receives. (2) It would ignore the fact that, in many instances, the developer and the city both can benefit from ad hoc exactions that are tailored specifically to the particular project and development site, rather than being limited to fees based on overall average impacts.

§ 14.2 *Fees Based on the* Dolan *Test Often Benefit Both Parties*

If the *Dolan* test is limited to ad hoc exactions, it will provide a strong incentive for cities to enact impact fees to reduce the risk associated with ad hoc exactions. However, it will encourage them to believe that they can pick any level of fee they choose because the *Dolan* test doesn't apply.[13] This is likely to produce fees that are unfair to some or all developers.

If the *Dolan* test applies to impact fees, however, and the cities believe they are subject to suit under section 1983 because the amount of the fee is a federal constitutional issue, they are likely to be fair to developers. Ironically, they may find that the fees based on the *Dolan* test raise more money than whatever fees they would have devised on their own. The reason is that the city is likely to retain one of the many consultants who are expert at setting fees according to the *Dolan* test, rather than picking numbers out of the air. Such fees will be fairer to developers because they will be based on the actual impact of the development.

However, although such fees treat developers more fairly, they do not necessarily reduce the developers' costs. Experience suggests that consultants often make cities aware that they have the ability to adopt impact fees that cover a wider range of services and a higher level of fees than the city would have anticipated if the consultant had not made a careful study of the fiscal impact of development.[14] Therefore, while legislatively adopted impact fees treat developers fairly and improve the developer's predictability,[15] the overall cost of exactions may increase. I have never seen reliable statistics about the overall amount of development exactions, but I would guess that they have gone up rather than down since *Dolan* was decided.

§ 14.3   *Exactions Tailored to Specific Projects Often Benefit Both Parties*

Although impact fees can provide a baseline that sets the exaction for an average development, most developments are not average. Each piece of land is different and relates, in its own particular way, to the services and facilities of the city. Fairness to both sides can be best achieved by allowing the developer and the city to negotiate exactions tailored specifically to the site. However, if the *Dolan* test does not apply to legislatively mandated fees, the city will be reluctant to allow itself much discretion in varying the fee to meet specific situations lest the fee be construed as a discretionary fee subject to the *Dolan* test. On the other hand, if the *Dolan* test applies to both impact fees and ad hoc exactions, the city will not have to worry if it bypasses the normal fee in favor of an exaction tailored to the site. In both cases, the same test will apply.

For example, the most common type of development exaction is probably a demand that the developer dedicate land for future widening of a two-lane road.[16] The *Dolan* test would say that the developer should only pay for the share of the road-widening cost that is proportional to the traffic generated by the development,[17] and that the money would be put into a fund to acquire land for widening streets in the general area.

That sounds fair, and in many cases it would be. But in many other cases, the developer would prefer to dedicate the land, and even pave the street, in exchange for a commitment by the city to widen the rest of the street. If the marketability of the property is improved by the wider street, the benefit of the wider street to the developer might far exceed the cost of the exaction. Moreover, the developer already may be building internal roads on the property and be able to pave the exterior street at a cost much lower than the city would have to pay.

I am not suggesting that the city should have the power to demand that the developer pave and dedicate the street rather than pay an impact fee that meets the *Dolan* test, but I think the city should have an incentive to negotiate an exaction that would benefit both parties. Ironically, if negotiating with the developer creates a risk of liability for the city that does not exist if the city imposes a flat fee, the city lawyer is likely to discourage such negotiations.[18] Therefore, I think it is in the best interest of both parties to apply the *Dolan* test equally to all types of development exaction.

The dicta in *Dolan v. City of Tigard,* suggesting that developers may be especially susceptible to disadvantage from ad hoc exactions,[19] simply reflects a failure of the Court to understand the way the development process operates. The relative negotiating power of the developer and the city depends on the perceived desirability of the developer's product to the city,[20] and the perceived desirability of the particular city to the developer.[21] In many cases, developers pay no exactions whatsoever and receive contributions from the city for blessing it with a desirable project for which other communities are competing.[22] To suggest that developers are typically at a disadvantage is unrealistic.

Developers whose projects are seen as undesirable would, of course, have a poorer negotiating position, but if cities find that, by adopting impact fees, they can avoid constitutional scrutiny of legislative exactions for development they don't want, it won't take them long to figure out how to play the game. They will simply adopt legislation imposing high fees on development they don't want.

To summarize, there is no logical reason why the form of the exaction should dictate the test that determines the fairness of it. Fairness to both the developer and the city depends on the cost-benefit ratio of the exaction, which has no relation to whether the exaction is in the form of land, cash, or services. Nor are ad hoc exactions necessarily more suspect than legislatively determined exactions. The courts should be encouraged to apply the same test to each kind of exaction.

§ 14.4 *The* Dolan *Test Has Been a Success*

The *Dolan* test is not only logical, it also works. The issue of development exactions is far less volatile today than it was 20 years ago. The *Dolan* test isn't broke, so it shouldn't be fixed by limiting its application.

As evidence that the test works, consider the change in attitude on the part of the development industry. Twenty years ago, the industry denied any responsibility for furnishing services or facilities outside the immediate development site and considered exactions to be blackmail.[23] Today, most elements of the industry accept the idea that development should pay its own way. Naturally, there are still disagreements over what that means, but they tend to be civilized disagreements among bean counters rather than ideological battles.[24] There are exceptions, of course, but I think the overall level of hostility over development exactions has declined.

With cities, as well, I believe there has been an equivalent change in attitude.[25] On the one hand, cities now recognize that if they try to discourage unwanted development through unreasonable ad hoc exactions, they run a risk of liability.[26]

On the other hand, the *Dolan* test has made cities realize that they have the constitutional authority to impose reasonable exactions that make development pay its own way. Until the Supreme Court made it clear that the cities had such authority, many local officials believed the development industry's arguments that they lacked the power to impose anything but the most minimal exactions.

Today, those cities that don't use their authority to impose development exactions face questions from taxpayer organizations asking why existing residences and businesses must absorb all of the cost of development. By imposing reasonable limits on the amount of the exactions, the *Dolan* test has muted developers' objections to the exactions because all developers receive more equitable treatment.

Further evidence that the *Dolan* test works is found in the large volume of state legislation that spells out the kinds of methodologies that meet the constitutional standard and often limits the standard further than the constitution requires.[27] The increasing similarity of this legislation from state to state illustrates the advantage of a uniform standard.

If the *Dolan* test is limited to certain forms of exaction, it won't work as well as if it applies to all exactions. I have already discussed how making illogical distinctions among exactions will create incentives for cities to set exactions inefficiently for both developers and themselves. In addition, the legal fees associated with litigating the boundary lines between the various categories of exaction will penalize both developers and cities.

For example, the Supreme Court may think there is a clean line between mandatory dedications of land and other types of exactions, but that merely illustrates the overall unfamiliarity of the Court with the land development process.[28]

Development negotiations can be very intricate. In many cases, negotiations between a developer and a city may involve a wide range of public service and facility issues. For example, any potential land dedication creates a whole new set of decisions about fees to be paid, the design of streets and sewers, the level of service that the city will provide, and many others. If the question of whether a particular city demanded a mandatory dedication of land from a particular developer becomes a jurisdictional one for purposes of the Civil Rights Act or state inverse condemnation law, there will be a parade of borderline cases in which the facts require detailed judicial analysis just to determine jurisdiction.

Even more difficult to define precisely is the distinction between legislatively imposed fees and fees determined on an ad hoc basis. Must legislative fees leave no room for discretion? If so, they are likely to produce a host of unfair results when applied to development that does not fit neatly into some average category. Consider, for example, the recent litigation over whether a particular mobile home park in Florida fit into a category that exempted it from paying a school impact fee because it did not produce school-age children.[29] The court's difficulty in determining whether the particular challenge to the fee was on its face or as applied is indicative of the many problems that would arise if such a distinction was jurisdictional.[30]

Deciding where regulation ends and exaction begins can be very complex.[31] It is frequently difficult to distinguish development exactions from land-use regulations to which the *Dolan* test doesn't apply. The history of the *Del Monte Dunes* litigation shows that the distinction between a development exaction and a denial of development approval isn't easy to make in complex cases. In that litigation, the Ninth Circuit treated the city's action as a development exaction to which the *Dolan* test applied,[32] but the Supreme Court held that it was a development denial to which the test did not apply.[33] In the *Dolan* case itself, the Court pointed out that if the city had required the property owner to maintain the floodway as private, open space rather than dedicating it to the public, it would not be considered a development exaction.[34]

§ 14.5 *Conclusion*

Lawyers and law professors have argued at great length over how and why the *Dolan* test relates to the rest of the body of constitutional doctrine that the Supreme Court has established. As I said in the introduction, this chapter doesn't deal with that issue. In practice, the *Dolan* test is logical and works well, not because of the brilliant constitutional analysis of the Supreme Court, but because the Court simply followed the body of law set down by most of the state courts before it.[35]

Whether the Supreme Court did developers a favor by taking up this issue is hard to say. Not only has the Court called attention to the authority of local governments to impose exactions, but by federalizing the issue, the Court has forced developers' lawyers to deal with issues of ripeness, abstention, removal, and the rest of the procedural traps that bedevil constitutional cases. I guess for those developers in California, where the state law was really hard on them,[36] it may have been worthwhile, but in the rest of the country, state land-use law may still provide a better recourse for developers than litigation under *Dolan*. The reasons are procedural, not substantive, because state courts are basically using the *Dolan* test as they always have—as state law.

The *Dolan* test is well established; it is logical in its outcome; and it seems to work reasonably well for both developers and local governments. Let's not complicate the legal picture unnecessarily by imposing illogical limitations on the type of exactions to which the *Dolan* test applies.

Notes

1. The Supreme Court's decision in *Dolan v. City of Tigard*, 512 U.S. 374 (1994), held that development exactions must have a logical nexus to the impact of the development and must be roughly proportional to that impact. In *Dolan*, the Court elaborated on an earlier test set forth in *Nollan v. California Coastal Commission*, 483 U.S. 825 (1987). The *Dolan* test has been more fully described in chapter 13, and the reader who is unfamiliar with it is referred to those pages for more detail.

2. A fine analysis of the bargaining process is in JOHN J. KIRLIN & ANNE M. KIRLIN, PUBLIC CHOICES—PRIVATE RESOURCES: FINANCING CAPITAL INFRASTRUCTURE FOR CALIFORNIA'S GROWTH THROUGH PUBLIC-PRIVATE BARGAINING (California Tax Foundation, 1982).

3. Subject to state and local rules, the developer may also choose to have services provided by some other public or private entity, but typically the local government is the provider.

4 *See, generally,* DEVELOPMENT EXACTIONS (James E. Frank & Robert M. Rhodes eds., 1987).

5. The intellectual origin of the modern law of development exactions is found in Ira Michael Heyman & Thomas K. Gilhool, *The Constitutionality of Imposing Increased Community Costs on New Suburban Residents Through Subdivision Exactions*, 73 YALE

L.J. 1119 (1964), which is still one of the best analyses of the policy issues relating to exactions.

6. *See, e.g.*, Nancy E. Stroud, *A Review of* Del Monte Dunes v. City of Monterey *and its Implications for Local Government Exactions*, 15 J. LAND USE & ENVTL. LAW 195 (1999).

7. *See, e.g.*, Inna Reznik, *The Distinction Between Legislative and Adjudicative Decisions in* Dolan v. City of Tigard, 75 N.Y.U. L. REV. 242 (2000).

8. For fairly recent reviews of some of the many court decisions that have taken one or both of these approaches, see Brett C. Gerry, *Parity Revisited: An Empirical Comparison of State and Lower Federal Court Interpretations of* Nollan v. California Coastal Commission, 23 HARV. J.L. & PUB. POL'Y 233 (1999); Richard D. Faus, *Exactions, Impact Fees, and Dedications—Local Government Responses to* Nollan/Dolan *Takings Law Issues*, 29 STETSON L.REV. 675 (2000).

9. Fred P. Bosselman, *Land as a Privileged Form of Property*, *in* TAKINGS: LAND-DEVELOPMENT CONDITIONS AND REGULATORY TAKINGS AFTER *DOLAN* AND *LUCAS* 29 (David E. Callies ed.,1996).

10. MARGARET JANE RADIN, REINTERPRETING PROPERTY 35-71 (1993).

11. DOUGLAS R. PORTER & LINDELL L. MARSH, DEVELOPMENT AGREEMENTS: PRACTICE, POLICY, AND PROSPECTS 31-33 (Urban Land Institute, 1989).

12. A classic example is *City of Monterey v. Del Monte Dunes at Monterey, Ltd.*, 119 S. Ct. 1624 (1999).

13. Of course, in many states their discretion would be limited by state law, but many cities may worry less about state law violations than federal civil rights violations.

14. Many local government officials are able to prepare excellent analyses themselves, but cities often like the sense of legitimacy that a consultant adds when litigation is likely. (I am now a full-time academic and don't do any consulting work.)

15. My experience suggests that although developers always say they want predictability, what they mean is "predictably low."

16. *See* JULIAN C. JUERGENSMEYER & THOMAS E. ROBERTS, LAND USE PLANNING AND CONTROL LAW 321-27 (1998).

17. Note that this is nothing new, but is consistent with the law of most states even before *Dolan*. *See* ROBERT R. WRIGHT & MORTON GITELMAN, CASES AND MATERIALS ON LAND USE 680-83 (5th ed. 1997). It is also one of the most widely ignored legal rules in practice.

18. Experience suggests that neither city engineers nor elected officials will necessarily follow their lawyer's advice in these situations when the logic of the rule is not apparent, but we should not encourage the use of rules that will regularly be ignored.

19. 512 U.S. 374, 385. *See also Nollan*, 483 U.S. at 837.

20. *See, e.g.*, ALAN A. ALTSHULER & JOSÉ A. GÓMEZ-IBÁÑEZ, REGULATION FOR REVENUE: THE POLITICAL ECONOMY OF LAND USE EXACTIONS 57-59 (1993).

21. *See, e.g.*, Stewart E. Sterk, Competition Among Municipalities as a Constraint on Land Use Exactions, 45 VAND. L. REV. 831 (1992).

22. The recent high-profile bidding process to attract Boeing's headquarters is repeated on a smaller scale every day all over the country.

23. For a principled argument to that effect, see Robert Ellickson, *Suburban Growth Controls*, 86 YALE L.J. 385, 475-76 (1977).

24. Even the National Association of Home Builders is now advising its members about the details of impact fee calculation rather than rejecting the concept out of hand. See BOB MCNAMARA, IMPACT FEE HANDBOOK (NAHB, 1997).

25. There are some high-end communities where the city's cachet is so valuable that developers will willingly pay fees that seem outrageous to most people elsewhere, but they are doing so because their profit is so great that they can afford it. These practices pose issues of exclusion, but such issues would have to be addressed by means other than giving the developer the right to attack a fee.

26. Under pressure from outraged voters they may sometimes be willing to run that risk, but unless we are prepared to abandon democratic government, we must expect that to happen occasionally.

27. *See, e.g.,* Daniel J. Curtin, Jr., Curtin's California Land Use and Planning Law 241 et seq. (20th ed., 2000); Bruce W. Bringardner, *Exactions, Impact Fees, and Dedications: National and Texas Law After* Dolan *and* Del Monte Dunes, 32 Urb. Law. 561 (2000).

28. Since the retirement of Justices Powell and Brennan, both of whom had considerable experience in local government matters, the Court lacks anyone who seems to have a feel for the land development process. In addition, potential applicants for Supreme Court clerkships are rarely encouraged to take an interest in such localized courses as local government or land use.

29. Volusia County v. Aberdeen at Ormond Beach, L.P., 760 So. 2d 126 (Fla. 2000).

30. For another example, see *Krupp v. The Breckenridge Sanitation District*, 19 P.3d 687 (Colo. 2001). The Colorado Supreme Court found that a plant investment fee was a legislatively established fee that was fairly calculated and rationally based and therefore not subject to a taking analysis. In effect, the court applied the substance of the *Dolan* test in order to determine that the *Dolan* test need not be applied. Alice's Red Queen would feel at home with law like this.

31. *See, e.g.,* Clark v. City of Albany, 904 P.2d 185 (Ore. App. 1985), *review denied,* 912 P.2d 375 (Ore. 1996).

32. Del Monte Dunes at Monterey, Ltd. v. City of Monterey, 95 F.3d 1422, 1428-30 (1996).

33. City of Monterey v. Del Monte Dunes at Monterey, Ltd., 119 S. Ct. 1624, 1631 (1999). For an analysis of the exaction/regulation distinction, *compare* Lee Anne Fennell, *Hard Bargains and Real Steals: Land Use Exactions Revisited*, 86 Iowa L. Rev. 1 (2000), *with* Richard J. Ansson, Jr., Dolan v. Tigard's *Rough Proportionality Standard: Why This Standard Should Not Be Applied to an Inverse Condemnation Claim Based Upon Regulatory Denial*, 10 Seton Hall Const. L.J. 417 (2000).

34. Dolan v. City of Tigard, 512 U.S. 374, 393-94 (1994).

35. Together with my former partner, Nancy Stroud, I wrote about the law of development exactions in 1987, just prior to the Supreme Court's *Nollan* decision. Reading today what we wrote then, one realizes that the Supreme Court's decisions have merely endorsed the body of substantive law that the great majority of states were applying anyway. Fred P. Bosselman & Nancy Stroud, *Legal Aspects of Development Exactions, in* Development Exactions 70 (James E. Frank & Robert M. Rhodes eds., 1987).

36. Even in California, however, the courts were evaluating impact fees according to standards similar to the *Dolan* test before the Supreme Court took up the issue. Russ Bldg. Partnership v. City and County of San Francisco, 199 Cal. App. 3d 1496 (1987). *See* Daniel J. Curtin, Jr., Curtin's California Land Use and Planning Law 243 (20th ed., 2000).

Impact Fees Should Not Be Subjected to Takings Analysis

15

Julian C. Juergensmeyer and James C. Nicholas

§ 15.0 Introduction

In our opinion, the *Nollan/Dolan* dispute—over whether the tests apply to impact fees or only to required dedications—misses the point.[1] No takings analysis of dual rational nexus-based impact fees is appropriate or necessary. If an impact fee is valid, i.e., it satisfies the dual rational nexus test, then it cannot destroy property rights. If an impact fee violates the nexus test—if those principles were not respected by those formulating and/or administering the impact fee program—it is invalid. Thus, there is no need to enter the takings labyrinth in order to make the determination of invalidity or to afford constitutional protection of a takings or due process nature to the fee payors. Furthermore, we would maintain that required dedications and "in lieu" payments should also be exempted from takings analysis and assimilated with impact fees by being subjected to the nexus test as well.

In fact, we would submit that the nexus test protects ownership interests more stringently and effectively than do takings principles. Rational nexus limits the amount of fees and dedications—and therefore the burden they can place on ownership interests—

357

more than do takings principles by requiring precise, not rough,[2] proportionality in calculating the amount of the fee and by requiring that the benefit be conferred back to the ownership interest from which it was collected. The nexus test also better directs governmental entities in terms of the principles they must follow to assure the validity of their infrastructure funding regulations. It also relieves them from the uncertainty of knowing when and if they have crossed the mystical "takings/eminent domain" line.

Lest readers be shocked by this thesis, let us hasten to say that we will not try to convince you that our position is strongly supported by judicial opinion. Frankly, we are unsure of the current law, because we believe that courts have largely ignored or misunderstood this aspect of the issue. Our thesis is a statement of what we think the law should and could be.

§ 15.1   Regulatory Takings Analysis and Impact Fees

The courts started applying takings analysis and principles to impact fees by reasoning: (a) impact fees are land-use regulations, (b) land-use regulations can go too far and become takings, (c) therefore, impact fees may constitute takings and must be analyzed from a takings perspective in order to prevent governmental entities from violating constitutionally protected private property rights by imposing excessive or unjustifiable impact fees.[3]

Perhaps the problem started with the need to "label" impact fees as land-use regulations so they would not be invalidated as unauthorized taxes. In an early impact fee case, the court found:

> The fee here is simply an exaction of money to be put in trust for roads, which must be paid before developers may build. There are no other requirements. There are no specifics provided in the ordinance as to where and when these monies are to be expended for roads, apparently this was to be left for future commission determination. This fee, therefore, is an exercise of the taxing power.[4]

Following this logic, if an impact charge was found not to be a permissible "fee," then it must be a "tax."

In the early days of impact fees, arguing that such fees were land-use regulations was both convenient and successful, because it allowed courts to approve impact fees as an evolution of monetary payments instead of physical dedications, i.e., "in lieu payments" rather than a new and different use of police power or a (partially disguised) use of the power of taxation.

Perhaps the original sin was to label required dedications and in lieu payments as land-use regulations rather than to extend the "privilege approach to subdivision approval" and then subject it to reasonableness requirements.[5] The court in *Hollywood Inc. v. Broward County*,[6] for example, noted the relevance of the privilege concept in connection with impact fees and required dedications in the following terms:

> The rationales of the cases affirming constitutionality indicate the dedication statutes are valid under the state's police power. They reason that the subdivider realizes a profit from governmental approval of a subdivision since his land is rendered more valuable by the fact of subdivision, and in return for this benefit the city may require him to dedicate a portion of his land for park purposes whenever the influx of new residents will increase the need for park and recreational facilities.[7]

The court, recognizing that subdividing is a profit-making enterprise, held that a jurisdiction could impose dedication or impact fee requirements in order to forestall the potential adverse effects of the development and to enable the jurisdiction to provide adequate public facilities for the new residents. After surveying constitutional tests used by courts in other states to evaluate subdivision exactions, the court enunciated a "rational nexus" or "reasonable connection" test.[8] The court held that dedication or impact fee ordinances are valid when there is a reasonable connection between the required dedication or fee and the anticipated needs of the community because of the new development:

> From the *City of Dunedin, Wald*, and *Admiral Development,* we discern the general legal principle that reasonable dedication or impact fee requirements are permissible so long as they offset needs sufficiently attributable to the subdivision and so long as the funds collected are sufficiently earmarked for the substantial benefit of the subdivision residents.[9]

Impact fees are in reality a very different approach to land development regulation than the use, height, and bulk restrictions approved in *Euclid*.[10] Impact fees stem more directly from impact analysis concepts[11] commonly found in environmental law than from land-use restrictions such as zoning. The issue is not how a landowner can or cannot use her land. The issue is how the infrastructure necessary to serve that use of land shall be provided and financed. This is a different issue with a different focus. As we understand the essence of takings jurisprudence, it is relevant to governments restricting the use of land, and thereby destroying a property right, that the public should provide compensation for those restrictions. To argue that validity of impact fees should be tested in the same way as land-use restrictions is beside the point. The issue is who should pay for infrastructure, not whether land can be used beneficially or whether compensation should be paid for lack of beneficial use.

Of course, all governmental power is subject to limits, or at least it should be. Consequently, if the landowner is required to pay an impact fee that exceeds the fee payor's proportionate share of the infrastructure cost, or if he is charged for infrastructure that is not provided to him, constitutional principles requiring fairness, equal protection, and due process should be available to him. As we have previously contended, that role should be played by the dual rational nexus test. That test affords better and clearer protection to fee payors than a contorted takings analogy they make to protect themselves from improperly formulated or administered impact fee programs.

§ 15.2   *Impact Fees and Required Dedications*

Fred Bossselman makes the point in his essay that "all forms of development exaction should be treated equally."[12] We agree with his conclusion although not with his approach. His concept is to treat them both equally by applying *Dolan* to impact fees, required dedications, and the like. Our counterproposal is to treat them equally by applying the dual rational nexus test to all of them and to then "exempt" them from takings analysis.

We believe, as did the *Hollywood, Inc.* court,[13] that required dedications and impact fees are indistinguishable in the land-use regulation context and should have been subjected to the requirement that they satisfy the dual rational nexus test. The failure of most courts to require this satisfaction has created the problem of needing to distinguish impact fees from required dedications for takings analysis purposes. The law should be revised so as to assimilate required dedications and impact fees for the applicability of the nexus test. Such assimilation would avoid the need for courts to struggle with the applicability of less clear and less stringent protection for property interests through regulatory takings analysis. Such an assimilation also would avoid the separation of two approaches, differing in method but identical in purpose, to developer-required funding of infrastructure and the resulting inconsistencies and confusion.

§ 15.3 *Impact Fees and the Dual Rational Nexus Test*

§ 15.3(a) *Defining and Applying the Dual Rational Nexus Test*

Having taken the position that the dual rational nexus test should be the sole determinant of the validity of impact fees in regard to their "fairness" and their effect on property interests, it seems incumbent on us to spend at least some space discussing that test in order to explain why, in our opinion, it makes takings analysis inappropriate and unnecessary as far as impact fees are concerned. We have written about impact fees and drafted and formulated impact fee programs for the last 30 years. On many occasions, we have expressed our opinion about the meaning and role of the dual rational nexus test,[14] and we maintain our position based on previously written materials.[15]

The initial formulation of the dual rational nexus test is usually attributed to statements made by the Wisconsin Supreme Court in 1965 in *Jordan v. Village of Menomonee Falls*.[16] That court expressed concern that the then popular, but now largely repudiated, "direct benefit"[17] and "specifically and uniquely attributable" tests[18] made it virtually impossible for governments to successfully defend monetary payment or land dedication requirements designed to require developer funding of infrastructure needs generated by subdivision development. Suggesting a substitute test, the court opined that monetary payment and dedication requirements for infrastructure should be considered a valid exercise of police power if there is a "reasonable connection" between the need for additional facilities and the growth generated by the subdivision. This first "rational nexus" was sufficiently established if the local government could demonstrate that a series of subdivisions had generated the need to provide educational and recreational facilities for this new stream of residents. In the absence of contrary evidence, such proof showed that the need for the facilities was sufficiently attributable to the developer's activity to permit the collection of fees to finance required improvements.[19]

The *Jordan* court also rejected the *Gulest* direct benefit requirement, declining to treat the fees as a special assessment. Therefore, it imposed no requirement that the ordinance restrict the funds to the purchase of facilities that would directly benefit the assessed subdivision. Instead, the court concluded that the relationship between the expenditure of funds and the benefits accruing to the subdivision providing the funds was a fact issue pertinent to the reasonableness of the payment requirement under police power.

The *Jordan* court did not expressly define the "reasonable-ness" required in the expenditure of extradevelopment capital funds; however, a second "rational nexus" was impliedly required between the expenditure of the funds and benefits accruing to the subdivision. The court concluded that this second "rational nexus" was met when the fees were to be used exclusively for site acquisition, and the amount spent by the village in constructing additional school facilities was greater than the amounts collected from the developments creating the need for additional facilities.

Therefore, this second "rational nexus" requirement inferred from *Jordan* is met if a local government can demonstrate that its actual or projected extradevelopment capital expenditures—ear-marked for the substantial benefit of a series of developments—are greater than the capital payments required of those developments. Such proof establishes a sufficient benefit to a particular subdivision in the stream of residential growth such that the extradevelopment payment requirements may be deemed reasonable under police power.

Hollywood Inc. provides an efficient, and our favorite, sum-mary of the dual rational nexus test:

> In order to satisfy these [nexus] requirements, the local government must demonstrate a reasonable connection, or rational nexus, between the need for additional capital facilities and the growth in population generated by the subdivision. In addition, the government must show a reasonable connection, or rational nexus, between the expenditures of the funds collected and the benefits accruing to the subdivision. In order to satisfy this latter requirement, the ordinance must specifically earmark the funds collected for use in acquiring capital facilities to benefit and serve new residents.[20]

§ 15.3(b) *Distinctions between Principles*

Having disagreed with Fred Bosselman's position that *Dolan* (and accompanying takings principles) should be applied to impact fees, have we really suggested an approach in impact fee law that will have practical significance? Depending upon one's view of exactly what difference it makes whether *Dolan* is applied to land dedication requirements and not impact fees, the answer may be "no." Dan Curtin and Cecily Talbert suggest that the practical difference is *heightened scrutiny* if *Dolan* applies.[21] Since we maintain that the dual rational nexus test is more stringent when properly applied to impact fees than the *Nollan/Dolan* takings principles, we cannot accept this as a practical difference.

A major point of difference for Curtin and Talbert is the legislative versus adjudicatively established fees distinction found in *Ehrlich*.[22] Fred Bosselman considers this distinction irrelevant.[23] In our view, the key to this alleged distinction is whether or not the fees (legislatively or adjudicatively determined) can satisfy the dual rational nexus test. If they do, then the distinction should be irrelevant. If they do not, they are not valid impact fees and their validity/invalidity must depend on other principles.[24]

Being dollar amounts, impact fees are calculated using principles of cost accounting. In the end, the resultant fee is adopted either legislatively or adjudicatively. Regardless of how they are adopted, the amount of the fee calculated must be no more than a proportionate share. For both required dedications and impact fees, a proportionate share is the upper limit, and no legislative or adjudicative decision can justify anything higher. In the vast majority of impact fees a legislative decision has been made to charge a fee less than what would be a proportionate share.[25] Certainly legislative bodies can choose to impose lesser fees, but not greater.

The lack of any justification for a distinction between required dedications and impact fees can be illustrated by again referring to *Hollywood Inc.*[26] The impact fee at issue was for public parks. The park requirement was imposed first as an option for the subdivider to dedicate land for parks at a standard of three acres per 1,000 projected subdivision occupants, or 128 square feet of land area per capita.[27] The impact fee that was an alternate means of meeting the requirement was based upon Broward County's historic cost of acquiring and developing parkland per acre.[28] This per acre cost was reduced to a cost per square foot, which was then multiplied by 128 to get cost per capita.[29] The arithmetic was the same for either the required dedication or the impact fee. The proportionality of a 1,000-person subdivision dedicating three acres of parkland would be exactly the same as the justification for the impact fee when multiplied by the number of home sites within the subdivision. Three acres of public parks would be needed to serve this hypothetical 1,000-person subdivision. The subdivider could dedicate three acres or pay an impact fee and Broward County would buy the three acres. Either way, the provision of three acres of parkland would happen, and it would be at the expense of the subdivider.   .

But what if Broward County was wrong? What if the required dedication should have been one acre per 1,000 instead of three? In this case, a required dedication at three acres per 1,000 would violate the proportionality requirement of *Dolan*. An impact fee calculated at three acres per 1,000 would violate the dual rational nexus test. Both the required dedication and the impact fee would be invalid. In the case of a dedication, some portion of the property would have been taken—two-thirds of that dedicated. In the case of an impact fee, the amount would be excessive and unreasonable. Presumably, the subdivider would be paid for the overage of land dedicated or the excess land would be returned. The fee payor would be refunded the impact fee excess. The "error" is the same but the solution would be different. Here, our argument is that the property owner receives the same protection from an application of the dual rational nexus test as from takings principles.

Continuing with the hypothetical error, let's now raise the question of damages. If an excessive dedication was required, either the property owner would receive payment for the excess or the excess property would be returned, thus raising the issue of damages for a temporary taking. In the case of an impact fee, the excess impact fee payment would be refunded and interest would be paid for the time the excess amount was held. Payment of interest on the excess impact fee payments constitutes compensation for payment of the excessive fee.[30] In the case of dedication, temporary taking damages would have to be paid, but what is the damage for a temporary taking? Interest. The damage to a property owner for a temporary taking is interest on the reasonable value of what had been taken for the period of the temporary taking.[31] The damage for a temporary taking resulting from an excessive dedication of property would be interest.[32] The damage resulting from an excessive payment of impact fees would be interest on the excess. The results would be the same. The appropriate damages payable to the property owner would be the same under principles of takings as under the principles of the dual rational nexus test.

While the legal bases of the protection afforded property owners are very different, there is no difference in the protection afforded or the anticipated results. If property is taken by an unreasonable exaction, compensation must be paid, including temporary damages. If excessive impact fees were paid, excesses must be refunded with interest. The net result is the same.

§ 15.4   Impact Fees and the Power of Taxation

§ 15.4(a) Distinguishing Impact Fees from Taxes

In the early days of impact fees, it was necessary to clarify their status with respect to taxes. Generally, local governments must be authorized to impose taxes. Simply put, on matters of taxation, Dillon's rule applied.[33] If impact fees were to be imposed as

taxes, local governments would have to be specifically authorized to impose them and such impositions would have to comply
with all legal requirements for taxes. Because local governments
had not been specifically authorized to impose "impact taxes,"
distinguishing impact "fees" from "taxes" was essential.

A general rule was developed: An impact assessment that complied with the dual rational nexus test was a permissible exercise
of police power and thus not a tax. It would follow that if an
impact assessment did not comply with the dual rational nexus
requirements, then it would be viewed as a tax. The Illinois Supreme Court explained the difference between a tax and a fee as
such:

> Taxes are an enforced proportional contribution levied
> by the State by virtue of its sovereignty for support of
> the government. [Citations omitted.] Service charges,
> tolls, water rates and the like are, on the other hand,
> contractual in nature, either express or implied, and are
> compensation for the use of another's property, or of an
> improvement made by another, and their amount is de-
> termined by the cost of the property or improvement
> and the consideration of the return which such an expen-
> diture should yield. [Citations omitted.] The charge is
> made, not by virtue of the sovereignty of the govern-
> mental unit, but in its business or proprietary capacity.[34]

Local governments argued that impact fees were more akin to
service charges in that they were charged in return for the provision of specific facilities, such as potable water infrastructure.
Impact fees were not supporting general government services,
and the amount to be paid was determined by the cost of providing the specified facilities. While impact fees are distinguishable
from taxes, there is still overlap and a great deal of confusion.
However, in designing impact fees that are distinguishable from
taxes, property owners are accorded a high degree of protection
from excessive or malproportioned impact fees.

§ 15.4(b) *Confusion between Fees and Taxes*

The primary goal of taxes is raising revenue to fund some governmental functions. Impact fees raise revenue to fund public
capital improvements. Thus, it would appear that this means of
revenue raising would bear some relationship to the broader subject of taxes. Perhaps confusion results from our public debates
about tax policy. Colloquially we view monetary payments to the

government as taxes, frequently employing the "duck test."[35] But there is a great difference between taxes and fees, not the least of which is that taxes require authorization and fees usually do not. As land regulatory and tax policies have evolved, the interface between the two had to be drawn by the courts. The Illinois court's distinctions quoted above are typical, but there are variations from state to state. For example, two identical school impact fees were prepared for St. Johns County, Florida, and Franklin, Massachusetts. In *St. Johns County v. North East Florida Home Builders*,[36] the "fee" was found to be a permissible exercise of the police power. In *Greater Franklin Developers Association v. Franklin*,[37] the same methodology was found to be an unauthorized tax.[38]

Taxes and taxation alternatives (fees) are politically sensitive, perhaps even explosive, subjects upon which there is little agreement. It would follow that the lack of agreement, political sensitivity, and confusion about taxes in general would spill over into discussions about alternatives to taxation, such as impact fees. There has been a national drift away from taxation and toward nontax revenues such as impact fees.[39] The courts are having to deal with the important distinctions between taxes and fees, the duck test notwithstanding. Moreover, it can be expected that both required dedications and impact fees will spread in usage and increase in amount or value. As these events unfold, the existing confusion would only be exacerbated by having two or more tests of the validity of land regulatory dedication requirements.

§ 15.5 Conclusion

It may seem odd in this era of heightened judicial and legislative interest in protecting private property rights to argue that impact fees and other developer funding "exactions" should be exempted from takings scrutiny. We maintain, however, that takings analysis is inappropriate and unnecessary for developer funding requirements.

It is inappropriate because takings cases and principles should and largely do focus on *use* restrictions placed on land. The basic takings principles established or recognized in *Pennsylvania Coal*,[40] *Penn Central*,[41] *Lucas*,[42] and *Palazzolo*[43]—as unclear and ad hoc as they may be—are intended to apply only to determination of whether restrictions on the use of land go "too far" and thereby constitute a taking (destruction) of property interests. Even though impact fees are commonly labeled land-use regulations, they have a totally different purpose than zoning, subdivision, and related land-use restrictions. The role and goal of impact fees is to resolve the issue of who pays for the public infrastructure necessary to serve whatever development is permitted pursuant to government regulations or the lack thereof.[44]

Takings analysis is unnecessary because the dual rational nexus test offers adequate and superior protection against unreasonable and excessive governmental interference with the land development process. As the need to distinguish impact fees from taxes indicates, impact fee programs raise different issues in regard to protection against excessive or inappropriate governmental actions than do land-use restrictions. The issues raised by impact fee programs relate not to how the land may or may not be used, but to whether the fee payor is being compelled to pay more than a proportionate or pro rata share of the public infrastructure costs necessitated by the development and whether the fees paid will be used to provide the infrastructure for which they are collected.

The practical differences that would result from impact fees (and required dedications) being exempted from takings analysis may not be that great from an outcome perspective. However, it would seem that any change in the law that would rescue landowners and governments from exhausting time and resources navigating the "takings maze" should be a welcome reform. Such a rescue would, of course, not be appropriate if it weakened the constitutional protection of property rights that allegedly underlies takings concepts, but no such sacrifice would result from the reform we advocate. In fact, the application of the dual rational nexus test that we advocate over takings analysis to impact fees (and required dedications) should only confirm the existing higher (than takings) standard, at least as far as impact fees are concerned. Furthermore, avoidance of the power of taxation further protects fee payors from having their fees misused. Governments, too, would profit by having the clearer principles of the dual rational nexus test.

Notes

1. Opposing views are presented in chapters 13 and 14.
2. In *Dolan* the Court established the standard for required dedications:

> We think a term such as "rough proportionality" best encapsulates what we hold to be the requirement of the Fifth Amendment. No precise mathematical calculation is required, but the city must make some sort of individualized determination that the required dedication is related both in nature and extent to the impact of the proposed development. Dolan v. Tigard, 114 S. Ct. 2309 (1994).

This standard may be contrasted with the requirements for an impact fee set out in one of our favorite impact fee decisions—*Hollywood Inc. v. Broward County,* 431 So. 2d 606 (Fla. 4th Dist. Ct. App. 1983), *cert. denied,* 440 So. 2d 352 (Fla. 1983):

[T]he local government must demonstrate a reasonable connection, or rational nexus, between the need for additional capital facilities and the growth in population generated by the subdivision. In addition, the government must show a reasonable connection, or rational nexus, between the expenditures of the funds collected and the benefits accruing to the subdivision. (*Id.* at 609).

3. In *Hollywood Inc.*, *supra* note 2, the court opined that if an exaction were too high it would be unreasonable, but did not label it a taking. In a footnote the court wrote:

Of course, a county could not require subdivision exactions which are so formidable as to deny the property owner of all reasonable use of the property. See *Graham v. Estuary Properties* [cite deleted]. Such an exaction would not be reasonable.

4. Broward County v. Janis Dev. Corp., 311 So. 2d 371 (Fla. Dist. Ct. App. 1975).

5. *See* Juergensmeyer & Roberts, Land Use Planning and Control Law § 7.8A (1998).

6. 431 So. 2d 606 (Fla. 4th Dist. Ct. App. 1983), *cert. denied*, 440 So.2d 352 (Fla. 1983).

7. 431 So. 2d 606, 610.

8. "This test was espoused, at least in part, in *Jordan v. Village of Menomonee Falls*, 28 Wis. 2d 608, 137 N.W.2d 442 (1965), *appeal dismissed*, 385 U.S. 4, 87 S. Ct. 36, 17 L. Ed. 2d 3 (1966), and described in Juergensmeyer & Blake, *Impact Fees: An Answer to Local Governments' Capital Funding Dilemma*, 9 Fla. St. U. L. Rev. 415, 430-33 (1981)." *Id.* at 611.

9. *Hollywood, Inc.*, 431 So. 2d at 609 (emphasis added). Note may be taken of the application of the rational nexus criteria by the court to both dedication requirements and impact fees, holding that in the view of that court there was no difference in the applicable law. We return to this point in § 15.03.

10. Euclid v. Ambler Realty Co., 272 U.S. 365 (1926).

11. The key role that impact analysis would come to play in land-use planning and control law was prophesized by Fred Bosselman back in 1985 in a short essay titled "Linkage, Mitigation and Transfer: Will Impact Analysis Become the Universal Antidote to Land Use Complaints?" *See* Juergensmeyer & Roberts, Land Use Planning and Control Law 5, 6 (1998).

12. *See* chapter 14.

13. *See supra* notes 2, 3, and 6.

14. Juergensmeyer & Blake, *Impact Fees: An Answer to Local Governments' Capital Funding Dilemma*, 9 Fla. St. U. L. Rev. 415 (1981); Juergensmeyer, *Drafting Impact Fees to Alleviate Florida's Pre-Platted Lands Dilemma*, 7 Fla. Envtl. & Urb. Issues 7 (Apr. 1980); Juergensmeyer, *Funding Infrastructure: Paying the Costs of Growth Through Impact Fees and Other Land Regulation Charges*, ch. 2 of The Changing Structure of Infrastructure Finance (J. Nicholas ed., 1985); Juergensmeyer & Wadley, *Florida Land Use and Growth Management Law* ch. 17 (looseleaf); James C. Nicholas, Arthur C. Nelson & Julian C. Juergensmeyer, A Practitioner's Guide to Development Impact Fees (1991); J. Juergensmeyer, *The Development of Regulatory Issues: The Legal Issues*, ch. 8 of Development Impact Fees (Nelson ed., 1988); Nicholas & Nelson, *The Calculation of Proportionate Share Impact Fees*, 408 A.P.A. Plan Advisory Ser. Rep. (1988); Nicholas, *Impact Exactions: Economic Theory, Practice and Incidence*, 50 Law & Contemp. Probs. 51 (1987).

15. The discussion of the dual rational nexus test that follows is based primarily upon the material found in JUERGENSMEYER & ROBERTS, LAND USE PLANNING AND CONTROL LAW, § 9.8 (1998).

16. 28 Wis. 2d 608, 137 N.W.2d 442 (1965).

17. Gulest Associates, Inc. v. Town of Newburgh, 25 Misc. 2d 1004, 209 N.Y.S.2d 729 (1960), *aff'd* 15 A.D.2d 815, 225 N.Y.S.2d 538 (1962).

18. Pioneer Trust and Savings Bank v. Village of Mount Prospect, 22 Ill. 2d 375, 176 N.E.2d 799 (1961).

19. It is somewhat ironic that the Illinois court has now interpreted the *Pioneer Trust* test to be met by impact fee programs that meet the rational nexus test. *See* Northern Ill. Home Builders v. County of Du Page, 165 Ill. 2d 25, 649 N.E.2d 384 (1995).

20. 431 So. 2d at 611. The Supreme Court of Florida accepted this explanation of the dual rational nexus test in *St. Johns County v. North East Florida Home Builders*, 583 So. 2d 635 (Fla. 1991), by saying:

> In essence, we approved the imposition of impact fees that meet the requirements of the dual rational nexus test adopted by other courts in evaluating impact fees. *See* Juergensmeyer & Blake, *Impact Fees: An Answer to Local Governments' Capital Funding Dilemma*, 9 FLA. ST. U.L. REV. 415 (1981). This test was explained in *Hollywood, Inc. v. Broward County*, 431 So. 2d 606, 611-12 (Fla. 4th Dist. Ct. App.), *review denied*, 440 So. 2d 352 (Fla. 1983). . . ."

Id. at 637.

21. *See* Curtin & Talbert, chapter 13.

22. Ehrlich v. . Culver City, 12 Cal. 4th 854, 911 P.2d 429 (1996).

23. *See* Bosselman, chapter 14.

24. Presumably matters of authority to impose such a requirement and also the consistency of the requirement with relevant law.

25. NICHOLAS, NELSON & JUERGENSMEYER, PRACTITIONERS' GUIDE, *supra* note 14, at 53.

26. Hollywood Inc. v. Broward County, 431 So. 2d 606 (Fla. 4th Dist. Ct. App. 1983), *cert. denied*, 440 So. 2d 352 (Fla. 1983).

27. 42,560 square feet in an acre times 3, divided by 1,000 equals 127.68, or 128 square feet per capita.

28. $34,000. This datum is from the files of the author, an expert witness in the case.

29. $0.80 per square foot parkland cost times 128 equals $102 per capita cost. This cost is multiplied by occupancy per dwelling unit to reach the final cost datum.

30. Three acres at $34,000 would be an impact fee of $102,000. If two-thirds of this payment were excessive, the excess would be $68,034. If this amount were held for one year at 6 percent, the interest payment would be $4,082.

31. The Wheeler cases are four cases dealing with the award of damages for a temporary taking of land. The final case dealt with the methodology of setting the amount of damages. This case is *Wheeler v. City of Pleasant Grove*, 896 F.2d 1347 (11th Cir. 1990). The upshot of these cases was an award of interest for the period of the temporary taking.

32. Assuming that the subdivider's land had the same $34,000 value as Broward County's cost, holding two acres at $68,034 in value for one year would require a payment of $4,082 in damages for a temporary taking, again applying 6 percent interest.

33. John F. Dillon, *Commentaries on the Law of Municipal Corporations* (1890). Simply stated, Dillon's rule is that local governments may exercise only those powers specifically delegated to them.

34. County of Du Page v. Smith, 21 Ill. 2d 572, 173 N.E.2d 485, 583 (1961).

35.   The essence of the duck test is that if it is yellow, swims, and has webbed feet, it is a duck. The result of the application of the duck test here is that if it is money paid to government, it is a tax regardless of the nomenclature attached. However, our yellow, web-footed swimmer could be a golden retriever. Sometimes simple rules aren't so simple.

36.   St. Johns County v. North East Florida Home Builders Ass'n, 583 So. 2d 635 (Fla. 1991).

37.   730 N.E.2d 900 (Mass. App. 2000).

38.   Having done both, we can assure the readers of the identical nature of the methodologies. The Massachusetts court's response was that Massachusetts employed a different test for what are permissible fees versus taxes requiring legislative authorization. *See id.*

39.   Bauman & Ethier, *Development Exactions and Impact Fees: A Survey of American Practices*, 50 Law & Contemp. Probs. 51 (1987).

40.   Pennsylvania Coal Co. v. Mahon, 260 U.S. 393 (1922).

41.   Penn Cent. Transp. Co. v. City of New York, 438 U.S. 104 (1978).

42.   Lucas v. South Carolina Coastal Council, 505 U.S. 1003 (1992).

43.   Palazzolo v. Rhode Island, 121 U.S. 2448 (2001).

44.   The takings issue is relevant to what development is allowed.

THE "SUBSTANTIALLY ADVANCE" QUANDARY: HOW CLOSELY SHOULD COURTS EXAMINE THE REGULATORY MEANS AND ENDS OF LEGISLATIVE APPLICATIONS?

16

DOUGLAS W. KMIEC

§ 16.0   Introduction

Is inquiring into the relationship between regulatory means and ends part of substantive due process or regulatory takings analysis? The U.S. Supreme Court in *City of Monterey v. Del Monte Dunes at Monterey, Ltd.*[1] wasn't prepared to say. Wrote Justice Kennedy, the Court has yet to supply "a thorough explanation of the nature or applicability of the requirement that a regulation substantially advance legitimate public interests outside the context of required dedications or exactions."[2]

If there is to be a "thorough explanation" forthcoming, there will need to be better resolution of the ongoing debate over how closely the judiciary should review land-use decisions. Landowners want close review; municipalities and other land-use regulators demand the opposite. As these pages reveal and as the above quotation from Justice Kennedy in *Del Monte* confirms, the Court has left the issue unsettled.

In *Agins v. City of Tiburon*,[3] the Court got the essentials right. A landowner is improperly singled out contrary to the Fifth Amendment Takings Clause *either* when he is confronted with regulation that does not substantially advance a legitimate governmental interest *or* when regulation deprives him of all economically viable use. There are litigable issues aplenty imbedded in both of these elements of general regulatory taking law, but it is useful at the outset to state plainly what some regulatory advocates forget and what some state courts continue to confuse: *either* element is sufficient to raise a taking concern.

In *Del Monte*, the U.S. Solicitor General effectively argued to the contrary by urging that the "substantially advance" prong was a due process concern and not part of takings. The object, of course, was to eliminate any meaningful judicial review of land-use decisions. In response, the landowner in *Del Monte* questioned whether throwing over established regulatory takings doctrine was within the grant of certiorari. In the end, the Court did not spend much time cogitating over the issue, stating only, "Given the posture of the case before us, we decline... to revisit the general test for regulatory takings liability outlined in *Agins*."[4] Nevertheless, the argument will undoubtedly continue to be pressed by the forces of pervasive, but unreviewed, regulation. And as noted, since even the Court observed in *Del Monte* that it has yet to provide "a thorough explanation" of the substantially advance prong "outside the context of required dedications or exactions," it is worthy of further comment.

§ 16.1   Substantive Due Process and the "Substantially Advance" Taking Inquiry

Substantive due process is properly highly deferential review. It merely seeks to ferret out arbitrary and capricious regulatory ends. In *Nollan*, for example, the Court made it abundantly clear that it had no desire to resurrect the so-called *Lochner* era and the discredited practice of judicial disagreement with legislatively chosen policy objectives. By contrast, the "substantially advance" inquiry in regulatory taking analysis articulated by the Court in *Agins*, and followed without exception thereafter, is—as the Court explained in *Nollan*—an inquiry into the causal connection or nexus between regulatory means and ends.

Justice Scalia patiently explained in *Nollan* that "there is no reason to believe (and the language of our cases gives some reason to disbelieve) that so long as the regulation of property is at issue the standards for takings challenges, due process challenges, and equal protection challenges are identical. . . ."[5] Similarly, in *Eastern Enters. v. Apfel*,[6] the Court invalidates a substantial imposition of retroactive liability for health care benefits as regulatory taking. It reasserted the basic distinctions between taking and due process analysis by highlighting the lack of required nexus between the liability imposed and the fact that Eastern never promised such benefits and had long ceased operations.

Acknowledging the substantially advance prong of *Agins* to be different from substantive due process is also consistent with the Court's stated view that where a claim can be brought under one of the explicit, separately stated guarantees in the Bill of Rights, there can be no claim for a substantive due process violation.[7] This view has been specifically applied to regulatory takings litigation in the Ninth Circuit.[8]

While seemingly admitting *Nollan's* means-end taking inquiry to be more searching than that pursued under substantive due process, the solicitor general in *Del Monte* proceeded to insist that the Court see these separate causes of action as one and apply deference to both. The solicitor general stated: "Our point is simply that where land-use regulation satisfies due process standards, it may not be deemed a taking, requiring the payment of compensation, based on a purportedly insufficient nexus between the governmental interest to be furthered and the means employed to advance that interest."[9] In affirming the monetary award in *Del Monte*, the Court did not accept the government's point, at least in a context where a local government repeatedly disregarded the general regulations it had legislatively put in place and made it impossible for a landowner to comply with announced standards.

In short, the Court in *Del Monte* did not change the regulatory taking rules. But the Court didn't improve them much either. True, the Justices didn't buy into the solicitor general's notion that because substantive due process asks a similar (but not identical) question to one-half of the *Agins* formulation that this due process similarity necessitates judicial deference to every particularized public imposition masquerading as a legislative policy choice. Yet, the Court in *Monterey* still failed to perceive how at least some types of legislative enactments in the land-use context can be fundamentally different than the fashioning of legislative policy outside the land-use context and merit heightened scrutiny.

§ 16.2   Dolan's *Misstep*

The problem goes back to *Dolan*. There, it will be recalled, the Chief Justice appropriately opined that heightened scrutiny would be misplaced for "legislative determinations classifying entire areas."[10] Far more questionably, he also seemed to deny a close look at *any* legislative enactment that did not require a conveyance of some portion of a claimant's property.[11] Rightly, the Court wants to avoid second-guessing legislative policy determination, especially on important environmental matters, but *Dolan* failed to fully apprehend that in land-use matters, unlike other legislative contexts, there are actually three steps:

1. enactment of general legislative policy;
2. application of that general policy to particular land parcels by means of a zoning map or similar enforcement device such as the excruciatingly extended site-planning review in *Del Monte;* and
3. administrative demands for particular land dedications.

Individualized assessment occurs in *both* of the latter two steps, not just by formally required conveyance, and therefore, the potential for the unconstitutional placement of disproportionate burdens—takings—exists in both of the latter contexts.

Justices Thomas and O'Connor seem to have grasped part of *Dolan's* missteps in their dissent to certiorari denial in *Parking Ass'n of Georgia, Inc. v. City of Atlanta.*[12] There, a general legislative enactment required parking lot owners to provide minimum barrier curbs, landscaping, and at least one tree to every eight parking spaces. The lower courts sustained this and the Supreme Court denied review. Justice Thomas questioned why the existence of a taking should depend on the "type of government responsible for the taking. A city council can take property just as well as a planning commission."[13]

Even the Thomas/O'Connor epiphany in *Parking Ass'n*, however, understates the importance of heightened review of regulatory means and ends because it is still unnecessarily wedded to some exaction demand. As the *Del Monte* facts reveal, this qualification yields inadequate constitutional principle. The disproportionate singling out of a landowner by quasi-exactions can be involved where the government asks not for title but merely requires inutility and open space. In *Del Monte*, the western third of the parcel had to be left undeveloped for public beach use and access. The only difference between a formal conveyance and such case is that the burden of taxation remains with the landowner.

§ 16.3   Is Dolan's Misstep Compounded in Del Monte?

Be that as it may, the city of Monterey in *Del Monte* did seemingly persuade the Court that rough proportionality analysis could not be applied that where there was no actual required conveyance. The city argued that the impact of private development can be measured, but there is nothing to compare it to when no dedication or exaction actually changes hands. The Court apparently accepted this. Justice Kennedy wrote in *Del Monte*, "[W]e have not extended the rough-proportionality test of *Dolan* beyond the special context of exactions. . . . The rule applied in *Dolan*. . . was not designed to address, and is not readily applicable to, the much different questions arising where the landowner's challenge is based not on excessive exactions but on denial of development."[14] The Court goes on to say that the "rough-proportionality test of Dolan is inapposite" outside the exaction context.[15] Did the Court mean "inapposite" for all time, or just in *Del Monte*?

Some academic critics of regulatory takings law lean toward forever, but in context it is not clear the Court fully thought the matter out. It would be an odd and ultimately unsatisfying position to put proportionality analysis forever off-limits in this way. What can (and constitutionally should) be measured is not merely whether particular conveyances demanded were proportionate to development externalities, but also whether customized requirements are being applied to a particular landowner in a disproportionate way. While *Dolan* was an example of how the concern with proportionality can be administered where there are required land dedications, proportionality was not invented in that case. Rather, it is at the heart of Fifth Amendment Takings law. Forty years ago, the Court observed that the amendment is "designed to bar Government from forcing some people alone to bear burdens which, in all fairness and justice, should be borne by the populace as a whole."[16]

Of course, even though the Court in *Del Monte* did not fully perceive the utility of proportionality analysis, it did not give total deference to the nexus between regulatory means and ends. In this sense, the heightened scrutiny of *Nollan*, rather than *Dolan*, governed the *Del Monte* outcome. Specifically, the Court affirmed a compensatory taking award in the absence of a reasonable relationship between the regulation imposed and "the city's proffered justifications."[17] *Del Monte* is thus an important extension of *Nollan* beyond the exaction setting. Yet the Court couched this result in multiple qualification. For example, the Court's analysis was done in light of "the tortuous and protracted history of attempts to develop the property," "the shifting nature of the city's demands and the inconsistency of its decision with the recommendation of its professional staff, as well as with its previous decisions," and even a "longstanding" interest on the part of the city to acquire the property.[18] What happens when these qualifications are not present? Will it be sufficient for regulatory taking analysis for a city merely to have any conceivable rational basis for disproportionately applied regulation?

§ 16.4 Heightened Review Is Appropriate for Specific Applications of General Policy

Deferential, rational-basis review should not be sufficient—at least in those contexts where it is not the adoption of a generally applicable policy that is challenged but an individualized application of it. To understand this better, it is worthwhile to briefly recount the *Del Monte* facts. They illustrate how site-plan review is not the equivalent of formulation of legislative policy—at least, not in any regular sense.

Del Monte involved a 37.6-acre rectangular parcel along the Pacific on the northern end of the city of Monterey. Originally owned and used by Phillips Petroleum for the storage of large oil tanks, the parcel has been zoned since 1981 for multifamily residential use and is surrounded by fully developed commercial, industrial, and multifamily uses. Theoretically, under the existing zoning ordinance (the general expression of legislative policy), 1,000 multifamily units could have been constructed on the parcel. However, five different housing proposals ranging in size from 344 units to 190 units were rejected over a five-year period. Under the last proposal, 17.9 of the 37.6 acres were to be left open in public open space, 7.9 acres left open as private landscaped areas, and 6.7 acres in public and private streets. This left roughly 5.1 acres of buildable space. Ultimately, the 5.1 acres, too, could not be developed, said the city, because that area had some natural buckwheat plants and buckwheat is the only known habitat of the endangered Smith Blue Butterfly (SBB).

Surely, as a policy choice, the city of Monterey's decision to have some multifamily zoning deserves judicial respect. It is also possible that a rezoning, narrowing options within that zone—so long as it is generally applicable to others and passed in accordance with the normal political process—would similarly be worthy of deference. But is there anything in constitutional law or separation of powers theory to explain giving deference to one interpretation after another making any reasonable investment expectation under the existing legislative plan impossible? The remainder of this chapter will illustrate how *Del Monte* is hardly an atypical example. The Supreme Court's use of the heightened review standard of *Nollan* in *Del Monte* should be understood as a continuation of the efforts of more than a few state and federal courts to recognize that some nominally legislative land-use actions are really administrative or adjudicatory in character and merit closer review or specialized procedural protections to avoid the disproportionate singling out of particular landowners.

§ 16.5 "Quasi-Adjudicative Rezoning"

The Oregon Supreme Court deserves credit for being the first to discern how legislative rezoning actions can actually be the particularized application of a general policy. Most states, of course, still give zone amendments or rezoning highly deferential review.[19] However, in *Fasano v. Board of County Comm'rs*,[20] the Oregon court reasoned,

> Ordinances laying down general policies without regard to a specific piece of property are usually an exercise of legislative authority, are subject to limited review, and may only be attacked upon constitutional grounds for an arbitrary abuse of authority. On the other hand, a determination whether the permissible use of a specific piece of property would be changed is usually an exercise of judicial authority and its propriety subject to an altogether different [and more demanding] test.[21]

Like the heightened review of *Nollan* and *Dolan*, *Fasano* asked whether regulatory means and legislative ends were well matched, specifically whether the Board of County Commissioners was able to rezone a parcel of property from single-family residential to planned residential (allowing for the construction of a mobile home park) without a showing of necessity. Neighboring homeowners argued that the rezoning did not align with the comprehensive plan and that there was no evidence that the residential character of the neighborhood required increased densities. The commission, on the other hand, argued that the homeowners must prove the rezoning action was wholly arbitrary. Moreover, the commission argued that it was not required to show proof of necessity or of compliance with the comprehensive plan. Agreeing with the neighbors, the Supreme Court of Oregon stated, "At this juncture we feel we would be ignoring reality to rigidly view all zoning decisions by local governing bodies as legislative acts to be accorded a full presumption of validity and shielded from less than constitutional scrutiny by the theory of separation of

powers. Local and small decision groups are simply not the equivalent in all respects of state and national legislatures."[22] The court,
therefore, placed the burden of proof upon the party seeking the
zoning change (the commission) to prove both the necessity of
rezoning and that changing the particular parcel in question best
served that need. Inquiring into necessity strays into forbidden
Lochner territory, but clearly assessing the change in relation to
the particular parcel does not.

Florida, Colorado, Illinois, and Michigan state courts all apply some variation of the quasi-judicial approach advanced in
Fasano. Florida, in *Board of County Comm'rs of Brevard County
v. Snyder*,[23] held that rezoning actions that involve the application
of general rules to specific individuals are quasi-judicial and therefore subject to a heightened level of judicial review. Drawing
upon *Fasano*, the Florida Supreme Court, in *Snyder,* proceeds in
three steps to analyze takings claims. First, a landowner must
show that the proposed use is compatible with the existing comprehensive plan and that the landowner has complied with all
existing procedural requirements of the zoning ordinance. Upon
this showing, the burden shifts to the governmental agency to
prove that denial of the application advances a legitimate public
purpose. Finally, and only if that nexus has been shown, the burden shifts back to allow the landowner to prove a taking based on
a denial of economic value.

Older cases in Colorado, Illinois, and Michigan make a similar point. See *City of Colorado Springs v. District Court in and
for County of El Paso*.[24] Illinois also holds that "[i]t is not a part
of the legislative function to grant permits, make special exceptions, or decide particular cases. . . . To put them in the hands of
legislative bodies, whose acts are not judicially reviewable, is to
open the door to arbitrary government." The Illinois Supreme
Court was particularly concerned with giving immunity to legislative actions, warning that "[i]f they undertake to confer upon
themselves authority to decide what in fact amount[s] to individual or particular cases, the foundations of our legal system
will fast disappear."[25] Michigan, too, holds that "an amendment
reclassifying particular land, [is] essentially an adjudication of
the rights of proponents and opponents of the proposed zoning
change, [and it] constitutes an administrative or adjudicatory act."[26]

Oregon, itself, has since modified *Fasano's* holding in
Neuberger v. City of Portland.[27] Legislation enacted in response
to *Fasano* requires any rezoning approval to comply with the
city's comprehensive plan. Nevertheless, Oregon courts still distinguish between general enactment and individual applications,
affording a heightened level of judicial scrutiny to landowners

affronted by particularized actions issued by legislative bodies. *Neuberger* held, "When a particular action by a local government is directed at a relatively small number of identifiable persons, and when that action also involves the application of existing policy to a specific factual setting, the requirement of quasi-judicial procedures has been implied from the governing law."[28]

§ 16.6 *Historic Landmark and District Designations*

Is heightened nexus or proportionality review warranted for other legislative actions beyond rezoning? Yes. Legislative determinations of historic landmark status also have the effect of singling out landowners. This was glossed over by a 6-3 majority in *Penn Central v. City of New York*,[29] where Justice Brennan assumed that there was an average reciprocity of advantage which offsets any disadvantage in being designated an historic landmark. However, as then Justice Rehnquist stated in dissent, "Where a relatively few individual buildings, all separated from one another, are singled out and treated differently from surrounding buildings, no such reciprocity exists."[30] Similarly, in *District Intown Properties Ltd. Partnership v. District of Columbia*,[31] property owners were denied from constructing townhouses on lots adjacent to an already established apartment complex (an historic designation). Pending permit approval, the District of Columbia Historic Preservation Review Board designated the property in its entirety an historic landmark. Dismissing the owner's takings challenge, the court mechanically followed the *Penn Central* reasoning even though the landmark designation effectively singled out the owner of the property for disfavored treatment.

The unfortunate implications of deferential review in historic designation cases are made plain in *Metropolitan Baptist Church v. District of Columbia*.[32] In *Baptist Church*, a church challenged a local legislative body (the Historic Preservation Review Board) when it included five church-owned rowhouses in a city historic district. The church argued that it had been denied a fair and full opportunity to be heard when the legislative body denied requests for a hearing continuance. The court stated that "there is no statutory or constitutional right to a hearing before the Board when it is in the process of designating historic districts."[33] Because there was no constitutional right to a hearing, said the court, the board's decision to deny continuation of the hearing was not a violation of the church's due process rights. The court reasoned, "Where a hearing is not required but is allowed by legislative grace, it need not be circumscribed by the legal formalities incident to a judicial proceeding." The drawing of historic district boundaries was claimed to be "legislative," as the board was "making a policy decision directed toward the general public," rather than an adjudicative process where the board "weigh[s] particular information and arriv[es] at a decision directed at the rights of specific individuals." The problem, of course, is that the legislation as applied was not directed at the "general public," but at the church's five rowhouses. The court deferred solely because of the "legislative" label and the claim that designation involves "digestion of various economic, environmental, and aesthetic considerations." The Constitution requires more, or at least it should.

§ 16.7   The Application of Ultra Vires Legislation—The "Normal Delay" Ruse

Beyond the site-plan context of *Del Monte,* the rezoning of specific parcels of *Fasano,* and landmark or historic designation, heightened review is also merited for those cases where legislative enactment is alleged to be ultra vires, or beyond the authority of the particular legislative body.

In *Del Oro Hills v. City of Oceanside,*[34] a landowner confronted legislation imposed by an invalid initiative, Proposition A, a growth control ordinance enacted in conflict with the general plan. Stating that "[a]n invalid regulation is not necessarily an unconstitutional one," the court declined to examine either the nexus or proportionality of imposing ultra vires legislation on a particular landowner.[35] Because the landowner in *Del Oro* was able to prove "only" a $2 million loss for development delay, the only available remedy was invalidation of the ordinance. Yet, it is hard to see how an *invalid* law advances a *legitimate* governmental purpose. Moreover, as the mere invalidation in *Del Oro* illuminates, failure to undertake a heightened nexus or proportionality inquiry can lead courts to overlook compensation due for temporary takings under *First English Evangelical Lutheran Church v. County of Los Angeles.*[36]

In actuality, the Supreme Court's direction that regulation substantially advance a legitimate end has been consistently disregarded by lower court rulings that delays resulting from regulatory mistakes do not amount to takings of property.[37]

In *Littoral,* the California Court of Appeals did suggest that "a transient and impermanent interference in real property use due to egregious bureaucratic overreaching may arguably constitute a compensable temporary taking. . . ."[38] The California Supreme Court made short work of that hope in *Landgate, Inc. v. California Coastal Comm'n,*[39] when another California landowner attempted to assert egregious bureaucratic overreaching in a case involving invalid assertions of authority in the denial of coastal building permits. The California court held that "an error by a governmental agency in the development approval process does not necessarily amount to a taking even if the error in some way diminishes the value of the subject property."[40] The court continued, "If the error is of a particular constitutional type—the passage and enforcement of a law or regulation that deprives property of all value—then the teaching of *First English* is that such an error is a compensable taking. But government land use regulations and decisions... which, despite their ultimately determined statutory defects, are part of a reasonable regulatory process designed to advance legitimate government interests, are not takings of property under the Supreme Court's doctrine...."[41] Accepting invalid authority as advancing legitimate governmental interests overrules the first part of the *Agins* taking standard. In essence, invalid assertions of authority are only compensable when a landowner meets the second and more difficult constitutional burden of proving that the invalidly asserted regulation deprives the owner of all value. *Landgate* feebly tries to cover its disregard of U.S. Supreme Court precedent by stating that "a government agency may not evade the takings clause by fabricating a dispute over the legality of a lot, or by otherwise arbitrarily imposing conditions on development in order to delay or discourage that development."[42] Nevertheless, as Justice Chin pointed out in dissent, "When a regulatory agency [wrongfully] prohibits all use of a particular property, and the property owner is forced to use the agency to get it to change its position, its stonewalling is not fairly characterized as a 'normal delay' in the permit approval process."[43]

Another California landowner attempted to recover compensation for wrongfully asserted governmental authority in *Buckley v. California Coastal Comm'n.*[44] The court of appeals affirmed that the Coastal Commission did not have jurisdiction over the lot but reversed a damage award on either a permanent or temporary taking theory. Perhaps the appellate court was right that the Buckleys could have submitted a revised grading plan, which would have been approved, and thus avoided a permanent taking. Again, however, failure to apply heightened scrutiny to the commission's lack of authority left the landowner without remedy for wrongfully and unlawfully imposed delay, even though both the "substantially advance" prong of *Agins* and arguably *First English* would support a temporary taking. The proposition is only arguable under *First English*, of course, because the factual context of that ruling was an alleged deprivation of all economic use. Does it make any sense, however, for temporary takings only to be recognized for one-half of the constitutional standard articulated in *Agins*?

Del Oro, Landgate, and Buckley leave California landowners without effective remedy for wrongful assertions of governmental jurisdiction over property. This was aptly recognized by the Supreme Court of Wisconsin in *Eberle v. Dane County Board of Adjustment*.[45] As the *Eberle* court noted, "the argument of the majority in Landgate was clearly considered and rejected by the U.S. Supreme Court in First English. . . ."[46] Even *Eberle*, however, fails to fully grasp how a regulatory taking can exist for *either* a failure to substantially advance a legitimate governmental interest *or* deprivation of all economically viable use, since it understates the holding of *Del Monte*. *Del Monte* held that jury determination of regulatory takings is appropriate for both alleged deprivation of all use and at least in the context of a "protracted. . . development application process,"[47] and whether a municipal decision "to reject a particular development plan bore a reasonable relationship to its proferred justifications."[48] By contrast, deferential review effectively immunizes governmental agencies by allowing for post hoc rationalization that illegal action somehow serves a legitimate governmental interest. Something is seriously amiss. As the Supreme Court also stated in *Del Monte*, "to the extent the city argues, as a matter of law, its land use decisions are immune from judicial scrutiny under all circumstances, its position is contrary to settled regulatory taking principles. We reject this claim of error."[49]

§ 16.8   Legislative Enactments Imposing Public Burdens on Specific Private Uses

Justice Thomas's dissent in *Parking Ass'n of Georgia, Inc. v. City of Atlanta*,[50] mentioned earlier, suggests an even broader application of heightened nexus or proportionality review. In *Parking Ass'n,* the city of Atlanta enacted an ordinance that required owners of parking lots (with more than 30 parking spaces) to provide minimum barrier curbs, landscaping, and at least one tree to every eight parking spaces. The Supreme Court of Georgia refused to apply heightened judicial review to the owners' claim for declaratory relief. The Georgia court deferred to the legislative classification, reasoning that the "[p]laintiff's reliance on *Dolan v. City of Tigard* is misplaced. . . . Here, the city made a legislative determination with regard to many landowners and it simply limited the use the landowners might make of a small portion of their lands."[51] Justice Sears of the Georgia Supreme Court stated in dissent, "*Dolan* lends support to the proposition that the city should bear the burden. In *Dolan*, the [U.S.] Supreme Court placed the burden on the city, because it had singled out a particular parcel to bear an extraction. Here, the city has singled out a particular use within the city to bear the extraction. Moreover, the city has retroactively imposed the extraction. These are persuasive reasons to require the city to justify the extractions."[52] Similarly, when the U.S. Supreme Court denied review in *Parking Ass'n*, Justice Thomas, for himself and Justice O'Connor, dissented, writing:

> It is hardly surprising that some courts have applied [*Dolan*'s] rough proportionality test even when considering a legislative enactment. It is not clear why the existence of a taking should turn on the type of governmental entity responsible for the taking. A city council can take property just as well as a planning commission can. Moreover, the general applicability of the ordinance should not be relevant in a takings analysis. . . . The distinction between sweeping legislative takings and particularized administrative takings appears to be a distinction without constitutional difference.[53]

Prior to the Supreme Court's disposition in *City of Monterey v. Del Monte Dunes at Monterey, Ltd.*,[54] a lower court gave emphasis to Justice Thomas's concern.[55] *Tahoe-Sierra* involved an ordinance that acted to prevent the eutrophication of Lake Tahoe. The court stated, "[T]here is yet no clear test for determining whether a regulation substantially advances a legitimate interest—at least in the type of situation involved here."[56] The court considered *Nollan* and *Dolan* but noted that "aside from one footnote in *Dolan*, these cases do not really indicate whether this test should also be applied to situations in which no concession is being sought by the government in return for the grant of a permit to a specific individual."[57] The court did take note of the Ninth Circuit's decision in *Del Monte Dunes at Monterey, Ltd. v. City of Monterey*.[58] Yet, a later Ninth Circuit decision in *Garneau v. City of Seattle*[59] refused to apply the "rough proportionality" test to a Tenant Relocation Assistance Ordinance requiring property owners to provide monetary relocation assistance to "low-income tenants" when there was a change in use of residential property.

§ 16.9   What Next for Heightened Scrutiny?

So then the issue is joined: Is the broader application of heightened review eliminated by Justice Kennedy's back-of-the-hand comment in *Del Monte* that the "rough proportionality test of *Dolan* is inapposite" outside the exaction (viz., the formal land dedication) context? As suggested here, the answer should be given in the negative, at least where what is being reviewed is not the formulation of general policy, but its specific application. Before the Supreme Court arrives at any conclusion of "inaptness," it would do well to consider the particularized contexts explored in this chapter: protracted and malleable site-plan review, particularized rezonings, historic/landmark designations, ultra vires assertions of authority, and the imposition of public burden on a small class of landowners. The U.S. Supreme Court would be assisted in this effort by taking heed of existing state precedents applying heightened nexus or proportionality review, some of which are noted immediately below.

For example, the Supreme Court of Michigan in *Peterman v. Department of Natural Resources*[60] held that the owner of beachfront property was entitled to compensation when his property was destroyed by the building of a boat launch by the Department of Natural Resources. The court cited *Dolan* for its essential nexus and rough proportionality requirements with the finding for compensation based on the nexus element. The court held that *Dolan* was not confined to cases involving the dedication of purely private property interests.[61] Similarly, Oregon, in *Clark v. City of Albany,*[62] held that "the fact that *Dolan* itself involved conditions that required a dedication of property interests does not mean that it applies only to conditions of that kind." The court continued, "For purposes of takings analysis, we see little difference between a requirement that a developer convey title to the part of the property that is to serve a public purpose, and a requirement that the developer himself make improvements on the affected and nearby property and make it available for the same purpose."[63]

Dolan was also given broad applicability to legislative actions by the New York Court of Appeals in *Manocherian v. Lennox Hill Hospital.*[64] *Manocherian* invalidated an ordinance requiring apartment owners to offer renewal leases under a rent stabilization program. The court held that the ordinance did not substantially advance a "closely and legitimately connected State interest," while the dissent argued that the rent control ordinance as a general enactment was not subject to the heightened scrutiny required by *Dolan.*[65] The majority reasoned that *Dolan* applied especially to legislative actions affecting individual landowners who are asked to bear the burden of supplying society's social welfare needs. This protects landowners from "nonproportional" actions, be they legislatively or administratively imposed. Other lower courts have reached a similar conclusion.[66]

Even the California Supreme Court, somewhat inconsistently given its holdings in *Del Oro*, *Landgate*, and *Buckley*, has occasionally seen the light. Dealing on remand from the U.S. Supreme Court after *Dolan* with a $280,000 public recreation fee for closing a *private* tennis court in *Ehrlich v. City of Culver City*,[67] the California Supreme Court held "[u]nder this view of the constitutional role of the consolidated "essential nexus" and "rough proportionality" tests, it matters little whether the local land use permit authority demands the actual conveyance of property or the payment of a monetary exaction."[68] Unfortunately, the California Supreme Court did not fully understand the import of Justice Thomas's dissent in *Parking Ass'n*, because it went on to deferentially sustain in *Ehrlich* a $33,200 required fee for "public art" merely because it was legislative in form. And after *Ehrlich*, the California Supreme Court reverted to total deference when in *Santa Monica Beach Ltd. v. The Superior Court of Los Angeles County*,[69] it held *Dolan* inapplicable to a rent control ordinance that seemed to undermine its own articulated legislative purpose. Justice Brown, in her dissent, argued, "The majority's call to deference thus rests on an unspoken and critical assumption: that property merits only an inferior level of protection. That conclusion, a historical artifact of the demise of the *Lochner* era, has no defensible constitutional provenance."[70] As Justice Scalia in *Pennell v. City of San Jose*[71] reflected:

> Singling out [individual landowners] to be the transferors may be within our traditional constitutional notions of fairness, [only when] they can plausibly be regarded as the source of the beneficiary of the [land-use] problem. Once such a connection is no longer required, however, there is no end to the social transformations that can be accomplished by the so-called "regulation," at great expense to the democratic process.[72]

A Washington court got it right when it applied heightened proportionality review to a plat approval condition outlined in a city ordinance. See *Benchmark Land Co. v. City of Battle Ground*.[73] The challenged condition required the landowner to make half-street improvements to a street adjoining the subdivision on one side, although the subdivision did not directly access the street. The city ordinance, said the court, which required that half-street improvements be based upon the "length of development adjoining the street," was not necessarily related to the actual increase of street usage the development would create. Empirical evidence proved that "there is no necessary correlation between the extent a development borders a street and the extent to which residents of the development will actually use the street."[74] Therefore, the court concluded that the city ordinance failed *Dolan's* roughly proportional inquiry "based upon a site-specific study."

§ 16.10   A Concluding Word

What do all of these circumstances have in common? Each involves a landowner with a specific project or parcel having that project or parcel individually reviewed, classified, or subject to customized requirements that, in fairness, ought to be borne by the public. The act of legislatively creating classifications, zones, or districts deserves judicial deference. Their application does not. An argument over the reasonableness of general regulation is analogous to a facial challenge in constitutional jurisprudence. In a facial challenge, it is not appropriate for the court to invalidate unless every conceivable application of a statute is unconstitutional. The U.S. Supreme Court enunciated the general rule for raising facial challenges in *United States v. Salerno*.[75] In *Salerno*, the Court stated, "A facial challenge to a legislative Act is, of course, the most difficult challenge to mount successfully, since the challenger must establish that no set of circumstances exists under which the Act would be valid. The fact that [a legislative Act] might operate unconstitutionally under some conceivable set of circumstances is insufficient to render it wholly invalid. . . . "[76] The constitutional principle of *Salerno* is well reflected in *Nollan* and *Dolan* since they avoid second-guessing general policy while potentially providing adequate safeguard for particularized land-use challenges. As the Court stated in *Del Monte*, courts and juries in takings cases are not asked to determine the substantive "reasonableness of general zoning laws or land-use policies," but only if there was "no reasonable relationship between the city's denial of the . . . proposal and legitimate public purpose."[77]

That potential will be realized, however, only when the heightened nexus and proportionality inquiries of *Nollan* and *Dolan* are extended beyond the exaction context to all "legislative" enactments that are applied to single out landowners disproportionately. The Court in *Del Monte*, by affirming a regulatory taking award for regulation that did not substantially advance a legitimate governmental interest, understood this. It was unnecessary for the Court in *Del Monte* to employ a proportionality analysis, but as the cases here illustrate, it is not unnecessary elsewhere. In other words, the Court should not be too quick to find a broader application of proportionality analysis to be "inapposite."

Notes

1. 119 S. Ct. 1624 (1999).
2. *See id.* at 1636.
3. 447 U.S. 255, 260 (1980).
4. *Citing* Dolan v. City of Tigard, 512 U.S. 374 (1994); Lucas v. South Carolina Coastal Council, 505 U.S. 1003 (1992); Nollan v. California Coastal Comm'n, 483 U.S. 825 (1987); Keystone Bituminous Coal Ass'n v. DeBenedictis, 480 U.S. 470 (1987); and United States v. Riverside Bayview Homes, Inc., 474 U.S. 121 (1985).
5. *See Nollan*, 483 U.S. at 836 n.3.
6. 118 S. Ct. 2131 (1998).
7. *See* Graham v. Connor, 490 U.S. 386 (1989).
8. *See* Armendariz v. Penman, 75 F.3d 1311 (9th Cir. 1994).
9. *See* Brief for United States at *22 & n.11, City of Monterey v. Del Monte Dunes at Monterey, Ltd., (submitted U.S. S. Ct., June 5, 1998) (No. 97-1235), *available in* 1998 WL 308006.
10. *See Dolan*, 512 U.S. at 385.
11. *See id.*
12. 450 S.E.2d 200 (Ga. 1994), *cert. denied*, 115 S. Ct. 2268 (1995).
13. *See id.* at 2268-69 (Thomas, J., dissenting).
14. *See Del Monte*, 119 S. Ct. at 1635.
15. *See id.*
16. *See* Armstrong v. United States, 364 U.S. 40, 49 (1960).
17. *See Del Monte*, 119 S. Ct. at 1627.
18. *See id.* at 1633-36.
19. *See, e.g.,* Arnel Dev. Co. v. City of Costa Mesa, 620 P.2d 565, 571-73 (Cal. 1980) (holding "no constitutional requirement compels us to depart from the California doctrine that rezoning is a legislative act," and further that "landowners retain constitutional protection against zoning which is arbitrary, unreasonable, or deprives them of substantially all use of their land").
20. 507 P.2d 23 (Or. 1973).
21. *Id.* at 26.
22. *Id.*
23. 627 So. 2d 469 (Fla. 1993).
24. 519 P.2d 325 (Colo. 1974) (en banc) (holding that the city council acts in quasi-judicial capacity when making rezoning decisions).
25. *See* Ward v. Village of Skokie, 186 N.E.2d 529, 533 (Ill. 1962) (holding that the board's decision to deny a special-use permit was arbitrary as applied to landowner's property; further, it is the nature of the zoning proceeding that should determine the necessary review standards, "[o]therwise basic constitutional protections can readily be circumvented by the simple expedient of placing quasi-judicial functions in a legislative body." *Id.* at 534).

26. *See* West v. City of Portage, 221 N.W.2d 303, 308 (Mich. 1974) (holding that rezoning particularized parcels of property is "administrative" and therefore not subject to referendum or initiative).

27. 603 P.2d 771 (Or. 1979); *see also* Menges v. Board of County Comm'rs of Jackson County, 606 P.2d 681 (Or. Ct. App. 1980).

28. *See Neuberger,* 603 P.2d at 775.

29. 438 U.S. 104 (1978).

30. *See id.* at 140.

31. 23 F. Supp. 2d 30 (D. D.C. 1998).

32. 718 A.2d 119 (D.C. 1996).

33. *See cf.* Donnelly Assoc. v. District of Columbia Historic Preservation Review Bd., 520 A.2d 270 (D.C. 1987) (holding there is no constitutional, nor statutory, right to a trial-type hearing when the board designates property a historic landmark).

34. 37 Cal. Rptr. 2d 677 (Cal. App. 1995).

35. *See id.* at 690.

36. 482 U.S. 304, 322 (1987) ("invalidation of the ordinance without payment of fair value for the use of the property during this period of time would be a constitutionally insufficient remedy").

37. *See also* Littoral Dev. Co. v. San Francisco Bay Conservation, 33 Cal. App. 4th 211 (1995) (holding that regulatory bodies' actions, although erroneous, were "facially valid" and therefore were not characteristic of "egregious bureaucratic overreaching" that may result in a temporary taking); Cannone v. Noey, 867 P.2d 797, 801 (Alaska 1994) (holding that "an arbitrary finding is not a substitute for the takings inquiry."); Dumont v. Town of Wolfeboro, 622 A.2d 1238 (N.H. 1993) (finding no taking when the town erroneously denied a site-plan application for proposed restaurant); Tabb Lakes, Ltd. v. United States, 10 F.3d 796 (Fed. Cir. 1993) (holding mistake by Army Corps of Engineers requiring property owner to submit to permit process did not result in compensable taking); Steinbergh v. City of Cambridge, 413 Mass. 736 (1992) (holding that although the imposed regulation was statutorily flawed, landowner failed to meet constitutional burden of proving that the regulation failed to advance a legitimate governmental interest); Smith v. Town of Wolfeboro, 615 A.2d 1252 (1992) (holding that planning board's improper application of a zoning ordinance did not result in a compensable taking); 1902 Atlantic Ltd. v. United States, 26 Cl. Ct. 575 (1992) (holding that "mere fluctuations in value during the process of government decision making, absent extraordinary delay, are 'incidents of ownership'. . . which cannot be considered a 'taking' in the constitutional sense"); Lujan Home Builders v. Orangetown, 150 Misc. 2d 547, 549 (1991) (holding that "as long as the land use decision-making process passes constitutional muster in the procedural sense and a full judicial mechanism exists to challenge the administrative determination, no cause of action exists for deprivation of use of the property for the period of time the property could not be used as requested by reason of administrative denial of relief").

38. 33 Cal. App. 4th at 221-22.

39. 953 P.2d 1188 (Cal. 1998), *cert. denied*, 119 S. Ct. 179 (1998).

40. *Id.* at 1020.

41. *Id.* at 1021.

42. *Id.* at 1029.

43. *Id.* at 1032.

44. 68 Cal. App. 4th 178 (Cal. App. 1998), *review denied* (Cal. Feb 24, 1999), *cert. denied*, 528 U.S. 816 (1999).

45. 595 N.W.2d 730, 742 n.25 (Wis. 1999) (finding a denial of a special exception permit for driveway access to be a temporary regulatory taking).

46. *Id.*

47. *See* City of Monterey v. Del Monte Dunes at Monterey, Ltd., 119 S. Ct. 1624, 1644 (1999).

48. *Id.*

49. *See Del Monte*, 119 S. Ct. at 1637.

50. 450 S.E.2d 200 (Ga. 1994), *cert. denied*, 115 S. Ct. 2268 (1995).

51. *See id.* at 203 n.3.

52. *See id.* at 204 n.5.

53. *Id.* at 2268-69 (Thomas, J., dissenting).

54. 119 S. Ct. 1624 (1999).

55. *See* Tahoe-Sierra Preservation Council, Inc. v. Tahoe Regional Planning Agency, 34 F. Supp. 2d 1226 (D. Nev. 1999).

56. *Id.* at 1239.

57. *Id.*

58. 95 F.3d 1422 (9th Cir. 1996), expanding application of *Dolan* beyond the exaction context.

59. 147 F.3d 802, 804 (9th Cir. 1998).

60. 521 N.W.2d 499 (Mich. 1994).

61. *See id.* at 512 n.34.

62. 904 P.2d 185 (Or. 1995).

63. *Id.* at 189.

64. 643 N.E.2d 479 (N.Y. 1994), *cert denied*, 115 S. Ct. 1961, *and cert. denied*, 115 S. Ct. 1962 (1995).

65. *See id.* at 480.

66. *See also* Carson Harbor Village Ltd. v. City of Carson, 37 F.3d 468 (9th Cir. 1994) (dismissing takings claim [challenging rent-control ordinance] on standing and ripeness issues, but stating in dicta that "the law is invalid if the required dedication of property is unrelated in nature, or disproportionate in extent, to the problem that the government seeks to mitigate or control"); Northern Ill. Home Builders' Ass'n v. County of Du Page, 649 N.E.2d 384, 388-90 (Ill. 1995) (applying rough proportionality test to development fees imposed pursuant to and established by county ordinances); Trimen Dev. Co. v. King County, 877 P.2d 187, 194 (Wash. 1994) (en banc) (applying rough proportionality standard to fee in lieu of dedication imposed pursuant to county ordinances); Kottschade v. City of Rochester, 537 N.W.2d 301, 307-08 (Minn. App. 1995) (applying rough proportionality test to land-use dedication requirement as set forth in city ordinance); Honesty in Envtl. Analysis and Legislation v. Central Puget Sound Growth Mgmt. Hearing Bd., 979 P.2d 864 (Wash. App. 1999) (holding that critical area policies and regulations under the Growth Management Act are subject to the *Dolan* rough proportionality analysis).

67. 911 P.2d 429 (Cal. 1996), *cert. denied*, 117 S. Ct. 299 (1996).

68. *See id.* at 444.

69. 968 P.2d 993 (Cal. 1999).

70. *See id.* at 1041.

71. 485 U.S. 1 (1988).
72. *Id.* at 22 (Scalia, J., concurring and dissenting).
73. 972 P.2d 944 (Wash. App. 1999).
74. *See id.* at 949.
75. 481 U.S. 739 (1987).
76. *Id.* at 745.
77. *See Del Monte*, 119 S. Ct. at 1628-34.

EMPERORS AND CLOTHES: THE GENEALOGY AND OPERATION OF THE *AGINS* TESTS

17

EDWARD J. SULLIVAN*

All lies and jest
Still a man hears what he wants to hear
And disregards the rest.
— Paul Simon, *The Boxer*
(Columbia Records, 1968)

§ 17.0   Introduction

In the January 2000 edition of *Land Use Law and Zoning Digest*,[1] John D. Echeverria wrote a devastating and incisive analysis of the so-called three-factor test for "regulatory takings" in *Penn Central Transportation Co. v. New York City*.[2] In particular, Echeverria exposed the lack of authority for the test, its vague and uncertain criteria, the way in which other courts have been unable to apply it, and its expansion of the takings doctrine well beyond a provision for compensation for direct physical appropriation. It is the purpose of this chapter to make a similar critique of the Supreme Court's decision in

*The author gratefully acknowledges the invaluable contribution of Nicholas De Marco, LL.B., University College, London, in the preparation of this chapter.

Agins v. City of Tiburon,[3] a case that has also been relied upon to expand the doctrine of takings as applied to land-use regulation.

The *Agins* two-prong test for a taking was whether a regulation substantially advanced legitimate state interests or whether it denied an owner economically viable use of land. I will demonstrate that the *Agins* Court failed to provide a narrower and more definite test than *Penn Central*. Rather, the *Agins* Court was just as prone to the same mistakes of vagueness, impracticability, and lack of authority on the one hand, while expanding the takings doctrine even further than had been done in *Penn Central* on the other.

In particular, this chapter will propose three principal arguments. The first is that the test in *Agins* has dubious parentage and that, in any event, it was, if not dicta, an unnecessary doctrinal excursion. Second, the result of the case has been the reemergence of substantive due process by another name; this point is most clear from the recent case of *Eastern Enterprises v. Apfel*.[4] Third, *Agins* demonstrates a fundamental problem of constitutional interpretation. The reason that it was so easy to transmogrify the law is that Americans view the Constitution in a quasi-religious way, as a form of natural law. If something is not actually in the Constitution but is felt to be desirable, then the Constitution is read and given effect as if it were really there.[5]

Instead, I suggest a positivist approach to constitutional theory over this version of American "natural law." One need not be a Marxist to appreciate the role of political, social, and economic views of those judges who purport to embrace a "value-free" reading of the federal Constitution.[6] Groucho Marx, rather than Karl Marx, is a better guide for American constitutional jurisprudence, in which it is easier to change direction by a new Court majority manipulating vague constitutional phrases. This is the same Court that decided that African-Americans were "property" in *Dred Scott v. Sanford* in 1856.[7] This same Court decided that these same persons, as citizens, were entitled to "separate but equal" treatment regarding governmental services in *Plessy v. Ferguson*[8] (which certainly turned out to be separate but not at all equal). This same Court does not appear to be bothered at all by the surging percentage of executions handed down upon these citizens' descendents.[9] While the current Court may not be as sympathetic about life and liberty, it is certainly more stimulated about property. And, while Groucho Marx, as a commentator, may have made observations on these circumstances, he might also have waxed humorously on the means by which the property rights agenda was advanced, i.e., by *Penn Central* and *Agins*.

In tracing the origins of *Agins*, you discover the emergence, basis, and rewriting of the takings doctrine in the Constitution and the effect of a substantive due process approach to land-use regulation. You then consider the way in which *Agins* reformulated the fundamental errors of 100 years into a two-factor test and an unexamined reliance on that test to develop takings law.

§ 17.1   *The Origins of* Agins

§ 17.1(a) *Takings and the Fifth Amendment*

The earliest American cases addressing the takings issue had no problem applying the words of the U.S. Constitution clearly and, presumably, as they were intended. The last 12 words of the Fifth Amendment read, "nor shall private property be taken for public use, without just compensation."[10] A taking occurred if there was direct physical appropriation of land for public use.

Historical reviews of land-use law before the ratification of the Constitution have demonstrated that land regulation (without compensation), rather than Fifth Amendment "direct occupation," was widespread and uncontroversial. J.F. Hart has concluded that:

> The historical records surveyed. . . show that the colonial experience of land use regulation cannot fairly be confined within the imagined boundary of nuisance control. The preferences of landowners were regularly subordinated to a vision of the public good that embraced many objectives beyond protecting health and safety. In regulating land e.g., the government sought benefits for the public, not just avoidance of harm.[11]

It was within such a context that the framers of the Constitution wrote. Their neglect to mention land-use regulation cannot reasonably be seen as an oversight. The Takings Clause of the Fifth Amendment was specifically limited to the direct physical appropriation of private land for public use.[12] This is clear also from the earliest American forays into constitutional construction, such as Article 2 of the Vermont Constitution of 1777,[13] Article 10 of the interim Massachusetts Constitution of 1780, and Madison's draft Bill of Rights.[14]

Yet, despite a complete absence of any evidence for the proposition that the Takings Clause was intended to cover regulation, some 20th-century courts have tried to impose their prejudices on history and insist the clause must encompass such regulation. The opinion of Chief Judge Smith of the Federal Claims Court in

Florida Rock Industries v. United States[15] is a particularly extreme example of this type of tautological "reasoning":

> To hold that property cannot be partially taken by a regulation . . . would be to hold that the need for government regulation trumps the Takings Clause. Yet, the need for government regulation is why the Takings Clause was enacted as a vital protection. Any other reading would make the clause a virtual nullity.[16]

A series of early state supreme court decisions recognized the legitimacy of land-use regulation, even if it caused substantial economic loss for the property owner.[17] In *Commonwealth v. Alger*,[18] Chief Justice Shaw of the Massachusetts Supreme Court distinguished regulation of land use from eminent domain, the latter of which alone entitled the owner to compensation:

> [e]very holder of property, however absolute and unqualified may be his title, holds it under the implied liability that his use of it may be so regulated. . . . This is very different from the right of eminent domain. . . . The power we allude to is rather the police power, the power vested in the legislature by the constitution, to make, ordain and establish all manner of wholesome and reasonable laws, statutes and ordinances, either with penalties or without, not repugnant to the constitution, as they shall judge to be for the good and welfare of the commonwealth, and of the subjects of the same. . . . It is not an appropriation of the property to a public use, but the restraint of an injurious private use by the owner, and is therefore not within the principle of property taken under the right of eminent domain.[19]

In 1887, the U.S. Supreme Court reiterated this distinction and the constitutionality of land-use regulation in *Mugler v. Kansas*.[20] In this case, a brewery had challenged a Kansas law that made its business operation unlawful on grounds of public health, safety, and morals. Justice Harlan, writing for the Court, rejected the plaintiff's challenge to the regulation under the Takings Clause of the Fifth Amendment. It is worth quoting his majority opinion at some length as it makes clear the fact that land-use regulations cannot be takings:

> A prohibition simply upon the use of property for purposes that are declared, by valid legislation, to be injuri-

ous to the health, morals, or safety of the community, cannot, in any just sense, be deemed a taking or an appropriation of property for the public benefit. Such legislation does not disturb the owner in the control or use of his property for lawful purposes, nor restrict his right to dispose of it, but is only a declaration by the state that its use by any one, for certain forbidden purposes, is prejudicial to the public interests. ... The power which the states have of prohibiting such use by individuals of their property, as will be prejudicial to the health, the morals, or the safety of the public, is not, and, consistently with the existence and safety of organized society, cannot be, burdened with the condition that the state must compensate such individual owners for pecuniary losses they may sustain, by reason of their not being permitted, by a noxious use of their property, to inflict injury upon the community. The exercise of the police power by the destruction of property which is itself a public nuisance, or the prohibition of its use in a particular way, whereby its value becomes depreciated, is very different from taking property for public use, or from depriving a person of his property without due process of law. In the one case, a nuisance only is abated; in the other, unoffending property is taken away from an innocent owner.[21]

For the same reasons, the Supreme Court in *Powell v. Pennsylvania*,[22] one year later, upheld that state's outlawing of oleomargarine on health grounds, thereby making several factories virtually useless. The plaintiff's takings claim in that case was dismissed as "without merit."

§ 17.1(b) *Rewriting the Constitution*—Pennsylvania Coal Co. v. Mahon

Consistent with laissez-faire ideals dominating in the United States, *Mugler* continued to be the principal case in this area throughout the 19th century. The revolution emerged with *Pennsylvania Coal*[23] when Justice Holmes "rewrote the Constitution"[24] that land-use regulation was to be judged under the Takings Clause. There was no previous authority for such an approach, and there had only been a few dicta remarks by Justice Holmes himself about the constitutionality of regulations being a "question of degree" before this remarkable decision. Essentially, Justice Holmes argued from a supposed commonsense standpoint that regulation of land use could only go "so far" (without being a taking of the property owner's interests), and whether it did so or not could only be determined on the circumstances of each case. Having recognized the general lawfulness of state regulation, even where it may cause diminution to the value of the private property involved, he suggested limits to this power:

> One fact for consideration in determining such limits is the extent of the diminution. When it reaches a certain magnitude, in most if not in all cases there must be an exercise of eminent domain and compensation to sustain the act. So the question depends upon the particular facts.[25]

Thus, Justice Holmes established that a regulation could be a taking and that a central factor in determining this issue was the degree to which it interfered with the property owner's profitable enjoyment of his land. Previous cases had not considered this factor, and it is hard to see how a case like *Mugler* could have possibly been decided the way it was if such interference were a factor. Rather, any judicial review of previous regulations was based on the extent to which they fulfilled a legitimate public need. An answer to this riddle may lie in Justice Holmes's reluctance to clothe his opinions in the constitutional mantle of substantive due process, against which he had long inveighed.[26]

§ 17.1(c) *Substantive Due Process*

Between *Pennsylvania Coal* in 1922 and *Penn Central* in 1978, there was little activity by the Court on the takings issue. In the 1920s, the Court, however, did use substantive due process to evaluate land-use regulations. Later, in seeking authority for one of the two tests developed in *Agins*, Justice Powell cited the 1928 substantive due process case of *Nectow v. Cambridge.*[27] He used *Nectow* as the basis for the proposition that the "application of a general zoning law to particular property effects a taking if the ordinance does not substantially advance legitimate state interests."[28] *Nectow* concerned the constitutionality of a city ordinance from the standpoint of substantive due process under the Fourteenth Amendment. *Agins* applied the test used in *Euclid v. Ambler Co.* as well.[29] The Court quoted the portion of *Euclid* that stated:

> [A] court should not set aside the determination of public officers in such a matter unless it is clear that their action "has no foundation in reason and is a mere arbitrary or irrational exercise of power having no substantial relation to the public health, the public morals, the public safety or the public welfare in its proper sense."[30]

In *Euclid*, local city ordinances were not found to be so unreasonable as to be unconstitutional under the due process clause of the Fourteenth Amendment, whereas in *Nectow,* not too dissimilar regulations failed to substantially advance state interests.

In the period after *Pennsylvania Coal,* it was substantive due process, the discredited device of the *Lochner* period, and not the Takings Clause in the Fifth Amendment, that was relied on by the Supreme Court as the constitutional test for the validity of regulations. Courts that approved of particular regulations could bend substantive due process in their direction, relying on *Euclid*; those that did not, could bend the doctrine the other way, relying on *Nectow*. *Agins*'s use of precedent in this instance was the mask for subjectivity.

§ 17.1(d) *The Resurrection of Pennsylvania Coal—The Case of Penn Central*

It was not until 1978 that the Supreme Court in *Penn Central* finally resurrected *Pennsylvania Coal* and extended it even further. *Penn Central* formulated a test to consider whether a regulation had gone "too far" from the standpoint of the property owner. A three-factor test was elaborated for determining whether a regulation amounted to a taking. That test was to consider the "economic impact" of the regulation, how it would affect "investment-backed expectations," and the "character of the governmental action."[31] It is not made clear to what extent and how a court is supposed to balance these often countervailing factors against each other. Echeverria is correct to criticize this vague and expansive test as one that ". . . invites unprincipled judicial decision making, conflicts with the language and original understanding of the Takings Clause, would confer unjust windfalls in many cases, and creates seemingly insurmountable problems in terms of defining an appropriate remedy."[32] That same criticism applies to the *Agins* tests.

The three-factor test in *Penn Central* was preceded by these remarks by Justice Brennan:

> . . . [T]his Court, quite simply, has been unable to develop any "set formula" for determining when "justice and fairness" require that economic injuries caused by public action be compensated by the government, rather than remain disproportionately concentrated on a few persons. . . . Indeed, we have frequently observed that whether a particular restriction will be rendered invalid by the government's failure to pay for any losses proximately caused by it depends largely "upon the particular circumstances [in that] case."[33]

Thus, it seems clear that there was no intention in *Penn Central* to create a ready-made formula to fit all cases. This itself should have served as a warning to future courts not to try to apply the generalizations in *Penn Central* as a "three-factor test" in a rigid manner.

§ 17.2 *The Supreme Court Decision in* Agins

The Aginses bought five acres of unimproved residentially desig-nated land in the city of Tiburon in a prime location overlooking San Francisco Bay. The city then revised its zoning ordinance, which made such development discretionary and allowed the Aginses to use their land for building between one and five single-family residences only. Without applying for approval for their own development plans, the Aginses challenged the ordinance on the grounds that it constituted a taking and thus was in breach of the Fifth Amendment. The Court found that, as there was no as-applied taking claim to consider, the only question was whether the mere enactment of the ordinance was a taking. In determin-ing this issue, the Court developed a new test for regulatory tak-ings:

> The application of a general zoning law to particular property effects a taking if the ordinance *does not sub-stantially advance legitimate state interests. . .* or *denies an owner economically viable use of his land. . . .* [34] (Em-phasis added.)

The first problem with this formulation is the Court's confusion between a facial and an as-applied challenge. While the Court seems to recognize the challenge was of the former type, it went on to formulate the test as if it were the latter, an "as-applied" challenge. If "the only question. . . is whether the mere enactment of the zoning ordinance constitutes a taking,"[35] then there is no need to apply that ordinance to a particular property. The mere enactment of an ordinance will be in breach of the Takings Clause and unconstitutional if it does not offer compensation for the taking of land. For example, if a city council enacts an ordinance allowing the confiscation of all land larger than ten acres without compensation, then we can deduce this is a facial violation of the Takings Clause of the Fifth Amendment. It is not necessary to consider the impact of the ordinance on particular property, or to wait until somebody with land of more than ten acres is affected to conclude the ordinance would be a taking. Once we consider an ordinance in terms of its specific impact on particular property, we are relying on an as-applied test; we are considering whether the particular features of an ordinance have such an effect on some unique property that they form a taking in those circumstances. The Court in *Agins* created such a test, but applied it in the context of a facial challenge.

The Court could simply have dismissed the challenge as unripe. This was the result in *Williamson County Regional Planning Commission v. Hamilton Bank of Johnson City.*[36] Justice Blackmun for the majority held that:

> As the Court has made clear in several recent decisions, a claim that the application of government regulations effects a taking of a property interest is not ripe until the government entity charged with implementing the regulations has reached a final decision regarding the application of the regulations to the property in issue.[37]

Indeed, he goes on to cite *Agins* as an example of a court not considering a claim because it is unripe.

The development of the two-prong test in *Agins* was unnecessary. If the Court had correctly described what it was doing, such a test would have properly been characterized as dicta. However, under the circumstances, it is questionable if the Court knew what it was doing when it, perhaps without sufficient consideration, developed what has become such an important test and has resulted in considerable confusion.

In *Keystone Bituminous Coal Ass'n v. DeBenedictis,*[38] Justice Stevens, for the majority, at first restates the *Penn Central* test as the one to rely on in as-applied challenges:

> [T]his Court has generally "been unable to develop any 'set formula' for determining when 'justice and fairness' require that economic injuries caused by public action be compensated by the government, rather than remain disproportionately concentrated on a few persons." Rather, it has examined the "taking" question by engaging in essentially ad hoc, factual inquiries that have identified several factors—such as the economic impact of the regulation, its interference with reasonable investment-backed expectations, and the character of the government action—that have particular significance. *Kaiser Aetna v. United States*, 444 U.S. 164, 175.

These "ad hoc, factual inquiries" must be conducted with respect to specific property and the particular estimates of economic impact and ultimate valuation relevant in the unique circumstances.[39]

Thus, the three-factor test should apparently apply to specific property, as applied. Justice Stevens goes on to say:

> Because appellees' taking claim arose in the context of a facial challenge, it presented no concrete controversy concerning either application of the Act to particular surface mining operations or its effect on specific parcels of land. Thus, the only issue properly before the District Court and, in turn, this Court, is whether the "mere enactment" of the Surface Mining Act constitutes a taking. See *Agins v. Tiburon*, 447 U.S. 255, 260. The test to be applied in considering this facial challenge is fairly straightforward. A statute regulating the uses that can be made of property effects a taking if it "denies an owner economically viable use of his land. . ." *Agins v. Tiburon*, *supra*. Petitioners thus face an uphill battle in making a facial attack on the Act as a taking.

The second part of the *Agins* test is relied on for facial challenges, and this is presented as causing an uphill battle for the plaintiff. It is impossible to consider whether a regulation "denies an owner economically viable use of his land" without an inquiry into the "specific property, and the particular estimates of economic impact and ultimate valuation relevant in the unique circumstances"—that is, without an as-applied test.

The confusion in *Agins* between facial and as-applied challenges has developed into an alleged basis for distinguishing between two types of tests that are essentially about the same thing—considering the economic impact of a regulation on a specific property. Furthermore, as argued below (and we will see that Justice Scalia agrees), properly considered, the test in *Agins* actually makes it easier to establish a takings claim than the three-factor balancing test in *Penn Central*. Far from creating an uphill struggle, this distinction would actually make it easier to establish a facial challenge than an as-applied challenge, giving a green light to landowners to use the courts against any regulation they think might potentially damage their interests before they have gone through the administrative and state court processes required for an as-applied challenge.

Without specifically criticizing or rejecting this confusion, there was some retreat from it in the case of *Pennell v. City of San Jose*.[40] In that case, landlords brought an action alleging as facially unconstitutional an ordinance that allowed a hearing officer to determine whether an annual rent increase in excess of 8 percent was reasonable, considering, inter alia, "the hardship of the tenant." They claimed this regulation was a taking in violation of the Fifth Amendment and that it violated the due process and equal protection clauses of the Fourteenth Amendment. The landlords had never faced such a hearing, nor did they allege they had any tenants who might, in the future, claim the required hardship. The Supreme Court found the landlords did have standing, but after consideration of the claims, dismissed this facial challenge under the Fourteenth Amendment. The majority held that the takings claim was premature:

> We think it would be premature to consider this contention on the present record. As things stand, there simply is no evidence that the "tenant hardship clause" has in fact ever been relied upon by a hearing officer to reduce a rent below the figure it would have been set at on the basis of the other factors set forth in the Ordinance. In addition, there is nothing in the Ordinance requiring that a hearing officer in fact reduce a proposed rent increase on grounds of tenant hardship. Section 5703.29 does make it mandatory that hardship be considered—it states that "the Hearing Officer shall consider the economic hardship imposed on the present tenant"—but it then goes on to state that if "the proposed increase constitutes an unreasonably severe financial or economic hardship . . . he may order that the excess of the increase" be disallowed. § 5703.29. Given the "essentially ad hoc, factual inquir[y]" involved in the takings analysis, *Kaiser Aetna v. United States*, 444 U.S. 164, we have found it particularly important in takings cases to adhere to our admonition that "the constitutionality of statutes ought not be decided except in an actual factual setting that makes such a decision necessary." *Hodel v. Virginia Surface Mining & Reclamation Ass'n, Inc.*, 452 U.S. 264, 294-95.[41]

It has been suggested that this is one example of the Court manipulating the facial and as-applied name tags based on whether they wish to address the merits of a takings claim.[42] While this may be true, the name tags have been manipulated in the other direction to consider such a claim, and such manipulation is greatly aided by the confusion in *Agins*. A clear rule, similar to the one stated in *Pennell*, is to be preferred, as it distinguishes between facial and as-applied on the only proper basis for such a distinction: whether the act complained of applies to the particular property of the complainant.

In the final analysis, like any other element of the takings issue, the issue boils down to one of judicial choice. Those who want to expand the takings doctrine to include all kinds of regulation want to make it easier for property owners to bring facial challenges against legislation.[43] It is not surprising, therefore, that Justice Scalia (Justice O'Connor concurring) expressed such a strongly worded dissent to this particular finding in *Pennell*:

> In sum, it is entirely clear from our cases that a facial takings challenge is not premature even if it rests upon the ground that the ordinance deprives property owners of all economically viable use of their land—a ground that is, as we have said, easier to establish in an "as-applied" attack. It is, if possible, even clearer that the present facial challenge is not premature, because it does not rest upon a ground that would even profit from consideration in the context of particular application. As we said in *Agins*, a zoning law "effects a taking if the ordinance does not substantially advance legitimate state interests. . . or denies an owner economically viable use of his land." The present challenge is of the former sort. Appellants contend that providing financial assistance to impecunious renters is not a state interest that can legitimately be furthered by regulating the use of property. Knowing the nature and character of the particular property in question, or the degree of its economic impairment, will in no way assist this inquiry. Such factors are as irrelevant to the present claim as we have said they are to the claim that a law effects a taking by authorizing a permanent physical invasion of property. See *Loretto v. Teleprompter Manhattan CATV Corp.*, 458 U.S. 419. So even if we were explicitly to overrule cases such as *Agins*, *Virginia Surface Mining*, and *Keystone*, and to hold that a facial challenge will not lie where the issue can be more forcefully presented in an "as-applied" attack, there would still be no reason why the present challenge should not proceed.[44]

Justice Scalia posits that a facial challenge should be and is easier to succeed than an as-applied challenge. He relies on the "substantive due process" part of the *Agins* test to establish this unique view and then, rather disingenuously, suggests that even if *Agins* were overruled, this would still be the case! In fact, as shown below, the Court was wrong to develop such a test for takings, and if *Agins* and the cases that followed this section of it were overruled, then, of course, this would not still be the case. However, to consider these issues further, it is necessary to move beyond the first major criticism of *Agins*—its confusion between as-applied and facial challenges and its thus totally unnecessary development of a test in the first place—to a more substantive critique of the two elements of the test itself.

§ 17.2(a) *The Alternative Tests of Agins*

This test places as alternatives both the substantive due process test borrowed from *Nectow* and the test of "economic impact" from *Penn Central*. The latter way in which a regulation can be deemed unconstitutional and a taking is where it "... denies an owner economically viable use of his land."[45] This seems to be a version of the test of "economic impact" and "investment-backed expectations" in *Penn Central*. Footnote 36 of *Penn Central* states that "if appellants can demonstrate at some point in the future that circumstances have so changed that the Terminal ceases to be 'economically viable,' applicants may gain relief."[46]

Commentators have argued about the extent to which *Agins* incorporated the test in *Penn Central*. Some have argued the *Agins* test replaces the test in *Penn Central*,[47] while some courts have said it includes the *Penn Central* test,[48] and others have said it only includes the economic impact and investment-backed expectations elements of that test.[49] This latter view seems the most accurate in that denial of economically viable use is obviously an economic impact and will be most profound where it affects investment-backed expectations; the economic character of the government action would fit more within the substantive due process test.

Thus, we can say that the Court in *Agins* created two alternative routes by which a taking could be found: the first—"if the ordinance does not substantially advance legitimate state interests"[50]—is based on substantive due process, the *Lochner* approach and the Fourteenth Amendment, and to some extent it may also incorporate the third factor of *Penn Central* (character of governmental action). The second, focusing on diminution of value, relies on the rewriting of the Fifth Amendment in *Pennsylvania Coal*, its resurrection in *Penn Central* in the form of the first two factors of the test (economic impact and investment-backed expectations), and an obscure footnote about hypothetical facts.

Agins combines the worst of both worlds: discredited substantive due process dug up from the *Lochner* period, with the spurious revision of the Fifth Amendment to encompass regulations that went "too far" from the standpoint of the landowner. What was novel about *Agins* was that it fashioned two ways to insist on governmental compensation for regulation in the alternative, as "two independent criteria,"[51] giving the landowner greater opportunity to obstruct government action. Pre-*Agins* courts had sought to justify their findings that a particular regulation was unconstitutional, alleging a substantive due process violation or a taking under *Pennsylvania Coal*, or, in the case of *Penn Central*, by balancing considerations of each against the other. *Agins* allows courts to "pick and choose" the easiest way to attack a regulation if so disposed.

§ 17.2(b) *Academic Criticism of* Agins

Compared to *Pennsylvania Coal*, *Penn Central,* or *Lucas*, the decision in *Agins* has attracted remarkably little academic criticism or discussion. Most references to it simply restate the test and do not even query its progeny. However, a number of articles search more deeply into the genealogy of *Agins* and its flaws, in particular, those by Byrne,[52] Echeverria,[53] Epstein,[54] McCaskey,[55] McUsic,[56] Peterson,[57] Summers,[58] and Wade.[59]

Byrne, Echeverria, McCaskey, McUsic, and Summers all comment on the incorporation of the *Lochner*-era substantive due process test via *Nectow* in *Agins*. By reintroducing this doctrine into takings law, Byrne argues, there is a "further blurring [of] the distinction between these constitutional doctrines."[60] Likewise, Echeverria talks of a "muddling of legal doctrines, not a considered analysis of whether, as a matter of first principles, takings law includes—or should include—a means-ends test."[61] McCaskey argues that Justice Scalia uses the *Agins* legitimate state interest test to adopt a "nexus test" in *Nollan v. California Coastal Commission*[62] based on the "means-ends" analysis in *Lochner*:

> [T]his standard is something more than the rational-basis analysis which merely maintains that government legislation be rationally related to a legitimate government purpose, and will afford more necessary protection for liberty of contract. . . [it] amounts to an intermediate level of review for liberty of contract and other economic rights.[63]

Summers concludes that the inclusion of the discredited and controversial substantive due process test into the definition of a taking in *Agins* causes intractable problems that can only be solved by an effective reversal of (at least that part of) *Agins*:

If the Court is now unhappy with the level of means-end scrutiny provided by due process, it should correct this problem at the source, rather than by making an end-run around due process via the Takings Clause. Such efforts not only "direct [. . .] attention away from the Court's deeper concern with fairness" and subject takings jurisprudence to the same criticisms which ultimately discredited *Lochner*-style substantive due process, but they also divert energy and attention away from the resolution of the most significant Takings Clause problem— the establishment of a principled and workable means of defining what constitutes a "taking."[64]

In an article by the author of this chapter on the decision in *Eastern Enterprises*,[65] it was argued that certain conservative members of the Supreme Court, in particular Justice Scalia, have relied on this back-door inclusion of substantive due process in the Takings Clause in order to both expand the takings doctrine to regulatory takings and, at the same time, diminish the scope of substantive due process, as this was the basis of the abortion decisions they are concerned to undermine (see, in particular, dissents of the Chief Justice, joined by Justices White, Scalia, and Thomas, and that of Justice Scalia, joined by the Chief Justice and Justices White and Thomas in *Planned Parenthood v. Casey*). [66]

Byrne goes on to criticize the second part of the *Agins* test, saying that it raised, but does not settle, the difficult issue of what kind of land uses are so fundamental that compensation must be provided:

In attempting to answer this question, the Court has stumbled into a thicket of natural law adjudication. The doctrinal confusion recounted here is neither incidental nor temporary. It arises from the immensity of the task that the Court has set for itself in regulatory takings cases: to mark as a matter of principle when limitation of property use becomes unfair. Not only have serious philosophers differed utterly in their approaches to these questions, but the trends of adjudication have changed so often over time that observers understandably view any answers as contingent. Moreover, the Constitution itself affords no guidance, except to proscribe outright confiscation. The Court simply does not have a basis in law, history, or consensual community standards to persuasively explain why one use restriction reflects the or-

dinary government adjustments of conflicting interests
and another violates fundamental fairness.[67]

§ 17.2(c) *Is a Natural Law Basis for Constitutional Law Effective?*

The American Constitution is neither sacrosanct nor beyond criticism. It is a product of a particular time and set of circumstances,
i.e., 18th-century rationalism, which saw itself as beyond time
and place. In other circumstances, it could have led to the up-
heaval and excesses of the French Revolution. However, circumstances change and the advent of fascism and socialism in time do
not bode well for those who see history as an unending scheme of
human progress. The rationalist structure of the Constitution
masked the social order it fixed and maintained that order until
change was forced, as in the case of domestic relations, with slavery and the inequality of women. The Constitution did not prohibit slavery—it took a civil war to do that. Not for nearly a
century did the Constitution prevent the effects of slavery from
being erased, if indeed that has ever happened. Nor does the Constitution prevent the political and social barriers to opportunity
today.

Instead, the Constitution has been an instrument of political
and social conservatism and, at times, the instrument of suppres-
sion. But, because the Constitution is vested as a quasi-religious
object in the American political psyche, it is largely beyond criticism or rarely considered in the context of its time, place, and
circumstances. Moreover, because American politics are less ideological and more pragmatic, little time is spent examining the
underpinnings that drive American political thought.

Only by demystifying the Constitution and understanding the
roles played by competing interests as extensions of various ideologies do we understand the impacts of those interests. Further,
only by understanding law as part of that competition, rather than
holy writ, will we be able to view law and politics more clearly.
The removal of the scales of received wisdom in the form of constitutional ideology is the task of positivists, who view judicial
opinions as part of the clash of these interests, to be dealt with as
such, rather than the rediscovery of some long-lost principle.

In political thought, there has always been tension between
those who believe the universe is ordered and that order can be
determined and shared, such as the idealistic traditions of Plato,
Aristotle, Aquinas, and Descartes, and those who believe that any
such order is fleeting and contingent, such as Augustine, Kelsen,
and Hart. While American constitutional law is identified with
the first school, American political thought is marked by the second. This dichotomy is manifested in the various views of *Agins*.

§ 17.3   *The Place of* Agins *in Subsequent Takings Cases*

Echeverria is correct to say that, while *Penn Central* has been cited more often in takings cases than *Agins*, it is the test in the latter case that has been most frequently relied upon by the Supreme Court.[68] Notwithstanding the cobbling together of a talismanic test from an amalgam of a series of more discredited and confused doctrines, the *Agins* alternative has provided an alternative takings precedent by the Court.

§ 17.3(a) *First Fruits:* Nollan *and* Dolan

The facts in *Nollan* were considerably different from those in most of the preceding takings cases. There was no question of a complete, or even substantial, denial of economic value. Rather, the California Coastal Commission granted a permit to the Nollans to allow them to replace a small bungalow on their beachfront lot with a larger house, which had the effect of blocking public views of the beach, only so long as, in return, they allowed an easement to the public to pass across their land, which was located between two public beaches. In other words, it was a situation where the commission offered to allow new development on the Nollans's land in return for a burden on it in favor of the public. The Nollans claimed such a condition was a taking, and the Supreme Court, Justice Scalia writing for the majority, agreed.

Justice Scalia relied on the first test in *Agins*, that a regulation must "substantially advance a legitimate state interest," to find the commission's action unlawful. He embellished the test with a new requirement: an "essential nexus" must exist between the interest relied upon by the state and the regulation made pursuant to that interest:

> The evident constitutional propriety disappears, however, if the condition substituted for the prohibition utterly fails to further the end advanced as the justification for the prohibition. . . . [t]he lack of nexus between the condition and the original purpose of the building restriction converts that purpose to something other than what it was. The purpose then becomes, quite simply, the obtaining of an easement to serve some valid governmental purpose, but without payment of compensation. Whatever may be the outer limits of "legitimate state interests" in the takings and land-use context, this is not one of them. In short, unless the permit condition serves the same governmental purpose as the development ban, the

building restriction is not a valid regulation of land use but "an out-and-out plan of extortion."[69]

If there were any doubt that the first test in *Agins* brought back the discredited doctrine of substantive due process, this use of the test must end that doubt. Not only does it mean that judges have the power to determine what is a "legitimate state interest," they can also determine whether this interest is properly pursued.[70] If, as here, the general interest is clearly public access to the beach, a regulation that seeks to enhance that interest in one way can be found unconstitutional where its precise requirements do not match its justifications to the satisfaction of the judge. Of course, the extent to which they do match will be an issue on which reasonable people will disagree, one that is best left to politicians and voters rather than judges. That is the problem with substantive due process.

In his strong dissent, Justice Brennan (with Justice Marshall concurring) advances many of these criticisms without quite grappling with the fundamental problem, the way in which the *Agins* Court reintroduced the substantive due process test. He argues that even if the essential nexus "cramped standard" is applied, the condition imposed corresponds to the type of burden created by the Nollans's development and that it does not raise the concerns underlying the development of the Takings Clause in previous cases (mostly *Pennsylvania Coal*). Fundamentally, he argues, the narrow concept of rationality advanced by Justice Scalia has long since been discredited as a judicial arrogation of legislative authority, citing Chief Justice Hughes in *Sproles v. Binford*:[71]

To make scientific precision a criterion of constitutional power would be to subject the State to an intolerable supervision hostile to the basic principles of our government.[72]

Sproles involved an unsuccessful substantive due process challenge to a Texas law regulating the maximum weight of vehicles to be allowed on Texas roads. It was, of course, decided during the *Lochner* period, in which the Supreme Court enthusiastically embraced the doctrine of substantive due process as a means to strike down judicially disfavored state action. Justice Brennan's reliance on the case in his dissent in *Nollan* illustrates the extent to which he perceives Justice Scalia not only resurrected but attempted to extend, with his "nexus" requirement, substantive due process even further than the *Lochner* Court had.

Yet, things were still to be taken one stage further. The Supreme Court in *Dolan v. City of Tigard*[73] upheld the test in *Nollan*, but added a further obstacle for government regulation. Even if an "essential nexus" had been achieved, the Court held there was a burden on government to show that the condition it imposed was "related both in nature and extent to the impact of the proposed development."[74] This "rough proportionality" test increases further the legislative power of the Court. The dissent of Justice Stevens (who was joined by Justices Blackmun and Ginsburg) argued that no takings had occurred in *Dolan*. The condition placed on the Dolans was in return for approval of their plans to develop, and that approval could be seen as compensation, but the Court did not scrutinize this element. Instead, there was a heightened scrutiny, of the substantive due process type, of the government conditions alone. The use of the Takings Clause against regulations dating back to *Pennsylvania Coal* and the discredited doctrine of substantive due process meet up to produce the same results:

> The so-called "regulatory takings doctrine that the Holmes" dictum kindled has an obvious kinship with the line of substantive due process cases that *Lochner* exemplified. Besides having similar ancestry, both doctrines are potentially open-ended sources of judicial power to invalidate state economic regulations that Members of this Court view as unwise or unfair.[75]

§ 17.3(b) *The Use of* Agins *in* Lucas

It was Justice Scalia, once again, who demonstrated the powerful impact of *Agins* in extending the uncertain doctrine of regulatory takings with his majority judgment in *Lucas*. In this case, it was the second test in *Agins* that was relied on to show a taking. This fact on its own highlights how the two tests in *Agins* became alternatives, dramatically expanding the scope of the Takings Clause. Just as *Nollan* had presented no question of the relevant condition denying the property owner all or substantially all the economically beneficial use of his land, there was no question in *Lucas* that the regulation did not substantially pursue legitimate state interests. Justice Scalia, for the 5-4 majority, stated:

> We think, in short, that there are good reasons for our frequently expressed belief that when the owner of real property has been called upon to sacrifice all economically beneficial uses in the name of the common good,

that is, to leave his property economically idle, he has suffered a taking.[76]

Lucas has become the leading case on "regulatory takings" and stands for the basic proposition that a regulation that denies the owner substantial economic use of his land will amount to a taking regardless of other concerns, such as legitimate public interests. At first, this test appears both broader and narrower than the three-factor test in *Penn Central*. On the one hand, the requirement that the regulation must eliminate all, or at least virtually all, the value of the land before it can be considered a taking creates a higher threshold than the economic impact one in *Penn Central*. Furthermore, it is irrelevant if it appears to be a taking based on the other factors of the test (particularly the character of the regulation), as it will only be compensable if it has an economically devastating consequence. On the other hand, it ignores the dicta in *Penn Central*, rejecting the idea that "diminution in property value, standing alone, can establish a 'taking.'"[77] The decision is the opposite, that diminution in property value standing alone, so long as it is a (near) total diminution, is the only way to certainly establish a taking. This shifts the ground toward an examination of the property owner's interest, which is easier for that owner to satisfy than the *Penn Central* test, which requires a balance between public and private interests. In so doing, it relies exclusively on the second test in *Agins*.

However, to some extent, *Lucas* incorporates the test in *Penn Central* for what Justice Scalia describes as landowners "whose deprivation is one step short of complete." In the now notorious footnote 8, he states:

> Such an owner might not be able to claim the benefit of our categorical formulation, but, as we have acknowledged time and again, "[t]he economic impact of the regulation on the claimant and . . . the extent to which the regulation has interfered with distinct investment-backed expectations" are keenly relevant to takings analysis generally. *Penn Central Transportation Co. v. New York City*. It is true that in *at least some* cases the landowner with 95 percent loss will get nothing, while the landowner with total loss will recover in full. But that occasional result is no more strange than the gross disparity between the landowner whose premises are taken for a highway (who recovers in full) and the landowner whose property is reduced to 5 percent of its former

value by the highway (who recovers nothing). Takings
law is full of these "all-or-nothing" situations.[78] (Emphasis added.)

Despite these all-or-nothing situations, what the note makes
clear is that after *Lucas*, landowners who suffer total loss in the
economic use of their land will automatically recover compensation for a taking, and landowners who have suffered great loss
have an opportunity to recover, applying the *Penn Central* test.
Thus, the effect of *Lucas* is to increase significantly the number
of claimants who will be successful in a takings claim.

Indeed, in *Florida Rock*,[79] the Court of Federal Claims understood that the *Lucas* test applied to total takings, whereas the
Penn Central test applied to "partial takings." Applying the three-
factor test in *Florida Rock*, the court held there had been a taking
even though the diminution of economic value was found to be
73.1 percent.[80]

Echeverria's analysis in his critique of *Penn Central* has a
somewhat different interpretation.[81] He argues that the effect of
the footnote means that those who have lost "substantially all" of
the economic value of their land may claim a regulatory taking.[82]
Thus he attempts to suggest, rather unpersuasively, that Justice
Scalia did not mean to apply the *Penn Central* test but meant to
include land-use deprivation of 95 percent within the category of
loss of total economic value. He then states:

. . . this relatively narrow, concise takings test avoids the
numerous problems created by the *Penn Central* three-
factor test.[83]

In one sense, this is true. The apparent "categorical" test based
on diminution of value is clearer than an uncertain balancing exercise between less definite factors. But it follows from a literal
interpretation of Justice Scalia's footnote that *Lucas* is in fact
broader than *Penn Central* in that it adopts the three-factor test
for "partial takings," while giving automatic relief where the loss
is 100 percent. Furthermore, the main problem with both tests is
the misuse of the Takings Clause in the Fifth Amendment against
otherwise valid regulations. Echeverria recognizes that regulations can positively affect the property value of the regulated
land by protecting services and amenities that help create property value.[84] This concept is ignored in *Lucas*.

Echeverria makes the same point in relation to the second test
in *Agins*:

> . . . Supreme Court regulatory takings precedents are generally consistent with the idea that takings doctrine should be limited to cases involving total (or near total) loss . . . this understanding of the basic test of a regulatory taking is similar to if not completely identical to the second prong of the *Agins* test, thereby offering at least a partial resolution of the confusion between the three-factor *Penn Central* test and the two-factor *Agins* test.[85]

Finally, he states that:

> Determining whether a regulation has eliminated all (or nearly all) economic value of a property presents a relatively simple and straightforward issue.[86]

I respectfully submit that this argument is misconceived. Does all the economic value include the value recoverable by sale of the land? If so, it is unlikely that a valid regulation will ever eliminate all economic value. Justice Scalia's formulation of "all economically beneficial use" of the land in *Lucas* and Justice Powell's use of the words "economically viable use of his land" in *Agins* suggest economic value only relates to the use the owner can make. But why should this be? If it were so, then surely the regulations in *Mugler* would be takings. This point was aptly made in the dissent of Justice Blackmun in *Lucas*:

> When the government regulation prevents the owner from any economically valuable use of his property, the private interest is unquestionably substantial, but we have never before held that no public interest can outweigh it.[87]

The failure to even consider the public interest in *Lucas* makes the takings doctrine broader rather than narrower. This expansion was made worse by Justice Scalia's rewriting of the nuisance exception to takings that turned 150 years of nuisance law on its head.

§ 17.4   Constitutional Interpretation and Doctrinal Consistency

It is my thesis that the central problem with the decisions on takings, particularly those based on the *Agins* analysis, is the way in which the discredited doctrine of substantive due process has been reintroduced. This is quite self-evident with the first test in *Agins*, the origins of which are indeed the substantive due process cases, but it is also the case with the second test, concerning the economic diminution of value. This test can be traced back, via *Penn Central* and *Nectow*, to Justice Holmes's decision in *Pennsylvania Coal* that a regulation becomes a taking when it goes "too far" in terms of the diminution of value. What constitutes "too far," just like what substantially advances a legitimate state aim, is a subjective, ultimately political, question. As Justice Blackmun stated in *Williamson County*:

> Those who argue that excessive regulation should be considered a violation of the Due Process Clause rather than a "taking" assert that *Pennsylvania Coal* used the word "taking" not in the literal Fifth Amendment sense, but as a metaphor for actions having the same effect as a taking by eminent domain.[88]

The blurring between substantive due process and the Takings Clause is not made clearer by the economic test in *Agins* or *Lucas*. What constitutes a total diminution of economically beneficial use is itself a subjective, vague, and value-laden test, which can be hard to calculate. Why must it be economically beneficial and not include the whole economic value? What about the fact that land-use regulation generally benefits the regulated land? The problem with the doctrine of regulatory takings, as it has emerged, is the way in which it masks essentially judicial preferences in constitutional language—the precise problem that existed with substantive due process.

Justice Scalia formally rejects the doctrine of substantive due process, both on grounds of its intellectual unsoundness and because it has been relied upon in the abortion decisions he opposes. Yet, as the chief champion and developer of the *Agins* reintroduction of substantive due process, his theory and practice are in conflict.

A consideration of his 1989 Oliver Wendell Holmes, Jr., lecture on "The Rule of Law as a Law of Rules" demonstrates this proposition.[89] Justice Scalia outlines an essentially orthodox theory of constitutional interpretation in favor of "general rules of law" and against a "discretion conferring approach." In so doing, he advances six core arguments: (1) *the Principle of Equality and Justice*: that like cases should be treated alike and not in a discriminatory fashion;[90] (2) *the Principle of Practicality:* the fact that the Supreme Court can only review an insignificant proportion of decided cases (1/20th of 1 percent of all cases decided by federal district courts; one-half of 1 percent of all cases decided by federal courts of appeal);[91] (3) *the Principle of Predictability:* that those subject to the law should know what it prescribes;[92] (4) *the Principle of Judicial Constraint:* for governing principle over arbitrary and subjective decision making;[93] (5) *the Principle of Emboldenment*—giving judges the courage to stand up to the majority will, because they rely on principle;[94] and (6) *the Pronouncement of Law over the Mere Finding of Fact*—the former being the proper function of the judge, the latter the main process involved in the discretion-conferring approach.[95]

Yet, if we consider these six laudable rationales for the general rule-of-law approach in relation to Justice Scalia's own reasoning on takings in *Lucas* in particular, and in relation to the same methodology in *Agins,* then it is apparent that the dangers of a masked discretion-conferring approach are very real.

In relation to:

1. *The Principle of Equality and Justice.* It is difficult to determine by Justice Scalia's test whether a taking has occurred. Some results will be neither predictable nor fair. In particular, a rigid application of the 100 percent beneficial-taking requirement, often suggested as the most consistent interpretation of *Lucas*, means that where a landowner suffers 95 or 99 percent beneficial loss because of regulations, she has no remedy. But where she suffers that extra 1 or 5 percent loss, she has a complete remedy. Justice Scalia addresses this very criticism in footnote 8 of *Lucas* and concludes that, "[t]akings law is full of these 'all-or-nothing' situations."[96] From the standpoint of justice and equality, a landowner should either be compensated for his loss, depending on the level of that loss, and not on whether it has been total or substantial, or he should not be compensated at all. To allow some to win "all" and many "nothing" simply because of incidental circumstances of the case is unjust and, yet, it follows directly from an application of the "categorical" test in *Lucas* and the second test in *Agins.*[97] The answer here may well be a political and legislative one, with the Court practicing restraint.

2. *The Principle of Practicality.* By allowing claims for regulatory takings, the quantity of litigation on behalf of landowners trying to obstruct any interference with the desired use of their land has dramatically increased. In particular, there have been a number of Supreme Court cases on the matter. Because of the vague and arbitrary approach inherent in the regulatory takings method (going back to the dictum of Justice Holmes in *Pennsylvania Coal* that regulation should not go "too far"), each case has been determined on its particular circumstances.

Therefore, new takings cases continue to take up Supreme Court time, and each particular case fails to lay down a principle that could stem this tide. Thus, after *Penn Central*, there were those cases, like *Williamson*,[98] that appeared to use ripeness devices to avoid considering takings claims. However, the confusion in *Agins* makes such control more difficult. *Nollan* arose out of the first test in *Agins*, and *Lucas* from the second test. Finally, there is the case of the utmost confusion, *Eastern Enterprises*, discussed below, where attempts were made to stretch the Takings Clause to all government regulations, not just those concerned with land use.

3. *The Principle of Predictability.* It follows that there is therefore no predictability. Which test applies? Does the test only apply to regulation of land use or is it primarily about regulation that leads to economic loss? How is economic loss measured? How can it be determined whether the property owner should have expected such regulation and, therefore, not have a legitimate claim for compensation? All these questions remain unanswered. Furthermore, it is government, in particular, that should be able to predict the legal consequences of the regulations as it is government that makes them. It is even more difficult for government to predict whether a particular regulation it makes will cause a particular landowner 100 percent loss, for instance. Must government ask the property owner first? If so, then it is pretty certain the property would always claim substantial loss, and the only "prediction" we could safely make is that land regulation would become either impossible or a legal minefield.

4. *The Principle of Judicial Constraint.* As already noted, the principle behind takings is to compensate for physical appropriation. Once this is replaced with compensating for loss caused as a consequence of something done in the interests of the general welfare, subjectivity is bound to become a problem. The reintroduction of substantive due process in defining the legitimacy of government action (*Agins*) and Justice Scalia's redefinition of the nuisance exception in *Lucas* are examples. To decide that certain types of regulation are not takings— because they made up part of the body of common-law nuisance in some bygone age—while deciding that others are, is not constraint. To hold that judges can burden government with liability to pay compensation to property owners if they think there is not a sufficient "nexus" between a government's regulation and its actual effect (*Nollan*) is the opposite of judicial constraint.

5. *The Principle of Emboldenment*. Judges ought to be more emboldened to challenge takings, even when carried out by an elected and accountable authority. They should do so when they clearly infringe the principle behind the doctrine (prohibition of physical appropriation without compensation), not when they decide the regulation goes too far in its effect on the property owner's economic beneficial use of the land. In such a case, their decisions appear much more political and can be interpreted as a much greater challenge to democracy. Judges truly sensitive to such concerns would not feel emboldened by being put in such a position.

6. *The Pronouncement of Law over the Mere Finding of Fact*. If the law had been pronounced, rather than judges engaging in an exercise of unprincipled fact-finding and relying on broadly based and discredited discretion-conferring doctrines of law to reinterpret the law of takings at every turning point, then the stream of takings cases to the courts would have ebbed a long time ago.

Justice Scalia's practice of discarding or twisting beyond recognition constitutional principles and longstanding precedent (as with the "nuisance exception") to fit particular circumstances where a property owner suffers as a result of legitimate government regulations is in sharp conflict with his theory of placing principle above a discretion-conferring approach.

The *Agins* test of whether a regulation substantially advances a legitimate state interest or denies an owner economically viable use of land is highly manipulable. In place of general rules of law, it allows the Constitution to be used and interpreted in a discretion-conferring manner that reflects the political leanings of the judges involved, yet provides the defense that the judge is the impartial applicator of the law.

§ 17.5   *The Circle Closes:* Eastern Enterprises v. Apfel

Eastern Enterprises should not have had anything to do with takings at all. It involved a challenge to a federal statute that made companies formerly engaged in mining liable for health care for their former employees. There was no question of land being taken or even regulated. Nevertheless, the Supreme Court struck down the statute as unconstitutional, although there was no majority as to the grounds for doing so. The plurality opinion (of Justice O'Connor, the Chief Justice, and Justices Scalia and Thomas) found a violation of the Takings Clause of the Fifth Amendment. They applied the three-factor test in *Penn Central* to find that the relationship between the black lung disease suffered by the former miners was not known at the time the various agreements were entered. Thus, the federal statute was retrospective legislation, and the Takings Clause was the remedy against such legislation. Furthermore, they found that there was no legitimate expectation of lifetime security arising out of union agreements or national legislation at the time the miners were employed by the company. They concluded that:

> In enacting the Coal Act, Congress was responding to a serious problem with the funding of health benefits for retired coal miners. While we do not question Congress' power to address that problem, the solution it crafted improperly places a severe, disproportionate, and extremely retroactive burden on Eastern. Accordingly, we conclude that the Coal Act's allocation of liability to Eastern violates the Takings Clause. . . . [99]

Four Justices dissented as to the holding and the analysis under the Takings Clause (Stevens, Souter, Ginsburg, and Breyer), while Justice Kennedy disagreed with the plurality opinion on the grounds that the statute could not be a taking, but agreed that the statute was unconstitutional on substantive due process grounds. Thus, the 5-4 final decision found the Coal Industry Retiree Health Benefit Act of 1992 (Coal Act) unconstitutional; however, five of the Justices also held it was not a taking.

This confused decision demonstrates the central argument made in this chapter. First, the plurality opinion's extension of takings to cover a regulation that imposed financial liability on the profits of a company shows just how far Justice Scalia and others are prepared to go in extending the takings doctrine (especially to avoid substantive due process). It had never been argued before that the Takings Clause of the Fifth Amendment applied to monetary property (in addition to real and perhaps intellectual property), and indeed by one vote, the Court in *Eastern Enterprises* did not feel able to extend the doctrine this far. Of course, such an extension makes clear the way in which the Takings Clause has simply become a substitute for substantive due process. If the kind of regulation at issue in *Eastern Enterprises* could be classified as a taking, then it is difficult to comprehend any kind of government regulation involving money that could not be so classified. A federal minimum wage law is a good example. Requiring a private employer to pay its employees more than is already being paid could be interpreted, applying the plurality opinion in *Eastern Enterprises*, as a monetary taking. And it was precisely this kind of use of substantive due process during the *Lochner* era that brought that doctrine and the courts into such disrepute.

In his dissent, Justice Kennedy argued that:

> If the plurality is adopting its novel and expansive concept of a taking in order to avoid making a normative judgment about the Coal Act, it fails in the attempt; for it must make the normative judgment in all events. The imprecision of our regulatory takings doctrine does open the door to normative considerations about the wisdom of government decisions. This sort of analysis is in uneasy tension with our basic understanding of the Takings Clause, which has not been understood to be a substantive or absolute limit on the government's power to act. The clause operates as a conditional limitation, permitting the government to do what it wants so long as it pays the charge. The clause presupposes what the government intends to do is otherwise unconstitutional.[100]

Justice Kennedy thus accuses the plurality of being just as subjective and normative in their use of the Takings Clause. However, Justice Kennedy could, in turn, be accused of the same subjective jurisprudence in relying on substantive due process. Justice Kennedy has at least the virtue of consistency in relying on the "well settled. . . principles" of this later doctrine![101]

This is the second point to come from *Eastern Enterprises*, and further reinforces the conclusion that the Takings Clause (as applied by Justice Scalia and as promulgated in the second test in *Agins)* and the discredited doctrine of substantive due process (promulgated in the first test in *Agins)* are but two different labels for the same exercise of judicial discretionary interference with government. In *Nollan* and *Lucas*, the different doctrines were used, both disguised as part of the Takings Clause to find a violation of the Constitution. In *Eastern Enterprises*, the Justices have a disagreement amongst themselves over how to label the process on which the Court was embarking. Justice Scalia's reticence to rely openly on substantive due process coincided with Justice Kennedy's lack of stomach to extend the Takings Clause so far from its constitutional roots. But the result is the same, and it is the modern application, partly under a different name, of *Lochner*'s substantive due process.[102]

One alternative to the unwelcome revival of substantive due process might involve a reconsideration of the Privileges and Immunities Clause based on the *Slaughterhouse* cases.[103] Justice

Miller, writing for the majority, said that the first sentence of the Fourteenth Amendment provided that "all persons born. . . in the United States. . . are citizens of the United States and of the state wherein they reside."[104] Thus, the Court reasoned, the Privileges and Immunities Clause referred to "citizens of the United States" and only pertained to aspects of national citizenship, such as access to the nation's seaports. That provision did not include rights to engage in a slaughtering business in New Orleans.

Such a proposed application has the benefit of most properly reflecting the intentions behind the Fourteenth Amendment (to guarantee protection for disadvantaged and potentially victimized citizens). Moreover, it offers special protection to the fundamental human rights of the individual, rather than operating as a tool for the more powerful, and avoidance of the kind of subjective judicial legislation that was associated with substantive due process. Such an approach would clearly separate out issues of takings from the Fourteenth Amendment and leave such issues to be dealt with under the Fifth Amendment, where again, it is argued, the original intention of which should be applied. After the *Slaughterhouse* cases, development of the Privileges and Immunities Clause ceased. This was a missed opportunity for protection of citizens against the states.

§ 17.6   Conclusion

A physical invasion of private property or acquisition of title by government should certainly be compensable. This is the purpose of the Takings Clause of the Fifth Amendment. But mere regulation of property—whatever the consequence of that regulation—is necessary for society to function and is not per se unconstitutional. An application of the "regulatory takings" doctrine to other spheres of social life would mean that the minimum wage, limitations on working hours, prohibitions on racial or sexual discrimination, all taxes, and so on may be construed as unconstitutional takings of private property under the Scalia approach, for which the state would have to compensate.[105] In Justice Stevens's dissent in *Lucas*,[106] he suggests that not so long ago slavery was considered a valid form of property within the United States. He goes on to say that society's common understanding and definition of property and what a property owner may legitimately do with his own property is subject to constant change. Justice Scalia's regulatory takings doctrine imposes a judicial veto over both the nature and extent of regulation, both as to its ends and means. To that extent, that doctrine is substantive due process in other garb, equally offensive to the relationship of the branches by whatever name. The result is self-evidently incompatible with a society that shares a flexible and evolving comprehension of property and property rights.

It must surely be true that not all state regulation is valid. There are, of course, those regulations that clearly infringe on the Constitution—for instance, a city council regulation saying that all properties that display Republican posters during an election will have to pay a special tax would be invalid as it would violate fundamental First Amendment rights. The argument against the Scalia doctrine of "regulatory takings" is that where there is no clear breach of the Constitution, it is unacceptable to rewrite the Constitution to suit a certain political ideology.

There also may be regulatory exercises that are invalid because they are outside the authority's competence to undertake them. Consider a regulation that prohibited owners from painting the outside walls of their property white within a one-mile radius of a city center. This may seem an obviously absurd example, but it illustrates the fact that there must be regulations that make distinctions without any basis, rational or otherwise. In that event, the Equal Protection Clause may be of some avail.[107] Of course, if all white paint were found to include a chemical that caused health problems, the regulation would no longer be so unreasonable. Even if the houses were part of a street of historic buildings that were traditionally painted red, a regulation meant to preserve such an historic site by prohibiting certain houses from being painted white or other clashing colors may be considered quite valid. Thus, one cannot determine a priori the specific type of regulation that may be lawful. Ultimately, whether a government can make such regulation depends on the authority the people have given it. If the majority of people in California want regulations to ban smoking in all property that has public access (that is, including private bars and restaurants), then prima facie, that regulation is reasonable, and the state is competent to make it. Chief Justice Shaw put it best over 100 years ago in the Massachusetts case of *Alger*[108] when he said public authorities had the power to:

> make, ordain and establish all manner of wholesome
> and reasonable laws, statutes and ordinances, either with
> penalties or without, not repugnant to the constitution,
> as they shall jud ge to be for the good and welfare of the
> commonwealth, and of the subjects of the same.[109]

Foreign jurisdictions do not have the problems we seem to have with government regulation. In fact, no other country's judiciary branch uses constitutionality as a device for judicial intervention against land-use regulation. As Byrne demonstrates in his thorough survey of international land-use law:

> Whether in the common law jurisdictions, European civil law jurisdictions, or the emerging nations of Eastern Europe and Asia, the law frankly accepts the necessity of extensive government regulation of land use. Other nations award compensation to owners only according to statutory standards or in cases of outright expropriation or reversal of site-specific planning permission. The peculiar importance of constitutional judicial review in general in the United States cannot explain the uniqueness of our approach to regulatory takings.[110]

But the "unique" American approach is itself an aberration. Regulatory takings were never mentioned in or dealt with by the Constitution. The early caselaw demonstrates that the Court did not assume the authority to intervene against legitimate government action. Justice Holmes's "rewriting" of the Constitution in *Pennsylvania Coal* was as uncharacteristic of the law at the time as it was of that eminent judge. It should never have been followed, as it never had a real constitutional basis.

The resurrection of *Pennsylvania Coal* and of substantive due process is a relatively recent phenomenon that began in cases that never found a taking. The vague dicta in *Penn Central* and the later unnecessary formulation of a test in *Agins*, which incorporated the fundamental error of *Pennsylvania Coal* and substantive due process, have since been relied on by those who seek to use the law against government. It may be time to take politics out of the hands of the judges and put it back where it belongs, in the hands of the people, except in the case of a clearly recognized constitutional error. Land-use regulation affects everyone in a given locality, and it must reflect the needs, wishes, and various trends of the particular population it seeks to serve. It is time to face *Agins* and this dressing-up of substantive due process for what it is and to reject it. Judicial activism is no more desirable because it has taken a turn to the right.

In the end, however, *Agins* is only a more recent example of how the courts use and manipulate vague phrases of the Constitution to meet their own ends. These manipulations are, in turn, used as a mask for advancement of a political or social agenda. By understanding judging as an extension of politics, we will be able to understand and confront our problems, rather than simply to accept judicial pronouncements as if they were commandments handed down from distant oracles.

Notes

1. J. Echeverria, *Is the* Penn Central *Three-Factor Test Ready for History's Dustbin?*, 1 LAND USE LAW & ZONING DIG. 3, Jan. 2000.

2. 438 U.S.104 (1978).

3. 447 U.S. 255 (1980).

4. 524 U.S. 498 (1998).

5. *See* Sullivan & Leeson, *Property, Philosophy and Regulation: The Case Against a Natural Law Theory of Property Rights*, 17 WILLAMETTE L. REV. 527 (1981).

6. See the videotaped statement of Justice Thomas, shortly after the Court decided *Gore v. Bush*, 121 S. Ct. 525 (2000), to the effect that the conservative majority of that Court decides cases without reference to politics, which may be the most recent and cynical unfurling of the banner of the value-free jurisprudence espoused by judges as a mask for deciding cases according to their own ideologies by "constitutional interpretation."

7. Dred Scott v. Sanford, 60 U.S. 393 (1856).

8. Plessy v. Ferguson, 163 U.S. 537 (1896).

9. Wainright v. Adams, 466 U.S. 964 (1984); Sullivan v. Wainright, 464 U.S. 109 (1983). The Court thought much better of the constitutional claim, however, when it was raised by the conservative political candidate in *Gore v. Bush, supra* note 6.

10. U.S. CONST. amend. V (Fifth Amendment to the Constitution of the United States of America, ratified on Dec. 15,1791). It is indeed surprising that in the 131 years between this ratification and *Pennsylvania Coal Co. v. Mahon*, 260 U.S. 393 (1922), no court discovered Justice Holmes's reasoning that regulatory takings were to be included within the Fifth Amendment, and even more surprising that no U.S. Supreme Court questioned Holmes's wisdom in that regard for another 56 years.

11. J.F. Hart, *Colonial Land Use and Its Significance for Modern Takings Doctrine*, 109 HARV. L. REV. 1252, at 1291 (1996).

12. *See* F. BOSSELMAN ET AL., THE TAKING ISSUE: AN ANALYSIS OF THE CONSTITUTIONAL LIMITS OF LAND USE CONTROL (COUNCIL ON ENVIRONMENTAL QUALITY 1973).

13. "That private property ought to be subservient to public uses when necessity requires it; nevertheless, whenever any particular man's property is taken for the use of the public, the owner ought to receive the equivalent in money."

14. "No person shall be subject, except in cases of impeachment, to more than one punishment or one trial for the same offense; nor shall he be compelled to be a witness against himself; nor be deprived of life, liberty, or property without due process of law; nor be obliged to relinquish his property, where it may be necessary for the public use, without a just compensation."

15. 45 Fed. Cl. 21 (1999).

16. *Id.* at 24-25.

17. *See* Presbyterian Church v. The City of New York, 5 Cow. 538 (New York 1826), Coates v. The Mayor, Alderman and Commonalty of New York, 7 Cow. 585 (New York 1827).

18. 61 Mass. 53 (1851).

19. *Id.* at 84-86. Compare this excerpt to the strikingly similar dissent of Justice Brandeis in *Pennsylvania Coal, supra* note 11, at 417-18:

Every restriction upon the use of property imposed in the exercise of the police power deprives the owner of some right theretofore enjoyed, and is in that sense, an abridgment by the state of rights in property without making compensation. But restriction imposed to protect the public health, safety or morals from dangers threatened is not a taking. The restriction here in question is merely the prohibition of a noxious use. The property so restricted remains in the possession of its owner. The state does not appropriate it or make any use of it. The state merely prevents the owner from making a use which interferes with paramount rights of the public. . . . The restriction upon the use of this property cannot, of course, be lawfully imposed, unless its purpose is to protect the public. . . . Restriction upon use does not become inappropriate as a means, merely because it deprives the owner of the only use to which the property can be profitably put. The liquor and the oleomargarine cases settled that.

20. 123 U.S. 623 (1887).

21. *Id.* at 668-69. Of course, that benighted Court could not have foreseen the blinding intellect of Justice Scalia, who disposed of this precedent in *Lucas v. South Carolina Coastal Council*, 505 U.S. 1003 (1992), while claiming to follow it. *See id.* at 1022-26.

22. 127 U.S. 678 (1888).

23. Pennsylvania Coal Co. v. Mahon, 260 U.S. 393 (1922).

24. Bosselman et al., *supra* note 12, at 124.

25. *Id.* at 413. Presumably, one can assume the power to make this distinction by donning black robes.

26. *See especially* Justice Holmes's dissent in *Lochner v. New York*, 198 U.S. 45, 64 (1905), at 75-76. *See also West Coast Hotel Co. v. Parrish*, 300 U.S. 379 (1937), and *United States v. Carolene Prods. Co.*, 304 U.S. 144, 153 n. 4 (1938), in which the Court distanced itself from the doctrine of substantive due process.

27. 277 U.S. 183 (1928).

28. Agins v. City of Tiburon, 477 U.S. 255, 260 (1980). The second test in *Agins* relates to "economically viable use of [the landowner's] land" and is dealt with below.

29. 272 U.S. 365 (1926).

30. *Nectow,* 277 U.S. at 187-88, *citing Euclid,* 272 U.S. 365.

31. *Penn Central*, 438 U.S. at 124.

32. J. Echeverria, *supra* note 1, at 10.

33. *Penn Central*, 438 U.S. 104 (1978).

34. *Agins*, 477 U.S. at 260.

35. *Id.*

36. 473 U.S. 172 (1985).

37. *Id.* at 186.

38. 480 U.S. 470 (1987).

39. *Id.* at 495. Note the similarity between the first paragraph cited and the excerpt from *Penn Central*, 438 U.S.

40. 485 U.S. 1 (1988).

41. *Id.* at 9-10, per Chief Justice Rehnquist (Justices Brennan, White, Marshall, Blackmun, and Stephens concurring).

42. R. Meltz, D. Merriam & R. Frank, The Takings Issue—Constitutional Limits on Land Use Control and Environmental Regulation 114 (Island Press 1999).

43. Note the scarcity of the choice of precedent in the years after *Euclid* and *Nectow* and until *Penn Central*.

44. *Pennell,* 485 U.S. at 18-19.

45. *Agins,* 477 U.S. at 260.

46. *Penn Central,* 438 U.S. at 138.

47. J. Byrne, *Ten Arguments for the Abolition of the Regulatory Takings Doctrine,* 22 ECOLOGY L.Q. 89, at 104 (1995); A. L. Peterson, *The Takings Clause: In Search of Underlying Principles,* 77 CAL. L. REV. 1299, at 1330-33 (1989); J. Echeverria, *supra* note 1, at 5.

48. Georgia Outdoor Advertising Inc. v. City of Waynesville, 900 F.2d 783, 787 (4th Cir. 1990).

49. Reahard v. Lee County, 968 F.2d 1131, 1136 (11th Cir. 1992).

50. *Agins,* 477 U.S. at 260.

51. J. Byrne, *supra* note 47.

52. *Id.*

53. J. Echeverria, *Does a Regulation That Fails to Advance a Legitimate Governmental Interest Result in a Regulatory Taking?,* 29 ENVTL. L. 853, Winter 1999, Takings Law Symposium.

54. R. Epstein, *Takings: Descent and Resurrection,* 1987 SUP. CT. REV. 1 at 5.

55. A.S. McCaskey, *Comment: Thesis and Antithesis of Liberty of Contract: Excess in Lochner and Johnson Controls,* SETON HALL CONST. L.J. 409, Fall 1993.

56. M.S. McUsic, *The Ghost of Lochner: Modern Takings Doctrine and Its Impact on Economic Legislation,* 76 B.U.L. REV. 605, Oct. 1996.

57. A.L. Peterson, *supra* note 47, at 1328-29.

58. G.E. Summers, Comment: *Private Property Without Lochner: Toward a Takings Jurisprudence Uncorrupted by Substantive Due Process,* 142 U. PA. L. REV. 837, Fall 1993.

59. W.W. Wade, *Penn Central's Economic Failings Confounded Takings Jurisprudence,* 31 URB. LAW. 277, Spring 1999.

60. J. Byrne, *supra* note 47, at 104.

61. J. Echeverria, *supra* note 53, at 858.

62. 483 U.S. 825 (1987).

63. McCaskey, *supra* note 55, at 473-74.

64. Summers, *supra* note 58, at 873.

65. E. Sullivan, *Reading the Entrails: Why the Supreme Court Did Not Strike Down Excessive Fees in* Ehrlich, 21 OR. REAL EST. LAND USE DIG., No. 3, 13 (July 1998).

66. 505 U.S. 833 (1992), at 944 and 979, respectively.

67. J. Byrne, *supra* note 47, at 104-06.

68. J. Echeverria, *supra* note 1, at 5.

69. *Nollan,* 483 U.S. at 837. For those many states that do not require findings to justify conditions requiring dedication of real property, *Nollan* appears to require such findings, thus imposing a procedural, as well as a substantive, burden on local governments.

70. Note that these are two parts of the three-part substantive due process test, *i.e.,* (i) legitimacy of the ends, (ii) legitimacy of the means, and (iii) whether the government's actions were unduly oppressive. Lawton v. Steele, 152 U.S. 133, 137 (1894).

71. 286 U.S. 374 at 388 (1932).

72. Cited in *Nollan,* 483 U.S. at 825 and 846.

73. 512 U.S. 374 (1994).

74. *Id.* at 391.

75. *Id.* at 406-07 (dissent).

76. *See Lucas*, 505 U.S. at 1019.

77. *Penn Central*, 438 U.S. at 131.

78. *Nollan*, 483 U.S. at 1019 n.8. *See also Florida Rock*, 45 Fed. Cl.

79. *Id.*

80. *Id.* at 76.

81. J. Echeverria, *supra* note 1.

82. *Id.* at 7.

83. *Id.* at 10.

84. *Id.* at 8.

85. *Id.* at 10.

86. *Id.* at 11.

87. *Lucas*, 505 U.S. at 1047.

88. *Williamson*, 473 U.S. at 198.

89. Scalia, A., *The Rule of Law as a Law of Rules*, 56 U. Chi. L. Rev. 1175 (1989).

90. *Id.* at 1178.

91. *Id.* at 1178-79.

92. *Id.* at 1179.

93. *Id.* at 1179-80.

94. *Id.* at 1180.

95. *Id.* at 1180-82.

96. *Lucas*, 505 U.S. at 1019 n.8.

97. Unless the Court decides to follow the interpretation of *Lucas* supported in *Florida Rock*, 45 Fed. Cl. 21 (1999).

98. *Williamson*, 473 U.S.

99. *Eastern Enterprises*, 524 U.S. at 538.

100. *Id.* at 544-45; *see also*, for a similar line of reasoning, S. Eagle, *Eastern Enterprises, Substantive Due Process, and a Coherent View of Regulatory Takings*, 51 Ala. L. Rev. 3 (Apr. 2000).

101. *Id.* at 547.

102. In an essay purportedly setting forth his own judicial philosophy, *The Rule of Law as a Law of Rules*, *supra* note 89, Justice Scalia suggests the elevation of principle judicial restraint, productivity, and pronouncement of law over fact-finding as paramount. *Id.* at 1178-82. Instead, the Court's recent takings cases appear to be result-driven and the product of judicial action in case selection. As Dwight Merriam has observed, perhaps it is mere coincidence that three of the most recent takings (*Dolan*, 512 U.S.; Suitum v. Tahoe Regional Planning Agency, 520 U.S. 725 (1997); and Village of Willowbrook v. Olech, 528 U.S. 562 (2000)) involved three widows, and their unique circumstances were used as a wedge to change takings law. The use of historical revisionism to demolish more than 100 years of the nuisance exception is more an exercise in raw power than respect for precedent.

103. 83 U.S. 36 (1872).

104. *Id.* at 80-81.

105. Indeed, if minimum wage laws were tested under Justice Scalia's test, they would almost inevitably be swept in by the Takings Clause. Is this not substantive due process in drag?

106. *Lucas*, 505 U.S. at 1068.

107.   The Court appears to have no difficulty in finding an equal protection violation when it is sufficiently offended by local land-use regulations. *Olech*, 528 U.S.; City of Cleburne v. Cleburne Living Center, 473 U.S. 432 (1985). However, as indicated above in notes 6 and 9, the Court's outrage is selective, and reliance upon it is akin to a "roll of the dice."

108   *Alger,* 61 Mass.

109.   *Id*. at 84-85.

110.   J. Byrne, *supra* note 47, at 106.

Defining the *Lucas* Box: *Palazzolo, Tahoe,* and the Use/Value Debate

18

Douglas T. Kendall*

§ 18.0　*Introduction*

The Supreme Court's ruling in *Lucas v. South Carolina Coastal Council*[1] creates a box: an (almost) categorical rule that regulations depriving landowners of "all economically beneficial uses" of their property constitute a taking.[2] Because landowners rarely prevail in takings claims evaluated under the multifactored inquiry established by *Penn Central Transportation Co. v. New York City,*[3] the dimensions of the *Lucas* box constitute an open takings question of the first magnitude. This question was at issue in the Supreme Court's last takings case, *Palazzolo v. Rhode Island,*[4] and it will be at the center of its next case, *Tahoe Sierra Preservation Council v. Tahoe Regional Planning Agency.*[5]

Government and developer advocates alike frame this debate in terms of whether *Lucas*'s per se rule is

---

* This chapter draws heavily from chapter 6 of Douglas T. Kendall, Timothy J. Dowling & Andrew W. Schwartz, Takings Litigation Handbook: Defending Takings Challenges to Land Use Regulations (American Legal Publishing, May 2000) (used with permission of the authors). To order the Handbook, call American Legal Publishing at 1-800-445-5588 or go to http://www.amlegal.com/tlh.htm.

about "use" or "value." Cognizant that even stringent regulation leaves land with some value, developer lawyers claim that *Lucas* is about "use" and, in particular, establishes some sort of right to develop vacant property. Recognizing that such a right to develop would be the death knell for many critical efforts to protect fragile ecosystems and open space, government advocates insist that *Lucas* is about protecting values, and significant value from any source will remove a claim from the confines of the *Lucas* box.

This purported dichotomy between "use" and "value" under *Lucas* is a false one. *Lucas* is not about use alone or value alone, it is about uses of property that create value. As a general matter, this is not a controversial proposition. The Supreme Court in *Lucas* and *Palazzolo*—the two cases that address the *Lucas* box— uses the terms use and value almost interchangeably. These cases make absolutely clear that *Lucas* applies only where a landowner is denied an "economically viable use" or, put more simply, where a landowner is denied a use that has value. Moreover, I presume that developer lawyers would argue that *Lucas* applies where developmental uses are permitted, but have little or no value.[6] In other words, at some level, I think everyone agrees that "value" is a factor in a *Lucas* analysis.

The real controversy about the size of the *Lucas* box concerns whether certain uses that create market value should nonetheless be excluded from the consideration of whether more than a "token" amount of market value remains. Developer lawyers argue that only "developmental uses" should be considered in evaluating whether a *Lucas* wipeout has transpired. Public-side advocates typically argue that any use—present, future, or speculative—that creates more than a token amount of market value defeats a *Lucas* claim.

Here again, I argue that there is less room for controversy than either side seems to think. For over two centuries, the Supreme Court has been deciding what uses can be examined in assessing value in the context of awarding just compensation under the Takings Clause. In cases such as *Olson v. United States*,[7] the Supreme Court has addressed whether:

> . . . the actual use and special adaptability of petitioners' shorelands. . . may be taken into consideration in ascertaining the just compensation to which petitioners are entitled.[8]

This is essentially the same question that faces the Supreme Court in cases such as *Tahoe Sierra Preservation Council (TSPC)*,[9] where developmental uses were prohibited during the course of two planning moratoria, but substantial value remained. In assessing TSPC's claim that this value should be ignored in evaluating its *Lucas* claim, the Supreme Court should look to its just compensation precedent.

The answer given by *Olson* and its progeny is a nuanced one that will not please developers or government lawyers all of the time. While most current and potential future uses must be considered, speculative, illegal, and governmental uses are frequently excluded even if there is evidence of remaining value for these purposes.

This chapter proceeds in three sections. First, it parses *Lucas* and *Palazzolo* and places these rulings in context within the Supreme Court's takings jurisprudence. This discussion highlights the logical and practical obstacles preventing adoption of either a developmental use only or a remaining value only touchstone in defining the *Lucas* box. The chapter then turns to *Olson* and the line of Supreme Court cases that address the question of what uses should be considered in ascertaining fair market value for the purposes of awarding just compensation. This discussion explains the relevance of these cases to the *Lucas* context and then summarizes the answers these cases provide for the most common *Lucas* use/value questions. The chapter concludes with an application of the *Olson* line of cases to the thorny *Lucas* questions raised (but not answered) in *Suitum v. TRPA*[10] and at issue in *TSPC*.

§ 18.1   *Overview of* Lucas

Under *Lucas*, a compensable taking occurs where government action denies a landowner all economically viable use of the land, unless the restrictions may be justified by reference to background principles of law.

The *Lucas* rule is a per se or categorical rule of liability because it requires compensation "without case-specific inquiry into the public interest advanced in support of the restraint."[11] In this respect, it is similar to the per se rule established in *Loretto v. Teleprompter Manhattan CATV Corp.*[12] for government-compelled, permanent physical occupations of property. Just as the *Loretto* Court described its per se rule as "very narrow,"[13] the *Lucas* Court characterized its per se rule as applying only in the "extraordinary circumstance" in which government action deprives land of all economically viable use.[14]

The legal authority and rationale for the *Lucas* per se rule remain somewhat clouded. Although the Court cited four cases as support for the rule, none of them actually applied such a rule to find a taking.[15] Nevertheless, the *Lucas* Court insisted that it was not inventing a new rule, but merely applying "a long established standard" of takings liability.[16] While acknowledging that it had never articulated a justification for this rule, the Court speculated that perhaps the rationale is "that total deprivation of beneficial use is, from the landowner's point of view, the equivalent of a physical appropriation."[17] *Lucas* also expressed concern that a complete deprivation of use creates "a heightened risk that private property is being pressed into some form of public service under the guise of mitigating serious public harm."[18] After noting that various federal and state statutes authorize eminent domain to acquire servitudes that prevent development, the Court concluded that these laws "suggest the practical equivalence in this setting of negative regulation and appropriation."[19] The Court further observed that because a total economic wipeout is "relatively rare," the per se rule does not threaten most government functions.[20]

Lucas limited its ruling in three important ways. First, the rule applies only where there has been a wipeout of *all* economically viable use.[21] *Lucas* makes clear that a landowner "whose deprivation is one step short of complete" (for example, a 95 percent loss of value) may not take advantage of the *Lucas* per se rule.[22]

Second, the *Lucas* per se rule applies only to alleged takings of *land*, not personal property.[23] Prior to *Lucas*, the Court ruled in *Andrus v. Allard*[24] that no taking occurred where federal law prohibited the sale of artifacts made from the feathers of federally protected birds, even though the ban might have left the owners without beneficial use of the artifacts. Although Justice Scalia previously had suggested that *Andrus* had been limited to its facts,[25] writing for the majority in *Lucas* he endorsed *Andrus* and specifically excluded personal property from the scope of the per se rule.[26]

Third, no taking occurs under *Lucas* (or any other test of takings liability) where background principles of law deprive the claimant of the property interest alleged to have been taken.[27]

§ 18.1(a) *Use and Value under Lucas*

The focus of this chapter is the question of whether the *Lucas* per se rule applies where regulation prohibits development, but the land retains substantial value. Land required to be left undeveloped may retain value from its potential use for a host of purposes including:

- agriculture, grazing, or timber production;
- recreation (including use for campgrounds, fishing stations, or playing fields);
- sale to abutting landowners wishing to enlarge their lot and protect their views;
- sale to land speculators hoping the development restrictions will be lifted someday or other uses will become profitable; and
- conservancy groups willing to purchase the property to guard against the possibility that the restrictions might be lifted.

Takings claimants argue that regulations that prohibit development effect a taking under *Lucas* even where substantial value remains. Supporting this "developmental use" interpretation, developers focus on portions of *Lucas* suggesting special concern for regulation that requires land to be left in its natural state.[28]

These references are isolated ones, however, best read as simply describing the specific factual situations before the Court, not as defining the parameters of the per se rule. Other portions of *Lucas,* analyzed in detail below, make clear that *Lucas's* per se rule is inapplicable where land retains more than token value, even where the challenged regulation prohibits development.

§ 18.1(b) *The Text of* Lucas

In fact, the concepts of use and value are so thoroughly linked in *Lucas* that the Court repeatedly employs the terms "use" and "value" as virtual synonyms. For example, in describing how to determine whether there is a denial of "all economically feasible *use,*" *Lucas* emphasized the importance of accurately defining "the 'property interest' against which the loss of *value* is to be measured."[29] This same footnote includes no less than five additional references to value in analyzing how to show denial of all economically feasible use.[30] The *Lucas* Court elsewhere combines the two phrases, describing the per se rule as applying where the government "eliminate[s] all economically valuable use."[31] And in explaining why total deprivation of value is the equivalent of a physical appropriation from the landowner's perspective, the *Lucas* Court equates land use with monetary gain, stating: "[F]or what is the land but the profits thereof [?]'"[32]

The *Lucas* Court's treatment of use and value as virtually synonymous reflects the Court's historic understanding of these concepts in takings analysis. *Lucas* relies heavily on *Agins v. City of Tiburon,*[33] where the Court was careful to stress that the "eco-

nomically viable use inquiry" requires examination of the "diminution in market value" caused by the regulation at issue.[34]

In addition to the Court's express equation of use and value,
Lucas provides other, overwhelming evidence that its per se rule is
limited to cases where remaining uses have no or virtually no market value. The very first paragraph recites the trial court's finding
that the challenged development ban rendered Mr. Lucas's land
"valueless," and it articulates the question: Does the development
ban effect a taking due to its "dramatic effect on the economic
value of Lucas's lots"?[35] The Court then described Lucas's complaint as rooted in the government's "complete extinguishment of
his property's value"[36] and characterized the ruling as finding no
taking "regardless of the regulation's effect on the property's value."[37]
It described the state supreme court dissent as concluding that a
taking occurred due to the government's "obliteration of the value
of petitioner's lots."[38] Thus, the record and posture of *Lucas* starkly
presented the U.S. Supreme Court with the issue of whether a complete obliteration of value effects a taking.

In delineating its per se rule of takings liability, the *Lucas*
opinion once again emphasized the key factual predicate that underlies the per se rule: the trial court's finding that the lots had
been "rendered valueless" by the regulation at issue.[39] The pivotal nature of this finding is evidenced by the majority's specific
justification for accepting it,[40] as well as the skepticism regarding
its accuracy expressed by each of the four separate opinions in
the case.[41] The critical role of the trial court's finding in the analysis
confirms that value is an essential component of the per se inquiry.

Lucas then emphatically addressed the precise question of
whether the per se rule applies to a near-complete, but not total,
deprivation of value. Responding to a hypothetical situation regarding a "landowner whose property is diminished in value
95%"—in language that could not be clearer—*Lucas* states that
"in at least *some* cases the landowner with 95% loss [in value]
will get nothing" under the Takings Clause because such an owner
would "not be able to claim the benefit of [the *Lucas*] categorical
formulation."[42] Of course, the landowner with a 95 percent loss
could argue a noncategorical claim under *Penn Central*, but both
the *Lucas* majority and Justice Stevens in dissent agree that only
"the landowner who suffers a complete elimination of value"[43]
recovers under the per se rule. This exchange shows that the per
se rule is inapplicable where land may be sold for 5 percent of its
original value, even where the land is required to be left vacant.[44]

To reinforce the centrality of value even further, the Court
distinguished several cases that found no taking because "[n]one

of them. . . involved an allegation that the regulation wholly eliminated the value of the claimant's land."[45] One of the cases so distinguished—*Hadacheck v. Sebastian*—involved a loss of value of 92.5 percent (from $800,000 to $60,000),[46] confirming that the *Lucas* per se rule applies only where land suffers a nearly complete loss of value.

§ 18.1(c) Palazzolo *and Other Post-*Lucas *Use/Value Cases*

Cases decided since *Lucas* reinforce the high court's special concern with regulation that strips all or nearly all value.

Just one year after *Lucas*, a unanimous Supreme Court cited with approval a case finding no taking despite losses of value exceeding 90 percent.[47]

More recently, in *Suitum v. Tahoe Regional Planning Agency*, the Court examined a takings claim based on a regulation that allegedly "deprived [the claimant] of 'all reasonable and economically viable use' of her property."[48] Although the agency argued that the claim was unripe because the claimant did not attempt to sell her transferable development rights (TDRs), the Court deemed the claim ripe because the trial court could determine a market value for the TDRs without an actual sale.[49] In other words, the lower court could determine whether the claimant lost all economically viable use because the record allowed for a determination of value. As in *Lucas*, evidence of value drove the "viable use" inquiry.

Finally, in *Palazzolo*, the Court again repeatedly emphasized the symbiotic relationship between use and value in finding that no *Lucas* taking had transpired, even though Palazzolo alleged a 94 percent diminution in the value of his land.[50]

In summarizing the case holding, the Court stated that the lower court was "correct to conclude that the owner is not deprived of all economic use of his property because the value of the uplands portions is substantial."[51] Later, in addressing ripeness, the Court made clear that remaining uses could be proven by showing the economic value stemming from those uses.[52] Finally in summarizing its conclusion, the Court describes the *Lucas* test in a way that suggests that remaining value is the only relevant consideration: "The court did not err in finding that petitioner failed to establish deprivation of all economic value, for it is undisputed that the parcel retains significant worth for construction of a residence."[53]

In short, value and use are inextricably linked in *Lucas* and in subsequent cases in a comprehensive manner that makes untenable the argument that *Lucas* applies whenever developmental uses are denied.

§ 18.2   Use/Value and the Role of Per Se Rules

The text of *Lucas* and its progeny is not the only roadblock facing developers in their effort to divorce use from value under *Lucas*. Even if a developmental use interpretation were consistent with *Lucas*, it could never be squared with the Supreme Court precedent from which the *Lucas* per se rule is carved.

To understand the force of this point it is necessary to reflect briefly on the role of per se rules. The per se rules established by the Court in *Loretto* and *Lucas* are not separate, independent tracks of takings analysis. Instead, they are specific applications of the multifactor test established by the Court in *Pennsylvania Coal v. Mahon*[54] and *Penn Central*. For example, the *Loretto* Court held that a government-compelled, permanent physical occupation is a per se taking, and it expressly tied this per se rule to the multifactor inquiry under *Penn Central*. After noting that *Penn Central* requires an examination of the character of the government action, the *Loretto* Court explained that "when the physical intrusion reaches the extreme form of a permanent physical occupation, . . . 'the character of the government action' not only is an important factor in resolving whether the action works a taking but also is determinative."[55] Such permanent occupations are a taking "without regard to whether the action achieves an important public benefit or has only minimal economic impact on the owner" under *Penn Central*.[56] Thus, the analytical relationship between *Loretto* and *Penn Central* is evident from the face of *Loretto*.

This is also true in *Lucas*. The *Lucas* Court articulated its per se rule within the general context of *Penn Central*, explaining that although *Penn Central* generally requires a multifactor inquiry, per se takings rules create liability "without case-specific inquiry [under *Penn Central*] into the public interest advanced in support of the restraint."[57] *Lucas* juxtaposes the per se and multifactor tests in a way that shows both their integration and mutual focus on value, stating that takings claimants must allege either "a diminution in (or elimination of) value."[58]

From the very first regulatory takings case through the modern era, the Supreme Court has evaluated takings liability by examining the regulation's effect on value.[59] *Lucas*'s per se rule does not shift the focus away from value, but simply abbreviates the traditional analysis in cases where land is rendered nearly valueless.

A developmental use interpretation of *Lucas* would throw a monkey wrench into takings jurisprudence by permitting per se takings claims to succeed where multifactored *Penn Central* takings claims would fail. The district court's ruling in *TSPC v. TRPA*[60] illustrates this incongruity. In evaluating a takings challenge to several planning moratoria, the court first evaluated the claim under *Penn Central* and concluded that all three *Penn Central* factors—expectations, economic impact, and the character of the government action—weighed in favor of TRPA.[61] Regarding economic impact in particular, the court emphasized the claimants' total failure to meet their burden of proving diminution in the value of the property at issue.[62] The court stressed that the plaintiffs' counsel evidently made a "calculated choice" not to offer the requisite proof on this element of their takings claim.[63] The court further found that the temporary moratoria did not interfere with any reasonable, investment-backed expectations.[64]

After disposing of the plaintiffs' claims under *Penn Central*, however, the court found a temporary, per se taking under *Lucas*. This unprecedented ruling not only ignores the analytical relationship between per se rules and the multifactor inquiry, but also ironically suggests that a landowner can prevail on a per se claim under *Lucas*—claims that are supposed to succeed only in the most "extraordinary circumstance[s]"[65]—with a showing on economic impact that did not support a taking finding under *Penn Central*.

§ 18.3   *Practical Problems with a Use-Only Standard*

Finally, a developmental use interpretation of *Lucas* raises a host of practical problems.[66] What, for example, does it mean to say that it is a taking if land cannot be developed? Do developer lawyers really think there should be a constitutional right to build a subdivision or a shopping mall? Over 75 percent of this country's land is intentionally devoted to nondevelopmental uses such as farming, timber harvesting, and recreational campsites.[67] In many cases, these nondevelopmental uses are the only economically viable use to which these lands can be put. It is hard to imagine the Supreme Court finding a *Lucas* taking where the highest and best use of the property is permitted under government regulations.

Of course, one potential response is that farming, timber harvesting, and commercial campsite operations are "developmental uses" in a way that other remaining uses such as gardening, hunting, tent camping, and use for a buffer zone are not. This line, however, is impossibly blurry. What if a parcel is extremely valuable as a hunting or fishing preserve and has few other potential uses? Is there really a constitutional difference between farming and gardening or between a commercial campsite and a hunting

reserve? Should the Supreme Court be in the business of divining
this line? Isn't the relevant question how much the property is
worth in the uses to which it may be put? Isn't *Lucas*, in other
words, also about value?

Another practical problem with a developmental use standard
concerns affirmative obligations. An alternative to any prohibition on development is an affirmative obligation that achieves
the same objective. For example, instead of prohibiting development in the Tahoe Basin in order to protect Lake Tahoe from
runoff, what if TRPA required developers to filter and remove
any sediment from their lot's runoff? Such an obligation could
easily make development prohibitively expensive and halt development as effectively as a development prohibition. Indeed, there
are cases in which affirmative obligations, such as the obligation
to clean up hazardous wastes, render property a sizeable liability.[68] It is hard to see any justification for a rule that treats a
development prohibition differently from an affirmative obligation that achieves the same effect.

Of course, developer advocates could respond by stating that
where affirmative obligations make developmental uses untenable, those uses are not "economically viable," and thus *Lucas*
should apply. But in making such an argument, these advocates
would be conceding that the value of the remaining uses matters,
at least in this context. If the viability or value of the use matters
where affirmative obligations are at issue, why should the viability or value of nondevelopmental uses be irrelevant in evaluating
the applicability of *Lucas*?

In sum, interpreting *Lucas* to establish some sort of right to
develop every vacant parcel in America would render the Court's
regulatory takings jurisprudence, already a mess, into an utterly
incomprehensible mishmash.

§ 18.4   *Problems with a Value-Only Standard*

Government-side advocates should also recognize that there are
some logical and practical difficulties with interpreting *Lucas* to
be only about value. For example, what if the only indication of
remaining value is an offer by the government to purchase property for use as parkland or a nature preserve? In such a case, a
court might well view the offer as an effort to avoid the constitutional obligation to pay full just compensation. For example, in
Del Monte Dunes at Monterey, Ltd. v. City of Monterey,[69] the
landowner argued that the city's denial of a development permit
extinguished all economically viable use of the property even

though the state of California bought the land for $4.5 million while the suit was pending. The Ninth Circuit rejected the suggestion that the government's purchase defeated a per se claim, stating:

> [A] landowner who believed that the government bought out his property at an unfairly low price might choose to bring an action for just compensation. The fact that he already received some money from the government in return for his property does not establish as a matter of law that economically viable uses for his property remain or that a taking did not occur.[70]

Similarly, what if land was valuable to land speculators only because of the slim possibility that the development prohibition would be struck down as a taking? If this form of speculative value was allowed to defeat a *Lucas* claim, then landowners would face a vicious circle. To establish a *Lucas* taking, landowners have to show a complete wipeout of uses creating significant market value. But wherever such a factual showing is possible, this very fact could encourage speculative holding to benefit from a takings verdict. If the value stemming from this type of speculative use defeated a *Lucas* claim, then the very strength of a takings claim would encourage speculation that would defeat the claim. Courts are unlikely to tolerate this outcome.

Finally, what if vacant land is valuable for uses that are illegal, but hard to police? For example, remote forests in California may be very valuable for use in marijuana cultivation. Remote land on the Mexican border may be valuable for illegal immigration. It seems perfectly appropriate for courts to decide on policy grounds that it is unfair to deny a *Lucas* claim on the grounds that the land is valuable to criminals seeking to violate the law.

§ 18.5   *Use and Value in Awarding Just Compensation*

The foregoing discussion makes two points. First, *Lucas* cannot plausibly be read to require consideration of only some narrow category of "developmental uses" in its total takings calculus. A broad range of present and future uses must be considered in evaluating whether enough value remains to place the claim within the confines of the *Lucas* box. Second, remaining value alone also should not be *Lucas*'s sole touchstone. Policy considerations make implausible the argument that value from sources such as government offers is enough to remove a takings claim from the

Lucas box. In short, both value and use must be considered. If more than a token amount of value stems from a nonprohibited use, a *Lucas* claim fails.

The tricky remaining question under *Lucas* is what uses should be considered and what uses should be excluded. The good news for courts considering this question is that they need not write on a blank slate. Indeed, the Supreme Court, lower federal courts, and state courts have been wrangling with this precise question for over two centuries in deciding what uses should be considered in determining fair market value for the purposes of awarding just compensation in successful takings claims.

These are several reasons why courts should look to these cases in defining the parameters of the *Lucas* box. Most obviously, these cases address a similar legal question under the same constitutional provision. While not binding on the *Lucas* question, just compensation cases are extremely relevant, persuasive authority.[71] Second, the interests of landowners and the government are flipped in *Lucas* cases from where they ally in just compensation cases. In just compensation disputes, landowners argue that a very wide range of uses should be considered if these uses result in a larger award of just compensation. What's good for the landowner's goose in awarding just compensation should be equally good for the government's gander in *Lucas* claims. Finally, as described below, just compensation cases lead to the answer that seems fair to both sides: Most uses are considered, but government, illegal, and overly speculative uses are excluded.

§ 18.5(a) *Overview of Just Compensation Cases*

In awarding just compensation for a taking, a court's task is to put the landowner in "the same position monetarily as he would have occupied if his property had not been taken."[72] Courts accomplish this goal by assessing the property's fair market value: the price that would be paid for the property at issue by a willing, informed, but unpressured buyer to an unpressured and informed seller.[73]

A determination of fair market value is usually based on an appraisal.[74] An appraisal is based on two essential steps. First, the appraiser must determine the "highest and best use" of the land: "the reasonably probable and legal use of vacant land or improved property, which is physically possible, appropriately supported, financially feasible, and that results in the highest value."[75] Second, the appraiser must estimate what the property is worth in that specified use.[76] As the Supreme Court stated in its landmark compensation ruling in *Monongahela Navigation Co. v. United States*: "the value of property, generally speaking, is determined by its productiveness—the profits which its use brings to the owner."[77]

§ 18.5(b) *Permissible Uses*

The Supreme Court considers most current and foreseeable future uses of land in evaluating just compensation. In *Olson v. United States*, the Court held that just compensation "includes all elements of value that inhere in the property, but it does not exceed market value fairly determined." This market value is to be determined by evaluating both existing uses and "all the uses for which it is suitable." Further refining this standard, the *Olson* Court stated that just compensation is determined by reference to the "highest and most profitable use for which the property is adaptable and needed or likely to be needed in the reasonably near future."[78]

Olson and other Supreme Court precedents establish that a wide range of present and foreseeable future uses should be considered in assessing the value of a parcel of land. For example, the uses valued for just compensation purposes in *Olson* were future, potential uses for farming and as a fishing station.[79] Other Supreme Court cases have awarded compensation based on property uses as varied as recreational camps,[80] landfilling,[81] cattle grazing,[82] timber production,[83] and constructing a boom to contain commercial lumber floated on rivers.[84]

§ 18.5(c) *Excluded Uses*

While most uses can be considered the "highest and best use" of property for appraisal purposes, the Supreme Court has ruled that certain uses that create value must nonetheless be excluded from consideration of what constitutes just compensation.

One bright line rule is that increased value or depreciation created by government use cannot be considered in awarding just compensation. As the Court stated in *United States v. Virginia Electric Co.*, the value of property "must be neither enhanced nor diminished by the special need which the government had for it."[85]

The Court in *United States v. Cors* explained why it is appropriate to ignore government-created increases in value:

> The special value to the condemnor as distinguished from others who may or may not possess the power to condemn has long been excluded as an element from market value. (Citation omitted). In time of war or other national emergency the demand of the government for an article or commodity often causes the market to be an

> unfair indication of value. The special needs of the gov-
> ernment create a demand that outruns the supply. The
> market, sensitive to the bullish pressure, responds with a
> spiraling of prices. The normal market price for the com-
> modity becomes inflated. And so the market value of the
> commodity is enhanced by the special need which the
> government has for it.[86]

As the Fifth Circuit has commented, "the Government's activity as purchaser or condemnor is more 'hold-up value' than 'fair market value.'"[87]

The Court in *Virginia Electric* added that it would also be "manifestly unjust to permit a public authority to depreciate prop-erty values by a threat... [of the construction of a government project] and then to take advantage of this depression in the price which it must pay for the property."[88]

Olson also establishes that overly speculative and illegal uses cannot be considered as the highest and best use of property.

Olson involved a Canadian dam that raised water levels and flooded properties bordering the Lake of the Woods in Minne-sota. In accordance with a treaty with Canada, the United States agreed to condemn and compensate Mr. Olson and similarly situ-ated property owners.

The issue in *Olson* was whether Mr. Olson and his neighbors should be compensated for the potential use of their property for reservoir purposes and the generation of power from water flow-age. Olson claimed that in reservoir use he and his neighbors could generate 200,000 continuous horse power with a market value of over $1 million annually.[89] The Supreme Court rejected Olson's claim, finding reservoir use wholly speculative, and awarded compensation based on Olson's ability to use his prop-erty for agriculture and fishing.[90]

Under *Olson,* potential uses cannot be considered in determin-ing just compensation where they are too speculative and depend on "events or combinations of occurrences which, while within the realm of possibility, are not fairly shown to be reasonably prob-able."[91] These uses are excluded to prevent "mere speculation and conjecture to become a guide for the ascertainment of value."[92]

Thus, for example, where property is zoned for one use (say agricultural or residential), but more valuable for a different use (say industrial), the property is valued for compensation purposes for the highest and best permissible use at the time of the taking unless the landowner can show that it was reasonably probable that the zoning authority would change the law to permit the more intensive use.[93]

§ 18.6   *Just Compensation Caselaw Meets Lake Tahoe*

Thus far, this chapter has demonstrated that *Lucas* is not about use or value alone, it is about both. Moreover, in the context of evaluating what can and cannot be considered the highest and best use in determining market value for just compensation awards, the Supreme Court has already answered many of the most important questions about the uses that can remove a landowner from the *Lucas* box.

Some tricky questions do remain, however, and one of them is whether the answers given by the Supreme Court's just compensation cases permit the Tahoe Regional Planning Agency to save Lake Tahoe. To conclude this chapter, I will apply the lessons of the Supreme Court's just compensation law to the novel *Lucas* claims articulated by property owners in *Suitum v. TRPA* and *TSPC v. TRPA*.

§ 18.6(a) Suitum v. TRPA

Suitum raised (but did not answer) one of the most important questions concerning the size of the *Lucas* box: Can the value of transferable development rights (TDRs) be considered in assessing whether a *Lucas* taking has occurred?

State and local governments around the country use TDRs to direct development away from farmland, historic structures, and environmentally sensitive land, and toward areas where growth is desired.[94] Through these TDR programs, local governments give owners of heavily restricted properties TDRs that can be sold or transferred to other, less sensitive parcels. TDR programs have successfully protected numerous historic landmarks and thousands of acres of critical open space.[95]

In *Suitum*, Pacific Legal Foundation (PLF), counsel for Ms. Suitum, argued that the value of TDRs cannot be considered in a *Lucas* analysis. The foundation was essentially asking the Supreme Court to overrule a portion of *Penn Central* where the Supreme Court relied in part on TDRs to reject a takings challenge to New York's historic preservation laws. In *Penn Central*, the Supreme Court ruled that TDRs are a use of property that must be taken into account in takings analysis, stating:

> [T]o the extent appellants have been denied the right to build above [Grand Central] Terminal, it is not literally accurate to say that they have been denied *all* use of even those pre-existing air rights. Their ability to use these rights has not been abrogated; they are made transferable to at least eight parcels in the vicinity of the Termi-

nal, one or two of which have been found suitable for the construction of new office buildings. . . . While these rights may well not have constituted "just compensation" if a "taking" had occurred, the rights nevertheless undoubtedly mitigate whatever financial burdens the law has imposed on appellants and, for that reason, are to be taken into account in considering the impact of regulation.[96]

Many (but not all) lower courts have similarly held that transferable development rights are a use of property that must be considered in evaluating a takings claim.[97]

The six-Justice *Suitum* majority expressly left unaddressed the question of how TDRs should be considered in assessing whether a taking has occurred, leaving *Penn Central* in place as binding precedent.[98] However, a three-Justice concurrence argued that *Penn Central*'s ruling on TDRs should be limited to situations where the claimant owns other nearby property subject to the challenged regulation that could benefit from the TDRs (as was the case in *Penn Central*).[99] If *Penn Central* could not be limited in this fashion, the concurrence argued, it should be overruled. To the concurring Justices, TDRs are analogous to a government offer for purchase, and for many of the policy reasons discussed above, the value stemming from their use should be excluded in considering whether a *Lucas* taking has occurred.

But TDRs are not the same as a purchase offer from the government. TDRs represent an interest in real property that can be devised, sold, and transferred.[100] The value of these interests fluctuates with the value of real estate, rising and falling with demand for real estate in the region. The value of TDRs is routinely considered in determining the fair market value of property for tax assessment and other purposes.[101] Moreover, the value of TDRs is not dictated by the government, rather their value is determined by the characteristics of the burdened lot and assessed in the market based on arms-length transactions. TDRs are essentially indistinguishable from other "sticks in the bundle" of real property. When a landowner uses these TDRs either on other parcels it owns or in a sale for value, the value in this use should be considered in assessing whether a *Lucas* taking has occurred.

To illustrate this point, consider what would happen if the federal government exercised eminent domain to acquire property in the Tahoe Basin. If the government acquired land that had TDRs attached to it, the landowners would surely argue that they must be compensated for the value of the TDRs. While the government might try to argue that these TDRs are "government-created" value that should be excluded under the *Cors* line of cases (discussed above), this argument should fail because the value of TDRs is based on their use to other property owners, it is not value "created by government demand." The same reasoning should convince courts to consider the value of TDRs in assessing a *Lucas* taking claim.

§ 18.6(b) TSPC v. TRPA

While arriving at the Supreme Court four years after *Suitum*, *TSPC* stems from an earlier regulatory action: TSPC is challenging a planning moratorium put in place by TRPA while formulating a permanent plan to protect Lake Tahoe.

TSPC landowners argue that they suffered a *Lucas* taking because they were deprived of all economically viable use of their property for the 32 months the planning moratorium was in place. Appraisal evidence relied upon by the district court, however, documents that during the entire period the lots retained substantial value both because of the usefulness of the property for sale to abutting landowners and because of the presumption that the moratoria would be lifted and additional uses would be permitted on the property.[102] TSPC is thus asking the Court to declare that both the current and future uses available to them should be excluded in evaluating their *Lucas* claim.

The Court should reject this invitation as to both sources of value. A vast amount of land in this country is employed gainfully as lawns, gardens, fields, view sheds, and buffer zones on the estates of wealthy landowners.[103] Courts, in turn, routinely consider the possibility of sale to a small class of abutting landowners in assessing just compensation.[104]

For example, in *Boom Co. v. Patterson*,[105] the Court determined that takings analysis must consider the potential uses of a parcel in conjunction with adjacent parcels. *Patterson* addressed the compensation due the owner of three unused islands in the Mississippi River. The Court awarded compensation based on the islands' potential use by timber companies along the riverbanks to form (in conjunction with riverfront lots) a natural boom to store harvested trees.[106] In *United States v. Fuller*,[107] then-Justice Rehnquist, writing for the Court, summarized the law by stating:

This court has held that generally the highest and best use of a parcel may be found to be a use in conjunction with other parcels, and that any increment of value resulting from such combination may be taken into consideration in valuing their parcel taken."[108]

Future uses must also be considered in evaluating a *Lucas* claim, at least where these uses meet the "reasonably probable" test established in *Olson*. In most fixed-duration moratoria cases, all parties will admit that it was reasonably probable that some development would be permitted once the moratorium expired. The only wrinkle in *TSPC* is the fact that the challenged moratoria ultimately replaced by very stringent development restrictions. TSPC may argue based on the ultimate outcome that it was not reasonably probable at the time the moratoria were passed to expect that at the expiration of the moratoria valuable future uses would remain.

There are several problems with this argument. First, the factual predicate for this argument—the assumption that the TSPC landowners ultimately suffered a complete wipeout—is false. As the *Suitum* case explains, each of the TSPC landowners retained at least the right to use their development rights on another parcel they owned in the region or for sale to other Tahoe Basin landowners. These TDRs are a valuable use that alone would have justified a significant purchase price during the moratoria.

Even if TSPC could show that no uses were permitted after the termination of the planning moratoria, it would still bear the burden of proving that future uses were not reasonably probable while the moratoria were in place. TSPC has not begun to meet this burden. Indeed, relying on the extreme notion that *Lucas* gives them the right to develop free even of temporary moratoria, TSPC refused to introduce evidence at trial detailing the uses permitted and value remaining in individual lots held by class members. This shortsighted legal strategy leaves TSPC utterly incapable of prevailing on its *Lucas* claim.

Finally, the evidence in the record shows that for at least some class members, there was every reason to believe that development would be permitted once the moratoria was lifted. Indeed, the plan adopted at the end of the moratorium in 1984 would likely have permitted development of land held by some class members. The more stringent development restrictions were put in place only after the 1984 plan was challenged by an environmental organization and enjoined by a federal court. There is, in short, no basis in the record before the Supreme Court to exclude future uses as too speculative under *Olson*.

§ 18.7   Conclusion

The discussion of the Tahoe cases illustrates why the use/value debate under *Lucas* is unlikely to go away any time soon. Developers and public-side officials will probably have to agree to disagree on close questions such as whether the sale of TDRs should be considered a prohibited source of value under *Lucas*. But this chapter also illustrates that the gulf between the opposing sides is, or should be, smaller than either side seems to think. Government advocates should be willing to recognize that at least some sources of value must be excluded in considering claims under *Lucas*. Property owners should similarly be willing to concede that logical and practical obstacles preclude a use-only standard. Both sides, in other words, should be able to agree that both use and value matter. Moreover, if fairness is the objective, then both sides should also be willing to live in *Lucas* by the rules they benefit from in just compensation cases.

Notes

1. 505 U.S. 1003 (1992).

2. *Id.* at 1019. The term "almost" reflects the fact that even complete wipeouts do not constitute takings where the proposed use was barred at the time of purchase by "background principles of the state's law of property and nuisance." *Id.* at 1029.

3. 438 U.S. 104 (1978).

4. 121 S. Ct. 2448 (2001).

5. 216 F.3d 764 (9th Cir. 2000), *cert. granted*, 121 S. Ct. 2589 (2001).

6. Developmental uses could be "valueless" in a number of circumstances. Consider, for example, a remote forest valuable only for the sale of lumber. Government entities concerned about protecting an endangered owl may decide to zone the property low-density residential, permitting a house or two to be built on the property but prohibiting logging. It is easy to imagine in this circumstance that the permitted developmental uses may be valueless (i.e., it may cost more to build a house on these remote properties than the house would be worth). It is hard to believe that in this circumstance Pacific Legal Foundation and other advocates for development interests would assert that *Lucas* was not applicable.

7. 292 U.S. 246, 248 (1934).

8. *Id.* at 248.

9. 216 F.3d 764 (9th Cir. 2000), *reh'g denied en banc*, 228 F.3d 998 (9th Cir. 2000), *cert. granted*, 121 S. Ct. 2448 (2001).

10. 520 U.S. 725 (1997).

11. *Lucas*, 505 U.S. at 1015.

12. 458 U.S. 419 (1982).

13. *Id.* at 441.

14. *Lucas*, 505 U.S. at 1017-18.

15. *See* Agins v. City of Tiburon, 447 U.S. 255, 260 (1980) (rejecting a facial takings challenge to zoning ordinances); Nollan v. California Coastal Comm'n, 483 U.S. 825, 837 (1987) (finding that a permit condition requiring the dedication of property constituted a taking because it utterly failed to address concerns raised by the proposed development); Keystone Bituminous Coal Ass'n v. DeBenedictis, 480 U.S. 470, 495 (1987) (rejecting a takings challenge to subsidence protections); Hodel v. Virginia Surface Mining & Reclamation Ass'n, 452 U.S. 264, 293-97 (1981) (rejecting a facial takings challenge to federal surface mining protections).

16. *Lucas*, 505 U.S. at 1016 n.6.

17. *Id*. at 1017.

18. *Id*. at 1018.

19. *Id*. at 1019.

20. *Id*. at 1018.

21. *Id*. at 1015, 1019.

22. *Id*. at 1019 n.8. The Court reiterated this point in *Dolan v. City of Tigard*, 512 U.S. 374, 385 n.6 (1994) (stating that the ability to derive *"some"* economic use of property precludes application of the *Lucas* categorical rule).

23. *Lucas*, 505 U.S. at 1015-19.

24. 444 U.S. 51, 66-68 (1979).

25. *Hodel v. Irving*, 481 U.S. 704, 719 (1987) (Scalia, J., concurring).

26. *Lucas*, 505 U.S. at 1027-28 ("And in the case of personal property, by reason of the State's traditionally high degree of control over commercial dealings, [the owner] ought to be aware of the possibility that new regulation might even render his property economically worthless. . . ").

27. *Lucas*, 505 U.S. at 1027-31.

28. *See id*. at 1018 ("[R]egulations that leave the owner of land without economically beneficial or productive options for its use—typically, as here, by requiring land to be left substantially in its natural state—carry with them a heightened risk that private property is being pressed into some form of public service under the guise of mitigating serious public harm."); *id*. at 1019 (statutes that authorize acquisition of servitudes to prevent development "suggest the practical equivalence in this setting of negative regulation and appropriation").

29. *Id*. at 1016 n.7 (emphasis added).

30. *Id*.

31. *Id*. at 1028.

32. *Id*. at 1017 (quoting 1 E. COKE, INSTITUTES, ch. 1 § 1 (1st Am. ed. 1812)).

33. 447 U.S. 255 (1980).

34. *Id*. at 262; *see also* Keystone Bituminous Coal Ass'n v. DeBenedictis, 480 U.S. 470, 502 n.29 (1987) (it could not be determined whether the claimants were denied "economically viable use" of their support estate in coal because "[t]here is no record as to what value" the support estate had); *accord* Park Ave. Tower Assocs. v. City of New York, 746 F.2d 135 (2d Cir. 1984), *cert. denied*, 470 U.S. 1087 (1985) (rejecting a takings claim where the owner could sell the property to someone else); Sadowsky v. City of New York, 732 F.2d 312, 318 n.3 (2d Cir. 1984) ("the court did not abuse its discretion in determining that, where appellants did not show unmarketability, sale of the properties was a possible use" that defeated takings liability); Pompa Constr. Corp. v. City of Saratoga Springs, 706 F.2d 418, 424 (2d Cir. 1983) (in determining whether a claimant can make beneficial use of land by selling it for religious use, the key question is not whether the use would be a profitable enterprise, but whether anyone would purchase the land for that purpose).

35. *Lucas*, 505 U.S. at 1007.

36. *Id*. at 1009.

37. *Id*. at 1010.

38. *Id*.

39. *Id*. at 1020.

40. *Id*. at 1020 n.9.

41. *Id*. at 1034 (Kennedy, J., concurring in the judgment) ("I share the reservations of some of my colleagues about a finding that a beachfront lot loses all value because of a

development restriction"); *id.* at 1043-44 (Blackmun, J., dissenting) ("The Court creates its new takings jurisprudence based on the trial court's finding that the property had lost all economic value. This finding is almost certainly erroneous."); *id.* at 1065 n.3 (Stevens, J., dissenting) (the "land is far from 'valueless'"); *id.* at 1076 (statement of Souter, J.) (the trial court's finding that the development ban rendered the land valueless is "highly questionable").

42. *Id.* at 1019-20 n.8.

43. *Id.* at 1019 n.8 (quoting Justice Stevens's dissent, 505 U.S. at 1064).

44. *See* District Intown Properties Ltd. P'ship v. District of Columbia, 198 F.3d 874, 882 (D.C. Cir. 1999) (*Lucas* makes clear that a 95 percent loss in value does not give rise to a per se taking).

45. *Lucas*, 505 U.S. at 1026 & n.13.

46. 239 U.S. 394, 405 (1915).

47. *See* Concrete Pipe and Prods. of Calif., Inc. v. Constr. Laborers Pension Trust, 508 U.S. 602, 645 (1993) (citing Hadacheck v. Sebastian, 239 U.S. 394 (1915) (92.5% diminution of value).

48. 520 U.S. 725, 731 (1997).

49. *Id.* at 740-42.

50. The Court's ruling on Palazzolo's *Lucas* claim is not particularly remarkable. The Court affirmed that no *Lucas* taking occurs where a property is worth more than $200,000 for use as a homesite. 121 S. Ct. 2448, 2464. In *Palazzolo*, in other words, there remained both use and value. The Court rejected without comment the unfounded argument of Palazzolo's counsel, Pacific Legal Foundation, that *Lucas* applies whenever a landowner is denied a "reasonable rate of return." *Id. See also* United States v. Powelson, 319 U.S. 266, 285 (1943) ("The Fifth Amendment allows the owner only the fair market value of his property; it does not guarantee him a return of his investment."). Responding to PLF's argument that the government could avoid a *Lucas* taking by "the simple expedient of leaving a landowner a few crumbs of value," the Court also clarified that "a State may not evade the duty to compensate on the premise that the landowner is left with a token interest." *Palazzolo*, 121 S. Ct. at 2464.

51. *Palazzolo*, 121 S. Ct. at 2457.

52. *Id.* at 2459-60.

53. *Id.* at 2465.

54. 260 U.S. 393 (1922).

55. *Loretto*, 458 U.S. at 426.

56. *Id.* at 434-35.

57. *Lucas*, 505 U.S. at 1015.

58. *Id.* at 1017 n.7.

The Supreme Court's use of per se takings rules tracks its use of per se rules in other areas of the law. In antitrust law, for instance, the Court employs a multifactor "rule of reason" to evaluate the reasonableness of a trade practice, but it has derived rules of per se liability, "[o]nce experience with a particular kind of restraint enables the Court to predict with confidence that the [multifactor] rule of reason will condemn it." Arizona v. Maricopa County Medical Soc'y, 457 U.S. 332, 344 (1982). In the same way, the Court derives per se rules of takings liability if a particular kind of land use restriction always leads to takings liability under the multifactor inquiry. The *Loretto* and *Lucas* per se rules are simply shorthand inquiries under certain *Penn Central* factors that dispense with the need to examine the other factors.

59. *Compare* Pennsylvania Coal Co. v. Mahon, 260 U.S. 393, 413 (1922) (diminution in value is relevant to takings analysis) *with Keystone*, 480 U.S. at 497 (regulatory takings analysis "requires us to compare the value that has been taken from the property with the value that remains").

60. 34 F. Supp. 2d 1226 (D. Nev. 1999), *rev'd*, 216 F.3d 764 (2000), *cert. granted*, 121 S. Ct 2589 (2001).

61. 34 F. Supp. 2d at 1240-42.

62. *Id.* at 1241.

63. *Id.*

64. *Id.* at 1240-41.

65. *Lucas,* 505 U.S. at 1017.

66. These and other practical obstacles to a "use" standard are masterfully detailed in Brief for Amicus Curiae State and Local Legal Center, *Suitum v. Tahoe Regional Planning Agency*, 520 U.S. 725 (1997) (No. 96-243).

67. *Id.* at 17.

68. *See, e.g., In re Dant & Russell, Inc.*, 853 F.2d 700, 702-03 (9th Cir. 1988) ("With cleanup costs estimated at $10-$30 million, the land has a substantial negative value no matter who ultimately takes possession.").

69. 95 F.3d 1422 (9th Cir. 1996), *aff'd on other grounds*, 526 U.S. 687 (1999).

70. *Id.* at 1432.

71. Notably, just last term in *Palazzolo*, the Court cited favorably the treatment given the use/value question in awarding compensation in cases such as *Olson*. 121 S. Ct. at 2461 ("When a taking has occurred, under accepted condemnation principles the owner's damages will be based upon the property's fair market value, *see, e.g.*, Olson v. United States, 292 U.S. 246, 255, 54 S. Ct. 704, 78 L. Ed. 1236 (1934); 4 J. SACKMAN, NICHOLS ON EMINENT DOMAIN § 12.01 (rev. 3d ed. 2000)—an inquiry that will turn, in part, on restrictions on use imposed by legitimate zoning or other regulatory limitations, *see id.*, at § 12C.03[1].").

72. United States v. Reynolds, 397 U.S. 14, 16 (1970).

73. United States v. Miller, 317 U.S. 369, 374-75 (1943).

74. Typically, in just compensation litigation both parties employ expert appraisers. The court awards just compensation after evaluating the opinions of each side's appraisers.

75. APPRAISAL INSTITUTE, THE APPRAISAL OF REAL ESTATE 50 (11th ed. 1996).

76. *See* United States v. Olson, 292 U.S. 246, 255-56 (1934); United States v. Fuller, 409 U.S. 488, 490 (1973). For a helpful overview of appraisal standards, see Interagency Land Acquisition Conference, Uniform Appraisal Standards for Federal Land Acquisitions (last modified Apr. 13, 1998), *available at* www.usdoj.gov/enrd/land-ack/.

77. 148 U.S. 312, 328 (1892).

78. 292 U.S. 246, 255 (1934).

79. *Id.* at 254 (Olson's property was lying fallow at the time of the taking).

80. United States v. 564.54 Acres of Land, 441 U.S. 506 (1979).

81. United States v. 50 Acres of Land, 469 U.S. 24 (1984).

82. United States v. Fuller, 409 U.S. 488 (1973).

83. Kirby Forest v. United States, 467 U.S. 1 (1983).

84. Boom Co. v. Patterson. 98 U.S. 403 (1878).

85. 365 U.S. 624, 636 (1960).

86. 337 U.S. 325, 333 (1949).

87. United States v. 320 Acres of Land, 605 F.2d 762, 782 (5th Cir. 1979).

88. *Virginia Electric*, 365 U.S. at 636 (quoting 1 ORGEL, VALUATION UNDER THE LAW OF EMINENT DOMAIN, § 105, 447 (2d ed. 1953).

89. *Olson,* 292 U.S. at 251.

90. *Id.* at 254.

91. *Id.* at 257.

92. *Id.*

93. United States v. Meadow Brook Club, 259 F.2d 41, 45 (2d Cir. 1958).

94. *See generally* RICK PRUETZ, SAVED BY DEVELOPMENT: PRESERVING ENVIRONMENTAL AREAS, FARMLAND AND HISTORIC LANDMARKS WITH TRANSFER OF DEVELOPMENT RIGHTS (Arje Press 1997) (listing more than 100 examples of successful TDR programs across the country).

95. *Id.*

96. *Penn Central*, 438 U.S. at 137.

97. *E.g.*, Good v. United States, 39 Fed. Cl. 81 (1997) (TDRs are a "use" of property relevant to evaluating a per se claim under *Lucas*), *aff'd*, 189 F.3d 1355 (Fed. Cir. 1999), *cert. denied,* 529 U.S. 1053 (2000); Deltona v. United States, 657 F.2d 1184, 1192 n.14 (Cl. Ct. 1981) (TDRs are relevant to economic impact); Aptos Seascape v. Santa Cruz City, 188 Cal. Rptr. 191, 198 (Cal. Ct. App. 1982) (TDRs may "preclude a finding that an unconstitutional taking has occurred"); Gardner v. New Jersey Pinelands Comm'n, 593 A.2d 251, 261 (N.J. 1991) (rejecting takings challenge due in part to TDRs); Fred F. French Investing Co. v. City of New York, 350 N.E.2d 381, 387 (N.Y. 1976) (TDRs "are an essential component of the value of the underlying property because they constitute some of the economic uses to which the property may be put . . . and may not be disregarded in determining whether the ordinance has destroyed the economic value of the underlying property." However, "development rights with uncertain and contingent market value did not adequately preserve" the claimant's property rights. *Id.* at 383.); Russo v. Beckelman, 611 N.Y.S.2d 869 (N.Y. App. Div. 1994) (rejecting a takings challenge due in part to TDCs); Shubert Org. v. Landmarks Preservation Comm'n, 570 N.Y.S.2d 504, 508 (N.Y. App. Div. 1991) (stating that "absent a successful challenge" the TDR "must be presumed to have economic benefit"); Fifth Avenue Corp. v. Washington County, 581 P.2d 50 (Or. 1978); Glisson v. Alachua County, 558 So. 2d 1030, 1036 (Fla. Ct. App. 1990) (same).

98. *Suitum*, 520 U.S. at 728.

99. *Id.* at 749 (Scalia, J., concurring).

100. Mitsui Fudosan (U.S.A.), Inc. v. City of Los Angeles, 268 Cal. Rptr. 356 (Cal. Ct. App. 1990).

101. *Id.* (considering TDRs for tax assessment); Security & Exchange Comm'n v. Am. Bd. of Trade, Inc., 829 F.2d 341 (2d Cir. 1987) (considering value of TDRs in assessing property value in bankruptcy proceeding).

102. TSPC v. TRPA, 34 F. Supp. 2d 1226, 1242-43 (1999) ("It is clear that the plaintiffs' properties—no matter how restricted their use—did retain some value during the period at issue. The defendants' appraiser, Mr. Johnson, testified to the fact that during the period at issue, some sales of Class 1-3 and SEZ properties did take place. Further, his testimony supports the proposition that all land in the Tahoe Basin has, and has always had, *some* value, no matter how limited its uses. In some instances that value may be minimal, but none of the land is completely 'valueless,' as was the case in *Lucas*.").

103. To cite just one example, see Peter Baker, *Saudi Prince Snaps Up Va. Mansion Next Door*, WASH. POST, Apr. 10, 1993, at A1 (discussing a McLean, Va., landowner who "bought the house in front of his house for $2 million—and then tore it down to provide more open space and a grander entrance from Chain Bridge").

104. Louisiana v. Nassar, 512 So. 2d 1221, 1224 (La. Ct. App. 1987) (compensation awarded based on potential sale of land to an abutting landowner); City of Lafayette v. Richard, 549 So. 2d 909, 911-12 (La. Ct. App. 1989) (same); *see also* Claridge v. New Hampshire Wetlands Board, 485 A.2d 287, 289 (N.H. 1984) (denying a takings claim due to "evidence in the record that tends to show that the land could be sold to abutters"). Courts award such compensation even where the land must be preserved in its natural state. *See* Assateague Island Condemnation Cases, 356 F. Supp. 357, 360-62 (D. Md.) (compensation awarded for nondevelopable marshland tract based on its value for use in assembly with adjacent property), *aff'd,* 487 F.2d 1397-99 (4th Cir. 1973) (unpublished table decisions).

105. Boom Co. v. Patterson, 98 U.S. at 403 (1878).

106. *Id.* at 408.

107. 409 U.S. 488 (1973).

108. *Id.* at 490 (citing *Olson*, 292 U.S. at 256).

CAN PROPERTY VALUE AVERT A REGULATORY TAKING WHEN ECONOMICALLY BENEFICIAL USE HAS BEEN DESTROYED? **19**

JAMES BURLING

§ 19.0   *Introduction*

It is already well established that government can take property through regulation as effectively as it can through more direct action. It is also well established that compensation must be paid when property is taken. But unlike a government taking through the filing of a condemnation action, or a taking through the physical invasion of real property, a regulatory taking is more difficult to recognize. Title ostensibly remains with the original owner, and a physical inspection of the land will often reveal little in the way of a governmental presence. Yet as Justice Brennan noted, it has been taken nevertheless: "From the property owner's point of view, it may matter little whether his land is condemned or flooded, or whether it is restricted by regulation to use in its natural state, if the effect in both cases is to deprive him of all beneficial use of it."[1]

Where the title has not been formally transferred and the government is not physically occupying or otherwise using the property directly, the question arises of how a court can best recognize property that has been taken through regulation. In *Agins v. City of Tiburon* the Court found that "[t]he application of a general zoning law to particular property effects a taking if the ordinance does not substantially advance legitimate state interests . . . or denies an owner economically viable use of his land. . . ."[2] But the answer of "denies an owner economically viable use of his land" only raises another question: When has there been a denial of economically viable use? In *Penn Central Transportation Co. v. New York City,*[3] the Court described takings in terms of an ad hoc, we-know-it-when-we-see-it formulation that depends on the economic impact of the regulation, the owner's investment-backed expectations, and the character of the governmental regulation. That formulation, of course, is not exactly a paradigm of bright-line guidance. Later, in *Lucas v. South Carolina Coastal Council,*[4] the Court described a "categorical" or "per se" taking—"where regulation denies all economically beneficial or productive use of land."

But did *Lucas* actually make it easier for government to survive a takings challenge? Critics of the doctrine of regulatory takings argue that the answer is "yes" because the touchstone, at least for a taking under *Lucas*, must be value: only when all value of a property has been destroyed can there be a regulatory taking.[5] Such arguments usually begin and end with an examination of *Lucas*. After noting the unique factual setting of that case, where the state of South Carolina conceded that there was no value to Mr. Lucas's property, the thesis is propounded that a taking was found in that case only because there was no value remaining in the property. Furthermore, because all land must have *some* value, and since no government lawyer will ever again be so foolish as to concede that a parcel has no value, it will be next to impossible for a court to find any regulatory taking in the future. Taking this syllogism one step further, critics continue by suggesting that, except for those "no-value" cases, that leaves only a "negative implication" wherein courts will presume no taking if some value remains.[6]

This syllogism is too facile. The doctrine of regulatory takings cannot be so easily relegated to the rare circus sideshow curiosity where land has no value.[7] Indeed, use and value in property are inseparable. Property does not exist in an abstract state; it must be used or useable to give value. And when the ability to use property is denied, its value is diminished. And when the diminishment of use and value is severe enough, compensation is owing.

The difficulty with the syllogism that compensation need rarely be paid unless *all* value is destroyed is that it fails to appreciate the fundamental nature of property and the place that property holds in the framework of the common law and constitutional theory. Although certain 19th-century theorists rejected the validity of private property, and while advocates of more expansive governmental regulation at the expense of private property rights rail against adherence to old doctrine,[8] that is not a view that animates the law today. While an extended discussion of the historical origins and philosophical defenses of western concepts of private property is well beyond the scope of this chapter, it is essential to know at least enough about those origins and defenses to understand what the Supreme Court thinks property is.[9] The Supreme Court does not define the nature of property on a clean slate with each new case; instead it relies on traditions that reach back to a time that predates the Constitution. Thus, in order to know in general what interests in property the Court will find are protected by the Constitution, and in order to know specifically whether the Court believes that the scope of a protected property interest is defined by its value, its use, or both, one must look not only at its more recent pronouncements in cases like *Lucas* and *Palazzolo v. Rhode Island,*[10] but also at the intellectual traditions that have resulted in the English and American common law's respect for rights in property.

This chapter will examine in brief the common-law tradition of property that was essential to the founders' settled understandings of the relationship between the state and the rights of individuals in property. Next, the guidance from the state and federal supreme courts from the 19th century to the present will be explored in light of these historical antecedents. The conundrum of use versus value will be examined in light of the most recent Supreme Court holdings, culminating in *Palazzolo*. What these sources reveal is that the solicitude given by the Court to the protection of rights in private property is based upon an understanding that the Constitution protects those rights not simply because property has "value" or even "use," but because the Court understands the interdependence between the utilitarian and moral justifications for private property. Whether one deals with a categorical taking, where all use has been destroyed, or a more traditional "balancing test" taking claim, where economic impacts, investment-backed expectations, and the character of the regulation must be weighed, the mere existence of some residual value in property should not be particularly dispositive if the landowner is unable to put the property to economically beneficial and productive *use*.

§ 19.1 *Rights in Property in the Common Law and Western Traditions*

Early writings on the nature of property certainly did not focus on the concept of "regulatory takings" and the question of whether there must be a deprivation of use, value, or both in order for a sovereign to have a duty to pay compensation. But with respect to direct condemnation or taking of property, the English common law has always been clear, since the days of the Magna Carta, that no amount of property can be taken unless compensation is paid. In the Magna Carta of 1215, two paragraphs in particular demonstrate the concern for property. First, chapter 39 states:

> No freeman shall be arrested, or detained in prison, or *deprived of his feehold*, or in any way molested; and we [the King] will not set forth against him, nor send against him, unless by lawful judgment of his peers or by the law of the land.[11]

And chapter 28 states:

> No constable and other bailiff of ours [the King] shall take corn, or other provisions from anyone without immediately tendering money therefor, unless he can have postponement thereof by permission on the seller.[12]

Chapter 39 is an obvious precursor of our Constitution's Due Process Clause's prohibition against deprivation of "life, liberty, or property without due process of law." And chapter 28 is a forerunner to the Takings Clause: "Nor shall private property be taken for public use without just compensation."

For purposes of this discussion, it is significant that, at least in the context of what we now characterize as direct condemnation cases, the Magna Carta required compensation for *partial* takings—that is, a taking of "corn or other provisions"—rather than requiring compensation only when the entire fee or property interest was taken. Furthermore, its protection against "*any* molestation" in the due process context is certainly consistent with a liberal reading of the charter's prohibition against a sovereign's interference with individual liberties.

The idea that there are limitations upon the sovereign's ability to take the property of his subjects was not unique to England. Hugo Grotius, the early-17th-century Dutch jurist, following a long line of continental property theorists, noted in *The Law of War and Peace*:

[A] right, even when it has been acquired by subjects, may be taken away by the king in two modes; either as a Penalty, or by the force of Eminent Dominion. But to do this by the force of Eminent Dominion, there is required, in the first place, public utility; and next, that, if possible, compensation be made, to him who has lost what was his, at the common expense.[13]

The focus here is on the taking of a "right"; the duty to compensate is not absolved if some value remains in the property.

Lord Coke, in a passage frequently cited by the Supreme Court and most recently in *Lucas,* finds:

[I]f a man seized of land in fee by his deed granteth to another the profits of those lands, to have and to hold to him and his heirs, and maketh livery secundum formam chartae, the whole land itself doth pass. For what is the land but the profits thereof; for thereby vesture, herbage, trees, mines, all whatsoever, parcel of that land doth pass.[14]

The Supreme Court cited a portion of this passage—"For what is the land but the profits thereof"—in *Lucas* to make the simple point that since David Lucas's property had lost all value, South Carolina had arguably taken his property. But one should not jump to the conclusion that the Court was endorsing the view that there can be a taking *only* when the "profits" or money value is taken.[15] To Coke, profits meant more than a cash profit in the contemporary vernacular. Instead, by including "vesture, herbage, trees, [and] mines" Cook was concerned with *use*—which is the only way for one to obtain the fruits.[16]

In his *Commentary on the Rights of Persons,* Blackstone makes plain the importance of property rights:

The third absolute right, inherent in every Englishman, is that of property: which consists in the free use, enjoyment, and disposal of all his acquisitions, without any control or diminution, save only by the laws of the land.

So great moreover is the regard of the law for private property, that it will not authorize the least violation of it; no, not even for the general good of the whole community. If a new road, for instance, were to be made through the grounds of a private person, it might perhaps be extensively beneficial to the public; but the law permits no man, or set of men, to do this without consent of the owner of the land. . . . [T]he legislature alone

can, and indeed frequently does, interpose, and compel
the individual to acquiesce... by giving him a full indemnification and equivalent for the injury thereby sustained.... All that the legislature does is to oblige the
owner to alienate his possessions for a reasonable
price.... [17]

There is nothing which so generally strikes the imagination and engages the affections of mankind, as the right
of property; or that sole and despotic dominion which
one man claims and exercises over the external things of
the world, in total exclusion of the right of any other
individual in the universe.[18]

In the quoted passages, Blackstone demonstrated solicitude
for "all" of a freeman's acquisitions against the "least violation."
Clearly, Blackstone does not temporize and cannot be read to
endorse the view that the government can take the use of a person's
property as long as some "value" remains.

Furthermore, as Professor Siegan notes, Blackstone's concerns
were quite similar to Lord Coke's:

[Blackstone's] enumeration is also quite inclusive, and
... covers entire and partial interests in property, such as
a restriction of land for the installation of a road.

Under the reasoning of both commentators, regulation causing a reduction in value would constitute a deprivation.[19]

Blackstone's commentary also provides insight into another
compelling thread of the common law's respect for rights in property: the belief that in property there is dominion and in dominion there is freedom. As noted often by the Supreme Court, in
English law, a man's home is his castle:

In 1604, an English court made the now-famous observation that "the house of every one is to him as his castle
and fortress, as well for his defence against injury and
violence, as for his repose." *Semayne's Case*, 77 Eng.
Rep. 194, 5 Co. Rep. 91a, 91b, 195 (K. B.).

In his *Commentaries on the Laws of England*, William Blackstone noted that

"the law of England has so particular and tender a regard
to the immunity of a man's house, that it stiles it his
castle, and will never suffer it to be violated with impu-

nity: agreeing herein with the sentiments of antient
Rome.... For this reason no doors can in general be bro-
ken open to execute any civil process; though, in crimi-
nal causes, the public safety supersedes the private."
William Blackstone, 4 Commentaries on the Laws of
England 223 (1765-1769).[20]

If dominion is a touchstone of the common law's respect for
property, then it stands to reason that the dominion extends to all
of the property and that the government cannot invade any of it
simply because some value remains in the property. Blackstone
was referring, of course, in this passage to the physical intrusion
of a person's home and estate by the sovereign, not to regulatory
takings. But if government could destroy most of the use and all
but a token value of property, then any concerns over dominion
would be hollow indeed.

No discussion of the preconstitutional law of property can be
complete without reference to John Locke's second treatise. Locke's
influence on Blackstone and the founding fathers was profound,
and that influence continues undimmed into the current Supreme
Court. Locke adopts a broad definition of property, that being which
men unite to preserve: "their Lives, Liberties and Estates, which I
call by the general Name, *Property*."[21] It is critical to Locke's natural law theory of government to note in this passage that property
came first and government second, and that property remains an
inherent right of the people. Indeed, Locke continues to note that
"[t]he great and *chief end* therefore, of Men's uniting into Com-
monwealths, and putting themselves under Government, *is the preservation of their Property*."[22] Because property is not a positivist
boon from the largesse of the sovereign, the sovereign cannot take
any part of that property away without consent. And like Blackstone,
Locke is emphatic about the relationship between liberty and property, arguing that when a government ceases to protect property,
but instead becomes an engine of its destruction, it has become an
illegitimate government, earning no allegiance from the people:

> Whenever the *legislators endeavor to take away, and
> destroy the Property of the People*... they put themselves
> into a state of War with the People, who are absolved
> from any farther Obedience.[23]

Plainly, one will not find support in the origins of the common
law's respect for property for the notion that as long as the sovereign leaves behind a few sticks in the bundle of rights, and as

long as some value remains, however inconsequential, the sovereign can take what it may with impunity.

§ 19.2 *Preservation of Property and the Origins of the Constitution*

The founders were deeply influenced by the writings on property by the likes of Locke and Blackstone. As many legal scholars have noted, Locke's idea that government is instituted to protect property, rather than the government being the source of property, deeply influenced the framers, especially James Madison, as they drafted the Constitution.[24]

The structure of the originally ratified Constitution was designed to protect property from, among other things, popular agitation for "an abolition of debts, for an equal division of property, or for any other improper or wicked project."[25] Later, the Fifth Amendment added an even more explicit protection of private property.

The most compelling defense of property by the drafters of the Constitution is found in Madison's "Essay on Property" from the *National Gazette*. Madison writes in the Lockean and Blackstonian tradition:

> This term [property] in its particular application means "that dominion which one man claims and exercises over the external things of the world, in exclusion of every other individual."
>
> In its larger meaning, it embraces every thing to which a man may attach a value and have a right; and which leaves to every one else the like advantage.
>
> In the former sense, a man's land, or merchandize, or money is called his property.
>
> In the latter sense, a man has property in his opinions and the free communication of them.
>
> He has a property of peculiar value in his religious opinions, and in the profession and practice dictated by them.
>
> He has a property very dear to him in the safety and liberty of his person.
>
> He has an equal property in the free use of his faculties and free choice of the objects on which to employ them.
>
> In a word, as a man is said to have a right to his property, he may be equally said to have a property in his rights.

> Where an excess of power prevails, property of no
> sort is duly respected. No man is safe in his opinions, his
> person, his faculties, or his possessions.
>
> . . . .
>
> That is not a just government, nor is property secure
> under it, where arbitrary restrictions, exemptions, and
> monopolies deny to part of its citizens that free use of
> their faculties, and free choice of their occupations, which
> not only constitute their property in the general sense of
> the word; but are the means of acquiring property strictly
> called. What must be the spirit of legislation where a
> manufacturer of linen cloth is forbidden to bury his own
> child in a linen shroud, in order to favor his neighbor
> who manufactures woolen cloth; where the manufacturer
> and wearer of woolen cloth are again forbidden the eco-
> nomical use of buttons of that material, in favor of the
> manufacturer of buttons of other materials![26]

This latter passage is most telling in that Madison is clearly
concerned not only with the possession of property in the abstract, but primarily in the ability to make beneficial use of, and
derive value from, property. The notion that government can forbid, *through regulation*, the use of property with impunity simply
because some underlying value remains has no place in Madison's
philosophy.

Perhaps the most relevant passage from the writings of the
founders on the narrow question of whether the Constitution protects the use or the value of property is a remark by Alexander
Hamilton, who asked, "what, in fact, is property but a fiction
without the beneficial use of it?" And he adds: "In many cases,
indeed, the income or annuity is the property itself."[27] To Hamilton,
use and value are inseparable; if the destruction of the use of
property makes that property "but a fiction," then so too should
the taking by government action of that same beneficial use.

§ 19.3   *Modern Jurisprudence and the Respected Place of Property in the Law*

Numerous decisions of the state and federal supreme courts are
consistent with the understanding that the Constitution is violated
when government takes not only property itself, but also the ability to use and extract a profit from it. In *Green v. Biddle*[28] the
Court had to decide whether a Kentucky statute that purported to
allow tenants to remain upon a lessor's property violated the Constitution. Citing to Lord Coke, the Court noted that:

A right to land essentially implies a right to the profits accruing from it, since, without the latter, the former can be of no value. Thus, a devise of the profits of land, or even a grant of them, will pass a right to the land itself.

It follows that when the use of property, or the profits from that use, are taken away from a landowner, it is the same as taking the land itself.

Professor Kobach notes that the doctrine of regulatory takings was first developed in the 19th century, primarily at the state law level in cases involving the interference with navigation rights.[29] For example, Chancellor Kent, in *Gardner v. Village of Newburgh*,[30] found that an owner of a riparian water right could not be deprived of the right to use his water, through a diversion, without the payment of just compensation because the "legislature [can] take private property for necessary or useful *public* purposes . . . a fair compensation must, in all cases, be previously made."[31] There was no argument that simply because the owner retained the land (and therefore much of the value) he was not entitled to compensation.

In *Yates v. Milwaukee*[32] the Court followed principles similar to those articulated by Chancellor Kent:

> This riparian right is property, and is valuable, and, though it must be enjoyed in due subjection to the rights of the public, it cannot be arbitrarily or capriciously destroyed or impaired. It is a right of which, when once vested, the owner can only be deprived in accordance with established law, and if necessary that it be taken for the public good, upon due compensation.

Similarly, in finding that restrictions on access to private property effected by a change in the grade of a street could constitute a taking, the Michigan Supreme Court, in *Thom v. State Highway Commissioner*, quoting an 1889 state supreme court case, stated:

> [T]he term "taking" should not be used in an unreasonable or narrow sense. It should not be limited to the absolute conversion of property, and applied to land only, but should include cases where the value is destroyed by the action of the government, or serious injury is inflicted to the property itself, or the owner is excluded from its enjoyment, or from any of the appurtenances thereto. In either of these cases it is a taking within the meaning of the constitution.[33]

While the language of *Thom* and *Pearsall* do refer to cases where "value is destroyed," it is not necessary that *all* value be destroyed, as the decision continues by noting that "[a] partial destruction or diminution in value is a taking."[34]

The U.S. Supreme Court also addressed regulatory takings *outside* the context of riparian rights when regulations threatened to deny the *use* of property even well before the Court's seminal opinion in *Pennsylvania Coal Co. v. Mahon.*[35] In *Curtin v. Benson,*[36] the Court struck down regulation of cattle grazing on private property within Yosemite National Park, finding:

> [T]he United States may exercise over the Park not only rights of a proprietor but the powers of a sovereign. There are limitations, however, upon both. Neither can be exercised to destroy essential uses of private property. . . . It is not a prevention of a misuse or illegal use but the prevention of a legal and essential use, an attribute of its ownership, one which goes to make up its essence and value. To take it away is practically to take his property away, and to do that is beyond the power even of sovereignty, except by proper proceedings to that end.

In other words, a regulation taking away the "essence and value" of property, here the right to graze cattle, could work an unlawful taking.

Similarly, in *Hudson County Water Co. v. McCarter*[37] the Court found that while a building height limitation may well be upheld as a valid exercise of the police power, if the regulation unduly trenched upon the *use* of the property, it would be a taking:

> For instance, the police power may limit the height of buildings, in a city, without compensation. To that extent it cuts down what otherwise would be the rights of property. But if it should attempt to limit the height so far as to make an ordinary building lot wholly useless, the rights of property would prevail over the other public interest, and the police power would fail. To set such a limit would need compensation and the power of eminent domain.[38]

Following the rationale of *McCarter,* in *Pennsylvania Coal* the Court struck down a statute prohibiting the mining of coal under structures on private property. In its oft-cited rationale, the Court held "that while property may be regulated to a certain extent, if regulation goes too far it will be recognized as a taking."[39] In neither the *McCarter* hypothetical nor in the actual facts of *Pennsylvania Coal* was *all* the value of the underlying property destroyed. There is nothing in the *McCarter* hypothetical that rules out there being some residual investment value in the property.[40]

And in *Pennsylvania Coal*, the Court struck down a statute, even though the coal owners could still mine considerable portions of their coal estates—the only exception being the coal underneath structures on private property.

While these examples show that the Court was ready to find a regulatory taking in instances where some value remains in the land, the clearest expression of what the Court had in mind may be found in *Agins v. City of Tiburon*, where the Court found: "The application of a general zoning law to particular property effects a taking if the ordinance does not substantially advance legitimate state interests ... or *denies an owner economically viable use of his land*."[41] Since 1980 the Court has affirmed this formulation in virtually every takings case that has come before it. Not once did the Court suggest that a taking, categorical or otherwise, requires a denial of all *value*. Instead the test has always been *economically viable use*. And in *Agins*, the Court based this "economically viable use" formulation on footnote 36 of *Penn Central*. The language of that footnote is telling because the Court noted that there was no taking, that its holding was

> based on Penn Central's present ability to *use* the terminal for its intended purposes and in a *gainful fashion*. The city conceded at oral argument that if appellants can demonstrate at some point in the future that circumstances have so changed that the terminal ceases to be "economically viable," appellants may obtain relief.[42]

In *Lucas, Del Monte Dunes*, and now *Palazzolo*, there are three reasons why mere residual value, such as the minimal value that property might retain through its sale, is insufficient to avoid or minimize a taking of property when government prohibits the beneficial use of that property. First, such a state of affairs is inconsistent with the facts of these cases. Second, it would be inconstant with the principles of regulatory takings as articulated by the Court in these cases. And third, it would be inconsistent with the Court's confirmation that our system of government is based on traditional understandings of property that are rooted in historic tradition—rather than a tradition redefined by changing regulatory regimes.

§ 19.3(a) *The Existence or Absence of Residual Value*

With respect to the facts, there is no indication that the Court's per se rule in *Lucas* was dependent solely upon the concession by South Carolina that Lucas's property had no value. Indeed, the skepticism of some of the members of the Court over whether Lucas's property had no value suggests that the Court's holding is grounded more upon the denial of beneficial use than the denial of all value. A more obvious indication that the Court is not beholden to the denial-of-all-value formulation in determining whether there has been a taking can be found in *City of Monterey v. Del Monte Dunes at Monterey, Ltd.,*[43] where the property in question had already been sold for a considerable sum. Again, what was relevant here was not that there was no value (there was), but that after five applications, each for a successively reduced development proposal, it was manifest that no use of the property would be allowed.[44]

Lastly, in *Palazzolo,* the petitioner was deprived of neither all use nor all value of his property. Mr. Palazzolo had argued that the remaining use and value, the ability to build a $200,000 home, was such an inadequate return on the potential investment that it was a categorical per se taking. The Court did not agree, finding that "[a] regulation permitting a landowner to build a substantial residence on an 18-acre parcel does not leave the property 'economically idle.'"[45]

Clearly, the Court did not reject the petitioner's taking claim merely because the property could be sold to a third party; it rejected the *categorical* claim because substantial use and value remained in the property. There is no reason to think that if the use of even the small upland portion had been denied, the Court would not consider that to be powerful evidence of a categorical taking—even if there was some remaining value in the property.

§ 19.3(b) *The Court's Articulation of Takings Principles if Marginal Value Remains*

The principles of takings law expressed in these recent cases also do not comport with the notion that the mere retention of some value, such as the value related to the ability to sell highly regulated property for a nonzero amount, will defeat a takings claim. First of all, the *Lucas* Court, in formulating its categorical rule, repeatedly focused on the question of use and repeatedly articulated the loss of use as being the touchstone of a regulatory taking.[46] Conversely, the Court's discussion of value is confined primarily to its description of the facts and legal arguments presented to it. Its discussion of value as a requirement for a taking is minimal.[47] In short, there is no indication that the existence of value alone could defeat a categorical regulatory takings claim. Since the existence of value will not defeat a categorical taking, there is no reason to think it would defeat a traditional regulatory takings claim in the *Penn Central* tradition because "value," under the rubric of the "economic impact" prong of the *Penn Central* test, is but one factor listed by the Court.

Some commentators suggest that *Lucas's* footnote 8, which addresses the situation where some residual value remains in property, supports the notion that all value must be destroyed for there to be a taking, at least under *Lucas*.[48] However, after reciting Justice Stevens's criticism that the case's formulation would leave uncompensated landowners who suffered "only" a 95 percent reduction in value, the Court quickly explained that "[t]his analysis errs in its assumption that the landowner whose deprivation is one step short of complete is not entitled to compensation."[49] The Court noted that the owner "might not be able to claim the benefit of our categorical formulation," but it does *not* say that the formulation is unavailable if all *use* is destroyed at the same time that some residual value remains. That question was left for another day, and to some degree the question was again addressed in *Palazzolo*.

The Court in *Palazzolo* emphatically agreed that mere nonzero value does not defeat a takings claim: "Assuming a taking is otherwise established, a State may not evade the duty to compensate on the premise that the landowner is left with a token interest."[50] Finding that there was significantly more than a "token interest," the Court remanded the case to the Rhode Island courts for a further analysis under *Penn Central*.[51] In other words, the answer to the question of takings and nonzero value is not yet settled. However, as shown next, if the past is any guide to the future, the Court's respect for traditional property rights bodes well for advocates of private property rights who suggest that a denial of economically viable use can lead to a taking in the tradition of *Agins* and *Lucas*, even when some putative value remains.

§ 19.3(c) *The Law's Adherence to Traditional Principles in Property Rights*

Lucas and *Palazzolo* also demonstrate the Court's endorsement of this nation's traditional common-law understandings of rights in property. *Lucas*, of course, referred to "background principles" in property,[52] and the Court pointedly noted that "the 'interest in land' that Lucas has pleaded (a fee simple interest) is an estate with a rich tradition of protection at common law."[53] While some have criticized the Court for its "nostalgic" views of property that really have no relationship to modern society,[54] and others

have criticized the Court for failing to embrace the need to abandon our "transformational economy" in favor of an "economy of
nature,"[55] the Court has declined these invitations. Among these
understandings is the idea that rights in property derive not from
the state, but are inherent rights that have always been owned by
the people.[56] When confronted by arguments that background
principles can be defined by newly adopted regulatory constraints,
the Court in both *Lucas* and *Palazzolo* was not impressed. *Lucas*
warned against states using the law as nuisance as a subterfuge to
"decree. . . anew" background principles of property.[57] Instead:

> Any limitation so severe cannot be newly legislated or
> decreed (without compensation), but must inhere in the
> title itself, in the restrictions that background principles
> of the State's law of property and nuisance already place
> upon land ownership.[58]

Similarly, in *Palazzolo*, when confronted with the suggestion
by amici and respondent that contemporary regulations changed
the background principles in Mr. Palazzolo's property—to the
extent that the regulations can make Mr. Palazzolo's former right
to use his property a postregulation benefit—the Court was un-
impressed: "The State may not put so potent a Hobbesian stick
into the Lockean bundle."[59]

This affirmation of Lockean principles is consistent with many
decades of takings jurisprudence where the Court has equated
property rights with liberty. In *Lynch v. Household Finance Corp.*,
the Court was emphatic:

> [T]he dichotomy between personal liberties and prop-
> erty rights is a false one. Property does not have rights.
> People have rights. The right to enjoy property without
> unlawful deprivation, no less than the right to speak or
> the right to travel, is in truth a "personal" right. . . . In
> fact, a fundamental interdependence exists between the
> personal right to liberty and the personal right in prop-
> erty. Neither could have meaning without the other. That
> rights in property are basic civil rights has long been
> recognized.[60]

In *Dolan v. City of Tigard*[61] the Court noted that property
rights are not a "poor relation" of other rights protected by the
Constitution. This is important not because the Court is enam-
ored with hoary abstract principles that some suggest are becoming increasingly irrelevant. It is important because the Court

recognizes that in order to guarantee liberty, a stable property rights regime must also be guaranteed, notwithstanding our evolution into a modern, complex, and ecologically enlightened society. As the Court has repeated in virtually every takings case since 1960: "The Fifth Amendment's guarantee ... [is] designed to bar Government from forcing some people alone to bear public burdens which, in all fairness and justice, should be borne by the public as a whole."[62] This is important because the preservation of property is consistent with the preservation of the dominion interests explicated by Blackstone. A right in property, no matter how humble that property may be, provides a sense of autonomy and security that is independent from the state. As affirmed in *Palazzolo*, rights to use property are not gifts of governmental largesse; they are, in the Lockean sense, rights that precede government. To suggest that government can destroy the uses of property, including the long-standing common-law right to develop it, leaving behind only the marginal value of the ability to resell useless property, is utterly inconsistent with these principles.

§ 19.4   *The Role of Value in Pursuing a Regulatory Takings Claim*

The practical implications to the practitioner should be an emphasis on the *uses* of the property. If a landowner can make a strong case that no economically beneficial use remains in the property, the landowner should be able to maintain an allegation that the categorical "per se" rule of *Lucas* applies, whether or not some residual value remains. To the extent that this "value" actually reflects a remaining "use," the landowner should be prepared to make an argument for a partial taking, using perhaps the template of *Florida Rock V.*[63]

If there are some significant uses remaining but those uses are severely reduced, then a landowner should be prepared to demonstrate the ways in which the use has been diminished through a comparison of the before and after condition of the property. The Court in *Palazzolo* would place such an analysis under the umbrella of *Penn Central*. Such considerations may include a before and after comparison of: (1) the various uses allowed on the property, (2) the real extent to which the land can be used, (3) the time horizons of the development, (4) the changes in the market risk of development caused by the restrictions, and (5) any changes in fair market value.

There is no doubt that ordinary market forces can affect each one of these factors. However, when a landowner can show that the regulatory restriction has caused a severe reduction in use and value, a reduction that is not caused by mere changes in the market, then considerations of fairness militate compensation. In other words, when a landowner is forced to "bear burdens which in all justice and fairness should be borne by the public as a whole," the landowner is owed compensation. The fact that some small value remains in the property is simply not a dispositive factor, if it is properly weighed in light of the overarching concerns that attach to rights in property. In other words, the loss of use, not the remainder of token value, should be the primary consideration.

Notes

1. San Diego Gas & Electric Co. v. San Diego, 450 U.S. 621, 652 (1981) (Brennan, J., dissenting).

2. 447 U.S. 255, 260 (1980) (citations omitted).

3. 438 U.S. 104, 124 (1978).

4. 505 U.S. 1003, 1015 (1992).

5. *See, e.g.*, Douglas T. Kendall, Timothy J. Dowling & Andrew W. Schwartz, Takings Litigation Handbook 196-204 (American Legal Publishing Corp. 2000).

6. *See, e.g.*, Richard J. Lazarus, *Putting the Correct "Spin" on Lucas*, 45 Stan. L. Rev. 1411, 1427 (1993) ("Instead, the negative implication of the category's nonapplicability will dominate the lower courts' takings analyses. These courts will likely apply the opposite presumption that no taking has occurred."). This is also, of course, what the Rhode Island Supreme Court essentially did in *Palazzolo* when it ended its evaluation of economic impact with its finding that some value remained in the property. *See* Palazzolo v. Rhode Island, 746 A.2d 707, 717 (R.I. 2000). *See also* Plantation Landing Resort, Inc. v. United States, 30 Fed. Cl. 63, 69 (1993) (because there was no denial of economically viable use, court need not explore other factors referred to in *Penn Central* and later cases).

7. Indeed, in his concurrence in *Lucas* Justice Kennedy had difficulty accepting the "curious" notion that Lucas's property retained no value. 505 U.S. at 1036 (Kennedy, J., concurring). About the only conceivable instance where land has no value, at least in the short term, might be where its liabilities—say, from toxic waste contamination—exceed its utility. (Such a result can only occur under a regime where retroactive liability attaches to purchasers of properties affected by past contamination; a state of affairs that in and of itself raises takings implications.)

8. *See, e.g.*, Tahoe-Sierra Preservation Council, Inc. v. Tahoe Regional Planning Commission, 911 F.2d 1331, 1338 n.5 (9th Cir. 1990) ("[T]he framers of the Fifth Amendment saw the wisdom of enumerating life, liberty, and property separately, and . . . few of us would put equal value on the first and third."); Lazarus, *supra* note 6, at 1424; Justice Philip A. Talmadge, *The Myth of Property Absolutism and Modern Government: The Interaction of Police Power and Property Rights*, 75 Wash. L. Rev. 857 (2000); Joseph L. Sax, *The Constitutional Dimensions of Property: A Debate*, 26 Loy. L.A. L. Rev. 23, 32-33 (1992) (argues the inadequacy of traditional property rights because of modern understanding that activities on any discrete parcel of property affect "everything else"); Joseph L. Sax, *Property Rights and the Economy of Nature: Understanding* Lucas v. South Carolina Coastal *Council*, 45 Stan. L. Rev. 1433 (1993) (calls for abandonment of traditional property rights law).

9.   For the reader interested in delving further into the origins of property, *see, e.g.*, BERNARD H. SIEGAN, PROPERTY RIGHTS: FROM MAGNA CARTA TO THE FOURTEENTH AMEND-MENT (Transaction Publishers 2001); RICHARD PIPES, PROPERTY AND FREEDOM (Alfred A. Knopf, Inc. 1999) (historical treatment of relationship between property rights and free-dom); ROBERT NOZICK, ANARCHY, STATE, AND UTOPIA (Basic Books 1974) (supplementing Lockean labor theory of property with libertarian historical rights theory); and, of course, JOHN LOCKE, *Second Treatise on Government*, in TWO TREATISES OF GOVERNMENT (Peter Laslett ed., Cambridge Univ. Press, 1967, amended 1970) (1690).

10.   121 S. Ct. 2448 (2001).

11.   Translation from Latin from SIEGAN, *supra* note 9, at 7 [galley proofs] (emphasis added). As Siegan notes, this chapter was expanded broadly in the Magna Carta of 1225 to include, in addition to imprisonment and deprivation of a feehold, protections for "liberties and free customs." *Id.* at 10 [galley proofs].

12.   Translation combined from SIEGAN, *supra* note 9, at 8, and from Ernest F. Henderson, *Select Historical Documents of the Middle Ages* (Stubb's Charters trans.), *in* THE CONSTI-TUTION OF THE UNITED STATES OF AMERICA AND THE CONSTITUTION OF THE STATE OF CALIFORNIA 6 (California State Senate 1993-1994).

13.   HUGONIS GROTII, DE JURE BELLI ET PACIS [THE LAW OF WAR AND PEACE] 118-19 (William Whewell trans., Cambridge University Press 1853).

14.   Lord Edward Coke, quoted in and cited as Co. LIT. 45 (4 b.) 1 Har. & But. ed. § 1 in Pollock v. Farmers' Loan & Trust Co., 158 U.S. 601, 667 (1895).

15.   *See, e.g.*, KENDALL ET AL., *supra* note 5, at 197. This rationale was also adopted by the Ninth Circuit in *Tahoe-Sierra Preservation Council, Inc. v. Tahoe Regional Planning Agency*, 216 F.3d 764, 781 (9th Cir. 2000) (equates "profits" with value), *cert. granted*, 150 L. Ed. 2d 749 (2001).

16.   A similar conclusion, that property must include its profits, can be found in the Napoleonic Code. In an appendix to *Green v. Biddle*, 21 U.S. (8 Wheat.) 1, 94 (1823), it is noted:

> So, also, the Napoleon code, which is in a great measure copied from the civil law, declares, that "the property of a thing, whether moveable or immoveable, gives a right to all which it produces, and to every thing which is inseparably united with it, whether naturally or artificially.
>
> . . . .
>
> . . . The natural or artificial fruits of the earth, the civil fruits, and the increase of animals, belong to the owner by right of accession.

(Citation omitted.)

17.   1 WILLIAM BLACKSTONE, COMMENTARIES *134-35.

18.   2 WILLIAM BLACKSTONE, COMMENTARIES *2.

19.   SIEGAN, *supra* note 9, at 40.

20.   Wilson v. Layne, 526 U.S. 603, 609-10 (1999).

21.   JOHN LOCKE, *Second Treatise on Government* § 123, in TWO TREATISES OF GOVERN-MENT (Peter Laslett ed., Cambridge Univ. Press, 1967, amended 1970) (1690).

22.   *Id.* § 124.

23.   *Id.* § 222.

24.   *See, e.g.*, BERNARD H. SIEGAN, PROPERTY AND FREEDOM: THE CONSTITUTION, THE COURTS, AND LAND-USE REGULATION 14-19 (Transaction Publishers 1997) (discusses Locke's influ-ence); DENNIS J. COYLE, PROPERTY RIGHTS AND THE CONSTITUTION: SHAPING SOCIETY THROUGH LAND USE REGULATION 228-30 (State University of New York Press 1993) (same); Harry V.

Jaffa, *What Were the "Original Intentions" of the Framers of the Constitution of the United States?*, 10 U. Puget Sound L. Rev. 351, 378-80 (1987) (same); *see also* Jack N. Rakove, Original Meanings: Politics and Ideas in the Making of the Constitution 41, 314-15 (Vintage Books 1996) (discusses Madison's growing concern over usurpation of property by local governments: "he understood 'that in all populous countries the smaller part only can be interested in preserving the rights of property'"); William B. Stoebuck, *A General Theory of Eminent Domain*, 47 Wash. L. Rev. 553, 554-55, 578-79 (1972) (discusses precursors to adoption of Lockean view in federal Constitution).

    25. The Federalist No. 10, at 49 (James Madison) (Bantam ed., 1982).

    26. James Madison, *National Gazette, March 29, 1792, in* Madison Writings (Literary Classics of the United States, Inc. ed., 1999).

    27. 3 Hamilton's Works 591 (Putnam's ed. 34), *as quoted in* Pollock v. Farmers' Loan and Trust Co., 157 U.S. 429, 591 (1895) (Fields, J., concurring).

    28. 21 U.S. (8 Wheat.) 1, 76 (1823).

    29. Kris W. Kobach, *The Origins of Regulatory Takings: Setting the Record Straight*, 1996 Utah L. Rev. 1211 (1996).

    30. 2 Johns. Ch. *162 (1816).

    31. *Id.* at *166.

    32. 77 U.S. (10 Wall.) 497, 504 (1870).

    33. Thom v. State Highway Commissioner, 138 N.W.2d 322, 324 (Mich. 1965) (quoting Pearsall v. Board of Supervisors of Eaton County, 42 N.W. 77, 77-78 (Mich. 1889)).

    34. 138 N.W.2d at 323 (citations omitted).

    35. 260 U.S. 393 (1922).

    36. 222 U.S. 78, 86 (1911).

    37. 209 U.S. 349, 355 (1908).

    38. Interestingly, the Court later cited this passage in *Penn Central Transportation Co. v. New York City*, 438 U.S. 104, 128 (1978)—thus acknowledging that an extreme regulatory impact would constitute a per se, categorical taking. Confirming this analysis, the majority opinion in *Penn Central* carefully noted that "nothing the Commission has said or done suggests an intention to prohibit *any* construction above the Terminal." *Id.* at 137.

    39. *Pennsylvania Coal*, 260 U.S. at 415.

    40. In *Florida Rock Industries, Inc. v. United States*, 791 F.2d 893, 902 (Fed. Cir. 1986), the Federal Circuit noted that even the most heavily regulated property still retains some value because of the possibility that the regulations will be changed in the future: "We do not perceive any legal reason why a well-informed 'willing buyer' might not bet that the prohibition of rock mining, to protect the overlying wetlands, would someday be lifted." *Accord* Florida Rock Industries, Inc. v. United States, 18 F.3d 1560, 1566 (Fed. Cir. 1994). Despite this residual value, the trial court on remand found that there had been a compensable partial taking of the property. Florida Rock Industries, Inc. v. United States, 45 Fed. Cl. 21 (1999) (Florida Rock V).

    41. 447 U.S. at 260 (emphasis added; citations omitted).

    42. 438 U.S. at 138 n.36 (emphasis added).

    43. 526 U.S. 687, 700 (1999).

    44. A consistent result, with opposite facts, was reached in *Andrus v. Allard*, 444 U.S. 51 (1979), where the right to sell eagle feathers was deemed to be a taking because the right to *use* the feathers, as a museum curiosity, for example, had not been denied.

    45. 121 S. Ct. at 2453 (quoting *Lucas,* 505 U.S. at 1019).

    46. 505 U.S. at 1012 ("temporary deprivations of use are compensable"); *id.* at 1013

("beneficial use of his land"); *id.* at 1014 ("If, instead, the uses of private property were subject to unbridled, uncompensated qualification under the police power, 'the natural tendency of human nature [would be] to extend the qualification more and more until at last private property disappeared.'" (quoting *Pennsylvania Coal*, 260 U.S. at 415)); *id.* at 1015 ("categorical treatment appropriate is where regulation denies all economically beneficial or productive use of land"); *id.* at 1016 (quotes *Agins* formulation); *id.* at 1016 n.6 (same) ("economically beneficial use of his land"); *id.* at 1016 n.7, 1017 ("deprivation of all economically feasible use" and "all economically beneficial use" and "total deprivation of beneficial use is, from the landowner's point of view, the equivalent of a physical appropriation" (quoting *San Diego Gas & Electric*, 450 U.S. at 652 (Brennan, J., dissenting)); *id.* at 1018 ("all economically beneficial uses" and "economically beneficial or productive options for its use"); *id.* at 1019 ("preventing developmental uses" and "sacrifice *all* economically beneficial uses in the name of the common good, that is, to leave his property economically idle, he has suffered a taking"); *id.* at 1027 ("all economically beneficial use"); *id.* at 1030 ("all economically productive or beneficial uses of land"); *id.* at 1031("common-law principles would have prevented the erection of any habitable or productive improvements on petitioner's land; they rarely support prohibition of the 'essential use' of land" (citing Curtin v. Benson).

47. 505 U.S. at 1007 (regulation has a "dramatic effect on the economic value"); *id.* at 1016 n.7 (discussing property interest "against which the loss of value is to be measured" and "unclear whether we would analyze the situation as one in which the owner has been deprived of all economically beneficial use of the burdened portion of the tract, or as one in which the owner has suffered a mere diminution in value of the tract as a whole"); *id.* at 1026 (regulation "wholly eliminated the value of the claimant's land").

48. *See, e.g.,* KENDALL, *supra* note 5, at 199.

49. 505 U.S. at 1019 n.8.

50. 121 S. Ct. at 2464.

51. 121 S. Ct. at 2464-65. Palazzolo argued that even the remainder of $200,000 could constitute a categorical taking when the uses and values of the property after the regulation are compared to the uses and values before the regulation. However, the Court chose to focus on the remainder amount and to leave the full comparison of before and after uses and values to a *Penn Central* analysis. 121 S. Ct. at 2465. Counsel for Palazzolo also had suggested that the petitioner might have suffered a partial taking. However, since this theory was not pled below, the Court declined to address it. *Id.*

52. 505 U.S. at 1029.

53. 505 U.S. at 1016. A more prosaic articulation is that property is "the group of rights inhering in the citizen's relation to the physical thing, as the right to possess, use and dispose of it." United States v. General Motors Corp., 323 U.S. 373, 378 (1945).

54. *See* Lazarus, *supra* note 6, at 1424.

55. Sax, *Property Rights and the Economy of Nature, supra* note 8.

56. *Accord* Nollan v. California Coastal Commission, 483 U.S. 825, 833 n.2 (1987) (ability to develop property a right, not a "governmental benefit").

57. 505 U.S. at 1028.

58. *Id.* at 1029.

59. 121 S. Ct. at 2462.

60. 405 U.S. 538, 552 (1972).

61. 512 U.S. 374, 392 (1994).

62. Armstrong v. United States, 364 U.S. 40 (1960).

63. 45 Fed. Cl. 21 (1999).

SHOULD LAND USE BE DIFFERENT? REFLECTIONS ON *WILLIAMSON COUNTY REGIONAL PLANNING BOARD V. HAMILTON BANK* 20

PETER A. BUCHSBAUM

§ 20.0 *Introduction*

No issue has bedeviled takings law more than ripeness—that is, when is it suitable to bring such a claim in federal court? Controversy over access to federal courts for property rights claims has been deep and prolonged. As noted in the preface to this book, even the idea for this publication derived from the controversies that arose over the report in Part III of this book, which was rendered by the retreat on takings cosponsored by the ABA Section of State and Local Government Law, the Rocky Mountain Law Institute.

The retreat report largely dealt with the ripeness issue. When presented with the report, the Council of the State and Local Government Law Section could not reach consensus on whether to publish the report resulting from the retreat, let alone agree on the substance of any of the ripeness issues set forth in the report. Further, at a meeting of the International Municipal Law Association (IMLA) about a year later, IMLA developed a vigorous critique of the retreat report, based largely on its recommendations about access to federal courts.

Beyond this ABA and IMLA involvement, ripeness issues have engendered a great deal of controversy in Congress—something very unusual for land-use issues. For the past several years the House of Representatives has considered and even passed legislation that would purportedly eliminate some of the barriers to bringing takings litigation to federal court by specifying when an application for development is ripe. It is almost incredible that the Congress would concern itself with the nitty-gritty of the local development process. Municipal groups have vigorously opposed this legislation. As a recently elected municipal official, I now receive every few months a pronouncement from one municipal organization or another stating that municipal governments will be severely hampered if there is easy access to federal courts for takings lawsuits that allege municipal incursions on property rights.

States have also been active. The well-known Bert J. Harris Jr. Private Property Rights Protection Act in Florida is largely designed to determine when a case becomes ripe to bring a takings claim in state court.[1] Other states have also passed legislation trying to define takings claims more closely so that it becomes easier to determine when such a claim may be brought.

§ 20.1   Treating Land-Use Cases Differently

Why all this fuss about bringing takings claims in federal court? For years, federal lawsuits telling state and local governments how to run their hospitals, jails, police forces, and mental institutions have been accepted as a matter of course.[2] Federal courts have run schools in desegregation cases and rendered decisions that totally reapportioned legislatures.[3] Under the Telecommunications Act of 1996,[4] they have ordered towns to accept towers, and under the Fair Housing Act Amendments Act of 1988[5] they have told localities to absorb group homes. Thus, federal courts have gotten into the land-use business.

So why the big controversy about bringing takings claims in federal court? Why is land-use litigation brought pursuant to 42 U.S.C. § 1983 different from any other form of invasive litigation—in fact, far more invasive litigation—that has been heard by the federal courts for years?

§ 20.1(a) Justifications for Different Treatment

There have been attempts to explain why takings are different. Tom Roberts, the editor of this book, has done the job perhaps better than anyone. The general rubric is that the takings claim is self-executing. The initial constitutional wrong occurs the moment the government takes your property or applies an excessive regulation. However, according to scholars,[6] the nature of the wrong is different from any other constitutional wrong. Unlike, for example, the First Amendment, where the government is forbidden to interfere with free speech, the Just Compensation Clause of the Fifth Amendment does not bar takings, it merely bars uncompensated takings. Accordingly, it is only the refusal to provide compensation, not the incursion on the property right, that triggers the constitutional violation.

Further, since the issue is compensation, the plaintiff cannot merely say that he or she has been deprived of a constitutional right until a request has been made to the state or local government for such compensation and has been denied. Thus, according to the theory, there must be an invasion of property rights and a consequent denial of compensation after request is made for the constitutional tort to have occurred.

In this way, it is asserted, takings are different. If a policeman bops you over the head, that cop has acted illegally; if the state or local government has invaded your right to use your property, you really don't know if it has acted illegally until you ask for compensation and it is denied.

§ 20.1(b) *Evaluating the Justifications*

This underlying premise is, of course, untrue. Assuming, as we must, after *First English Evangelical Lutheran Church of Glendale v. County of Los Angeles*[7] and *Lucas v. South Carolina Coastal Commission*,[8] that there is a right to recover money where the regulation transcends the—take your pick—*Penn Central* three-part test,[9] *Agins v. Tiburon* two-part test,[1] or *Lucas* deprivation of all beneficial/economic/etc. use, and further assuming that you have sought to make use of your land and have been told no, then, from the moment you receive that denial, you have been deprived of your right to compensation. The result is in concept no different from the policeman bopping you over the head. After he is done, and assuming he is not repeating the attack, then the only issue is compensation for the violation of your right not to have your body attacked by an official. Yet you do not have to ask for money before suing.

The same should be true, one would think, where the government tells you you can't do something to or with your land; at that point the right to compensation should vest, just as your right to equal protection of the laws would vest where the denial of use is discriminatory, or your right to substantive due process of law would vest if the denial were arbitrary and capricious.[11] Yet if the

claim is for a taking, the denial itself does not result in the right
to go to federal court, even though, if your claim is right on the
merits, the government has, by its denial, invaded your property
by excessive regulation and not provided compensation for that
invasion.

So we return to the question of what makes land use different.
Further, why did the modest recommendations of the retreat report concerning access to federal court engender such controversy?

§ 20.1(c) *The Real Reason for Different Treatment*

The answer that should be acknowledged is not based on any substantial analytical difference between takings claims and other kinds
of claims, but is really more of a substantive reaction to litigation
of land-use issues in federal court. *Williamson County Regional
Planning Board v. Hamilton Bank*[12] was not the first case to treat
land-use claims in a fashion almost totally different from that accorded to other claims. In fact, the federal courts have done a similar hands off for exclusionary zoning litigation, which has been
intensely debated throughout state courts in this country.

In the case of *Warth v. Seldin*,[13] decided in the 1970s, the
Supreme Court was confronted by a claim by lower-income people
that, but for the defendant's (a Rochester suburb) tight zoning,
they would have been able to find housing in that suburb. Virtually every state court that has examined the issue has found standing. However, the Supreme Court decided that the gap between
exclusionary zoning and the actual receipt of housing was too
great, even though the plaintiffs had alleged that, but for the zoning, housing would have been made available by someone. The
Court essentially ignored this allegation and held that the plaintiffs did not have standing, since the provision of housing to them
was not sufficiently connected to the exclusionary zoning that
they had alleged. To be sure, the Supreme Court later backtracked
somewhat from this viewpoint in the *Village of Arlington Heights*
case,[14] where there was at least a prospective developer of low- or
moderate-income housing on the scene. Yet *Warth v. Seldin* had
the fundamental effect of essentially taking federal courts out of
the exclusionary zoning litigation arena. In effect, through the
standing device, the Supreme Court decided that this one type of
civil rights claim would not be heard in federal court.

§ 20.2 Williamson County's *Exhaustion Barrier*

Viewed from this perspective, the Supreme Court's decision in
Williamson County to impose a twofold barrier to litigation of

takings claims in federal court becomes more comprehensible as a substantive reaction to land-use claims, rather than an accurate analysis of any difference between such claims and ordinary civil rights damage claims. The Court first required exhaustion of remedies, which is not typically required in cases under 42 U.S.C. § 1983. Between *Williamson County* and its later cousin, *McDonald, Sommer and Frates v. Yolo County*,[15] the Court required an actual decision denying a use before a takings claim could ripen sufficiently for federal court review. Moreover, the use requested could not be grandiose—whatever that means—but rather had to be reasonable.[16]

Contrast this situation with a First Amendment allegation. Ordinances can easily be attacked on their face if, for example, they do not allow certain types of protests on city streets. No one thinks to suggest that a First Amendment litigant cannot even be in court unless he or she has requested only a reasonable parade permit and then only after the request for that reasonable parade has been specifically rejected. Even though Chief Justice Rehnquist in *Dolan v. City of Tigard*[17] stated that the Fifth Amendment is not to be considered a poor relation and is as much a part of the Bill of Rights as the First Amendment, this procedural hurdle is exactly what the federal courts require in takings cases alone.

§ 20.2(a) *The Impact of* Palazzolo *as to the First* Williamson *Prong*

As a result, someone who proposes a 100-lot development in an area zoned for 10 lots cannot even get to court. Rather than simply rejecting the request on the grounds that it was substantively absurd and that the substantive decision making of the locality merited deference, the federal courts engage in a turgid analysis as to whether the proposal was reasonable enough even to be considered for federal court. The court would also inquire as to whether the locality actually did take a position on how much development it would allow. While the recent *Palazzolo v. Rhode Island*[18] decision does clear up this prong of the *Williamson County* analysis somewhat—if an agency says it will allow nothing, then the federal court is reasonably bound by that statement—*Palazzolo* does not and cannot lay this problem to rest. True, when a governmental entity makes its position reasonably clear, as Rhode Island did by saying there could be no development in wetlands, the property owners are under no obligation to keep changing and resubmitting development proposals.

Yet *Palazzolo*, even as to finality, leaves a great deal of uncertainty. Take the property owner seeking a tenfold increase in density. The community simply tells him no—we will consider something, but not tenfold. What happens then? Suppose further it is totally unclear, as it is in New Jersey, my home state, in many cases as to whether a variance is even obtainable where someone seeks increased density.[19] Suppose further that the locality refuses to give any guidance as to what it will accept by way of a changed zoning. In such a case, it will still, notwithstanding *Palazzolo*, be difficult to determine whether there has been a final decision denying a reasonable request for an alteration of current zoning restrictions.

§ 20.2(b) *Let the Cases Be Heard on the Merits*

The retreat report suggested several options for dealing with the first Williamson prong. It required that an application actually conform to the existing zoning to ripen an obligation to respond. It also stated that if government gave guidance, the landowner had to respond to that guidance before the claim would be ripe. Nonetheless, even this limited proposal was found to be too radical for publication as a stand-alone document.

But the retreat report did not get to the heart of the issue. It would be far simpler to develop a substantive doctrine of deference to local decision making and dismiss cases on the merits, as will probably happen when the *Olech* equal protection claim finally goes to trial.[20] But to tell a litigant who is faced with a land-use restriction that may violate *Agins*, or *Lucas*, or *Penn Central* to go through intense procedural wrangling before even finding out if the federal court door is open—that makes no sense.

In some fashion the Supreme Court seems to have realized the fallacy of the *Williamson County* first prong when it decided *Village of Willowbrook v. Olech*.[21] In *Olech*, the Court allowed an equal protection claim to proceed where a landowner claimed that the village had required a greater dedication of right-of-way from her than from other landowners. The Court in that situation made no comment about seeking a final decision from the locality or seeking a variance from the exaction mandate. Instead, it treated the case like it treats every other civil rights damage claim. Namely, the initial municipal decision to impose the exaction was enough to trigger a federal case, period. *Williamson County* et al. were not even mentioned. In general, substantive due process cases are treated the same way, although there is a great split in the circuits as to the extent to which a property right must actually exist before substantive due process will lie. The Supreme Court has not spoken to this issue yet.

However, nothing in *Olech* suggests that the Supreme Court or other federal courts are going to start willy-nilly striking down local land-use decisions. Instead, the *Olech* approach simply says you can be in court; we will deal with the merits. This approach seems far preferable to the wrangling that currently occurs as to predicate issues, namely, whether an application is really reasonable and whether there was some hope somewhere that a municipality or state government could be inveigled into granting a variance before a federal action lies.

§ 20.3   Williamson County's Forum Barrier—the Second Prong

Williamson County even more closely emulated *Warth* in its second prong regarding exhaustion of state judicial compensation remedies. As Professor Roberts has pointed out, this second prong, holding that state compensation remedies must be exhausted before a case can be brought into federal court, virtually closes the federal courthouse door. It thus functions like the denial of standing in *Warth v. Seldin*. I must admit, when I first read that aspect of *Williamson County*, I thought the Supreme Court must have meant only state compensation remedies that were in the nature of particular administrative proceedings would have to be exhausted before a litigant could proceed in federal court. That is not the case. As Professor Roberts has further argued,[22] once the *First English* case was decided in 1987, every state had to provide some remedy in compensation for taking.[23] The essential holding of this decision was that mere invalidation of a regulation was not a sufficient remedy for a taking. Thus, after 1987, every state perforce had to have a compensation remedy.

However, such compensation remedies in most states come in the form of civil actions that look, taste, feel, and smell exactly like federal civil actions. These are not specialized procedures involving compensation claims; instead they are general pieces of civil litigation, essentially identical to federal court suits.

In almost all other areas of civil rights endeavor, 42 U.S.C. § 1983 functions as a fully supplemental remedy allowing access to federal court. This much was determined more than 40 years ago in *Monroe v. Pape*.[24] Thus, for almost any other type of federal civil rights claim, the existence of a parallel state procedure has no bearing whatsoever on the right to get to federal court.

Moreover, for all other civil actions there is no need to find out what the highest court of a state thinks before first pursuing a federal claim. That much was determined by that noted radical, Chief Justice White, in the 1913 decision in *Home Telephone and Telegraph Co. v. City of Los Angeles*.[25] In that case Los Angeles had adopted a rate regulation that was allegedly a taking of property repugnant to the Fourteenth Amendment. The district court had dismissed the action for want of jurisdiction. On appeal, the U.S. Supreme Court held that the claim, which was essentially under the Fifth Amendment since it alleged that the rate regulation was confiscatory, should be heard in federal court.[26] It rejected, 88 years ago, the defendants' claim that a federal takings action would be cognizable only if the Supreme Court of California had determined that the ordinance was valid. It held that the Fourteenth Amendment was not limited to wrongs authorized by a state but was designed to limit abuse of power by officers of the state, and that claims could be pursued directly in federal court without resort to state procedures.[27]

The issue was further raised in the infamous case of *Screws v. United States*.[28] In that case, a white sheriff had beaten a black prisoner. In his defense, in a federal court action, the sheriff stated that he was not acting under color of state law since, if the beating was unlawful, it violated Georgia law. Justice Frankfurter, in a dissenting opinion that has bothered me since I first read it in law school, found this reasoning perfectly appropriate. There could be no federal constitutional violation, according to him, by a state officer whose conduct violated state law. Fortunately, the majority rejected that view, stating that Screws had acted under color of state law in arresting the victim. It made no difference whether the Supreme Court of Georgia would have eventually approved his conduct or not. He was the state when he took his victim into custody and beat him, just as Los Angeles was the state when it levied rate regulation on the local telephone company.

The doctrine of these cases cannot be squared with *Williamson County*. State officers have, in the allegations so typical of many takings claims, violated the Constitution by invading property rights without paying, just as they allegedly violated the Takings Clause in *Home Telephone and Telegraph* by an unduly restrictive rate regulation. That invasion is an ongoing one—the use of the property is stymied without any payment being made. During the period when the regulations are in effect, the property cannot be used as the plaintiff would like, yet he or she has received no money.

However, when it comes time for the plaintiff to seek compensation, the plaintiff is told that he or she has no access to federal courts until the supreme court of the state determines what compensation is due. This result makes no sense. The constitutional violation, even if cast as failure to provide compensation, exists and is ongoing upon application of the regulation and the refusal by a responsible officer to pay. Nothing more would be required for any other constitutional wrong.

Unless there is some clear ground for treating land-use cases differently, there should be access to federal court without the need for preliminary state proceedings. Since no such ground exists, it is clear that *Williamson County* represents for land-use cases only a rather careless and offhanded exception to Supreme Court doctrine allowing immediate access to federal court when officers misbehave, which has been settled since 1913 and was reaffirmed in both *Screws v. United States* in 1945 and *Monroe v. Pape* in the early 1960s.

What is disturbing is that most defenders of the second prong couch their arguments in terms of state's rights. Usually sound lawyers express outrage that anyone could consider the state courts incapable of dealing with takings claims. Yet that outrage does not extend to any other form of federal claim.

Further, it is clear that suspicion of state courts is built right into the Constitution. The Diversity Clause has no other basis. It should be remembered, in this connection, that diversity jurisdiction was virtually the only jurisdiction, along with admiralty, exercised by the lower federal courts until 1875. Thus, our lower federal court system was for 85 years administered primarily in cases based on the suspicion of local courts.

In addition, federal question jurisdiction was extended to federal courts in 1875 because the Congress finally decided that state courts were inhospitable to federal claims. Likewise, the supplemental remedy doctrine of *Monroe v. Pape* developed during the 1960s just because there were problems in state courts. Given these historical precedents, it is simply too late in the day to argue that granting federal courts review of a particular substantive area constitutes an insult to state courts. For better or for worse, our dual system of justice was firmly established in 1789. Only land use is made different.

Aside from its anomaly as a matter of jurisprudence, the second prong of *Williamson County* regarding exhaustion of state judicial remedies engenders a whole range of oddities that could be eliminated. First, there is a question on which Professor Roberts has eloquently expounded concerning relitigation of cases brought in state court. As he points out, the designation of the issue as ripeness is misleading.[29] In the course of litigation on the merits in state court, the federal takings claim does not merely ripen, it is fully litigated. Although it is possible that theoretical reservations of rights may be allowed, similar to the *England* reservation[30] of the right to return to federal court on federal issues where abstention is found and a controlling state issue must first be litigated, it is unlikely that the federal courts would ever allow litigation of the same factual issues already dealt with in state court. And in fact, the leading takings case on this subject, *Dodd v. Hood River County*,[31] just so holds; in the course of ripening a matter in state court, the plaintiff lost its right, under doctrine of collateral estoppel, to relitigate the same factual issues in federal court.

It is this combination of ripeness and issue preclusion that makes *Williamson County* in its second prong, judicial remedy exhaustion, the functional equivalent of *Warth v. Seldin*—that is, an effective dismissal of a whole class of land-use litigation from federal court—albeit in this instance takings rather than exclusionary zoning. The misleading character of the so-called ripeness doctrine could be eliminated if the second prong of *Williamson County* were eliminated.

The other critical oddity caused by the second prong came when the Supreme Court decided in *City of Chicago v. International College of Surgeons*[32] that a municipality had the right to remove takings claims brought in state court to federal court. As a result of the combination of *Williamson County* and *College of Surgeons*, even the plaintiff who brings a takings claim in state court is subject to an incredible burden. Assume he or she has read *Williamson County* and sued in state court. Nonetheless, the municipal defendant can—and many of them do, owing to the better summary judgment procedures in federal court—remove the case to federal court. The same defendant can then claim that the federal takings claim, once removed, is not ripe, so that it has to be dismissed, while the rest of the case, perhaps alleging substantive due process, equal protection, or other violations, may remain in federal court to be disposed of in accordance with the more streamlined federal summary judgment procedures. Thus, while municipal lobbyists rail against the horror of federal judicial intervention into local land-use cases, their constituents are scurrying into federal court because they feel they are more likely to win land-use cases quickly there.

There is a one-word description for that sort of result—nonsense. Land-use cases are the only ones in which the defendant gets to determine the forum.[33] In what other area of endeavor besides land use does the defense and only the defense decide on the forum? Again, this anomaly results solely from *Williamson County*'s second prong and would vanish if that second prong were eliminated.[34]

§ 20.4 *Conclusion*

Clearly, under *Williamson County*'s two prongs, even as mitigated in *Palazzolo*, land-use cases are treated in a fashion that differs from that accorded to any other litigation. Yet there is no principled distinction between takings litigation and other civil rights litigation. While the takings claims may be self-executing, clearly they are founded on a violation of the Fifth and Fourteenth Amendments and actionable under 42 U.S.C. § 1983, just like any other damage claim for violation of constitutional rights.[35] The only viable conclusion is that federal courts simply do not want to hear land-use cases. Be it claims by pesky excluded people for access to the goods of suburbia, or claims by property owners seeking fair treatment from those same suburban jurisdictions, the Supreme Court has clearly come down in favor of the middle and upper middle, home-owning class that runs our suburbs.[36]

There is nothing all that surprising in this. One of my law school professors remarked in describing an old English construction case that was decided in favor of the homeowner rather than the repairman that the judge in question—an English lord—had a lot more in common with the property owner than with the tradesman. Judges, especially federal judges, are drawn from that class of people who largely benefit from strict land-use regulation. The notion that they will have to adjudicate cases involving such regulations, as contrasted with the drug cases many of them typically now have, does not meet with their favor.

The above is facetious. It is, however, suggested by an utter inability to find any rational reason why the federal courts have granted land use an exception from judicial review under 42 U.S.C. § 1983 and the Fourteenth Amendment.

There seems to be some feeling in the Supreme Court that land use is different, even though this feeling has never been explained or justified. In its holding in *Solid Waste Agency of Northern Cook County v. Army Corps of Engineers*,[37] restricting federal authority to regulate wetlands, the Supreme Court did refer to the traditional deference accorded to local land-use regulation. And in *Romer v. Evans*,[38] where the Court struck down the results of an anti-gay referendum, it did advert to the referendum's effect of preventing people from petitioning local governments to establish pro-gay rights legislation. Thus, the Court seems to be evolving some as-yet inchoate doctrine according some place in the constitutional firmament to local government, with particular emphasis on land use.

Yet in the course of evolving some theory of local governance, in the case of land use the Court has acted in a thoroughly confusing fashion by emphasizing the substantive rights of landowners in such cases as *City of Monterey v. Del Monte Dunes*[39]—right to jury trial; *Dolan v. City of Tigard*[40] and *Nollan v. California Coastal Commission*[41]—right to be free of unreasonable land-use exactions; *Lucas v. Carolina Coastal Commission* and *First English*—right to a compensation remedy; while at the same time, through *Williamson County* and *McDonald, Sommer and Frates*, undermining the procedural rights of landowners to those very substantive claims it has been enunciating. The resulting procedural morass has caused thoroughly unnecessary conflict and confusion.

The Supreme Court could and should straighten out the morass. Litigants have a right to know that they can be in court. Moreover, there is no justification for treating land-use cases differently from police cases, or personnel cases, or education cases, all of which involve arguably more important functions of local government. The Supreme Court should thus overrule *Williamson County*.

The Court can protect local prerogative, as it has in other areas and even in equal protection for local use claims, by imposing, if it wishes to preserve local home rule, an appropriately deferential standard for substantive review of local decisions, as it appeared to do in *Olech*. In this way, litigants could argue about the merits, not about who belongs in what court. Also, such an approach would preserve the essential concept that the federal courthouse door is open to those who claim their constitutional rights have been violated. That critical concept, which has been essential to the protection of civil rights and civil liberties in our country, becomes weakened by arbitrary exceptions to federal court authority, such as now exists with respect to land use. It should be remembered that the brutal sheriff, Claude Screws, was tried federally and not in the Georgia courts for good reason.

As treasured as local home rule is, there is no justification for different constitutional *procedural* treatment of it; protection of local prerogatives can come through an appropriate level of federal judicial deference to local discretion. The same Court that has engaged in reapportionment, restructured local government and state government in countless ways, and has afforded broad federal court protection for a variety of constitutional guarantees should not treat land use as a special case where federal courts need not apply. Land use is only one of many local government functions and not nearly as important as voting districts, schools, or police, which the Court has constitutionally regulated. Therefore, *Williamson County* should be discarded.

Notes

1. FLA. STAT. ANN. § 70.001 (2).

2. A representative sample of such cases is collected in *Southern Burlington County NAACP v. Mt. Laurel Twp.*, 92 N.J. 151, 456 A.2d 102 (1983).

3. Shaw v. Hunt, 517 U.S. 899 (1996); Baker v. Carr, 369 U.S. 186 (1962).

4. 47 U.S.C. § 332.

5. 42 U.S.C. § 3604.

6. Thomas E. Roberts, *Procedural Implications of Williamson County/First English in Regulatory Takings Litigation*, 31 ENVTL. L. REP.10,353 (2001) (hereinafter Roberts).

7. 482 U.S. 304 (1987).

8. 505 U.S. 1003 (1992).

9. 438 U.S. 104 (1978).

10. 447 U.S. 255 (1980).

11. *See* Village of Willowbrook v. Olech, 528 U.S. 562 (2000) (no ripeness requirement imposed on an equal protection claim alleging a discriminatory land-use exaction of land). The situation with substantive due process is somewhat more complex because many courts insist that only deprivation of a firmly vested right to develop can trigger substantive due process review, but even there the issue is usually, but not in all circuits, related to the existence of a property right, not the ripeness of the federal claim.

12. 473 U.S. 172 (1985).

13. 422 U.S. 490 (1975).

14. 429 U.S. 252 (1977).

15. 477 U.S. 340 (1986).

16. *Id.*

17. 512 U.S. 374 (1994).

18. 121 S. Ct. 2448 (2001). *See* discussions *infra* chapters 3 and 8 for details of the ripeness issue in *Palazzolo.*

19. *See, e.g.*, Dover Twp. v. Board of Adj. of Dover Twp., 158 N.J. Super. 401, 386 A.2d 421 (1978).

20. *See* discussion of *Olech, infra* chapters 22 and 23.

21. 528 U.S. 562 (2000).

22. Roberts, *supra* note 6.

23. *First English, supra* note 7.

24. 365 U.S. 167 (1961).

25. 227 U.S. 278 (1913).

26. The Fifth Amendment had been found applicable to the states through the Fourteenth Amendment a few years before in *Chicago Burlington & Quincy R. Co. v. Chicago*, 166 U.S. 226 (1897).

27. 227 U.S. 278 (1913).

28. 325 U.S. 91 (1945).

29. Roberts, *supra* note 6 and writings cited therein at 10,354 n. 5.

30. England v. Board of Medical Examiners, 375 U.S. 411 (1964). *See* Field v. Sarasota Manatee Airport Authority, 953 F.2d 1299, 1307-09 (11th Cir. 1992) (holding open the possibility of a similar reservation of federal rights in a takings lawsuit).

31. 136 F.3d 1219 (9th Cir. 1998).

32. 522 U.S. 156 (1997).

33. I do some municipal work. I was chastised by an insurance carrier lawyer, who got a land-use work that I had answered in state court, for not removing that case to federal court, since the carrier lawyer always removed land-use cases to federal court to take

advantage of the summary judgment procedures. Yet even while municipal defendants are rushing to federal court, it has somehow become a matter of near destruction of local government if the plaintiff's choice to sue in federal court is respected.

34. The retreat report had suggested a moderate position—that a government entity that removed a case to federal court waived the right to assert that the takings claim should be dismissed as unripe. This theory has not yet been litigated. But a recent decision holding that a state does not waive its sovereign immunity by removing a case to federal court suggests that the a ripeness defense will also be found not to be waived by removal. *See* Lapides v. Board of Regents, 251 F.3d 1372 (11th Cir. 2001).

35. *See* Azul-Pacifico, Inc. v. City of Los Angeles, 973 F.2d 704 (9th Cir. 1992), *cited in* Roberts, *supra* note 6, at 10,356 n. 31.

36. *Compare* Sheryll D. Cashin, *The Tyranny of the Favored Quarter*, 88 GEO. L. J. 1985 (2000). Prof. Cashin argues that the fragmented politics of most American metropolitan areas allow upper-middle-class homeowners in outlying suburbs to gain more than their fair share of economic goods while diverting social problems and social expenses elsewhere.

37. 531 U.S. 159 (2001).

38. 517 U.S. 620 (1996).

39. 526 U.S. 687 (1999). This case is particularly fascinating. It found that a jury should hear the takings claim in federal court while all but explicitly holding that no other takings case would ever get such a federal trial because *Williamson County* mandated resort to state courts. *Williamson County* was found inapplicable in this one unique situation because the filing of this case had preceded the Supreme Court's mandate in *First English* that all states make a compensation remedy available. See Note, *Paving a Road, Reaffirming a Roadblock: City of Monterey v. Del Monte Dunes at Monterey Inc.*, 21 PUB. LAND & RESOURCES L. REV. 145 (2000).

40. 512 U.S. 374 (1994).

41. 487 U.S. 825 (1987).

THE FINALITY REQUIREMENT IN TAKINGS LITIGATION AFTER *PALAZZOLO*

21

VICKI BEEN

§ 21.0   *Introduction*

In its 1985 decision in *Williamson County Regional Planning Commission v. Hamilton Bank of Johnson City*,[1] the United States Supreme Court severely limited property owners' access to federal courts to litigate Fifth Amendment takings challenges to environmental and land-use regulations. The developer in *Williamson County* claimed that denial of approval for the last stages of its 676-acre subdivision had effected a taking of its property, and sought both an injunction ordering the local government to approve the proposal and compensation for the "temporary taking" of its property. The Supreme Court granted certiorari in the case to address the then-unanswered question of whether the Fifth Amendment required compensation for temporary "regulatory" rather than "physical" takings.[2] The Court found itself unable to reach that question, however, because the takings claim was not yet "ripe." The Court gave two reasons: first, the Court held that a takings challenge is not ripe until the landowner has received a "final decision regarding how it will be allowed to develop its property."[3] Second, the Court held that "if a State provides an adequate procedure for seeking just compensation, the property owner cannot claim a violation of the Just Compensation Clause until it has used the procedure and been denied just compensation."[4]

Property rights advocates and developers revile *Williamson County*.[5] This chapter focuses on the controversy generated by the opinion's finality requirement.[6] The Court's insistence on a "final decision" is said to fundamentally misunderstand the nature of the land-use process.[7] It is accused of driving up the cost of litigation and thus discouraging potential litigants with valid claims. It is lamented as giving federal judges, some of whom have admitted their dislike for land-use controversies, an opportunity to avoid their duty to hear property owners' claims.[8] It is bemoaned as giving local governments an opportunity to "string out" developers, hoping that delay will wear them down.[9]

Criticism of *Williamson County* reached fever pitch in the last few years, as property rights advocates pushed the Private Property Rights Implementation Act though the House of Representatives.[10] The proposed legislation has stalled in the Senate,[11] but property rights advocates continue to try to chip away at *Williamson County* in the courts. The Supreme Court has shown little sympathy for criticism of either prong of *Williamson County*, however, and has held fast to its finality and state compensation requirements. In its most recent discussion of the finality rule, *Palazzolo v. Rhode Island*,[12] the Court again showed no willingness to back away from *Williamson County*. The Court addressed what lower courts have sometimes referred to as a "futility" exception to the finality rule, but did so in an unusual factual context that will severely limit the reach of the Court's holding to very few takings claims. At the same time, the Court was careful to leave room for the states to impose their own finality and exhaustion rules, a development that property rights advocates may find quite troublesome. The Court's strong reiteration that the finality rule is essential to the constitutional determination of whether a regulation has effected a taking also may render the decision an annoyance to property rights advocates' efforts to overturn *Williamson County* in Congress.

The following sections review *Williamson County*'s finality requirement, as developed by the Court's later cases and the lower courts; explore how *Palazzolo* is likely to affect the application of that requirement; and examine the criticisms of the finality requirement.

§ 21.1   *The Finality Requirement*

§ 21.1(a) *The Genesis of the Requirement*

Penn Central Transportation Co. v. City of New York[13] is known primarily for the Court's confession of inability to precisely define a regulatory taking, and its adoption instead of "ad hoc, factual inquiries" to determine when a regulation goes so far as to effect a taking. But *Penn Central* also planted the seed for *Williamson County*'s finality requirement. Although the *Penn Central* Court reached the merits of the claim that the landmark preservation law had effected a taking by interfering with Penn Central's plans to build a 55-story building on top of Grand Central Station, the Court found Penn Central's claims unpersuasive, in part because the property owner had not sought approval for a smaller structure. The Court reasoned that the record therefore did not establish whether Penn Central would be "denied any use of any portion of the airspace above the Terminal."[14]

Two years later, in *Agins v. City of Tiburon*,[15] the Court again invoked notions of finality when confronted with a takings claim. In *Agins*, property owners challenged zoning ordinances restricting the development of their land to between one and five single-family residences, claiming that the ordinances had "completely destroyed the value of [the] property for any purpose or use whatsoever."[16] The Court affirmed the California Supreme Court's holding that the zoning ordinances did not on their face take the property and refused to reach the as-applied challenge: "Because the appellants have not submitted a plan for development of their property as the ordinances permit, there is as yet no concrete controversy regarding the application of the specific zoning provisions."[17]

Similarly, in *Hodel v. Virginia Surface Mining & Reclamation Ass'n*,[18] the Court rejected a claim that the Surface Mining Control and Reclamation Act of 1977 effected a taking, holding that because the property owners had not "availed themselves of the opportunities provided by the Act to obtain administrative relief by requesting either a variance ... or a waiver" of the restrictions, the case was not ripe.[19]

§ 21.1(b) Williamson County

In *Williamson County*, the developer submitted a preliminary plat for a large cluster development in 1973. After the preliminary plat was approved, the developer invested approximately $3.5 million in the golf course that was the central amenity of the development and in other infrastructure. It submitted final plats for each section of the project as it was ready to begin construction and received approvals for about one-third of the units it planned. In 1977, however, the county changed its zoning ordinance in ways that would reduce the project's density. Initially, the planning commission exempted the project from the new rules, but in 1979 the commission reversed course and decided that plats submitted for renewal should be evaluated by the regulations in effect at the time the renewal was sought. In 1980, the developer submitted a revised preliminary plat. Upon review, a special committee appointed to work with the developer identified eight problems with the revised plat, some (but not all) of which were occasioned by changes in the regulations in the intervening years. The special committee recommended a waiver of the regulations giving rise to three of the objections, but the commission denied approval of the plat, citing two problems with the project's density for which no waiver had been suggested. The developer appealed to the Board of Zoning Appeals, which ordered the commission to apply the density regulations that had been in effect in 1973. The commission declined to follow that decision because it believed that the board had no authority to hear appeals from the commission, and denied approval of the plat for all eight of the reasons identified by the special committee.

Although the developer claimed that it had done everything possible to resolve the conflict with the commission,[20] the Court held that the claim was not ripe. It noted that, unlike the claimant in *Agins*, the property owner in *Williamson County* had submitted a development plan. But like the claimant in *Hodel*, the property owner had not sought variances, even though "it appears that variances could have been granted to resolve at least five of the Commission's eight objections."[21] The property owner thus had "not yet obtained a final decision regarding how it will be allowed to develop its property."[22] The Court explained that its insistence on a final decision was "compelled by the very nature of the inquiry required by the Just Compensation Clause" because elements of that inquiry, such as the "economic impact of the challenged action and the extent to which it interferes with reasonable investment-backed expectations... simply cannot be evaluated until the administrative agency has arrived at a final, definitive position regarding how it will apply the regulations at issue to the particular land in question."[23]

§ 21.1(c) *The Requirement That Applications Be "Meaningful"*

The Court elaborated further on its finality requirement in *McDonald, Sommer & Frates v. Yolo County*.[24] The landowner in *McDonald* sought permission to subdivide its tract into 159 single-family and multifamily lots, and when its application was denied, challenged the rejection as a taking, alleging that "any application for a zone change, variance or other relief would be futile."[25] The Court again relied upon *Penn Central* and *Agins* to hold that the challenge was premature: "Our cases uniformly reflect an insistence on knowing the nature and extent of permitted development before adjudicating the constitutionality of the regulations that purport to limit it."[26] *MacDonald* elaborated that "[i]t follows from the nature of a regulatory takings claim that an essential prerequisite to its assertion is a final and authoritative determination of the type and intensity of development legally permitted on the subject property. A court cannot determine whether a regulation has gone 'too far' unless it knows how far the regulation goes."[27] Indeed, "no answer is possible until a court knows what use, if any, may be made of the affected property."[28]

The Court acknowledged that, unlike the situation in *Agins,* the property owner had submitted a proposal and had received a response to that proposal. But the possibility that some development would still be permitted remained, because the property owner had "alleged the denial of only one intense type of residential development"[29] and "rejection of exceedingly grandiose development plans does not logically imply that less ambitious plans will receive similarly unfavorable reviews."[30]

The dissent argued that the property owner's allegation that any further proposals would be futile rendered the case ripe. The majority countered, however, that the state courts had rejected the claim of futility and had found instead that the owner's proposal was so intensive that "a meaningful application has not yet been made."[31] The majority apparently understood the possibility of abuse in the requirement of a meaningful plan, because it noted that a property owner could not be required "to resort to piecemeal litigation or otherwise unfair procedures in order to obtain this determination."[32] The Court left it to the lower federal courts and state courts, however, to define the line between appropriately insisting that a developer submit realistic proposals and inappropriately forcing the developer into exercises in futility.[33]

§ 21.1(d) *The Reach of the Finality Requirement*

The Court made clear in *Yee v. City of Escondido*[34] that *Williamson County*'s finality requirement does not apply to facial challenges. The Court has not addressed whether the finality requirement applies to claims that the government has physically occupied property, nor whether it applies to claims that the government has taken property by conditioning the grant of a permit on dedication of land. The lower federal courts and state courts have not reached consensus on either of those issues.[35]

The Supreme Court also has not addressed whether the finality requirement applies to a landowner's substantive due process, procedural due process, or equal protection claims. Many lower federal and state courts apply the finality requirement to substantive due process and equal protection claims, while many have held the requirement inapplicable to procedural due process claims; but again there is no consensus.[36]

§ 21.2   Palazzolo

In 1959, Anthony Palazzolo and a friend bought a plot of land adjacent to Winnapaug Pond that consisted primarily of salt marsh and transferred the land to Shore Gardens, Inc. (SGI). Palazzolo then became SGI's sole shareholder.[37] In 1962, SGI applied to the Rhode Island Division of Harbors and Rivers (DHR) for permission to dredge Winnapaug Pond and to fill the salt marsh "to make it adaptable for useful development." The following year, after DHR returned the application because it was incomplete, SGI submitted another application, seeking permission to dredge the pond, fill the property, and construct a bulkhead. In 1966, SGI submitted yet another application, again to dredge and fill, this time for the purpose of constructing a private beach club. In 1971, DHR first approved the applications, then quickly revoked that approval, citing the proposal's adverse environmental impact.

In 1978, Palazzolo became the owner of the property because the Rhode Island Secretary of State revoked SGI's corporate status. In the intervening years, DHR's successor agency, the Coastal Resources Management Council (CRMC), adopted a Coastal Resources Management Program, which generally prohibited the filling of coastal wetlands. The regulations gave CRMC very little flexibility to grant a "special exception" to the prohibitions against fill: an applicant for such an exception must demonstrate that "[t]he proposed activity serves a compelling public purpose which provides benefits to the public as a whole as opposed to individual or private interests,". . . and is either related to a public infrastructure project, "a water-dependent activity that generates substantial economic gain to the state," or "an activity that provides access to the shore for broad segments of the public." Further, the applicant must show that "all reasonable steps shall be taken to minimize environmental impacts" and that "[t]here is no reasonable alternative means of, or location for, serving the compelling public purpose."

Palazzolo sought a special exception from CRMC in 1983, submitting an application nearly identical to SGI's 1963 applications.[38] CRMC denied the permit, noting that it was "vague and inadequate for a project of this size and nature," finding a "complete lack of evidence demonstrating to this Council the need and demand for the proposed activity," and finding that the proposed project would have "significant impacts" on the waters and wetlands of the pond.[39] Palazzolo reapplied in 1985, proposing a 50-car parking lot, along with picnic tables, barbecue pits, and a trash dumpster, to form a private beach club, along the lines that SGI had requested in 1966. Again, CRMC denied the application. Palazzolo appealed to the Rhode Island courts, but lost the appeal.

Palazzolo then filed an inverse condemnation claim in the Rhode Island courts, alleging that the denial of the permit constituted a taking by destroying "all economically beneficial use of the property." He sought compensation of $3.15 million, the profits he alleged he would earn by filling the wetlands and developing 74 single-family homes on the property. None of Palazzolo's applications had sought approval for single-family residential use, and, indeed, Palazzolo had denied in hearings on his applications for a special exception that he planned to develop the land for residential use. The trial judge rejected the takings claim, finding first that the proposal would constitute a public nuisance. He also found that the state's uncontradicted evidence about the value of the uplands on the property demonstrated that "the plaintiff did not lose all beneficial use" of the property and that Palazzolo would be "able to pursue a smaller and more appropriate proposal to develop the subject property."

The Rhode Island Supreme Court affirmed, on somewhat different grounds.[40] The court first found that the claim was not yet ripe. After discussing the general concept of ripeness, relying on both federal and state precedents, the court emphasized that the "concept of ripeness looms large in the jurisprudence of takings because for a court to determine whether a taking has occurred, the court must be able to ascertain 'the nature and extent of permitted development' on the subject property."[41] The court determined that the claim was not ripe for two reasons. First, although Palazzolo based his takings claim on denial of permission to develop a 74-lot subdivision, he never applied for permission to develop such a subdivision. Second, the court noted that Palazzolo's applications had been to fill all, then nearly all, of the wetlands, and held that "[u]ntil Palazzolo has explored development options less grandiose than filling eighteen acres of salt marsh, he cannot maintain a claim that the CRMC has deprived him of all beneficial use of the property."[42] In an unfortunately overbroad footnote, the court stated:

> This holding leads to the self-evident conclusion that a landowner who is denied regulatory approval to use his or her property in a particular way must file additional applications seeking permission for less ambitious uses before a takings claim may be sustained.[43]

Although the ripeness determination should have been dispositive, the Rhode Island Supreme Court then "briefly discuss[ed] the merits of Palazzolo's claim."[44] It either held in the alternative, or opined in dicta, first that Palazzolo's claim under *Lucas* that he had been deprived of all beneficial use was defeated by the undisputed evidence that the property had at least $200,000 in value because of the potential for development on its uplands. Further, the court held (or opined) that because the challenged regulations were in effect at the time Palazzolo succeeded to SGI's interest in the property, "the right to fill wetlands was not part of the title he acquired."[45] Third, because Palazzolo had acquired his legal interest after the regulations went into effect, he could have no "reasonable investment-backed expectations" in developing the land under the *Penn Central* takings test.[46]

The U.S. Supreme Court's interest in the case undoubtedly was generated by the Rhode Island court's adoption of the so-called "notice" rule that one who buys property subject to pre-existing regulations cannot claim that those regulations constitute a taking. But the imprecise and overbroad wording of the Rhode Island court's ripeness ruling also presented the property rights bar an opportunity to seek to cabin the "less grandiose" application language in *McDonald*. The state and its amici,[47] on the other hand, sought to show that, despite their number, the poorly developed and diffuse character of Palazzolo's applications left the courts unable to determine what value the regulations left in the property.

In an opinion handed down on the last day of its term, the Supreme Court reversed the Rhode Island Supreme Court on both ripeness grounds and the notice rule.[48] The Supreme Court affirmed the state court's holding that the value left in the property defeated the *Lucas* claim, however, and remanded for further consideration of the *Penn Central* claim.[49] The holdings on the merits are discussed elsewhere in this volume,[50] so the following discussion focuses only on the ripeness issue.

The Court began its ripeness discussion by reemphasizing the critical role that the finality requirement plays in takings jurisprudence:

A final decision by the responsible state agency informs the constitutional determination whether a regulation has deprived a landowner of "all economically beneficial use" of the property, *see Lucas,* or defeated the reasonable investment-backed expectations of the landowner to the extent that a taking has occurred, *see Penn Central.* These matters cannot be resolved in definitive terms until a court knows "the extent of permitted development" on the land in question.[51]

The Court rejected the Rhode Island Supreme Court's holding that no final determination had been reached, however, because the Court believed the regulations unequivocally prohibited development of the type Palazzolo proposed, even if he were to scale back the proposal to fill fewer wetlands. The Court noted that the *Williamson County* rule was necessary because of the "high degree of discretion characteristically possessed by land-use boards,"[52] but reasoned that "once it becomes clear that the agency lacks the discretion to permit any development, or the permissible uses of the property are known to a reasonable degree of certainty, a takings claim is likely to have ripened."[53] The Court distinguished *McDonald, Williamson County,* and *Agins,* which it characterized as involving denials of "substantial" projects that left doubt whether a "more modest submission" might be accepted. In contrast, the Court emphasized that Rhode Island candidly admitted that it would not allow fill of the wetlands for any "likely or foreseeable use."[54]

The Court then turned to the real question, which was whether there had been a final decision on the extent to which the upland portions of the property could be developed. Palazzolo had never applied to develop the uplands; indeed, the record failed to reveal even how many acres of uplands existed. The state argued that Palazzolo's *Penn Central* claim was not ripe because the courts could not determine the value of the uplands given the ambiguity in the record about how many acres of uplands existed and how many homes would be allowed on those uplands. The Court considered that argument to have been waived, however, by the state's failure to contest the statement in Palazzolo's petition for certiorari that the uplands had an estimated worth of $200,000 as the site for one home.[55] The Court's reliance on that misstep was presaged at oral argument, when Justice Scalia impatiently remarked that the state's argument came too late in the day because the Court might not have granted certiorari had the Court thought that the value of the uplands was in dispute.[56] The Court asserted that, in any event, there was no "genuine" ambiguity in the record because testimony suggesting that there were enough uplands to support more than the one home was countered by one of the state's witnesses, who suggested that the additional uplands might not be reachable without filling some wetlands.[57]

Justice Ginsburg's dissent lambasted the Court's decision, arguing that Palazzolo had engaged in "bait-and-switch" by turning the state's use of the $200,000 figure as a defense against a

Lucas claim into an admission that the uplands property was worth *only* $200,000 for the purposes of a *Penn Central* analysis, even though Palazzolo had never raised or argued the *Penn Central* issue in the state courts.[58] The dissent argued that because the state offered the $200,000 figure only as a defense to Palazzolo's argument that there was no value left in the land, the state did not need to "pursue further inquiry into potential upland development."[59] The state's evidence should be read as establishing "only a floor, not a ceiling" on the value of the permissible development.[60] The majority retorted that the state "was aware of the applicability of *Penn Central*."[61]

The majority then addressed the Rhode Island Supreme Court's holding that the claim was not ripe because Palazzolo based his claim for compensation on a right to develop a 74-unit residential subdivision, but had never applied for permission to develop such a project. The state and its amici argued that Palazzolo's strategy of seeking compensation for a project for which no application had been made was designed to hide the fact that the subdivision project would have been stopped by the town's zoning ordinances or by the Rhode Island Department of Environmental Management's sewage disposal regulations long before it ever reached the CRMC. The Court acknowledged the validity of the concern, but said it was not encompassed by *Williamson County*'s finality requirement. Because the Rhode Island Supreme Court had relied upon *Williamson County* rather than on state law exhaustion or permitting requirements:

> The instant case does not require us to pass upon the authority of a state to insist in such cases that landowners follow normal planning procedures or to enact rules to control damage awards based on hypothetical uses that should have been reviewed in the normal course, and we do not intend to cast doubt upon such rules here.[62]

Given that the state agency had entertained the application and had made clear the extent of development permitted, without citing "non-compliance with reasonable state law exhaustion or pre-permit processes," the Court ruled that federal ripeness rules did not require an application for the subdivision upon which the claim for compensation was based.[63]

§ 21.2(a) *The Narrowness of* Palazzolo's *Holding*

The Court's ripeness ruling was cited by property rights lawyers as a major victory. Jim Burling of the Pacific Legal Foundation, counsel for Palazzolo, for example, called the decision "an important achievement" because "it removed a bizarre roadblock that has stood in the way of landowners seeking payment for their property after government has regulated the value out of it. No longer can government require landowners to pursue meaningless permit applications purely for the purpose of delay and to drive up the litigation costs."[64]

A simplistic view of the decision may lead property owners to file more litigation, thinking that the finality barrier has been lowered. More litigation undoubtedly will have some chilling effect upon land-use and environmental regulators. But when the dust settles, the decision may have very little impact. As the majority itself highlighted, the facts in Palazzolo were "quite unlike" the normal case in which the environmental or land-use agency "has discretion in considering development plans for the property, including the opportunity to grant any variances or waivers allowed by law."[65] The special exception provision of the Rhode Island regulations was extraordinarily stringent, and there is no evidence that the state led Palazzolo to believe that it had flexibility to accept applications that differed only in the number of wetlands destroyed. Indeed, at trial, Mr. Palazzolo testified that CRMC had informed him that any proposal involving the filling of wetlands would be denied.[66] Where the variance or special exception provision of a zoning ordinance or land-use or environmental regulation is more open-ended, as most are, *Palazzolo*'s reasoning simply won't apply.

Further, because drafters of such provisions may view *Palazzolo* as a reason to give regulators more discretion,[67] the end result of *Palazzolo* could be to introduce more discretion, and therefore more difficulty in identifying the point when a decision maker has reached a final determination, rather than less. Of course, the Court reiterated the warning first issued in *McDonald* that government could not burden property owners with "repetitive or unfair land-use procedures" and emphasized that point by citing *Monterey v. Del Monte Dunes at Monterey, Ltd.*[68] The government could not, therefore, disingenuously represent that it has discretion that it did not, in fact, possess.

The Court's holding that the case was ripe, even though no application had ever been submitted for development of the uplands, also is of quite limited reach because the case is so idiosyncratic. The state itself put into evidence the fact that it would allow at least one home on the uplands portion and introduced evidence regarding the value of the land with one home. Its strategy was to defeat the *Lucas*[69] claim by showing that the property retained substantial value even without development of the wetlands. In the future, governments rejecting a proposal that involves only a portion of the land should be careful to specify that the denial does not necessarily preclude development on the remainder of the land. The government's response to alternative claims under *Lucas* and *Penn Central* should clearly indicate whether evidence that the government introduces about the value remaining in the land establishes a minimum or a maximum. Finally, one of the primary sources of confusion in the case, highlighted at oral argument when one Justice bemoaned the lack of a proper map in the record, was the fact that Palazzolo's applications had never specified the size of the total parcel or disclosed which portions were uplands. The staff recommendations on the applications noted those deficiencies; in the future, agencies would be well advised to reject applications without such crucial information as incomplete, rather than trying to address the merits of the application.

§ 21.2(b) *Finality and the Relevant Parcel Debate*

One aspect of *Palazzolo* that may work to the government's favor is the potential relationship it reveals between the finality requirement and the problem of how to define the property, the $64,000 question[70] that the Court has repeatedly avoided.[71] Rhode Island asserted at oral argument that Palazzolo had applied for permission to develop only the wetlands in an effort to establish that the regulated wetlands alone were a separate property interest.[72] It pointed out that the finality rule is intended to reveal the value left in the property, but the value is "always going to be 100 percent as to the burden[ed] part of the parcel. . . . There's a whole parcel violation that underlies the ripeness problem."[73] Most developers want to build, not litigate, so presumably they won't put forward proposals for less than their whole parcel just to manufacture a takings claim. But careful agencies will guard against the risk of abuse by insisting that a proposal encompass all the land that the agency believes makes up the whole parcel, and by making clear that denial of a proposal for development of less than all the parcel is not a decision as to the remainder of the parcel. By revealing the link between ripeness and the definition of the relevant parcel, *Palazzolo* can be used to validate reasonable permitting requirements that regulatory authorities adopt to thwart manipulation of the property interest.

§ 21.2(c) *Using State Law to Protect Permitting Processes*

The most important sword *Palazzolo* provided to regulatory agencies, however, lies in the Court's acknowledgment that state law principles might appropriately have precluded Palazzolo's litigation. Rhode Island and its amici argued that Palazzolo's application for fill to construct a beach club could not ripen a claim that the state took his right to construct a 74-unit residential subdivision. They pointed out that the CRMC would not have entertained an application for residential use until Palazzolo had obtained the appropriate zoning permits from the town of Westerly and sewage disposal permits from the state's Department of Environmental Resources. By short-circuiting those processes and preventing the state from using them to develop a record about the potential harms of such intensive use, they argued, Palazzolo's gambit would leave the Court reviewing the takings claim unable to assess whether the project lacked viability apart from the wetlands regulations.

The Court granted the validity of that concern and disclaimed any intent to "cast doubt upon" the authority of a state "to insist ... that landowners follow normal planning procedures or to enact rules to control damage awards based on hypothetical uses that should have been reviewed in the normal course."[74] The Court noted, however, that the state court did not rely on "state law ripeness or exhaustion principles," and "neither the agency nor a reviewing state court has cited non-compliance with reasonable state law exhaustion or pre-permit processes." The Court declined to read *Williamson County* to reach the application-sequencing problem.[75]

Regulatory agencies should respond to the Court's discussion by strictly enforcing their rules about the sequencing of reviews where more than one agency has an interest in a proposed development, and by insisting on meticulous adherence to all requirements for a permit application. Rhode Island might have avoided this whole controversy, for example, by rejecting Palazzolo's applications because of their incompleteness and poor quality,[76] or by invoking state law principles of administrative res judicata because of the proposals' similarity to those that had already been denied.[77] Government defendants in takings cases also should respond to *Palazzolo* by focusing on their state's ripeness and exhaustion precedents, rather than relying solely on *Williamson County*.

§ 21.3   *Legitimacy of the Finality Requirement*

Palazzolo accordingly left *Williamson County*'s finality requirement alive and well, much to the disappointment of many critics. The criticisms leveled, however, do not withstand scrutiny.[78] The most serious criticism is that the finality requirement is subject to abuse.[79] Knowing the substantial harm that delay can cause a developer and the substantial cost of repeated proposals, local governments are said to be prone to "string out" applicants by insisting that the developer jump through unnecessary hoops before receiving the inevitable denial. Faced with the threat of costly and time-consuming procedures, the developer may give in to unreasonable demands in order to secure development permission, or may forego litigation over valid claims because of the expense of ripening the claim.

The finality requirement admittedly poses a risk of abuse. But the risk is constrained by the threat that the government will be held liable for interfering with the property owner's rights during the permitting process, if the developer eventually proves that the permit denial effected a taking.[80] It is not yet settled whether any eventual takings award would include compensation for the deprivation of property during the time spent securing a final determination. The Court said in *First English* that its rule requiring compensation for temporary regulatory takings did not "deal with the quite different questions that would arise in the case of normal delays in obtaining building permits, changes in zoning ordinances, variances, and the like."[81] A court would certainly be justified in considering delays to be other than "normal" if they were caused by unfair demands that a developer submit to unnecessary procedures. Indeed, the courts could decide that procedures required to obtain a final decision will not be considered "normal" if they result in a taking.[82] Most important, however, a local government seriously compromises its credibility on the merits of the takings claim if it can be portrayed as acting in bad faith by insisting that developers submit to procedures that the government knew or should have known would be futile. The decision and the size of the award in *Del Monte Dunes*, for example, was no doubt seriously influenced by the evidence that the city of Monterey encouraged the developer to file five different applications, successively reducing density from 344 to 190 units, but the city nevertheless denied permission to build.[83]

The threat of liability may be insufficient to constrain the risk of abuse efficiently if the probability of an award against the government is too low. Ultimately, that is an empirical question, which requires far greater attention from scholars and policy analysts. However, the empirical evidence that does exist certainly does not support the allegation of widespread abuse. Two studies were relied upon during congressional hearings on the Private Property Rights Implementation Act.[84] The most recent, conducted by a law firm retained by the National Association of Home Builders (NAHB), examined takings cases decided by the lower federal courts between 1990 and 1998 in which property owners sought development approval.[85] It found that the majority of those takings cases were dismissed for failure to meet at least one of the *Williamson County* requirements or on abstention grounds, and therefore concluded that the "ripeness rules have become stumbling blocks" for property owners.[86] The NAHB study was cited during the hearings for the proposition that "it took property owners, on the average, 9.6 years to have an appellate court reach its determination."[87]

The NAHB study does not demonstrate, however, any evidence of widespread abuse of the finality requirements. Of the 79 cases studied, 25 involved dismissals for lack of a final decision.[88] The study provides no systematic review of the nature of those dismissals. It does not indicate whether the property owners had submitted one or several applications, or provide any other information about the finality determination that could serve as evidence that the finality requirement is being abused. Indeed, although the study was conducted to bolster the claim that congressional action was warranted, the study does not even question how many of the finality determinations would have been different under the standards of finality imposed by the proposed legislation.[89] The study's statement that "landowners thus endured almost a decade of negotiation and litigation to obtain a judicial determination" is based on a subset of only 14 cases in which the takings claims were heard on the merits by appellate courts. But even if credited, that conclusion does nothing to reveal the length of time required to satisfy the finality requirement.[90]

In the second study, Brian Blaesser analyzed land-use decisions in the lower federal courts from 1983 to 1988.[91] He found that in 36 district court cases where ripeness was an issue, 94 percent were decided against the plaintiff. Of the dismissed cases, 24 percent did not meet the finality requirement, 56 percent fell under the state remedies prong, and 18 percent failed to satisfy both requirements.[92] Again, however, Blaesser failed to probe whether the cases in which the finality requirement was invoked reveal evidence that the requirement is being abused by regulatory authorities. Both the NAHB study and Blaesser document that a significant number of takings plaintiffs failed to satisfy the finality requirement; they tell us nothing about whether the requirement is being misused to force property owners to waste time in futile procedures. The studies seem to assume that the property owner never seeks to short-circuit legitimate procedural requirements, so that any dismissal on finality grounds must be wrong, and any invocation of the finality requirement by regulatory officials must be abuse. There is simply no reason to believe that is true. Indeed, the fact that the Private Property Rights Imple-

mentation Act largely tracks the finality rules that the lower federal courts and state courts have adopted[93] belies the assumption.

The other primary criticism of the finality requirement is that
it misunderstands the nature of land-use decision making. Gideon
Kanner laments, for example, that *Williamson County* "giv[es]
no inkling that the Court ... was aware of how variances are
applied in state land-use law, and that on these facts, in particular,
a variance would have been factually and legally inappropriate."[94]
It is undoubtedly true that the courts know less about land-use
law than practitioners in the field would like (as is true of every
field). Courts surely have at times misunderstood local regulatory structures. But the finality requirement stems from the flexibility that marks the current regulatory system. Some critics
would prefer a world in which land-use regulation was a simple
matter of rubber-stamping a developer's plans, rather than the
complex back-and-forth between developers and the community
that defines the current system. The certainty of rigid command-
and-control regulatory schemes comes, however, at the price of
the fairness and efficiency that flexibility may promote. Variances, for example, are expressly intended to give local governments a "safety valve" to avoid harsh results when generally valid
regulations work a special hardship on a particular landowner.

No doubt many critics of the finality requirement have as
their real complaint the Court's substantive takings doctrine. Simplistic "per se" rules of takings, however, often are unable to
achieve the fairness that the Takings Clause was intended to ensure. The best we've been able to do in searching for the right
balance between the property owner's desire to use her land as
she wishes and the community's desire to protect against pollution and misuse of the environment and other common property
is a test that takes into account the extent of the owner's loss. As
long as that is an element of the test, the finality requirement will
be necessary.

Notes

1. 473 U.S. 172 (1985).

2. *Id.* at 185. The Court finally resolved the question in *First English Evangelical
Lutheran Church of Glendale v. County of Los Angeles*, 482 U.S. 304 (1987).

3. 473 U.S. at 186.

4. *Id.* at 195.

5. *See, e.g.*, Michael M. Berger, *The "Ripeness" Mess in Federal Land Use Cases or
How the Supreme Court Converted Federal Judges into Fruit Peddlers*, 1991 INST. ON
PLAN. ZONING & EMINENT DOMAIN, ch. 7; Timothy V. Kassouni, *The Ripeness Doctrine
and the Judicial Relegation of Constitutionally Protected Property Rights*, 29 CAL. W. L.
REV. 1 (1992).

6. The second prong of *Williamson County* is even more controversial than the finality requirement. For excellent overviews of that controversy, *see* Thomas E. Roberts, *Procedural Implications of* Williamson County/First English *in Regulatory Takings Litigation: Herein of Reservations, Removal, Diversity, Supplemental Jurisdiction, Rooker-Feldman, and Res Judicata,* 31 ENVTL. L. REP. 10,353 (April 2001); Thomas E. Roberts, *Ripeness and Forum Selection in Land-Use Litigation, in* Takings: Land Development Conditions and Regulatory Takings After *Dolan* and *Lucas* 46 (David L. Callies ed., 1996); *see also* Kathryn E. Kovacs, *Accepting the Relegation of Takings Claims to State Courts: The Federal Courts' Misguided Attempts to Avoid Preclusion under* Williamson County, 26 ECOLOGY L.Q. 1 (1999).

7. Gideon Kanner, *Hunting the Snark, Not the Quark: Has the U.S. Supreme Court Been Competent in Its Effort to Formulate Coherent Regulatory Takings Law?* 30 URB. LAW. 307 (1998).

8. *See, e.g.,* Gregory Overstreet, *The Ripeness Doctrine of the Taking Clause: A Survey of Decisions Showing Just How Far Federal Courts Will Go to Avoid Adjudicating Land-Use Cases,* 10 J. LAND USE & ENVTL. L. 91 (1994).

9. *See, e.g.,* S. REP. No. 105-242, at 8-19 (1998); H.R. REP. No. 105-323, at 4-5 (1997).

10. H.R. 1534, 105th Cong. (1997).

11. S. 2271, the companion bill to H.R. 1534, failed to muster the required three-fifths vote for a motion to "proceed to consideration." Versions of the bill have been reintroduced in successive years, but none has been reported out of committee. For discussions of the bills, *see, e.g.,* Max Kidalov and Richard H. Seamon, *The Missing Pieces of the Debate over Federal Property Rights Legislation,* 27 HASTINGS CONST. L.Q. 1 (1999); Robert Meltz, *Property Rights Legislation: Analysis and Update,* CA 24 ALI-ABA 17 (1996); Frank I. Michelman, *A Skeptical View of "Property Rights" Legislation,* 6 FORDHAM ENVTL. L.J. 409 (1995); Carol M. Rose, *A Dozen Propositions on Private Property, Public Rights and the New Takings Legislation,* 53 WASH. & LEE L. REV. 265 (1996): Lois J. Schiffer, *Taking Stock of the Takings Debate,* 38 SANTA CLARA L. REV. 153 (1997); Glenn P. Sugameli, *Takings Bills Threaten People, Property, Zoning, and the Environment,* 31 URB. LAW. 177, 182-83 (1999); *see also* Michael M. Berger & Gideon Kanner, *The Need for Takings Law Reform: A View from the Trenches—A Response to Taking Stock of the Takings Debate,* 38 SANTA CLARA L. REV. 837 (1998).

12. 533 U.S. __ , 121 S.Ct. 2448 (2001).

13. 438 U.S. 104 (1978). *Penn Central's* ad hoc test no longer applies if a regulation deprives an owner of all economically beneficial uses of its property. Lucas v. South Carolina Coastal Council, 505 U.S. 1003 (1992).

14. 438 U.S. at 136-37.

15. 447 U.S. 255 (1980).

16. *Id.* at 258 (quoting the complaint).

17. *Id.* at 260 (citations omitted).

18. 452 U.S. 264 (1981).

19. *Id.* at 297.

20. 473 U.S. at 188.

21. *Id.*

22. *Id.* at 190.

23. *Id.* at 190-91.

24. 477 U.S. 340 (1986).

25. *Id.* at 344.

26. *Id.* at 351.

27. *Id.* at 348.

28. *Id.* at 350.

29. *Id.* at 352 n.8.

30. *Id.* at 352-53 nn.8-9.

31. *Id.*

32. *Id.* at 350 n.7.

33. For representative cases, *see, e.g.*, Greenbrier (Lake County Trust Co. No. 1391) v. United States, 40 Fed. Cl. 689, 702 (1998), *aff'd*, 193 F.3d 1348 (Fed. Cir. 1999), *cert. denied*, 530 U.S. 1274 (2000); Southview Assocs. v. Bongartz, 980 F.2d 84, 98 (2d Cir. 1992), *cert. denied*, 507 U.S. 987 (1993); Gilbert v. Cambridge, 932 F.2d 51, 61 (1st Cir. 1991), *cert. denied*, 502 U.S. 866 (1991); Herrington v. County of Sonoma, 857 F.2d 567 (9th Cir. 1988), *cert. denied*, 489 U.S. 1090 (1989); Kinzli v. City of Santa Cruz, 818 F.2d 1449 (9th Cir. 1987), *amended*, 830 F.2d 968 (9th Cir. 1987), *cert. denied*, 484 U.S. 1043 (1988).

34. 503 U.S. 519, 533-34 (1992); *see also* Suitum v. Tahoe Regional Planning Agency, 520 U.S. 725, n.10 (1997) ("'facial' challenges to regulation are generally ripe the moment the challenged regulation or ordinance is passed").

35. One lower federal court has held that the finality requirement does not apply to physical occupations, Sinaloa Lake Owners Ass'n v. City of Simi Valley, 882 F.2d 1398, 1402 (9th Cir. 1989), *amended*, 882 F.2d 1398 (9th Cir. 1989), *cert. denied*, 494 U.S. 1016 (1990), *overruled on other grounds*, Armendariz v. Penman, 75 F.3d 1311, 1325 (9th Cir. 1996). But another court stated, in dicta, that the issue was unclear. Harris v. City of Wichita, 862 F. Supp. 287, 291 (D. Kan. 1994), *aff'd*, 74 F.3d 1249 (10th Cir. 1996). For a review of decisions regarding the applicability of the finality requirement in challenges to physical dedications, *see* Roberts, *Ripeness and Forum Selection, supra* note 6, at 49-52.

36. For substantive due process claims, *compare* Taylor Inv., Ltd. v. Upper Darby Township, 983 F.2d 1285 (3d Cir.) (final determination requirement applies), *cert. denied*, 510 U.S. 914 (1993), *with* Restigouche, Inc. v. Town of Jupiter, 59 F.3d 1208, 1212 (11th Cir. 1995) ("Because substantive due process and takings challenges to the zoning process scrutinize that process in slightly different ways, . . . [the] claims mature at different points in the process."). *See also* David S. Mendel, *Note, Determining Ripeness of Substantive Due Process Claims Brought by Landowners Against Local Governments*, 95 MICH. L. REV. 492 (1996).

For equal protection claims, *compare* Christopher Lake Dev. Co. v. St. Louis County, 35 F.3d 1269 (8th Cir. 1994) (yes), *with* P.L.S. Partners, Women's Med. Ctr. of R.I., Inc. v. City of Cranston, 696 F. Supp. 788 (D.R.I. 1988) (no).

For procedural due process claims, *compare, e.g.*, Nasierowski Bros. Inv. Co. v. City of Sterling Heights, 949 F.2d 890 (6th Cir. 1991) (no final detrmination requirement), *with* Rocky Mountain Materials & Asphalt, Inc. v. Board of County Comm'rs, 972 F.2d 309 (10th Cir. 1992) (applying both prongs of *Williamson County* to a procedural due process claim).

37. The initial acquisition and transfers of the land were referred to by the trial court as a "title examiner's nightmare," so who owned what when is less than crystal clear. The best description is in Dwight H. Merriam and Bryan W. Wenter, Palazzolo *Promotes Property Rights*, 24 ZONING & PLAN. L. REP. 45 (2001).

38. Palazzolo v. Rhode Island, 746 A.2d 707, 711 (R.I. 2001).

39. 121 S. Ct. at 2456.

40. 746 A.2d at 713-17.

41. *Id.* at 713 (citations omitted).

42. *Id.* at 714.

43. *Id.* at 714 n.6.

44. *Id.* at 714.

45. *Id.* at 716.

46. *Id.* at 717.

47. The author was of counsel to the National Wildlife Federation and other environmental and land-use organizations in their amicus brief in *Palazzolo*.

48. The decision included six separate opinions. Justice Kennedy's majority opinion was joined by Justices Rehnquist, O'Connor, Scalia, and Thomas; Justice O'Connor concurred but wrote separately to set forth her understanding of how the state court should interpret the majority opinion when it applied the *Penn Central* test on remand; Justice Scalia concurred but disagreed with Justice O'Connor's interpretation; Justice Stevens concurred with the majority's ripeness decision but dissented as to the remaining issues; Justice Ginsburg dissented, joined by Justices Souter and Breyer, arguing that the case was not ripe; Justice Breyer dissented separately to set forth his views on the notice issue.

49. 121 S. Ct. at 2457.

50. *See*, in particular, chapters 2 and 3 with respect to the notice rule, and chapters 8, 9, and 10 with respect to partial takings.

51. 121 S. Ct. at 2458 (citations omitted).

52. *Id.* at 2459 (quoting Suitum v. Tahoe Regional Planning Agency, 520 U.S. 725, 738 (1997)).

53. 121 S. Ct. at 2459.

54. *Id.*

55. *Id.* at 2460.

56. Justice Scalia jumped into a discussion between James Burling, representing Palazzolo, and another justice about whether more than one house might be allowed on the uplands as follows:

> Question: Twice in the brief in opposition they acknowledge that the CMRC would have approved a single home site, which would have netted greater proceeds, i.e., $ 200,000 at less risk; they say that on page four, and again at, say, page 19, they say specifically the Council would be happy to have petitioner situate a single home thus allowing petitioner to realize $200,000. So I, you know, I thought that was not in the case when we took it.
>
> Mr. Burling: That is correct, Your Honor.
>
> Question: We might not have taken it had I thought it was in the case.

Transcript, Palazzolo v. Rhode Island, 2001 WL 196990, at *7 (transcript does not indicate the identity of the Justice asking the question, but the author was present during oral argument). Later, Justice Scalia again made his point in an exchange between Justice Kennedy and counsel for Rhode Island:

> Question: Can we take the case on the assumption that the only likely permitted use of the property in question is to build one residence on the upland area leaving the 18 or so wetlands area unimproved?
>
> General Whitehouse: I do not believe, Justice Kennedy, that that would be consistent with the decisions of either the Rhode Island Superior Court or the Rhode

Island Supreme Court, which both indicated that there were additional economically viable uses available, and they did not refer to those as the building of a
house.

Question: It seems to me odd then that they would get to the question of a *Lucas*
taking, etc.

General Whitehouse: Well, there are three categories of information here. There is
the established, and what we referenced, Your Honor, in our memorandum in
opposition; there was the established, and established in the Superior Court,
proposition that at least one house worth at least $200,000 can be built. Then there
is the uncertainty as to what additional upland there is and how many other
houses can be built.

Question [by Justice Scalia]: Did you reference that in your brief in opposition?
I mean that might have made a big difference as to whether we wanted to take this
case. Did you make any reference to the fact that there was uncertainty as to how
much additional use could be made of the property?

General Whitehouse: No, Your Honor.

Question: Well, it's too late now.

Id. at *26-27.

57. 121 S. Ct. at 2460.
58. *Id.* at 2474-75 (Ginsburg, J., dissenting).
59. *Id.* at 2475.
60. *Id.* at 2476.
61. *Id.* at 2461.
62. *Id.*
63. *Id.* at 2462.
64. Press Release, Pacific Legal Foundation, Pacific Legal Foundation Scores Landmark Victory for Private Property Rights Advocates in the U.S. Supreme Court (June 28,
2001), *available at* http://www.aboutpalazzolo.com/news/prma/062801.htm (visited Aug.
30, 2001).
65. 121 S. Ct. at 2459.
66. Palazzolo v. Coastal Res. Mgmt. Council, 1997 WL 1526546, at *3 (R.I. Super.
1997).
67. Merriam and Wenter point out that government runs a risk in "loosen[ing]" up
variance and special exception provisions because the less stringent standards would then
open the door to more claims for relief. Merriam and Wenter, *supra* note 37. *See also*
Merriam's discussion *infra* chapter 8. The drafter will have to weigh the advantages of
discretion, including the effect greater discretion may have on ripeness determinations,
against the disadvantages.
68. 526 U.S. 687 (1999). *Del Monte* involved a horrendous record, in which the
developer submitted a proposal for 344 units; then after being told that 264 units would be
favorably received, submitted a second proposal for 264 units; then after being told that
224 units would be favorably received, submitted a third proposal for 224 units; then after
the city council overturned denial of that proposal with instructions to approve a 190-unit
proposal, submitted a fourth proposal for 190 units, which was conditionally approved;
then submitted a fifth proposal for 190 units that met all the conditions imposed, but
nevertheless was denied permission to build. Although the district court held that the
application was nevertheless not ripe, the Ninth Circuit reversed. 920 F.2d 1496 (9th Cir.
1990). Ripeness was not at issue in the Supreme Court's decision in *Del Monte*, but the

Court made its outrage at the process clear. *See, e.g.,* 526 U.S. at 698 (noting that the record reflected "five years, five formal decisions, and 19 different site plans").

69. By making very clear that the *Lucas* per se rule for regulations that destroy "all economically viable use" really means *all, Palazzolo* may limit the number of *Lucas* claims asserted.

70. For good discussions of the so-called denominator question, *see, e.g., infra* chapters 4 and 5; ROBERT MELTZ ET AL., THE TAKINGS ISSUE 144-54 (1999); Robert H. Freilich et al., *Regulatory Takings: Factoring Partial Deprivations into the Taking Equation, in* TAKINGS: LAND-DEVELOPMENT CONDITIONS AND REGULATORY TAKINGS AFTER *DOLAN* AND *LUCAS* 165 (David L. Callies ed., 1996); Marc R. Lisker, *Regulatory Takings and the Denominator Problem,* 27 RUTGERS L.J. 663 (1996); Daniel Mandelker, *New Property Rights under the Taking Clause,* 81 MARQ. L. REV. 9 (1997); Margaret Jane Radin, *The Liberal Conception of Property: Cross Currents in the Jurisprudence of Takings,* 88 COLUM. L. REV. 1667, 1676 (1988); Courtney C. Tedrowe, *Note, Conceptual Severance and Takings in the Federal Circuit,* 85 CORNELL L. REV. 586 (2000).

71. *See, e.g., Lucas,* 505 U.S. at 1016 n.7.

72. 2001 WL 196990, at *34-35.

73. *Id.* at *37; *see also id.* at *35-41.

74. 121 S. Ct. at 2461.

75. *Id.* at 2461-62. The Court's several references to state law "exhaustion" requirements are particularly interesting. In *Williamson County,* the Court went to great pains to distinguish its finality requirement from exhaustion requirements, because it had earlier held in *Patsy v. Florida Board of Regents,* 457 U.S. 496 (1982), that a plaintiff need not exhaust administrative remedies before bringing a suit predicated on 42 U.S.C. § 1983. The Court noted that exhaustion and finality are "conceptually distinct," reasoning that:

> [w]hile the policies underlying the two concepts often overlap, the finality requirement is concerned with whether the initial decisionmaker has arrived at a definitive position on the issue that inflicts an actual, concrete injury; the exhaustion requirement generally refers to administrative and judicial procedures by which an injured party may seek review of an adverse decision and obtain a remedy if the decision is found to be unlawful or otherwise inappropriate.

473 U.S. at 192. For discussions of the distinction, *see also* Roberts, *Ripeness and Forum Selection, supra* note 6, at 52-54; Berger, *supra* note 5, at 7-15. Whether the *Palazzolo* Court's reference to exhaustion reflected the Court's own confusion of the two concepts or signaled an interest in retreating from *Patsy* in the takings context is unclear.

76. The CRMC's denial of Palazzolo's 1983 proposal, for example, noted that the application was "vague and inadequate for a project of this size and nature." 121 S. Ct. at 2456.

77. Indeed, the Rhode Island Supreme Court invoked the state's Administrative Procedures Act in warning that Palazzolo should not continue to submit repetitive applications: "The doctrine of administrative finality dictates that an applicant may not challenge administrative action by filing identical repetitive applications, but must bring any challenge in Superior Court in accord with the Administrative Procedures Act." 746 A.2d at 714 n.6 (citations omitted).

78. For views of the finality requirement more sympathetic than the critiques explored here, *see* R. Jeffrey Lyman, *Finality Ripeness in Federal Land-Use Cases from Hamilton Bank to Lucas,* 9 J. LAND USE & ENVTL. L.101 (1993); Michael K. Whitman, *The Ripeness*

Doctrine in the Land-Use Context: The Municipality's Ally and the Landowner's Nemesis, 29 URB. LAW.13 (1997).

79. *See*, *e.g.*, Berger, *supra* note 5.

80. Of course, informal norms about fair play also may serve to constrain regulatory officials.

81. 482 U.S. at 321.

82. *See* Gregory M. Stein, *Regulatory Takings and Ripeness in the Federal Courts*, 48 VAND. L. REV.1, 59-61 (1995).

83. *See* Douglas T. Kendall et al., *Choice of Forum and Finality Ripeness: The Unappreciated Hot Topics in Regulatory Takings Cases*, 33 URB. LAW. 405, 427-28 (2001).

84. *See* S. REP. No. 105-242, at 45 (1998); H.R. REP. No. 105-323, at 5 (1997); *see also Amendment to the Webb-Kenyon Act and Private Property Implementation Act of 1997: Hearings on H.R. 1063 and H.R. 1534 Before the Subcomm. on Courts and Intellectual Property of the House Judiciary Committee*, 105th Cong. 69 (1997).

85. John J. Delaney & Duane J. Desiderio, *Who Will Clean Up the "Ripeness Mess"? A Call for Reform So Takings Plaintiffs Can Enter the Federal Courthouse*, 31 URB. LAW. 195 (1999).

86. *Id.* at 202.

87. *Id.* at 205.

88. *Id.* at 206-31.

89. The Private Property Rights Implementation Act would have required an applicant to submit "one meaningful application, as defined by applicable law," and if rejection of that application was not accompanied by a written explanation, would require the applicant to apply for "one appeal or waiver." If an application was rejected with explanation, the applicant would be required to submit "another meaningful application taking into account the terms of the disapproval," and if that were disapproved, to apply "for one appeal and one waiver with respect to the disapproval." H.R. 1534, 105th Cong. § 6(c) (1997).

90. Delaney & Desiderio, *supra* note 85, at 205.

91. Brian W. Blaesser, *Closing the Federal Courthouse Door on Property Owners: The Ripeness and Abstention Doctrines in Section 1983 Land Use Cases*, 2 HOFSTRA PROP. L.J. 73 (1988).

92. *Id.*

93. *See* Kidalov and Seamon, *supra* note 11, at 21.

94. Kanner, *supra* note 7, at 331.

PROTECTING PROPERTY FROM UNJUST DEPRIVATIONS BEYOND TAKINGS: SUBSTANTIVE DUE PROCESS, EQUAL PROTECTION, AND STATE LEGISLATION

22

STEVEN J. EAGLE

§ 22.0   Introduction

This chapter considers means of protecting individual property rights other than the Takings Clause. These include the doctrines of substantive due process and equal protection in ensuring that individuals are not unjustly deprived of their property,[1] and also state protective legislation. The chapter begins with a review of why private property was so important to the framers and how they structured the Constitution and Bill of Rights to protect it. It then considers how substantive due process was the basis of the Supreme Court's regulatory takings jurisprudence.

While the Court previously had regarded property and contract as fundamental rights, in the late 1930s it shifted abruptly to a model that regarded political and social rights as fundamental. In line with this inversion of preferred rights, it created a revisionist history that recasts earlier substantive due process cases as takings cases. Indeed, federal courts have ruled that cases more easily perceived as involving *deprivations* of property must be treated under the rubric of *takings* of property.

Those changes affect our view in subtle ways. Cases decided before the late 1930s simply referred to "due process of law." The expression "substantive due process" was not used by the Supreme Court until 1948[2] and followed from the insistence of Progressives that due process was a guarantee of procedural regularity only.[3] However, according to a study by Professor James Ely, "due process was fashioned in part to protect the rights of property owners, and ... judicial decisions placing property in a subordinate constitutional category are historically unsound.... [The term 'substantive due process'] is misleading and betrays a tendency to read history backward."[4]

Since 1987, the Supreme Court has vindicated property rights claims in a number of cases in which it purported to utilize Takings Clause analysis only. Yet it has maintained an ambivalence toward substantive due process that it has refused to clarify. At the same time, substantive due process concepts have infused takings cases.

This chapter reviews these developments and notes two situations in which the Court's regulatory takings jurisprudence seems awkward and inadequate. The Court's equation of "just compensation" with "fair market value"[5] provides no relief to owners deprived of property that is of intense value to them but of no value to others. Also, owners who have been deprived of property arbitrarily or capriciously cannot prevail under the Takings Clause unless the asset is converted to public use.[6] Closely related to deprivation of property through arbitrary rules is deprivation of equal protection of the laws that results in one individual losing property rights that may continue to be asserted by others similarly situated.

The Supreme Court's failure to develop a coherent theory of property rights contributes heavily to these difficulties. In recent years, however, many states have passed some form of property rights protective legislation. Some of those statutes show promise of providing meaningful protection for individual rights.

Strengthened and more explicit use of substantive due process analysis is not incompatible with energetic application of the Takings Clause. While due process and equal protection analysis might afford better doctrinal fit and more effective relief in some cases, these clauses have considerable overlap with the Takings Clause. Furthermore, the Supreme Court has "rejected the view that the applicability of one constitutional amendment preempts the guarantees of another."[7]

§ 22.1 A Historical Analysis of American Property Rights Jurisprudence

§ 22.1(a) **Why and How the Framers Sought to Protect Private Property**

The framers were imbued with the English and Scottish Enlightenment understanding that government was a compact among individuals for the protection of their liberties. When James Madison wrote that "[a]s a man is said to have a right to his property, he may be equally said to have a property in his rights,"[8] he was echoing John Locke's *Second Treatise of Government*, which declaimed, "Lives, Liberties, and Estates, which I call by the general Name, *Property*."[9] John Adams wrote that "[p]roperty must be secured or liberty cannot exist,"[10] and Madison declared that "[g]overnment is instituted to protect property of every sort...."[11] Given the importance of private property in creating general prosperity and buttressing individual liberty, it follows that protecting property rights was the "great focus" of the framers.[12] These property rights did not spring from an act of positive law, but rather arose through evolution of the common law:

> In the concrete taking case the court must initially decide if the plaintiff has an actual property interest, if this is a point of dispute. This determination is based upon long and venerable case precedent, developed over the last two centuries. It is further clarified in the light of our law's Common Law antecedents. The Anglo-American case precedent is literally made up of tens of thousands of cases defining property rights over the better part of a millennium. The legal task is very unlike legislative policy-making because judicial decision-making builds historically and logically upon past precedent in narrow cases and controversies rather than current general exigencies or sweeping political mandates. The genius of our Framers' tripartite division of constitutional power is the creation of separated institutions that each best deal with different categories of governmental decisions.[13]

The Constitution and the Bill of Rights contained a number of provisions explicitly and implicitly designed to protect property and to facilitate its use. The states were proscribed from interfering with agreements affecting transfers of property by the Contract Clause,[14] and from interfering with a new national common market by the Interstate Commerce Clause.[15]

At the same time, the new national government was made subject to many restrictions that made it difficult for Congress to interfere with property. Some were structural, such as those dividing the powers of the national government among its branches.[16] Some cabined the role of the national government. The doctrine of enumerated powers limited the permissible ends of federal legislation[17] with other powers being retained by the states or by the people.[18] Also, the permissible ends of federal spending were limited to activities that benefit the "general Welfare of the United States."[19] This provision has been rendered ineffective by the Supreme Court,[20] although scholars recently have urged its revival.[21] Similarly, the Privileges and Immunities Clause[22] was intended, in the words of Justice Bushrod Washington, to protect privileges that are "fundamental" and "belong, of right, to the citizens of all great governments [including] the right to acquire and possess property of every kind."[23]

The framers also designed provisions more directly protective of property rights. The Fifth Amendment Takings Clause declares: "[N]or shall private property be taken for public use, without just compensation."[24] This implicitly acknowledges that the power of eminent domain devolved from the British Crown to the federal government as well as the states. It also explicitly limits the exercise of that power to condemnation for "public use"[25] and where "just compensation" is provided.[26] Also, the Fifth Amendment Due Process Clause provides that the federal government cannot deprive individuals of due process of the laws.[27]

§ 22.1(b) *The Supreme Court's Property Jurisprudence before the New Deal*

Prior to the Civil War, the federal government did not attempt significant regulation of private land use. Its acquisition of private land for such uses as forts and post offices clearly required owner consent or the explicit exercise of eminent domain. The Supreme Court held in 1833 that the Fifth Amendment did not protect against state interference with private property.[28]

The post–Civil War Fourteenth Amendment evidenced Congress's distrust of the willingness of states to protect the liberties of newly freed slaves or others. It proscribed the states from making and enforcing measures that "shall abridge the privileges or immunities of citizens of the United States."[29] Furthermore, it made the due process language of the Fifth Amendment applicable to the states,[30] and mandated that no state shall "deny to any person within its jurisdiction the equal protection of the laws."[31]

In the watershed *Slaughter-House Cases*,[32] a closely divided Court held that the Due Process Clause of the Fourteenth Amendment required procedural due process only,[33] and that the Privileges or Immunities Clause pertained only to aspects of national citizenship such as free access to ports and not to the right to earn a livelihood in one's craft or profession.[34] Only very recently has the Court begun to infuse the Privileges or Immunities Clause with new life.[35]

Late in the 19th century, the influential treatise of Thomas Cooley,[36] together with calls from the growing national business community, led the Supreme Court toward renewed interest in the protection of property rights through substantive due process. This process began with qualifications in the language of cases in which regulations were sustained. In *Munn v. Illinois*,[37] the Court upheld state regulation of grain elevators, but on the basis of the fact that such economically vital businesses were "affected with a public interest."[38] Likewise, in *Mugler v. Kansas*,[39] it upheld a Prohibition statute resulting in large economic losses to a brewery, but on the grounds that Prohibition was imposed "to guard the community against the evils attending the excessive use of such liquors."[40] Thus, at the same time the Court was upholding the states' police power, it was making independent judgments about the appropriateness of its use.

The mere invocation of the police power by regulators was insufficient to circumvent judicial review. In 1890, in *Chicago, Milwaukee & St. Paul Railway Co. v. Minnesota*,[41] the Court held that railroads had a due process right to judicial review of rate regulations to ensure that they could achieve a fair return on their investments. The Court's balancing of asserted police power ends against the effects of regulation on affected individuals was made clear in *Lawton v. Steele*,[42] where the Court declared: "To justify the State in this interposing its authority in behalf of the public, it must appear, first, that the interests of the public . . . require such interference; and, second, that the means are reasonably necessary for the accomplishment of the purpose and not unduly oppressive upon individuals."[43]

In 1905, in *Lochner v. New York*,[44] the Court struck down a statute prescribing maximum hours for bakers on the grounds that the state did not offer sufficient support for its assertion that longer hours would adversely affect their health. *Lochner* became emblematic of economic substantive due process and the popular myth that the Court used substantive due process to invalidate health and safety legislation wholesale.[45] Substantive due process review in fact helped the poor and immigrants to compete against dominant interests in the marketplace.[46] It also was the basis for the Court's invalidation of racial zoning in *Buchanan v. Warley*.[47]

§ 22.1(c) *The Classic Property Deprivation/Takings Cases*

Between 1897 and 1928, the Supreme Court decided four cases that are now generally regarded as the foundation of modern regulatory takings jurisprudence. In *Chicago, Burlington & Quincy R.R. v. City of Chicago*,[48] it reviewed a claim that the payment of only nominal consideration for the condemnation of land used to extend a public street violated the Due Process Clause of the Fourteenth Amendment. The Court explained that the state might provide full procedural due process "and yet it might be that its final action would be inconsistent with [the Fourteenth] amendment."[49]

> [A]s this court has adjudged, a legislative enactment, assuming arbitrarily to take the property of one individual and give it to another individual, would not be due process of law, as enjoined by the fourteenth amendment, it must be that the requirement of due process of law in that amendment is applicable to the direct appropriation by the state to public use, and without compensation, of the private property of the citizen. The legislature may prescribe a form of procedure to be observed in the taking of private property for public use, but it is not due process of law if provision be not made for compensation.[50]

Pennsylvania Coal v. Mahon[51] generally is regarded as the genesis of the Court's modern regulatory takings doctrine, although that label might be a later recharacterization.[52] While the common law recognizes rights to the surface and to underground minerals as estates in land, Pennsylvania law recognized a third estate, the right to support of the surface. The sale by the coal company of the surface rights to Mahon explicitly provided that the company retained the right of support as well as the mineral interest. In an attempt to protect their homes from possible subsidence resulting from mining, landowners who had not purchased the right of support subsequently obtained state legislation precluding mining that might result in the sinking of lots on which private structures were located. They obtained an injunction, which was sustained by the state courts.[53] The result was that much valuable coal had to be left in place as support pillars.

The enigmatic heart of Justice Holmes's opinion reads: "[W]hile property may be regulated to a certain extent, if regulation goes too far it will be recognized as a taking."[54] However, Holmes never mentioned the Fifth Amendment Takings Clause. For him, the central issue was: "As applied to this case the statute is admitted to destroy previously existing rights of property and contract. The question is whether the police power can be stretched so far."[55] Furthermore, in language reminiscent of *Lawton v. Steele*,[56] Holmes added: "We are in danger of forgetting that a strong public desire to improve the public condition is not enough to warrant achieving the desire by a shorter cut than the constitutional way of paying for the change."[57]

Four years after *Pennsylvania Coal*, the Supreme Court gave its imprimatur to comprehensive zoning in *Village of Euclid v. Ambler Realty Co.*[58] *Euclid* was viewed as a test case of zoning by both commercial real estate owners and Progressive Era reformers. Hence, the landowner did not apply for a building permit nor did it seek any kind of administrative relief. Rather, it asserted that it was holding the land for sale and that this precluded any relief short of invalidation of the ordinance.[59]

The Court's opinion was written by Justice Sutherland, who generally supported economic substantive due process. However, Sutherland held strong and idiosyncratic views about contagion of disease and the propensity to violence in densely packed cities.[60] Largely on this account, he was inclined to give full play to the police power justification for zoning.[61] He wrote that "with the great increase and concentration of population, [urban] problems have developed ... which require ... additional restrictions in respect of the use and occupation of private lands in urban communities. Regulations, the wisdom, necessity, and validity of which, as applied to existing conditions, are so apparent that they are now uniformly sustained, a century ago, or even half a century ago, probably would have been rejected as arbitrary and oppressive."[62] Adding little more than a casual analogy to the law of nuisance,[63] he concluded: "If the validity of the legislative classification for zoning purposes be fairly debatable, the legislative judgment must be allowed to control."[64] Sutherland made no mention of the Takings Clause, nor of *Pennsylvania Coal*.

Two years after *Euclid*, Sutherland wrote for the Court in *Nectow v. City of Cambridge*.[65] That case presented an "as applied" challenge to the residential zoning of a strip of a larger parcel located in an industrial area. The trier of fact had determined that there was no police power justification of the zoning, and that the formerly valuable strip was rendered unusable. "The attack upon the ordinance is that ... it deprived [the plaintiff] of his property without due process of law in contravention of the Fourteenth Amendment."[66] Sutherland cited *Euclid* for the proposition that the power of the government "to interfere by zoning regulations with the general rights of the land owner by restricting the character of his use, is not unlimited, and other questions aside, such restriction cannot be imposed if it does not bear a substantial relation to the public health, safety, morals, or general welfare."[67] *Nectow* concluded that "the action of the zoning authorities comes within the ban of the [Due Process Clause of the] Fourteenth Amendment and cannot be sustained."[68] The Court did not decide another takings case for 50 years.[69]

§ 22.1(d) *The New Deal Revolution*

Based on public suspicion of large-scale business and demands to alleviate the Great Depression, during the 1930s Congress passed redistributive legislation and the Supreme Court was induced to uphold it. In a stream of cases, the Court pulled back from economic substantive due process.[70] Finally, in 1938, in *United States v. Carolene Products Co.*,[71] the Court established the now-familiar dichotomy whereby fundamental rights and rights of discrete and insular minorities receive heightened scrutiny, while economic and social legislation are presumed constitutional so long as there is plausibly a rational relationship between it and achievement of a legitimate government end.[72]

While the cases culminating in *Carolene Products* often are regarded as repudiating substantive due process, they instead transformed its content and nomenclature. *Carolene Products* "brilliantly endeavored to turn the Old Court's recent defeat into a judicial victory" by turning from property and contract to making "the ideals of the victorious activist Democracy serve as a primary foundation for constitutional rights in the United States."[73] Although purporting to substitute a "process model"[74] for a substantive one, *Carolene Products* might be viewed more accurately as substituting one set of preferred rights for another. Given the emphasis that the framers placed on property as an integral component of liberty,[75] its subordination under a model premised on fundamental rights is inexplicable.[76] Given the Court's continued unwillingness to utilize economic substantive due process as such, its enhanced regard for the need to protect property rights during the past 15 years has been expressed through the Takings Clause.

§ 22.1(e) *A Revisionist History Transmutes Substantive Due Process into Takings*

The Supreme Court's recent property rights cases have demonstrated its proclivity to use substantive due process analysis while steadfastly refusing to confront the fact that it is doing so. In

Dolan v. City of Tigard,[77] for instance, Justice Stevens wrote a spirited dissent[78] reviewing the substantive due process origins of *Chicago, Burlington & Quincy.*[79] He asserted that it "applied the same kind of substantive due process" as gave rise to *Lochner v. New York.*[80] Stevens also found an "obvious kinship" to *Lochner* in Justice Holmes's regulatory takings analysis in *Pennsylvania Coal Co. v. Mahon.*[81] This invocation of the "specter" of *Lochner*[82] alludes to the "Victorian melodrama"[83] of economic substantive due process, in which the case constitutes the "centerpiece in this tale of wickedness."[84]

Chief Justice Rehnquist's majority opinion responded only by brusquely pronouncing *Chicago, Burlington & Quincy Railroad*[85] as incorporating the Fifth Amendment Takings Clause into the Fourteenth Amendment.[86] This still is the Court's articulated position.[87]

§ 22.2   *The Takings Clause and Its Limitations*

The Takings Clause of the Fifth Amendment provides: "[N]or shall private property be taken for public use without just compensation."[88] In the Supreme Court's often-quoted phrase in *Armstrong v. United States,*[89] the Takings Clause "was designed to bar Government from forcing some people alone to bear public burdens which, in all fairness and justice, should be borne by the public as a whole."[90]

"Just compensation" rarely is "full compensation."[91] Also, the use of eminent domain for private purposes results in pernicious rent-seeking behavior.[92] I assert that for these reasons the Fifth Amendment limited eminent domain to instances where the property thus obtained would be limited to "public use."[93]

The Takings Clause does not purport to authorize or to forbid acts of eminent domain. Rather, in the words of Justice Kennedy:

> The Clause operates as a conditional limitation, permitting the government to do what it wants so long as it pays the charge. The Clause presupposes what the government intends to do is otherwise constitutional.[94]

In many cases the Takings Clause is a satisfactory vehicle for vindicating citizens' rights, but it is an awkward mechanism for rectifying some deprivations of private property. The Clause may offer no protection to owners who have demonstrable subjective value in their property but no market value. It also is not well suited to protecting government deprivations of nonspecific property.

§ 22.3   Embedded Due Process in the Court's Recent Takings Cases

While the Supreme Court purports to deal with deprivations of property through takings analysis only, some of its cases utilize substantive due process nested inside takings nested inside substantive due process.[95] The outer layer is the orientation of results toward fairness and respect for property as a fundamental constitutional norm. The middle layer is the Takings Clause, as applicable to the states through incorporation within the Fourteenth Amendment Due Process Clause. The inside layer is due process, which manifests itself through the "substantial advancement" prong of *Agins*,[96] through proportionality in *Dolan*,[97] and through an expansion of the "character of the governmental regulation" test of *Penn Central*.[98]

§ 22.3(a) *The* Agins *Substantial Advancement Test*

The case most notably imparting substantive due process underpinnings is *Agins v. City of Tiburon*,[99] where the Court enunciated a two-prong test:

> The application of a general zoning law to particular property effects a taking if the ordinance does not substantially advance legitimate state interests, see *Nectow v. Cambridge*, . . . or denies an owner economically viable use of his land, see *Penn Central Transp. Co. v. New York City*. . . . [100]

What is referred to as the "first prong" of *Agins*, the "substantially advance legitimate state interests" test, cites *Nectow* but obscures that it was a substantive due process case.[101] In 1999, the Court decided *City of Monterey v. Del Monte Dunes at Monterey, Ltd.*,[102] the subtext of which was municipal disingenuousness that in every instance met developer compliance with stated conditions for permission to develop with a new round of demands.[103] The Court upheld the trial judge's decision, made over the city's objection, to allow the jury to determine liability under Del Monte's takings claim, which included ascertaining whether the city's permit denials substantially advanced the stated purposes of its regulations. The solicitor general's brief rehearsed the substantive due process roots of *Agins* in *Euclid* and *Nectow*,[104] and then launched into a frontal assault on the legitimacy of the first prong of *Agins* as a component of the Takings Clause.[105] Since the city itself initially had proposed the essence of the jury instructions, the Court "decline[d] the suggestions of amici" to revisit the matter.[106]

§ 22.3(b) *Deprivation of Wealth as a Taking*—Eastern Enterprises

In *Eastern Enterprises v. Apfel*,[107] the petitioner formerly engaged in coal mining. It asserted that a federal Coal Act, designed to bail out a financially troubled health plan for retired miners and their families,[108] violated the Due Process and Takings Clauses of the Fifth Amendment. The act required that Eastern make cumulative payments to the plan of some $50 million to $100 million.[109] Eastern was not a party to the collective bargaining agreement that significantly expanded benefits and led to the plan's financial difficulties. Under the act, liability had been assigned to Eastern with respect to miners it had last employed many years earlier.[110]

Justice O'Connor, writing for a plurality of the Court, concluded that the act "imposes severe retroactive liability on a limited class of parties that could not have anticipated the liability, and the extent of that liability is substantially disproportionate to the parties' experience."[111] The fact that Eastern departed from the coal industry before benefit expectations rose and before plan funding fell was stressed both in the plurality opinion[112] and in Justice Kennedy's concurrence.[113] On the other hand, Justices Stevens, Souter, Ginsburg, and Breyer joined in two dissenting opinions in which Stevens asserted that Eastern had been party to an "implicit understanding" regarding benefits,[114] and Breyer emphasized that Eastern's burden had been moderated by other aspects of the Coal Act and was reasonable.[115]

The *Eastern Enterprises* Court was marked by different five-to-four splits on the judgment and on the constitutional provision that the Court should apply in reaching the judgment. Justice O'Connor's plurality opinion, joined by Chief Justice Rehnquist and Justices Scalia and Thomas, deemed the act unconstitutional under the Takings Clause.[116] Justice Breyer's dissent, joined by Justices Stevens, Souter and Ginsberg, deemed the act constitutional under the Due Process Clause.[117] Justice Kennedy, concurring in the judgment and dissenting in part, deemed the act unconstitutional under the Due Process Clause.[118] Thus, the plurality plus Kennedy judged the act unconstitutional as applied, but the dissent plus Kennedy constituted a majority for a due process analysis.

Both Justice Kennedy's swing opinion[119] and Justice Breyer's dissent[120] argued (1) a Due Process analysis is correct and (2) a Takings Clause analysis is incorrect. Justice O'Connor's plurality opinion argued (1) a Takings Clause analysis is correct and (2) a Due Process Clause analysis need not be considered.[121]

Kennedy reasoned that since the statute's constitutionality "appears to turn on the legitimacy of Congress's judgment rather than on the availability of compensation . . . the more appropriate constitutional analysis arises under general due process principles."[122] He also deemed the plurality's Takings Clause analysis to be "incorrect and quite unnecessary for decision of the case."[123] Justice Breyer asserted not only that the issue of retroactive liability "finds a natural home in the Due Process Clause,"[124] but also that he "agree[s] with Justice Kennedy that the plurality views this case through the wrong legal lens. The Constitution's Takings Clause does not apply."[125]

Justice O'Connor's plurality opinion asserted the correctness of a Takings Clause analysis and the lack of need to consider a Due Process Clause analysis.[126] On the first point, she stated:

> That Congress sought a legislative remedy for what it perceived to be a grave problem in the funding of retired coal miners' health benefits is understandable; complex problems of that sort typically call for a legislative solution. When, however, that solution singles out certain employers to bear a burden that is substantial in amount, based on the employers' conduct far in the past, and unrelated to any commitment that the employers made or to any injury they caused, the governmental action *implicates fundamental principles of fairness underlying* the Takings Clause. Eastern cannot be forced to bear the expense of lifetime health benefits for miners based on its activities decades before those benefits were promised. Accordingly, in the specific circumstances of this case, we conclude that the Coal Act's application to Eastern effects an unconstitutional taking.[127]

While "fundamental principles of fairness" might "underlie" the Takings Clause, those principles are at the heart of due process. Furthermore, the unfairness in the sovereign seizing property without compensation sometimes resides in the lack of compensation and sometimes in the seizure itself.

Significantly, Justice O'Connor refused to analyze the case beyond the Takings Clause at the price of converting what might have been a majority opinion into a plurality opinion that lower courts must parse for meaning. One Court of Federal Claims case has deemed *Eastern Enterprises* of no precedential value.[128] Others have ruled that "a majority of the Supreme Court held that a regulation must relate to a specific interest for the Takings Clause to apply."[129]

In some cases resembling *Eastern Enterprises*, it might be possible to discern that the retroactive obligation has a sufficient nexus to a discrete asset so that application of the Takings Clause is the more natural recourse.[130] In a broader sense, however, *Eastern Enterprises* might serve as a catalyst for a reappraisal of substantive due process. The U.S. Court of Appeals for the Third Circuit declared in *Unity Real Estate Co. v. Hudson*,[131] for instance, that "[t]he splintered nature of the Court makes it difficult to distill a guiding principle from *Eastern*."[132] However, "[t]o the extent that *Eastern* embodies principles capable of broader application, we believe that due process analysis encompasses the relevant concerns."[133]

Perhaps the most fruitful avenue for vindicating the "fundamental principles of fairness"[134] that the *Eastern Enterprises* plurality acknowledged was "correlated to some extent"[135] with due process would be the infusion of the latter concept into the *Penn Central* "character of the governmental action" test.[136]

§ 22.4 *"Character of the Governmental Action"—An Expanding Test*

In 1978, in *Penn Central Transportation Co. v. City of New York*,[137] Justice Brennan confessed for the Court that it, "quite simply, has been unable to develop any 'set formula' for determining when 'justice and fairness' require that economic injuries caused by public action be compensated by the government, rather than remain disproportionately concentrated on a few persons."[138] He added:

> In engaging in these essentially ad hoc, factual inquiries, the Court's decisions have identified several factors that have particular significance. The economic impact of the regulation on the claimant and, particularly, the extent to which the regulation has interfered with distinct investment-backed expectations are, of course, relevant considerations. So, too, is the character of the governmental action. A "taking" may more readily be found when the interference with property can be characterized as a physical invasion by government than when interference arises from some public program adjusting the benefits and burdens of economic life to promote the common good.[139]

§ 22.4(a) *"Character" as Physical vs. Regulatory Taking*

Based on the juxtaposition previously noted,[140] the "character of the governmental action" test conventionally has been described in terms of physical invasions versus economic regulations.[141]

Under that interpretation, however, the test's utility terminated after four years when, in *Loretto v. Teleprompter Manhattan CATV Corp.*,[142] the Court held that "when the physical intrusion reaches the extreme form of a permanent physical occupation, a taking has occurred. In such a case, 'the character of the government action' not only is an important factor in resolving whether the action works a taking but also is determinative."[143] In *Lucas v. South Carolina Coastal Council*,[144] the Court suggested that "total deprivation of beneficial use is, from the landowner's point of view, the equivalent of a physical appropriation."[145] It established the categorical rule that the imposition of regulation constitutes a compensable taking when it "denies an owner economically viable use of his land."[146] The effect of the categorical rule in *Lucas* is to limit *Penn Central* analysis to partial takings only.[147] The effect of the categorical rule in *Loretto* is to limit *Penn Central* to regulatory takings.

§ 22.4(b) *"Character" as Comprehensive Balancing*

The idea of a "character of the governmental action" test being more comprehensive than the physical versus regulatory taking dichotomy was implicit in *Penn Central*,[148] and was utilized explicitly by the California Court of Appeal on remand from the U.S. Supreme Court in *First English Evangelical Lutheran Church of Glendale v. County of Los Angeles*.[149]

> In *Agins* the public purpose advanced was the interest in preventing premature urbanization.... The Supreme Court might have difficulty finding that this public purpose would justify depriving a landowner of *"all* use" of his property. However, the Supreme Court recognized the public purpose in *First English* is far different—the preservation of lives and health. It would not be remarkable at all to allow government to deny a private owner "all uses" of his property where there is no use of that property which does not threaten lives and health. So it makes perfect sense to deny compensation for the denial of "all uses" where health and safety are at stake but require compensation for the denial of "all uses" where the land use regulation advances lesser public purposes.[150]
>
> *On balance*, the public benefits this regulation confers far exceed the private costs it imposes on the individual property owner (especially after factoring in the public benefits this property owner shares).[151]

Similarly, the U.S. Court of Appeals for the Federal Circuit stated in *Creppel v. United States*[152] that, under the "character of the governmental action" test, "the courts must inquire into the degree of harm created by the claimant's prohibited activity, its social value and location, and the ease with which any harm stemming from it could be prevented."[153]

§ 22.4(c) *"Character" as Targeted Retroactivity*

Two recent Court of Federal Claims cases discuss the "character of the governmental action" test in light of the Supreme Court's decision in *Eastern Enterprises v. Apfel.*[154] In *American Pelagic Fishing Co., L.P., v. United States*,[155] legislation was passed, apparently at the behest of competitors, that uniquely precluded the *Atlantic Star* from fishing for Atlantic mackerel in the Exclusive Economic Zone (EEZ) of the United States.[156] The *Atlantic Star* had been specially fitted for mackerel fishing at a cost of $40 million, and could not be put to an alternative economically beneficial use.[157] The court found that fishing in the EEZ was highly regulated and the owners could have foreseen future regulations of general applicability that might limit fishing. "The targeted revocation of existing permits, however, and the targeted denial of future permits by Congress were not events any citizen in a constitutional republic could have reasonably expected."[158]

The court noted that, "[d]espite the plurality in *Eastern Enterprises*, . . . the Takings Clause only protects juridically recognized property interests."[159] However, use rights in the *Atlantic Star* constituted such an interest, which was taken by dint of divestment of any profitable economic use.[160]

American Pelagic also asserted that *Eastern Enterprises* changed the "character of governmental action" test. It began by observing that the plurality opinion "suggests that, in considering the character of a governmental action alleged to constitute a taking, at least two other factors are also relevant: (1) whether the action is retroactive in effect, and if so, the degree of retroactivity; and (2) whether the action is targeted at a particular individual. Both factors are present here."[161] Justice Kennedy was "troubled by the retroactive, targeted nature of the legislation" as well.[162]

> The plurality's discussion of retroactivity seems to bridge its analysis of reasonable, investment-backed expectations and its analysis of the character of the governmental action. Because the question of whether plaintiff could have reasonably expected retroactive legislation and the

question of whether retroactive legislation is of such a character as to support the finding of a taking appear to us to be two sides of the same coin, we discuss both retroactivity and targeting in our analysis of the character of the governmental action."[163]

Another recent Court of Federal Claims case, *Walcek v. United States*,[164] stated that the "character of the governmental action" test "requires the court to consider the purpose and importance of the public interest underlying the regulatory imposition, focusing, in particular, on whether the challenged restraint would constitute a nuisance under state law."[165]

The common thread in cases like *First English* on remand, *Eastern Enterprises, American Pelagic,* and *Walcek* is that the judges who decided them undertook to balance the degree of harm to the public that motivated the regulation against the losses to the landowner. And that is precisely what the courts did under the rubric of economic substantive due process. The following is an example of explicit balancing in *Lawton v. Steele*,[166] an 1894 case discussed earlier:[167]

> If the property were of great value, as, for instance, if it were a vessel employed for smuggling or other illegal purposes, it would be putting a dangerous power in the hands of a custom officer to permit him to sell or destroy it as a public nuisance, and the owner would have good reason to complain of such act as depriving him of his property without due process of law. But where the property is of trifling value, and its destruction is necessary to effect the object of a certain statute, we think it is within the power of the legislature to order its summary abatement.[168]

§ 22.4(d) *"Character" as Good Faith*

Even as the Supreme Court rejected the assertion that comprehensive zoning was unconstitutional on its face in *Village of Euclid v. Ambler Realty Co.*,[169] it observed that ordinances would face more specific challenges in subsequent cases and that "some of them, or even many of them, may be found to be clearly arbitrary and unreasonable."[170]

The lack of good faith suggested in the phrase "arbitrary and unreasonable" was a crucial element in the Court's recent decision in *City of Monterey v. Del Monte Dunes at Monterey, Ltd.*[171] Del Monte Dunes had sought to develop 344 residential units on a site zoned for more than 1,000 units. The city made serial demands that the number of units be cut, that they be moved to a different location on the parcel, and that other modifications be made. As the developer made the requested changes, it learned that the city would not take "yes" for an answer. After five years of administrative review, the submission of no fewer than 19 different site plans, and after five formal decisions had been obtained, Del Monte filed suit in 1986 in a federal district court under 42 U.S.C. § 1983.[172]

Justice Kennedy, writing for the Court, summarized the facts in a way that seemed to incorporate Del Monte's view of the "tortuous and protracted history of attempts to develop the property, as well as the shifting and sometimes inconsistent positions taken by the city throughout the process."[173]

Although Kennedy's opinion was in other respects written for a unanimous Court, the Justices were split over whether a jury trial could be granted over the city's objection.[174] The trial court had reserved for itself the landowner's due process claim, but had submitted the takings claim to the jury. "At the close of argument, the District Court instructed the jury it should find for Del Monte Dunes if it found either that Del Monte Dunes had been denied all economically viable use of its property or that 'the city's decision to reject the plaintiff's 190-unit development proposal did not substantially advance a legitimate public purpose.'"[175]

As Justice Souter noted in dissent on the jury issue, substantive due process claims generally are reserved for the court.[176] Here, the court did reserve the substantive due process claim and found for the defendant. However, the jury was permitted to find for the plaintiff on the takings claim, with its due process–based component of substantial advancement. Justice Kennedy responded:

> [T]he jury was instructed to consider whether the city's denial of the final proposal was reasonably related to a legitimate public purpose. Even with regard to this issue, however, the jury was not given free rein to second-guess the city's land-use policies. Rather, the jury was instructed, in unmistakable terms, that the various purposes asserted by the city were legitimate public interests.
>
> The jury, furthermore, was not asked to evaluate the city's decision in isolation but rather in context, and, in particular, in light of the tortuous and protracted history of attempts to develop the property.... [D]espite the protests of the city and its amici, it is clear that the Court of Appeals did not adopt a rule of takings law allowing

> wholesale interference by judge or jury with municipal
> land-use policies, laws, or routine regulatory decisions.[177]

§ 22.5   The Possible Retreat from Legislative Redefinition of Property

§ 22.5(a) Rights and Adjudications under Common Law and Statutes

Property rights in the United States were not created by the Constitution, but were part and parcel of the historic "rights of Englishmen."[178] They grew by accretion of the common law.[179]

A number of recent cases have suggested the outlines of a possible shift from interpreting fundamental rights through the lens of legislation toward again viewing those rights from the perspective of their common-law origins. The Supreme Court, for instance, recently has reinforced the difference between retroactive statutes and retrospective changes of interpretation in the common law. In *Landgraf v. USI Film Products*,[180] it declared that "the presumption against retroactive legislation is deeply rooted in our jurisprudence, and embodies a legal doctrine centuries older than our Republic."[181] On the other hand, in *Rogers v. Tennessee*,[182] the Court deemed constitutional the retroactive application of a judicial decision abolishing the common-law rule that no defendant could be convicted of murder unless his victim had died by the defendant's act within a year and a day of the act.

§ 22.5(b) Rejection of the "Positive Notice Rule" in Palazzolo v. Rhode Island

In the Supreme Court's most recent property rights case, *Palazzolo v. Rhode Island*,[183] it rejected the state's assertion that a landowner purchasing after the enactment of a statute could not challenge that statute under the Takings Clause.[184] Justice Kennedy, writing for the Court, characterized the state's argument as follows: "Property rights are created by the State. ... [B]y prospective legislation the State can shape and define property rights and reasonable investment-backed expectations, and subsequent owners cannot claim any injury from lost value. After all, they purchased or took title with notice of the limitation."[185] He responded:

> The State may not put so potent a Hobbesian stick into
> the Lockean bundle. The right to improve property, of
> course, is subject to the reasonable exercise of state au-
> thority, including the enforcement of valid zoning and
> land-use restrictions. ... The Takings Clause, however,
> in certain circumstances allows a landowner to assert that

a particular exercise of the State's regulatory power is so unreasonable or onerous as to compel compensation. Just as a prospective enactment, such as a new zoning ordinance, can limit the value of land without effecting a taking because it can be understood as reasonable by all concerned, other enactments are unreasonable and do not become less so through passage of time or title. Were we to accept the State's rule, the postenactment transfer of title would absolve the State of its obligation to defend any action restricting land use, no matter how extreme or unreasonable. A State would be allowed, in effect, to put an expiration date on the Takings Clause.[186]

Both Locke and Hobbes believed in the importance of property and that men entered into society for their mutual protection. However, there was a profound difference between them, as Justice Kennedy suggested. Hobbes saw property as subject to moral disagreement, and secure rights in property established only by the positive act of an unquestioned political sovereign.[187] Locke, on the other hand, expansively defined "Property" as the "Lives, Liberties, and Estates" of individuals, the protection of which constitutes the basis of government and government's continuing obligation.[188]

§ 22.5(c) *The Court's Possible Retreat from Circularity*

In 1967, in *Katz v. United States*,[189] the Supreme Court held that electronic eavesdropping upon private telephone conversations within a glass-walled telephone booth in a public place constitutes a search and seizure and must meet Fourth Amendment requirements. While the parties contested whether the phone booth was a place in which the defendant might expect privacy, the Court declared that "the Fourth Amendment protects people, not places."[190] It was left to the concurring opinion of Justice Harlan to point out that what protection people are accorded is a function of the extent to which their expectations of privacy are regarded as reasonable, and that, in turn, is largely a function of where they are located.[191]

The Supreme Court's "reasonable investment-backed expectations" test for partial regulatory takings, introduced in *Penn Central*[192] and restated in *Lucas*,[193] is subject to a similar problem. As Justice Kennedy noted in his concurrence in *Lucas*: "There is an inherent tendency toward circularity in this synthesis, of course; for if the owner's reasonable expectations are shaped by what courts allow as a proper exercise of governmental authority, property tends to become what courts say it is."[194] Put another way, "regulation begets regulation."[195] Indeed, the U.S. Court of Appeals for the Federal Circuit has stated that property rights are limited not only by existing regulations but also by the "regulatory climate" at the time of purchase.[196]

Recently, however, the Court has decided cases that may pare back on the circularity evident in both *Katz* and *Lucas*. In *Kyllo v. United States*,[197] Justice Scalia declared:

> The *Katz* test—whether the individual has an expectation of privacy that society is prepared to recognize as reasonable—has often been criticized as circular, and hence subjective and unpredictable. While it may be difficult to refine *Katz* when the search of areas such as telephone booths, automobiles, or even the curtilage and uncovered portions of residences are at issue, in the case of the search of the interior of homes—the prototypical and hence most commonly litigated area of protected privacy—there is a ready criterion, with roots deep in the common law, of the minimal expectation of privacy that *exists,* and that is acknowledged to be *reasonable*. To withdraw protection of this minimum expectation would be to permit police technology to erode the privacy guaranteed by the Fourth Amendment. We think that obtaining by sense-enhancing technology any information regarding the interior of the home that could not otherwise have been obtained without physical "intrusion into a constitutionally protected area" constitutes a search—at least where (as here) the technology in question is not in general public use. *This assures preservation of that degree of privacy against government that existed when the Fourth Amendment was adopted.* On the basis of this criterion, the information obtained by the thermal imager in this case was the product of a search.[198]

This notion of a core of protected fundamental rights surrounded by an area in which balancing is appropriate comports both with the categorical rules of *Loretto*[99] and *Lucas*[200] and with *Lucas*'s notion of "background principles" itself. In *Palazzolo v. Rhode Island*,[201] in the course of striking down the positive notice rule's assertion that all promulgated restrictions were "background principles" of law against subsequent purchasers,[202] the Court observed:

> [A] regulation that otherwise would be unconstitutional absent compensation is not transformed into a background

principle of the State's law by mere virtue of the passage of title. This relative standard would be incompatible with our description of the concept in *Lucas,* which is explained in terms of those common, shared understandings of permissible limitations derived from a State's legal tradition. A regulation or common-law rule cannot be a background principle for some owners but not for others. The determination whether an existing, general law can limit all economic use of property must turn on objective factors, such as the nature of the land use proscribed.[203]

Like the "degree of privacy against government that existed when the Fourth Amendment was adopted" in *Kyllo,* the "shared understandings . . . derived from a State's legal tradition" in *Palazzo* requires the kind of examination of what is fundamental and what is arbitrary that is at the heart of substantive due process methodology. Furthermore, *Palazzolo* reinforces the idea that a doctrine cannot be the law "for some . . . but not for others." The belief that "due process mandated general, not special, laws" has strong roots as a substantive limit imposed by state courts on legislative power in the pre–Civil War era.[204]

§ 22.6   *Preventing or Compensating Property Deprivations beyond "Takings"*

§ 22.6(a) *The Commandeering of Private Property of No Monetary Value*

Every state has mandated that lawyers place sums entrusted to them by clients that are too small to generate interest in separate accounts within pooled interest on lawyers trust accounts (IOLTA accounts).[205] These funds are used to support legal agencies representing indigents and other law-related public purposes.[206] The total amount of monies entrusted in IOLTA accounts is great. The lawyer does not, of course, possess a right to retain the interest. In an era of computerized accounting, it would be easy to attribute pro rata shares of interest to the legal clients whose small, short-term deposits make up the lawyer's single trust account. Rather, the problem stems from the juxtaposition of ethical rules that require lawyers to keep such funds in demand accounts[207] and banking regulations that preclude the payment of interest on pooled demand accounts but which make an exception for IOLTA deposits.[208]

The U.S. Supreme Court reviewed the constitutionality of mandatory IOLTA programs in 1998, in *Phillips v. Washington Legal Foundation*.[209] It held that interest on a client's trust account was the property of the client. The Court relied on the fact that Texas follows the general rule that "interest follows principal" and determined that the adoption of the Texas IOLTA program did not alter this general rule. Quoting from its decision in *Webb's Fabulous Pharmacies, Inc. v. Beckwith*,[210] it stated, "As we explained, 'a State, by ipse dixit, may not transform private property into public property without compensation' simply by legislatively abrogating the traditional rule that 'earnings of a fund are incidents of ownership of the fund itself and are property just as the fund itself is property.'"[211] Having determined that "the interest income generated by funds held in IOLTA accounts is the 'private property' of the owner of the principal," the Court left the issues of takings and just compensation to be addressed on remand.[212]

In its remand opinion, *Washington Legal Foundation v. Texas Equal Access to Justice Foundation*,[213] the U.S. District Court held that there had not been a taking. The plaintiffs had asserted that a per se test was appropriate, since the state had invaded or appropriated private property and had deprived them of their right to exclude others from making beneficial use of their property.[214] The court rejected this analysis on the grounds that *Webb's Fabulous Pharmacies* was not a per se case. Furthermore, the "appropriation of money does not qualify as a physical appropriation of property, since money is fungible, 'unlike real or personal property'";[215] and the Supreme Court's per se cases "all differ from this case because those cases involve the physical invasion of real property."[216]

Applying a *Penn Central* balancing test, the court concluded that there was no economic loss, since the IOLTA deposits could not have generated net interest. "Plaintiffs in the instant action cannot maintain they are being unfairly singled out to bear a burden, when they are in fact bearing no burden at all."[217] Finally, it asserted that "[t]he IOLTA Program is not in any way unfair to Plaintiffs. 'It cannot be said that the Takings Clause is violated whenever legislation requires one person to use his or her assets for the benefit of another.'"[218] The court added that there was no showing that IOLTA had cost clients direct interest receipts,[219] and that consideration of any indirect benefit to the client from having the lawyer retain interest from a client trust fund was foreclosed by the Canon of Professional Ethics.[220]

The district court's view ignores the common-law notion of "relativity of title." While the lawyer has no property right to assert, and the client's property right is so small as to be incapable of capture for direct monetary gain, each has a better claim to the interest than does a stranger. It is not unreasonable for both the lawyer and the client to assume that if the lawyer retains the tiny sums involved, ultimately they will redound to the benefit of the client in the form of a marginally smaller fee somewhere down the line. IOLTA, on the other hand, reflects a distrust of private ordering and private charity. It relies upon the assumption that all items that are of some value to it, and to the owner, but not to the market, are fair game for a variant of escheat for a worthy purpose. As this book was going to press, the U.S. Court of Appeals reversed the district court, finding a per se taking and remanding for declaratory and injunctive relief.[221]

In *Washington Legal Foundation v. Legal Foundation of Washington*,[222] the U.S. Court of Appeals for the Ninth Circuit found, under similar circumstances, that there had been a per se taking[223] and remanded for a determination of the net amount of interest, if any, that the client could have obtained in the absence of IOLTA.

Whether mandatory IOLTA programs are "unfair" to clients depends on one's perspective. The plaintiffs in the Texas case contended that interest on their monies was put to uses that were "ideological and/or political in nature."[224] In the Washington case, the Ninth Circuit quoted an affidavit from one of the plaintiffs stating that "it is not so much that I want the $20 [in lost interest], though I do, as that I don't want the Legal Foundation's donees to get it, because I don't like what they do with it."[225]

As Professors Heller and Krier have noted, "IOLTA programs compromise the expressive and liberty interests of depositing clients, but conventional takings analysis is not very responsive to these concerns. The majority in *Phillips*, for example, focused on monetary injuries that were trivial at best, yet ignored the denial of voice that motivated the case in the first place."[226] It would seem that better solutions to the commandeering of client funds in *Phillips* and the other IOLTA cases lie in an application of substantive due process.

§ 22.6(b) *Deprivation of Property with No "Public Use"*

In *Christy v. Hodel*,[227] the Ninth Circuit upheld the criminal conviction of a Montana rancher for killing a grizzly bear in violation of the Endangered Species Act. Bears had killed 20 of Christy's sheep and ultimately drove the rancher out of business.[228] The court averred that the regulations were governmental actions, but left the plaintiffs with "full . . . property rights to their sheep. . . . Undoubtedly, the bears have physically taken plaintiffs' property, but plaintiffs err in attributing such takings to the government."[229]

Dissenting from the denial of certiorari in *Christy*,[230] Justice White observed:

> Christy's claim of a constitutional right to defend his property is not insubstantial. The right to defend one's property has long been recognized at common law and is deeply rooted in the legal traditions of this country. Having the freedom to take actions necessary to protect one's property may well be a liberty "deeply rooted in this Nation's history and tradition," and, therefore, entitled to the substantive protection of the Due Process Clause. In any event, Christy's claim to such protection presents an interesting and important question—the proper resolution of which is not altogether clear—that merits plenary review.
>
> Even more substantial is Christy's claim that the Endangered Species Act operates as a governmental authorization of a "taking" of his property; leaving him uncompensated for this taking violates the Fifth Amendment, Christy contends. There can be little doubt that if a federal statute authorized park rangers to come around at night and take Christy's livestock to feed the bears, such a governmental action would constitute a "taking.". . . [P]erhaps a Government edict barring one from resisting the loss of one's property is the constitutional equivalent of an edict taking such property in the first place.[231]

Justice White's views seem in accord with the Supreme Court's earlier determination in *Armstrong v. United States*[232] that the government's complete destruction of a materialman's lien in certain property constituted a taking, and with its more recent holding in *Dames & Moore v. Regan*[233] that the availability of compensation was a prerequisite for the seizure of the claims of contractors against the government of Iran as part of the settlement of the embassy hostage crisis.[234]

In all of these cases, the government acted in such a way as to have incurred liability if it had been a private actor. Its actions seemed more directed at extracting resources from immediate targets of opportunity than in imposing a broad sharing of public burdens. In each case as well, the government's act resulted in the indirect deprivation of a valuable right, instead of its taking, and in no direct use by the sovereign. Recognition that the arrogation by government of owners' traditional rights to take reasonable steps to defend their property deprives them of due process of law, as suggested by Justice White in *Christy*, seems the just way to solve this deprivation problem.

§ 22.7 *Due Process Requires Meaningful Scrutiny*

A revival of substantive due process is dependent upon an adequate level of scrutiny of governmental regulations. I use the term "meaningful scrutiny" for this purpose, because it is not a term of art existing in the Supreme Court's lexicon, and because, in any event, the existing terms of art are increasingly imprecise.

In addition to "rational basis" review for the general run of economic and social legislation,[235] there is "strict scrutiny" for "fundamental" rights.[236] Supplementing this two-tiered scheme is "mid-level" review for gender and illegitimacy.[237] Perhaps Justice Marshall was prescient in 1973 when he advocated variable review[238] since, as Professor Richard Fallon has noted, the Court's articulated framework both reflects and invites confusion."[239] Fallon attributes this to the Court's tendency to give the rational basis test "enhanced bite" where classifications are apt to stigmatize or come close to trenching on protected rights.[240] He also cites, inter alia, the Court's "ad hoc balancing of 'the liberty [interest] of the individual' against 'the demands of an organized society.'"[241] Furthermore, in some cases identifying substantive due process rights, the Court "has not even tried to fit [those rights] into a two-tiered model."[242]

"Meaningful scrutiny" stands here for the proposition asserted by the Court in another context that "[t]here must be a congruence and proportionality between the injury to be prevented or remedied and the means adopted to that end."[243] Similarly, the Court used the term "rough proportionality" in *Dolan v. City of Tigard.*[244] There, it examined whether the demanded exaction "substantially advance[d] legitimate state interests"—whether it was a rational means to achieve a legitimate end and also whether the regulation properly placed a burden upon the landowner.[245]

"Meaningful scrutiny" also encompasses the serious type of rational basis review used by the Court in *City of Cleburne v. Cleburne Living Center.*[246] There, the zoning ordinance required a special-use permit for a group home for the mentally retarded, notwithstanding that hotels, fraternity houses, and similar intense uses could locate in the same residential district as a matter of right.[247] The Court carefully reviewed the proffered reasons for the requirement and concluded that it was not "rationally related to a legitimate governmental purpose."[248]

Professor Tribe has referred to the Court's review in *City of Cleburne* as "covertly heightened scrutiny,"[249] but his contrast is with maximum deference to legislative decisions, comporting with his characterization of the "rational basis" test as a "conceivable basis test."[250] Tribe warns:

> The lack of openly acknowledged criteria for heightened scrutiny permits arbitrary use of the type of inquiry undertaken in *Cleburne*, for which courts will remain essentially unaccountable. With no articulated principle guiding the use of this more searching inquiry, even routine economic regulations may from time to time succumb to a form of review reminiscent of the *Lochner* era.[251]

It is inescapable, however, that legitimate "rational basis" review does require judges to make substantive evaluations about legislative goals and their conformity with the states' police powers.[252]

§ 22.8   *Equal Protection*

As the Supreme Court declared in *City of Cleburne v. Cleburne Living Center*,[253] "[t]he Equal Protection Clause of the Fourteenth Amendment commands that no State shall 'deny to any person within its jurisdiction the equal protection of the laws,' which is essentially a direction that all persons similarly situated should be treated alike."[254]

The immediate object of the Clause was the protection from state interference of the rights of newly freed slaves, a task shared in no clearly apportioned way with the Fourteenth Amendment Due Process and Privileges or Immunities Clauses.[255] Early equal protection cases ensured that the states accorded to corporations the same economic rights enjoyed by natural persons.[256] During the *Lochner* era, the Supreme Court used equal protection analysis to strike business tax classifications[257] and state laws that discriminated against black citizens in a political primary.[258]

Modern land-use regulations are given considerable latitude under *Euclid*,[259] and also under *Carolene Products*,[260] so that economic and social legislation will be presumed constitutional as long as there is plausibly a rational relationship between it and a legitimate government end sought to be achieved.[261] Where the land-use regulation allegedly derogates from a fundamental right or harms a suspect class, however, the presumption that the ordinance or rule accords equal protection is not applicable. Even in a case of alleged racial bias, *Village of Arlington Heights v. Metropolitan Housing Development Corp.*,[262] the Court held that "[d]isproportionate impact is not irrelevant,"[263] but that "[p]roof of racially discriminatory intent or purpose is required to show a violation of the Equal Protection Clause."[264]

Under the Supreme Court's rational basis test for general economic and social legislation, courts have been even more reluctant to find invidious discrimination where the regulations seemed logical and their application did not involve a protected class.[265] However, in recent years the courts have accorded equal protection claims more hospitable treatment, culminating in the Supreme Court's recent decision in *Village of Willowbrook v. Olech*.[266] In *WHS Realty Co. v. Town of Morristown*,[267] for instance, local regulations were held to be arbitrary. Residents of certain multifamily buildings, when occupied by a preponderance of tenants, were denied municipal garbage collection. The court found no factual basis for the town's claim that its policy fostered home ownership and that it was violative of equal protection.

In *Forseth v. Village of Sussex*,[268] the U.S. District Court had dismissed for want of *Williamson County* ripeness[269] the landowners' contention that the village board president had coerced them to transfer land to him for his own private use as a condition for approval of development. The U.S. Court of Appeals for the Seventh Circuit held that "bona fide equal protection claims arising from land-use decisions can be made independently from a takings claim and without being subject to *Williamson [County]* ripeness."[270] Furthermore, the plaintiffs had asserted that the defendants had acted "maliciously," thus comporting with the standard the court enunciated in *Esmail v. Macrane*.[271]

Similarly, in *Thomas v. City of West Haven*,[272] the Connecticut Supreme Court held that a showing of personal animus by planning officials in connection with the denial of an application for a zone change established a prima facie case that the plaintiff landowners were victims of selective treatment in violation of the Equal Protection Clause.

Against this background, the Supreme Court's holding in *Village of Willowbrook v. Olech*[273] is particularly significant. The respondent, Grace Olech, had asked the village to connect her property to the municipal water supply. It refused to do so for three months because she would not grant it a 33-foot easement. Other property owners requesting water connections were asked for only a 15-foot easement. The district court dismissed her claim, but the Seventh Circuit, quoting *Esmail*, held that a plaintiff can allege an equal protection violation by asserting that state action was motivated solely by a "'spiteful effort to "get" him for reasons wholly unrelated to any legitimate state objective.'"[274]

The Supreme Court held that it had "recognized successful equal protection claims brought by a 'class of one,' where the plaintiff alleges that she has been intentionally treated differently from others similarly situated and that there is no rational basis for the difference in treatment."[275] It concluded:

> That reasoning is applicable to this case. Olech's complaint can fairly be construed as alleging that the Village intentionally demanded a 33-foot easement as a condition of connecting her property to the municipal water supply where the Village required only a 15-foot easement from other similarly situated property owners. The complaint also alleged that the Village's demand was "irrational and wholly arbitrary" and that the Village ultimately connected her property after receiving a clearly adequate 15-foot easement. These allegations, quite apart from the Village's subjective motivation, are sufficient to state a claim for relief under traditional equal protection analysis. We therefore affirm the judgment of the Court of Appeals, but do not reach the alternative theory of "subjective ill will" relied on by that court.[276]

In a short opinion concurring in the result, Justice Breyer reiterated the solicitor general's concern about refashioning the Equal Protection Clause in "a way that would transform many ordinary violations of city or state law into violations of the Constitution. It might be thought that a rule that looks only to an intentional difference in treatment and a lack of a rational basis for that different treatment would work such a transformation."[277] Breyer emphasized that he joined in the judgment only because Olech *had* been subjected to vindictive action and illegitimate animus.[278]

In a sense, the Breyer concurrence in the judgment hit home that the other eight Justices apparently *had* adopted an approach that regards "irrational and wholly arbitrary" governmental action violative of equal protection, without the need for a showing of "subjective ill will." In addition, the Court let stand without comment the Seventh Circuit's holding that the *Williamson County* ripeness rules do not apply to equal protection cases. Should the Court continue to adhere to these principles in the cases that undoubtedly will follow, property owners will be able to assert in federal court that they were the victims of arbitrary conduct, without having to undergo prolonged state proceedings and issue and claim preclusion in the process.[279] Perhaps Professor Joseph Sax's early admonition that an "equal protection element" within takings law "prevent[s] discriminatory restriction of any one of a number of identically situated owners"[280] was a prescient statement of the law.

§ 22.9 *State Property Rights Protective Legislation*

By the end of the 1990s, at least 22 states had enacted property rights protection statutes.[281] While these differ in important details, they may be categorized roughly into "takings impact assessment statutes" and "compensation statutes."[282] All operate prospectively only.

Many of the statutes provide for takings impact assessment (TIA) only. They mandate that state agencies review their rules or contemplated actions to ensure that they do not constitute uncompensated "takings," as defined in U.S. Supreme Court decisions. TIA statutes might be inspired by the assessment mechanism in the National Environmental Policy Act of 1969 (NEPA),[283] or by the Reagan Administration's Executive Order 12,630, "Governmental Actions and Interference with Constitutionally Protected Property Rights."[284] While the sufficiency of NEPA assessments has been outcome determinative in many cases, E.O. 12,630 precluded citizen enforcement and generally has been disregarded by federal officials.[285]

Some TIA statutes permit blanket certification of compliance, others permit informal agency determinations. More rigorous statutes require agencies to prepare formal, written analyses that must include assessments of alternative actions that might have less impact on property rights. A few states limit the assessment process to specified agencies. About half of the states with TIA statutes impose their requirements on all state agencies, but not political subdivisions. Four states include both state agencies and all or most local governments.[286]

Compensation statutes are intended to provide monetary relief to landowners who have suffered regulatory takings. They rightly preclude compensation where the proscribed use constituted a common-law nuisance, but otherwise they seek to make owners whole when regulations reduce the value of their property in order to provide the public with various goods.

Five states have enacted compensation statutes. Arizona has enacted an administrative appeals process that is limited to the removal or modification of exactions imposed by a city or county in connection with the granting of a permit.[287] Mississippi requires that just compensation be paid for regulation of agricultural and forest land causing a 40 percent diminution in value.[288] The similar law in Louisiana is triggered by a 20 percent diminution.[289] Both statutes refer to the "affected" land or "part" of land. The two state laws having the greatest potential for property rights protection are those of Texas and Florida. Both are too new, however, for a meaningful assessment of their costs or benefits. Also, in 2000 the voters of Oregon approved an amendment to the state constitution that provides broad protection for property rights, Initiative Measure 7. A trial court has found the measure invalidly adopted.[290]

§ 22.9(a) *Texas*

The 1995 Texas Private Real Property Rights Preservation Act[291] provides that an owner may sue for takings damages when an act of the state or a political subdivision results in at least a 25 percent diminution in the value of real property.[292] However, the provision is hedged with broadly defined exceptions for actions to regulate floodplain development, to carry out federal mandates, and the like. In what might be the only reported case to date, a municipal utility district prevailed because the court determined that the standby fee it levied against undeveloped property came under the exception for localities acting responsibly to fulfill state mandates.[293]

§ 22.9(b) *Florida*

Florida's Bert J. Harris, Jr., Private Property Rights Protection Act[294] is the most innovative of the state property rights statutes. Compensation is triggered not by a set percentage of loss—25 percent of the value of the property, for example—but by the imposition of an "inordinate burden."[295]

> The terms "inordinate burden" or "inordinately burdened" mean that an action of one or more governmental entities has directly restricted or limited the use of real property such that the property owner is permanently unable to attain the reasonable, investment-backed expectation for the existing use of the real property or a vested right to a specific use of the real property with respect to the real property as a whole, or that the property owner is left with existing or vested uses that are unreasonable such that the property owner bears permanently a disproportionate share of a burden imposed for the good of the public, which in fairness should be borne by the public at large. The terms "inordinate burden" or "inordi-

nately burdened" do not include temporary impacts to real property; impacts to real property occasioned by governmental abatement, prohibition, prevention, or remediation of a public nuisance at common law or a noxious use of private property; or impacts to real property caused by an action of a governmental entity taken to grant relief to a property owner under this section.[296]

This provision tracks the Supreme Court's caselaw, in part, particularly the "investment-backed expectations" language of *Penn Central.*[297] However, the "disproportionate share of a burden imposed for the good of the public" language is new. While its rhetoric tracks the previously quoted "fairness and justice" language of *Armstrong v. United States,*[298] the language of the Florida act seems to go beyond mere "aspiration" by establishing explicit legal rights. It declares that "it is the intent of the Legislature that, *as a separate and distinct cause of action from the law of takings*, the Legislature herein provides for relief, or payment of compensation, when a new law, rule, regulation, or ordinance of the state or a political entity in the state, as applied, unfairly affects real property."[299]

The Florida statute also contains innovative and potentially important procedural reforms. The first is its careful provision for the award of damages. The trial court is charged with ascertaining whether the owner had a property right that was inordinately burdened. If so, it would ascertain the percentage of compensation due from each governmental entity involved, if there is more than one.[300] At that point a jury is empanelled to determine the amount of compensation owed.[301] The act has been the subject of substantial scholarly commentary.[302] One case has been reported under the act, dismissing the landowner's complaint for failure to supply a required appraisal.[303]

The act also provides for the apportionment of damages among agencies involved in a joint statutory taking.[304] More important, it mandates that the agency issue to the owner a "ripeness decision."

During the 180-day notice period [prior to the owner being permitted to file an action]. . . each of the governmental entities. . . shall issue a written ripeness decision identifying the allowable uses to which the subject property may be put. The failure of the governmental entity to [comply shall] operate as a ripeness decision that has been rejected by the property owner. The ripeness decision, as a matter of law, constitutes the last prerequisite to judicial review, and the matter shall be deemed ripe or final for the purposes of the judicial proceeding created by this section, notwithstanding the availability of other administrative remedies.[305]

§ 22.9(c) *Oregon*

In November 2000, the voters of Oregon passed Initiative Measure 7. This ballot measure would amend article I, section 18 of the state constitution to require the state or a political subdivision to pay just compensation equal to the full reduction in value caused by the enforcement of a regulation adopted after the owner has purchased the private real property in question. Excepted are regulations imposed to implement a requirement of federal law[306] and regulations discontinued within 90 days after a claim is filed.[307]

However, the "adoption or enforcement of historically and commonly recognized nuisance laws shall not be deemed to have caused a reduction in the value of a property. The phrase 'historically and commonly recognized nuisance laws' shall be narrowly construed in favor of a finding that just compensation is required under this section."[308] In other words, the measure requires that government pay for diminution of the value of land caused by regulations that extend beyond traditional nuisance law.

On February 22, 2001, a circuit court judge ruled that Ballot Measure 7 was not validly adopted[309] on the grounds that it failed to give voters the "full text" on the measure, interpreted to mean inclusion of the present constitutional provisions affected.[310] Also, the measure contained multiple amendments to the state constitution that were required to be voted upon separately.[311] Both appeals and attempts at a substitute legislative compromise are in progress.[312]

Notes

1. The material in this chapter draws from Steven J. Eagle, *Substantive Due Process and Regulatory Takings: A Reappraisal*, 51 ALA. L. REV. 977 (2000).

2. Republic Natural Gas Co. v. Oklahoma, 334 U.S. 62, 90 (1948) (Rutledge, J., dissenting).

3. *See, e.g.*, EDWARD S. CORWIN, COURT OVER CONSTITUTION 107 (1938).

4. James W. Ely, Jr., *The Oxymoron Reconsidered: Myth and Reality in the Origins of Substantive Due Process*, 16 CONST. COMMENT. 315, 319 (1999).

5. *See* United States v. 50 Acres of Land, 469 U.S. 24 (1984). "The Fifth Amendment requires that the United States pay 'just compensation'—normally measured by fair market value—whenever it takes private property for public use." *Id.* at 25-26. *See also* United States v. Miller, 317 U.S. 369, 374 (1943) ("what a willing buyer would pay in cash to a willing seller").

6. *See infra* § 22.23.

7. United States v. James Daniel Good Real Property, 510 U.S. 43, 49 (1993).

8. James Madison, *Property*, NATIONAL GAZETTE, Mar. 29, 1792.

9. JOHN LOCKE, *The Second Treatise of Government, in* TWO TREATISES OF GOVERNMENT, § 123 (Peter Laslett, ed.1965) (1690) (emphasis in original).

10. 6 JOHN ADAMS, THE WORKS OF JOHN ADAMS 280 (Charles Francis Adams ed.) (1850) (quoted in JEAN EDWARD SMITH, JOHN MARSHALL: DEFINER OF A NATION 388 (1996)).

11. Madison, *supra* n.8.

12. JENNIFER NEDELSKY, PRIVATE PROPERTY AND THE LIMITS OF AMERICAN CONSTITUTIONALISM 92 (1990). "The great focus of the framers was the security of basic rights, property in particular, not the implementation of political liberty." *Id.*

13. Hage v. United States, 35 Fed. Cl. 147, 151 (1996) (citing THE FEDERALIST No. 47 (James Madison)).

14. U. S. CONST. art. I, § 10. "No State shall. . . pass any. . . Law impairing the Obligation of Contracts. . . ." *Id.*

15. *Id.*, art. I, § 8. "The Congress shall have Power. . . To regulate Commerce. . . among the several States. . . ." *Id.* After long being moribund, the clause recently has been utilized by the Supreme Court to curtail extensions of federal power. *See, e.g.*, United States v. Lopez, 514 U.S. 549 (1995); Solid Waste Agency of N. Cook County v. United States Army Corps of Eng'rs, 121 S. Ct. 675 (2001).

16. *Id.*, arts. I, II, and III (setting forth powers of the legislative, executive, and judicial branches, respectively).

17. *Id.*, art. I, § 8. The doctrine has enjoyed a considerable resurrection in recent years, with the Supreme Court striking down acts of Congress that "commandeered" state officials. *See* New York v. United States, 505 U.S. 144, 146 (1992); Printz v. United States, 521 U.S. 898 (1997).

18. *Id.*, amend. X.

19. *Id.*, art. I, § 8. "The Congress shall have Power to lay and collect Taxes, Duties, Imposts and Excises, and to pay the Debts and to provide for the common Defence and general Welfare of the United States." *Id.*

20. *See, e.g.*, United States v. Butler, 297 U.S. 1 (1936) (treating the spending power as essentially non-justiciable); Massachusetts v. Mellon, Frothingham v. Mellon, 262 U.S. 447 (1923) (consolidated actions) (severely restricting taxpayer standing to challenge spending).

21. *See, e.g.*, John C. Eastman, *Restoring the "General" to the General Welfare Clause*, 4 CHAPMAN L. REV. 63 (2001) (stating that until the mid-19th century, the clause was viewed "as a limitation on the powers of Congress, not as a grant of plenary power"). *Id.* at 87. *See also* Lynn A. Baker, *The Spending Power and the Federalist Revival*, 4 CHAPMAN L. REV. 195 (2001) (asserting that the spending power is the greatest threat to state autonomy).

22. U.S. CONST. art. IV. "The Citizens of each State shall be entitled to all Privileges and Immunities of Citizens in the several States." *Id.*

23. Corfield v. Coryell, 6 F. Cas. 546, 551-52 (C.C.E.D. Pa. 1823).

24. U. S. CONST. amend. V.

25. *Id.* The "public use" requirement is important because of the mischief that would occur if government officials could take private property from some and transfer it to others. Also, "just compensation" is almost never full compensation, since the benefits that most owners derive from their property exceed the fair market value that would be offered by a stranger. *See* Coniston Corp. v. Village of Hoffman Estates, 844 F.2d 461 (7th

Cir. 1988). Nevertheless, the Public Use Clause was vitiated in Hawaii Hous. Auth. v. Midkiff, 467 U.S. 229 (1984), where the Court declared it "coterminous" with the police power. *Id.* at 240.

26.   The requirement that compensation be paid has a "self-executing" character. Clarke v. United States, 445 U.S. 253, 257 (1980).

27.   U.S. CONST. amend V. "[N]or shall any person. . . be deprived of life, liberty, or property, without due process of law." *Id.*

28.   Barron v. Mayor & City Council of Baltimore, 32 U.S. (7 Pet.) 243 (1833).

29.   U.S. CONST. amend. 14, § 1.

30.   *Id.* ("nor shall any State deprive any person of life, liberty, or property, without due process of law. . .").

31.   *Id.*

32.   83 U.S. (16 Wall.) 36 (1872).

33.   *Id.* at 80-81. *See also* Davidson v. New Orleans, 96 U.S. 97 (1877).

34.   *Id.* at 79.

35.   *See* Saenz v. Roe, 526 U.S. 489 (1999).

36.   THOMAS M. COOLEY, A TREATISE ON THE CONSTITUTIONAL LIMITATIONS WHICH REST UPON THE LEGISLATIVE POWER OF THE STATES OF THE UNION (1868). Cooley encouraged an expansive reading of the Fourteenth Amendment and "linked the Jacksonian principles of equal rights and opposition to special economic privileges with due process protection of property." JAMES W. ELY, JR., INTRODUCTION TO PROPERTY RIGHTS IN THE AGE OF ENTERPRISE vii, xii (1997).

37.   94 U.S. 113 (1876).

38.   *Id.* at 126.

39.   123 U.S. 623 (1887).

40.   *Id.* at 662.

41.   134 U.S. 418 (1890).

42.   152 U.S. 133 (1894).

43.   *Id.* at 137.

44.   198 U.S. 45 (1905).

45.   *See* David Currie, *The Constitution in the Supreme Court: The Protection of Economic Interests, 1889-1910*, 52 U. CHI. L. REV. 324, 381 & n. 341 (1985) (showing that the Court sustained more such statutes than it struck down).

46.   *See* Herbert Hovenkamp, *The Political Economy of Substantive Due Process*, 40 STAN. L. REV. 379, 387-88 (1988).

47.   245 U.S. 60 (1917). "We think this attempt to prevent the alienation of the property in question to a person of color was not a legitimate exercise of the police power of the State, and is in direct violation of the fundamental law enacted in the Fourteenth Amendment of the Constitution preventing state interference with property rights except by due process of law." *Id.* at 82.

48.   166 U.S. 226 (1897).

49.   *Id.* at 234-35.

50.   *Id.* at 236 (citing Davidson v. New Orleans, 96 U.S. 97 (1877)).

51.   260 U.S. 393 (1922).

52.   *See, e.g.*, Robert Brauneis, "The Foundation of Our 'Regulatory Takings' Jurisprudence": *The Myth and Meaning of Justice Holmes's Opinion in* Pennsylvania Coal Co. v. Mahon, 106 YALE L.J. 613, 666 (1996).

53.   260 U.S. at 412.

54.   *Id.* at 415.

55. *Id.* at 413.

56. 152 U.S. 133 (1894). See text accompanying note 42, et seq.

57. 260 U.S. at 416.

58. 272 U.S. 365 (1926). *See* Steven J. Eagle, Regulatory Takings § 4-2, et seq. (2d ed. 2001).

59. See Arthur V.N. Brooks, *The Office File Box—Emanations from the Battlefield, in* Zoning and the American Dream: Promises Still to Keep 3, 3-4 (Charles M. Haar & Jerold S. Kayden eds., 1989).

60. *See* Hadley Arkes, *Who's the Laissez-Fairest of Them All*, Pol'y Rev., Spring 1992, at 78, 84-85.

61. *See Euclid*, 272 U.S. at 394-95 (stressing that apartment houses were "very near to being nuisances"). Also, an apartment building often constituted "a mere parasite." *Id.* at 394. Revealingly, apartment use was neither intended by the landowner nor implicated in the zoning of the parcel.

62. *Id.* at 386-87.

63. *Id.* at 387-88.

64. *Id.* at 388.

65. 277 U.S. 183 (1928).

66. 277 U.S. at 185.

67. *Id.* at 188 (citing *Euclid*, 272 U.S. at 395).

68. *Id.* at 189.

69. Penn Central Transp. Co. v. City of New York, 438 U.S. 104 (1978).

70. *See, e.g.*, Nebbia v. New York, 291 U.S. 502 (1934) (upholding state regulatory scheme for milk production); West Coast Hotel v. Parrish, 300 U.S. 379 (1937) (minimum wage).

71. 304 U.S. 144 (1938).

72. *See id.* at 152-53 n.4 ("There may be narrower scope for operation of the presumption of constitutionality when legislation appears on its face to be within a specific prohibition of the Constitution, such as those of the first ten amendments, which are deemed equally specific when held to be embraced within the Fourteenth. . . ").

73. Bruce A. Ackerman, *Beyond* Carolene Products, 98 Harv. L. Rev. 713, 714-15 (1985).

74. See John Hart Ely, Democracy and Distrust (1980) (advocating the Court's role in enhancing democratic processes).

75. *See supra* § 22.02.

76. *See, e.g.*, United States v. Carlton, 512 U.S. 20, 41-42 (1994) (Scalia, J., concurring) ("The picking and choosing among various rights to be accorded 'substantive due process' protection is alone enough to arouse suspicion; but the categorical and inexplicable exclusion of so-called 'economic rights' (even though the Due Process Clause explicitly applies to 'property') unquestionably involves policymaking rather than neutral legal analysis.").

77. 512 U.S. 374 (1994).

78. *Id.* at 396 (Stevens, J., dissenting).

79. Chicago, Burlington & Quincy R.R. v. Chicago, 166 U.S. 226 (1897).

80. *Id.* at 407 (Stevens, J., dissenting) (citing *Lochner*, 198 U.S. 45 (1905)).

81. *Id.* at 406-07 (Stevens, J., dissenting) (discussing *Pennsylvania Coal*, 260 U.S. 393 (1922)). Holmes had declared: "The general rule at least is that while property may be regulated to a certain extent, if regulation goes too far it will be recognized as a taking." 260 U.S. at 415.

82. *See* Cass R. Sunstein, Lochner's *Legacy,* 87 COLUM. L. REV. 873, 873 (1987) (characterizing *Lochner* as a "specter" that "has loomed over most important constitutional decisions").

83. *See* James E. Fleming, *Constructing the Substantive Constitution,* 72 TEX. L. REV. 211, 211-12 (1993).

84. *See* James W. Ely, Jr., *Economic Due Process Revisited,* 44 VAND. L. REV. 213 (1991) (reviewing PAUL KENS, JUDICIAL POWER AND REFORM POLITICS: THE ANATOMY OF *LOCHNER V. NEW YORK* (1990)).

85. 166 U.S. 226 (1897). *See supra* text accompanying n.48 et seq.

86. 512 U.S. at 384 n.5 (asserting "there is no doubt that later cases have held that the Fourteenth Amendment does make the Takings Clause of the Fifth Amendment applicable to the States. . . . Nor is there any doubt that these cases have relied upon *Chicago, B. & Q. R.R. Co. v. Chicago. . .* to reach that result." *Id.*

87. *See* Palazzolo v. Rhode Island, 121 S. Ct. 2448, 2457 (2001).

88. U.S. CONST. amend. V.

89. 364 U.S. 40 (1960).

90. *Id.* at 49.

91. *See* Coniston Corp. v. Village of Hoffman Estates, 844 F.2d 461 (7th Cir. 1988). *See also supra* note 25 and accompanying text.

92. Firms seeking to acquire lands owned by others would be encouraged to utilize the political process rather than the market, "buying" utilization of eminent domain and subsequent reconveyance for "redevelopment" rather than approaching the owner and attempting to negotiate a price. Likewise, gains to be derived by legislators from "selling" such rights in exchange for campaign contributions and other incentives would distort their perception of the public interest. On rent seeking in the property rights context, *see* EAGLE, REGULATORY TAKINGS, *supra* note 58, at § 1-4 et seq.

93. The Supreme Court essentially abrogated the public use requirement by deeming it "coterminous" with the police power. Hawaii Hous. Auth. v. Midkiff, 467 U.S. 229, 240 (1984). *See also* Poletown Neighborhood Council v. City of Detroit, 304 N.W.2d 455 (Mich. 1981). However, there has been a modest trend toward less deferential scrutiny of "public use" justifications in the lower federal courts and in state courts. *See, e.g.,* 99 Cents Only Stores v. Lancaster Redevelopment Agency, ___ F. Supp.2d ___, 2001 WL 811056 (C.D. Cal. June 26, 2001); Casino Reinvestment Dev. Auth. v. Banin, 727 A.2d 102 (N.J. Super. 1998); Friends of Mammoth v. Town of Mammoth Lakes Redevelopment Agency, 98 Cal. Rptr. 2d 334 (Cal. App. 2000). *Cf.* Dean Starkman, *More Courts Rule Cities Misapply Eminent Domain,* WALL ST. J., July 23, 2001, at B1.

94. Eastern Enters. v. Apfel, 524 U.S. 498, 545 (1998) (Kennedy, J., concurring in the judgment and dissenting in part).

95. Steven J. Eagle, Del Monte Dunes, *Good Faith, and Land Use Regulation,* 30 ENVTL. L. REP. 10,100, 10,105 (2000).

96. Agins v. City of Tiburon, 447 U.S. 255 (1980). *See supra* § 22.01.

97. Dolan v. City of Tigard, 512 U.S. 374 (1994). *See infra* text accompanying note 243, et seq.

98. Penn Central Transp. Co. v. City of New York, 438 U.S. 104, 124 (1978). *See supra* § 22.01.

99. 447 U.S. 255 (1980).

100. *Id.* at 258 (citation omitted) (alteration in original).

101. *See supra* text accompanying note 65, et seq.

102. 526 U.S. 687 (1999).

103. *See id*. at 706 ("Although *Del Monte Dunes* was allowed to introduce evidence challenging the asserted factual bases for the city's decision, it also highlighted the shifting nature of the city's demands and the inconsistency of its decision with the recommendation of its professional staff, as well as with its previous decisions. *See, e.g., id*. at 1300. *Del Monte Dunes* also introduced evidence of the city's longstanding interest in acquiring the property for public use.") *See also* Eagle, *supra* note 95, at 10,100; *infra* text accompanying note 171 et seq.

104. Brief for the United States as Amicus Curiae Supporting Petitioner, 1998 WL 308006 *22-24 (1998).

105. *Id*. at 27-28.

106. 526 U.S. at 704.

107. 524 U.S. 498 (1998).

108. Coal Industry Retiree Health Benefit Act of 1992, 26 U.S.C. §§ 9701-9722.

109. 524 U.S. at 529.

110. *Id*. at 509-11

111. *Id*. at 528-29.

112. *Id*. at 530.

113. *Id*. at 550 (Kennedy, J., concurring in judgment and dissenting in part) ("Eastern was once in the coal business and employed many of the beneficiaries, but it was not responsible for their expectation of lifetime health benefits or for the perilous financial condition of the 1950 and 1974 plans. . . . ").

114. *Id*. at 551 (Stevens, J., dissenting).

115. *Id*. at 560-61 (Breyer, J., dissenting).

116. *Id*. at 553.

117. *Id*. at 558 (Breyer, J., dissenting).

118. *Id*. at 568 (Kennedy, J., concurring in judgment and dissenting in part).

119. *Id*.

120. *Id*. at 553 (Breyer, J., dissenting).

121. *Id*. at 538.

122. *Id*. at 545 (Kennedy, J., concurring in judgment and dissenting in part).

123. *Id*. at 539.

124. *Id*. at 556 (Breyer, J., dissenting).

125. *Id*. at 554.

126. *Id*. at 538 ("Because we have determined that the. . . allocation scheme violates the Takings Clause as applied to Eastern, we need not address Eastern's due process claim.").

127. *Eastern Enters.*, 524 U.S. at 537 (emphasis added).

128. Commonwealth Edison Co. v. United States, 46 Fed. Cl. 29, 39 (2000).

129. Florida Rock Indus., Inc. v. United States, 45 Fed. Cl. 21, 43 n.13 (1999). *See also* American Pelagic Fishing Co., L.P. v. United States, 49 Fed. Cl. 36, 46 (2001), and *infra* text accompanying note 155, et seq.

130. American Pelagic Fishing Co., L.P. v. United States, 49 Fed. Cl. 36, 46 (2001). A more problematic example is *United States Fidelity & Guaranty Co. v. McKeithen*, 226 F.3d 412 (5th Cir. 2000) (holding that, in the case of retroactive liability imposed on insurance companies cutting back on underwriting within the state, assessments arise from a "specific fund of benefits" for claimants and are charged "against the fund of reserves set aside from the premiums collected under specific insurance policies"). *Id*. at 420.

131. 178 F.3d 649 (3d Cir. 1999).

132. *Id*. at 658.

133.   *Id.* at 659.

134.   *Eastern Enters.*, 524 U.S. at 537.

135.   *Id.*

136.   Penn Central Transp. Co. v. City of New York, 438 U.S. 104 (1978).

137.   438 U.S. 104 (1978).

138.   *Id.* at 124.

139.   *Id.* (internal citations omitted).

140.   *See supra* text accompanying note 139.

141.   *See, e.g.*, American Pelagic Fishing Co., L.P. v. United States, 49 Fed. Cl. 36 (2001). "The factor of 'the character of the governmental action' has been cast in terms of whether the government physically appropriates the res or comes close to doing so." *Id.* at 50.

142.   458 U.S. 419 (1982) (holding the government-authorized installation of wires and a small hook-up box on the plaintiff's apartment building without her consent a compensable taking).

143.   *Id.*

144.   505 U.S. 1003 (1992).

145.   *Id.* at 1017.

146.   *Id.* at 1016 (quoting Agins v. City of Tiburon, 447 U.S. 255, 260 (1980)).

147.   However, the issue of whether an owner's lack of "reasonable investment-backed expectations" trumps the otherwise categorical rule of *Lucas* remains unsettled. *See* Good v. United States, 189 F.3d 1355, 1361 (Fed. Cir. 1999) (yes); Palm Beach Isles Associates v. United States, 208 F.3d 1374, 1379 (Fed. Cir. 2000), *aff'd on reh'g*, 231 F.3d 1354 (2000); *reh'g en banc denied*, 231 F.3d 1365 (2000) (no). *Palazzolo* did not speak to this issue, since the Court found that substantial value remained in the parcel. Palazzolo v. Rhode Island, 121 S. Ct. 2448. 2464-65 (2001).

148.   Penn Central Transp. Co. v. City of New York, 438 U.S. 104 (1978). The Court noted that "in instances in which a state tribunal reasonably concluded that 'the health, safety, morals, or general welfare' would be promoted by prohibiting particular contemplated uses of land, this Court has upheld land-use regulations that destroyed or adversely affected recognized real property interests." *Id.* at 125.

149.   258 Cal. Rptr. 893, 905 (Cal. App. 1989).

150.   *Id.* at 901-02 (discussing Agins v. Tiburon, 598 P.2d 25(1979), *aff'd on other grounds*, 447 U.S. 255 (1980).

151.   *Id.* at 905 (emphasis added).

152.   41 F.3d 627 (Fed. Cir. 1994).

153.   *Id.* at 361.

154.   524 U.S. 498 (1998). *See supra* text accompanying note 107 et seq.

155.   49 Fed. Cl. 36 (2001).

156.   *Id.* at 40-44.

157.   *Id.* at 46.

158.   *Id.* at 49-50.

159.   *Id.* at 46.

160.   *Id.* ("from the standpoint of traditional property concepts, the res potentially taken by the government was the ship itself").

161.   *Id.* at 50 (internal citation to *Eastern Enters.*, 524 U.S. at 532-37 omitted).

162.   *Id.* at 46 (citing *Eastern Enters.*, 524 U.S. at 549 (Kennedy, J., concurring in the judgment and dissenting in part)).

163.   *Id.* at 50 note 19.

164. 49 Fed. Cl. 248 (2001).

165. *Id.* at 270.

166. 152 U.S. 133 (1894).

167. See *supra* note 42 and accompanying text.

168. 152 U.S. at 141.

169. 272 U.S. 365 (1926).

170. *Id.* at 395.

171. 526 U.S. 687 (1999).

172. *Id.* at 698.

173. *Id.* at 700.

174. The split was 4-1-4. Justice Kennedy wrote that a jury trial was available, given the nature of *Del Monte*'s § 1983 claim. 526 U.S. at 707-18. Justice Scalia wrote that a jury trial always is available for § 1983 claims. *Id.* at 723-32 (Scalia, J., concurring in part and concurring in the judgment). Justice Souter dissented, concluding that there was neither a statutory nor a constitutional basis for a jury trial. *Id.* at 733-55 (Souter, J., concurring in part and dissenting in part).

175. 526 U.S. at 700.

176. *Id.* at 753 (Souter, J., concurring in part and dissenting in part).

177. *Id.* at 706-07.

178. Forrest McDonald, Novus Ordo Seclorum: The Intellectual Origins of the Constitution 13 (1985).

179. *See supra* § 22.01 and the quotation accompanying note 13.

180. 511 U.S. 244, 265 (1994).

181. *Id.* at 265.

182. 121 S. Ct. 1693 (2001).

183. 121 S. Ct. 2448 (2001)

184. A number of jurisdictions had adopted the positive notice rule. *See, e.g.,* Gazza v. New York State Dept. of Envtl. Conserv., 679 N.E.2d 1035 (N.Y. 1997); Hunziker v. State, 519 N.W.2d 367 (Iowa 1994); and City of Virginia Beach v. Bell, 498 S.E.2d 414 (Va. 1998). See detailed discussion *supra* chapters 2 and 3.

185. 121 S. Ct. at 2462 (citation omitted).

186. *Id.* at 2462-63. However, five Justices deemed the preexistence of a regulation to have some (undetermined) bearing on whether a prospective owner could form a reasonable investment-backed expectation regarding the proscribed use. *See id.* at 2465-67 (O'Connor, J., concurring); *id.* at 2468 (Stevens, J., concurring in part and dissenting in part); *id.* at 2477 n. 3 (Ginsburg, J. dissenting) (joined by Souter and Breyer, JJ.); *id.* at 2477 (Breyer, J., dissenting).

187. *See* Thomas Hobbes, Leviathan 179 (Richard Tuck ed., 1991); Jeremy Waldron, *Supply Without Burthen Revisited*, 82 Iowa L. Rev. 1467, 1467 (1997).

188. *See* John Locke, *The Second Treatise of Government* § 123, in Two Treatises of Government (Peter Laslett ed., 1965) (1690).

189. 389 U.S. 347 (1967).

190. *Id.* at 351.

191. *Id.* at 360.

192. Penn Central Transp. Co. v. City of New York, 438 U.S. 104, 124 (1978). *See supra* § 22.01.

193. Lucas v. South Carolina Coastal Council, 505 U.S. 1003 (1992). Justice Scalia suggested that it is unclear how the relevant parcel in a takings inquiry might be deter-

mined. "The answer to this difficult question may lie in how the owner's reasonable expectations have been shaped by the State's law of property—i.e., whether and to what degree the State's law has accorded legal recognition and protection to the particular interest in land with respect to which the takings claimant alleges a diminution in (or elimination of) value. . . . " *Id.* at 1016 n.7.

194.   505 U.S. at 1034 (Kennedy, J., concurring). Citing *Katz*, he added: "Some circularity must be tolerated in these matters, however, as it is in other spheres." *Id.*

195.   District Intown Properties L. P. v. District of Columbia, 198 F.3d 874, 887 (D.C. Cir. 1999).

196.   Good v. United States, 189 F.3d 1355, 1361 (Fed. Cir. 1999) (upholding denial of development permit and observing that at time of purchase landowner should have anticipated that Endangered Species Act would later be enacted).

197.   121 S. Ct. 2038 (2001)

198.   121 S. Ct. at 2043 (internal citations omitted) (emphasis in original except for penultimate sentence).

199.   Loretto v. Teleprompter Manhattan CATV Corp., 458 U.S. 419 (1982). *See supra* text accompanying note 142 et seq.

200.   Lucas v. South Carolina Coastal Council, 505 U.S. 1003 (1992). *See supra* text accompanying note 144 et seq.

201.   121 S. Ct. 2448 (2001).

202.   *See supra* § 22.01. In Lucas v. South Carolina Coastal Council, 505 U.S. 1003 (1992), the Court excepted from the rule that complete deprivations of economically beneficial use constituted categorical takings that deprivation of uses in which the owner was not free to engage as a result of "restrictions that background principles of the State's law of property and nuisance already place upon land ownership." *Id.* at 1029.

203.   121 S.Ct. at 2464 (citing *Lucas,* 505 U.S. at 1029-30).

204.   *See* James W. Ely, Jr., *The Oxymoron Reconsidered: Myth and Reality in the Origins of Substantive Due Process*, 16 CONST. COMMENT. 315, 336 (1999).

205.   *See* Washington Legal Found. v. Legal Found. of Washington, 236 F.3d 1097, 1102 n.8 (9th Cir. 2001).

206.   *See* Phillips v. Washington Legal Found., 524 U.S. 156, 159 n.1, 159-60 (1998).

207.   *See, e.g.*, Washington Legal Found. v. Texas Equal Access to Justice Found., 86 F. Supp. 2d 624, 628 (W.D. Tex. 2000) (citing Tex. Disciplinary R. Prof. Conduct 1.14, *reprinted in* TEX. GOV'T CODE ANN., tit 2, subtit. G app. A (Vernon's Supp. 1998) (TEX. State Bar R. art. X, § 9).

208.   *See Phillips*, 524 U.S. at 161.

209.   524 U.S. 156 (1998).

210.   499 U.S. 155 (1980).

211.   524 U.S. at 167 (quoting *Webb's Fabulous Pharmacies*, 449 U.S. at 164).

212.   *Id.* at 172.

213.   86 F. Supp. 2d 624 (W.D. Tex. 2000).

214.   *Id.* at 644.

215.   *Id.* (quoting United States v. Sperry, 493 U.S. 52, 62 n.9 (1989)).

216.   *Id.* (citing Loretto v. Teleprompter Manhattan CATV Corp., 458 U.S. 419 (1982); Lucas v. South Carolina Coastal Council, 505 U.S. 1003 (1992); and Kaiser Aetna v. United States, 444 U.S. 164 (1979)).

217.   *Id.* at 646.

218.   *Id.* at 647 (quoting Connolly v. Pension Benefit Guarantee Corp., 475 U.S. 211, 223 (1986)).

219. *Id.* at 638-43.

220. *Id.* at 642.

221. Washington Legal Found. v. Texas Equal Access to Justice Found., __ F.3d __, 2001 WL 1222105 (5th Cir. 2001).

222. 236 F.3d 1097 (9th Cir. 2001).

223. *Id.* at 1111.

224. 86 F. Supp. 2d at 635.

225. 236 F.3d at 1105.

226. Michael A. Heller & James E. Krier, *Making Something Out of Nothing: The Law of Takings and* Phillips v. Washington Legal Foundation, 7 Sup. Ct. Econ. Rev. 285, 300-01 (1999) (footnotes omitted).

227. 857 F.2d 1324 (9th Cir. 1988).

228. *Id.* at 1326.

229. *Id.* at 1334. The court cited numerous cases that have considered, and rejected, the argument that destruction of private property by protected wildlife constitutes a governmental taking. *See, e.g.*, Bishop v. United States, 126 F. Supp. 449, 452-53 (Ct. Cl. 1954) (damage done to crops by geese protected under the Migratory Bird Treaty Act); Sickman v. United States, 184 F.2d 616 (7th Cir. 1950) (rejecting similar claim under the Federal Tort Claims Act). *See also* Mountain States Legal Found. v. Hodel, 799 F.2d 1423 (10th Cir. 1986) (no taking when wild horses ate privately owned forage).

230. Christy v. Lujan, 490 U.S. 1114 (1989).

231. *Id.* at 1115-16 (White, J., dissenting) (internal citations omitted).

232. 364 U.S. 40 (1960).

233. 453 U.S. 654 (1981) (upholding the federal seizure of contract claims against the government of Iran).

234. *Id.* at 688-89 (citations omitted).

235. *See, e.g.*, Allied Stores v. Bowers, 358 U.S. 522, 530 (1959) (upholding any classification based "upon a state of facts that reasonably can be conceived to constitute a distinction, or difference in state policy").

236. *See, e.g.*, Roe v. Wade, 410 U.S. 113, 155 (1973) (abortion rights); *see also* Gerald Gunther, *The Supreme Court, 1971 Term—Forward: In Search of Evolving Doctrine on a Changing Court: A Model for a Newer Equal Protection*, 86 Harv. L. Rev. 1, 8 (1972) (referring to "strict scrutiny" as "'strict' in theory and fatal in fact").

237. *See, e.g.*, Perry Educ. Ass'n v. Perry Local Educators Ass'n, 460 U.S. 37, 45 (1983) (providing that legislation must be "narrowly tailored to serve a significant government interest").

238. *See* City of Cleburne v. Cleburne Living Center, 473 U.S. 432, 460 (1984) (Marshall, J., dissenting).

239. Richard A. Fallon, Jr., *Some Confusions About Due Process, Judicial Review, and Constitutional Remedies*, 93 Colum. L. Rev. 309, 315 (1993).

240. *Id.* at 316-17.

241. *Id.* at 317 (alteration in original) (citing Youngberg v. Romeo, 457 U.S. 307, 320 (1982) (quoting Poe v. Ullman, 367 U.S. 497, 542 (1961) (Harlan, J., dissenting))).

242. *Id.* (citing rights pertaining to "minimum contacts" requirements for a state's assertion of personal jurisdiction).

243. City of Boerne v. Flores, 521 U.S. 507, 520 (1997) (holding that the Religious Freedom Restoration Act exceeded congressional powers).

244. 512 U.S. 374, 391 (1994).

245. *Id.* at 385.

246. 473 U.S. 432 (1985).

247. *Id.* at 435-39.

248. *Id.* at 446.

249. LAURENCE H. TRIBE, AMERICAN CONSTITUTIONAL LAW 1612 (2d ed. 1988).

250. *Id.* at 1443.

251. *Id.* at 1445 (internal footnote omitted).

252. *See, e.g.*, Texas Manufactured Housing Ass'n Inc. v. City of Nederland, 101 F.3d 1095, 1106 (5th Cir. 1996).

253. 473 U.S. 432 (1985).

254. *Id.* at 439 (citing U.S. CONST. amend. XIV, § 1).

255. U.S. CONST. amend. XIV, § 1 ("No State shall make or enforce any law which shall abridge the privileges or immunities of citizens of the United States; nor shall any State deprive any person of life, liberty, or property, without due process of law. . . .").

256. Santa Clara County v. Southern Pac. R.R., 118 U.S. 394 (1886).

257. *See, e.g.*, Quaker City Cab Co. v. Pennsylvania, 277 U.S. 192 (1928).

258. Nixon v. Herndon, 273 U.S. 536 (1927).

259. Village of Euclid v. Ambler Realty Co., 272 U.S. 365 (1926). "If the validity of the legislative classification for zoning purposes be fairly debatable, the legislative judgment must be allowed to control." *Id.* at 388.

260. United States v. Carolene Products Co., 304 U.S. 144 (1938). *See supra* note 72 and associated text.

261. *See, e.g.*, Allied Stores v. Bowers, 358 U.S. 522 (1959) (upholding classification based "upon a state of facts that reasonably can be conceived to constitute a distinction, or difference, in state policy." *Id.* at 530.).

262. 429 U.S. 252 (1977).

263. *Id.* at 265 (quoting Washington v. Davis, 426 U.S. 229, 242 (1976)).

264. *Id.*

265. *See, e.g.*, Nordlinger v. Hahn, 505 U.S. 1 (1992) (property tax disparities caused by California Proposition 13 not violative of Equal Protection Clause); Colorado Manufactured Housing Ass'n v. City of Salida, 977 F. Supp. 1080 (D. Co. 1997) (holding zoning ordinances restricting location of manufactured homes not violative of the Equal Protection Clause if based on public perception of disadvantages of mixing mobile homes and other types of buildings, whether such perceptions are rational or not). *Cf.* Bannum, Inc. v. City of Louisville, 958 F.2d 1354 (6th Cir. 1992) (holding special permit for group home violates Equal Protection Clause).

266. 528 U.S. 562 (2000).

267. 733 A.2d 1206 (N.J. Super. Ct. App. Div. 1999).

268. 199 F.3d 363 (7th Cir. 2000).

269. *See* Williamson County Regional Planning Comm'n v. Hamilton Bank, 473 U.S. 172 (1985) (imposing "final decision" and "denial of compensation" ripeness requirements on plaintiffs asserting regulatory takings claims against states and localities in federal court). *See supra* chapters 20 and 21 dealing with ripeness.

270. *Id.* at 370 (citing Hager v. City of West Peoria, 84 F.3d 865, 872 (7th Cir. 1996)).

271. 53 F.3d 176, 180 (7th Cir.1995).

272. 734 A.2d 535 (Conn. 1999).

273. 528 U.S. 562 (2000).

274. *Id.* at 563-64.

275. *Id.* at 564 (citations omitted).

276. *Id.* at 565 (citation omitted).

277. *Id*. (Breyer, J., concurring in the result).

278. *Id*.

279. The Supreme Court stated in *Williamson County* that the landowner's takings claim in federal court was "premature." Williamson County Regional Planning Commission v. Hamilton Bank, 473 U.S. 172, 185 (1985). While this leads to the inference that the landowner had the right to return after its takings claim had been "ripened" in state court, some commentators have disagreed. *See, e.g.*, Thomas E. Roberts, *Fifth Amendment Taking Claims in Federal Court: The State Compensation Requirement and Principles of Res Judicata*, 24 URB. LAW. 479 (1992). "Under well-established procedural rules, use of the state courts to litigate the demand for compensation ends the matter. Res judicata will bar relitigation of the claim. Even if the federal claim is viewed as not arising until compensation has been denied, the rule of issue preclusion will prevent relitigation in federal court. *Id*. at 483. The Supreme Court denied certiorari in a case that squarely raised the issue, *Rainey Bros. Construction Co. v. Memphis and Shelby County Board of Adjustment*, 528 U.S. 871 (1999).

280. Joseph L. Sax, *Takings, Private Property and Public Rights*, 81 YALE L.J. 149, 166 n. 32 (1971).

281. *See* ARIZ. REV. STAT. ANN. § 9-500.12 (1996) (city), § 11-810 (West Supp. 1997) (county); DEL. CODE ANN. tit. 29, § 605 (Supp. 1996); FLA. STAT. ANN. § 70.001 (West Supp. 1997); IDAHO CODE §§ 67-8001 to 67-8004 (1995); IND. CODE ANN. §§ 4-22-2-31 to 4-22-2-32 (West Supp. 1996); KAN. STAT. ANN. §§ 77-701 to 77-707 (Supp. 1995); LA. REV. STAT. ANN. § 3:2609, 3622.1 (West Supp. 1997); ME. REV. STAT. ANN. tit. 5, § 8056(1)(A) (West 1989); MICH. COMP. LAWS ANN. § 24.241:245 (West Supp. 1997); MISS. CODE ANN. §§ 49-33-1 to 49-33-19 (Supp. 1996); MO. ANN. STAT. § 536.017 (West Supp. 1996); MONT. CODE ANN. §§ 2-10-101 to 2-10-105 (1995); N.D. CENT. CODE § 28-32-02.5 (Supp. 1995); N.C. G.S. § 113-206; OR. REV. STAT. § 197.772; TENN. CODE ANN. §§ 12-1-201 to 12- 1-206 (Supp. 1996); TEX. GOV'T CODE ANN. §§ 2007.041 to .045 (West 1996); UTAH CODE ANN. §§ 63-90-1 to 63-90-4 (Supp. 1996); VA. CODE ANN. § 9-6.14:7.1(G); WASH. REV. CODE § 36.70A.370 (West Supp. 1997); W. VA. CODE §§ 22-1A-1 to 22-1A-3 (1994); WYO. STAT. ANN. §§ 9-5-301 to 9-5-305 (Michie 1995). *See* Mark W. Cordes, *Leapfrogging the Constitution: The Rise of State Takings Legislation*, 24 ECOLOGY L. Q. 187, 190 n.16 (1997); Marilyn F. Drees, *Do State Legislatures Have a Role in Resolving the "Just Compensation" Dilemma? Some Lessons from Public Choice and Positive PoliticalTheory*, 66 FORDHAM L. REV. 787 (1997). *See also* Lynda J. Oswald, *Property Rights Legislation and the Police Power*, 37 AM. BUS. L.J. 527 (2000).

282. *See* Mark W. Cordes, *Leapfrogging the Constitution: The Rise of State Takings Legislation*, 24 ECOLOGY L. Q. 187, 190 n.16 (1997).

283. 42 U.S.C.§§ 4321, 4332 (2)(C). *See* 40 C.F.R. § 1500.2.

284. 53 C.F.R. 8859 (1988), *reprinted in* 5 U.S.C. § 601.

285. *See, e.g.*, Hertha L. Lund, *The Property Rights Movement and State Legislation, in* LAND RIGHTS, 199, 219 (Bruce Yandle ed., 1995).

286. *See* STEVEN J. EAGLE, REGULATORY TAKINGS § 13-9(b) (2d ed. 2001).

287. ARIZ. REV. STAT. ANN. § 9-500.12 (1996) (city), § 11-810 (West Supp. 1997) (county).

288. MISS. CODE ANN. §§ 49-33-1 to -19 (Supp. 1996).

289. LA. REV. STAT. ANN. §§ 3:3601 to 02 (West Supp. 1997).

290. McCall v. Kitzhaber, No. 00C19871 (Marion Cty. Circuit Ct., Feb. 22, 2001).

291. TEX. GOV'T CODE ANN. § 2007.001 et seq.

292. The government action that would constitute a "taking" is limited to that which

"affects an owner's private real property that is the subject of the governmental action, in whole or in part or temporarily or permanently. . . and is the producing cause of a reduction of at least 25 percent in the market value of the affected private real property. . . ." § 2007.002 (5)(B). It is unclear whether the 25% diminution could be applied to the affected segment of the parcel or must be applied to the parcel as a whole. *See* Jerome M. Organ, *Understanding State and Federal Property Rights Legislation*, 48 OKLA. L. REV. 191, 214 (1995).

293. McMillan v. Northwest Harris County Mun. Utility Dist. No. 24, 988 S.W.2d 337 (Tex. App. 1999).

294. FLA. STAT. ANN. § 70.001 (West Supp. 1997).

295. *Id*. at § 70.001 (2).

296. *Id*. at § 70.001(3)(e).

297. Penn Central Transp. Co. v. City of New York, 438 U.S. 104, 124 (1978).

298. 346 U.S. 40, 49 (1960). *See supra* text accompanying note 89 et seq.

299. FLA. STAT. ANN. § 70.001(1) (emphasis added).

300. *Id*. at § 70.001 (6)(a).

301. *Id*. at § 70.001 (6)(b).

302. *See, e.g.*, Julian C. Juergensmeyer, *Florida's Private Property Rights Protection Act: Does It Inordinately Burden the Public Interest?*, 48 FLA. L. REV. 695 (1996); Nancy E. Stroud & Thomas G. Wright, *Florida's Private Property Rights Act—What Will It Mean for Florida's Future?*, 20 NOVA L. REV. 683 (1996); Vivien J. Monaco, *The Harris Act: What Relief from Government Regulation Does It Provide for Private Property Owners?*, 26 STETSON L. REV. 861 (1997).

303. Sosa v. City of West Palm Beach, App. 4 Dist., 762 So. 2d 981 (2000).

304. *Id*. at § 70.001(6)(a).

305. *Id*. at § 70.001(5)(a).

306. Measure 7 (c).

307. Measure 7 (e).

308. Measure 7 (b).

300. McCall v. Kitzhaber, No. 00C19871 (Marion Cty. Circuit Ct., Feb. 22, 2001).

310. *Id*. at 11-12.

311. *Id*. at 23.

312. *See* Peter Livingston, *Measure 7 and Property Rights: Pretty Simple? Pretty Fair?*, 61 OR. ST. B. BULL. 9 (June 2001).

Alternatives to Takings: Procedural Due Process, Equal Protection, and State Law Doctrine

23

Susan L. Trevarthen

§ 23.0 Introduction

Often the dissatisfaction a claimant feels with governmental regulation of land might be better addressed by some theory of liability other than the Fifth Amendment Takings Clause. With many regulatory takings cases, one gets the sense that the claimant, and sometimes the court, is struggling to force the square peg of a particular case into the round hole of regulatory taking doctrine. Alternatively, one sees a laundry list of federal and state claims, often including regulatory taking, equitable estoppel, due process, equal protection, and even First Amendment, reflecting the lack of clarity in the governing caselaw about the distinctions between these claims.[1] This chapter focuses on some alternatives that are most frequently available in the factual situations typical of regulatory takings claims. They fall into two categories: an equitable claim of estoppel or vested rights, and a legal claim under 42 U.S.C. § 1983 for damages for violation of one's constitutional rights.[2]

It is important to note that these other claims may not be easier to establish than a regulatory taking nor more likely to result in significant monetary compensation. There is a reason that most challenges to local land use regulation and permitting are difficult and rarely successful: the separation of powers doctrine underlying all judicial review of local government decision making. In their zeal to invoke the individual rights provided by the founding fathers, the advocates of private property rights overlook this most fundamental tenet of our system of government.[3] Quite simply, the courts are not charged with, and are institutionally incapable of, responding to citizen input and enacting and applying police power regulations to protect the public health, safety, and welfare. Courts are not policy-making bodies. The adversary process we rely on to reveal the factual truth about a dispute between two parties is poorly suited to determine complex policy decisions with diffuse impacts over many different individuals and interest groups. Ultimately, if one is dissatisfied with local government policy, the remedy is at the ballot box where it belongs.

§ 23.1 Equitable Estoppel and Vested Rights Claims

The most persistent dissatisfaction with takings jurisprudence arises from equitable concerns. Private property rights advocates highlight anecdotal stories of governmental regulation run amok over a sympathetic property owner as evidence of the need for reform.[4] Underlying these appeals to emotion is an argument about the equity of governmental regulation. The argument is perhaps most frequently supported and succinctly stated by the famous quote from *Armstrong v. United States*: The Just Compensation Clause was designed to bar a government from "forcing some people alone to bear public burdens, which, in all fairness and justice, should be borne by the public as a whole."[5]

Because the underlying concern is equitable, it is logical to examine other equitable remedies that may apply in these cases. Principal among these alternatives are the doctrines of vested rights and equitable estoppel. Equitable estoppel focuses on whether it would be inequitable to allow the government to repudiate its prior conduct.[6] The vested rights doctrine is grounded in common law and constitutional principles, and questions whether an owner's property rights can be deprived or frustrated by government regulation.[7] Despite the subtle distinctions between their bases, the doctrines are often applied interchangeably, for example, as they are in the common law in the state of Florida.[8] Other jurisdictions, such as New York and Washington, address the theoretical and practical differences between these two doctrines.[9] For purposes of this chapter, they will be treated as interchangeable.

§ 23.1(a) *Estoppel vs. Taking as a Remedy*

The most significant advantage of the estoppel remedy for the typical takings claimant is that it is well equipped to deal with concerns about fairness. Back when law and equity were distinct courts, equity was explicitly authorized to deal with arguments of fairness and recognized such doctrines as unclean hands. It fixed injustice, for example, by awarding specific performance or enjoining conduct rather than merely awarding money damages. When a taking case grapples with issues of "bad faith," as is done, for example, in *City of Monterey v. Del Monte Dunes*,[10] it is straying into the territory of equity. The basis for doing so is highly questionable given the historical basis and literal language of the Takings Clause, which does not outlaw takings but rather simply requires the payment of compensation for them.

There are also many drawbacks, from the private property owner's perspective, to relying on these equitable doctrines to address the shortcomings of takings jurisprudence. First, it is rare that a government will be estopped against a legitimate exercise of the police power, just as it is rare that it will be found to have worked a regulatory taking of property.[11] Another shortcoming is that equitable remedies are by their very nature not monetary. They thus form a poor substitute if a plaintiff is most concerned with monetary compensation for the government's action. In that event, the claims discussed below would be more appropriate, as they seek monetary damages.

§ 23.1(b) *Good-Faith Reliance and the Pre-acquisition Notice Rule*

There are several similarities in the analysis applicable to the regulatory taking claim and that of the estoppel or vested rights claim, as is demonstrated most recently in the U.S. Supreme Court decision in *Palazzolo v. State of Rhode Island*.[12] The first element of equitable estoppel is that the plaintiff must have relied in good faith on official government action. The property owner must show that its good-faith reliance was on a specific governmental act or omission, such as a permit or approval. Evidence of the right must be clear, complete, and specific.[13]

One of the only clear rulings in *Palazzolo* is that the majority of the Court will not bar a property owner from seeking compensation for a taking solely because the owner acquired the property after the enactment of the offending regulation.[14] By repudiating this "pre-acquisition notice" rule, at least as a threshold matter, the Court has opened the door to more takings claimants. Property owners may have acquired property with full knowledge of the limitations on its use and, regardless of the depressed price they may have paid as a result, still be able to later attack those regulations. In equitable terms, one might say that there is no good-faith reliance on the absence of regulation in such a transaction. Regardless, *Palazzolo* indicates that it is possible to claim just compensation and force the government to defend a suit.

A corollary of the good-faith reliance standard of equitable estoppel is that, where the property owner either knows or has good reason to believe that the official governmental position will soon change, equitable estoppel may not be justified.[15] Similarly, if there is a pending change in the regulations, if there are active and documented efforts by those authorized to develop and prepare such changes, including presentation of the issue to the local governing board or planning commission, then the applicant may be deemed to have constructive knowledge of the changes and may not be entitled to a permit under the existing regulations.[16] However, consistent with the equitable basis of this doctrine, if the government has engaged in intentional delay or arbitrary and capricious action, the applicant will not be estopped from relying on its rights.[17]

Palazzolo makes it clear that a lawsuit can survive despite pre-acquisition notice. Still, the inquiry does not end there, because the determinative vote (Justice O'Connor, in concurrence) strongly emphasized that such notice was relevant and should be considered in the facts of each case.[18] In *Del Monte Dunes*,[19] the Supreme Court addressed allegations of bad faith in governmental conduct from a property owner that it clearly accepted was acting in good faith. Future cases will have to flesh out whether the bad faith of the owner is ever relevant to the regulatory takings inquiry, or only the bad faith of the government. The pending-change doctrine of Florida estoppel law described above sets out one model of how the owner's knowledge or lack thereof might be analyzed.

§ 23.1(c) *Detriment and Reasonable Investment-Backed Expectations*

Estoppel jurisprudence focuses on what the property owner has at stake. The property owner must show that it has changed its position substantially to its detriment, for example, by incurring extensive obligations or expenses in good-faith reliance on the governmental action.[20] Cases have found that mere acquisition of the property and payment of property taxes are not detriment, but that the detrimental reliance (for example, soft development costs) need not be extensive in amount.

This reliance requirement is like a "no harm, no foul" rule. If a property owner knew of the government's action but did nothing concrete to act in response to it, then there is no harm in a legally recognizable sense. Even the law of equity does not address a purely subjective disappointment in another party's action.[21]

The regulatory takings analysis looks at what property is being regulated and tries to define the precise extent of the owner's rights. Background principles of property law and nuisance law must be considered in determining whether the governmental regulation should result in a taking. As examined in greater detail elsewhere in this book, property cannot be segmented to create a taking but rather must be considered as a whole.[22] *Palazzolo's* dicta on the "property as a whole" doctrine raises doubts concerning this previously settled point of law.

Palazzolo breathes new life into the reasonable investment-backed expectations doctrine.[23] The investment-backed expectation issue is discussed purely in terms of acquisition costs. Palazzolo acquired his property by operation of law when his closely held corporation was dissolved for nonpayment of taxes; he never even applied for the residential subdivision that was the basis for his valuation, making this a poor factual case for exploring the investment-backed expectations doctrine in any event.[24] However, even if there had been no change of ownership, the corporation's investment in the property was less than 10 percent of the current value of the property as understood by the Supreme Court.[25]

Unlike the concept of detrimental reliance, the takings concept of reasonable investment-backed expectation frequently focuses on the acquisition and ownership costs of the property. The problem with focusing on the difference between acquisition costs and current value in isolation is that the analysis may miss such factors as the lack of a fully arm's-length transaction or changing market conditions.

Takings doctrine should not, as a matter of good public policy, require the taxpayers to pay for an alleged diminution in value resulting from the owner's overpayment for the property. Yet a simple "before and after" calculation of value may do just that and not have anything to do with the government's action. Property values fluctuate as a function of market conditions. Should an owner who bought at the height of a real estate boom automatically be able to establish a regulatory taking merely because he or she sues after the bubble bursts? In those factual circumstances, experienced most recently with the bubble of the late 1980s and the market correction of the early 1990s, anything a government does to change its regulatory scheme could be "proven" to result in a large decline in value.

Another issue relevant to the equity of takings damages is the exact effect of the governmental action. If a taking is alleged based on the government's refusal to consider the project at all, as, for example, by the refusal to amend the comprehensive plan or zoning classification to allow it, the claimant will usually base the calculation of damage on the value of the property as developed for that use. Implicit in that calculation is an important assumption that subsequent approvals will be granted. For example, even if the zoning would allow the use, the particular site plan yielding the alleged value might be certain to be denied because it violates environmental or building regulations.

Some courts have already begun to address this speculative aspect of damages awards in unconstitutional land-use regulation cases. In *Herrington v. Sonoma County*,[26] the Ninth Circuit upheld the district court's assessment of taking damages that included just such a factor for the likelihood of the claimant receiving all development approval and obtaining the alleged "after" value. The comprehensive plan approval at issue in that case was just the beginning of the process, and several other discretionary development approvals would have to be obtained before development could proceed.[27]

As a rule, damages issues are not well developed in regulatory takings cases, as most cases are resolved on other legal grounds or settled before such matters are litigated. The detrimental reliance model suggests that, as a matter of fairness, the cause of the owner's alleged losses needs to be proven to result from the government's action.

§ 23.1(d) *Takings of Vested Rights?*

At least one claimant has attempted to meld equity with takings and argue that the taking of a vested right to development is something separate and independent from a regulatory taking claim stemming from the interest in the property itself. This attempt to multiply the interests subject to takings protection was rejected by the Eleventh Circuit,[28] which stated:

> Restigouche argues that its 'vested rights' claims are federal claims in and of themselves. Whether Restigouche has any 'vested rights,' i.e., protected property interests, is relevant to the determination of whether Restigouche has stated a federal constitutional claim. . . . However, proof of some vested right by itself does not state a federal claim independent of the constitutional claims already raised and addressed in this opinion. Although some of Restigouche's 'vested rights' claims may be pendent state law claims, their dismissal by the court below was well within its discretion.

Thus, although a vested right to development under an earlier set of regulations cannot provide an independent basis for a taking claim, it may form the basis for the section 1983 claims discussed below.[29]

§ 23.2 *Claims for Compensation under 42 U.S.C. § 1983*

Section 1983 is a remedial statute that permits a claimant to seek monetary compensation from a local government for the violation of his or her federal constitutional rights, if the elements of state action (usually referred to as acting "under color of law" in these cases), causation, and damage can be proven.[30] In addition to any damages that are proven, a successful claimant under section 1983 is entitled to an award of attorney's fees. Section 1983 is considered to be a species of tort liability.

The claims most frequently associated with land use are equal protection and due process. More recently, creative claimants have also been exploring First Amendment–based claims on the theory that governmental action has singled them out for harsher treatment due to their political views. Other chapters in this book delve into the quandary of substantive due process, whether of the rational basis or the "substantially advance"[31] variety, so this discussion will focus on equal protection, procedural due process, and First Amendment–based claims under section 1983.

§ 23.3 *Procedural Due Process*

This right protects procedural fairness, which is often an issue raised by claimants with regard to the ripeness doctrine applicable to regulatory takings claims. Unfortunately for these claimants, the constitutional standard for procedural due process is quite minimal for the many land-use decisions that are legislative, such as the adoption or amendment of a comprehensive plan, a change to the development standards for a particular district, or a comprehensive rezoning of property.[32] By statute, most states require that the local government provide only advertised notice and a public hearing on a legislative change.[33] Actual legislative motive, even if it is alleged to be suspect, is irrelevant.[34] Most local governmental processes can easily meet this standard.

However, where the decision is quasi-judicial under the relevant state law, procedural due process may offer a more viable alternative for relief. Issues such as the length of the hearing, witness qualifications, sworn testimony, cross-examination, ex parte contacts, and bias of the decision maker become relevant.[35] Where the decision maker is a collegial elected body, these questions can become quite thorny as one struggles to apply judicial constructs based on a courtroom to a political reality of elected officials being asked not to be responsive to constituent desires and focus only on the evidence presented at a hearing.

Even so, the effectiveness of a procedural due process claim is practically limited. A property interest must be established. There may be difficult questions of whether the claimant is required to resort to any postdeprivation remedies.[36] Also, the primary relief for denial of procedural due process is equitable, which may not be satisfactory to many property owners.[37] The old maxim is that the remedy for procedural defects is more procedure. Because of separation of powers constraints that prevent a reviewing court from simply rezoning property or issuing a development permit, the remedy for a procedural due process claim may simply be another hearing before the decision maker. Although legally correct, this outcome may not mollify an aggrieved claimant suspicious of the local decision-making process. Also, in most cases, only minimal damages are caused by the denial of procedural due process, and the courts will not award additional damages for the intrinsic value of this or any other constitutional right under section 1983.[38]

§ 23.4   Equal Protection

This discussion of equal protection will focus on the standards applicable to economic regulation of an applicant who is not part of a suspect class. Issues such as claims of racial discrimination in permit decisions are beyond the scope of this book and are amply treated elsewhere.

§ 23.4(a) Rational Basis Review of Economic Regulation

The purpose of the Equal Protection Clause is to secure every person within the state's jurisdiction against intentional and arbitrary discrimination, whether occasioned by the express terms of a statute or by its improper execution through duly constituted agents.[39] It requires a showing of differential governmental treatment of similarly situated persons without a rational basis. This in itself can be a challenging requirement because each development site has both natural characteristics and characteristics of the surrounding built environment that may influence whether the government's action was rational. Thus, development projects are often legitimately distinguishable on their facts.

An equal protection claim can be an attractive alternative to a takings claimant because it has the virtue of avoiding many of the thorniest issues in takings jurisprudence. First, it is not necessary to demonstrate a property interest, as is required for a due process or taking claim.[40] Second, the only ripeness required is a final decision from the local government; there are no issues of exhausting state court remedies for compensation. Third, because a properly alleged equal protection claim turns on the very specific facts applicable to that claimant, the claim is far more likely to survive a summary judgment motion and get to a jury or judge on the merits.

Regardless, some difficulties remain. The standard for judging whether equal protection rights have been violated by the enactment of an economic regulation is the same as for due process claims: is there a rational basis for the regulation? If so, it stands. Moreover, the rational basis supporting the government's enactment need not have actually motivated it; it is sufficient if the basis *could have* supported the action. Aggrieved developers and property owners have historically had a difficult time overcoming this standard. Where the claim was against the application of a governmental regulation to a particular property, these claimants fared no better because many courts refused to recognize that there could be a "class of one" applicant that is entitled to greater scrutiny as would be given to a member of a larger protected class such as race or alienage.

One of the only rational basis cases of the Supreme Court to have found a violation is *City of Cleburne v. Cleburne Living Center*.[41] There, the Court overturned a special-use permit requirement for a group home for the mentally retarded, which was not also required of hotels, fraternity houses, and other intense residential uses. The accepted explanation of why this case found a violation, when legions of other rational basis cases do not, is that the Court has treated the mentally retarded akin to a protected class without explicitly denominating them as such.

At least one state has recently signaled its willingness to consider equal protection claims in the land-use context. The Supreme Court of Wisconsin decided that the rezoning of property to agricultural could be a violation of equal protection where it was alleged that numerous other properties in the community that were more suitable for the agricultural classification had not been rezoned.[42] Under the selective enforcement line of cases, which recognize that a government program may be implemented over time without necessarily being discriminatory, a potential defense would be proof that this was just the first rezoning and that the other suitable properties would also be rezoned.

§ 23.4(b) *"Ill Will" or "Class of One" Equal Protection Claims*

Equal protection claims became more attractive with last year's unanimous U.S. Supreme Court decision in *Village of Willowbrook v. Olech*.[43] The case arose out of the U.S. Circuit Court of Appeals for the Seventh Circuit, which for several years has been developing a body of caselaw recognizing that a property owner, as a "class of one," could attempt to prove that he or she had been singled out by the government for adverse treatment out of ill will or malice.[44]

The village, in response to Olech's request to connect to the municipal water supply, initially required her to dedicate a road-widening easement more than twice as large as that demanded of other applicants. Ultimately, it relented and was able to connect her property to the water supply while accepting only a standard-sized easement. Olech claimed that the requirement of a larger easement was irrational because it was motivated by ill will due to an unrelated lawsuit she had successfully brought against the village.[45] The Seventh Circuit reversed the dismissal of her claim, stating that if the village's action was motivated solely by a spiteful effort to get her, for reasons wholly unrelated to any legitimate state objective, then an equal protection claim could be alleged on that basis. It specifically found that the mere fact of differential treatment with regard to the easement did *not* violate equal protection, and reinstated the claim only because she could also allege ill will.[46]

The Supreme Court affirmed, though the majority explicitly reserved judgment on the "ill will" theory, and relied instead on the allegation that a larger easement was required when events subsequently demonstrated that the smaller easement was adequate, suggesting that the requirement was arbitrary and irrational.[47] In a footnote, the majority did recognize that Olech could be considered part of a larger class of owners who were part of the litigation against the village and were also subject to a similar easement condition, but instead concluded that the number of individuals in a class is immaterial for equal protection analysis and affirmed that a "class of one" was sufficient. Justice Breyer went further, emphasizing in his opinion (concurring in the result) that *Olech* did not raise the "simple and common instance of a faulty zoning decision" but rather involved "vindictive action," "illegitimate animus," or "ill will" as variously styled by the Seventh Circuit.[48]

Subsequently, the Seventh Circuit has had occasion to address the Supreme Court's *Olech* decision. In an opinion authored by the same judge as the original *Olech* decision, Judge Posner, the court interpreted the decision as did Justice Breyer, reinstating its original "ill will" requirement for such claims.[49] In another recent case, the Seventh Circuit once again reinstated an equal protection claim against a local government's requirement that a real estate developer sell a buffer zone of property to the president of the village board (an abutting landowner) for below-market value as a condition of approval for his subdivision. The court held the requirement was malicious, corrupt, and wholly unrelated to any legitimate state objective.[50] However, *Olech*-style claims have yet to survive in other circuits, raising doubt as to the eventual significance of this case.[51]

One of the problems with an "ill will" claim is how to defend such an equal protection case in a community that is strongly growth control–oriented. Local elections are often decided by issues such as the candidate's vision for the future development of the city, in terms of both amount and quality of development. That is a legitimate policy direction for a city council to determine, based on substance and not on illegitimate issues such as distaste for a particular applicant. Even if the record establishes that there is no love lost between the applicant and a majority of the governmental actors, the Constitution should be satisfied if the application is considered on its merits and the decision is based on uniformly applied policy concerning the merits. There is no constitutional right to be liked. Litigation strategy may become dispositive if it is possible to show that all applicants are given a uniformly difficult time, but the trial judge considers it irrelevant that other similarly situated persons were also treated badly.

§ 23.5   First Amendment

Some courts conceive of the bad-faith claim as a form of retaliation for the exercise of First Amendment rights. If such an approach were applied in *Olech*, then the theory of the case might be that the excessive easement requirement was retaliation for Olech having exercised her right of access to the courts and criticized the village, in violation of her First Amendment rights. Such retaliation claims appear to have derived from the employment law cases that prohibit retaliation against an employee for his or her exercise of free speech.[52] These cases recognize that if there is an independent justification for the adverse action, then any facts regarding retaliatory motive become irrelevant. For example, if the employee is stealing from the employer, discharge may be appropriate even though the record may clearly evidence that the employer was unhappy with the employee's exercise of his or her free speech rights against the employer, giving rise to a potential retaliatory motive. Similarly, in the land-use context, if an application clearly violates the governing law, then allegations as to the possibility of a retaliatory motive for the denial should be irrelevant and should not prevent the grant of summary judgment for the government.

One such land-use claim of political retaliation is *Reserve,*

Ltd. v. Town of Longboat Key.[53] Reserve claimed that the town's revocation of a building permit was based on the personal animus between town officials and its general partner, due to the partner's involvement in local politics advocating looser growth controls and greater development.[54] His original claims of equitable estoppel, substantive and vagueness/procedural due process, and taking were eliminated through the town's summary judgment motions, and only the First Amendment and equal protection claims survived. Such claims have been recognized as viable by the First and Fifth Circuits.[55]

Most of these decisions are on summary judgment motions at the pretrial stage, so the details of how to prove and defend a land-use retaliatory motive case under the First Amendment are rather sketchy. Although few of these claims have resulted in reported decisions after trials, the theory could become an important alternative on the right facts. From a defense perspective they are problematic, because most developers are involved to some extent in local political matters or at least have expressed opinions in favor of certain growth policies. If any developer can get to a jury on a First Amendment claim merely by establishing a history of political donations, public support for increased growth in the community, and the denial of an application, then local governments may need to increase their litigation budgets substantially.

§ 23.6   Conclusion

A concern for fairness and equity seems to underlie most of the complaints about current regulatory takings caselaw. In general, the U.S. Constitution is neutral on the equity or morality of takings, and merely requires payment of compensation for them. However, regulatory taking is not the only theory by which a property owner may challenge the fairness of the government's treatment.

State law claims such as equitable estoppel are designed to address fairness issues and thus may better satisfy an aggrieved applicant's sense of justice. Estoppel law raises important questions regarding the relative equities of the parties and suggests a framework for examining the actions of the applicant as well as the government. A drawback is that equitable claims yield little in the form of monetary compensation.

If the focus of the claim is compensation, then a property owner may seek compensation under a variety of constitutional theories, including due process, equal protection, and First Amendment, using 42 U.S.C. § 1983. Whatever the theory of liability, claims for compensation against the impacts of a governmental land-use decision raise important policy issues regarding the speculativeness and avoidability of harm. These issues have not been resolved or even addressed by most jurisdictions, and thus there is a great deal of uncertainty for litigants in this arena.

Notes

1. *See, e.g.,* Martin County v. Section 28 Partnership, Ltd., 772 So. 2d 616 (Fla. 4th Dist. Ct. App. 2000); Restigouche, Inc. v. Town of Jupiter, 59 F.3d 1208 (11th Cir. 1995); Reserve, Ltd. v. Town of Longboat Key, 933 F. Supp. 1040 (M.D. Fla. 1996); and Villas of Lake Jackson, Ltd. v. Leon County, 121 F.3d 610 (11th Cir. 1997), all of which involved multiple claims and even multiple lawsuits in federal and state court.

2. Because I practice in Florida and because the Florida land-use cases are fairly well developed, I will frequently refer to Florida and Eleventh Circuit law as examples.

3. A recent and interesting assessment of the responsibilities that accompany the right of property ownership in the American tradition is Donovan D. Rypkema, Property Rights and Public Values, Lecture at the National Building Museum (June 13, 2001) (transcript available at www.envpoly.org/takings/prypkema.htm, the web site of the Environmental Policy Project of Georgetown University Law Center).

4. *See, e.g.,* Suitum v. Tahoe Regional Planning Agency, 520 U.S. 725 (1997) and Vatalaro v. Dept. of Envtl. Protection, 601 So. 2d 1223 (Fla. 2d Dist. Ct. App. 1992), *rev. den.,* 613 So. 2d 3 (Fla. 1992) for just two of the many elderly widows who populate the regulatory taking cases.

5. 364 U.S. 40, 49 (1960).

6. Heeter, *Zoning Estoppel: Application of the Principles of Equitable Estoppel and Vested Rights to Zoning Disputes,* 1971 URB. L. ANN. 63, 64-65.

7. *Id.*

8. *See, e.g.,* City of Hollywood v. Hollywood Beach Hotel Co., 283 So. 2d 867 (Fla. 4th Dist. Ct. App. 1973), *rev'd in part,* 329 So. 2d 10 (equitable estoppel will be applied to government regulation of land use if a property owner, in good-faith reliance on some act or omission of the government, has made a substantial change in position or has incurred extensive obligations and expenses, making it inequitable and unjust to destroy the right).

9. *See* 4 ZIEGLER, RATHKOPF'S THE LAW OF ZONING AND PLANNING, § 50.05 for a detailed discussion of the doctrines nationwide.

10. 526 U.S. 687 (1999).

11. *See, e.g.,* Tri-State Sys., Inc. v. Department of Transp., 500 So. 2d 212, 215 (Fla. 1st Dist. Ct. App. 1987), *rev. den.,* 502 So. 2d 1041.

12. 121 S. Ct. 2448 (2001).

13. Harbour Course Club, Inc. v. Department of Cmty. Affairs, 510 So. 2d 915 (Fla. 3d Dist. Ct. App. 1987).

14. Compare Metropolitan Dade County v. Fontainebleau Gas & Wash, Inc., 570 So. 2d 1006 (Fla. 3d Dist. Ct. App. 1990) (owners are deemed to purchase property with constructive knowledge of applicable land-use regulations, and subsequent purchaser could not detrimentally rely on mistaken governmental actions in violation of such regulations).

15. Sharrow v. City of Dania, 83 So. 2d 274 (Fla. 1955). *See also* Miami Shores Village v. William N. Brockway Post No. 124 of American Legion, 24 So. 2d 33 (Fla.

1945) (impending election and possible change of officers can nullify reliance on act of current governing body, on the theory that the "red flags" flying in a "hot municipal campaign" give notice that certain candidates, if elected, may alter the voting pattern of the governmental body). *Compare* Bregar v. Britton, 75 So. 2d 753 (Fla. 1954), *cert. den.,* 348 U.S. 972 (red flags or political protest occurring *after* the property owner's reliance does *not* prevent the application of estoppel).

16. Franklin County v. Leisure Props., Ltd., 430 So. 2d 475 (Fla. 1st Dist. Ct. App. 1983), *rev. den.,* 440 So. 2d 352; and Smith v. City of Clearwater, 383 So. 2d 681 (Fla. 2d Dist. Ct.App. 1980), *rev. den.,* 403 So. 2d 407. *Compare* Gardens Country Club, Inc. v. Palm Beach County, 712 So. 2d 398 (Fla. 4th Dist. Ct.App. 1998) (doctrine of zoning in progress not applicable to comprehensive plan changes).

17. City of Margate v. Amoco Oil Co., 546 So. 2d 1091 (Fla. 4th Dist. Ct.App. 1989) (finding that city had denied site plan in order to gain time to pass new laws that would prevent the proposed construction).

18. 121 S. Ct. 2448, 2466 (2001).

19. City of Monterey v. Del Monte Dunes at Monterey, Ltd., 526 U.S. 687 (1999).

20. Gross v. City of Riviera Beach, 367 So. 2d 648 (Fla. 4th Dist. Ct.App. 1979), *cert. den.,* 378 So. 2d 345.

21. *Compare* City of Pompano Beach v. Yardarm Restaurant, Inc., 509 So. 2d 1295 (Fla. 4th Dist. Ct.App. 1987) (holding that city's early obstructionist tactics did not estop city from later repealing controversial special height exception, where property owner failed to make any real effort to construct in the five years after the city backed off). The Florida courts later denied an inverse condemnation claim on these facts, at 641 So. 2d 1377 (Fla. 4th Dist. Ct.App. 1994), *rev. den.,* but a subsequent federal claim resulted in a finding that there was a taking and substantial damages. That unpublished trial court decision is currently on appeal in the Eleventh Circuit.

22. See *supra* chapter 4.

23. *See* Kaiser-Aetna v. United States, 444 U.S. 164, 175 (1979).

24. Interestingly, the Court states that the lack of an application for the subdivision would be relevant to calculation of damages, but it does not indicate how that fact should be taken into account. Perhaps it is relevant to a determination of whether the proof is too speculative to support an award of damages.

25. Palazzolo had claimed the property could be developed into a subdivision worth over $3 million if the wetlands could be filled and developed. Based on arguably incomplete evidence and findings below, the Supreme Court concluded that the allowable use of the uplands on Palazzolo's property was only one dwelling unit worth $200,000 (in 1986 dollars).

26. Herrington v. Sonoma County, 790 F. Supp. 909, 925 (N.D. Cal. 1991) (as amended), *aff'd,* 12 F.3d 901, 904-06 (9th Cir. 1993).

27. *Compare* Jacobi v. City of Miami Beach, 678 So. 2d 1365 (Fla. 3d Dist. Ct. App. 1996), stating:

> In sum, the property owners may not recover for the harm caused by the decision-making process pursuant to the asserted claims. We are cognizant that the property owners were unable to proceed unhindered in the development of their property. They experienced delays and incurred expenses awaiting resolution of the neighbors' appeal to the Board and their successful appeal to the circuit court. However, there is no guarantee that regulatory bodies will not become embroiled in disputes with property owners in which the owners ultimately will prevail. In

addition, there is no concomitant guarantee that property owners may recover for harm caused by these disputes. Every time a property owner is successful. . . in a challenge to a governmental regulation. . . he is almost certain to suffer some temporary harm in the process. At the least, he will incur significant litigation expenses and frequently will incur substantial revenue losses because the use of his property has been temporarily curtailed while the dispute is being resolved. The Due Process Clause of the Fourteenth Amendment requires a State to employ fair procedures in the administration and enforcement of all kinds of regulations. It does not, however, impose the utopian requirement that enforcement action may not impose any[ ] cost upon the citizen unless the government's position is completely vindicated. Williamson County Reg'l Planning Comm'n v. Hamilton Bank of Johnson City, 473 U.S. 172, 204-05, 105 S. Ct. 3108, 3126, 87 L. Ed. 2d 126, 150 (1985) (Stevens, J., concurring). *See* Boatman v. Town of Oakland, 76 F.3d 341, 346 (11th Cir. 1996) ("The notion that the Constitution gives a property owner a substantive right to a correct decision from a government official. . . is novel indeed.").

28.   Restigouche, Inc. v. Town of Jupiter, 59 F.3d 1208 (11th Cir. 1995) (also refusing to recognize claims categorized as "fails to substantially advance" takings and "justice and fairness" takings as distinct, viable federal constitutional claims in the zoning context).

29.   Gardens Country Club, Inc. v. Palm Beach County, 712 So. 2d 398 (Fla. 4th Dist. Ct. App. 1998); Henniger v. Pinnellas County, 7 F. Supp. 2d 1334 (M.D. Fla. 1998).

30.   *See generally* City of Monterey v. Del Monte Dunes at Monterey, Ltd., 526 U.S. 687, 707 (1999). One excellent source for detailed information on section 1983 law is the treatise by SHELDON NAHMOD, CIVIL RIGHTS AND CIVIL LIBERTIES LITIGATION: THE LAW OF SECTION 1983.

31.   See *supra* chapters 16 and 17.

32.   Some states still treat any rezoning as legislative; Florida has joined Oregon and the growing ranks of states that consider site-specific rezonings to be quasi-judicial. Board of County Commr's of Brevard County v. Snyder, 627 So. 2d 469 (Fla. 1993). Generally, state law determines in which category a decision will fall.

33.   *See, e.g.,* Section 166.041(3), Florida Statutes, setting out procedures for adoption of any ordinance. Federal procedural due process cases do not even require this minimal procedure for a legislative determination. *See, e.g.,* Missouri v. Jenkins, 495 U.S. 33, 66 (1990) (Kennedy, J., concurring in part and in the result), emphasizing that notice and a hearing for legislative action are provided through the representative form of government.

34.   *See, e.g.,* Bogan v. Scott-Harris, 118 U.S. 966 (1998).

35.   *See, e.g.,* Jennings v. Metropolitan Dade County, 589 So. 2d 1337 (Fla. 3d Dist. Ct. App. 1991), *rev. den.,* 598 So. 2d 75 (Fla. 1992); Broward County v. G.B.V. Int'l, Ltd., 787 So. 2d 838 (Fla. 2001).

36.   Zinermon v. Burch, 494 U.S. 113 (1990); Coletta v. City of North Bay Village, 962 F. Supp. 1486 (S.D. Fla. 1997).

37.   McKinney v. Pate, 20 F.3d 1550 (11th Cir. 1994).

38.   Carey v. Piphus, 435 U.S. 247 (1978); and Memphis Cmty. Sch. Dist. v. Stachura, 477 U.S. 299 (1986).

39.   Village of Willowbrook v. Olech, 120 S. Ct. 1073, 1075 (2000).

40.   Kantner v. Martin County, 929 F. Supp. 1482 (S.D. Fla. 1996); and Front Royal and Warren County Indus. Park Corp. v. Town of Front Royal, 135 F.3d 275, 290 (4th Cir. 1998) (where governmental action does not burden a fundamental right or employ a suspect classification, equal protection turns on whether the officials could reasonably

have believed that the action was rationally related to a legitimate governmental interest).

41.   City of Cleburne v. Cleburne Living Center, 473 U.S. 432 (1985).

42.   Thorp v. Town of Lebanon, 612 N.W.2d 59 (Wis. 2000).

43.   Village of Willowbrook v. Olech, 120 S. Ct. 1073 (2000) (per curiam).

44.   *See, e.g.,* Esmail v. Macrane, 53 F.3d 176 (7th Cir. 1995).

45.   *Olech,* 120 S. Ct. at 1074.

46.   Olech v. Village of Willowbrook, 160 F.3d 386, 388 (7th Cir. 1998).

47.   *Olech,* 120 S. Ct. at 1074.

48.   *Id.* at 1075.

49.   Hilton v. City of Wheeling, 209 F.3d 1005, 1007-08 (7th Cir. 2000). The concern was that, if a claimant could establish a prima facie case merely by alleging an unexplained difference in the government's treatment of similarly situated persons, then the federal courts would potentially face an avalanche of cases concerning "local enforcement of petty state and local laws."

50.   Forseth v. Village of Sussex, 199 F.3d 363 (7th Cir. 2000).

51.   Greenspring Racquet Club, Inc. v. Baltimore County, 2000 WL 1624496 (4th Cir. 2000) (unpublished) (relying on the equal protection standard of its earlier *Front Royal* case, *supra* at note 40, to uphold dismissal, and stating that *Olech* did not change the result where an obvious legitimate purpose is evident on the face of a challenged law); Bryan v. City of Madison, 213 F.3d 267 (5th Cir. 2000) (a claim of selective prosecution or enforcement must demonstrate a motive involving a suspect class or fundamental right; "personal vindictiveness" might be a sufficient basis on the right facts, but a municipal response to public outcry was not personal vindictiveness); and Alsenas v. City of Brecksville, 2000 WL 875717 (6th Cir. 2000) (unpublished).

52.   *See, e.g.,* Tindal v. Montgomery County Comm'n, 32 F.3d 1535 (11th Cir. 1994) (First Amendment retaliatory discharge cases are generally analyzed under the following four-part test: (1) whether the employee's speech involved a matter of public concern; (2) whether the employee's interest in the speech outweighed the government's legitimate interest in promoting efficient public service; (3) whether the speech played a substantial part in the challenged employment decision; and (4) whether the employer would have made the same employment decision regardless of the protected speech).

53.   Reserve, Ltd. v. Town of Longboat Key, 933 F. Supp. 1040, 1046-47 (M.D. Fla. 1996).

54.   The permit was revoked after 60 days' failure to complete substantial work on the construction of the project (the time provided by code was 30 days). The requirement was interpreted by the building official to apply to each situation and survived the vagueness challenge. It was designed to avoid abandoned construction sites and their concomitant danger to public health and safety, particularly in light of the oceanfront location of most construction on the island.

55.   Rolf v. City of San Antonio, 77 F.3d 823, 827-28 (5th Cir. 1996) (a landowner states a First Amendment claim against a city for a condemnation proceeding allegedly brought in retaliation for the owner's opposition to city policy); Nestor Colon Medina & Sucesores, Inc. v. Custodio, 964 F.2d 32, 40-41 (1st Cir. 1992) (denial of land-use permit in unjustifiable retaliation for the applicant's expression of his political views is a First Amendment violation).

APPENDIX

Introduction

This section consists of two reports. The first, mentioned in the Preface, is the report of a retreat held at the University of Denver Law School in June 1999. The second report, issued by the International Municipal Lawyers Association (IMLA), is a response to the retreat report.

While the Section of State and Local Government Law of the ABA was a cosponsor of the retreat, the Section did not endorse or adopt the retreat report. Neither, of course, did the American Bar Association. Thus, the retreat report should not be cited as reflecting the position of the ABA or the ABA Section of State and Local Government.

When the Section received the report and circulated it, as the Preface to this book notes, many comments were received. The IMLA response was one such comment. Since it offers views at odds with the retreat report, it is published here to carry out this book's effort at presenting both sides of the various takings issues. It is published with the permission of IMLA.

The retreat report and the comments from IMLA and others were the catalyst to the development of this book.

REPORT OF RETREAT ON TAKINGS JURISPRUDENCE

Jointly sponsored by
The American Bar Association
Section of State and Local Government Law and
The Rocky Mountain Land Use Institute

University of Denver Law School
June 24–27, 1999

Commentary by:
Peter A. Buchsbaum, Esq.
Greenbaum, Rowe, Smith, Ravin, Davis & Himmel LLP
P. O. Box 5600
Woodbridge, NJ 07095
(732) 549-5600
Pbuchsbaum@greenbaumlaw. com
Retreat Co-Coordinator

Introduction

The complexities of takings jurisprudence as developed by the United States
Supreme Court, the lower federal courts, and state courts have posed a
dilemma for lawyers, local governments, state governments and the private
sector. As a result of the ferment in this field of law, most recently evidenced by the May 24, 1999 Supreme Court ruling in *City of Monterey v.
Del Monte Dunes*, 119 S. Ct. 1624 (1999), the Section of State and Local
Government of the American Bar Association and The Rocky Mountain
Land Institute decided jointly to sponsor a Retreat on the subject. The
purpose of the Retreat was to determine whether a group of knowledgeable
and concerned lawyers and law professors with different points of view
could agree on some propositions relating to takings jurisprudence. The
hope was that if consensus could be reached, law reform positions so agreed
on could be presented by the State and Local Government Section or other
sections of the ABA for action by the House of Delegates.

The Retreat did convene at the University of Denver Law School between June 24 and June 27, 1999. In attendance were 24 individuals representing a spectrum of views. These individuals essentially came on their
own expense, although the ABA had offered scholarships to those among
the approximately 55 invitees who were from the public sector or academia
in order to encourage a wide range of participation.

What follows is the report of this Retreat group. It is not a unanimous
consensus. Of the 24 attendees (see list Exhibit A attached), approximately
four, including Tim Dowling of Community Rights Counsel, Vicki Been,

professor at the New York University Law School, and Ed Sullivan, a private practitioner in Oregon who has helped implement its innovative planning system, dissented. Those who favored the report included the two co-chairs of the Retreat, Ed Ziegler, a professor at the University of Denver Law School and chairman of the Rocky Mountain Land Use Institute, and Peter Buchsbaum, chair of the ABA Section on Local Government Law's committee on land use, planning and zoning. Also favoring the report were Dwight Merriam, former president of the American Planning Association and now a practitioner in private practice; Daniel Mandelker, professor at the Washington University St. Louis and an author of well-known land use texts; and Gideon Kanner, along with his partner, Michael Berger, who argued the *Del Monte Dunes* case for the plaintiff, as well as Thomas Pelham, a former ABA land use committee chair and a former secretary of community affairs for the state of Florida. Charles Siemon, a coauthor of *The White River Junction Manifesto*, which favored strong land use regulation, likewise supported the Report.

The initial Retreat report stirred a great deal of controversy and interest, as demonstrated by articles by one of the dissenters, Tim Dowling, in the *National Law Journal* and replies by Mr. Siemon and by Sholem Friedman, chair of the ABA State and Local Government Law Section, in that same publication.

An initial question raised was why the ABA should be involved in such a controversial topic. The Retreat Report answers this question, particularly with respect to the ripeness issues which involved a great deal of the Retreat's efforts. According to most of the Retreat participants, the ripeness issue is one of judicial administration—when can a litigant be in court. On this issue, the ABA has every right to get involved, they urge. The Supreme Court in the *Williamson County* case, 473 U. S. 172 (1985), determined that before a federal takings claim is ripe, a landowner or developer must show that he or she has received a final decision from the state or local agency. Further case law has attempted to define what is meant by a final decision. Some of this case law has focused, not just on the decision, but on whether the development proposal being submitted was realistic. In general, case law holds that when a local government rejects a proposal which is so far-fetched as to be unrealistic, that rejection does not trigger a right to judicial review. Only the submission and rejection of realistic proposals does so.

To this is added the further doctrine that the initial rejection of even a realistic proposal may not suffice to ripen a claim. Instead, the developer must request either a variance or some other form of relief in order to insure that the local government or state government's rejection of the claim is really final for purposes of ripening a takings claim.

The bulk of Retreat participants believed these ripeness criteria have tended to confuse the issue of jurisdiction over a claim with its merits. If a claim is substantively ridiculous—by requesting far more density than any would find reasonable—it should be rejected on its merits. However, to make that substantive judgment also a determinant of whether a plaintiff has the right to be in court in the first place can cause great confusion. When into this mix is added the confusion as to how many times a land owner must appear before a local body in order to obtain a truly final position, we have then a potentially mind-numbing fog enveloping a question that should have a clear answer: Does a particular individual have a right to be in court?

And this is where the ABA does potentially have a role, according to the Report. It does have a legitimate interest in lawyers being able to tell clients with some clarity that a particular forum is or is not open to litigation and when that forum can be accessed.

This matter has not been alleviated by the *Del Monte Dunes* case. Although the Court did hold in *Del Monte Dunes* that five rejections were sufficient to ripen that particular dispute, it explicitly declined to clarify the rules any further. And for better or for worse, not every case can get to the United States Supreme Court. Thus, as a result, the ordinary government or private lawyer, when confronted with a potential takings claim, still cannot really advise his or her client as to whether the claim is ripe for judicial review or whether still another approach must be made to the local governing body before constitutional litigation can be commenced. It is this effort to clarify a very fundamental issue—when one can be in court— that could justify ABA involvement. The Retreat Report assumes that some greater clarity in the law would benefit all concerned, not merely the private sector, since attorneys on any side of a land use dispute can benefit if they clearly can advise clients on the likelihood of success of a claim that could involve millions of dollars in damages and maybe a million dollars or more in legal expenses.

A further note. The Retreat effort did not advocate change in the essentials of the *Williamson County* ripeness requirements. There was no consensus on such changes. Nor is the Report any part of any legislative strategy in Washington with respect to the so-called ripeness bill, H. R. 2372, now before the House of Representatives. In fact, the Retreat Report endorses no legislation, since there was no consensus whatsoever at the Retreat about any particular piece of legislation. Instead, this Report should be read as a statement of general principles to be developed with respect to the law of takings.

Moreover, an effort was made at the Retreat to avoid participation directly by interest groups, although outside counsel who are involved in the lobbying on H. R. 2372, and who were involved in the lobbying on H. R. 1534, the predecessor to H. R. 2372, were at the Retreat. It is recognized that the congressional approach has spurred a great deal of controversy, and the effort in the Retreat was to see if a consensus could be found. For that reason, the Retreat Report is more general than any piece of legislation. It is not intended to endorse or oppose any particular bill in Congress.

Finally, all the Retreat participants recognized that the four areas addressed in the Report—ripeness, segmentation, realistic investment-backed expectations, and temporary takings—cover a lot of ground. It was not intended that action be taken by the State and Local Government Law Section or the ABA as a whole on all of them at any particular time. In fact, the ripeness portion of the Report, which is the most complete, was probably the highest priority of the Retreat, since it involved the greatest deal of discussion during the Retreat, and most purely involves judicial administration, which is or should be the greatest concern of the American Bar Association and its constituent parts.

The Retreat having concluded, the Section of State and Local Government Law has authorized release of this Report for general comment. The Section Council at its meeting in May 2000 intends to examine all the commentary and decide whether to adopt the Retreat report, or any part thereof, in its initial form or as amended. Readers of the report should be aware that the Council has not endorsed the Report or determined at this point whether it is in agreement with these recommendations. There are already the beginnings of a lively debate in the Council about the recommendations. Nonetheless, Council does feel that the Retreat effort was a valuable one, involving as it did a significant portion of the takings bar; that the issues involved are of paramount public importance; and that the Section has an obligation to present this Report generally and to see if the law in this critical area can be improved.

With this introduction having hopefully set forth the context and purposes of the Report, and why ABA action in the areas covered by the report may be appropriate, the actual text of the recommendations follows.

Retreat Report

I. Ripeness

A. Introduction

As set forth in the Introduction to the report as a whole, the ripeness issue has probably most bedeviled litigants seeking to raise takings claims, particularly in federal court, but also in state court so far as a final decision is required before a takings claim is considered to be ripe for judicial review. Accordingly, the meaning and potential improvements in the law of ripeness as established in *Williamson County Regional Planning Commission v. Hamilton Bank*, 473 U. S. 172 (1985), became a key focus of the Retreat. In fact, it was in this area, controversial though it be, that the Retreat organizers hoped to be able to achieve consensus so that the threshold question of when a litigant is properly in court could be addressed in a clear and consistent fashion.

B. *Williamson County* First Prong—Final Decision on a Reasonable Proposal

These recommendations have been divided into general principle and specific implementation. There was more consensus at the Retreat on the general principle than on the specific implementation. It was also felt that the general principle was more important although somewhat more generally expressed. It was the intention of the Retreat to bring clarity to when litigants have provided a final application that must be acted upon. The general principle of providing guidance to land use applicants is therefore critical. The principle is embodied in #1.

With respect to the specific implementation, the Retreat recognized that a number of different avenues might suffice. Further, it did not want to be bound by a specific legislative proposal. Therefore, the Retreat established the recommendation as a bright-line test for determining when ripeness had occurred, without necessarily precluding other implementation devices that conform to the general principle. Accordingly, there is an interplay between items 1 and 2 in which item 1 is the guiding overall approach that is being recommended.

1. Ripeness and Final Decisions—General Principle:

Where government has discretion in the review of a development proposal, and a developer has provided sufficient information as required by the authority about its proposal, government should provide guidance to help an applicant determine what will be a compliant application, and should not simply treat proposals as unreasonable without suggesting the further information and substantive parameters that would be acceptable for the rendering of a final decision on the application. This guidance could be provided by a ripeness statement, or some other suitable expression from the regulatory authority.

2. Specific Implementation

A taking claim is ripe if:

a. A meaningful—that is, one which at least facially complies with local requirements—and complete application as defined by the reviewing authority has been submitted;

b. That application has been rejected by the final regulatory authority, and the rejection is accompanied by guidance regarding the additional information or changes in the substance of the proposal required to make an alternative development proposal approvable;

c. The landowner/developer has responded to the regulatory authority s statement of additional information and/or changed the proposal to conform to the guidance provided.

d. Provided however, if the government fails to provide guidance, the claim is ripe for review

Commentary: The range of development options for a particular piece of property is identified in the locally legislatively adopted land use regulations. Accordingly, development applications submitted at intensities consistent with these locally adopted zoning regulations are appropriate. However, there may be local reasons why development at a higher development intensity authorized under the zoning code may not be appropriate. When this occurs, the regulating authority should identify its concerns and the parameters of acceptable development to provide meaningful guidance to the land use applicant. The regulating authority should not simply reject proposals as unreasonable without suggesting what parameters would be reasonable and send an applicant on an odyssey that lasts several years. Guidance can solve this problem.

There is a distinction between ripeness and the merits of a taking claim. There may be reasons why an applicant may choose to pursue further alternative development proposals even though his taking claim may be ripe. We observe that taking claims may arise out of the bad faith of either or both the applicant and local government that could benefit from clarification of the baseline ripeness principles and, therefore, this is the spirit in which these suggestions are offered.

Non-constitutional Approaches: The kinds of conflicts that lead to takings cases are best resolved non-constitutionally through improvements in the local planning process. If regulatory authorities understand that private property owners have protectable property interests that courts will enforce, then there exist incentives for realistic regulatory reforms. If landowners understand that government requires adequate information on which to base a decision, they will not be tempted to submit proposals that are not thought through and then run to court claiming a constitutional violation. Therefore, it is recommended not only that the courts continue to refine takings law but also that lawyers provide leadership in achieving meaningful regulatory reform.

Further, officials who are regulatory decision-makers should be the focus of significant educational efforts regarding the confluence of constitutional rights and community planning and political objectives. However, this kind of an initiative only works when the judiciary interprets constitutional protections in a clear and consistent manner.

C. *Williamson County* Second Prong—Exhaustion of State Judicial Remedies

Purpose of the recommendations: Recommendation #1 discusses whether a takings claim, once raised in state court, can ever be litigated in federal court. The ripeness doctrine suggests, by its very term, that once a request for compensation for an alleged taking has been ripened for bringing the matter to state court, then the claim so "ripened" can be brought in federal court. However, there is authority in *Dodd v. Hood River County*, 136 F. 3d

1219 (9th Cir. 1998) that preclusion bars relitigating the takings claim in federal court. Under this doctrine, ripening the issue in state court at the same time precludes it ever being raised in federal court. There are, however, indications to the contrary at least where federal rights have been specifically reserved for later litigation in federal court. *Fields v. Sarasota Manatee Airport Authority*, 953 F. 2d 1299, 1307-09 (11th Cir. 1992). It is obviously of critical importance that a takings plaintiff and a takings defendant know whether there is ultimately a resort to federal court after a takings issue is initially litigated in state court.

The second and third recommendations deal with the apparent anomaly in effect, though probably not in intent, when *Williamson* is juxtaposed against *Chicago v. City of Chicago v. International College of Surgeons*, 522 U. S. 156 (1997). Under *City of Chicago,* governmental defendants can, and frequently do, remove takings claims initiated in state court to federal court under the federal removal statute. At the same time, under *Williamson*, plaintiffs who bring those very same claims in federal court are told they must litigate in state court. As a result, the defendants in takings claims have a choice of forum—state or federal—while takings plaintiffs under *Williamson* are apparently required to go only to state court. This apparent anomaly and unfairness is the subject of recommendations 2 and 3.

Recommendations—Second Prong

1. There is an inconsistency among the circuits which should be resolved by the Supreme Court as to whether a federal claim which is ripened in state court may be ultimately brought in federal court.
2. *Chicago College of Surgeons'* holding that a government can remove a takings claim to federal court creates unfairness if, under *Williamson*, a plaintiff cannot also sue for a takings in federal court; either both sides or neither side of a takings lawsuit should be allowed to go to federal court.
3. Also, after it removes a takings claim to federal court, a government defendant should not then be allowed to challenge the claim on state judicial exhaustion grounds.

II. Reasonable investment-backed expectations

A. Introduction

The question of whether a particular government action interferes with a landowner's reasonable investment-backed expectations has been a feature of takings jurisprudence at least since *Penn Central Transportation Company v. City of New York*, 438 U. S. 104 (1978). The apparent idea behind the concept is that a landowner who never had a realistic prospect for development in the first instance should not complain when a government regulation restricts the opportunity for development. The idea has been used, most recently, to support holdings that a property owner who bought after environmental regulation was in place knew or should have known that regulation would restrict development. Therefore, any claim that such regulation is a "taking" should be rejected because there was no realistic expectation of ability to develop at the time the purchase was made.

There is another school of thought on this subject. If a government regulation is duly harsh and oppressive, and thus constitutes a taking, that harshness should not, it is argued, be alleviated simply because the property in question was sold after the alleged improper regulation was adopted. The law with respect to variances appears to track this chain of logic— there is decisional support for the proposition that denial of a land use variance can constitute a taking, even when the complaint is raised by a purchaser who bought after the zoning restriction in question was adopted.

The Retreat wrestled with the confusion concerning this area of the law and determined that the concept of investment-backed expectations can be useful as a factor, but certainly not a sole factor, in determining whether a regulation has effectuated a taking. (See Recommendation #1.) The group also felt that greater clarity in state law as to vested rights would help in determining what reasonable investment backed expectations could be. (See Recommendation #2.)

Finally, the Retreat felt that investment-backed expectations as a factor was not normally useful in determining whether just compensation has been provided by the government, although it could be used, following a determination that just compensation has not been provided for a taking, in determining the extent of damages. Damages, almost as in a contract case, could be measured by what the government allowed versus what the owner expected in terms of the value of the property (see Recommendations 3 and 4). There was a dissent on this subject from Professor Jan Laitos of the Denver University Law School, who felt that realistic investment-backed expectations did not go to define a property right, but should really be used in determining what notice of regulations defeats a takings claim.

B. Recommendations

1. Although application of the reasonable investment-backed expectations concept can be confusing, an owner's reasonable expectations, as defined by state law, are useful to determine whether there are constitutionally protected property interests. The issue of whether a property owner has notice of preexisting rules or understandings may also be relevant to determining the existence of such protected property interests;

2. An owner's reasonable investment-backed expectations which are a protected vested right under state law should be recognized as a distinct protected property interest. A model vested rights law could provide useful clarification of what rights are vested under local law.

3. The concept of reasonable investment-backed expectations is useful in determining compensatory damages.

III. Segmentation

A. Introduction

A key issue besetting takings jurisprudence is determining the appropriate unit of property to measure the extent of loss. Many land use cases involve a part of an existing vacant tract, or the portion of the tract left over after the balance of the property has been previously developed. It then becomes critical whether a court should focus on particular portions of a vacant property, if not all is developed, and, if a property has been developed over time, whether it is justifiable to ignore the portion which has been developed while potentially finding a taking of the undeveloped remainder. This latter situation can occur where, for example, stringent wetlands regulations in particular have rendered undevelopable a portion of a property which had been built on before the regulations were imposed.

Also in play here is Justice Scalia's cryptic footnote 7 in the *Lucas* case, *Lucas v. South Carolina Coastal Council*, 505 U. S. 1003 (1992). There he stated that he was not sure whether a taking of 90 percent of a piece of property would be reviewed as a total taking of the 90 percent or as a partial taking of the entire amount. Given that the Supreme Court is uncertain on this issue, it seemed appropriate for the Retreat group to try to address it.

In dealing with this issue, the Retreat group in Recommendation #1 first tried to ensure that there was no artificial manipulation of the amount of land considered in determining whether a taking has occurred. Therefore, assuming the numerator in a takings claim is the amount of value lost, and this can be determined relatively objectively through appraisals, the Retreat group asked that there be a neutral method for determining the denominator, which is the value of the totality of the land considered to be affected by the regulation. The term segmentation involved an effort by a landowner to artificially divide the land into smaller segments to produce a smaller denominator which would result in a potentially artificially high fraction of the land value being lost to a regulation. The term agglomeration was intended to deal with equally artificial potential efforts by government to include in the denominator the value of lands which should not be included in the parcel under consideration.

The substantive recommendations in this section of the Retreat report are intended largely to track factors set forth in two leading cases on the subject, *Zealy v. City of Waukesha*, 548 N. W. 2d 528 (Wis. S. Ct. 1996) and *Ciampitti v. United States*, 22 Cl. Ct. 310 (1991). The Retreat group was relatively content with these factors and thus did not suggest new law in this area.

Finally, the Retreat asked, but did not answer, the question of whether the availability of transferrable development rights (TDRs) should be included in the takings equation. In *Suitum v. Tahoe Regional Planning Commission*, 520 U. S. 725 (1997), the Supreme Court split on whether TDRs were a form of compensation, to be credited against damages due from the government if a taking had been found, or whether a TDR could actually ward off a finding that a taking had occurred. The Retreat did not answer this question. The recommendations in this area follow.

B. Recommendations

1. Courts should use a neutral measure to determine the denominator which is not malleable by either the property owner (segmentation) or by the government (agglomcration).
2. We recommend that a court, when faced with a parcel-as-a-whole issue, consider the following factors:

   a. Degree of contiguity (horizontal or vertical).
   b. Treatment by owner in its planning for the land.
   c. Treatment by government in its existing regulation.
   d. Date parcels acquired.
   e. Extent to which restrictions benefit other areas of property.
   f. Size and character of parcels customarily traded in the community (Commercial Unit).
   g. Reasonable expectations of property owner.
   h. Whether parcels have been combined for purposes other than takings.

3. These factors are similar to the factors used in the *Ciampitti* and *Zealy* decisions.

IV. Temporary takings

A. Introduction

Finally, the Retreat grappled with an issue addressed in *Del Monte Dunes*, which is when delay in approval of a development, or a moratorium on construction, constitutes a temporary taking.

This issue distinguished itself from permanent takings caused by regulations that permanently deprive a property owner of the use of land. The Retreat Report findings assume, based on *First English* and *Del Monte Dunes*, that unreasonable delay can cause a taking. Essentially, the first recommendation adopted established law that normal time delays in obtaining a particular land use determination do not constitute a taking. The second recommendation asserts that normal delay in reviewing a land use application is not compensable as a taking, although it may be compensable on other grounds, even where the application is denied and such denial is found to be a taking. Thus, assuming normal processing, a land use denial found to be a taking is only compensable from the time of the actual denial, not from the time the application is made.

Further, the group felt (see recommendation #3) that time spent litigating should be compensable up to the time of the court decision finding a taking. The fourth recommendation reflects the Retreat's agreement that denials of approvals which are invalid for state law reasons should not be compensated as a taking. Such invalid denials might conceivably be compensated under Section 1983 as substantive due process or equal protection violations, but they are not takings.

Finally, the group considered moratoria and suggested, as it had with vested rights statutes in the realistic investment-backed expectation area, that state legislation clearly defining criteria for moratoria would be very helpful in achieving non-constitutional resolution of the takings issues concerning moratoria. See Recommendation #5. The group also felt that bad faith moratoria should be compensated as a taking. This last subject may be further explicated by the Supreme Court, which appeared to be concerned with the city's bad faith in *Del Monte Dunes*. It is bad faith in denying an approval which is the subject of a recent land use decision on which certiorari has been granted, *Olech v. Village of Willowbrook*, 160 F. 3d 386 (7th Cir. 1998), *cert. granted*, 9/28/99, so that the Supreme Court may be speaking to the bad faith issue in the near future. Recommendations in this area follow.

B. Recommendations
1. Normal time spent seeking land use approvals, the denial of which is valid, is not a taking.
2. As to time spent seeking approval, where the denial of the approval is found to be a taking, the taking starts only at the time of denial, although the delay may be compensable on other grounds.
3. Time spent litigating a takings claim where there is a judgment that a taking has occurred is compensable from the time of denial up to the time of the court decision finding the taking.
4. Time spent litigating a denial that is invalid for reasons other than a taking, such as lack of authority or other reasons, is not compensable as a taking.
5. Moratoria. A moratorium is not necessarily a temporary taking provided, however, that a moratorium is a taking where it is objectively demonstrable that it was enacted in bad faith as a means of preventing economically beneficial use of the subject property. Further, state legislatures should consider the enactment of authorizations including clear requirements for land use moratoria, and local governments should apply such requirements.

ABA RETREAT ATTENDEE LIST
Vicki Been
Professor of Law
New York University Law School

Michael M. Berger, Esq.
Berger & Norton
Santa Monica, California

Peter A. Buchsbaum, Esq.
Greenbaum, Rowe, Smith, Ravin, Davis & Himmel LLP
Woodbridge, New Jersey

David Cardwell, Esq.
Holland & Knight LLP
Orlando, Florida

Thomas R. Curry, Esq.
City Attorney
City of Livermore
Livermore, California

Daniel J. Curtin, Esq.
McCutchen, Doyle, Brown, Enersen, LLP
Walnut Creek, California

John J. Delaney, Esq.
Linowes & Blocher, LLP
Silver Spring, Maryland

Timothy J. Dowling, Esq.
Community Rights Council
Washington, D. C.

Christopher J. Duerksen, Esq.
Clarion Associates of Colorado LLC
Denver, Colorado

Professor Steven J. Eagle
George Mason University School of Law
Arlington, Virginia

Richard Hluchan, Esq.
Levin & Hluchan
Voorhees, New Jersey

Gideon Kanner, Esq.
Berger & Norton
Santa Monica, California

Cornelia Wyma Keatinge, Esq.
Lakewood, Colorado

Wendie L. Kellington, Esq.
Schwabe, Williamson & Wyatt, P. C.
Portland, Oregon

Professor Jan Laitos
University of Denver College of Law
Denver, Colorado

J. Thomas McDonald, Esq.
Otten, Johnson, Robinson, Neff & Ragonetti, P. C.
Denver, Colorado

Professor Daniel R. Mandelker
Washington University Law School
St. Louis, Missouri

Dwight Merriam, Esq.
Robinson & Cole
Hartford, Connecticut

Professor Lynda Oswald
University of Michigan Business School
Ann Arbor, Michigan

Thomas G. Pelham, Esq.
Apgar & Pelham
Tallahassee, Florida

R. S. Radford
Pacific Legal Foundation
Sacramento, California

Charles L. Siemon, Esq.
Siemon, Larsen & Marsh
Boca Raton, Florida

Edward Sullivan, Esq.
Preston Gates & Ellis LLP
Portland, Oregon

Professor Edward H. Ziegler
University of Denver College of Law
Denver, Colorado

RESPONSE TO THE REPORT OF THE RETREAT ON TAKINGS JURISPRUDENCE

Prepared by:
International Municipal Lawyers Association
1100 Vermont Avenue N.W.
Suite 200
Washington, D.C. 20005
(202) 466-5424

Introduction

In June 1999, the Section of State and Local Government Law of the American Bar Association (ABA) and The Rocky Mountain Land Institute jointly sponsored a retreat on the subject of takings jurisprudence. "The purpose of the Retreat was to determine whether a group of knowledgeable and concerned lawyers and law professors with different points of view could agree on some propositions relating to takings jurisprudence. The hope was that if consensus could be reached, law reform positions could be presented by the State and Local Government Law Section or other sections of the ABA for action by the House of Delegates. "[1] The retreat led to the preparation of the Report of Retreat on Takings Jurisprudence (Report). Four lawyers in attendance at the Retreat dissented. Subsequent to the Report's preparation, and after considerable discussion within the legal community about the proposals contained in the Report, the Section of State and Local Government Law requested comments and responses for consideration before a decision is made regarding whether the ABA should adopt the recommendations of the Report. This paper constitutes the International Municipal Lawyers Association's (IMLA) response to that request and strongly cautions against ABA endorsement or even involvement.

This Response was drafted this spring by the current and former officers of IMLA's Land Development, Planning and Zoning Section. The Response was then presented to and endorsed by the IMLA Board of Directors at their mid-year meeting on April 8, 2000. On April 9, IMLA hosted a forum for attendees of its Mid-Year Seminar, at which attorney Peter Buchsbaum of New Jersey, the principal draftsman of the Report, and Professor Daniel Mandelker of Washington University School of Law, a Retreat participant, explained the Report and commented on IMLA's draft

Response. Subsequently, this Response was modified to address comments made by attorney Buchsbaum and Professor Mandelker.

As the basis for its recommendations, the Report takes the position that several cases in the takings arena have fundamental shortcomings and create confusion in the law. This response addresses that position, recognizing that differences of opinion will continue to exist regarding whether current cases provide adequate guidance to local governments, landowners, and citizens impacted by local land use decisions. This response also focuses on the specific recommendations made by the Report and explains why the proposals essentially constitute a legislative push to reform developing constitutional law, fail to clarify any alleged confusion in the law, and even compound problems. Worse, the Report may even create problems where none existed. In addition, this response also sets forth reasons why it is inappropriate for the ABA to take a stance, particularly the stance advocated in the Report, with regard to the development of takings law.

Although, as Attorney Buchsbaum and Professor Mendelker reiterated, the Report endorses no bill and is meant to be a statement of general principles, its recommendations are very similar to the Private Property Rights Implementation Act of 1999 and other federal "property rights" legislation, which are generally recognized as being actively and aggressively supported by the National Association of Home Builders and which IMLA strongly opposes. Numerous editorials have been written criticizing the bill for, among other things, being unconstitutional and unfairly shifting the balances struck by courts between private and public sector interests and between property rights and smart-growth advocates. The bill clearly would shift the balance in favor of private sector interests and property rights advocates' positions. IMLA is concerned that the Report will be used by supporters of H.R. 2372 to move the debate out of the Courts and from among practitioners into the political arena where well-financed interests have a better opportunity to shape the outcome.

Takings law is complex and uncertain. The Supreme Court itself has said that it "has generally eschewed any set formula for determining how far is too far, preferring to engage in essentially ad hoc, factual inquiries."[2] The complexity and uncertainty of takings law, however, does not dictate the course taken by the Report—recommendations that, by their nature, will undoubtedly be pursued through legislative efforts to change the Constitution to the benefit of some, and to the detriment of others. This approach is in fact doomed to fail because it is founded on the misguided belief that the Congress has the authority to interpret the Constitution.[3]

The Report states that clarification of issues would benefit all sides equally; however, issues of law remain unresolved because multiple possible outcomes exist. Resolution of uncertainties in the law inevitably and necessarily benefits one side at the expense of another. Any attempt to resolve these issues prematurely—through other than the appropriate common-law method of resolution of constitutional issues—will unjustifiably and prematurely foreclose more analytical solutions and refinements. Such an attempt violates the fundamental principle of constitutional jurisprudence that constitutional law should develop incrementally, through decisions in actual, concrete cases.

It is also important not to ignore the impact of the propositions advocated by the Report on takings jurisprudence beyond federal law. Although state courts have typically followed our federal courts' analyses on major takings principles, the role of state courts in defining parallel state constitutional provisions is significant. Considerable variation exists among the states in their takings jurisprudence. For example, states that have constitutional provisions that require compensation for a "taking or damaging" of property may or may not have developed state takings jurisprudence that closely parallels that of the Fifth Amendment. The Report's recommendations, though they could arguably resolve federal issues, may create more confusion and protracted litigation by creating inconsistencies and contrasts between federal and state takings jurisprudence.

If local land use procedures need to be improved in a particular community, the appropriate response is to reform those procedures at the state and local level. That solution does not involve the imposition of a one-size-fits-all mandate through changes in takings jurisprudence that would severely tilt the playing field in favor of developers in every community in the country. The ABA should not associate itself with controversial proposals designed to advance the agendas of special interests. Nor should the ABA attempt to freeze-frame an area of constitutional law, which will evolve naturally over time as new issues and different nuances to existing issues are highlighted and given focus by events in our ever-changing society. The recent Supreme Court decision in *Eastern Enterprises v. Apfel*[4] makes clear that our highest court is not yet of one mind on such critical issues as the relationship between the takings clause and due process clause. Given the changing course of constitutional opinion in these areas, and given that interpretation of the Constitution should evolve through the courts, the ABA should not seek codification of one version of constitutional precepts over others.

I. Ripeness

The Report asserts that the issue of ripeness is one of judicial administration, leading to the conclusion that on such matters the ABA has a right to be heard and present solutions to perceived problems.[5] However, the courts have made it clear that ripeness is a matter of constitutional law.[6] Article III of the United States Constitution demands that a case or controversy exists before a federal court has subject matter jurisdiction over an action.[7] Federal courts may not render advisory opinions. Until a claim is ripe for review, pursuant to federal court established precedent, no case or controversy exists.[8] Accordingly, courts, as they have in the past, should be the entities to define ripeness based on their interpretation of the Constitution. Disagreement by segments of the Bar concerning the courts' interpretations of when a claim is "ripe" does not make legislative reform of the Constitution proper, or for that matter possible. Additionally, the ABA, as a membership organization representing lawyers of diverse interests and backgrounds, specifically local governments, private individuals, developers, and commercial interests, should not put forth and endorse legislative proposals that conflict substantially with interests of a significant segment of its membership. Nor should it endorse legislative proposals that alter the interpretation of the Constitution. In our system of government it is the courts' role to interpret the Constitution.

A. Williamson County: *Final Decisions and Exhaustion of State Remedies*

The Report suggests that the first prong of *Williamson County Regional Planning Comm'n v. Hamilton Bank*,[9] the requirement of a final decision to a reasonable development proposal, be embodied by a "bright line test for determining when ripeness has occurred. . . ."[10] The Report badly misconstrues *Williamson County*. Under that decision, ripeness for federal takings jurisdiction is determined through the application of the following tests: (a) rejection of a (complete) development application by the local government; (b) denial of a request for a variance or other form of relief available under local regulations; (c) denial of a subsequent application, if the first application was not a final proposal; and (d) utilization of available state procedures for obtaining just compensation. These tests are clearly conjunctive. However, the Report appears to assume that these tests are disjunctive: that is, that *Williamson County* stands for the proposition that if federal takings are to be avoided, there must necessarily be a uniform measure, throughout the United States, of what constitutes a "final" local decision.

1. The First Prong: Finality

Over the years, the Supreme Court has carefully developed reasonable "ripeness" rules that conserve judicial resources; provide guidance, if not absolute answers, for determining when claims may be brought in federal court; avoid premature and perhaps futile decisions; and prevent developers from improperly escalating every land use dispute into a federal takings lawsuit. Under *Williamson County* and its progeny, before suing in federal court, a developer must ripen a takings claim by obtaining a final local decision from local officials regarding how the land may be used. The Court unanimously reaffirmed a line of finality ripeness case law only three years ago in *Suitum v. Tahoe Regional Planning Authority*.[11]

These established ripeness principles are logical because a regulation effects a taking only when it goes "too far" and has "very nearly the same effect" as an expropriation.[12] As explained in *MacDonald, Sommer & Frates v. County of Yolo*,[13] a court cannot determine whether a regulation has gone too far unless it knows how far the regulation goes.[14] Federal courts also recognize that land use issues are quintessentially local issues, that land use agencies are "singularly flexible institutions"[15] and that developers should work closely with local planners before running to federal court, lest they turn the federal judiciary into a board of zoning appeals.

The Supreme Court has made clear that a property owner need not resort to piecemeal litigation or unfair local procedures.[16] In that context, it is appropriate to address, as a part of a takings analysis, on a case-by-case basis, whether local procedures unfairly prevent an applicant from obtaining a final decision. Existing jurisprudence adequately addresses this concern. By the same token, it is also appropriate to consider whether the owner may be required to submit more than one development plan because rejection of a single plan may not automatically suggest that a less ambitious plan will be denied.[17]

The Report proposes a new definition of ripeness for takings claimants, one that is inconsistent with settled ripeness jurisprudence. Under the Report's definition, a developer's takings claim would be ripe for adjudication in federal court after a single application "has been rejected by the final regulatory authority."[18] Because the definition does not define the term "final regulatory authority," it is unclear whether the developer would be required to pursue a variance, waiver, or other local procedures before suing in federal court. This ambiguity alone renders the definition fatally flawed, for it would allow developers to argue that they should be permitted to side-step important local processes. These local procedures often are the most convenient and inexpensive forums for neighbors and other community residents to voice concerns with a development project. Moreover, even where developers do not actually file suit in federal court, they could threaten early federal court litigation and, thus, exert undue pressure on local officials to approve inappropriate development proposals. The definition of ripeness proposed by the Report would give a developer a ripe takings claim after the rejection of one development plan, no matter how harmful it would be to the local community, even if local officials would approve a less harmful plan. Local communities cannot afford this threat of premature litigation.

Recognition of an applicant's ability to pursue relief mechanisms provided in a local ordinance is perhaps the most significant omission in the Report. That pursuit may be the most important element of the Supreme Court's formulation of local ripeness requirements. Those mechanisms may include a variance, as in *Williamson County*, or an adjustment, or exception. The Supreme Court has made it abundantly clear that the failure to pursue such local relief is jurisdictionally fatal to a regulatory takings claim. There is nothing vague about this requirement and it is understood by every prudent developer. If such relief mechanism is unavailable or inadequate under local law, then this element is satisfied.

The Report, however, apparently in an effort to preclude the "subsequent application" requirement announced in *MacDonald,* would totally undermine the local relief requirement of *Williamson County.* It would do so by substituting a vague two-part test following denial of the initial application: first, the burden shifts to the local government to provide "guidance" regarding additional information or changes to the substance of the proposal; second, the landowner must "respond" to such "guidance."[19] This formulation, by its vagueness, invites, rather than reduces, the prospect of litigation.

Moreover, even where developers do not actually file suit in federal court, they may nevertheless threaten federal court litigation and, thus, exert undue pressure on local officials to approve otherwise inappropriate development proposals. The definition of ripeness proposed by the Report would give a developer a ripe takings claim after the rejection of one development plan, no matter how grandiose or harmful to the community.

Under the Report's definition of ripeness, a local community could avoid the threat of litigation only if it could demonstrate precisely how the owner's development proposal could be made acceptable. This extraordinary proposal would shift onto local government the burden of taking on a task above and beyond their normal planning responsibilities, to prepare site-specific plans for a developer regardless of the seriousness or economic viability of the proposed project. In other words, to avoid immediate federal court litigation, the local community would need to assume the burden and expense of doing the developer's planning work.

Moreover, the suggestion that the local government provide local guidance for developers and that their regulatory decision makers "should be the focus of significant educational efforts regarding the confluence of constitutional rights and community planning and political objectives" is both insultingly offhanded and unrealistic. If local land use procedures need to be improved in a specific community, the solution is to reform those procedures at the state and local level. Indeed, many states and localities are doing just that by enacting permitting deadlines, streamlining procedures, and implementing other reforms to expedite the application process. The ABA, however, should not endorse a proposal that is tantamount to a federal legislative proposal which would constitutionalize a "one-size-fits-all" mandate and severely tilt the playing field toward developers in every community in the country.

2. The Second Prong: State Remedies

The Report next focuses on the second prong of *Williamson County,* the exhaustion of state remedies. The Report's three propositions set forth in Section I.C of the document are designed to undermine the requirement to seek compensation in state court. They are baseless and should be rejected.

Proposition I.C.1 purports to identify an alleged circuit conflict regarding a developer's ability to re-litigate issues in federal court after seeking compensation in state court.[20] However, the circuits uniformly have ruled that developers and other takings claimants are subject to the federal "full faith and credit" statute[21] where appropriate. Just last term, the Court denied a petition for a writ of certiorari in *Rainey Bros. Construction Co., Inc. v. Memphis and Shelby County Bd. of Adjustment*.[22] In that case, the petitioners argued, similarly to the Report, that the Sixth Circuit's application of res judicata to the state court's decision on the merits of petitioners' takings claim "intensifies" the conflict among federal circuits.

In arguing that there is a circuit conflict, the Report cites cases in which courts have held that a property owner may "reserve" the federal constitutional claim while litigating state compensation claims in state court as required by *Williamson County*.[23] Such reservations are not unusual and are the proper way to ensure that a federal court is provided an opportunity to consider federal claims. Making the requisite reservation does not, however, authorize courts to ignore the federal "full faith and credit" statute. Instead, such reservations preserve claimants' rights to return to federal court to litigate unresolved issues. This is precisely what happened in *Dodd v. Hood River County*,[24] where the Ninth Circuit *allowed* the owner to reserve the federal takings claim while litigating state claims in state court.

The question in *Dodd* was whether issue preclusion—commonly referred to as collateral estoppel—prevented the plaintiffs from litigating the federal takings claim after the facts underlying the state takings claim had been resolved against them. The Ninth Circuit determined that issue preclusion should be applied when the owner returned to federal court, and that full faith and credit should be given to the state court's determination regarding the economic impact of the challenged environmental safeguards. Otherwise, the Ninth Circuit fully considered the federal takings claim on the merits, rejecting it because the environmental protections at issue were reasonable and the owners lacked investment-backed expectations to use their property in a manner that contravened pre-existing rules.[25]

Contrary to the assertion of the Report, no conflict exists between *Dodd* and *Fields v. Sarasota Manatee Airport Authority*.[26] The Eleventh Circuit, in *Fields*, also held that "one need only 'reserve her constitutional claims for subsequent litigation in federal court' by 'making on the state record a reservation as to the disposition of the entire case by the state courts' to preserve access to a federal forum."[27] In *Fields*, however, the court found that the plaintiff had failed to make a reservation and, therefore, was barred by merger and res judicata principles from relitigating the claims. *Dodd* and *Fields* both stand for the proposition that a plaintiff may reserve federal claims while engaged in state court litigation. *Dodd* simply explains that to the extent the state court addresses issues relevant to the federal claim, the federal court must give the state court decision preclusive effect.

Proposition I.C.1 is premised on a mistaken view of the federal court system which assumes that claimants have a right of unfettered access to the federal courts. In *Allen v. McCurry*,[28] the Supreme Court expressly rejected this contention. There, a criminal defendant unsuccessfully relied on an alleged violation of the Fourth Amendment in a state court criminal trial, and subsequently brought an action in federal court under Section 1893.[29] to recover damages for the alleged violation. The Supreme Court ruled that the state court's rejection of the allegation precluded re-litigation of the matter in federal court under the federal "full faith and credit" statute and generally applicable principles of res judicata and collateral estoppel. After concluding that the "full faith and credit" statute applies in Section 1983 cases, the *Allen* Court wrote:

> The actual basis of the Court of Appeal's holding appears to be a generally framed principle that every person asserting a federal right is entitled to one unencumbered opportunity to litigate that right in a federal district court, regardless of the legal posture in which the federal claim arises. But the authority for this principle is difficult to discern. It cannot lie in the Constitution, which makes no such guarantee, but leaves the scope of the jurisdiction of the federal district courts to the wisdom of Congress.

* * *

There is, in short, no reason to believe that Congress intended to provide a person claiming a federal right an unrestricted opportunity to relitigate an issue already decided in state court simply because the issue arose in a state proceeding in which he would rather not have been engaged at all.[30]

After having rejected the contention that constitutional claimants are always entitled to "a second bite at the apple" in federal court, the Supreme Court reaffirmed the ability of state courts to address federal claims:

> The only other conceivable basis for finding a universal right to litigate a federal claim in a federal district court is hardly a legal basis at all, but rather a general distrust of the capacity of the state courts to render correct decisions on constitutional issues. It is ironic that *Stone v. Powell*, 428 U.S. 465 (1976) provided the occasion for the expression of such an attitude in the present litigation, in view of this Court's emphatic reaffirmation in that case of the constitutional obligation of the state courts to uphold federal law, and its expression of confidence in their ability to do so.[31]

Some have argued that *Allen* is distinguishable because the criminal defendant had the opportunity to litigate the federal constitutional issue, whereas a takings claimant must pursue state claims in federal court and might subsequently be precluded from ever litigating the federal claim. In fact, however, under the concept of "full faith and credit" and the doctrines of claim and issue preclusion, a takings claimant will be precluded from relitigating only those matters that were (or could have been) raised in state court.[32] If the state court has not fully resolved the federal claim, federal courts will entertain unlitigated issues.[33] Where the claimant did not have a full and fair opportunity to litigate an issue in state court, the federal court will hear the claim.[34]

Application of the doctrines of claim and issue preclusion in actions under Section 1983 reduces wasteful re-litigation and "'promotes' the comity between state and federal courts that has been recognized as a bulwark of the federal system. "[35] By suggesting that these doctrines should be relaxed in takings cases, the Report's proposals effectively seek preferential treatment for developers and land owners—a chance to get two bites at the apple—that has been denied to constitutional claimants. To urge a relaxation of generally applicable rules of *res judicata* is to ignore the federal "full faith and credit" statute, to marginalize the vital role of state courts in our federal system, and to promote special treatment of property owners not afforded to claimants under other constitutional provisions. The ABA should do none of these.

Propositions I.C.2 and I.C.3 likewise are designed to undermine the state compensation requirement by suggesting that an "unfairness" was created by *City of Chicago v. International College of Surgeons.*[36] *International College of Surgeons* allows a municipality to remove certain state law claims to federal court under the federal "supplemental jurisdiction" statute.[37] In *International College of Surgeons*, however, the Court was silent regarding the ability to remove a federal takings claim to federal court. The district court in that case apparently erred in allowing a federal takings claim to proceed in federal court since, under *Williamson County*, no violation of the Takings Clause could have occurred until the claimant was denied compensation in state court. The Supreme Court's ruling, however, does not address (and certainly does not endorse) the district court's error in this regard. Even in the vigorous dissent in *International College of Surgeons*, the dissenters did not cite *Williamson County*, much less suggest any tension or unfairness arising from the two rulings. The Report essentially asks the ABA to address an apparent error by a single district court, and there is no compelling need to do so. More importantly, the ABA should not be made a partner to the attempt to misuse *International College of Surgeons* in a backdoor attempt to undercut *Williamson County*, the essential role of state courts, and the language of the Takings Clause.

II. Reasonable Investment-Backed Expectations

Proposition II.B.1 states that an owner's expectations, as defined by state law, are useful in determining the existence of protected property interests. While this assertion undoubtedly is true, it suggests that only state law defines expectations and property interests. Expectations also may be shaped by federal law and other sources.[38]

The Report, however, attempts to "federalize" property law by a "one size fits all" approach to investment-backed expectations. While that approach may be more convenient for lawyers or some constitutional scholars, it fails to recognize the diverse views of property law in the several states.

In particular, Proposition II.B.2 states that vested rights should be recognized as a distinct property interest. Although the proposition does not expressly indicate whether such interests should be compensable under the Takings Clause, it is likely that this proposition would be interpreted as requiring compensation (at least for a temporary taking) in these instances because the retreat was limited to takings issues. The result would be that, if one's expectations of building a 70-story building are frustrated by a change of the height regulations to a maximum of 50 stories, the land owner would be able to claim compensation. This is a result the landowner would not have otherwise been entitled to under current takings law. The various states have different views of vested rights. It is far better for those states to develop their own jurisprudence on the subject than to have it accomplished by a national council of *experts*, selected for that purpose and reflecting only the views of those assembled.

The vested rights doctrine, however, was developed from the Due Process Clause and generally has been viewed as giving rise to equitable relief.[39] Indeed, the terms "vested rights" and "estoppel" often are used interchangeably.[40] Where government officials violate a vested right, the property owner is entitled to injunctive relief. This proposition would not clarify or enhance the law, but would instead create confusion by suggesting that the owner is automatically entitled to compensatory relief as well. Developers could exploit this confusion at the expense of neighboring property owners, and the community at large, by threatening a suit for compensation whenever there is disagreement over whether a vested right exists. In that case, the developer could exert undue pressure on local officials to approve development proposals even where a legitimate dispute exists over the developer's right to pursue the project.

Proposition II.B.2 is designed to promote the use of vested right statutes. Developer associations across the country are pursuing these statutes to strengthen their negotiating position in local land use disputes. Courts are fully able to determine whether a vested right exists. It would be inappropriate for the ABA to endorse a legislative vehicle that would federalize a judicial determination that is essentially a matter of state law, and that would give developer interests an unwarranted advantage over local citizen interests. Moreover, this proposition could be read to suggest that the role of expectations is limited to defining property interests, which is wrong. Under longstanding precedent, an owner's expectations, as shaped by federal and state law, may preclude takings liability even where the underlying property interest remains unaffected.[41] Accordingly, this proposition would not clarify and enhance takings jurisprudence, but instead muddy the waters.

Further, it is curious to see the focus in the Report on property owner expectations. There is much less of the other side of the coin, i.e., one who buys or elects to build upon land with actual or constructive knowledge of proposed changes or other background property or use constraints being limited by this principle. No "multi-factor inquiry" can obviate the unfairness of such a landowner "having it all" through manipulation of "reasonable investment-backed expectations."

III. Segmentation

Proposition III.B.1 states that in defining the relevant parcel for takings analysis (the so-called "denominator" issue), courts should use a standard that is "not malleable by either the property owner (segmentation) or by the government (agglomeration)."[42] The proposal to prevent segmentation by the owner is already entirely consistent with established black letter law, a principle often referred to as the non-segmentation principle.[43] It is not at all clear why it is either necessary or appropriate to seek legislative restatement and ratification of long-established principles of takings jurisprudence.

On the other hand, the proposal to disallow agglomeration by the government is unclear. The term "agglomeration" does not appear in Supreme Court takings case law and is not generally used in takings jurisprudence. Because the term is unfamiliar and undefined, the proposition could be construed to conflict with the bedrock principle that courts should consider a takings claimant's entire parcel, or what the Supreme Court calls the "parcel as a whole."[44] If the proposition is intended to mean simply that the government should not be allowed unfairly to bundle property interests in defining the relevant parcel, it should be rewritten to state this expressly. However, there is no evidence in existing case law that courts need additional guidance from the ABA on such an obvious point.

Propositions III.B.2 and III.B.3 list various factors that courts consider in defining the relevant parcel, a list derived in part from *Zealy v. City of Waukesha*.[45] But the proposed laundry list is far less sophisticated and developed than that which can easily be ascertained from a review of existing case law because it ignores certain presumptions and other principles that courts have developed. For example, contiguous property under common ownership generally should be treated as a single relevant parcel.[46] Moreover, a takings claimant who treats property as a single parcel for purposes of purchase and financing should not be allowed to segment the property for purposes of takings analysis.[47] By ignoring the dispositive nature of certain factors and other governing principles developed by the courts, the Report's laundry list could inject confusion into an area of takings analysis that already contains sufficiently clear guidance for practitioners.

IV. Temporary Takings

Proposition IV.B.5 states that a planning moratorium is a compensable taking where it is implemented in bad faith. This "bad faith" standard raises the question of whether government action is compensable in instances where it does not "substantially advance legitimate state interests," one of two tests articulated in *Agins v. City of Tiburon*.[48] In 1998, however, five Justices strongly questioned the viability of *Agins'* "substantially advance" test to determine takings liability.[49] Because the Takings Clause requires compensation only where property is taken for a public use, it is not appropriate to impose takings liability for government action taken in bad faith or that otherwise fails to advance a legitimate public interest. In these instances, invalidation is the appropriate remedy. In view of *Eastern Enterprises*, developers have good reason to believe that the Supreme Court soon will formally repudiate the much-criticized *Agins* theory of takings liability, and they evidently hope that an ABA endorsement of the theory will help resuscitate it. The ABA should refuse to do so.

Conclusion

IMLA urges the ABA not to adopt the recommendations of the Report. Interpretation of the Constitution should be left to our courts. For segments of the ABA to push for action that is designed to alter or modify existing constitutional law disregards the separation of powers principles that are hallmarks of our system of government. Where members of the ABA can be most useful is at the local level in drafting legislation to deal with problems that may arise in their own communities. Legislation can be particularly important in areas of comprehensive planning, adherence to comprehensive plans, procedural reforms, and the like. While less glamorous than constitutional speculation, that effort is more likely to achieve distributive justice. Should various special interests be successful in their attempt to legislate changes in takings jurisprudence, the obvious result would be further time-consuming and expensive litigation that will unnecessarily consume already overburdened federal judicial resources, and all to no avail, as such legislative action would be clearly unconstitutional.

Notes

1. Report at 2.
2. Penn Central Transp. Co. v. New York City, 438 U.S. 104, 124 (1978).
3. *See* City of Boerne v. Flores, 117 S. Ct. 2157, 2168 (1997)("If Congress could define its own power by altering the Fourteenth Amendment's meaning, no longer would the Constitution be 'superior paramount law, unchangeable by ordinary means.' It would be 'on a level with ordinary legislative acts, and like other acts, . . . alterable when the legislatures should please to alter it.'").
4. 118 S. Ct. 2131, 2157 (1998).
5. Report at 3.

6. *See* Suitum v. Tahoe Regional Planning Agency, 520 U.S. 725, 733 n.7 (1997). ("We have noted that ripeness doctrine is drawn from both Article III on judicial power and from prudential reasons for refusing to exercise jurisdiction." (quoting Reno v. Catholic Social Services, Inc., 509 U.S. 43, 57 n.18, 113 S. Ct. 2485, 2496 n.18, (1993))). *See also* City of Monterey v. Del Monte Dunes at Monterey, Ltd., 119 S. Ct. 1624, 1639 (1999) (unless and until the state court denies compensation for a taking, the landowner "suffer[s] no constitutional injury from the taking alone").

7. Allen v. Wright, 468 U.S. 737, 750 (1984).

8. *See* St. Clair v. City of Chico, 880 F.2d 199, 201 (9th Cir.), *cert. denied*, 493 U.S. 993 (1989).

9. 473 U.S. 172 (1985).

10. Report at 7.

11. 520 U.S. 725, 735-39 (1997).

12. Pennsylvania Coal Co. v. Mahon, 260 U.S. 393, 414-15 (1922).

13. 477 U.S. 340 (1986).

14. *Id*. at 348.

15. *Id*. at 350.

16. *Id*. at 350 n.7.

17. *Id*. at 353 n.9.

18. Report at 8.

19. Report at 8.

20. Report at 10.

21. 28 U.S.C. 1738 (1948).

22. 178 F.3d 1295 (6th Cir. 1999), *cert. denied*, ____ U.S. ____, 120 S. Ct. 172 (1999).

23. Report at 10.

24. 59 F.3d 852, 862 (9th Cir. 1995).

25. Dodd v. Hood River County, 136 F.3d 1219, 1229-30 (9th Cir. 1998).

26. 953 F.2d 1299 (11th Cir. 1992).

27. *Id*. at 1303 (citing Jennings v. Caddo Parish School Bd., 531 F. 2d 1331 (5th Cir.), *cert. denied*, 429 U.S. 897 (1976)).

28. 449 U.S. 90 (1980).

29. 42 U.S.C. § 1983.

30. *Allen*, 449 U.S. at 103-04 (footnotes omitted).

31. *Id*. at 105.

32. *Id*. at 94.

33. *E.g., Dodd*, 136 F.3d at 1229-30.

34. *Allen*, 449 U.S. at 95.

35. *Id*. at 95-96.

36. 522 U.S. 156 (1997).

37. 28 U.S.C. 1367(a)(1990).

38. *E.g.,* Lucas v. South Carolina Coastal Council, 505 U.S. 1003, 1028-29 (1992) (federal navigational servitude shapes owners' expectations and property interests).

39. J. JUERGENSMEYER & T. ROBERTS, LAND USE PLANNING AND CONTROL LAW 227-28 (1998).

40. *Id*.

41. *E.g.,* Ruckelshaus v. Monsanto Co., 467 U.S. 986, 1006-07 (1984) (preexisting federal pesticide statute that permits disclosure of trade secrets submitted with a registra-

tion application shapes the expectations of the owner of the trade secrets in a way that precludes takings liability, notwithstanding the owner's cognizable property interest).

42. Report at 14.

43. *E.g.,* K & K Construction, Inc. v. Department of Natural Resources, 456 Mich. 570, 575 N.W.2d 531 (Mich. 1998).

44. *E.g.,* Keystone Bituminous Coal Ass'n v. DeBenedictis, 480 U.S. 470, 498-501 (1987); Penn Central Transp. Co. v. New York City, *supra* note 2, at 130-31.

45. 548 N.W. 2d 528 (Wis. 1996), and Ciampitti v. United States, 22 Cl. Ct. 310 (1991).

46. *Zealy,* 548 N.W.2d at 532.

47. *Ciampitti,* 22 Cl. Ct. at 320.

48. 447 U.S. 255, 260 (1980).

49. *See* Eastern Enterprises v. Apfel, 118 S. Ct. 2131, 2157 (1998) (Kennedy, J., dissenting in part) (the *Agins* "substantially advance" test "is in uneasy tension with our basic understanding of the Takings Clause"); *id.* at 2161 (Breyer, J., with Stevens, Souter, and Ginsburg, JJ. dissenting) (the Takings Clause does not apply to a challenge to arbitrary or unfair government action, but instead provides compensation for legitimate government action).

INDEX

Note: References are to sections; page numbers are in brackets [ ].

V

W